GeoTol Pro 2020 - About this Workbook

This GeoTol Pro 2020 workbook is part of a profess
dimensioning and tolerancing (GD&T). It covers the
or specialized concepts of the ASME Y14.5-2018
The program approaches the subject from the "practical world" with the use of both 2D and 3D graphics of the drawing symbols and figures for explanation. This program has been presented and refined over the past 35 years to approach the subject from three different perspectives: design, manufacturing, and inspection. Some explanations and exercises will be specific to each of these groups so everyone can learn each other's role and communicate better with the concepts and language. How to apply, read, inspect, and report the tolerances will be addressed in these lessons and exercises.

This workbook is programmed to accompany either live training or the GeoTol Pro Online/ Video Series to the ASME Y14.5-2018. The program materials contain a variety of computer color animated graphics, video clips, wood and plastic model demonstrations to keep participants engaged throughout the program. As an option, a color animated PowerPoint presentation and a wood/plastic model set are available to assist a program leader in live training. The model set is comprised of parts, assemblies, and inspection equipment shown in this workbook.

A typical unit consists of the participant viewing the video or live training and following along in the workbook. During and after units, workshop exercises are completed. The solutions to the exercises are presented and discussed by a program leader. A separate solutions guide book is available. The workbook will provide a good reference to the concepts covered in training, but may also be used as self-study or for more practice afterwards. An index is provided at the back of the book for quick reference to any topic.

Customizing the Program - The workbook is split into 14 units. The first 6 units are considered the core concepts that cover the basics from symbols, terms, definitions to the fundamentals of datum reference frames, position and profile tolerances. We encourage everyone to go thru these first 6 units in chronological order. The remaining units cover more detailed and specialized concepts in ASME Y14.5. These units do not necessarily need to be done in order and select units may be chosen to create a custom lesson plan.

Geometric tolerancing is a broad subject and can be used on a variety of applications with different geometry from large parts to small parts, machined parts, plastic, sheet metal, composites, turned parts, castings, additive manufacturing, weldments, etc. While the fundamental concepts of the tolerancing will remain the same, each of these applications may have its own special treatments. This program has a variety of specialty applications to allow the program leader to skim or skip some subjects while concentrating on the more applicable topics for a targeted training approach.

Lots of Exercises - Exercises are the key to really understanding a subject. This program is loaded with practical exercises to drive home the concepts and encourage questions and effective discussions. After each topic and throughout the units are exercises varying from design application to manufacturing and verification techniques. We encourage everyone to try the exercises to provide in-class feedback to both the instructor and student for the level of knowledge retained over each topic. Not every exercise may need to be completed during the training and some may be saved for practice or self-study later.

Practical Application Practice - Unit 14 consists of a series of application problems for designers to practice applying GD&T to an empty drawing based on functional requirements. These problems may be interspersed in the training anytime after unit 6. These problems are made for design personnel but may be helpful for people in manufacturing and inspection to see the perspective of how datum features are selected and how the tolerance values are calculated/determined.

GeoTol is a new language, and like any new language, it will take time and practice. The more you use it, the more you will understand it. Suggestions for improvement are welcome and encouraged. Send us an e-mail with your comments and visit our website at www.geotol.com. Good Luck.

Note: The information in this text is the authors' interpretation of geometric dimensioning and tolerancing based on ASME and ISO standards and though deemed to be correct, must be considered as advisory and to be used at the discretion of the user.

In some instances, figures show added detail for emphasis. In other cases, figures are incomplete by intent. Numerical values of dimensions and tolerances are illustrative only. Be sure to consult national and international standards for more information on the subject.

Advanced Books on GD&T:

Our advanced workbook called **GeoTol Applications and Tolerance Stacks** goes beyond the symbols and definitions in this book. The first half of the advanced book is a series of case-study examples to practice problems on applying GD&T. The second half is an in-depth study into tolerance stack-ups: when multiple tolerances accumulate in an assembly. This course can be taken as a next step for design engineers and others doing GD&T application and analysis.

Acknowledgements:

The father/son authors of Al Neumann and Scott Neumann would like to acknowledge the support and patience from wife/mother, Kathy Neumann, daughter/sister, Holly Neumann, and daughter in-law/wife Kayla Neumann.

We dedicate this book to the newest member of our family grandson/son, Liam Neumann born in March 2020.

Acknowledgement is given for references and definitions derived from the ASME Y14.5-2018 and ASME Y14.5.1-2019 standards published by the American Society of Mechanical Engineers (ASME), New York, NY.

The authors would like to express their appreciation and gratitude to the many professional associates and friends on the standards committees, schools, colleges, universities, companies and professional organizations, both nationally and internationally, who provided technical input and draft review of this workbook.

About the Authors

Al Neumann (father) in 1983, founded Technical Consultants Incorporated (rebranded as GeoTol in 2021). Al has been devoted to education and training in geometric tolerancing and product definition. Al Neumann is a graduate of Central Michigan University. He has worked in a variety of engineering and manufacturing firms related to automotive, aircraft, medical and the defense industry.

Al Neumann is a recognized international expert in geometric dimensioning and tolerancing. He has written many books and has produced four video training programs on the subject. Mr. Neumann has presented hundreds of training programs to people throughout the US and worldwide over 35 years.

He served as a member on the ASME Y14.5, Dimensioning and Tolerancing committee for 35 years. He was section sponsor on the Datum Reference Frame section for the ASME Y14.5-2009 standard, and vice chairman for ASME Y14.5-2018. He was a member on the ASME Y14.5.1, Mathematical Definitions of Dimensioning and Tolerancing for 25 years. He also served as chairman on the US TAG to ISO TC213 on Dimensioning and Tolerancing.

Scott Neumann (son) is President of GeoTol. He graduated from The University of Florida with a bachelor's degree in Mechanical Engineering. He specializes in geometric tolerancing product definition, tolerance stack-up analysis, measurement data and inspection techniques.

Scott has presented hundreds of geometric tolerancing training programs to engineering, manufacturing, and quality personnel at major corporations in the US and worldwide since 2007. He has also practiced consulting and mentoring to improve product documentation and inspection methods on a variety of products. The industries include aerospace, defense, automotive, medical, industrial, and consumer products. He has coauthored two other textbooks and video programs on the subject: *GeoTol Pro to Y14.5-2009* and *GeoTol Applications and Tolerance Stacks*. Scott is 2009 Senior Level GDTP certified to ASME Y14.5.2 and is an active member of the following committees related to GD&T:

ASME Y14.5 Dimensioning and Tolerancing Support Group member
ASME Y14.5.1 Mathematical Definitions of Dimensioning and Tolerancing
ASME Y14.5.2 Certification of Dimensioning and Tolerancing
ASME Y14.45 Measurement Data Reporting
AED Assembly Level Tolerancing
Y14 US TAG Support Group in the ISO-GPS and ISO-TPD committees

Al Neumann, Scott Neumann, and their expert team at GeoTol, travel worldwide presenting on-site, virtual, and online training and consulting on geometric tolerancing and related subjects. They work with large and small companies customizing training and education to meet particular needs.

Geo Tol Pro 2020

A Practical Guide to Geometric Tolerancing

Table of Contents and Training Program Outline

Unit 1

Introduction - Symbols and Terms

Introduction to Geometric Dimensioning and Tolerancing
A Brief History
ASME Standards related to Product Definition and Metrology
ISO Standards related to Product Definition and Metrology
Common Symbols
Common Symbol Application
Millimeter vs. Inch Conventions
Tolerances in Perspective
Features of Size and Features without Size
Geometric Tolerancing Characteristic Symbols
Feature Control Frame
Geometric Tolerance Zone Shapes
Geometric Tolerance Categories
Symbols Associated with a Feature Control Frame
Symbols Related to Datum Identification
Index Plate - Practical Example
Index Plate - Matching a Perfect DRF to an Imperfect Part
Index Plate - Practical Example in 3D
Definitions
Fundamental Rules
Material Conditions - MMC and LMC
Workshop Exercise 1.1
Workshop Exercise 1.2
Workshop Exercise 1.3

Introduction to Geometric Tolerancing

Geometric Dimensioning and Tolerancing (GD&T) is an international engineering language that is used on drawings to express the allowable geometry of a part. It uses a series of symbols and feature control frames, rather than words, to describe the worst-case limits of a product. These symbols and frames are applied to the features and provide a clear definition of design intent. Quality control also uses these limits to develop a plan for verification, set rigid accept/reject criteria, and guides the reporting of the measurement data.

The buzz term "GD&T" is often thought of as one set of concepts, however it can be separated into two ideas: dimensioning and tolerancing. Dimensions are used to describe the perfect geometry of a part including distances, sizes, and angles of features. Because of slight manufacturing defects, no part could ever be made to this theoretically perfect geometry. Therefore, tolerances are added to a drawing to define the worst-case variations of these defects while still allowing part function.

Dimensioning has been used in the mechanical engineering world for hundreds and even thousands of years to describe the geometry of a part. It is also used in civil engineering and architecture for layouts of buildings and bridges. Tolerancing is not necessary in applications with artisan/craftsman-style manufacturing. Cut-to-match, file-to-fit, match drilling, shim packing are all methods to work around the manufacturing defects. However, this custom fitting often leads to more costly and time-consuming production. Serviceability can also be difficult because a replacement part must be custom-made again by a skilled craftsman. Tolerancing is a somewhat unique concept implemented to mechanical engineering drawings for two reasons: part interchangeability and quality control.

There are two different tolerancing systems: plus/minus tolerancing and geometric tolerancing (GeoTol). Plus/minus tolerancing was the original dimension-based tolerancing system with somewhat arbitrary definitions not backed by any official standard. Geometric tolerancing a more modern feature-based tolerancing system with definitions defined in an industry and government backed set of standards (Y14.5 and ISO-GPS). It describes the form, orientation and location of part features within theoretical tolerance zones relative to a defined coordinate system.

The GeoTol system is an engineering language with a strong mathematical base which is essential for parts with precise and complicated geometry. This exact language also becomes more necessary as the design, manufacturing, and inspection team gets bigger and more separated with more diverse supply chains. GeoTol is similar to any other language such as French, German, or Spanish, and therefore there are certain grammar and punctuation rules that must be learned and practiced. This is important because we want to avoid "slang" in communication which could lead to incorrect interpretations of the design intent and accepting nonfunctional parts. Because of the mathematical base, the language is machine readable and many verifications may become more automated. Like any language, it takes a while to learn the GD&T system. People from various companies and backgrounds possess different knowledge levels. There are some personnel who might be considered conversational, others can read it but not write it, and others might be linguistic experts. It takes time, practice and effort to thoroughly understand the GD&T system.

A Brief History of Tolerancing

The plus/minus tolerancing system

Prior to the 1800s, manufacturing of parts was done in artisan/craftsman style. There were no tolerances and assembly relied on human skill to hand-file machined parts to match-to-fit sizes for precision use like in military weapons. Parts were generally not interchangeable.

Although small degrees of interchangeability have been used since medieval times, more robust approaches to the concepts started on military components in France in the late 1700's. General Jean-Baptiste de Gribeauval started his "system of uniformity" with standardized weapons using standardized parts. He tasked his general inspector for the French arsenal, Honore Blanc, to reduce the time and cost of producing muskets with less skilled labor. Borrowing from the ideas of go/no-go gages for measuring cannon balls, Blanc was able to create 50 gun locks within plus/minus tolerances and demonstrated interchangeability. The idea never took off in France however, as fellow gunsmiths were skeptical and maybe even fearful of loosing their livelihood. Unfortunately Blanc's workshop and most samples were lost in the French revolution. However, one witness to his demonstration in 1785 was the American ambassador to France, Thomas Jefferson (also later the 3rd president of the US). He took Blanc's samples and the tolerance idea back to the US as a way to promote interchangeability back home.

In the US, the interchangeability idea was approached by many independent gunsmiths supplying weapons to the US army with varying levels of success in small batches throughout the late 1700's and early 1800's. The problem was eventually tasked to two US armories, Harpers Ferry Armory and Springfield Armory. John Hall at an independent workshop inside Harpers Ferry achieved interchangeability in gun locks in 1825. He collaborated with fellow gunsmith Simeon North, who ran a small workshop at Springfield Armory, to expand interchangeability at two different workshops in 1834. Although it took time (another 60-70 years), tolerancing eventually spread beyond military weapons to other industries including sewing machines, typewriters and automotive.

Another notable story is with Eli Whitney, a firearms manufacturer that is sometimes falsely credited with the invention of interchangeability. In 1799 before US congress, he made a presentation of assembly with ten sets of musket parts and claimed the same parts and mechanisms through the use of tolerancing. Although Whitney did secure a contract for 10,000 muskets, he struggled with that order and never achieved the concept of interchangeability himself. It was later found that his presentation was faked and the pieces were not fully interchangeable. Even though Whitney did not implement the concept, the idea of plus/minus tolerancing and interchangeability was brought further to the forefront at that time. The idea was simple: dimensions have a plus/minus tolerance and gages are used to verify them within the limits. The difficult problem was the precision required for interchangeability was beyond manufacturing and inspection abilities at the time. Full widespread use of tolerancing didn't happen before the invention of mechanized manufacturing equipment such as the lathe and milling machines, better inspection equipment such as the micrometer and the dial test indicator, and more precise US standards for length.

The Start of Geometric Tolerancing

Plus/minus tolerancing with a mix of artisan-style no-tolerance manufacturing was used thru the early 1900s and World War 1. It wasn't until the ramp up to World War 2, Stanley Parker from the Royal Torpedo Factory in Scotland realized there were problems with the plus/minus tolerancing system for locating holes. Parker was one of the first people to initiate the use of round tolerances for holes rather than square zones. Although symbols were not used on the drawing, the concept of position tolerance was written in notes.

The United States Department of Defense saw a need for more robust standardization of drawings including dimensioning and tolerancing after World War II. Military parts were made for the war effort by many outside manufacturers from automotive to consumer products. They did not have the tribal knowledge that was needed with the plus/minus tolerances to understand the design intent. The DOD mandated the use of the early Mil standard 8 for drawings of military parts where interchangeability was essential. The Mil standards eventually merged with the SAE Aero/Auto, and ASA Y14.5 to create the USASI Y14.5-1966 standard.

This standard is now written by the Y14.5 committee comprised of industry experts from US government agencies, universities, and companies in defense, aerospace, automotive, medical, consumer products, measurement devices and software. The meetings are coordinated and standards published by ASME (American Society of Mechanical Engineers) with ANSI (government body) approval. The committee roster has rotated through the years to create a standard that is in constant flux. A new edition is released about every 10 years with each edition clarifying concepts and adding new symbology as technology and knowledge improves.

Evolution of Dimensioning and Tolerancing Standards in the USA:

Mil Std 8 from 1949-1963 | ASA Y14.5-1957 | SAE/Aero from 1946-1963

USASI Y14.5-1966 (one unified national standard)
ANSI Y14.5-1973
ANSI Y14.5M-1982
ASME Y14.5M-1994
ASME Y14.5-2009
ASME Y14.5-2018

The latest American National Standard on dimensioning and tolerancing is the ASME Y14.5-2018. There have been many clarifications, enhancements, and a few new concepts over past standards. In Appendix A of this book you will find a list of the major changes from the previous ASME Y14.5-2009 and ASME Y14.5M-1994 standards.

There is a standard on the Mathematical Definitions of Dimensioning and Tolerancing: ASME Y14.5.1-2019. This document is primarily used in the development of software and provides a clear mathematical definition to the worded concepts of Y14.5. There is also a certification program and standard on the subject called the ASME Y14.5.2-2017, Certification of Geometric Dimensioning and Tolerancing Professionals.

There are other Y14 drawing standards written by different subcommittees that define drawing views (Y14.3), line conventions (Y14.2), casting symbols (Y14.8), Digital Product Definition Data Practices (Y14.41) to name a few. The Y14 standards are all about product definition and documentation. There is a separate group of subcommittees that writes the B89 series of standards on metrology and measurement of the specifications. See the next page for a list.

The ISO-GPS standards

There is also a competing series of geometric tolerancing standards called ISO-GPS (International Organization for Standardization - Geometrical Product Specification). ISO combines tolerancing with measurement in the GPS series of documents written by the Technical Committee (TC) 213. The ISO dimensioning and presentation in the drawing is covered by the TPD (Technical Product Documentation) series written by TC/10. See the next pages for a list of these standards.

The ISO working groups consist of people representing standards institutes from different countries (the countries are called member bodies). The US is a member body in these ISO standards called the US TAG (Technical Activity Group) through ASME and ANSI.

The definitions of most dimensioning and tolerancing symbols are similar between ASME and ISO, with only slight differences. For consistency, this book will show examples and give definitions of symbols from ASME Y14.5. However, any major differences are highlighted in the units with a full summary in Appendix B of this book.

ASME Standards Related to Product Definition and Metrology

The following is a reference list of ASME standards that are related to product definition (Y) and metrology (B) that are active at the print date of this book. The date of publication must be listed when referencing these documents. The notation *(R2018)* after is the reaffirmed date. Standards must be either revised or reaffirmed every 5 years or are withdrawn. The (rev) after shows these standards are currently in the process of being reaffirmed or revised. For more detailed information on the status and current available standards, see the ASME website: www.asme.org

ASME Y14.1-2012 (rev), Decimal Inch Drawing Sheet Size and Format
ASME Y14.1M-2012 (rev), Metric Drawing Sheet Size and Format
ASME Y14.2-2014 (R2020), Line Conventions and Lettering
ASME Y14.3-2012 (R2018), Orthographic and Pictorial Views
ASME Y14.5-2018, Dimensioning and Tolerancing
ASME Y14.5.1-2019, Mathematical Definition of Dimensioning and Tolerancing Principles
ASME Y14.5.2-2017, Certification of Geometric Dimensioning and Tolerancing Professionals
ASME Y14.6-2001 (R2018), Screw Thread Representation
ASME Y14.8-2009 (R2014) (rev), Castings, Forgings, and Molded Parts
ASME Y14.24-2012 (rev), Types and Applications of Engineering Drawings
ASME Y14.31-2014 (R2019), Undimensioned Drawings
ASME Y14.34-2013 (R2018), Associated Lists
ASME Y14.35-2014 (R2019), Revision of Engineering Drawings and Associated Documents
ASME Y14.36-2018, Surface Texture Symbols
ASME Y14.37-2019, Composite Part Drawings
ASME Y14.38-2019, Abbreviations and Acronyms for Use on Drawings and Related Documents
ASME Y14.39 Draft, Preferred limits and fits (consolidating B4.1 and B4.2)
ASME Y14.41-2019, Digital Product Definition Data Practices
ASME Y14.43-2011 (rev), Dimensioning and Tolerancing Principles for Gages and Fixtures
ASME Y14.44-2008 (R2014) (rev), Designations for Electrical and Electronics Parts and Equip
ASME Y14.45-2021, Measurement Data Reporting
ASME Y14.46-2017, Product Definition for Additive Manufacturing
ASME Y14.47-2019, Model Organization Practices
ASME Y14.48 Draft, Universal Direction and Load Indicators
ASME Y14.100-2017, Engineering Drawing Practices
ANSI B4.1-1967 (R2009) (rev), Preferred Limits and Fits for Cylindrical Parts
ANSI B4.2-1978 (R2009) (rev), Preferred Metric Limits and Fits

ASME B1.1-2003 (R2008), Unified Inch Screw Threads
ASME B1.13M-2005 (R2015), Metric Screw Threads: M Profile
ASME B5.10-1994 (R2013), Machine Tapers — Self Holding and Steep Taper Series
ASME B46.1-2009, Surface Texture, Surface Roughness, Waviness, and Lay
ASME PDS-1.1–2013, Dimensioning, Tolerancing, Surface Texture, and Metrology Standards - Rules for Drawings With Incomplete Reference to Applicable Drawing Standard
ASME B89.1.10-2013, Dial Indicators for Linear Measurements
ASME B89.1.13-2013, Micrometers
ASME B89.1.14-2018, Calipers
ASME B89.3.7-2013, Granite Surface Plates
ANSI B89.3.1-1972 (R2003), Measurement of Out-of-Roundness
ASME B89.4.10360.2-2008 Acceptance Test and Reverification Test for Coordinate Measuring Machines (CMMs) Part 2: CMMs Used for Measuring Linear Dimensions (Technical Report)
ASME B89.4.21.1 - 2020, Environmental Effects on Coordinate Measuring Machine Measurements [Tech Report]
ASME B89.4.22 - 2004, Methods for Performance Evaluation of Articulated Arm Coordinate Measuring Machines
ASME B89.6.2-1973 (R2017), Temp and Humidity Environment for Dimensional Measurement
ASME B89.7.2-2014 Dimensional Measurement Planning
ASME B89.7.3.1-2001 Considering Measurement Uncertainty for Conform To Specs
ASME B89.7.3.2-2007 Guidelines for Evaluation of Dimensional Measurement Uncertainty

ISO Standards Related to Product Definition and Metrology

ISO-GPS (Geometrical Product Specification) is the system used to define the geometrical requirements of parts in engineering specifications, and the requirements for their verification.

ISO-TPD (Technical Product Documentation) includes standards for technical drawings, model based (3D), computer based (2D) or manually produced for technical purposes.

Below are the notable standards that define general ISO-TPD and ISO-GPS concepts. ISO standards are noted with the ISO number, colon and then year of publication:

ISO 128-1 (TPD) General principles of representation Part 1: Intro and fund requirements
ISO 128-2 (TPD)General principles of representation Part 2: Basic conventions for lines
ISO 128-3 (TPD) General principles of representation Part 3: Views, sections and cuts
ISO 128-100 (TPD) General principles of representation — Part 100: Index
ISO 129-1:2018/AMD 1:2020 (TPD) Presentation of dims and tols Part 1: General principles
ISO 6410-1:1993 (TPD) - Screw threads and threaded parts — Part 1: General conventions
ISO 16792:2015 (TPD)- Digital product definition data practices

ISO 1:2016 Standard temperature for spec of geometrical and dimensional properties
ISO 8015:2011 Fundamentals -- Concepts, principles and rules
ISO 286-1 and ISO 286-2:2010 Tolerance classes and fits
ISO 1101:2017 Geometrical tolerancing -- Tolerances of form, orientation, location, and runout
ISO 1660:2017 Geometrical tolerancing -- Profile tolerancing
ISO 2692:2014 Geometrical tolerancing -- Maximum material requirement (MMR), least material requirement (LMR) and reciprocity requirement (RPR)
ISO 5458:2018 Geometrical tolerancing -- Pattern and combined geometrical specification
ISO 5459:2011 Geometrical tolerancing -- Datums and datum systems (under development)
ISO 2768-1:1989 General tolerances -- Part 1: Tolerances for linear and angular dimensions without individual tolerance indications
ISO 2768-2:1989 General tolerances -- Part 2: Geometrical tolerances for features without individual tolerance indications
ISO 14405-1:2016 Dimensional tolerancing -- Part 1: Linear sizes
ISO 14405-2:2018 Dimensional tolerancing -- Part 2: Dimensions other than linear sizes
ISO 14405-3:2016 Dimensional tolerancing -- Part 3: Angular sizes
ISO 14406:2010 Extraction
ISO 16610-1:2015 (many in this series): Filtration -- Part 1: Overview and basic concepts
ISO 17450-1:2011 General concepts Part 1: Model for geometrical specification and verification
ISO 17450-2:2012 General concepts Part 2: Basic tenets, specifications, operators, uncertainties
ISO 17450-3:2016 General concepts Part 3: Toleranced features
ISO 17450-4:2017 General concepts Part 4: Geometrical characteristics for quantifying GPS deviations

ISO 14638 is the matrix model that provides an overview of the structure of the ISO GPS system. Most of the basic principles and tolerancing concepts are found in ISO 8015 and ISO 17450 but the basic geometric tolerancing principles are in ISO 1101.

There are many other GPS standards that cover inspection of the specifications and measuring equipment not listed here. For a full and current list, www.iso.org/committee/54924/x/catalogue/

Common Symbols

The table below shows dimensioning symbols found on drawings. Note the comparison with the ISO standards. Most symbols have been in Y14.5 since at least 1994. Newer symbols introduced in Y14.5-2009 are indicated with 09 next to them. There were no new symbols in the dimensioning section in Y14.5-2018.

	ASME Term	Symbol	ISO Term	Symbol
	Basic Dimension	[12]	Theoretically Exact Dimension (TED)	[12]
	Reference Dimension	(12)	Auxiliary Dimension	(12)
	Number of Places	3X	Repeated Dimension	3X
	Diameter	Ø	Diameter	Ø
	Radius	R	Radius	R
	Controlled Radius	CR	None	None
	Spherical Diameter	SØ	Spherical Diameter	SØ
	Spherical Radius	SR	Spherical Radius	SR
	Square	□	Square	□
	Counterbore	⌴	Cylindrical Counterbore	⌴
09	Spotface	⌊SF⌋	None	None
	Countersink	⌵	Countersink	⌵
	Depth	↧	Depth	↧
	Arc Length	⌒18	Arc Length	⌒18
	Slope	⌳	Slope	⌳
	Conical Taper	⌲	Conical Taper	⌲
	Dimension Origin	⌖→	Dimension Origin	⌖→
	Dimension not to scale	23 (underlined)	Out-of-scale dimension	23 (underlined)
09	Continuous Feature	⟨CF⟩	Common Tolerance Feature of Size	CT
	Statistical Tolerance	⟨ST⟩	None	None
09	Independency	Ⓘ	None (default)	None
	None (default)	None	Envelope Principle	Ⓔ

Common Symbol Application

Many of the common dimensioning symbols from the chart on the previous page are shown on the drawing below. The symbols are a standard method of describing part geometry and specifying requirements without the use of words. Most of these symbols are used on example drawings throughout this book.

Drawing with practical application of common dimensioning symbols

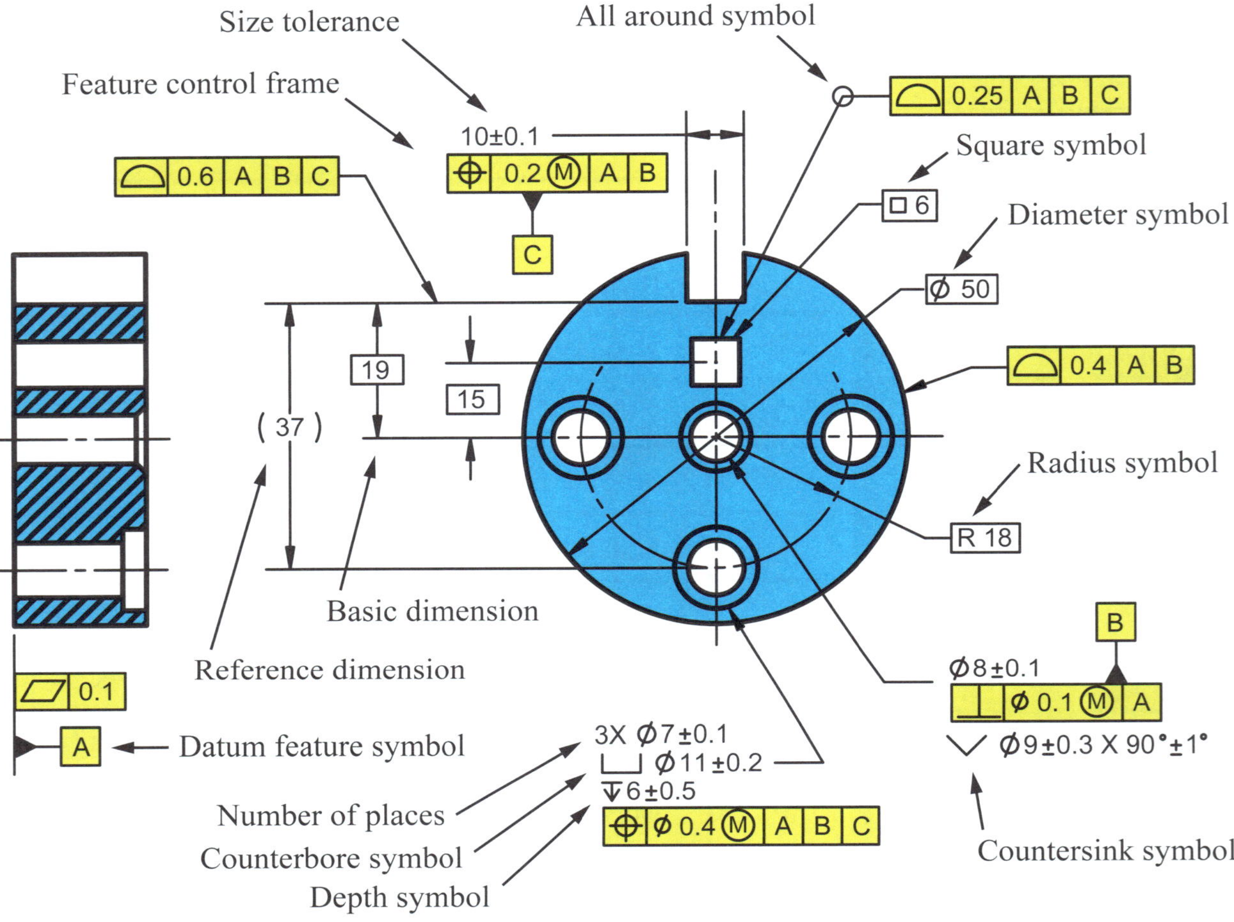

Basic dimensions are theoretically exact and define the perfect geometry of a feature. Reference dimensions are repeats of dimensions or are derived from other values shown on the drawing or related drawings. Reference dimensions are auxiliary information.

Repetitive features, such as holes, may be specified by stating the number of places and an "X". Where used with a basic dimension, the number of places and the X may be placed either inside or outside the basic dimension box. Note the X is also used as "by" when specifying a countersink with diameter 9 by 90 degrees or a slot width 10X20.

The countersink, counterbore, and depth symbols could be defined with normal dimensioning techniques. However, these symbols organize a set of coaxial features on the drawing and make it easier to read.

The details of size tolerance, the datum feature symbol, feature control frame, and basic dimensions will be explained later in this unit.

Millimeter vs. Inch Units

Although the ASME Y14.5 (and most other ASME standards) use millimeter (mm) values for dimensions and tolerances, inches (in) may also be used. On drawings where all dimensions are in millimeters or all dimensions are in inches, individual identification of linear units is not required. However, the drawing shall contain a note stating UNLESS OTHERWISE SPECIFIED, ALL DIMENSIONS ARE IN MILLIMETERS (or IN INCHES, as applicable). This book will use a variety of both units in examples because of the wide range of industry audience. The book will adhere to the following rules set by section 4.3 of Y14.5 when switching units:

Millimeter Dimensioning

(a) Where the dimension is less than 1 mm, a zero shall precede the decimal point.	0.5 not .5
(b) Where the dimension is a whole number, neither the decimal point nor a zero shall be shown	12 not 12.0
(c) Where the dimension exceeds a whole number by a decimal fraction of 1 mm, the last digit to the right of the decimal point shall not be followed by a zero.	0.5 not 0.500
NOTE: This practice differs for tolerances expressed bilaterally or as limits.	$\varnothing 12^{+0.25}_{-0.10}$ $\varnothing\begin{matrix}12.25\\11.90\end{matrix}$

Inch Dimensioning

(a) A zero shall not be used before the decimal point for values less than 1 in.	.5 or .500 not 0.5
(b) A dimension shall be expressed to the same number of decimal places as its tolerance. Zeros are added to the right of the decimal point where necessary.	.500±.005 not .50±.005

The tolerancing "lingo"

Tolerances are often small values with a lot of zeros in front. It can be difficult to speak about these numbers quickly. Here are a few semi-standard ways to talk about these numbers:

.005 inch "point-zero-zero-five" can instead be said as "five thousandths" or "five thou"

.020 inch "twenty thousandths" or "twenty thou"

.0002 inch "two ten-thousandths" or "two tenths"

Inch values are expressed in thousandths of an inch (not tenths or hundredths)

Note: in some industries .005 is expressed as "5 mills" This comes from the prefix "milli-" which refers to thousandths of something (5 milli-inches). However, mills often gets mixed up with millimeters and is not recommended. Paint thickness and coatings are still often expressed in "mills".

0.005 mm "zero-point-zero-zero-five" can instead be said as "five microns"

0.02 mm "twenty microns"

A micron is short for a micrometer. This is only necessary when the tolerances get small enough that the number of zeros makes them hard to say. Note that this "lingo" is not documented in Y14.5 but rather is "shop talk" and slang that could be helpful to know.

Tolerances in Perspective

Tolerances values on engineering drawings can be very small and difficult to keep in perspective. Small tolerances can be compared to germs. Our parents always told us to wash our hands to stay free of germs so we don't get sick. But when we look at our hands, we do not see any germs. Tolerances are also often small and not visible with the naked eye. Holding a machined part, the surfaces look flat and square, but if you view the parts with precise inspection equipment such as micrometers, dial indicators, or CMMs, you would find that there are differences from the dimensions on the drawing and from one manufactured part to the next. The engineer designs the parts with perfect geometry in CAD, but the produced parts are never perfect. To understand geometric tolerancing, you must think of all parts being imperfect to some degree.

The produced parts shown in this book are drawn with exaggerated error, to help the user understand how to match perfect tolerance zones with the imperfect geometry of the part. Some form of imagination is required when visualizing these small tolerances.

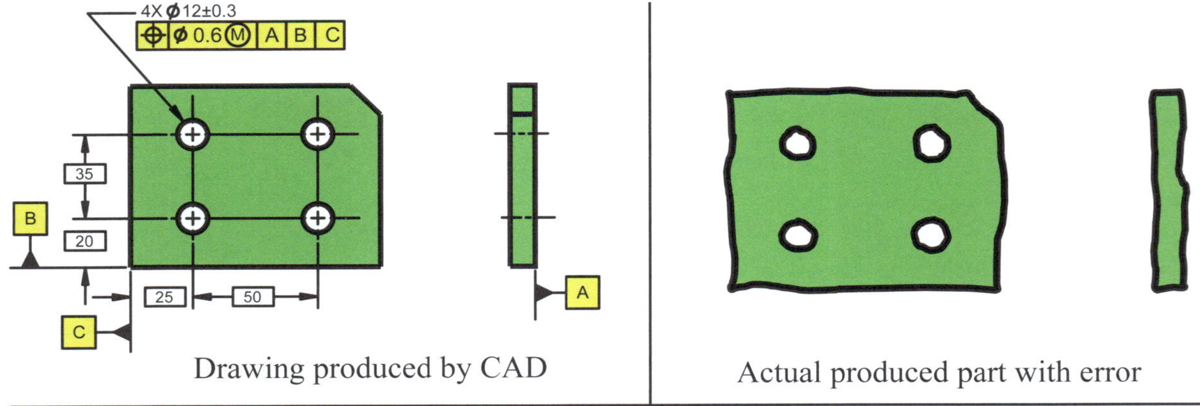

The illustration below provides a perspective of tolerance values with a magnified whisker from a common house cat. Note that a flatness tolerance of .001 inch (0.025 mm) is holding the surface to a tolerance of one quarter the size of the whisker. These tight tolerances are often necessary, but important to keep in perspective.

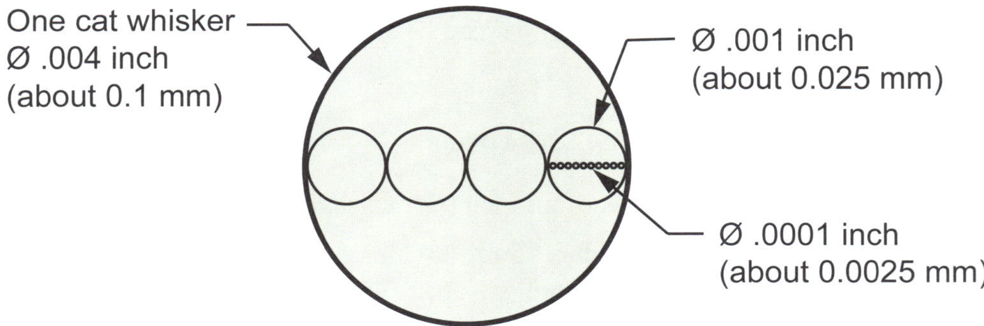

Small tolerances can increase cost in the manufacture, inspection and tooling of parts. Tooling tolerances are generally 30% of part tolerances, and quality strives for measurement uncertainties of 10% of part tolerances. Tolerances applied to the design push even tighter requirements through the manufacturing and verification process. The two goals of a designer: allow tolerances as large as possible while preserving the function of the part.

Features of Size and Features without Size

Geometric tolerancing is a feature based system. A feature is a general term applied to a physical portion of a part such as a surface, pin, tab, hole or slot. Parts are composed of many features.

There are two types of features: Features of size and features without size (surfaces). This is an important distinction in geometric tolerancing.

Examples of features without size: (Surfaces)

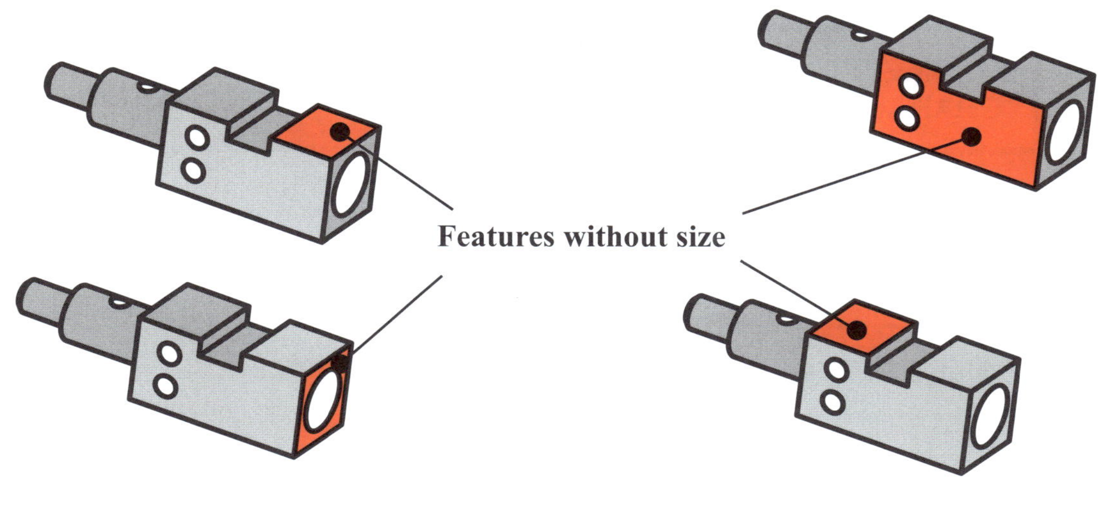

Examples of features of size

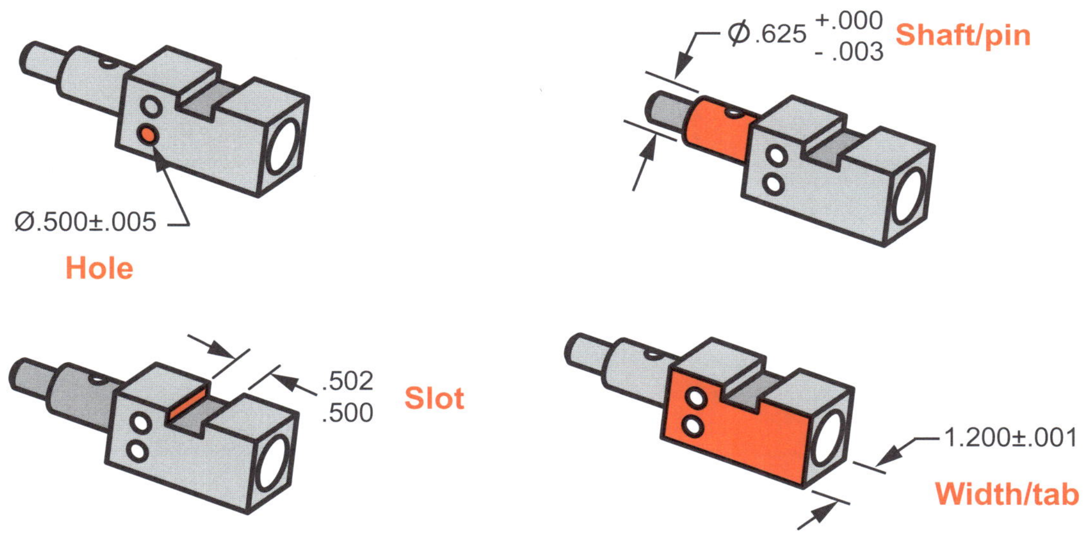

Regular features of size are usually controlled with a size tolerance and have an easily determined axis or median plane (through the unrelated actual mating envelope).

Geometric Tolerancing Characteristic Symbols

There are 12 geometric tolerancing characteristics with the corresponding symbols shown below. These symbols are placed in the first compartment of a feature control frame and define the geometry characteristic of the feature that is to be controlled.

The characteristics are grouped into four types of tolerance: form, orientation, location, and runout. The general primary control with a few notes is also shown. This is only a quick summary and a more complete definition can be found later in the text.

SYMBOL	GEOMETRIC CHARACTERISTIC	TYPE OF TOLERANCE	PRIMARY CONTROL
⏥	FLATNESS	Form	Controls shape of a surface or feature of size Datum feature reference not allowed Does not control relationship between features
—	STRAIGHTNESS		
⌭	CYLINDRICITY		
○	CIRCULARITY		
⊥	PERPENDICULARITY	Orientation	Controls tilt/angle of a surface or feature of size Datum feature reference required *Optional: Angularity symbol may be used for all orientation controls*
//	PARALLELISM		
∠	ANGULARITY		
⌖	POSITION	Location	Locates features of size Also controls orientation
⌓	PROFILE OF A SURFACE		Locates surfaces Also controls form and orientation Can also control size
⌒	PROFILE OF A LINE		
⌰	TOTAL RUNOUT	Runout	Centers a surface of revolution around a datum axis Also controls form and orientation
↗	CIRCULAR RUNOUT		

Note: Geometric characteristic symbols of concentricity and symmetry were removed in ASME Y14.5-2018. See unit 13 for more explanation.

Feature Control Frame

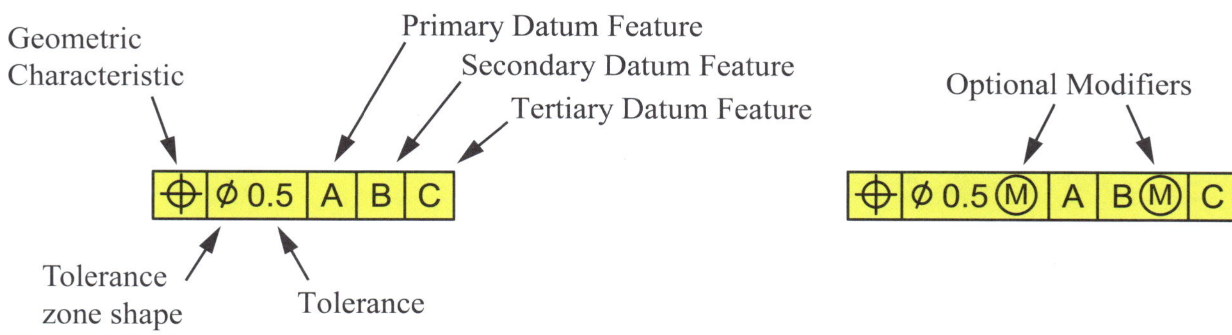

The feature control frame (in ASME) or tolerance indicator (in ISO) is the symbolic means of expressing the tolerance requirements for a feature or set of features. The frame is divided into rectangular compartments:

The first compartment contains one of the 12 geometric characteristic symbols.

There can never be more than one of these symbols in one frame. Multiple feature control frames or a composite tolerance are used for multiple requirements.

The second compartment contains the shape of the tolerance zone followed by the tolerance.

The default tolerance zone shape (without a symbol) is parallel planes/total wide zone. A diameter symbol (Ø), or spherical diameter symbol (SØ) may be added to change the tolerance zone to a cylindrical or spherical shaped zone.

The tolerance is expressed as a total value and never a plus/minus.

Modifiers may be added behind the tolerance value. These modifiers can be MMC, LMC, projected tolerance zone, free state, tangent plane, statistical tolerance, unequally disposed profile, and dynamic profile. See later units for detailed explanations.

The third, fourth, and fifth compartments contain the datum feature reference(s) to create the datum reference frame. Depending on the specification, these compartments are not always necessary.

The alphabetical order of the datum references has no significance but rather the order of precedence reading from left to right as primary, secondary and tertiary. These compartments define the datum reference frame and represent the constraints for the tolerance zone. See unit 4 for detailed explanations.

Modifiers for the datum features may be added behind each datum feature letter. These modifiers can be MMB, LMB, [BSC], and translation. See unit 7 for detailed explanations.

Other aspects of the feature control frame contain other information about the tolerance.

The tolerance controls the surface when the frame is attached to the surface thru extension lines or leader lines. The tolerance controls the axis, center plane, or center point of the feature when the frame is placed under the size tolerance.

Features may be grouped into a pattern with notations nX, INDICATED, multiple leader lines, all around symbol, or all over symbol. Symbols of "between" or "from-to" may be used to indicate the extent of the control. See units 11 and 12 for detailed explanations.

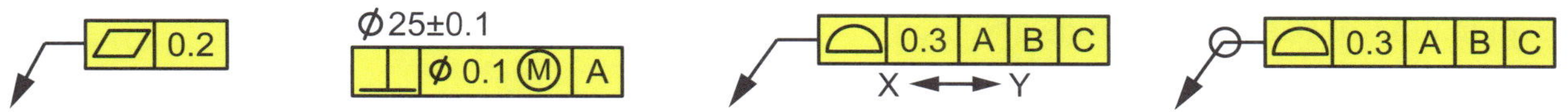

Geometric Tolerance Zone Shapes

A feature control frame creates a geometrically shaped **tolerance zone** within which the feature must lie. The tolerance zones may be a variety of shapes usually defined by the geometric characteristic in the first compartment and other symbology in the second compartment. The tolerance zone may or may not be constrained relative to a datum reference frame. While 3D tolerance zones are the most common, 2D tolerance zones may also be used for cross-sectional control of a feature.

Common tolerance zone shapes:

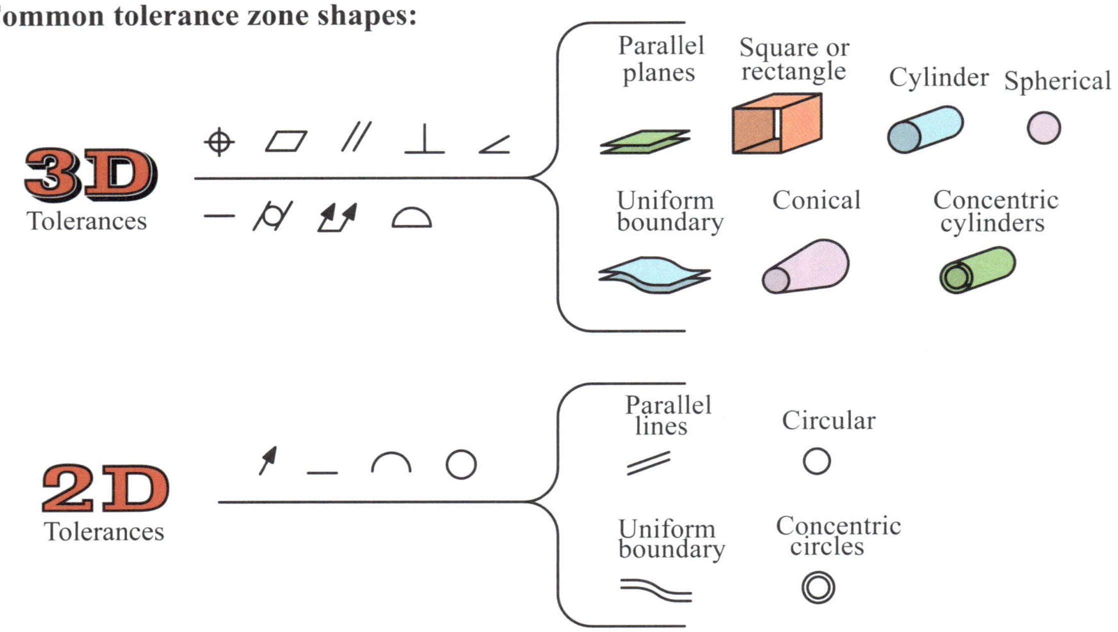

3D Tolerances

Parallel planes, Square or rectangle, Cylinder, Spherical, Uniform boundary, Conical, Concentric cylinders

2D Tolerances

Parallel lines, Circular, Uniform boundary, Concentric circles

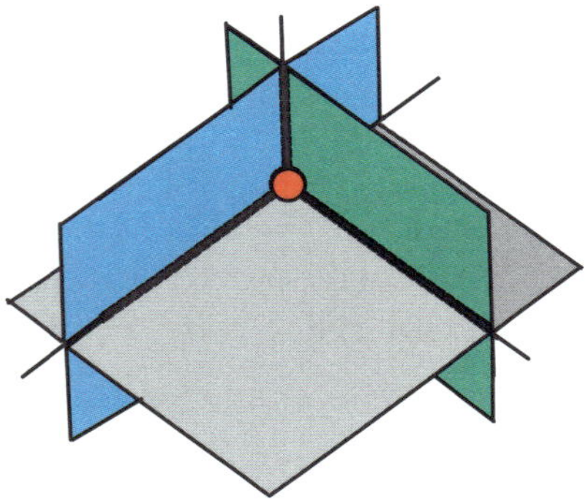

The **Datum Reference Frame** is a coordinate system used to constrain tolerance zones and establish the origin of measurement. All basic dimensions will be defined from this datum reference frame.

Basic Dimensions (in ASME) or Theoretically Exact Dimensions (in ISO)

Basic dimensions are theoretically exact dimensions used to define the perfect location of a feature. Dimensions are indicated as basic dimensions by a rectangular box around the value or by a general note on the drawing such as: ALL DIMENSIONS ARE BASIC. The default tolerances (±) stated in the title block of a drawing do not apply to basic dimensions. There will be more explanation of basic dimensions and their use in unit 3.

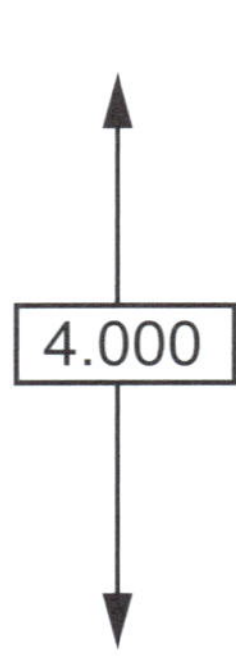

Geometric Tolerance Categories

Geometric tolerancing is a feature-based tolerancing system and the tolerances are divided into three main types: form, orientation, and location.

Form tolerances control the "shape" of a feature (to itself) and are often used as a refinement of size.

Orientation tolerances control the "tilt/angle" of a feature to a datum reference frame and are associated with basic angle dimensions. They are often used as a refinement to location. If applied to surfaces, orientation tolerances also control form.

Location tolerances control location/distance of features to each other or to a datum reference frame and are associated with basic linear dimensions.

Position locates the center plane or axis of a feature of size. Position also controls orientation.

Profile locates a surface. Profile also controls orientation and form. It can also control size.

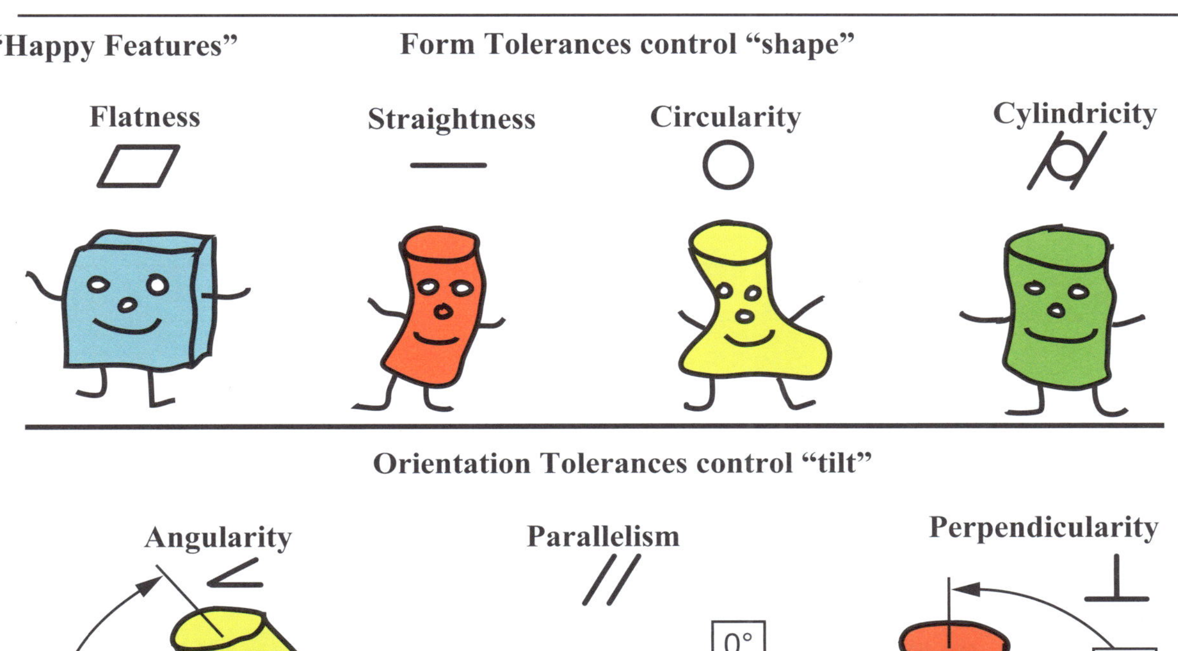

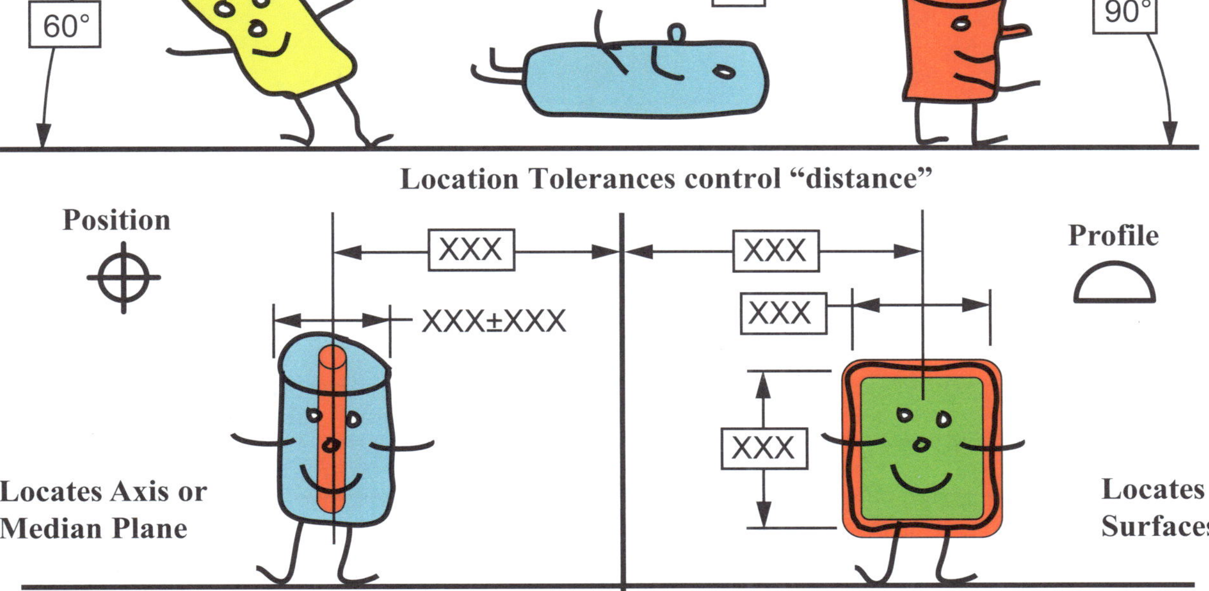

Symbols associated with a Feature Control Frame

The table below lists symbols that may be placed inside or associated with a feature control frame. It also compares terms and symbols with the ISO-GPS standards. Most symbols have been in Y14.5 since at least 1994. Symbols with 09 next to them were first introduced in Y14.5-2009. Symbols with 18 were first introduced in Y14.5-2018.

	ASME Term	ASME Symbol	ISO Term	ISO Symbol
09	Maximum Material Condition (MMC) (when applied to a tolerance) Maximum Material Boundary (MMB) (when applied to a datum reference)	Ⓜ	Maximum Material Requirement (MMR)	Ⓜ
09	Least Material Condition (LMC) (when applied to a tolerance) Least Material Boundary (LMB) (when applied to a datum reference)	Ⓛ	Least Material Requirement (LMR)	Ⓛ
	Diameter	⌀	Diameter	⌀
	Spherical diameter	S⌀	Spherical diameter	S⌀
	Projected tolerance zone	Ⓟ	Projected tolerance zone	Ⓟ
	Free state	Ⓕ	Free state condition	Ⓕ
	Tangent plane	Ⓣ	Tangent feature	Ⓣ
09	Translation	▷	(default) Distance variable	[DV]
09	Unequally disposed profile	Ⓤ	Specified tolerance zone offset	UZ
18	Dynamic profile	Δ	Unspecified tolerance zone offset	OZ
	All around	↙○—	All around	↙○—
09	All over	↙◎—	All over	↙◎—
	Between	↔	Between	↔
18	From-to	→	None (proposed)	None
	Major diameter	MAJOR	Major Diameter	[MD]
	Minor diameter	MINOR	Minor Diameter	[LD]
	Pitch diameter	PITCH	Pitch Diameter	[PD]
	None	None	Combined zone	CZ
	None (default)	None	United feature	UF
	None	None	Orientation only constraint	><
	None	None	Any cross-section	ACS

Note: There are many more modifiers in ISO-GPS standards. This list shows equivalent concepts with ASME Y14.5 plus a few other notable symbols. See the appendix on ISO differences.

Symbols Related To Datum Feature Identification

This table identifies terms and symbols that are associated with establishing datums from datum features. A more complete definition and description of each these specifications can be found later in units 4 and 8. The movable datum target symbol marked with 09 was new for the ASME Y14.5-2009 standard.

TERM	SYMBOL ASME Y14.5	SYMBOL ISO
Datum Feature	 A	 A
Datum Feature ANSI Y14.5M-1982 (former standard)	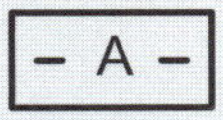 - A -	None
Datum Target	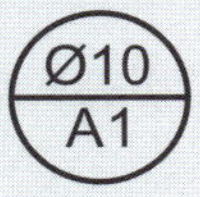 Ø10 A1	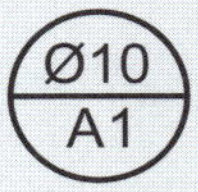 Ø10 A1
Datum Target Point	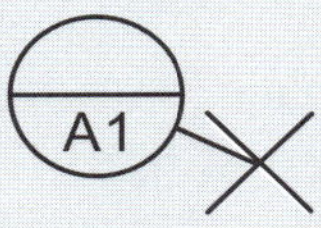 A1	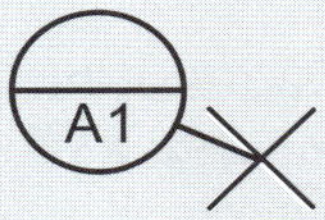 A1
Datum Target Line	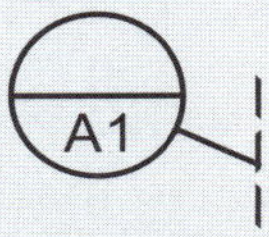 A1	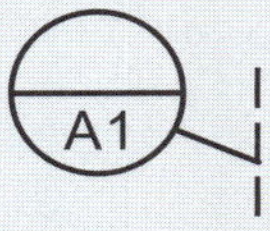 A1
Datum Target Area	 Ø20 A1	 Ø20 A1
09 Movable Datum Target	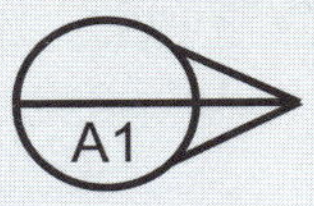 A1	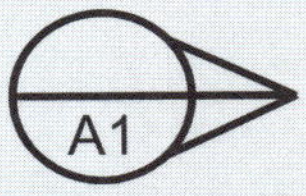 A1
Dimension Origin		

Index Plate - Practical Example

The establishment of a Datum Reference Frame (DRF) and geometric tolerances are based on functional design requirements. An index assembly is shown below. The top index plate clamps on its face and is centered by the pilot pin. The plate is rotationally aligned with the side planar surface and secured with three screws. Study the functional requirements below.

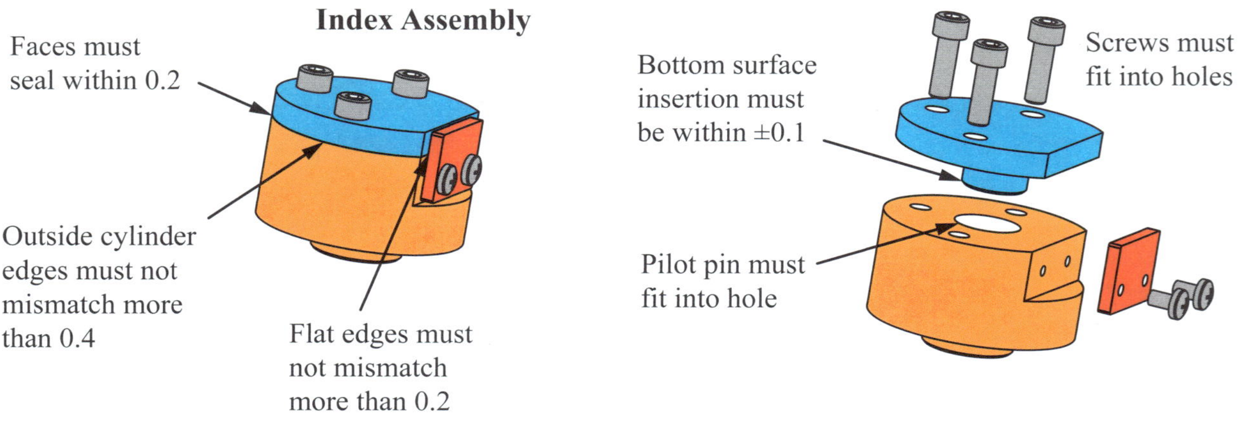

The ABC DRF is established from datum features based on mating conditions.

The primary datum feature A is the large planar face, and its form is qualified with a flatness.

The secondary datum feature B is the pilot pin, and its orientation relationship to datum A is controlled with a perpendicularity tolerance.

The tertiary datum feature C is the planar surface to stop rotation and its location relationship to AB is controlled with a profile tolerance of 0.2 for the mismatch with the mating part.

The three holes are given a size tolerance and position of 0.4 to the ABC DRF to align with the mating tapped holes and accept the screws.

The top surface of the pilot pin is located with a profile tolerance of 0.2 for the insertion depth requirement. The outside diameter surface is located with a profile tolerance of 0.4 for the mismatch on the outside edges. The last surface is toleranced with large profile tolerance of 0.6 because it is relatively unimportant.

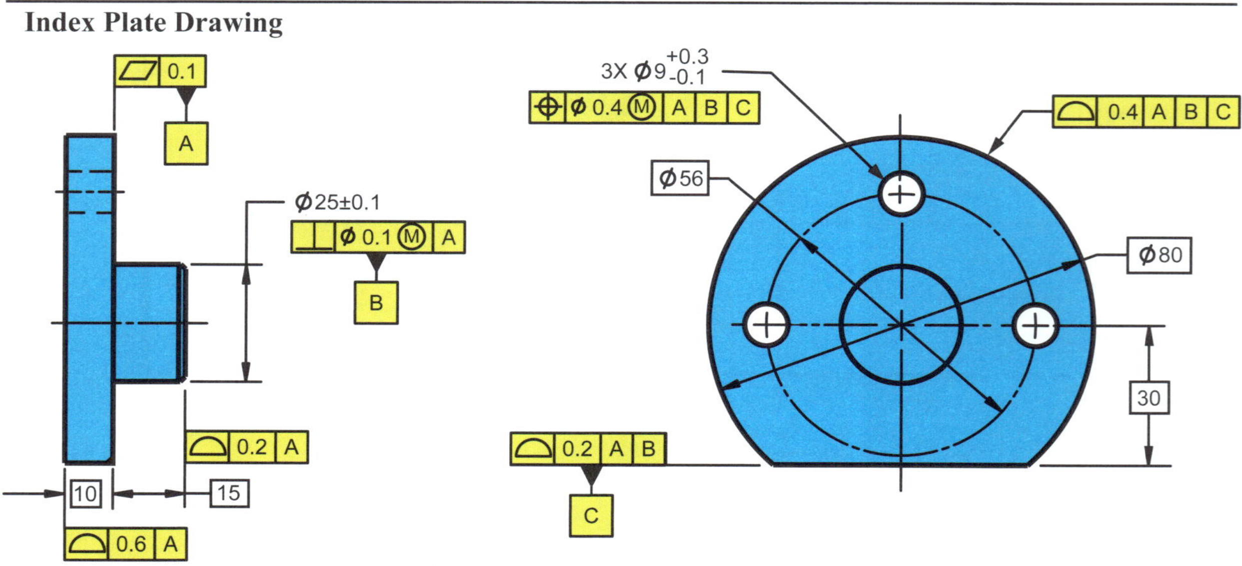

Index Plate - Matching a Perfect DRF to an Imperfect Part

The produced index plate is shown below with exaggerated variation from manufacturing. The perfect geometry of the DRF, true geometric counterparts and tolerance zones are mated to the imperfect geometry of the produced part. The construction of the DRF and corresponding terminology is shown below. This example is only meant to be an initial introdcution to the subject. More detail on the establishment of a DRF and these terms can be found later in unit 4.

Establishment of ABC DRF on the produced index plate.

Datum A is a perfect plane established by the high points of datum feature A. Measurements originate from this plane.
Datum Feature A is the imperfect surface on the part. Variations of the feature are controlled with a flatness tolerance.
Datum Feature B is the imperfect pilot dia on the part. Its axis is oriented to datum plane A with a perpendicularity tolerance.
True Geometric Counterpart (TGC) B (related actual mating envelope) is the smallest circumscribed cylinder perpendicular to datum plane A that contacts the high points of datum feature B.
Datum B (Related) is the axis of the TGC. This is the axis of the AB DRF. Measurements originate from this axis.
Feature Axis is the axis of the **unrelated actual mating envelope**. The unrelated AME is the smallest circumscribed cylinder unrelated to any datums.
0.1
Flatness tolerance zone
Perpendicularity Tolerance Zone is a 0.1 cylindrical tolerance zone that is perpendicular to datum plane A. The feature axis must fall within this zone.
30
0.2 Profile tolerance zone locates the surface.
Datum Feature C is the imperfect planar surface on the part. It is located to the AB DRF with a profile tolerance.
True Geometric Counterpart C is a perfect plane perpendicular to datum plane A that progresses towards datum B axis to make maximum contact with datum feature C and constrain rotation. This plane sets the orientation planes of the DRF around datum axis B.
0.2 Profile tolerance zone locates the surface relative to datum A.
15
Datum A

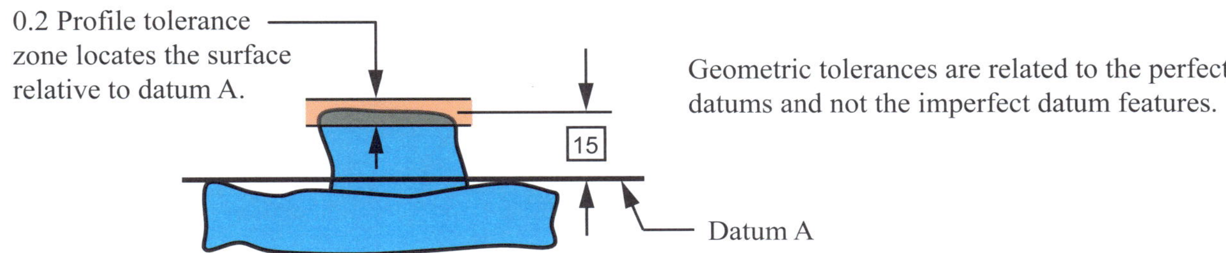

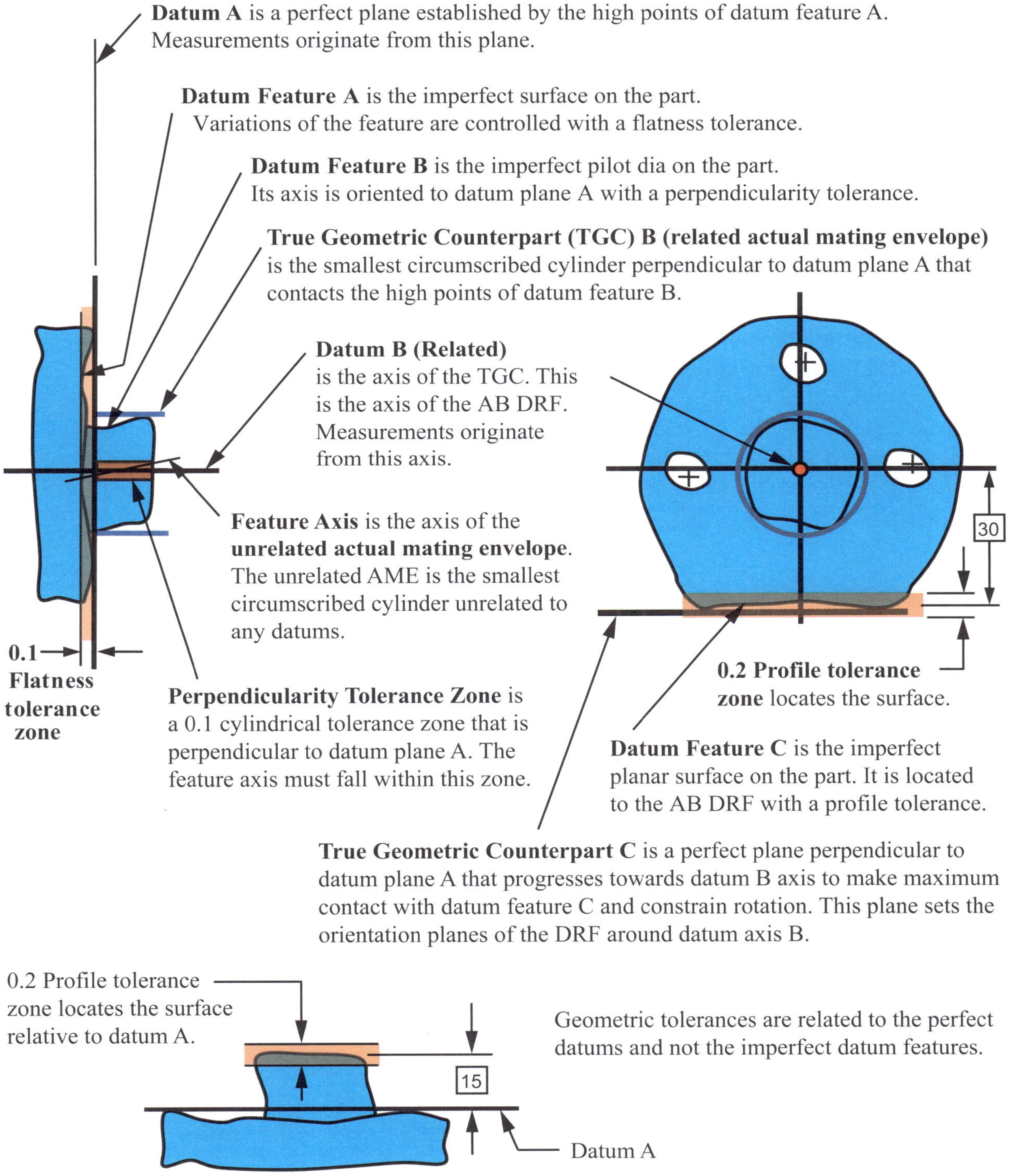

Geometric tolerances are related to the perfect datums and not the imperfect datum features.

Index Plate - Practical Example in 3D

3X ∅9 +0.3 -0.1
∅ 0.4 Ⓜ A B C
0.1
A
∅25±0.1
∅ 0.1 Ⓜ A
B
0.4 A B C
0.6 A
0.2 A B
C
0.2 A

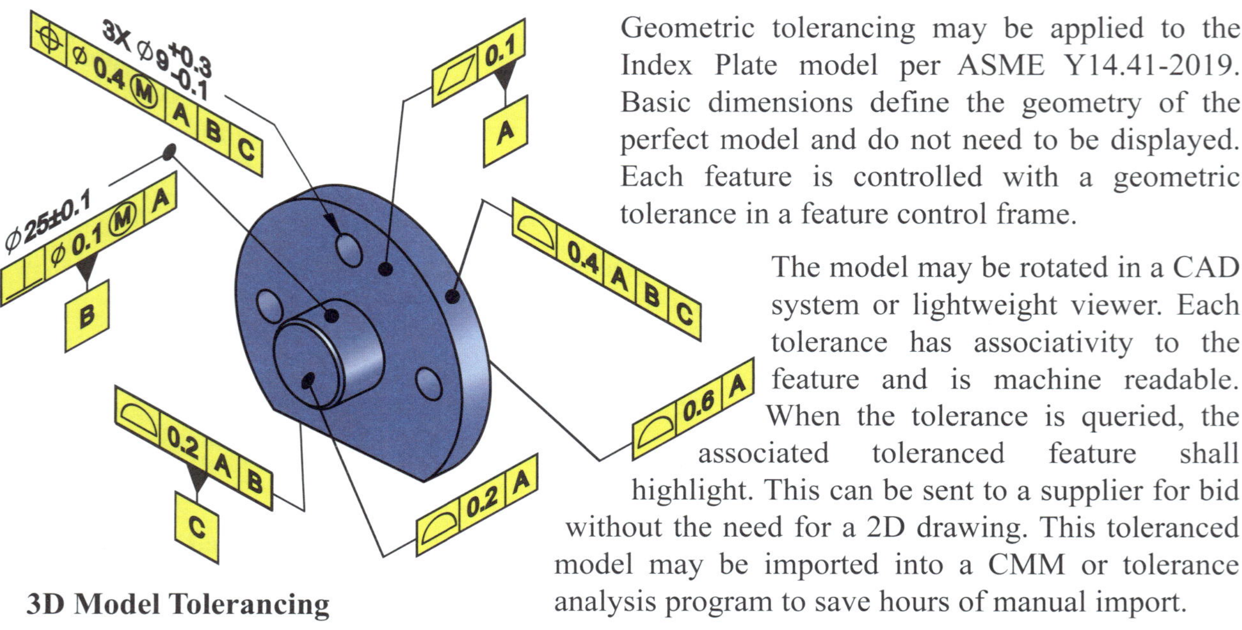

3D Model Tolerancing

Geometric tolerancing may be applied to the Index Plate model per ASME Y14.41-2019. Basic dimensions define the geometry of the perfect model and do not need to be displayed. Each feature is controlled with a geometric tolerance in a feature control frame.

The model may be rotated in a CAD system or lightweight viewer. Each tolerance has associativity to the feature and is machine readable. When the tolerance is queried, the associated toleranced feature shall highlight. This can be sent to a supplier for bid without the need for a 2D drawing. This toleranced model may be imported into a CMM or tolerance analysis program to save hours of manual import.

Features are the building blocks of a part, and GeoTol is a feature-based tolerancing system. The variation on these surfaces, holes, pins, slots are controlled with size and geometric tolerances. Three features are selected as datum features (A,B,C) that constrain the part and create a datum reference frame. Other features are located to this DRF with position and profile tolerances.

Every feature shall have a tolerance.

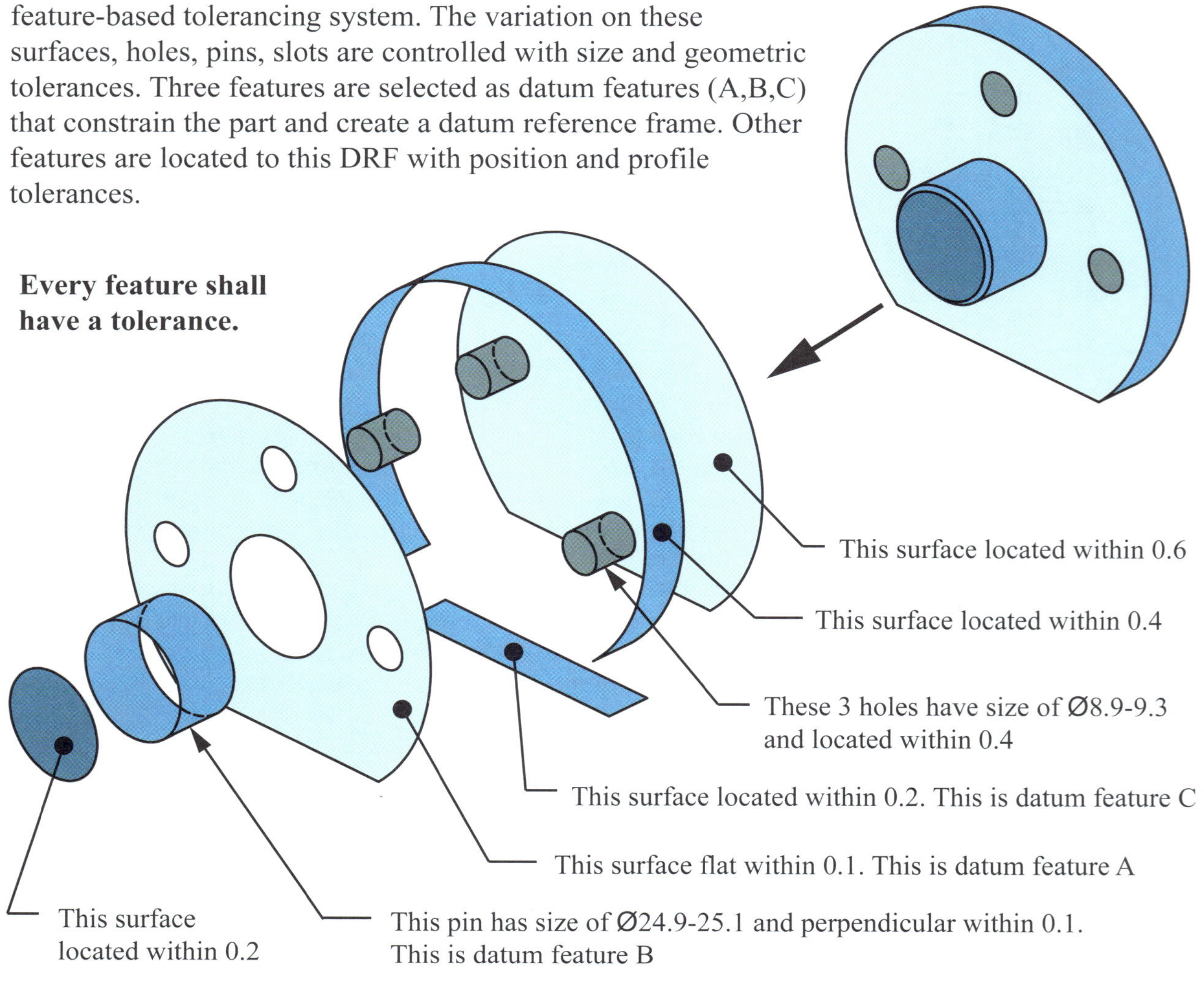

This surface located within 0.6
This surface located within 0.4
These 3 holes have size of Ø8.9-9.3 and located within 0.4
This surface located within 0.2. This is datum feature C
This surface flat within 0.1. This is datum feature A
This surface located within 0.2
This pin has size of Ø24.9-25.1 and perpendicular within 0.1. This is datum feature B

Definitions

The definitions below are terms used in this text and the ASME Y14.5-2018 standard.

Feature - A physical portion of a part such as a surface, pin, hole, or slot or its representation on drawings, models, or digital data files.

Feature Axis - The axis of the unrelated actual mating envelope of a feature.

Feature Center Plane - The center plane of the unrelated actual mating envelope of a feature.

Actual Mating Envelope (AME) - A similar perfect feature(s) counterpart of smallest size that can be contracted about an external feature(s) or of largest size that can be expanded within an internal feature(s) so that it coincides with the surface(s) at the highest points. This envelope is on or outside the material. There are two types of AMEs, as described below.

a. **Unrelated Actual Mating Envelope** (Unrelated AME) - A similar perfect feature(s) counterpart expanded within an in internal feature(s) or contracted about an external feature(s) and **not constrained** to any datum(s).

b. **Related Actual Mating Envelope** (related AME) - A similar perfect feature(s) counterpart expanded within an in internal feature(s) or contracted about an external feature(s) **while constrained** either in orientation or location or both to the applicable datum(s).

Geometric tolerances applied to a hole or pin at MMC or RFS control the feature axis.

The feature's axis is established from the unrelated actual mating envelope (largest inscribed cylinder for a hole)

The related AME is the orientation constrained or location constrained mating envelope. This term is used to explain other concepts including the establishment of secondary and tertiary datums, also in the evaluation of the MMB boundaries. See unit 4 and unit 7.

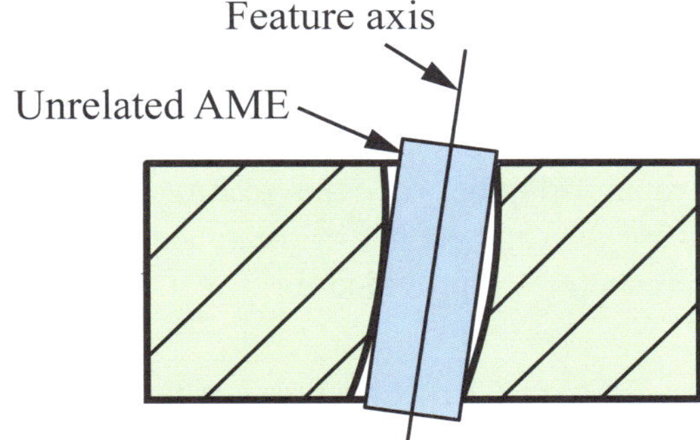

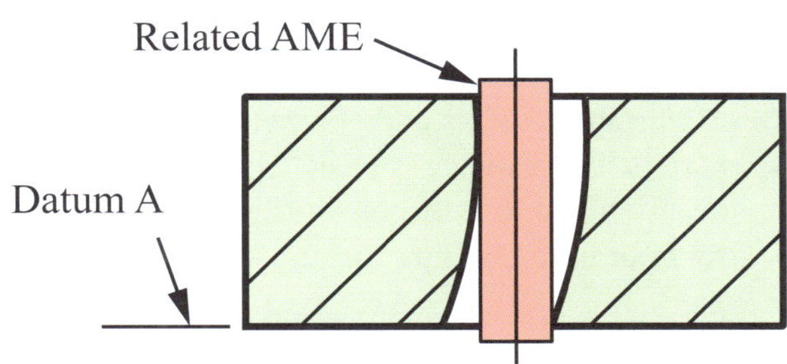

Note: Geometric tolerances with LMC modifiers control the axis of the **unrelated actual minimum material envelope**. This is a similar perfect feature(s) counterpart contracted about an internal feature(s) or expanded within an external feature(s), and not constrained to any datums. See unit 3 for more information.

Note: Straightness of a median line controls the derived median line and not the axis. Flatness of a median plane controls the median plane and not the center plane. See unit 10.

Fundamental Rules

Section 4.1 of Y14.5-2018 defines fundamental rules of dimensioning and tolerancing. Most of the rules are carry overs from the 2009 version with small updates/clarifications to include model based practices. Rules (q) and (s) are new for 2018. The statements below represent a shorter list of the most notable rules with some truncated for clarity. See Y14.5-2018 for the full list:

(a) Each feature shall be toleranced. Tolerances may be applied directly to size dimensions. Tolerances shall be applied using feature control frames when feature definition is basic. Tolerances may also be indicated by a note or located in a block of the drawing format.

(b) Dimensioning and tolerancing shall be complete so there is full understanding of the characteristics of each feature. Values may be expressed in an engineering drawing or in a CAD definition data set.

(c) Each necessary dimension of an end product shall be shown or defined by model data. No more dimensions than those necessary for complete definition shall be given. The use of reference dimensions on a drawing should be minimized.

(d) Dimensions shall be selected and arranged to suit the function and mating relationship of a part and shall not be subject to more than one interpretation.

(e) The drawing should define a part without specifying manufacturing methods. Thus, only the diameter of a hole is given without indicating whether it is to be drilled, reamed, punched, or made by another operation. However, in those instances where manufacturing, information is essential to the definition of engineering requirements, the information shall be specified.

(h) Dimensions in orthographic views should be shown in true profile views and refer to visible outlines. When dimensions are shown in models, the dimensions shall be applied in a manner that shows the true value.

(j) An implied 90° angle shall apply where center lines and lines depicting features are shown on orthographic views at right angles and no angle is specified. The applicable tolerance is the same as for all other angular features shown on the field of the drawing governed by general angular tolerance notes or general tolerance block values.

(k) An implied 90° basic angle shall apply where center lines of features or surfaces shown at right angles on an orthographic view are located or defined by basic dimensions and no angle is specified. The applicable tolerance(s) are provided by a feature control frame or note that governs the orientation of features.

(l) A zero basic dimension shall apply where axes, center planes, or surfaces are shown coincident on orthographic views and geometric tolerances establish the relationship between the features. On CAD models, the distance is basic when queried model distances are zero and geometric tolerances establish the relationship between the features. The applicable tolerance(s) are provided by a feature control frame or note that governs the location of features.

(m) UOS, all dimensions and tolerances are applicable at 20°C (68°F) in accordance with ASME B89.6.2. Compensation may be made for measurements made at other temperatures.

(n) UOS, all dimensions and tolerances apply in a free state condition.

(o) UOS, all tolerances and datum features apply for full depth, length, and width of the feature.

(p) Dimensions and tolerances apply only at the drawing level where they are specified. A dimension specified for a given feature on one level of drawing (e.g., a detail drawing) is not mandatory for that feature at any other level (e.g., an assembly drawing).

(q) UOS by a drawing/model note or reference to a separate document, the as-designed dimension value does not establish a functional or manufacturing target.

(s) UOS, elements of a surface include surface texture and flaws (e.g., burrs and scratches). All elements of a surface shall be within the applicable specified tolerance zone boundaries.

Material Conditions - MMC and LMC

Features of size (such as holes, slots, tabs and pins) have size tolerance that allow them to be large or small within the tolerance limits. There is often a need to refer to a feature at a specific size limit. Maximum Material Condition (MMC) and Least Material Condition (LMC) are terms for the worst-case size limits of a hole, pin, slot, or width.

Maximum Material Condition (MMC) - The condition where the feature contains the maximum material within the stated limits of size. For example: **the smallest hole or biggest pin.**

Least Material Condition (LMC) - The condition where the feature contains the least material within the stated limits of size. For example: **the smallest pin or biggest hole.**

MMC and LMC examples:

The MMC and LMC is shown for each feature of size.

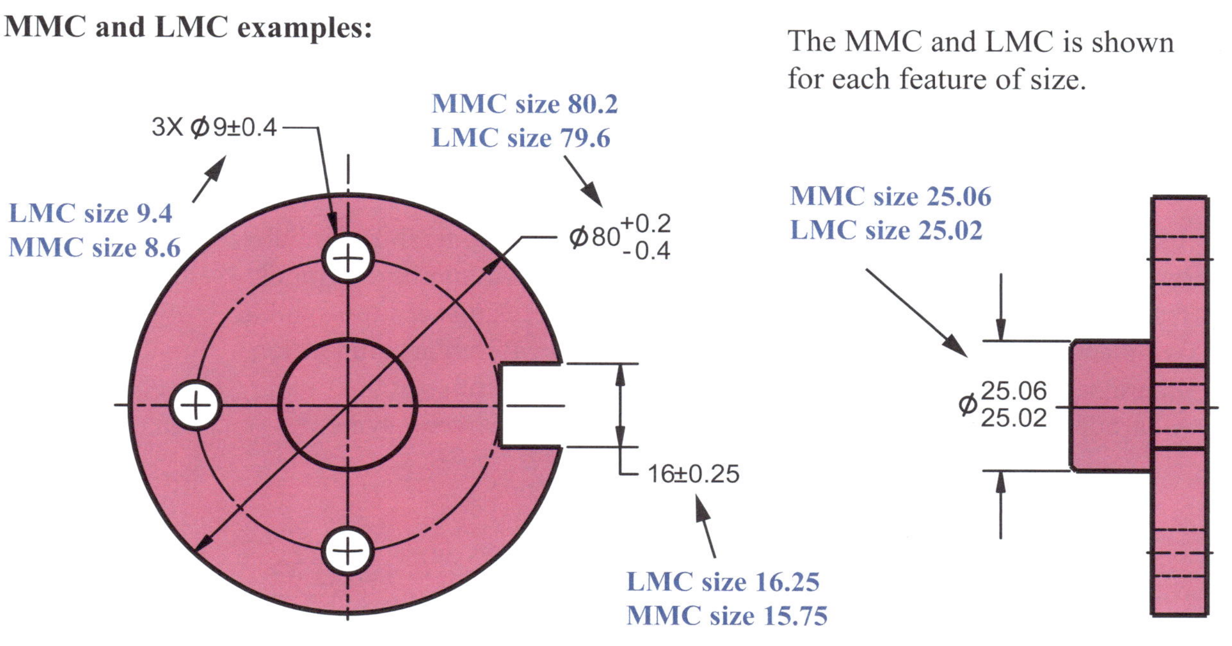

Limit vs. Unilateral vs Bilateral Tolerancing

The size tolerance of a Ø15 mm or Ø.500 inch hole may displayed in a variety of ways shown below. Each of these display methods has the same meaning with two worst case limits of MMC and LMC. It is a matter of preference which display method is used.

	Limit		Bilateral Equal	Bilateral Unequal	Unilateral
mm	Ø$^{15.3}_{14.9}$	Ø14.9-15.3	Ø15.1±0.2	Ø15$^{+0.3}_{-0.1}$	Ø14.9$^{+0.4}_{0}$
inch	Ø$^{.504}_{.500}$	Ø.500-.504	Ø.500±.002	Ø.501$^{+.003}_{-.001}$	Ø.500$^{+.004}_{-.000}$

Note: the term nominal is sometimes confused in these designations. From ASME Y14.5-2018: *Nominal size: the designation used for purposes of general identification. (USAS B4.1).*

Therfore, any number between .500 to .504 could be called the nominal size of the hole above.

Also note rule (q) from the fundamental rules: *UOS, the as-designed dimension value does not establish a functional or manufacturing target.*

Workshop Exercise 1.1

1. What is the name and date of the latest American National Standard on dimensioning and tolerancing?

2. What is the name and date of the latest American National Standard on mathematical definitions of dimensioning and tolerancing?

3. What is the name and date of the latest American National Standard on certification of dimensioning and tolerancing professionals?

4. In ISO, there are many documents that cover geometric tolerancing. What is the number and date of the ISO standard that covers the generalities of geometric tolerancing? Tolerancing of form, orientation, location and runout?

On the drawing below, find and label the following symbols.

5. Feature control frame
6. Radius symbol
7. Basic dimension
8. Two places designation
9. Square symbol
10. All around symbol
11. Countersink symbol
12. Counterbore symbol
13. Datum feature symbol
14. Reference dimension
15. Depth symbol
16. Diameter symbol

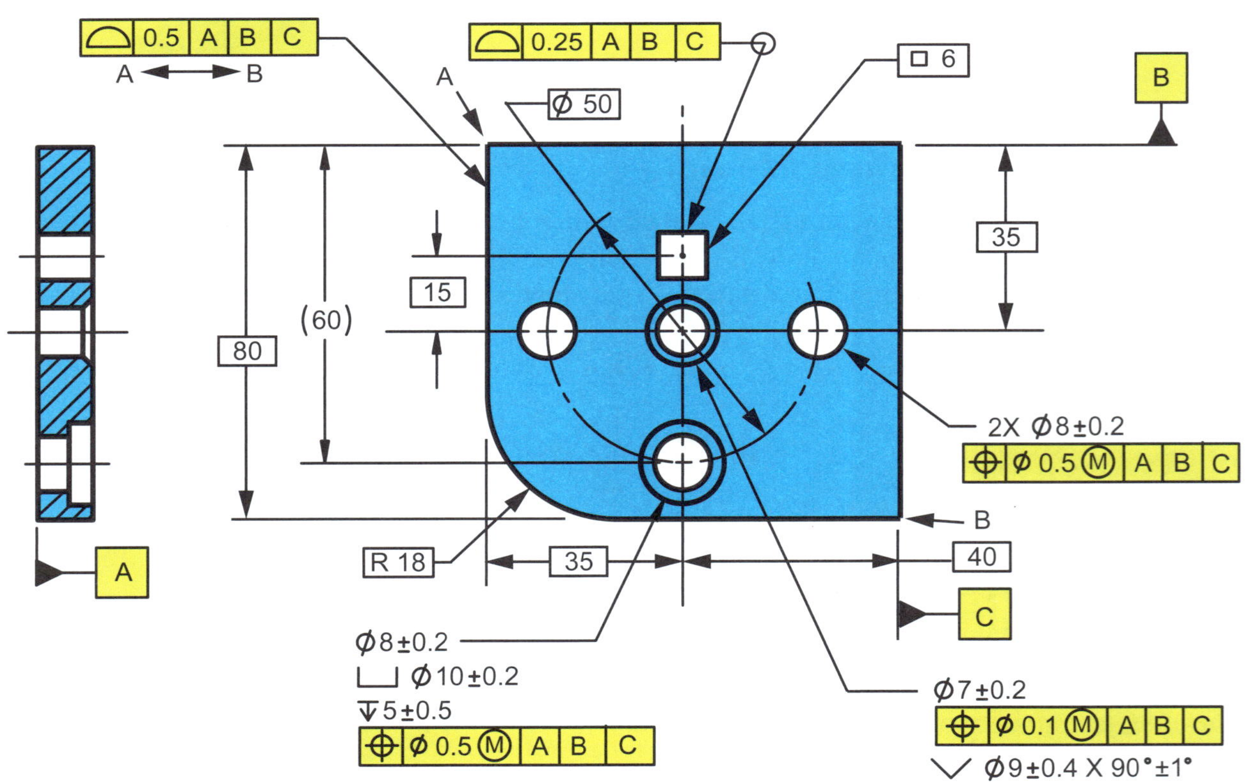

Workshop Exercise 1.1

17. In the table below, sketch the proper symbol next to the geometric characteristic term. Select from the symbols shown below. Also, identify the type of tolerance such as: form, orientation, location, and runout.

SYMBOL	GEOMETRIC CHARACTERISTIC	TYPE OF TOLERANCE
	FLATNESS	
	STRAIGHTNESS	
	CYLINDRICITY	
	CIRCULARITY	
	PERPENDICULARITY	
	PARALLELISM	
	ANGULARITY	
	POSITION	
	PROFILE OF A SURFACE	
	PROFILE OF A LINE	
	TOTAL RUNOUT	
	CIRCULAR RUNOUT	

Workshop Exercise 1.2

Label the terms for the symbols shown in the table. Choose from the terms listed below.

Free State

Spherical Radius

Projected Tolerance Zone

Tangent Plane

Least Material Condition

Unequally Disposed Tolerance

Translation

Spherical Diameter

Dynamic Profile

All Over

All Around

Continuous Feature

Maximum Material Condition

Term	Symbol ASME Y14.5
	SØ
	SR
	 (all around symbol: circle on leader)
	 (all over symbol: double circle on leader)
	Δ
	<CF>
	Ⓜ
	Ⓛ
	Ⓕ
	Ⓟ
	Ⓣ
	▷
	Ⓤ

Workshop Exercise 1.3

1. Next to the dimensions, write the Maximum Material Condition (MMC) and Least Material Condition (LMC) of the five features of size below.

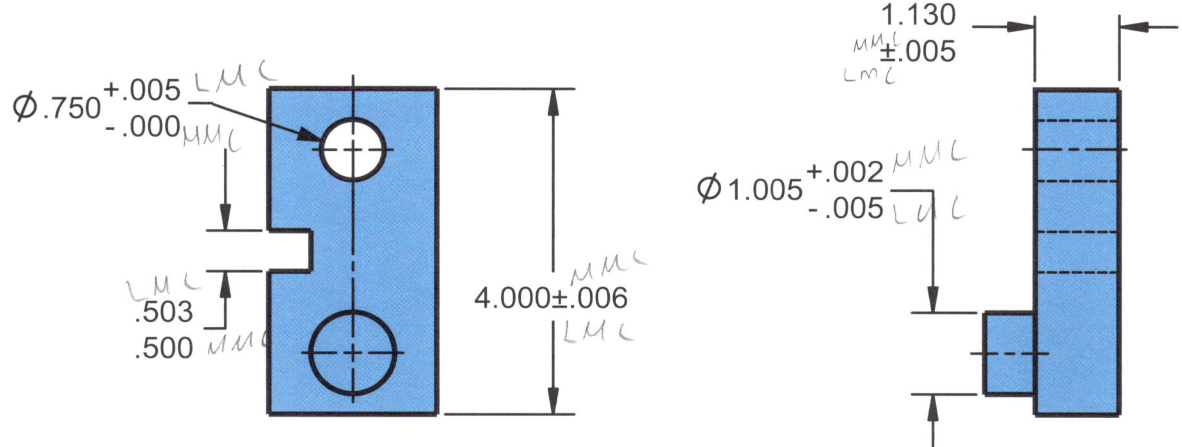

2. The following five dimensions/tolerances use unit conventions from ASME Y14.5-2018. Label which are in inches and which are in millimeters.

Ø.250 $^{+.002}_{-.000}$ 0.4 ± 0.06   6.000 ± .002   Ø 0.85 / 0.80   ⏥ | 0.01

3. Label the parts of the feature control frame. Choose from the terms below.

Shape of tolerance zone	Primary datum feature
Tertiary datum feature	Geometric characteristic
Secondary datum feature	Feature tolerance
Material condition modifier	

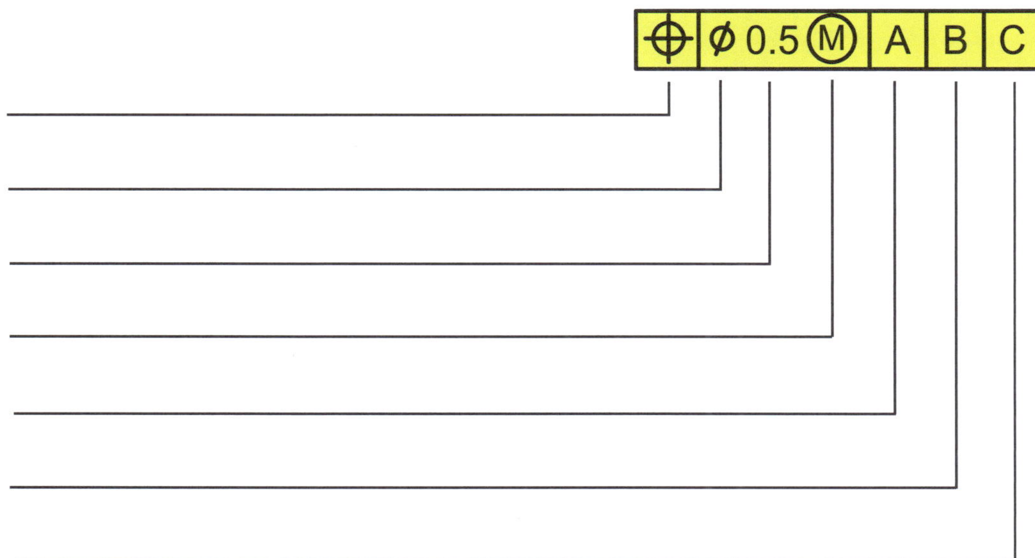

Unit 2

Limits of Size

Limits of Size - Rule #1, Envelope Principle
Limits of Size also Controls Form
Two Requirements for a Size Tolerance - Shaft
Two Requirements for a Size Tolerance - Hole
Local Size per Y14.5.1
Exceptions to Rule #1, ISO Independency
Size Does Not Control Interrelationship Between Features
Plus/Minus Dimensions Are Not Clear for Locating Surfaces
Profile Tolerance Is Used to Locate Surfaces
Size Tolerance vs. Location Tolerance
Dimension Origin Symbol
Workshop Exercise 2.1
System of Limits and Fits
Limits and Fits Tables
Workshop Exercise 2.2

Limits of Size: Rule #1 - The Envelope Principle

Regular Feature of Size definition from the Y14.5 standard:
One cylindrical surface, spherical surface, or opposed parallel surfaces, each of which is associated with a directly toleranced dimension.

(A feature of size is a hole, pin, sphere, slot, or width defined with a plus/minus tolerance.)

Rule #1: The Envelope Principle - The surface or surfaces of a feature of size shall not extend beyond a boundary of perfect form at MMC. Each local size must also be within the size limits.

Drawings of a pin and a hole are shown below with size tolerances. Rule #1 requires features of size to have perfect form at MMC. This insures that the pin will fit in the hole.

(MMC is the smallest hole or biggest pin)

This on the drawing

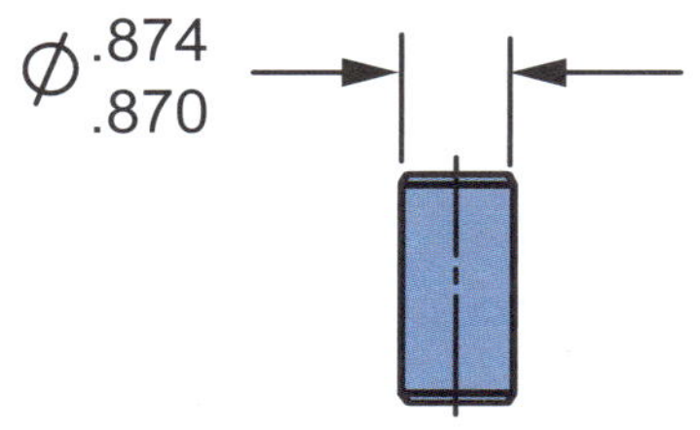

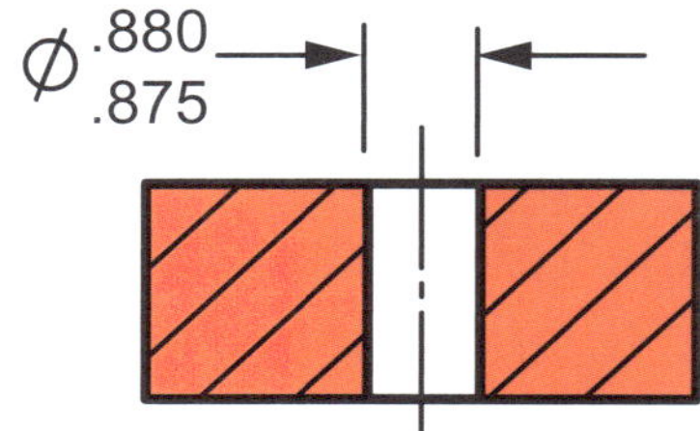

The min clearance is calculated as MMC hole - MMC pin .875 - .874 = .001

The max clearance is calculated as LMC hole - LMC pin .880 - .870 = .010

Means this

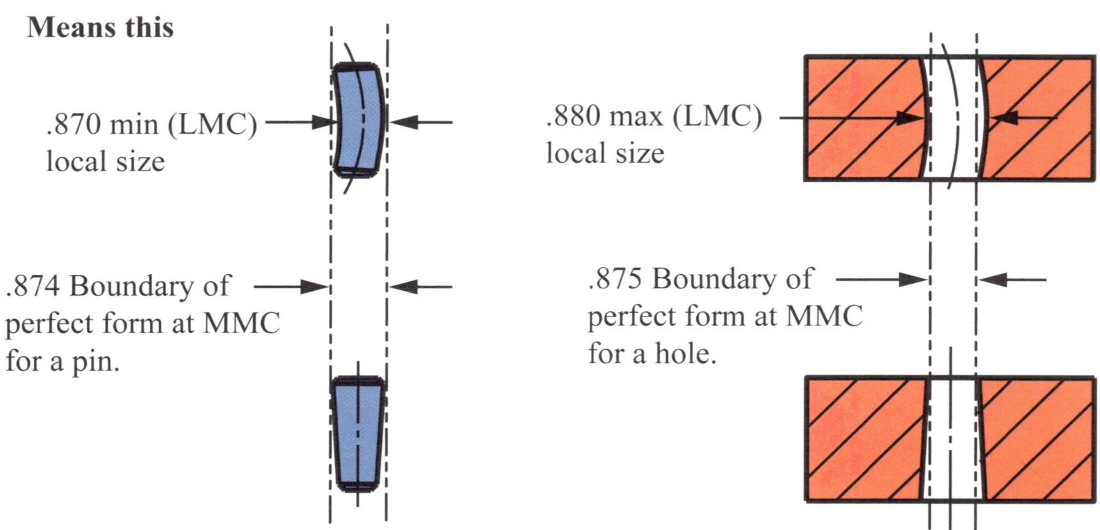

There is no default requirement for perfect form at LMC. Thus, a feature produced at its LMC limit is permitted to vary from true form to the maximum variation allowed by the size tolerance.

The Limits of Size Control Form

This on the drawing

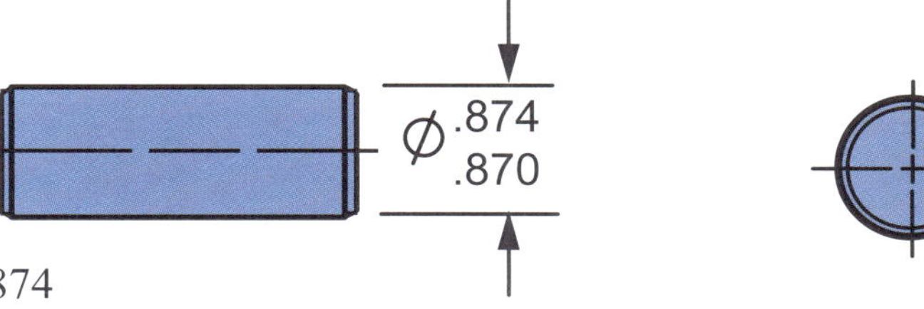

Because of rule #1, the .870-.874 size tolerance also controls its form.

Means this

.870 Min

Ø.874 Max

The pin can be waisted within .004.

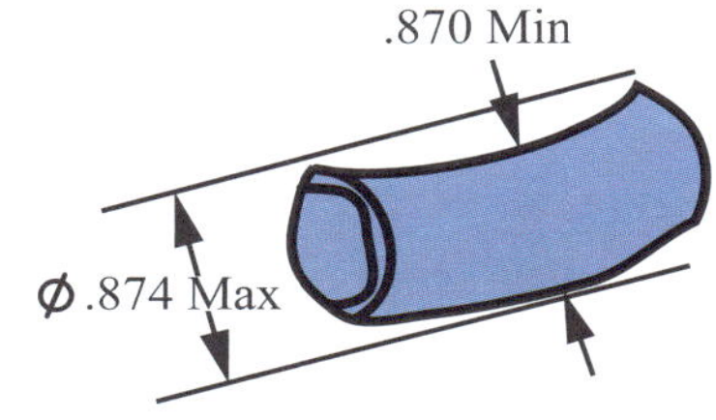

The pin can be bent within .004.

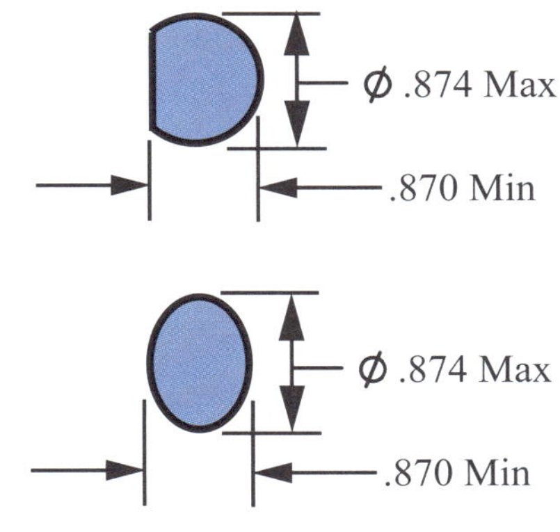

The pin can be “D” shaped, oval, or out-of-round within .004.

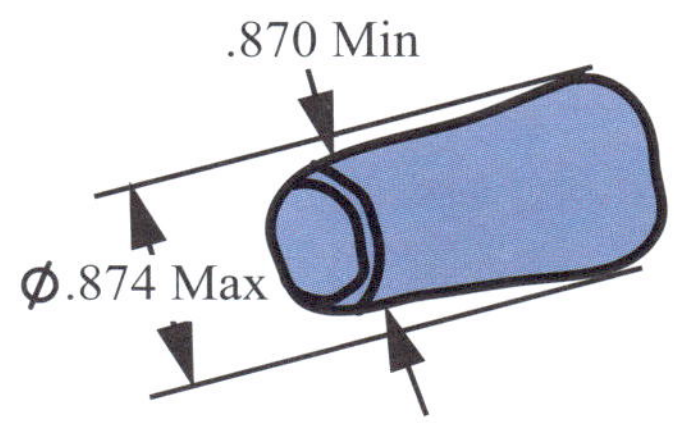

The pin can be tapered within .004.

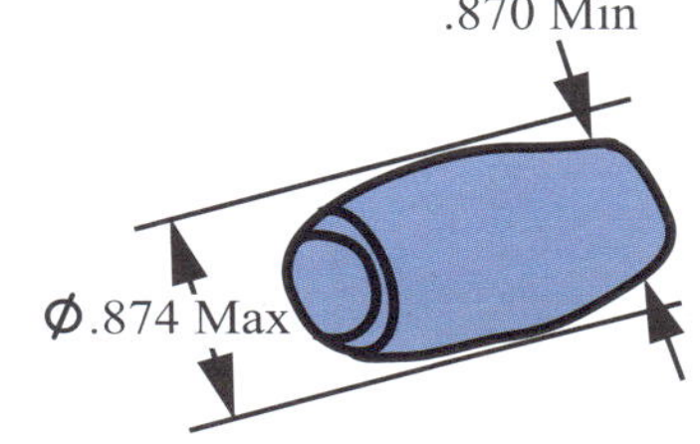

The pin can be barreled within .004.

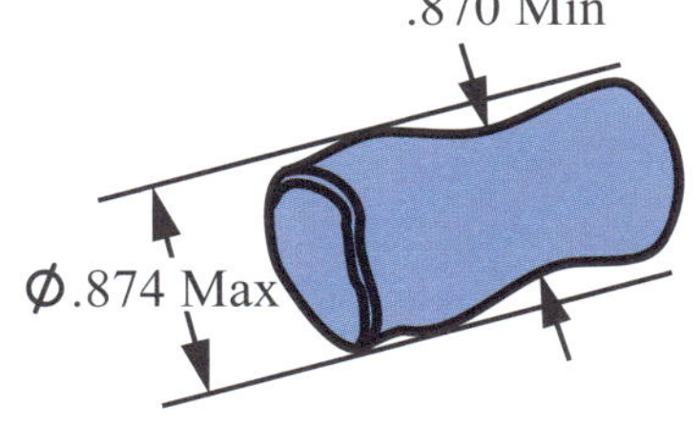

The pin can have a combination of form error within .004.

If it is necessary to refine the form of a feature of size, a form tolerance such as straightness, circularity, or cylindricity may be applied. See unit 10 for more information.

If it is necessary to relax the form defined by rule #1 and still retain the local size requirements, independency symbol, derived median line straightness, or median plane flatness may be applied. See exceptions to rule #1 in this unit and unit 10 for more information.

Two Requirements for a Size Tolerance - Shaft

By default, every feature of size must not extend beyond a boundary of perfect form at MMC in addition to the local size. The ASME Y14.5.1-2019 Mathematical Definitions standard provides two actual values for size, one for the MMC limit and one for the LMC limit. These are called the ***mating envelope*** and ***local size*** respectively.

For a shaft or pin feature of size:

The ***mating envelope*** is defined as the smallest circumscribed cylinder. This cannot be larger than the MMC value.

The ***local size*** is the smallest individual distance along the feature. This cannot be smaller than the LMC value.

This on the drawing

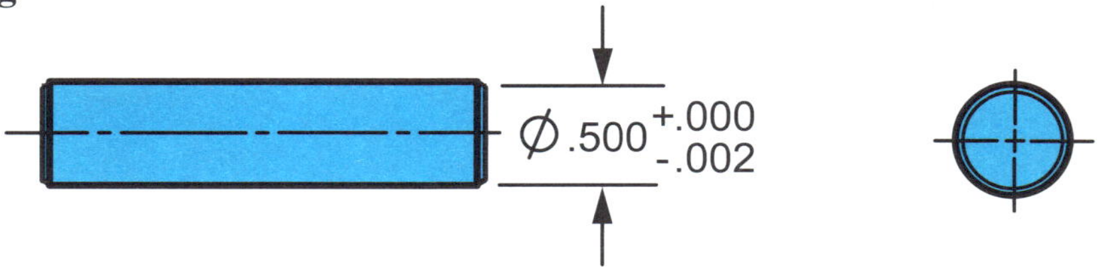

Means this

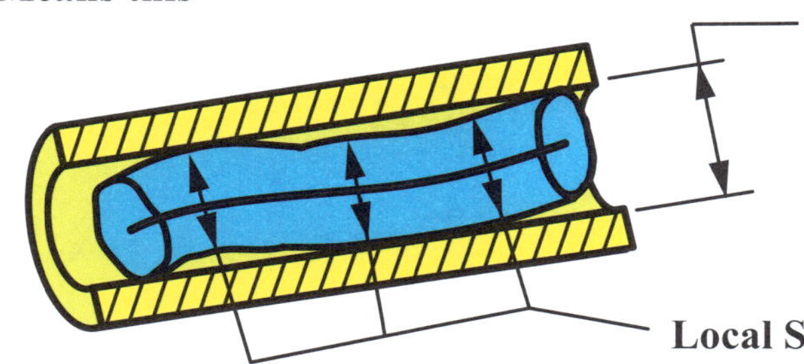

Mating Envelope
The surface or surfaces shall not extend beyond a boundary of perfect form at MMC (Ø.500)

Local Size
The local size at each cross-section shall not be smaller than the LMC value (Ø.498).

Measured part

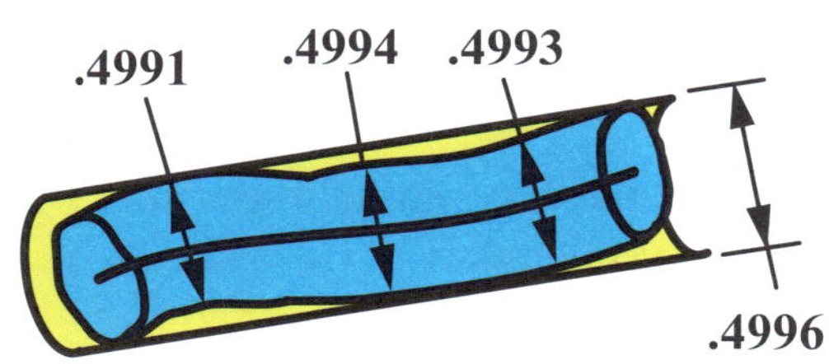

ASME Y14.45 Measurement Data Reporting method B requires the two worst-case size values (mating envelope and local size) to be reported. Other measured local size values in addition to the worst-case may also be recorded.

ID# is floated next to the size specification to match inspection report

Sample Measurement Report

ID#	Tolerance Type	Allowed	Measured Value	Pass/ Fail	Comments
1	MMC	Ø.5000	.4996	Pass	mating env
1	LMC	Ø.4980	.4991	Pass	local size

Two Requirements for a Size Tolerance - Hole

This on the drawing

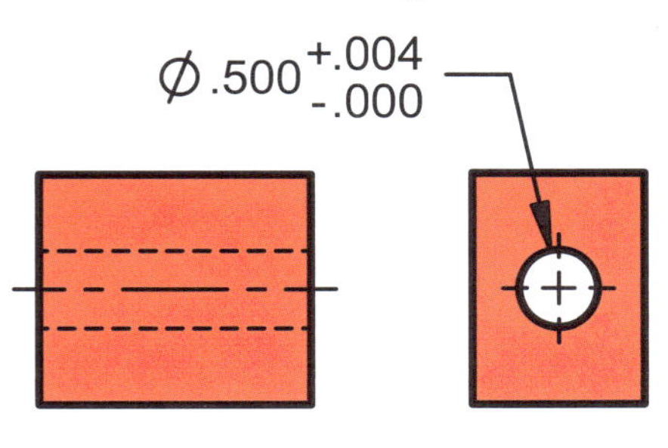

Actual hole with exaggerated form error

What is the size of this hole?

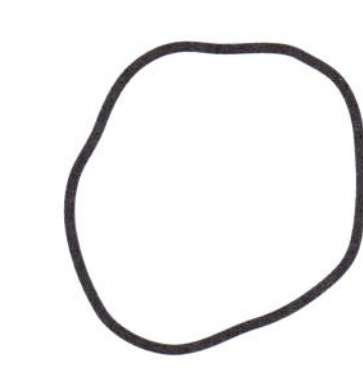

Since the actual size of an imperfect feature cannot be defined by only one number, the ASME Y14.5 creates two worst-cases: ***mating envelope*** and ***local size***.

Means This

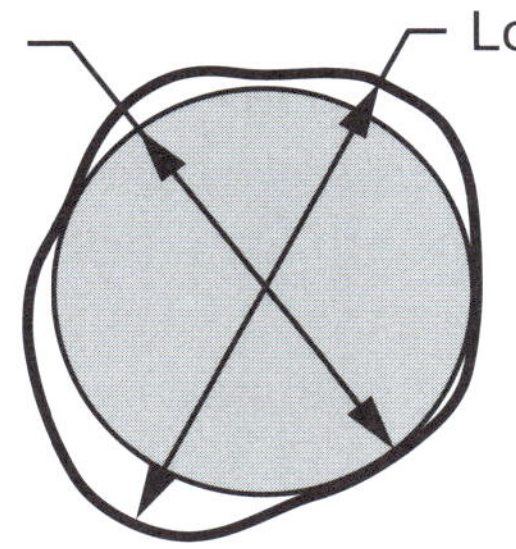

The mating envelope (largest inscribed cylinder) shall be no smaller than .500 (MMC).

Common measurement tool: gage pin (go gage), CMM

The worst local size shall be no larger than .504 (LMC).

Common measurement tool: gage pin (no-go gage) calipers, bore gage, CMM

ID#	Tolerance Type	Allowed	Pass/ Fail	Comments
1	MMC	Ø.500	Pass	gage pin
1	LMC	Ø.504	Pass	calipers

Sample measurement report for size as pass/fail only

ID#	Tolerance Type	Allowed	Measured Value	Pass/ Fail	Comments
1	MMC	Ø.5000	.5010	Pass	mating env
1	LMC	Ø.5040	.5035	Pass	local size

Sample measurement report including measured size values

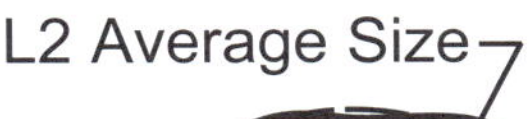

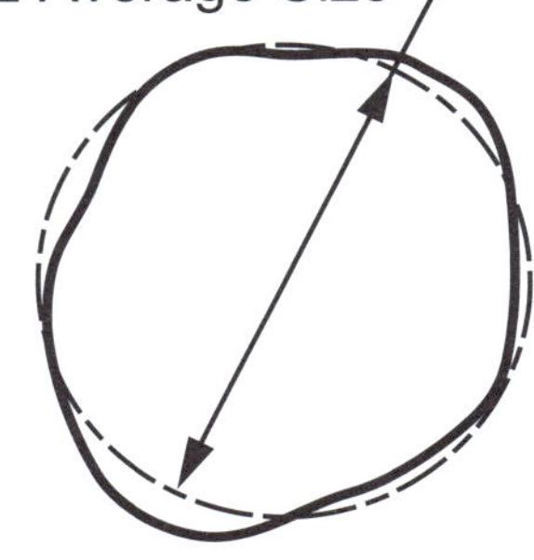

Caution: CMM programs often have the default algorithm set to least squares (L2) to measure the average size and report one value. However, the hole's actual local size is larger and the actual mating envelope is smaller than this average.

The CMM algorithm for determining the mating envelope of a hole is the largest inscribed cylinder (LIC). However, with a low number of measurement points, LIC may give repeatability problems. L2 is used by CMM programmers to give a more repeatable result by filtering the form error. This may be satisfactory if the form error on the feature is small and the tolerance is loose enough. However, if the measurement must be more accurate, take more data points and use the LIC algorithm to be closer to the design intent defined by the MMC requirement. The drawing only defines the theoretical specification. The quality plan determines the measurement procedure. Determining how to measure any tolerance is based on many factors including balancing the risk with time, cost, and equipment available. See unit 5 for more on the quality plan.

Local Size per Y14.5.1

The pin has a size tolerance of .498-.500. The pin will have two checks:

1. Mating envelope (insuring the boundary of perfect form at MMC limit)
2. Local size (insuring the LMC limit)

Notice that a two-point micrometer does not verify the mating envelope. The pin could be bent beyond its perfect form at MMC envelope and still pass a micrometer check. A functional cylindrical go-gage for a shaft, or pin gage for a hole, should be used to verify the MMC boundary.

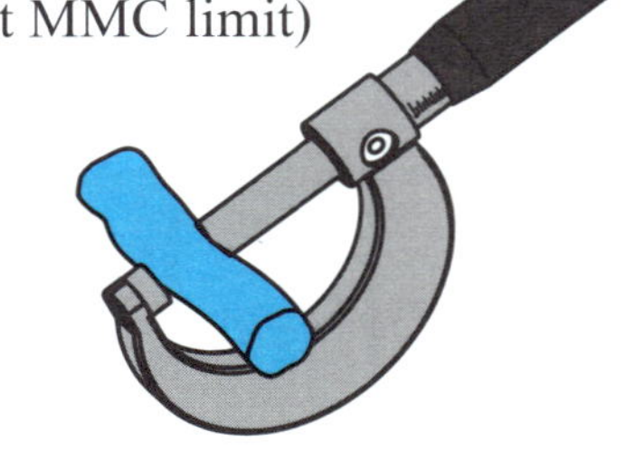

A two-point micrometer may be used to measure local size.

Y14.5.1 conformance to local size

The definition of **local size** is defined in the ASME Y14.5-2018 standard as "any individual distance at any cross-section" it is also referred in other places of the text as "circular elements of the feature at any cross-section". Because of these conflicting definitions, the ASME Y14.5.1-2019 gives two definitions for conformance to local size: one as local distances and another as a floating sphere. Measuring local size of a pin with a micrometer or calipers is sufficient in most cases, but the engineer/inspector should realize that in extreme cases, a two-point check verification could pose conformance issues. See ASME Y14.5.1-2019 for more information.

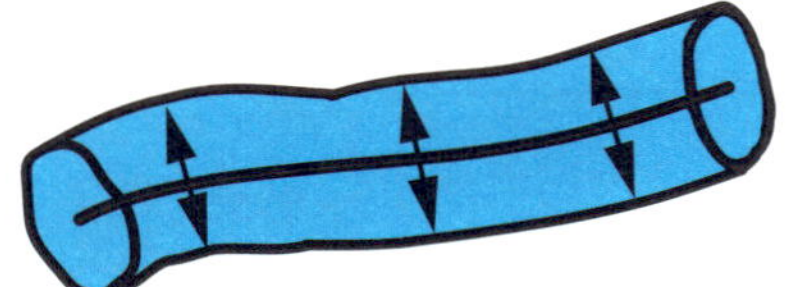

Opposing points definition: Feature conforms to local size if each line distance at each cross-section is larger than LMC. All line distances at each cross section must pass thru a common center point.

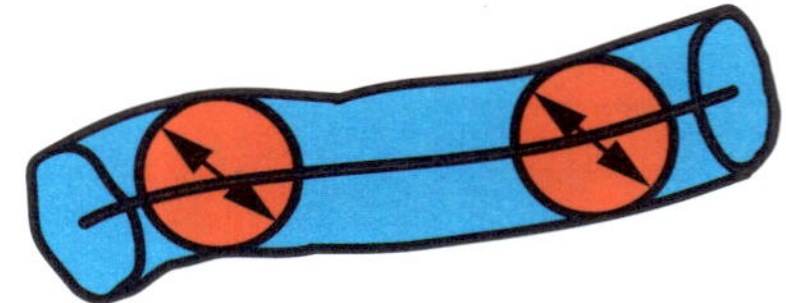

Circular cross-section definition: Feature conforms to local size if an LMC size sphere may be pulled along some spine without exiting the material.

How these definitions can be different: Shafts/holes (especially thin-walled parts) can be unintentionally produced with lobes or flat spots (center-less grinding manufacturing processes or diameters clamped too tightly in a 3-jaw chuck). This odd lobed shape will yield different results when measuring the local size as a 2-point distance versus a spherical cross-section.

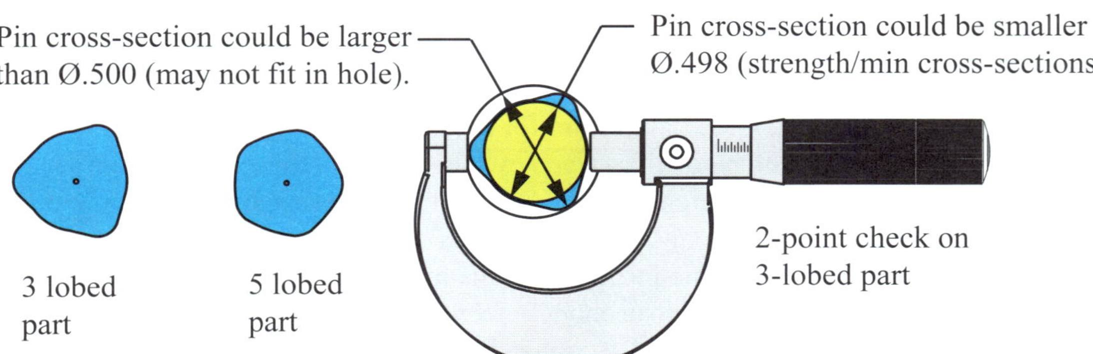

The graphics above illustrate how a measuring device using two opposed points will not necessarily insure a circular cross section at LMC. This does not mean calipers or a micrometer can not be used, but risk is possible when demanding restrictive tolerances. In some cases, a more a stringent inspection procedure may be necessary such as a CMM.

Exceptions to Rule #1 and ISO definitions

Exceptions to Rule #1 in ASME Y14.5

Perfect form at MMC does not apply in the following cases:

a. when items are identified as stock, such as bars, sheets, tubing, structural shapes, and other items produced to established industry standards that prescribe form limits.

b. when the free state modifier is specified on the size tolerance. See unit 8.

c. when form tolerances of median-line straightness and median-plane flatness are applied. See unit 10.

d. when average diameter is specified on the size tolerance. See unit 10.

e. when the feature of size has a geometric tolerance specified with an LMC modifier. Instead perfect form at LMC is required. See unit 3.

f. when the **independency symbol**, "circle I", is placed next to the size tolerance.

Application of the independency symbol in ASME Y14.5

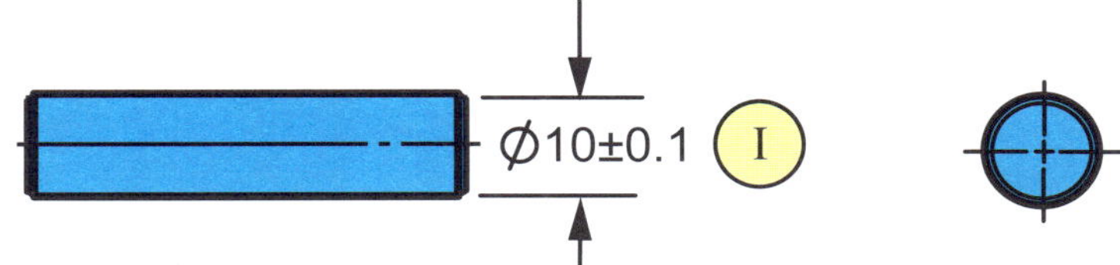

This may be used to control thickness only and other specifications control the form (example: thin plate with a flatness specification).

ISO 8015, 2011 -Fundamental Tolerancing Principle

In ISO standards, the default requirements for features of size are opposite the ASME Y14.5 requirements. ISO standards use the ***Principle of Independency*** defined in ISO 8015: 2011.

Principle of Independency (ISO):

By default, every GPS specification for a feature or relation between features shall be fulfilled independent of other specifications except when it is stated in a standard or by special indication as part of the actual specification.

This means perfect form at MMC is not required for a feature of size by default in ISO standards. If it is necessary to directly invoke the envelope principle, then the circle E symbol Ⓔ is placed next to the size tolerance or as a global notation on the drawing outlined by ISO 14405-1.

The global note to envoke perfect form at MMC for all features of size: "Size ISO 14405 Ⓔ "

Application of the envelope symbol in ISO 14405-1

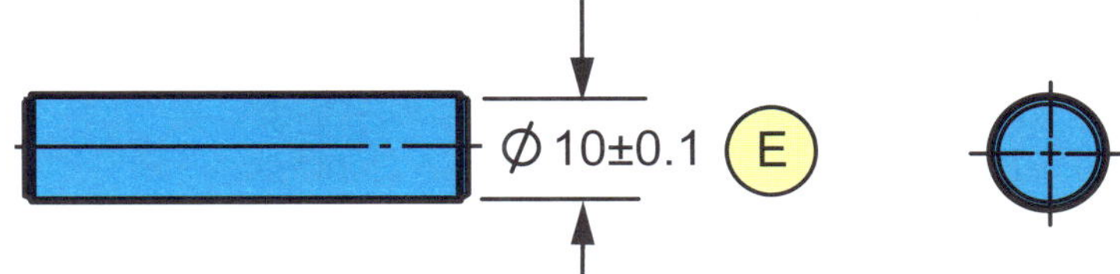

The default size requirement in ISO 14405-1 is 2-point size but many modifiers may be applied.

Note: The ISO 1101 definition for position and perpendicularity controls the derived median line (different than ASME Y14.5). This will control the straightness on a feature. Therefore, the form is somewhat controlled even if the envelope principle is not invoked (see differences in the ISO standards in Appendix B).

Size Does Not Control Interrelationship Between Individual Features

The **limits of size** (rule #1) only controls the size and form of individual features. The limits of size does not control the orientation or location relationship between features. Features shown perpendicular to each other must be toleranced for orientation to avoid incomplete drawing requirements.

The drawings below have size tolerances that appear like they will fit together, but since there is no tolerancing relationship shown between the features, they may not assemble.

Mating parts

This on the drawing

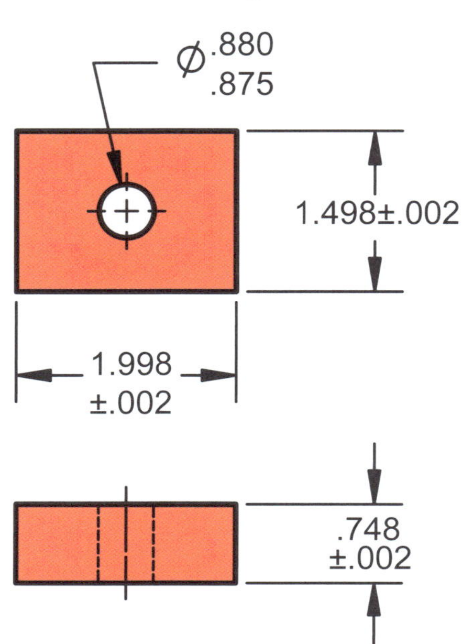

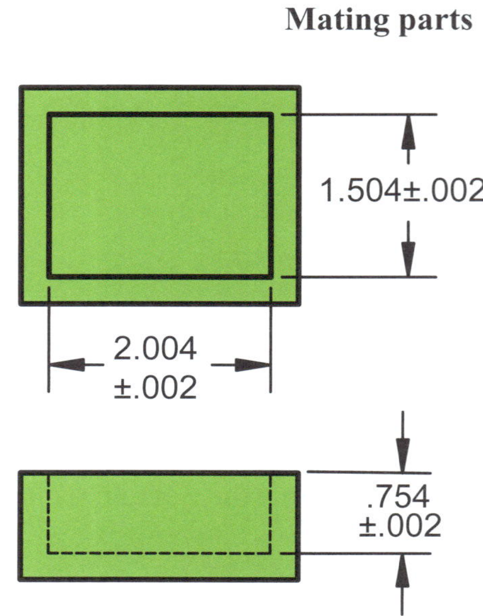

UNLESS OTHERWISE SPECIFIED: ALL ANGLES ± 1°

Means this

The width features may be produced out of square and the part as a parallelogram. The hole will not be perpendicular to any surface. Each individual feature must be within size limits but there is no implied relationship between the features.

The only relationship between the features is the specified ±1° angle tolerance. This angle tolerance is also vague, as there are many implied angles on the parts.

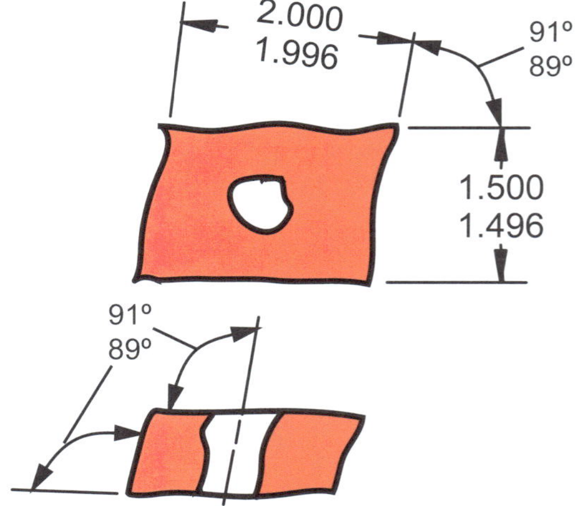

Controlling the relationship between the features may be accomplished by specifying a perpendicularity, position or profile tolerance. See the next page for the part controlled with profile tolerance.

Size Does Not Control Interrelationship Between Individual Features

This on the drawing

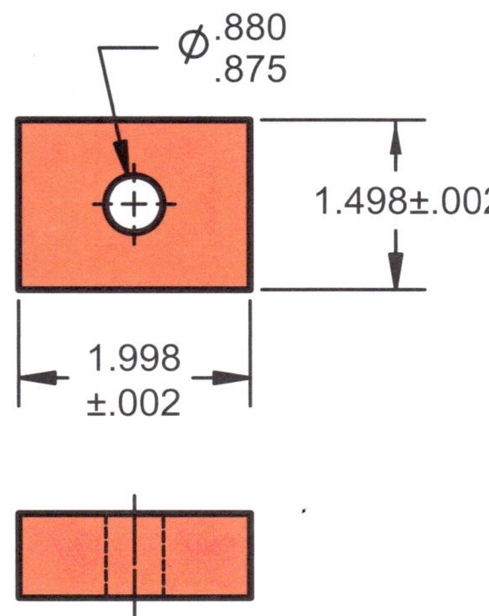

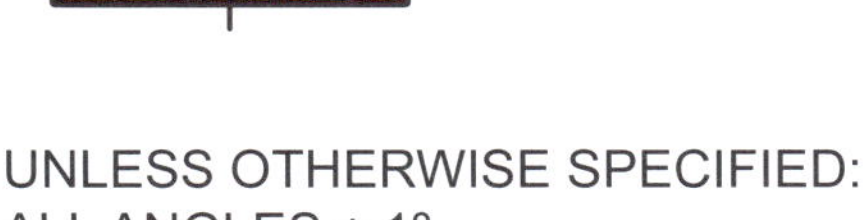

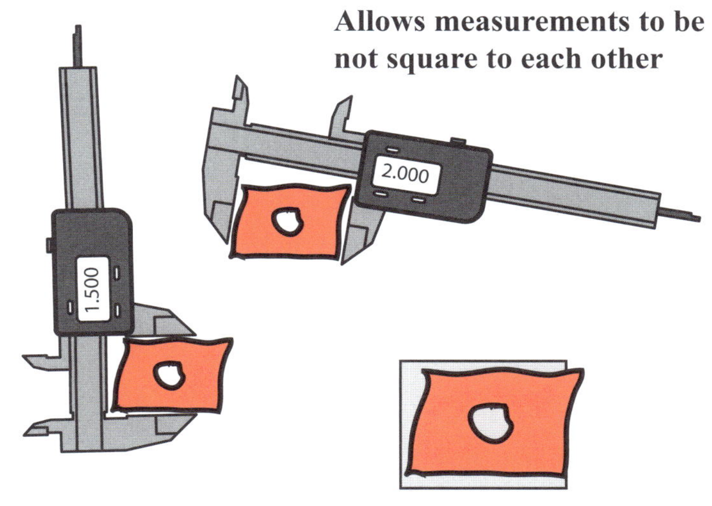

The ±1° angle tolerance between the features of size allow the part to be a parallelogram and may not fit in a 1.500 X 2.000 perfect rectangular box.

There is no implied relationship between the size toleranced features except the specified angle tolerance. The part could be a parallelogram. Perfect form at MMC controls individual features, but not the interrelationship between features.

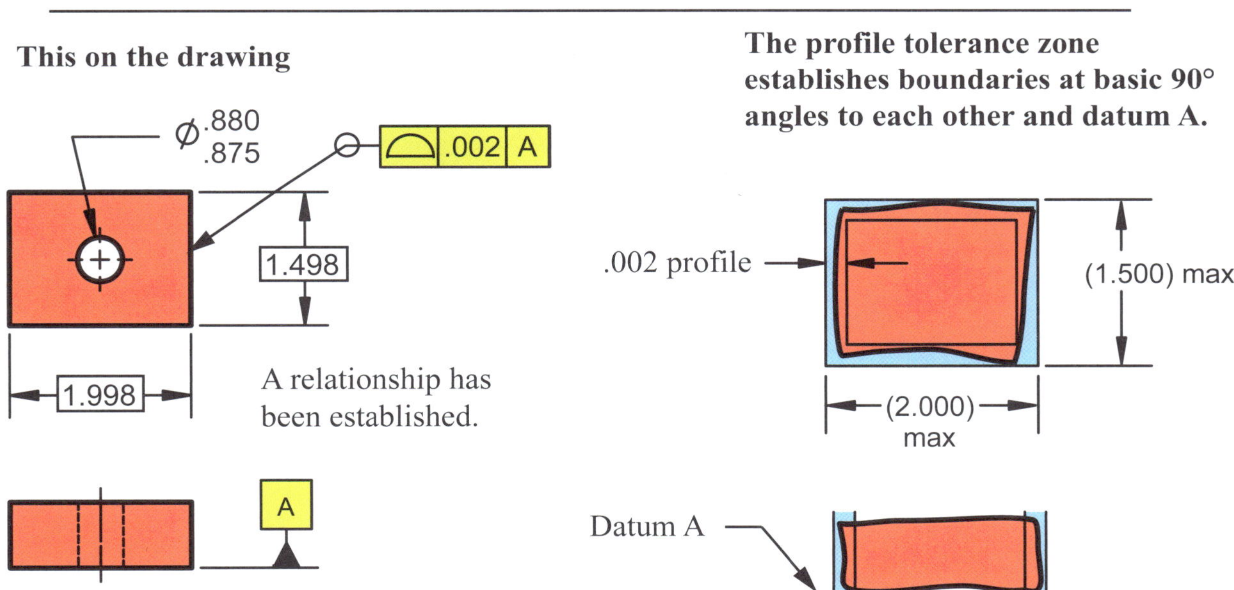

The drawing above has the surfaces defined by the basic linear dimensions and the implied basic 90° angles. The profile tolerance is applied all around and referenced to datum feature A. The tolerance zone is set by these basic dimensions and allows size, form, and orientation variations within its boundaries. This relates the surfaces to each other and will insure the part will fit in a 1.500 X 2.000 rectangular box. A profile tolerance is shown but other geometric controls could be used as well. Profile tolerance is explained in detail later in unit 3.

Size Does Not Control Interrelationship Between Individual Features

There is no tolerancing relationship between part features implied in the ASME Y14.5 standard. The limits of size (rule #1) only control the size and form of individual features but not the relationship between features. Features shown perpendicular, coaxial, or symmetrical to each other must be controlled with tolerances. A datum reference frame needs to be defined and location/orientation controls applied to avoid incomplete drawing requirements.

The shaft drawing below displays four cylindrical features with a center line. All of the diameters are shown on center, so manufacturing tries to make all diameters on the same center. The problem is the tolerance and verification; the drawing does not define the allowed coaxiality tolerance. How much are the centers allowed to be off to each other? It is not defined.

This on the drawing

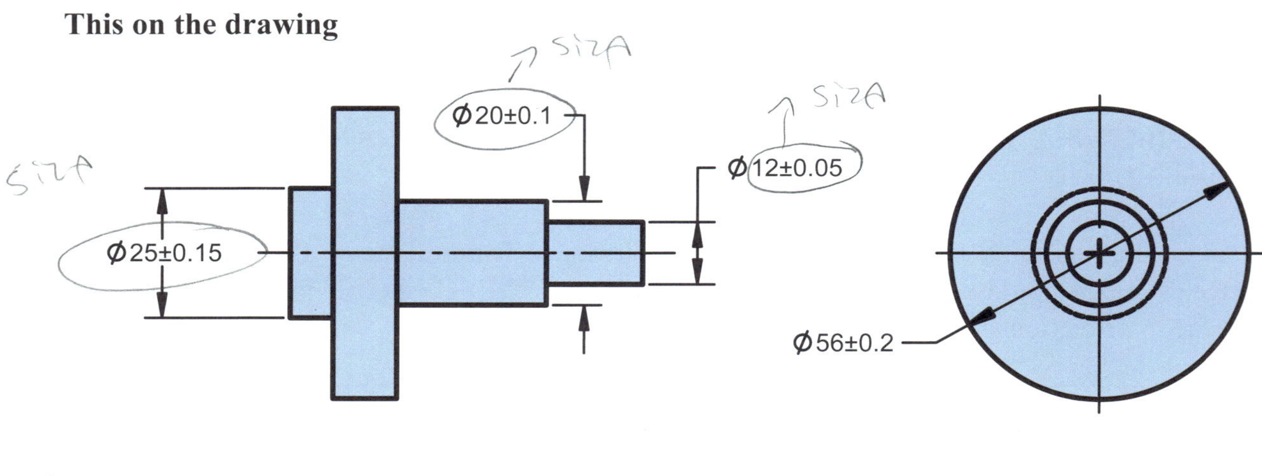

Produced part with error

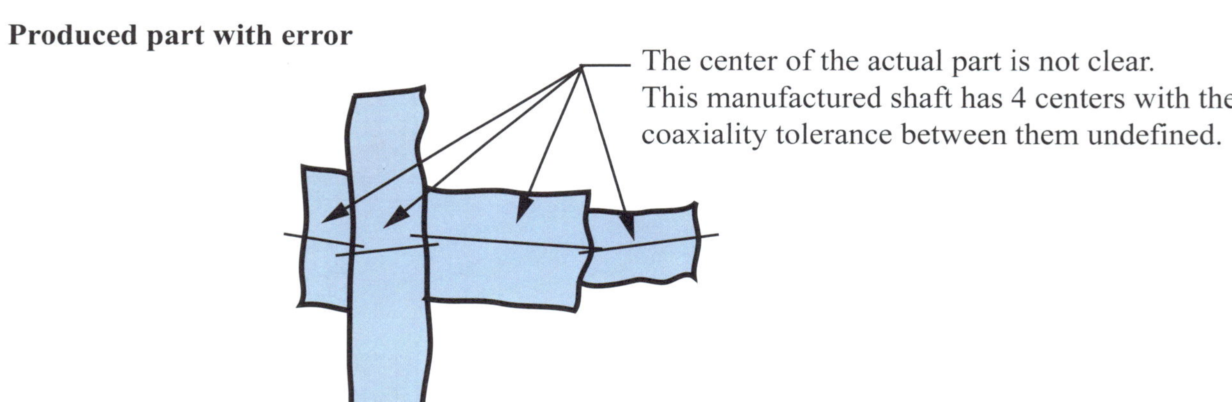

The center of the actual part is not clear. This manufactured shaft has 4 centers with the coaxiality tolerance between them undefined.

The actual produced part has error, exaggerated here for clarity. Centerlines only exist on drawings, not on parts. There is no way to establish center of the part unless a feature is selected. The actual part above has four axes derived from the four separate features. As you can see, an inspector would get a different center depending on which diameter is indexed. The datum reference on this part and the relationship between the features is unclear.

Size Does Not Control Interrelationship Between Individual Features

To control the relationship between features, a datum reference frame (DRF) is first established from specific datum features on the part. Then symbols such as perpendicularity, position, profile, or runout are applied to control variation of the remaining features.

In this case, the large face is identified as the primary datum feature A and the 25 mm pilot diameter is selected as datum feature B. Datum feature B is related to datum A with a perpendicularly tolerance. The remaining features are located to this DRF with position tolerances. (Runout and profile tolerances could be used as well depending on functional requirements.) This makes the relationship between the features fully defined.

This on the drawing

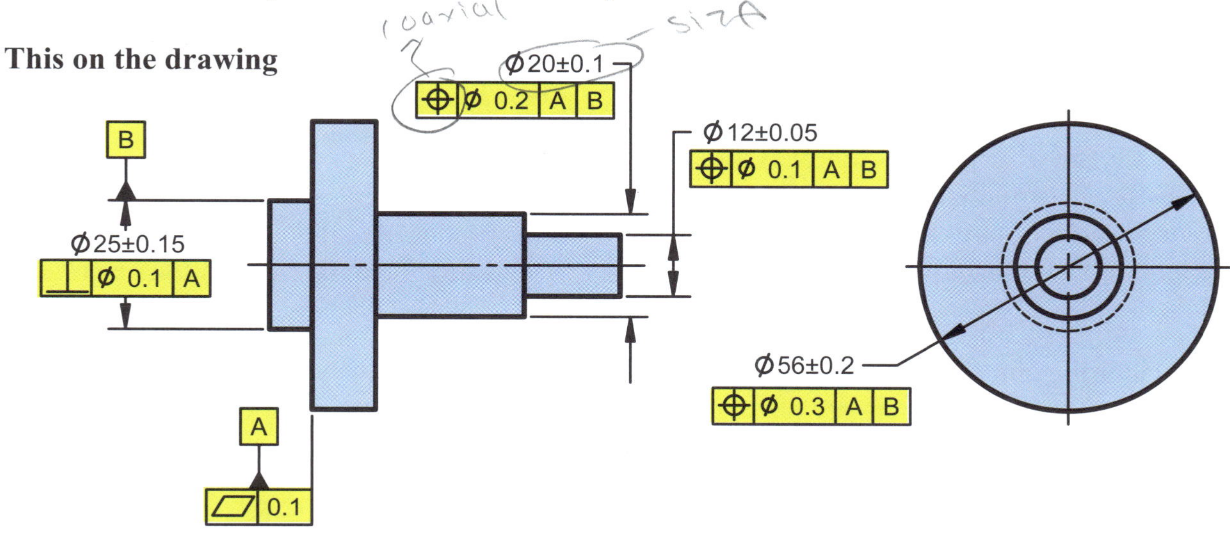

Produced part

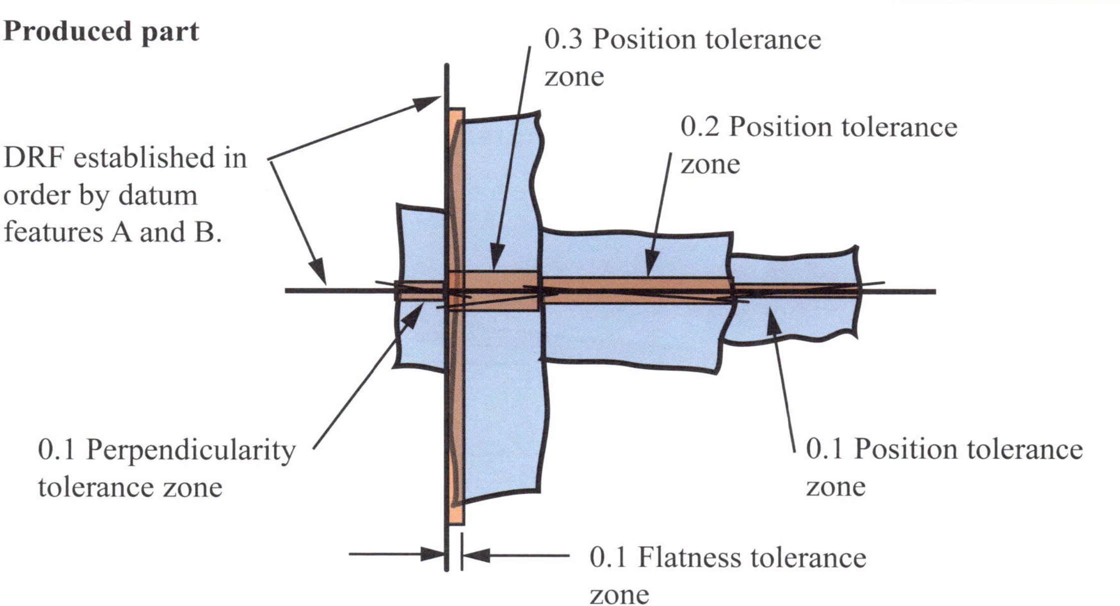

The drawing of the produced part above shows the established DRF and the position tolerance zones for each of the diametrical features. The axis of the features must fall within their respective perpendicularity and position tolerance zones. There is additional detailed information on coaxial tolerances shown later in unit 13.

Plus/Minus Dimensions Are Not Clear for Locating Surfaces

Plus/minus tolerances are used to define size, not location

Plus/minus tolerances define features of size according to the limits of size (rule #1). A feature of size must have opposing elements in to order to verify the cross-section.

As you can see from the geometry on this part, it is impossible to verify a two point caliper check because the surfaces do not have opposing elements. Instead, one surface must be set as zero and the distance verified with a height gage or CMM. The 20±0.3 distance between the surfaces is not a size dimension, it is a location dimension. Plus/minus tolerances on dimensions locating surfaces are not clear, and multiple interpretations of the tolerance are possible.

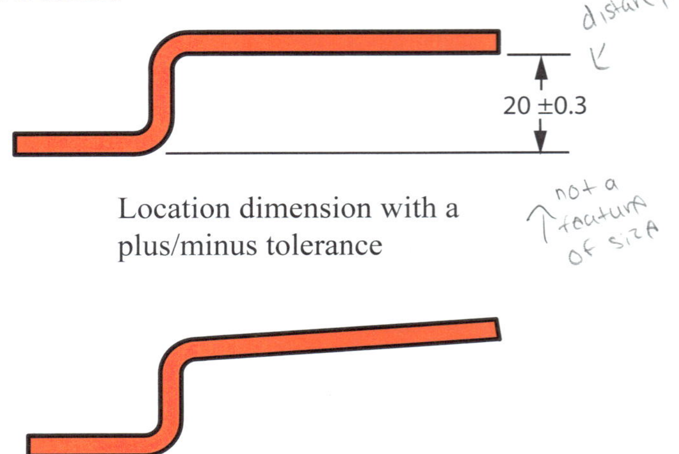

Location dimension with a plus/minus tolerance

Produced part is imperfect and is just a little bent. Is it within tolerance?

Manufacturing aims for the mean dimension. However, there will always be some variance in the process, and the two surfaces are never exactly parallel. Plus/minus dimensions do not define an origin. When the height is verified, the inspector must choose which surface is set up as the datum. Since one surface is longer than the other, different results will be obtained depending on which surface is selected. There can be multiple interpretations as to what constitutes a maximum height.

Note: A dimension origin symbol could be used to help define the origin, but most parts are not this simple and require a 3D datum reference frame to locate additional features on the part.

Plus/minus tolerances that locate surfaces do not provide a clear origin of measurement.

Leveling the short end and checking the long end will show the part bad.

20.3 Max

Leveling the long end and checking the short end will show the part good.

20.3 Max

Tipping the part in some orientation will show the part very good.

20.3 Max

Profile Tolerance Is Used to Locate Surfaces

Profile tolerance replaces the traditional plus/minus tolerancing for the location of surfaces. The two examples below illustrate a sheet metal part mounted in an assembly. Datums are selected based on functional mounting conditions and in each case the design intent and definition of the tolerance is clear.

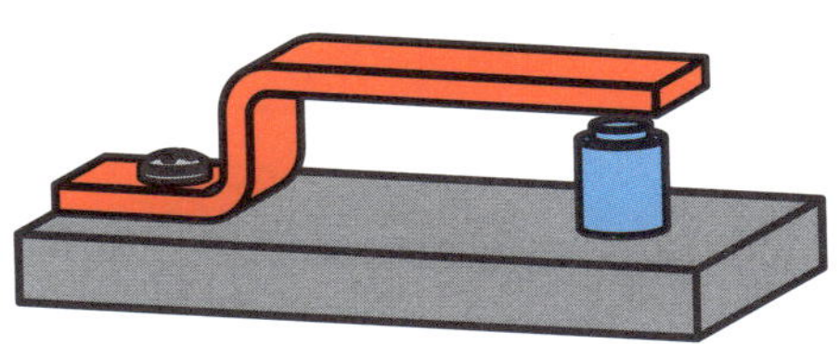

This application

In this assembly, the short face mounts to the base and the longer face must clear the pin. The short surface is identified as the datum feature and qualified with a flatness tolerance. The long surface is located to the datum with a 0.6 profile tolerance. To inspect, mount on the short surface and indicate the longer surface within a distance of 20±0.3.

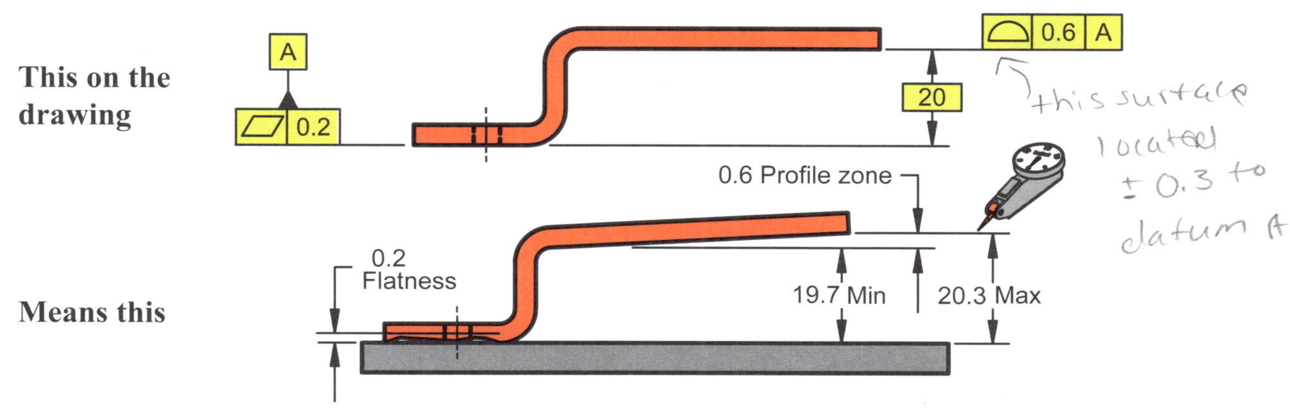

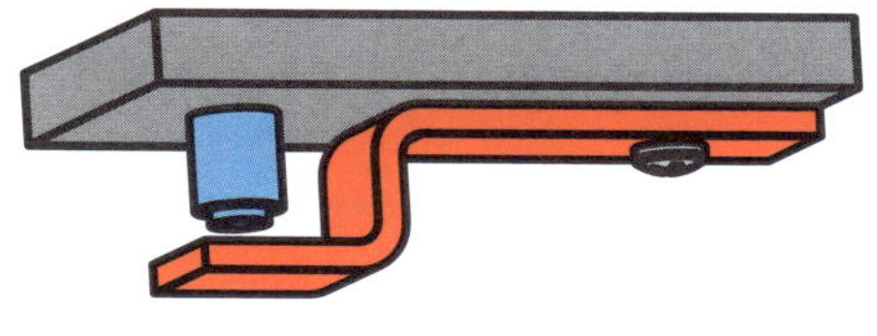

This application

In this assembly, the long face mounts to the base and the shorter face must clear the pin. The long surface is identified as the datum feature and qualified with a flatness tolerance. The short surface is located to the datum with a 0.6 profile tolerance. To inspect, mount on the long surface and indicate the shorter surface within a distance of 20±0.3.

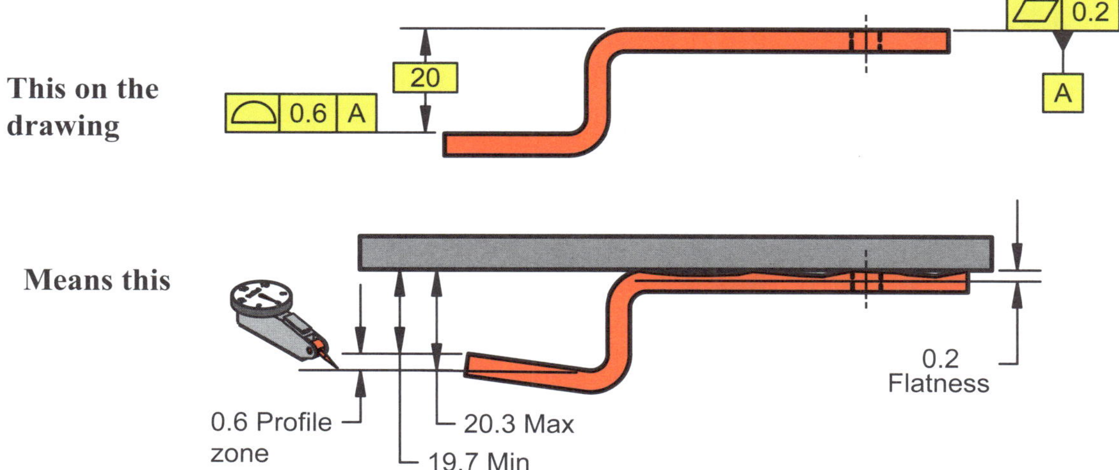

Size Tolerances Versus Location Tolerance

This on the drawing

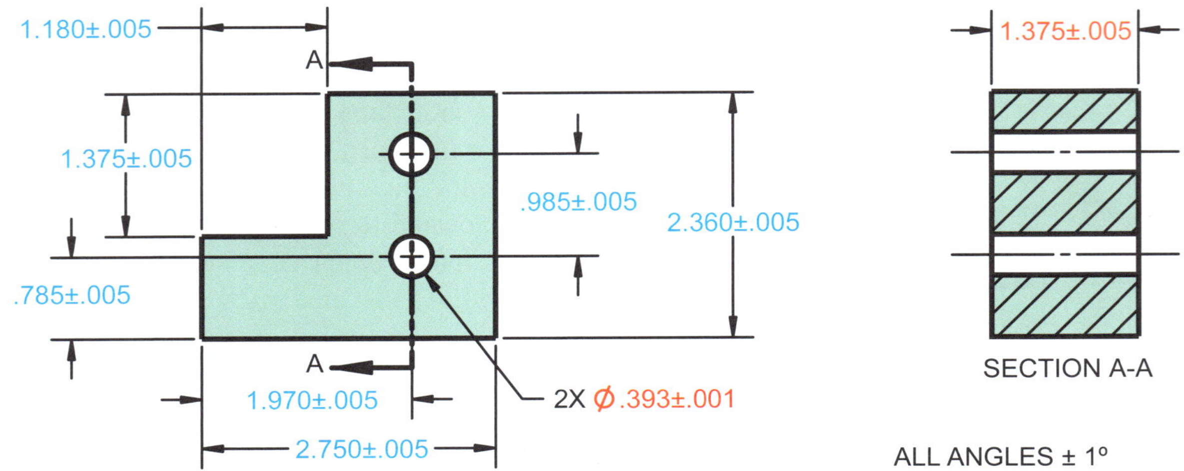

The dimensions in red define size tolerances and control how large or small the feature may be. Size tolerances are well defined in the ASME Y14.5 standard (limits of size: rule #1) and are used on holes, shafts, slots, and widths.

The dimensions in blue define location tolerances and show vague relationships between features. Without a clear datum reference frame, plus/minus tolerances on location dimensions are ambiguous and not defined in the ASME or ISO standards. Instead, these dimensions should be basic (without tolerance) and the symbols of position and profile should control the tolerancing relationship of the holes and surfaces to the datum reference frame. See unit 3 for more info on how the geometric tolerancing system works.

Could Mean This?

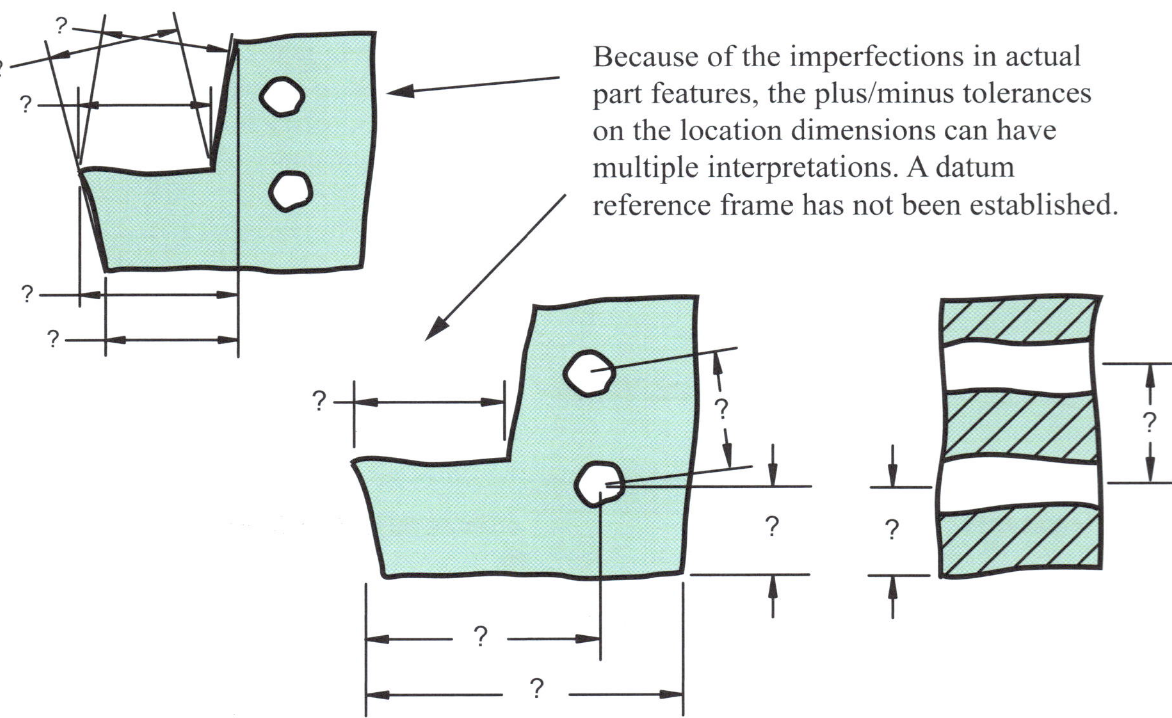

Workshop Exercise 2.1

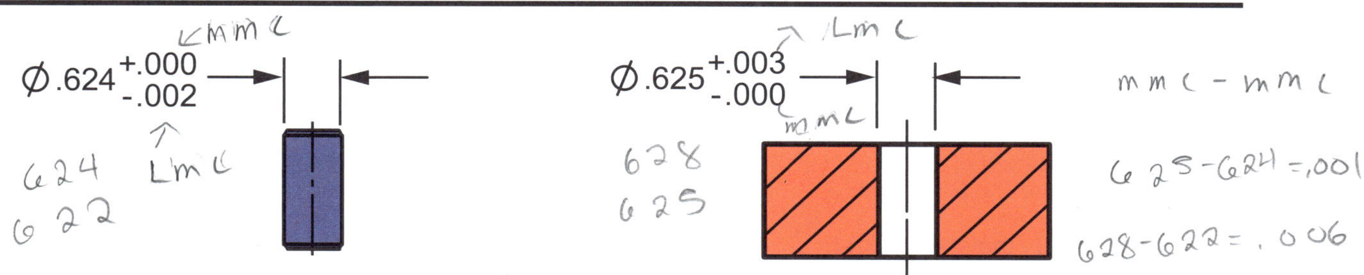

1. What is the min and max clearance between the pin and hole above? ____________

2. According to the limits of size, also known as Rule #1, the size tolerance applied to a feature controls the size and ________ of the feature.

A: Orientation B: Location C: Form D: Runout

3. What is the maximum amount of straightness tolerance allowed on the pin below?

A: .001

B: .002

C: .004

D: Not defined

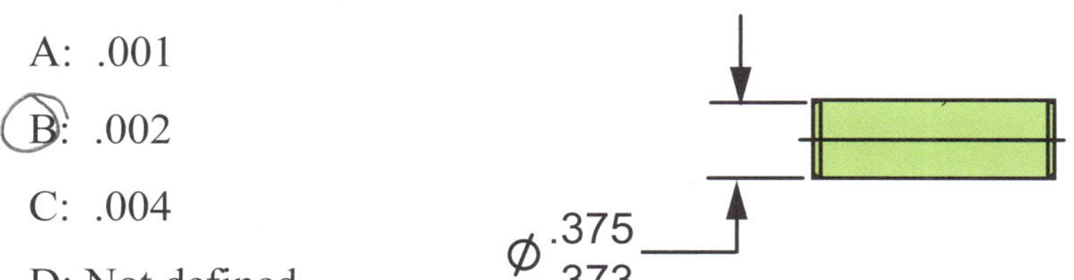

INTERPRET PER
ASME Y14.5-2018

4. If all cross-sections of the pin above were produced at a local size of .375, what is the maximum straightness variation possible?

A: .000 B: .001 C: .002 D: Not defined

5. A feature of size will have two measured size values: **mating envelope** and **local size**. The measured part is shown below. On the report, fill out the measured values and mark pass or fail.

Measured part

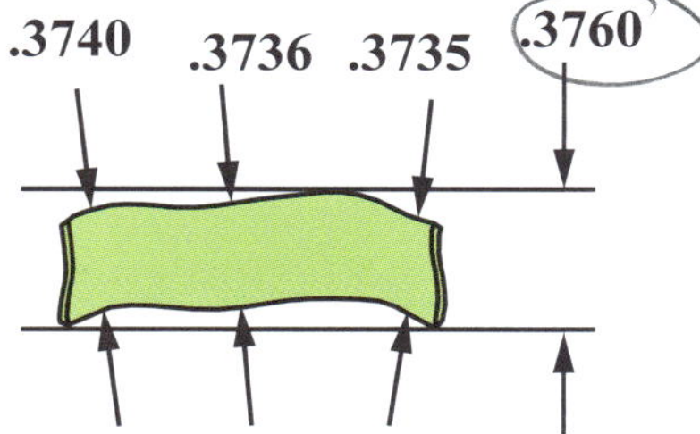

Measurement Report

ID#	Tolerance Type	Allowed Limit	Measured Value	Pass/ Fail
1	MMC	.375		
1	LMC	.373		

6. If a gage pin were used to verify the size of a hole, does it measure the mating envelope or the local size?

____

7. If calipers were used to verify the size of a hole, do they measure the mating envelope or the local size?

____

Workshop Exercise 2.1

8. On the shaft below, with only the limits of size defined, what coaxiality tolerance is implied among the three diameters?

A: Within the size tolerance

B: Within half the size tolerance

C: Not defined

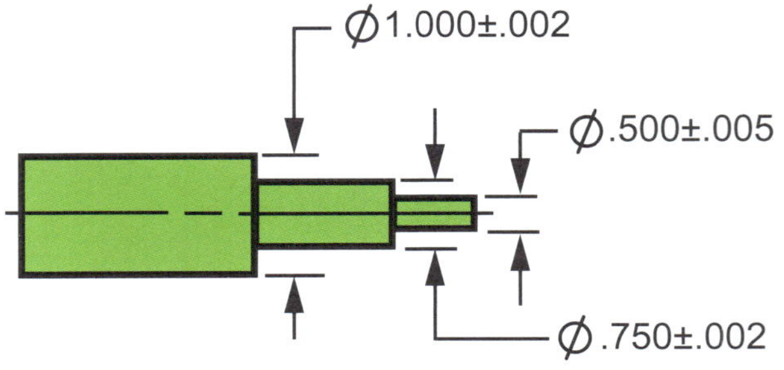

9. On the pin below, with only the limits of size defined, what perpendicularity tolerance is implied between the pin and right surface?

A: .006

B: .005

C: .001

D: Not defined

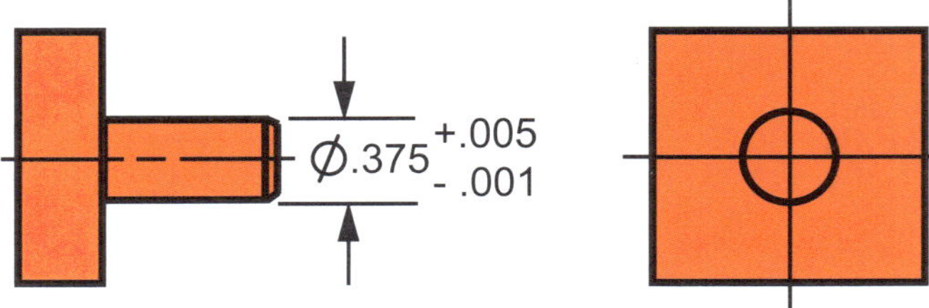

10. On the part below, circle only dimensions defining features of size.

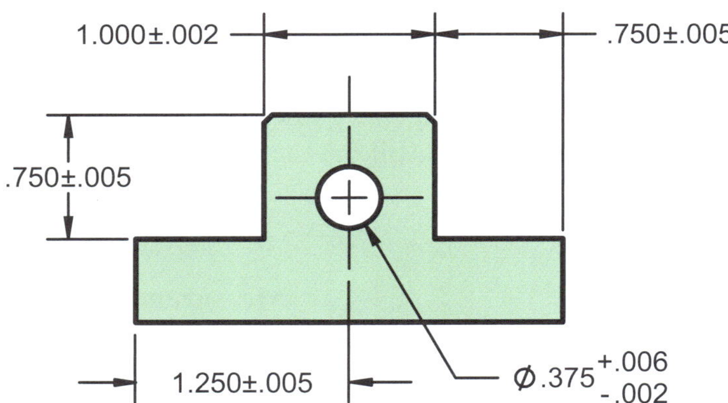

11. On the part above, you circled the size dimensions. Explain the difference between the dimensions you circled and the dimensions you did not.

____

____

____

System of Limits and Fits

In order to determine mating fit tolerances between features like pins and holes or bearings and shafts etc., the engineer must define size tolerances to obtain proper functional requirements. There are standards to provide the engineer with guidelines for selecting size tolerances. The ANSI B4.1-1967 (R2004) Preferred Limits and Fits for Cylindrical Parts and ANSI B4.2-1978 (R2004) Metric Limits and Fits defines 5 main types of fits. This information can also be found in The Machinery's Handbook.

Note: This is only a brief explanation of the fits with a few sample charts and examples of how to use them. For a full description of each fit and application, consult the appropriate standard.

Running and Sliding Fits (RC) are intended to provide a similar running performance with suitable lubrication allowance, throughout the range of sizes.

•Always have positive min clearance for lubrication
•Applications: Translating shafts, bushings, bearings

RC1 thru RC9 RC 1 – Close Sliding Fit RC 9 – Loose Running Fit

Locational Clearance Fits (LC) are intended for parts which are normally stationary, but which can be freely assembled or disassembled. They range from snug fits for parts requiring accuracy of location, to the looser fastener fits where freedom of assembly is of prime importance.

•Range from line-to-line min clearance for better alignment, to significant min clearance for ease of assembly
•Snug fit applications: pilots, dowels, and other alignment features
•Loose fit applications: clearance holes for fasteners

LC 1 thru LC11 LC 1 - Snug Fit LC11 - Loose Fit

Locational Transition Fits (LT) are a compromise between clearance and interference fits, for application where accuracy of location is important, but either a small amount of clearance or interference is permissible.

•Applications: pilots, dowels, and other alignment features

LT 1 thru LT6

Locational Interference Fits (LN) are used where accuracy of location is of prime importance but with no special requirements for bore pressure.

•Applications: fits for a no "slop" alignment application
•Can be harder to assemble and disassemble

LN 1 thru LN 3

Force Fits (FN) constitute a special type of interference fit, normally characterized by maintenance of constant bore pressures throughout the range of sizes.

•High bore pressures needed for high forces and/or torsion stress

FN1 thru FN5 FN1 – Light drive fits FN 5 – Heavy force fits

Example problem:
Application: A pilot shaft and hole
Nominal Size: 1.8 in.
Fit: locational clearance, class LC3

H8 +1.6 / 0 Hole size 1.8016 / 1.8000

h7 0 / -1 Shaft size 1.800 / 1.799

Use sample chart to find hole and shaft tolerances.

Min clearance = .0000
Max clearance = .0026

Table 5. American National Standard Clearance Locational Fits ANSI B4.1-1967 (R2004)

Nominal Size Range, Inches	Class LC 1			Class LC 2			Class LC 3			Class LC 4			Class LC 5		
		Standard Tolerance Limits			Standard Tolerance Limits			Standard Tolerance Limits			Standard Tolerance Limits			Standard Tolerance Limits	
Over To	Clearance[1]	Hole H6	Shaft h5	Clearance[1]	Hole H7	Shaft h6	Clearance[1]	Hole H8	Shaft h7	Clearance[1]	Hole H10	Shaft h9	Clearance[1]	Hole H7	Shaft g6
	Values shown below are in thousandths of an inch														
0– 0.12	0 0.45	+0.25 0	0 −0.2	0 0.65	+0.4 0	0 −0.25	0 1	+0.6 0	0 −0.4	0 2.6	+1.6 0	0 −1.0	0.1 0.75	+0.4 0	−0.1 −0.35
0.12– 0.24	0 0.5	+0.3 0	0 −0.2	0 0.8	+0.5 0	0 −0.3	0 1.2	+0.7 0	0 −0.5	0 3.0	+1.8 0	0 −1.2	0.15 0.95	+0.5 0	−0.15 −0.45
0.24– 0.40	0 0.65	+0.4 0	0 −0.25	0 1.0	+0.6 0	0 −0.4	0 1.5	+0.9 0	0 −0.6	0 3.6	+2.2 0	0 −1.4	0.2 1.2	+0.6 0	−0.2 −0.6
0.40– 0.71	0 0.7	+0.4 0	0 −0.3	0 1.1	+0.7 0	0 −0.4	0 1.7	+1.0 0	0 −0.7	0 4.4	+2.8 0	0 −1.6	0.25 1.35	+0.7 0	−0.25 −0.65
0.71– 1.19	0 0.9	+0.5 0	0 −0.4	0 1.3	+0.8 0	0 −0.5	0 2	+1.2 0	0 −0.8	0 5.5	+3.5 0	0 −2.0	0.3 1.6	+0.8 0	−0.3 −0.8
1.19– 1.97	0 1.0	+0.6 0	0 −0.4	0 1.6	+1.0 0	0 −0.6	0 2.6	+1.6 0	0 −1	0 6.5	+4.0 0	0 −2.5	0.4 2.0	+1.0 0	−0.4 −1.0
1.97– 3.15	0 1.2	+0.7 0	0 −0.5	0 1.9	+1.2 0	0 −0.7	0 3	+1.8 0	0 −1.2	0 7.5	+4.5 0	0 −3	0.4 2.3	+1.2 0	−0.4 −1.1
3.15– 4.73	0 1.5	+0.9 0	0 −0.6	0 2.3	+1.4 0	0 −0.9	0 3.6	+2.2 0	0 −1.4	0 8.5	+5.0 0	0 −3.5	0.5 2.8	+1.4 0	−0.5 −1.4
4.73– 7.09	0 1.7	+1.0 0	0 −0.7	0 2.6	+1.6 0	0 −1.0	0 4.1	+2.5 0	0 −1.6	0 10.0	+6.0 0	0 −4	0.6 3.2	+1.6 0	−0.6 −1.6
7.09– 9.85	0 2.0	+1.2 0	0 −0.8	0 3.0	+1.8 0	0 −1.2	0 4.6	+2.8 0	0 −1.8	0 11.5	+7.0 0	0 −4.5	0.6 3.6	+1.8 0	−0.6 −1.8
9.85– 12.41	0 2.1	+1.2 0	0 −0.9	0 3.2	+2.0 0	0 −1.2	0 5	+3.0 0	0 −2.0	0 13.0	+8.0 0	0 −5	0.7 3.9	+2.0 0	−0.7 −1.9
12.41– 15.75	0 2.4	+1.4 0	0 −1.0	0 3.6	+2.2 0	0 −1.4	0 5.7	+3.5 0	0 −2.2	0 15.0	+9.0 0	0 −6	0.7 4.3	+2.2 0	−0.7 −2.1
15.75– 19.69	0 2.6	+1.6 0	0 −1.0	0 4.1	+2.5 0	0 −1.6	0 6.5	+4 0	0 −2.5	0 16.0	+10.0 0	0 −6	0.8 4.9	+2.5 0	−0.8 −2.4

[1] Pairs of values shown represent minimum and maximum amounts of interference resulting from application of standard tolerance limits.

Table 3. American National Standard Running and Sliding Fits ANSI B4.1-1967 (R2004)

Nominal Size Range, Inches	Class RC 1			Class RC 2			Class RC 3			Class RC 4		
		Standard Tolerance Limits			Standard Tolerance Limits			Standard Tolerance Limits			Standard Tolerance Limits	
Over To	Clearance[1]	Hole H5	Shaft g4	Clearance[1]	Hole H6	Shaft g5	Clearance[1]	Hole H7	Shaft f6	Clearance[1]	Hole H8	Shaft f7
	Values shown below are in thousandths of an inch											
0 – 0.12	0.1 0.45	+0.2 0	−0.1 −0.25	0.1 0.55	+0.25 0	−0.1 −0.3	0.3 0.95	+0.4 0	−0.3 −0.55	0.3 1.3	+0.6 0	−0.3 −0.7
0.12 – 0.24	0.15 0.5	+0.2 0	−0.15 −0.3	0.15 0.65	+0.3 0	−0.15 −0.35	0.4 1.12	+0.5 0	−0.4 −0.7	0.4 1.6	+0.7 0	−0.4 −0.9
0.24 – 0.40	0.2 0.6	+0.25 0	−0.2 −0.35	0.2 0.85	+0.4 0	−0.2 −0.45	0.5 1.5	+0.6 0	−0.5 −0.9	0.5 2.0	+0.9 0	−0.5 −1.1
0.40 – 0.71	0.25 0.75	+0.3 0	−0.25 −0.45	0.25 0.95	+0.4 0	−0.25 −0.55	0.6 1.7	+0.7 0	−0.6 −1.0	0.6 2.3	+1.0 0	−0.6 −1.3
0.71 – 1.19	0.3 0.95	+0.4 0	−0.3 −0.55	0.3 1.2	+0.5 0	−0.3 −0.7	0.8 2.1	+0.8 0	−0.8 −1.3	0.8 2.8	+1.2 0	−0.8 −1.6
1.19 – 1.97	0.4 1.1	+0.4 0	−0.4 −0.7	0.4 1.4	+0.6 0	−0.4 −0.8	1.0 2.6	+1.0 0	−1.0 −1.6	1.0 3.6	+1.6 0	−1.0 −2.0
1.97 – 3.15	0.4 1.2	+0.5 0	−0.4 −0.7	0.4 1.6	+0.7 0	−0.4 −0.9	1.2 3.1	+1.2 0	−1.2 −1.9	1.2 4.2	+1.8 0	−1.2 −2.4
3.15 – 4.73	0.5 1.5	+0.6 0	−0.5 −0.9	0.5 2.0	+0.9 0	−0.5 −1.1	1.4 3.7	+1.4 0	−1.4 −2.3	1.4 5.0	+2.2 0	−1.4 −2.8
4.73 – 7.09	0.6 1.8	+0.7 0	−0.6 −1.1	0.6 2.3	+1.0 0	−0.6 −1.3	1.6 4.2	+1.6 0	−1.6 −2.6	1.6 5.7	+2.5 0	−1.6 −3.2
7.09 – 9.85	0.6 2.0	+0.8 0	−0.6 −1.2	0.6 2.6	+1.2 0	−0.6 −1.4	2.0 5.0	+1.8 0	−2.0 −3.2	2.0 6.6	+2.8 0	−2.0 −3.8
9.85 – 12.41	0.8 2.3	+0.9 0	−0.8 −1.4	0.8 2.9	+1.2 0	−0.8 −1.7	2.5 5.7	+2.0 0	−2.5 −3.7	2.5 7.5	+3.0 0	−2.5 −4.5
12.41 – 15.75	1.0 2.7	+1.0 0	−1.0 −1.7	1.0 3.4	+1.4 0	−1.0 −2.0	3.0 6.6	+2.2 0	−3.0 −4.4	3.0 8.7	+3.5 0	−3.0 −5.2
15.75 – 19.69	1.2 3.0	+1.0 0	−1.2 −2.0	1.2 3.8	+1.6 0	−1.2 −2.2	4.0 8.1	+2.5 0	−4.0 −5.6	4.0 10.5	+4.0 0	−4.0 −6.5

[1] Pairs of values shown represent minimum and maximum amounts of clearance resulting from application of standard tolerance limits.

Workshop Exercise 2.2

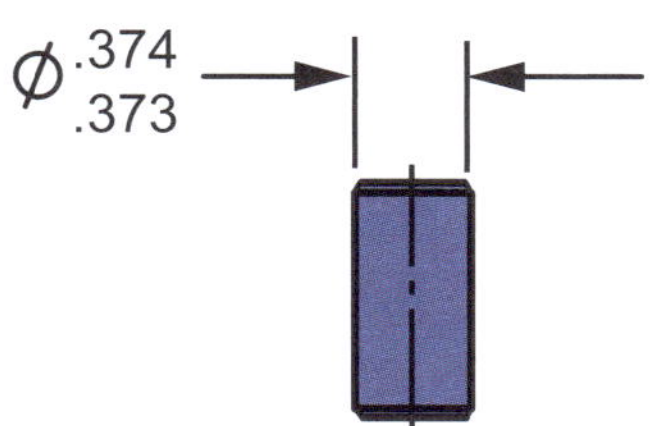

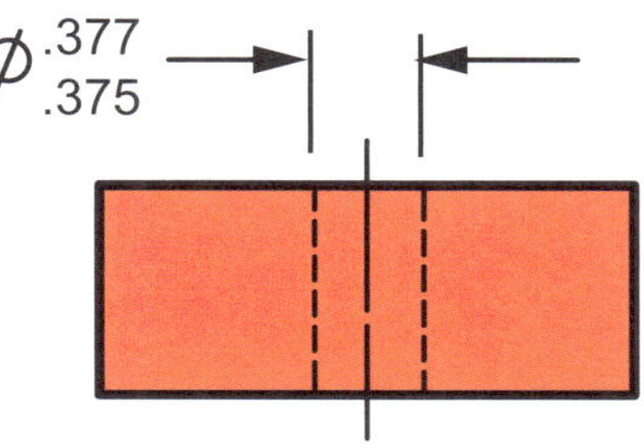

1. What is the min and max clearance between the pin and hole above? ______________

2. Name an application for a running and sliding fit.

____

3. What type of fit would be best for an application with a pilot hole and shaft that must be freely assembled and disassembled?

____

4. Which would provide more interference, a locational interference fit or force fit?

____

5. Which would be a tighter fit, an LC3 or an LC9?

____

Use sample charts on the previous page to find hole and shaft limits for the following nominal sizes and fits. Write your answers as min and max hole and shaft sizes. Also include the min/max clearance between the parts.

6. Application: dowel alignment pin and hole
Nominal Size: .375 in.
Fit: locational clearance, class LC3

Min clearance = _____
Max clearance = _____

Hole size: _____
_____

Shaft size: _____
_____

____

7. Application: shaft in bushing
Nominal Size: 1 in.
Fit: close running fit, class RC4

Min clearance = _____
Max clearance = _____

Hole size: _____
_____

Shaft size: _____
_____

____

8. Application: spool valve with translating shaft
Nominal Size: 1.2 in.
Fit: sliding fit, class RC2

Min clearance = _____
Max clearance = _____

Hole size: _____
_____

Shaft size: _____
_____

Unit 3

How the Geometric Tolerancing System Works

Plus/Minus Tolerancing to Locate Features Is Not Clear

The drawing below is defined with plus/minus toleranced dimensions. The plus/minus tolerances for the size of the holes and size thickness of the bar have a clear definition in the ASME Y14.5 standard. The remaining plus/minus dimensions describe vague relationships between features and are subject to misinterpretations.

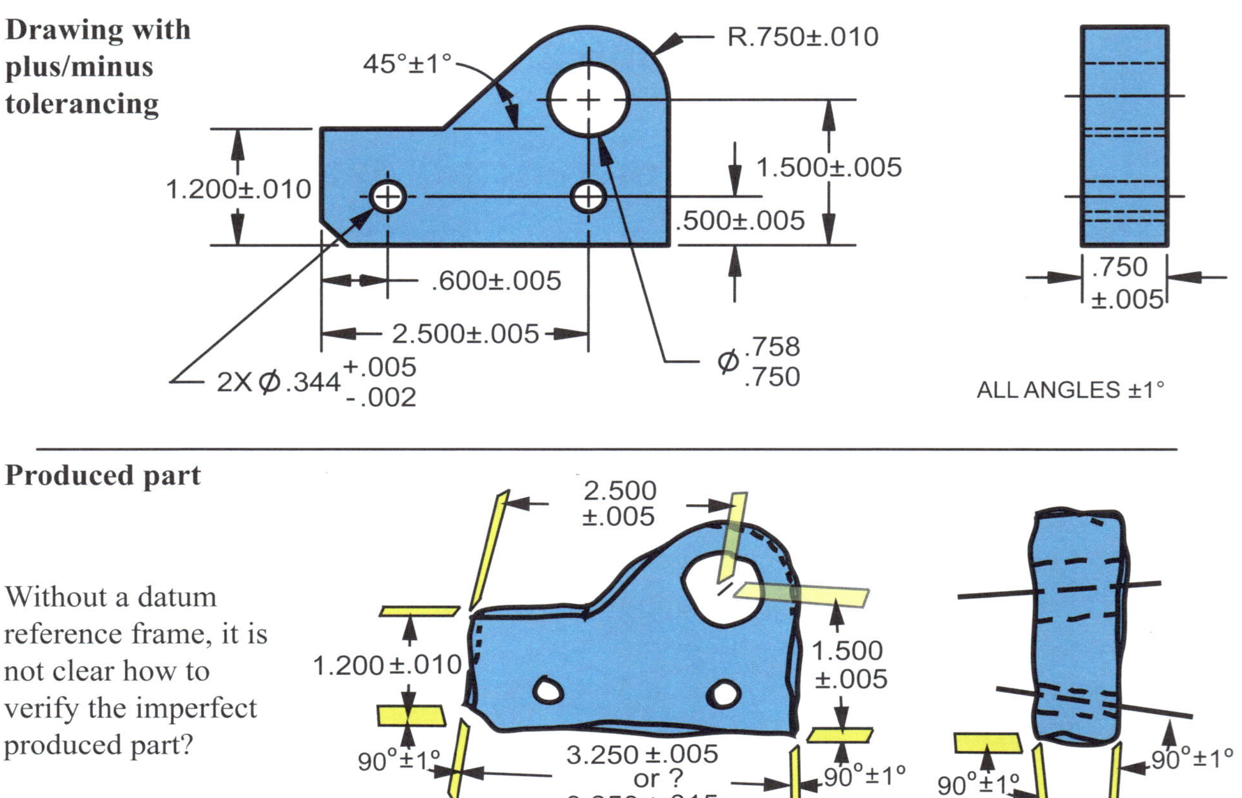

We have a drawing without clear definitions of the tolerances. There are no datums established. The features on the part are not flat, perpendicular or parallel. The holes are out of location and are not perpendicular or straight. All features have implied 90° and 0° angles to each other with a tolerance of ±1°.

Despite the ambiguous definition of these tolerances, manufacturing does its best to produce the part to the mean of the toleranced dimensions. The problem lies with inspection procedures. How do we verify conformance? Do we measure square to one preselected edge, or like a parallelogram? What is the order of the datums? How square do the holes measure, and relative to which datum? Some of the surfaces do not oppose each other. If we measure from the long surface to the short surface, we will get a different answer than if we measure from the short surface to the long surface.

The surfaces are not flat. Do we measure from the high points, low points or median points? What is the location of the .750 radius? Is it the same as the hole? What if we wanted it different? What is the tolerance on the overall length of the part? Do we add the ±.005 tolerance from the 2.500 dimension plus the ± .010 tolerance on the .750 radius? Do the angle tolerances contribute to this overall length? In order to develop an inspection procedure, we need a clear 3D mathematical definition of the product. We need geometric tolerancing.

Comparison - Position Tolerancing vs. Plus/Minus Tolerancing

There are two drawings shown below. In the top drawing, the large hole is located with plus/minus tolerances. In the bottom drawing, the hole is located with a position tolerance. The comparison of the two methods below show position tolerancing to provide an increase in location tolerance for the hole, while establishing a datum reference frame and clearly defining design intent. Position tolerancing is a superior method for the location of holes.

Plus/minus tolerancing

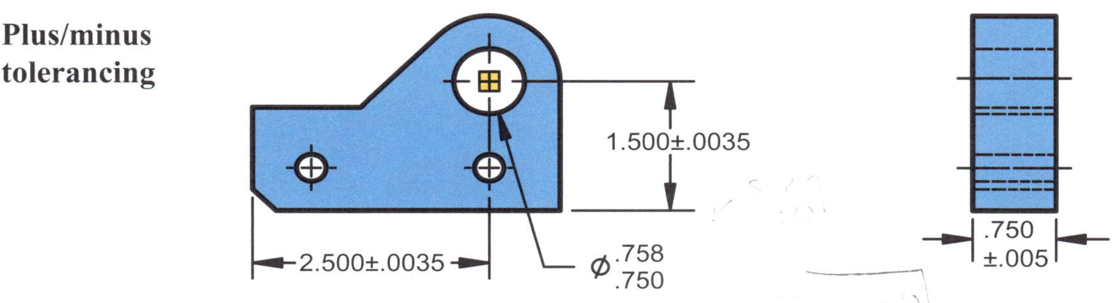

The hole has ±.0035 tolerances on the X/Y dimensions. This locates the hole within a square tolerance zone of .007, which is approximately .010 across the corners. This allows the axis of the hole to be off in a diagonal direction more than in the horizontal or vertical. Tolerances of ±.0035 in the X and Y allows the hole to be off center as much as ±.005.

Position tolerancing

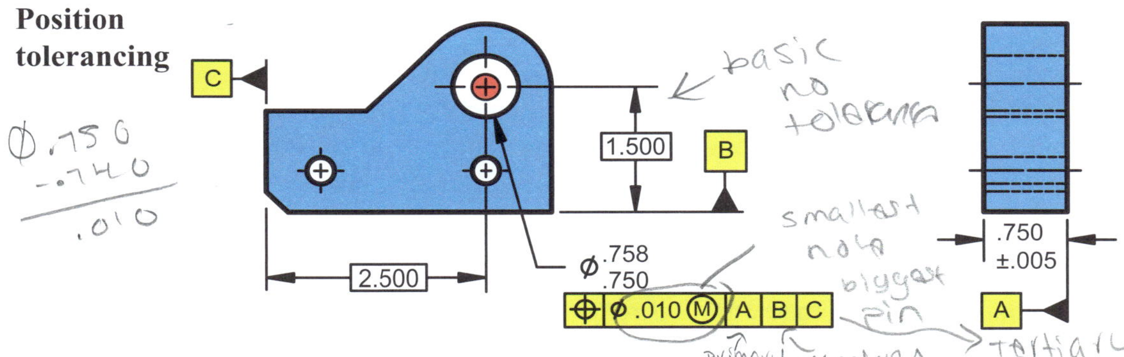

The hole is located with a position tolerance. Theoretically exact basic X/Y dimensions (enclosed in a box) locate the Ø.010 cylindrically shaped tolerance zone. The axis of the hole must fall in this zone and allows the same deviation in any direction.

Position tolerancing provides an increase in location tolerance over plus/minus tolerancing.

.018 dia position at LMC

.007

.010 dia position at MMC

Tolerance increase zone

.007 sq tol zone

The position tolerance zone provides an increase in location tolerance in the horizontal and vertical directions over the plus/minus tolerancing, while still ensuring the hole location is never more than .010 total. If the hole is a clearance hole, the MMC modifier specification following the position tolerance will allow additional location tolerance, up to .018 as the hole departs from MMC to LMC. See the rest of this unit for more explantion on MMC modifers.

How the Geometric Tolerancing System Works

Before controlling relationships between features, first define the size tolerance of holes, slots, tabs, and pins with plus/minus dimensions.

There is a three step process to apply a geometric tolerancing scheme to a part:

1. Identify the datum features in their order of precedence to establish a Datum Reference Frame (DRF) based on mating conditions.
2. Qualify the datum features with form, orientation, or location tolerances as necessary.
3. Locate all other features:

   Apply position tolerances to locate features of size

   Apply profile tolerances to locate surfaces

   Make all dimensions locating these features basic

The next page shows geometric tolerancing applied to the Hole Bar. It mounts on the back, bottom and side surfaces shown, and it is kept in place by the two mounting screws. The location of the large hole is important, but its function will be kept vague at this point and will be discussed later.

The size of two .344 clearance holes are defined by a standard drill (11/32). They are oversized by 1/32 to clear a .3125 (5/16) screw. The size tolerance is determined by standard drill tolerance to allow economical production. The large hole is defined with a size and tolerance of .750/.758. The thickness of the bar is also defined with a size tolerance (could also be profile).

1. The datum features are selected in an order of precedence by how the part mounts in the assembly. The back face is the primary datum feature (A) because the bolts pull it up tight to this face a full 3 points of contact. The bottom surface is the secondary datum feature (B) because this surface is long and provides a more reliable mount than the shorter left-side surface. It makes 2 points of contact. The left end surface is the tertiary datum feature (C) and makes 1 point of contact.

2. The imperfect datum features are qualified to the theoretically perfect DRF. Datum feature A is related to itself with flatness. Datum feature B is related to A with a perpendicularity. Datum feature C is related to A and B with a perpendicularity. In this step, the lower precedence datum features are related to the higher precedence datum features. These tolerances determine the stability of the imperfect part in its mounted condition.

3. Position tolerance is applied to the two holes. The tolerance is calculated using the fixed fastener formula and an MMC modifier is added. This ensures the holes will always clear the mating screws. (More on the MMC modifier later in this unit and the fastener formulas later in unit 12.)

Profile tolerances are applied to the surfaces between points X and Y. The tolerance in the profile feature control frame defines a total wide zone that is equally disposed about the true profile. The feature surfaces must fall within this zone. The profile tolerance is a relatively large tolerance at .020 to indicate the outside surface is relatively unimportant.

The location of the features to the DRF are defined with theoretically-exact basic dimensions that are enclosed in a box. These basic dimensions locate the position and profile tolerance zones within which the features axes or surfaces must lie.

Geometric Tolerancing Applied to the Hole Bar

Geometric tolerancing is a clear and concise three dimensional, mathematical engineering language for communicating design intent based on functional requirements. A fully geometrically toleranced product drawing is shown based on assembly mounting conditions.

The datum reference frame is established by datum features A, B and C. The basic dimensions locate the center of the position and profile tolerance zone. The surfaces and hole axes must lie within the specified geometric tolerance zones.

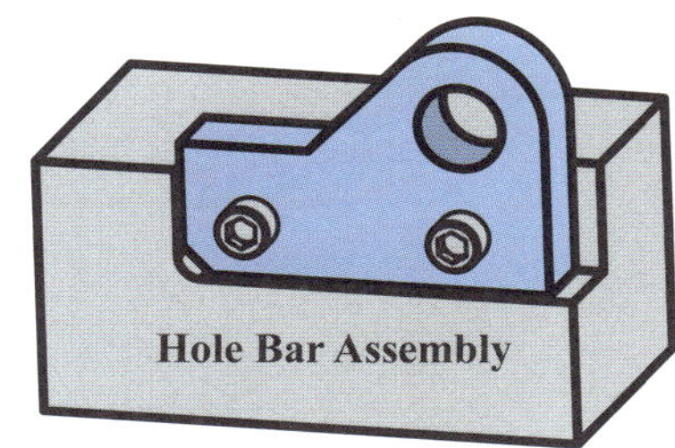

This on the drawing

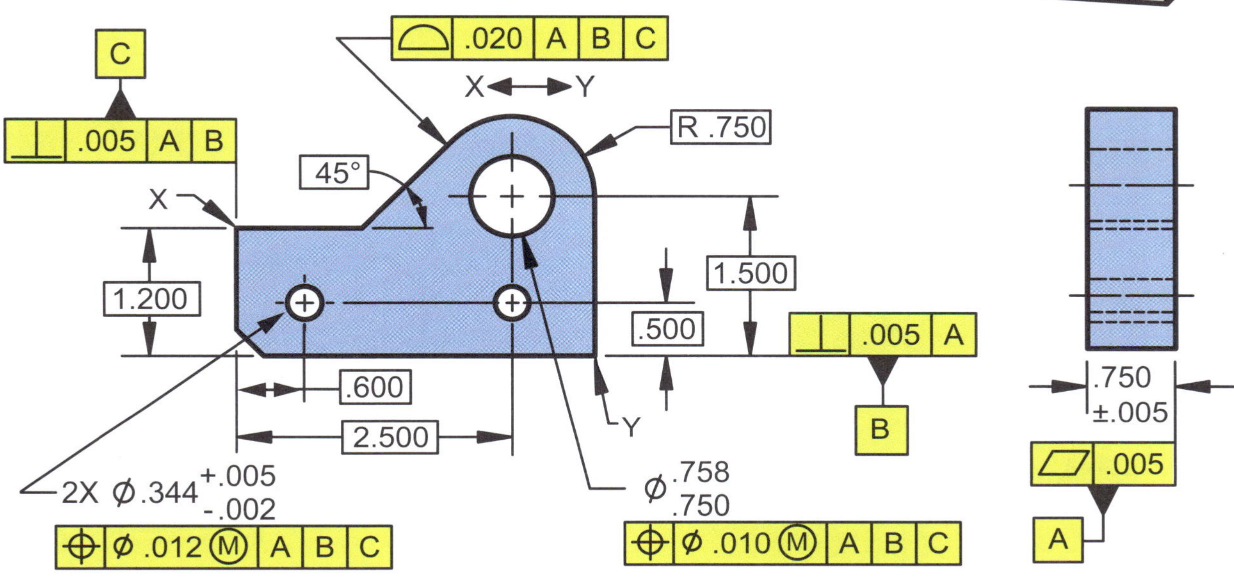

Means this on produced part

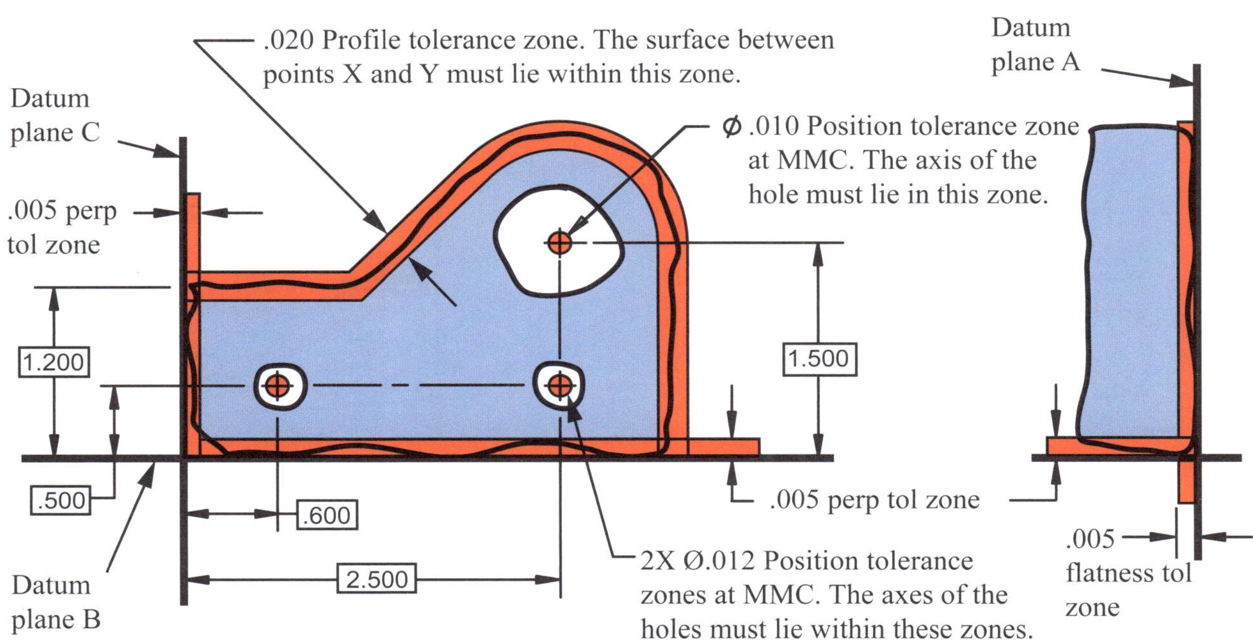

Geometric Tolerancing Applied to the Hole Bar

This on the drawing

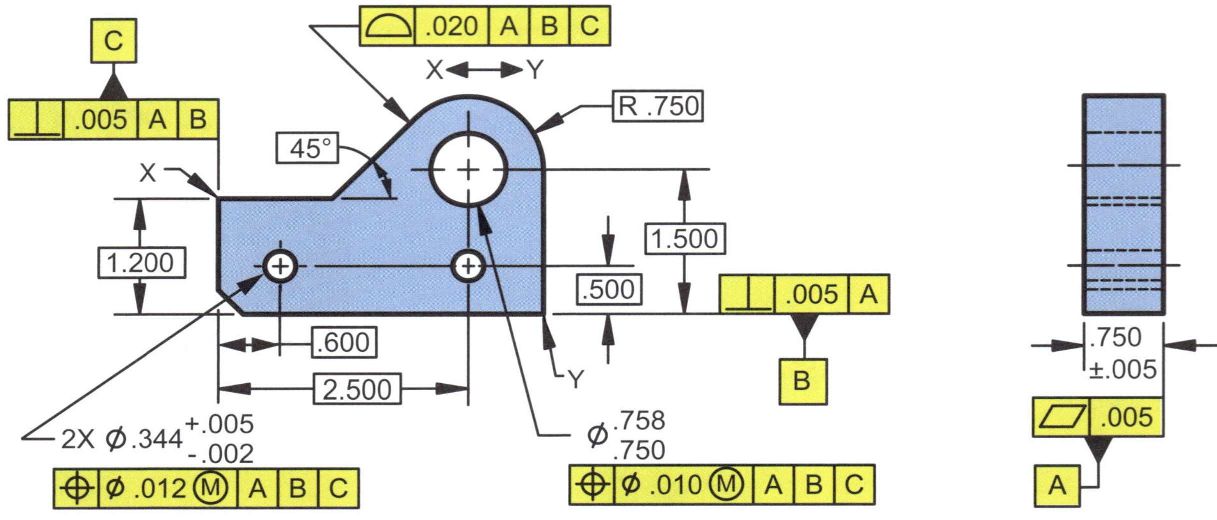

Means this

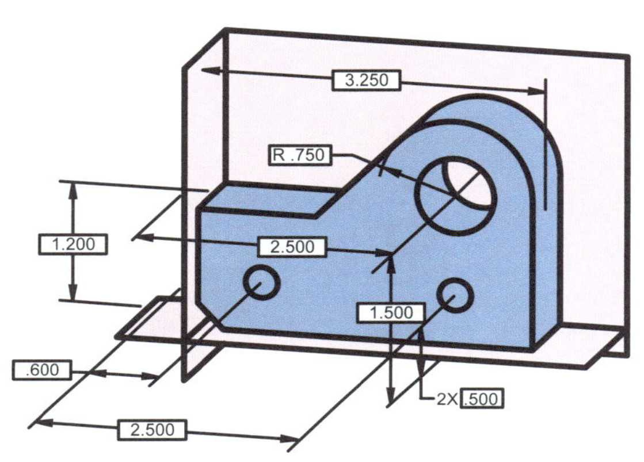

The theoretical part is shown with basic dimensions that define the true position and true profile of the features relative to the DRF.

The position and profile tolerance zones are centered about the true position and true profile. The width and diameters of the zones set by the tolerance values.

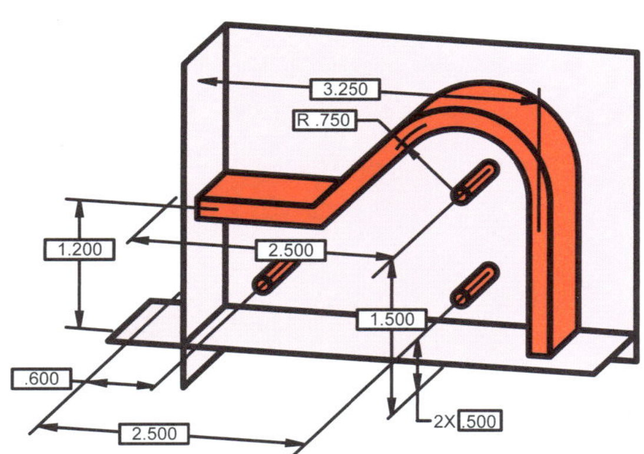

The tolerance zones represent the worst case boundaries for the features and are fixed relative to the DRF.

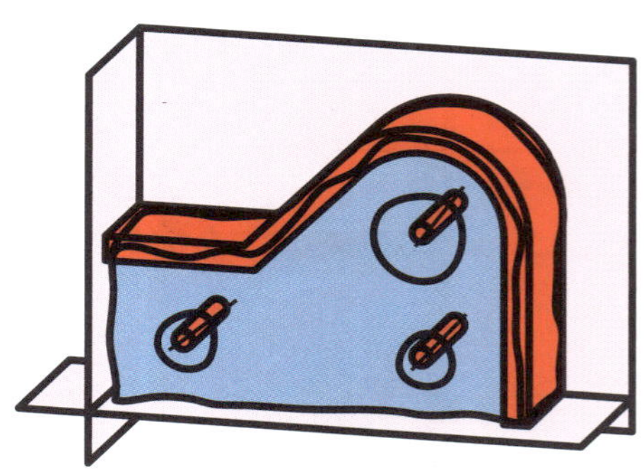

The produced part is mated, in order of precedence, to the DRF. The part features must lie within the designated tolerance zones.

Geometric Tolerancing Applied to the Hole Bar 3D

The 3D model may be toleranced in the CAD system according to ASME Y14.41-2012. All annotations are specified in one or more annotation planes. As the 3D model is rotated, the text rotates along with the model. The text rotation will update with each rotation of the model so the text will not appear backwards or upside-down.

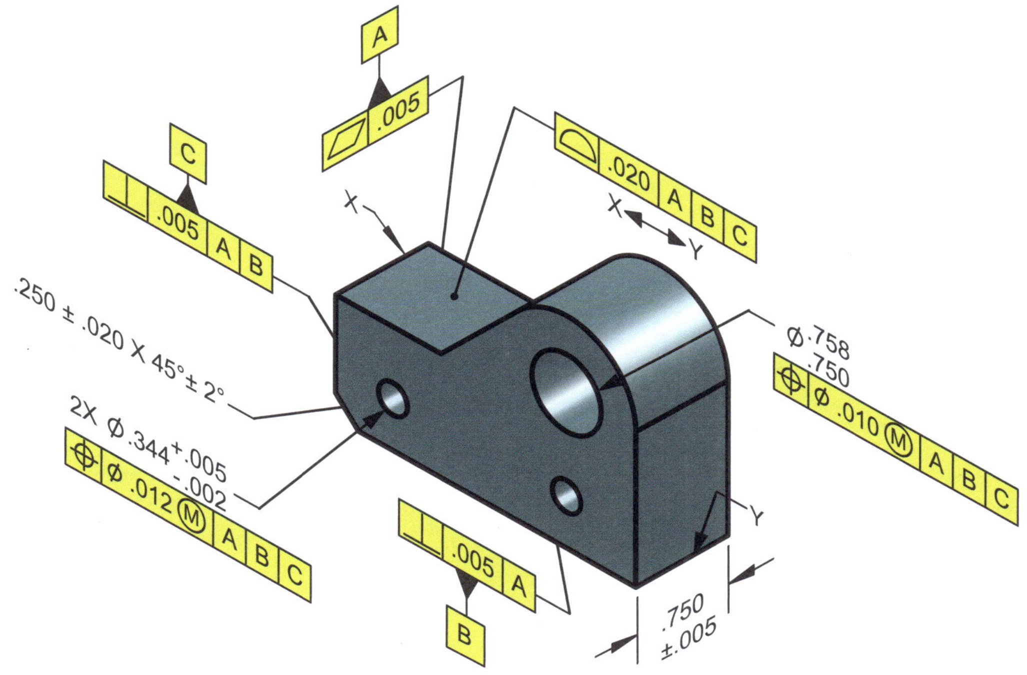

The 3D annotated model includes the ability to enable or disable the display of all annotations or selected annotations. This means the user can choose to show all the feature control frames and dimensions, or they can select and show individual feature annotations on demand.

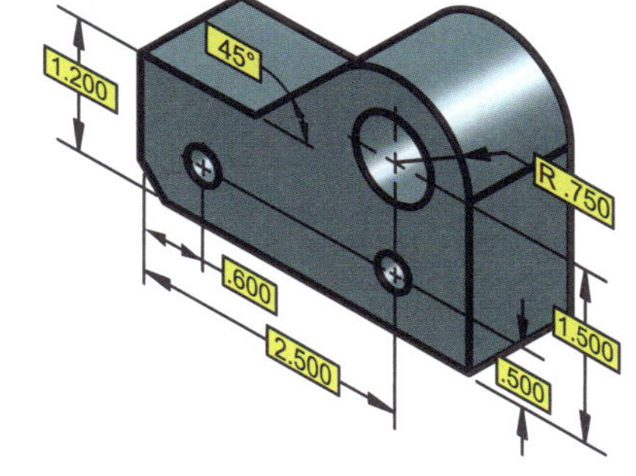

When a feature control frame is queried, the corresponding feature(s) shall highlight to show associativity.

When multiple features have a single annotation, the features are grouped into a pattern in the CAD system before the geometric tolerancing is applied to ensure associativity.

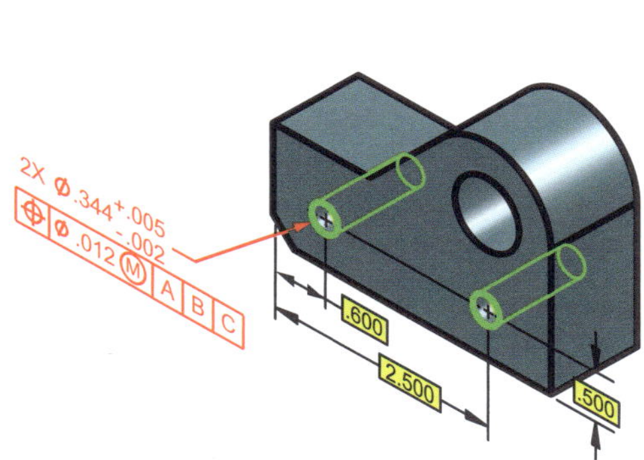

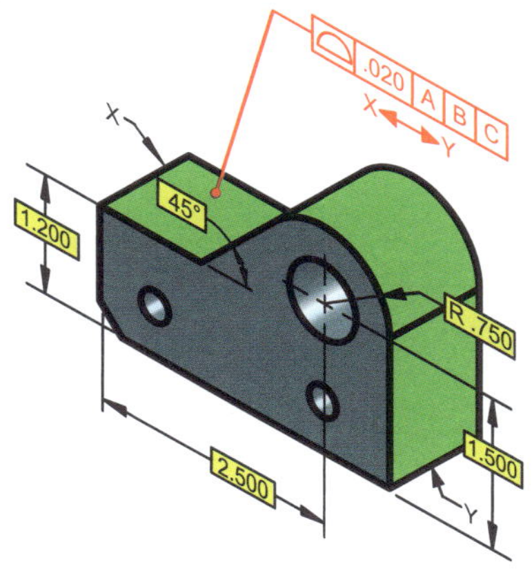

Selecting Position Tolerances with Modifiers

The large hole below has a position tolerance applied. Below are three different functional scenarios for different material condition modifiers. See the following pages for explanations of material condition modifiers and revisit these scenarios.

A press fit pin mounts in the hole. The size tolerance on the hole is tight because of the required press fit. The position tolerance defines the location of the pin. The size tolerance and location tolerance are unrelated. The feature has an RFS modifier applied.

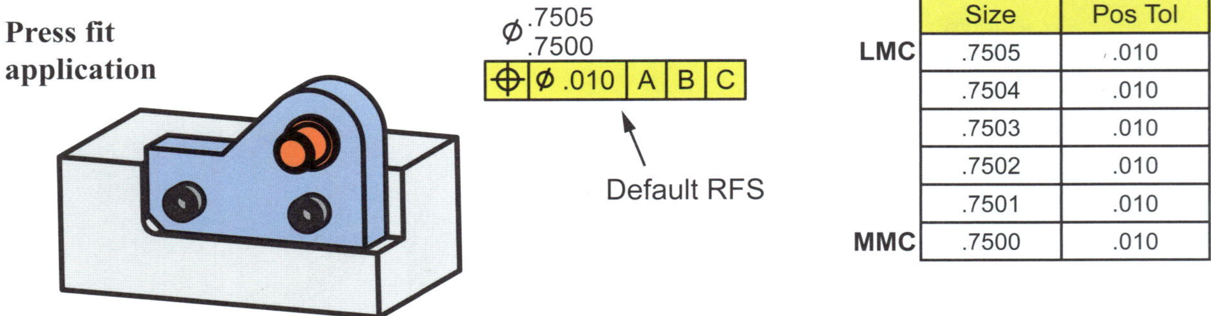

	Size	Pos Tol
LMC	.7505	.010
	.7504	.010
	.7503	.010
	.7502	.010
	.7501	.010
MMC	.7500	.010

The hole clears a .740 **fixed pin**. The size tolerance on the hole is large because it is used for clearance and does not have a fitting requirement. The position tolerance is calculated by the clearance with the MMC hole and MMC pin. The feature has an MMC modifier applied.

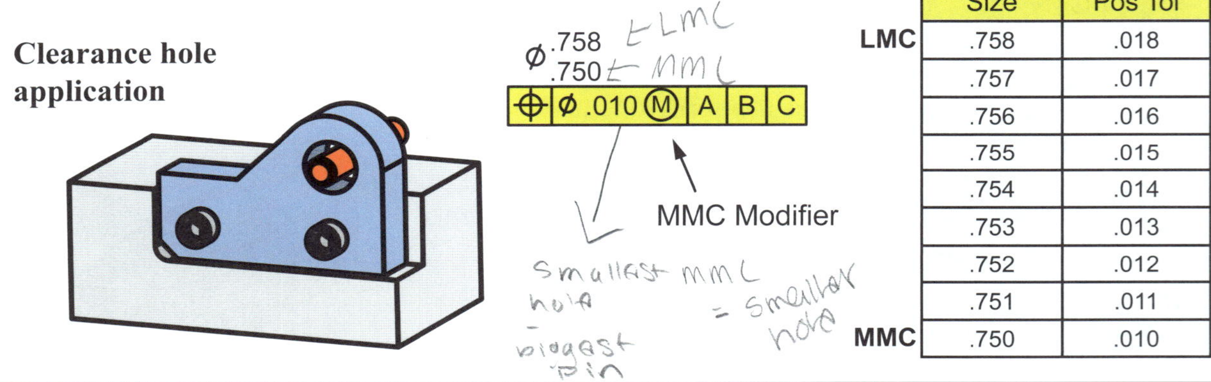

	Size	Pos Tol
LMC	.758	.018
	.757	.017
	.756	.016
	.755	.015
	.754	.014
	.753	.013
	.752	.012
	.751	.011
MMC	.750	.010

The part is a lifting lug and a hook fits through the hole to lift the entire assembly. The size tolerance on the hole is large because it does not have a tight fitting requirement. The wall thickness is important for the strength and prevent a crack or breakthrough. Both the LMC size and location tolerance is used for strength analysis. The feature has an LMC modifier applied.

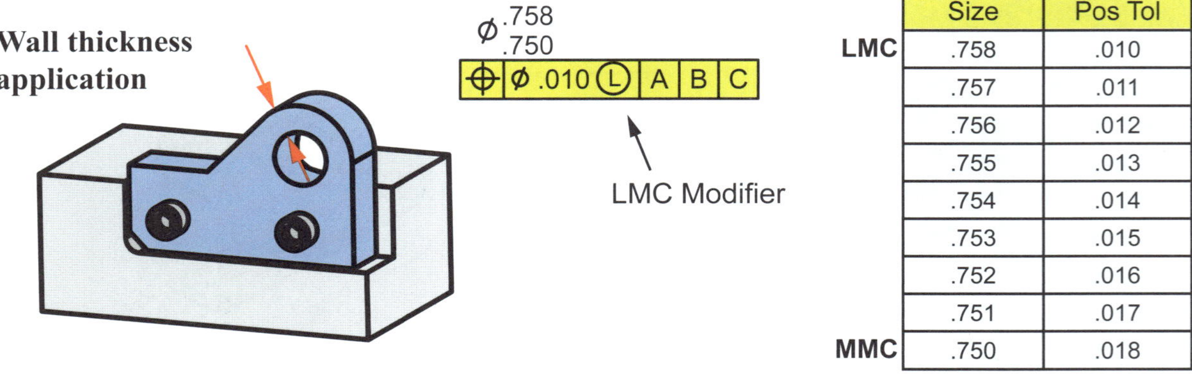

	Size	Pos Tol
LMC	.758	.010
	.757	.011
	.756	.012
	.755	.013
	.754	.014
	.753	.015
	.752	.016
	.751	.017
MMC	.750	.018

Modifier Rules - Applicability of RFS and MMC/LMC Modifiers

Material condition modifiers may be found behind the tolerance in a feature control frame. If applicable, the default condition is Regardless of Feature Size (RFS). The circle M, for Maximum material condition, or circle L, for Least material condition, may be specified instead.

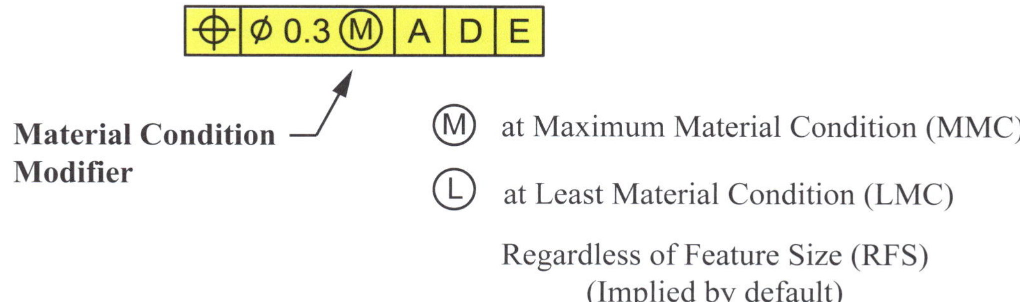

Material condition modifiers are only applicable for features of size (holes, slots, pins, widths). These modifiers may not be applied to symbols controlling surfaces. The modifiers are always applicable to position tolerance but never with a profile tolerance. Perpendicularity, parallelism, angularity may have a modifier if they are controlling a feature of size. Median plane flatness and median line straightness may also have a modifier.

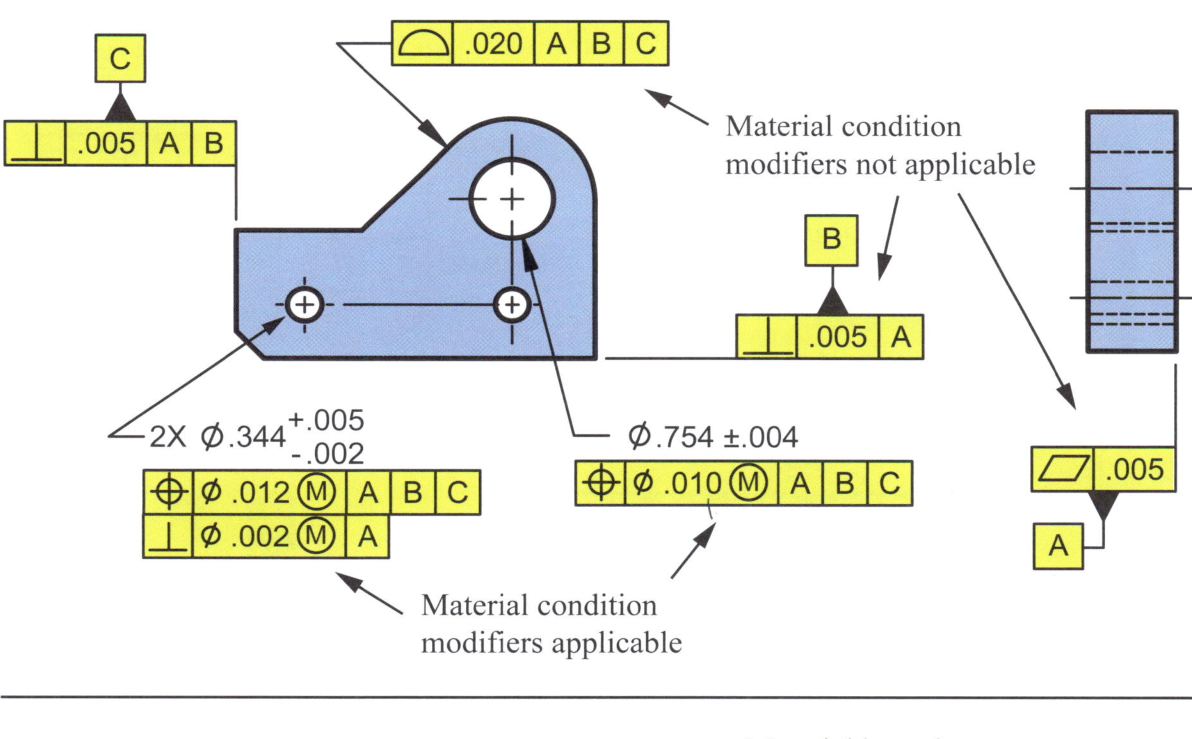

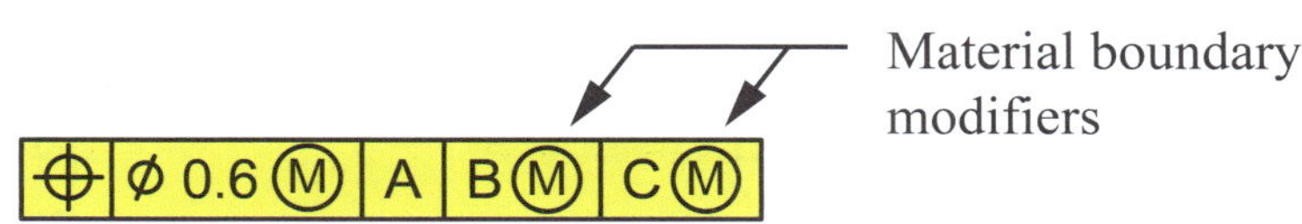

Material boundary modifiers are sometimes added behind the datum feature references. Although they look the same as material condition modifiers, they invoke a different concept and will be talked about more in unit 7.

Position Tolerance Applied Regardless of Feature Size (RFS)

A position tolerance is used to locate features of size. It defines a tolerance zone within which the feature axis or center plane must lie. The size of this zone determines the amount of variation allowed from true (theoretically exact) position. Basic dimensions establish the true position from the specified datums as well as the interrelationship between the features. See the next page for an pictorial view of the tolerance zones.

If there is no material condition modifier following the feature tolerance, the geometric tolerance applies regardless of feature size (RFS). When RFS applies, the specified geometric tolerance is independent of the actual size of the feature. The allowable geometric tolerance is limited to the specified value in the feature control frame (regardless).

The feature control frame below states that the holes must be positioned within a 0.6 diameter tolerance zone. Since there is no material condition modifier following the feature tolerance, it is implied to apply RFS. This requires the axis of each hole to be positioned within a 0.6 diameter position zone despite the feature's size. There is no additional position tolerance allowed as the holes get larger or smaller.

Position tolerance applies RFS

	Diameter Feature Size	Diameter Position Tolerance Allowed
LMC	12.3	0.6
	12.2	0.6
	12.1	0.6
	12.0	0.6
	11.9	0.6
	11.8	0.6
MMC	11.7	0.6

The default RFS requires the axis of the features to be positioned within a 0.6 diameter tolerance zone regardless of the feature size.

Position tolerance applies RFS

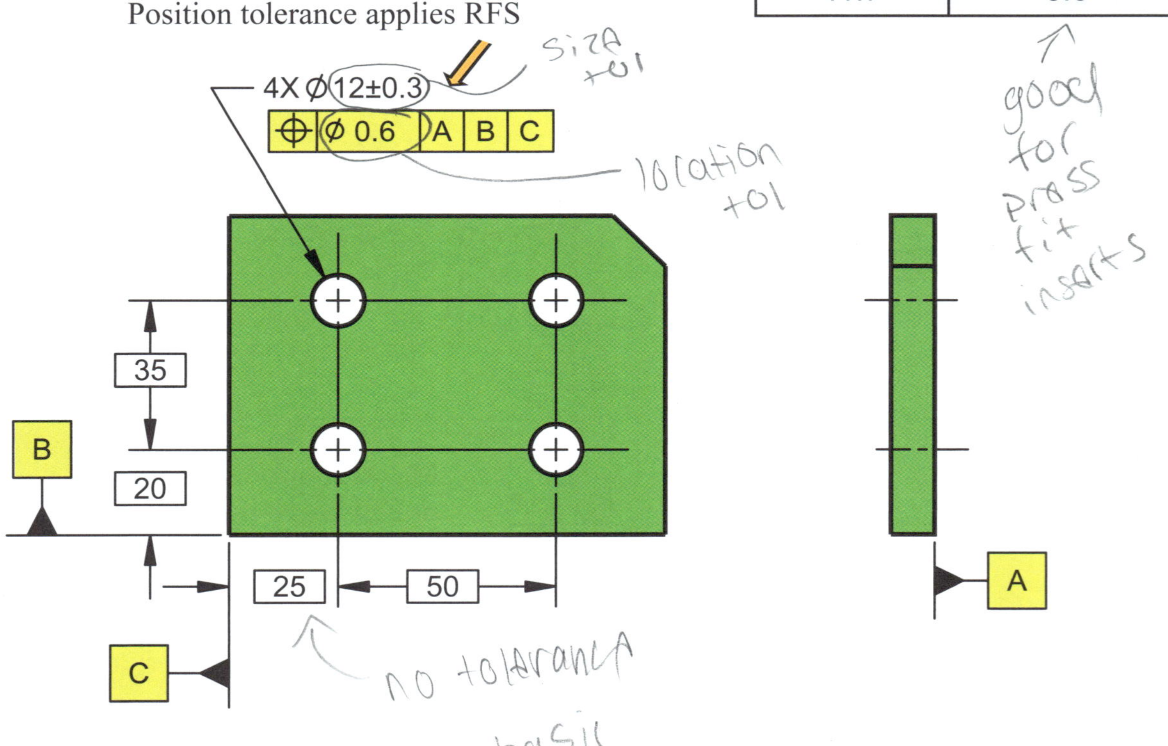

Position Tolerance Applied Regardless of Feature Size (RFS)

The graphic below shows the imperfect part from the drawing on the previous page. The tolerance zones (enlarged for clarity) are theoretical and perfectly located by the basic dimensions from the datum reference frame.

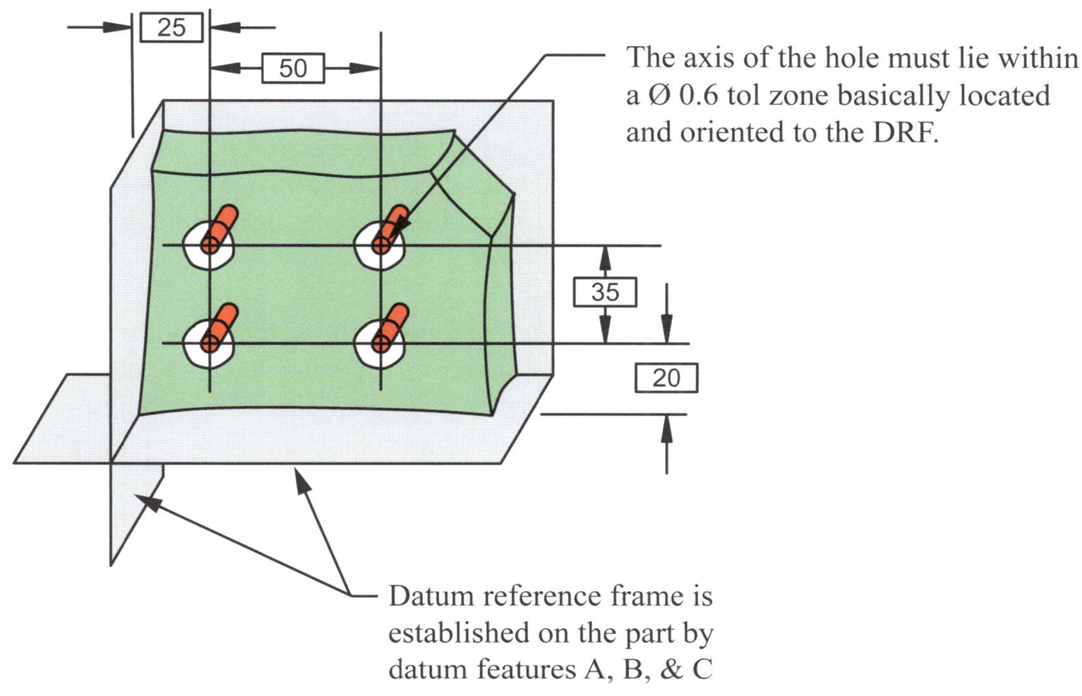

Section view of above part

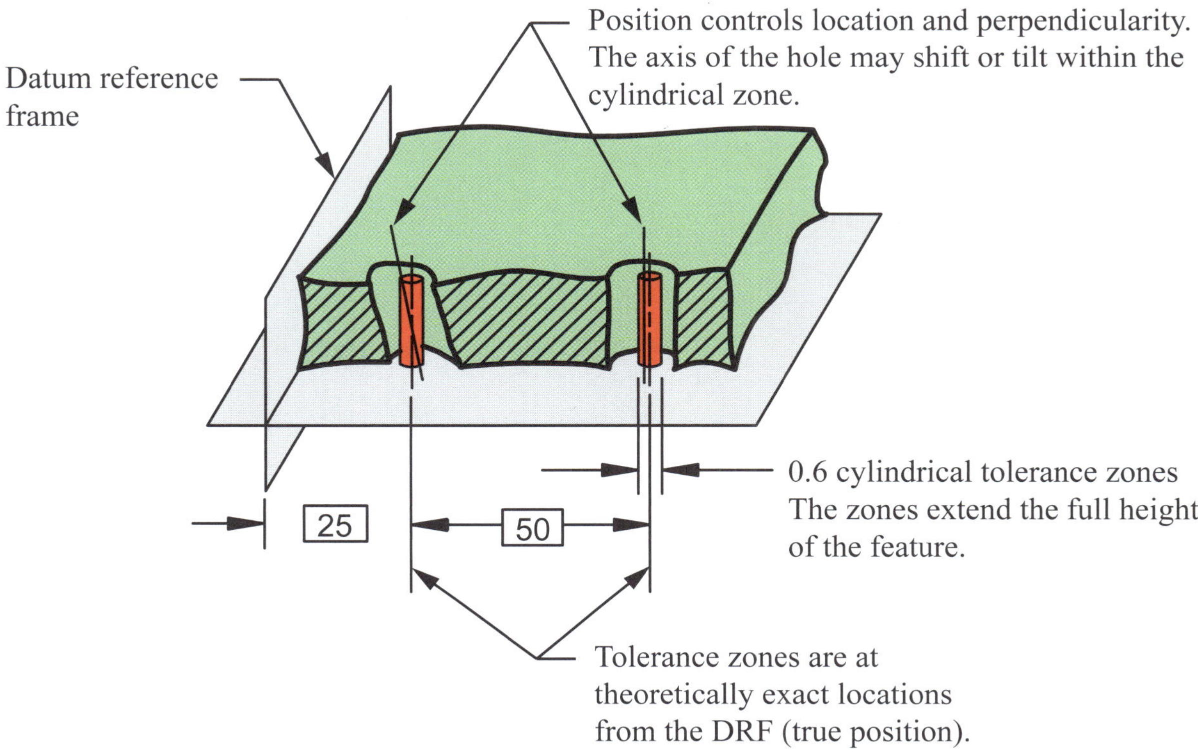

Effect of the Maximum Material Condition (MMC) Modifier

The maximum material condition (MMC) of a feature is the smallest hole or biggest pin. An MMC modifier may be applied by placing the circle M symbol in the feature control frame following the feature tolerance. This allows additional geometric tolerance as the feature's size departs from its MMC. The MMC modifier may only be applied to features of size.

The feature control frame below states that the holes must be positioned within 0.6 at the feature's MMC. The MMC for the hole is 11.7 diameter; the 0.6 position tolerance applies at this size. As the hole departs (gets larger) from its MMC size, it is allowed additional position tolerance equal to its departure from MMC. Industry often calls this departure from MMC "bonus tolerance". The holes could have as much as 1.2 diameter position if they are produced at their LMC size of 12.3. See table below.

The size of the hole for the bonus tolerance is determined by the unrelated actual mating envelope. The bonus tolerance is always one-for-one because the hole size is a diameter value and the position tolerance is a diameter zone. The MMC modifier principle applies to each hole individually and each hole may have a different position tolerance.

Position tolerance at MMC

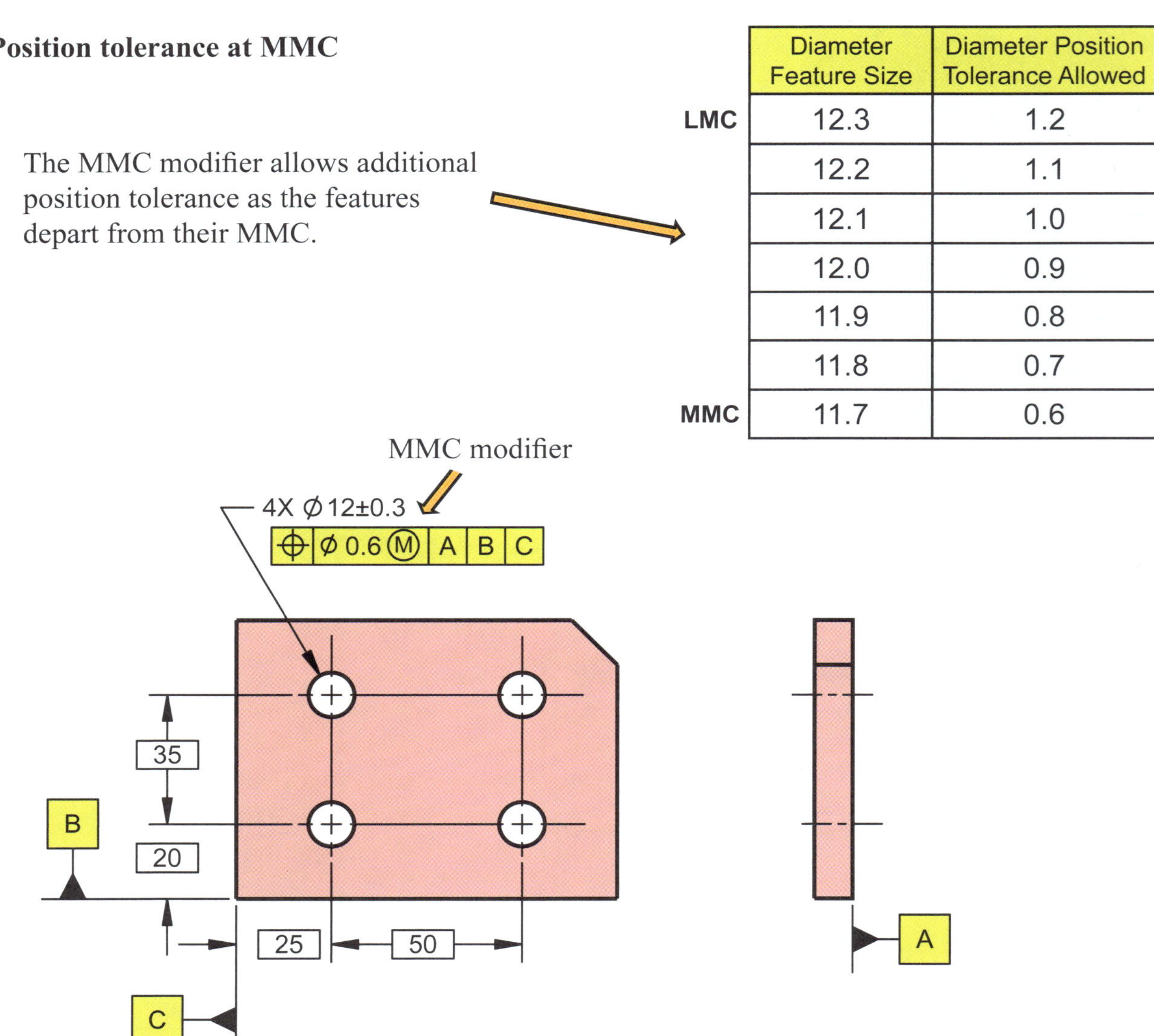

	Diameter Feature Size	Diameter Position Tolerance Allowed
LMC	12.3	1.2
	12.2	1.1
	12.1	1.0
	12.0	0.9
	11.9	0.8
	11.8	0.7
MMC	11.7	0.6

Zero Tolerancing at MMC

The example below illustrates holes positioned with zero tolerance at MMC. As each hole departs from MMC, additional position tolerance is allowed equal to this departure. If the hole is produced at MMC of 11.1, it must be perfectly located. If the hole is produced at the mean value of 11.7, it is allowed 0.6 position. The hole is allowed as much as 1.2 diameter position tolerance if it is produced at the LMC size of 12.3.

If you compare this drawing with the drawing on the previous page, you will see the tables are the same from 11.7 up. Zero tolerancing at MMC allows additional size tolerance while maintaining the same position tolerance and worst case boundaries.

Zero tolerancing at MMC or LMC is not often used with features produced with standard size tools such as drilled holes. Its best use is for manufacturing processes with tools that can easily vary the size of the hole such as cast holes, milled holes, lathe turning. The increase in size tolerance while maintaining the same position tolerance and boundaries can make a part more economical to produce. Also see zero perpendicularity at MMC in unit 7.

Any geometric control that allows a material condition modifier may be toleranced with a zero tolerance at MMC or LMC. (Zero tolerance regardless of feature size is not possible).

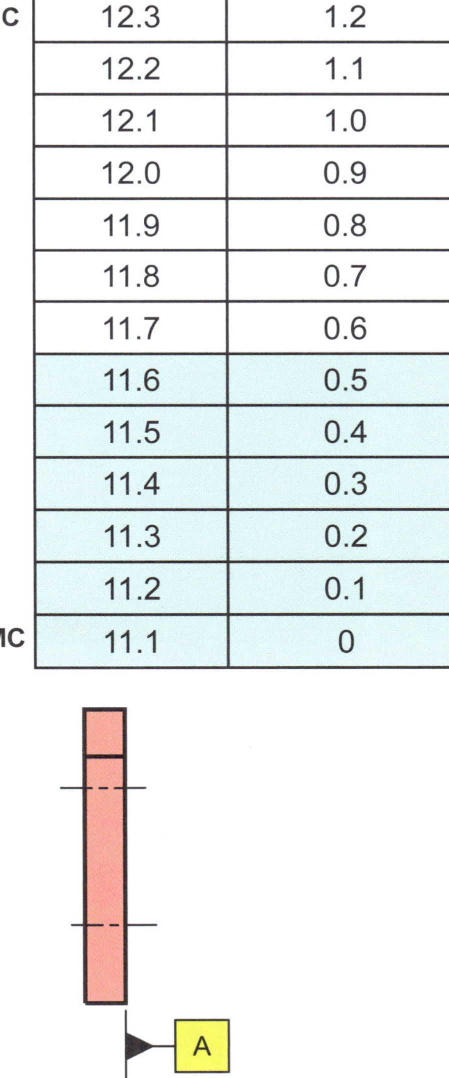

	Diameter Feature Size	Diameter Position Tolerance Allowed
LMC	12.3	1.2
	12.2	1.1
	12.1	1.0
	12.0	0.9
	11.9	0.8
	11.8	0.7
	11.7	0.6
	11.6	0.5
	11.5	0.4
	11.4	0.3
	11.3	0.2
	11.2	0.1
MMC	11.1	0

Zero position tolerance at MMC

The MMC modifier allows additional position tolerance as the features depart from their MMC.

4X Ø 12.3 / 11.1

| ⌖ | Ø 0 Ⓜ | A | B | C |

35 20 25 50 B C A

Effect of the Least Material Condition (LMC) Modifier

The least material condition (LMC) of a feature is the biggest hole or smallest pin.

An LMC modifier may be applied by placing the circle L symbol in the feature control frame following the feature tolerance. This allows additional geometric tolerance as the feature's size departs from its LMC. The LMC modifier may only be applied to features of size.

The feature control frame below states that the holes must be positioned within 0.6 at the feature's LMC. The LMC for the hole is 12.3 diameter; the 0.6 position tolerance applies at this size. As the hole departs (gets smaller) from its LMC size, it is allowed additional position tolerance equal to its departure from LMC. Industry often calls this departure from LMC "bonus tolerance". The holes could have as much as 1.2 diameter position if they are produced at their MMC size of 11.7. See table below.

The size of the hole for the bonus tolerance is determined by the unrelated actual minimum material envelope. The bonus tolerance is always one-for-one because the hole size is a diameter value and the position tolerance is a diameter zone. The LMC modifier principle applies to each hole individually and each hole may have a different position tolerance.

Note: The LMC modifier unlocks the perfect form at MMC requirement set by the limits of size (rule#1). The LMC modifier instead requires perfect form at LMC.

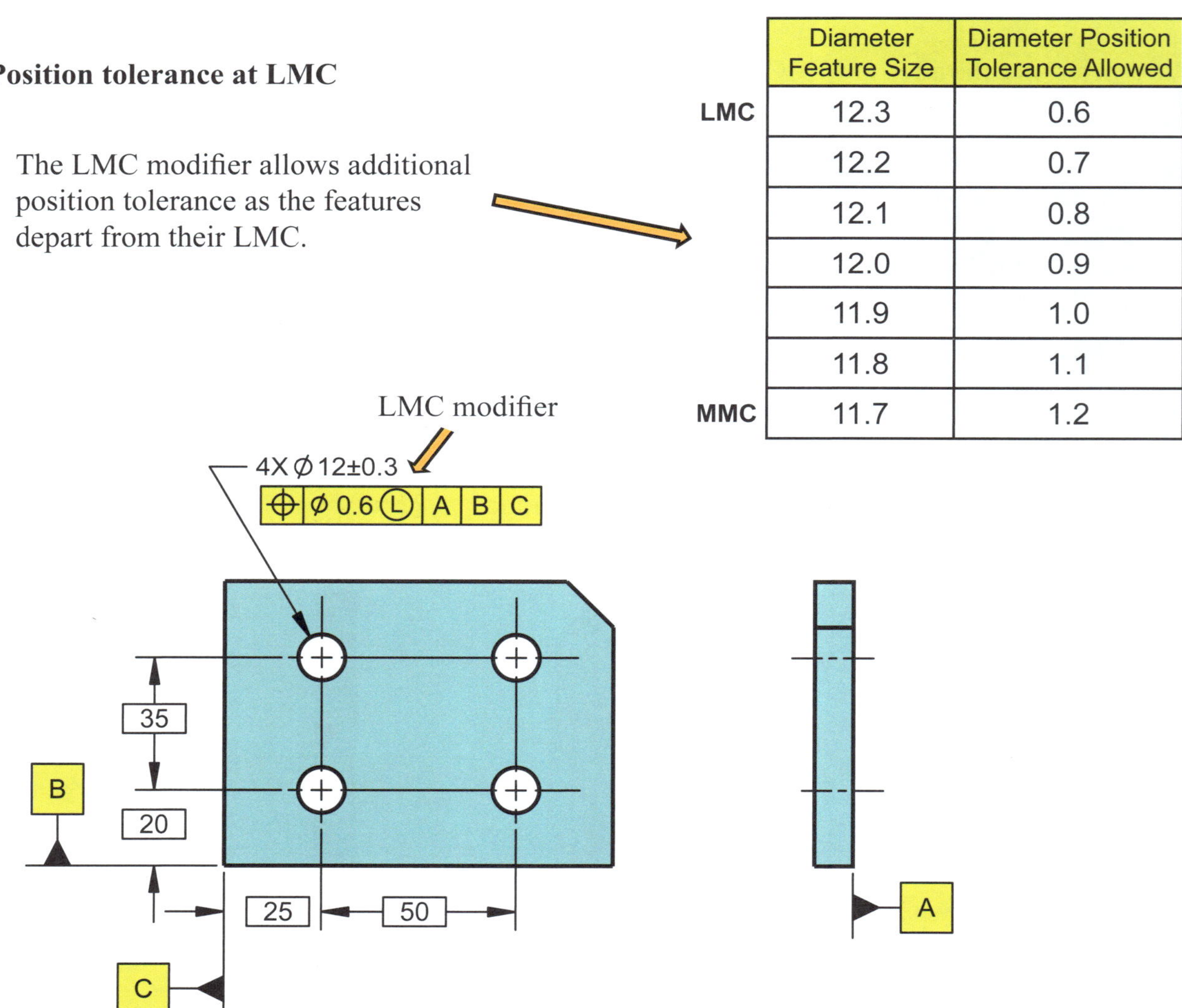

	Diameter Feature Size	Diameter Position Tolerance Allowed
LMC	12.3	0.6
	12.2	0.7
	12.1	0.8
	12.0	0.9
	11.9	1.0
	11.8	1.1
MMC	11.7	1.2

Modifier Rules - Former Practices

ASME Y14.5M-1994 and ASME Y14.5-2009 (no change)

The ASME Y14.5-2009 and ASME Y14.5M-1994 standards state that RFS is implied for all applicable geometric tolerances.

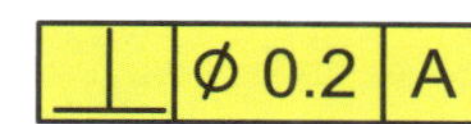

Datum feature symbol

If MMC or LMC modifiers are required, they must be specified.

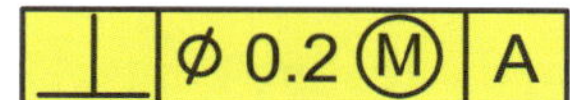

ANSI Y14.5M-1982 (former practice)

The ANSI Y14.5M-1982 standard states that RFS, MMC, and LMC must be specified for position tolerances. RFS is indicated with the symbol circle S.

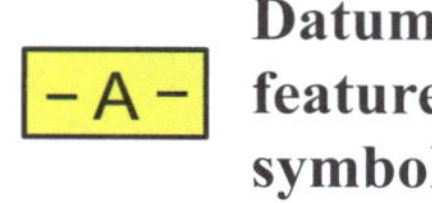

Datum feature symbol

RFS is implied for all other geometric tolerances. If MMC or LMC modifiers are required, they must be specified.

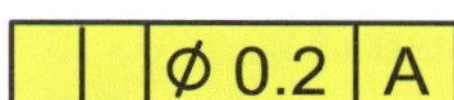

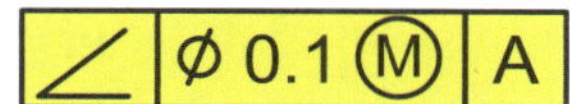

ANSI Y14.5M-1973 (former practice)

The ANSI Y14.5M-1973 standard states that MMC is implied for position tolerances. Notice the datum feature references preceed the tolerance in this standard.

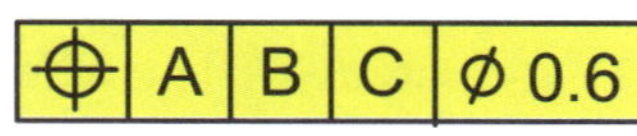

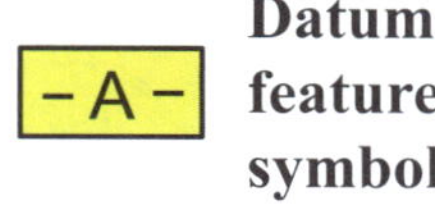

Datum feature symbol

If RFS or LMC modifiers are required, they must be specified.

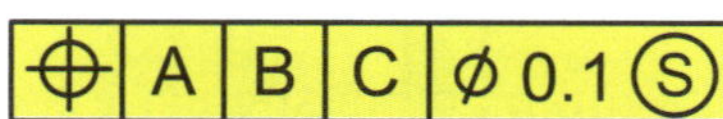

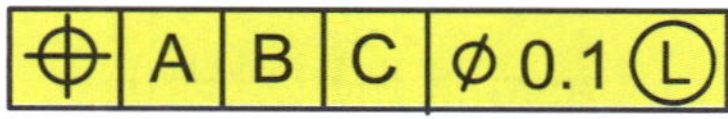

RFS is implied for all other geometric tolerances. If MMC or LMC modifiers are required, they must be specified.

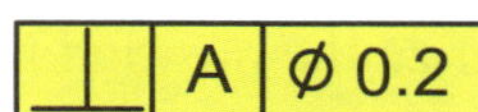

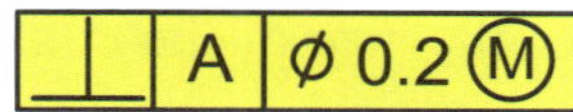

When to Use MMC, LMC and RFS Modifiers - Guidelines

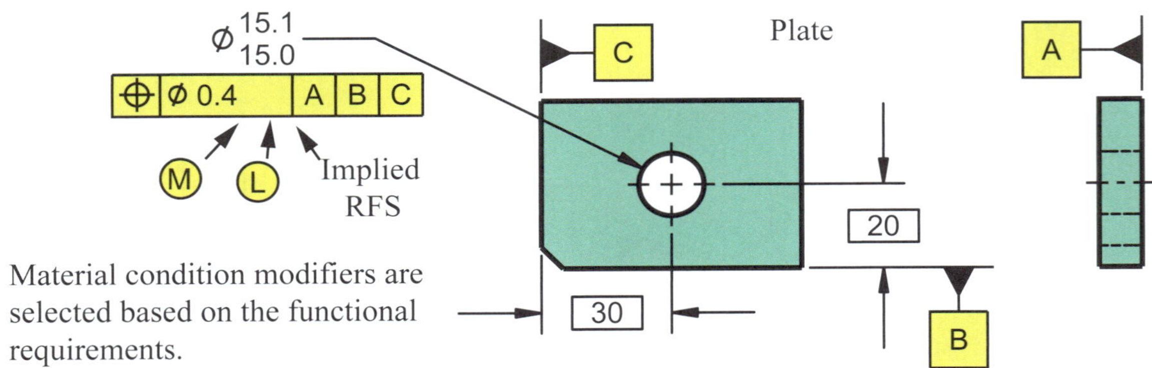

Material condition modifiers are selected based on the functional requirements.

Material condition modifiers are shown in the feature control frame following the feature tolerance. At some companies in the past, it seemed that all holes were positioned at MMC regardless of hole function. We generally understood that MMC provided more tolerance and allowed the use of functional gages. This allowed designers to get by without really thinking about material condition modifiers.

In reality, the hole function should determine the choice of a material condition modifier. Generally, if the hole is being used to clear a mating part, then the MMC modifier is applied. If the hole is being used to locate a mating part, then RFS or LMC is applied. Sometimes a larger position RFS can be a better application than a smaller position with an MMC modifier. A properly applied modifier achieves the design requirements and allows maximum manufacturing tolerance.

The following three examples show a rectangular top plate that mounts in the bottom left corner and forms an assembly with the base plate. The datum reference frame (DRF) applied represents this mounting condition in each of the three applications. Note: The mounting condition and the value of the size and position tolerances are only shown for illustrative and comparison purposes.

MMC modifier is applied when the feature is used for clearance applications.

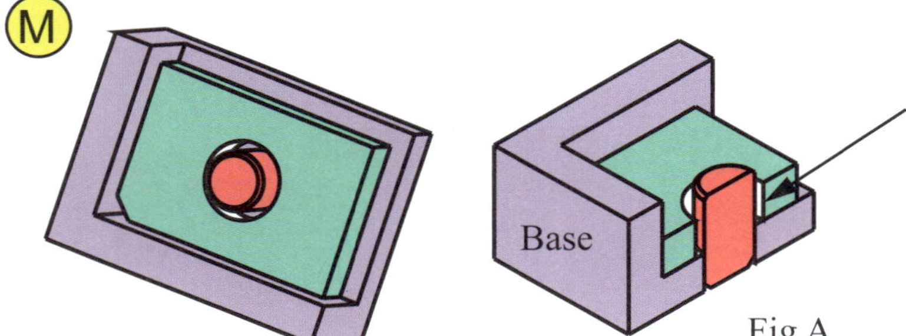

Fig A

The hole in the plate must clear the pin pressed in the base. As the hole gets larger, additional clearance is created. The MMC modifier allows additional position tolerance as the hole gets larger.

With the part mounted in the DRF, the Ø15-15.1 hole in the top plate must clear a fixed pin in the mating part. In this application, both the size and location of the hole are interrelated to the amount of clearance available. The MMC modifier states: as the hole gets larger in size (and provides more clearance) its center is allowed to be off position more by an equal amount. This creates a Ø14.6 inner boundary (virtual condition) of which no portion of the surface of the feature may enter. Manufacturing may adjust the size of the cutting tool to optimize the position and size tolerance of the hole as needed.

When to Use MMC, LMC and RFS Modifiers - Guidelines

LMC modifier is used for location applications when the effect of the hole's size tolerance also contributes to the location.

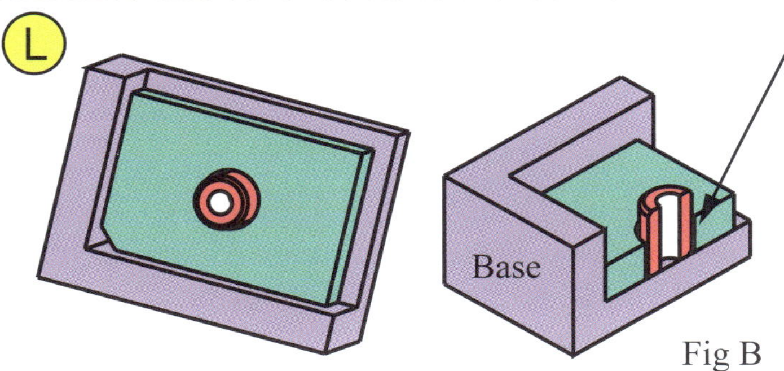

Fig B

The hole in the plate locates a bushing. The bushing fits with some clearance (it is not pressed). The hole's size tolerance also contributes to the location error ("slop"). As the hole gets smaller, less slop is possible. The LMC modifier provides additional position tolerance as the hole gets smaller. RFS may also be used instead.

With the part mounted in the DRF, the Ø15-15.1 hole in the top plate must locate a floating pin that fits in the hole. The size and position of the hole are interrelated and both will have an effect on the location of the mating part. A large hole allows the mating pin to "rattle". The LMC modifier states: as the hole gets smaller in size (and provides a better fit with the mating pin), its center is allowed to be off position more by an equal amount. This creates a Ø15.5 outer boundary (virtual condition) of which no portion of the surface may extend beyond. Manufacturing may adjust the size of the cutting tool to optimize the position and size tolerance of the hole as needed.

RFS is used for location applications when the size tolerance has no relation to the location.

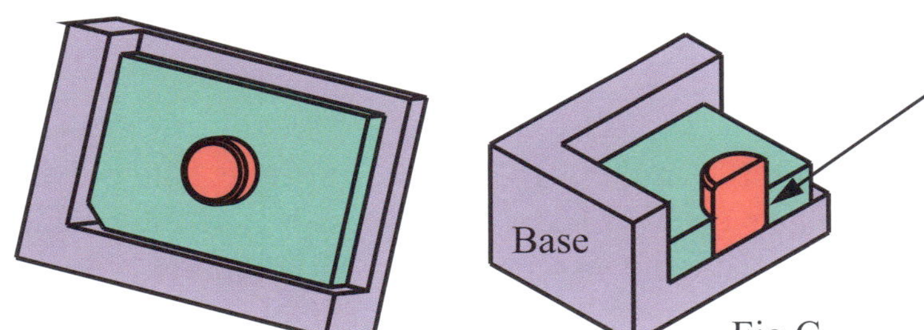

Fig C

The hole in the plate locates a press fit pin. The hole size has no effect on the location of the pin. The hole is located regardless of feature size.

With the part mounted in the DRF, the Ø15-15.1 hole in the top plate must locate a pin that is pressed (interference fit) with the hole. The press-fit pin will always center itself in the hole (no "slop"), and its possible location variation is solely determined by the hole's position tolerance. (The hole's size tolerance will not contribute to the location). This RFS specification states that if the hole gets larger or smaller in size, it allows no additional positional tolerance. Manufacturing should process the size and position of the feature as individual unrelated requirements.

More LMC Modifier Applications

It can be difficult to recognize applications for LMC modifiers, and they are less common than applications for RFS or MMC modifiers. Below are a few places where they could be used.

Note: Use caution in the application of LMC modifiers, as they can cause interference problems if they are improperly used for clearance applications. If in doubt, use RFS rather than LMC.

LMC Modifier used to locate

Holes for self-piloting weld nuts in a sheet metal part could be an application for an LMC modifier. The holes fixture the pilot of the weld nut for welding. Both the size and position tolerance on the hole determine the final location of the thread. The LMC size hole will have the most clearance ("rattle") on the mating pilot. The LMC modifier gives a tighter position tolerance at this LMC size. As the hole is produced smaller, the rattle on the mating part is reduced, therefore more position tolerance is permissible.

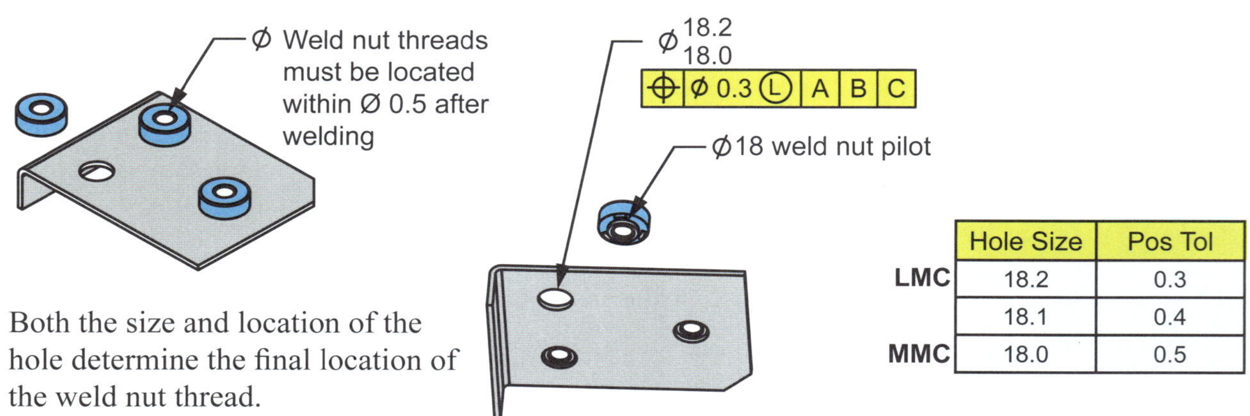

	Hole Size	Pos Tol
LMC	18.2	0.3
	18.1	0.4
MMC	18.0	0.5

Both the size and location of the hole determine the final location of the weld nut thread.

In the assembly above, the Ø18 pilot will rattle 0.2 in the Ø18.2 LMC size hole. The position tolerance is only 0.3 at this size. As the hole gets smaller, less rattle is possible, so the position tolerance could be greater without making the final alignment worse. The LMC modifier keeps the same worst-case final thread alignment while also maximizing manufacturing tolerance (allowing bonus tolerance).

Note: According to ASME Y14.5-2018 standard, a position tolerance at LMC requires perfect form at LMC, and perfect form at MMC is not required. Extreme form deviation could cause a fit problem for a mating part (no rule #1). If the feature depth is minimal, as in sheet metal or other thin material, this is not a problem. If the feature depth is significant, and it requires a fit with a mating part, a note may be added: perfect form at MMC is required. Another option is an additional requirement of perpendicularity of zero at MMC. This would invoke rule#1 and ensure the perfect form at MMC for the fit.

LMC Modifiers on Cast Holes

LMC modifiers are also used for locating holes on a casting that will be machined at the next level. LMC modifiers provide tighter position when the hole is at its largest size (LMC), but more position when the hole is smaller, thus preserving a boundary of guaranteed machine stock. See the cast pillow block part in unit 8 for an example.

Workshop Exercise 3.1

Study the drawing below and answer the following questions.

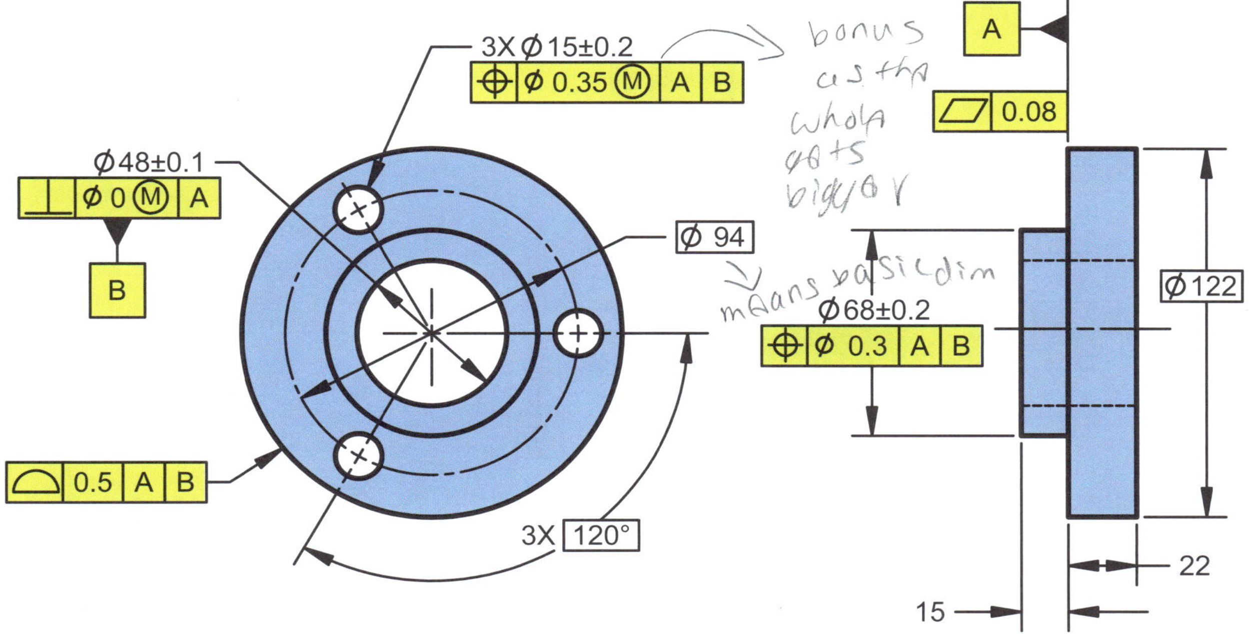

UNLESS OTHERWISE SPECIFIED:
ALL DIMENSIONS ±0.3
ALL ANGLES ±1°

1. What is the MMC of the Ø68 mm boss?

   68.2

2. Is the position tolerance on the boss referenced at MMC, LMC, or RFS?

   RFS

3. How much position tolerance is allowed on the boss if it is produced at a size of 68.1 mm?

   +0.3

4. What is the MMC of the 3 holes?

   14.8

5. How much position tolerance is allowed if the 3 holes are produced at a size of 14.8 mm?

   0.35 →

6. How much position tolerance is allowed if the 3 holes are produced at a size of 15 mm?

   0.55

7. What is the perpendicularity tolerance to datum A for the 3 holes?

   same as the position tolerance

8. What could be the maximum perpendicularity tolerance on the center hole?

   0.2

9. Does the 94 mm bolt circle dimension have tolerance? If so, what is it?

   no, its a basic dimension

Profile Tolerance

Profile tolerance controls the location of a surface to the datum reference frame. In the example below, it is also controlling the form, orientation, and size of the feature between points X and Y.

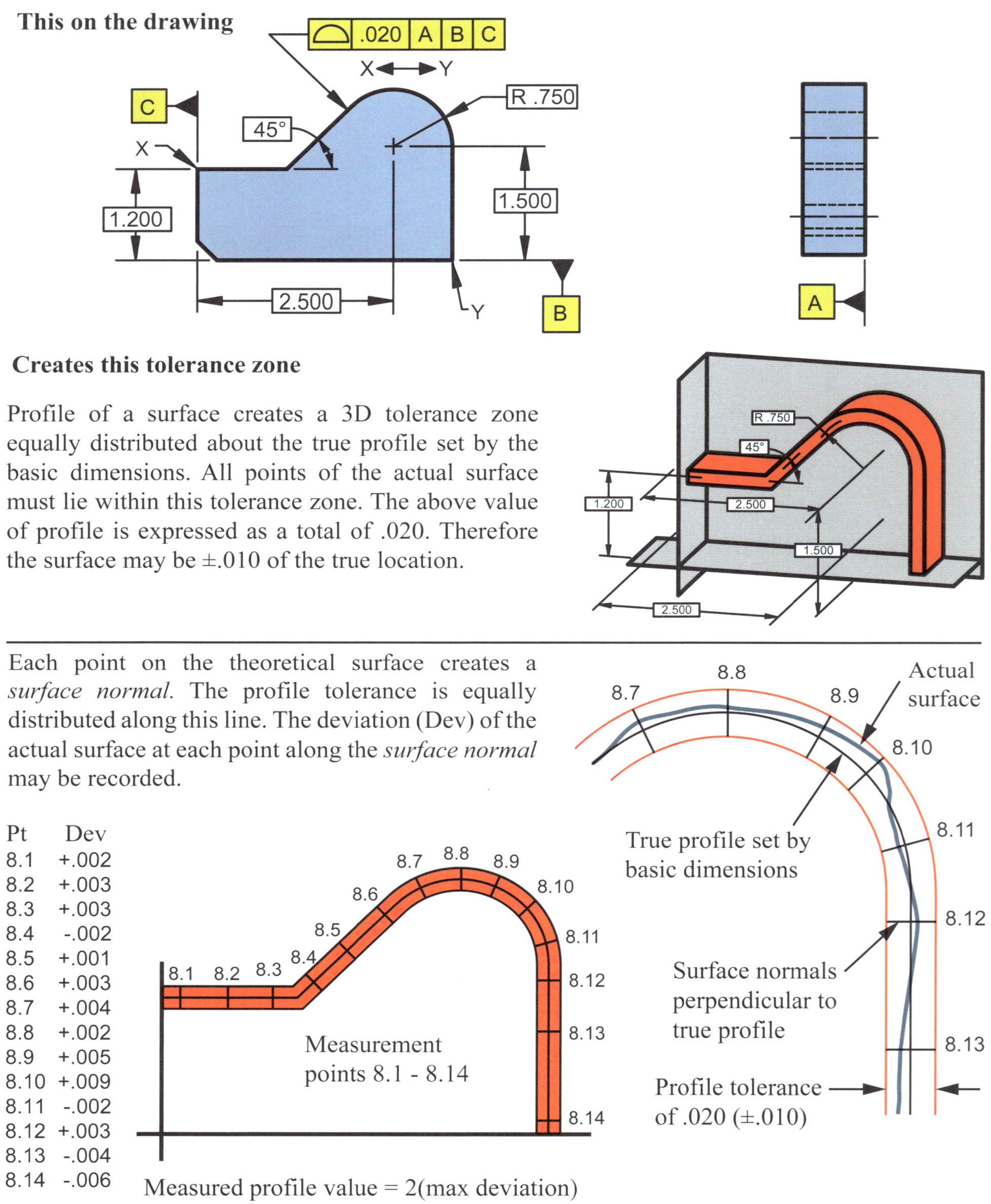

This on the drawing

Creates this tolerance zone

Profile of a surface creates a 3D tolerance zone equally distributed about the true profile set by the basic dimensions. All points of the actual surface must lie within this tolerance zone. The above value of profile is expressed as a total of .020. Therefore the surface may be ±.010 of the true location.

Each point on the theoretical surface creates a *surface normal.* The profile tolerance is equally distributed along this line. The deviation (Dev) of the actual surface at each point along the *surface normal* may be recorded.

Pt	Dev
8.1	+.002
8.2	+.003
8.3	+.003
8.4	-.002
8.5	+.001
8.6	+.003
8.7	+.004
8.8	+.002
8.9	+.005
8.10	+.009
8.11	-.002
8.12	+.003
8.13	-.004
8.14	-.006

Measured profile value = 2(max deviation)

Measured profile zone = .018

*The location and number of measurement points are set by the dimensional measurement plan.

Workshop Exercise 3.2

This exercise provides experience in applying and interpreting geometric tolerancing symbology. Apply geometric tolerancing to the drawing according to the instructions below. If you have trouble applying the symbols, page through this unit looking for similar examples. The Hole Bar in this unit is a good reference. Draw the symbols and feature control frames clearly and neatly.

1. Establish the right face in the side view as datum feature A. Qualify this feature with a flatness of .005.

2. Establish the top surface in the front view as datum feature B. Qualify this feature with a perpendicularity of .005 to datum feature A.

3. Establish the left surface in the front view as datum feature C. Qualify this feature with a perpendicularity of .005 to datum features A and B.

4. Position the .250 hole within a diameter of .005 RFS relative to datum features A, B, C.

5. Position the three holes within a diameter of .012 at MMC relative to datum features A, B, C.

6. In the front view, identify the upper right corner as point “Y” and the lower left corner as point “X”. Apply a profile tolerance of .020 between points X and Y relative to datum features A, B, C.

7. Establish all necessary dimensions as basic.

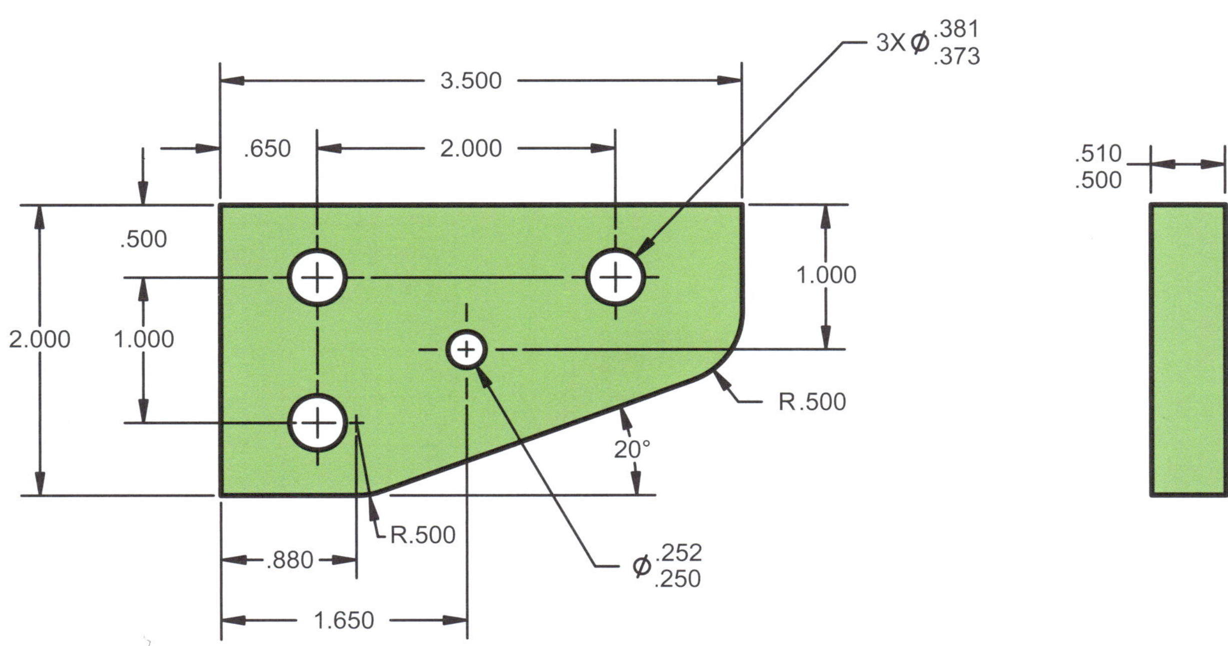

Front View

Side View

datum → theoretical plane
datum feature → actual part

Workshop Exercise 3.2

8. The produced part from the previous page is mated to the datum reference frame below. Draw and shade in the geometric tolerance zones created in the previous problem. Show the flatness, perpendicularity, profile, and position zones. Exaggerate the size but show the zones neatly.

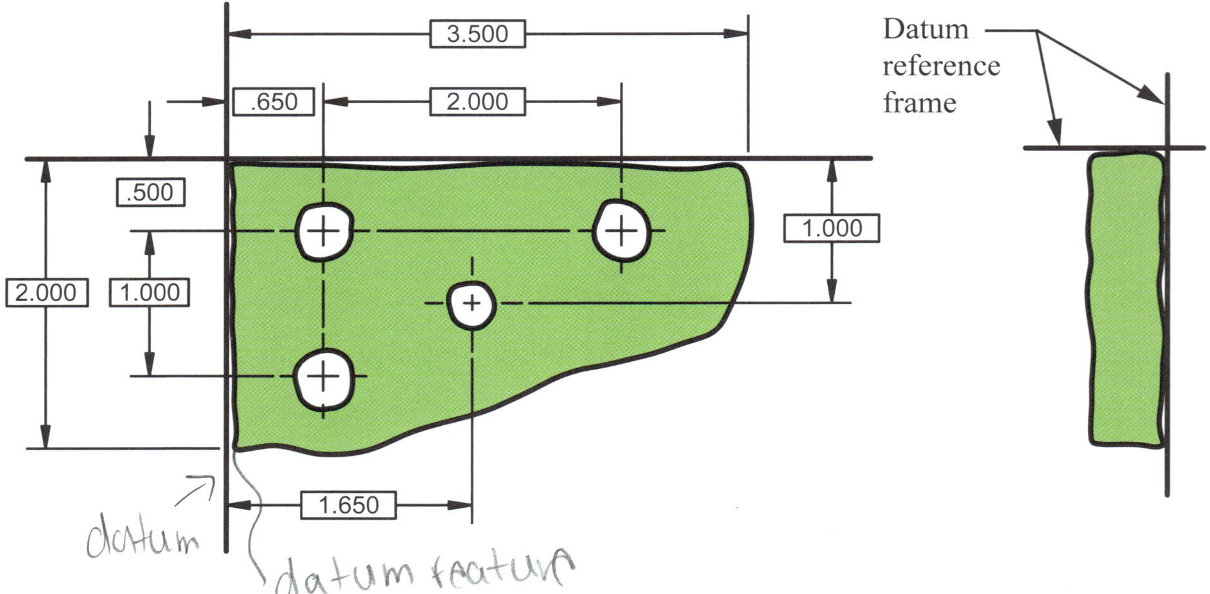

9. The datum reference frame is established and profile tolerance applied. What would be the maximum length of the part?

A: 3.505 B: 3.510 C: 3.515 D: 3.520 E: 3.525

10. A position tolerance and MMC modifier is applied to the four holes below. The MMC modifier allows additional position tolerance as the features depart from their MMC. Complete the table below to show the allowed position tolerance for the range of hole sizes.

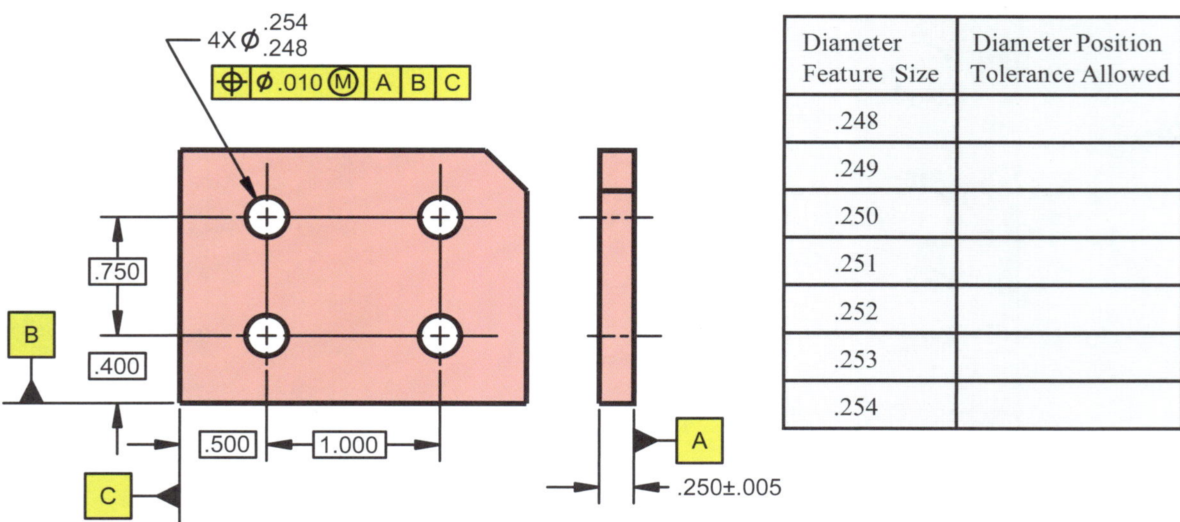

Diameter Feature Size	Diameter Position Tolerance Allowed
.248	
.249	
.250	
.251	
.252	
.253	
.254	

11. If the MMC modifier were removed from the feature control frame in the drawing above, how would the table on the right change?

Full Geometric Tolerancing

Below is a drawing with full geometric tolerancing. Plus/minus size tolerances are applied to the holes. All other dimensions are declared basic with the UOS note. Three surfaces are used as datum features and qualified with flatness and perpendicularity. All other features are located with position and profile tolerances.

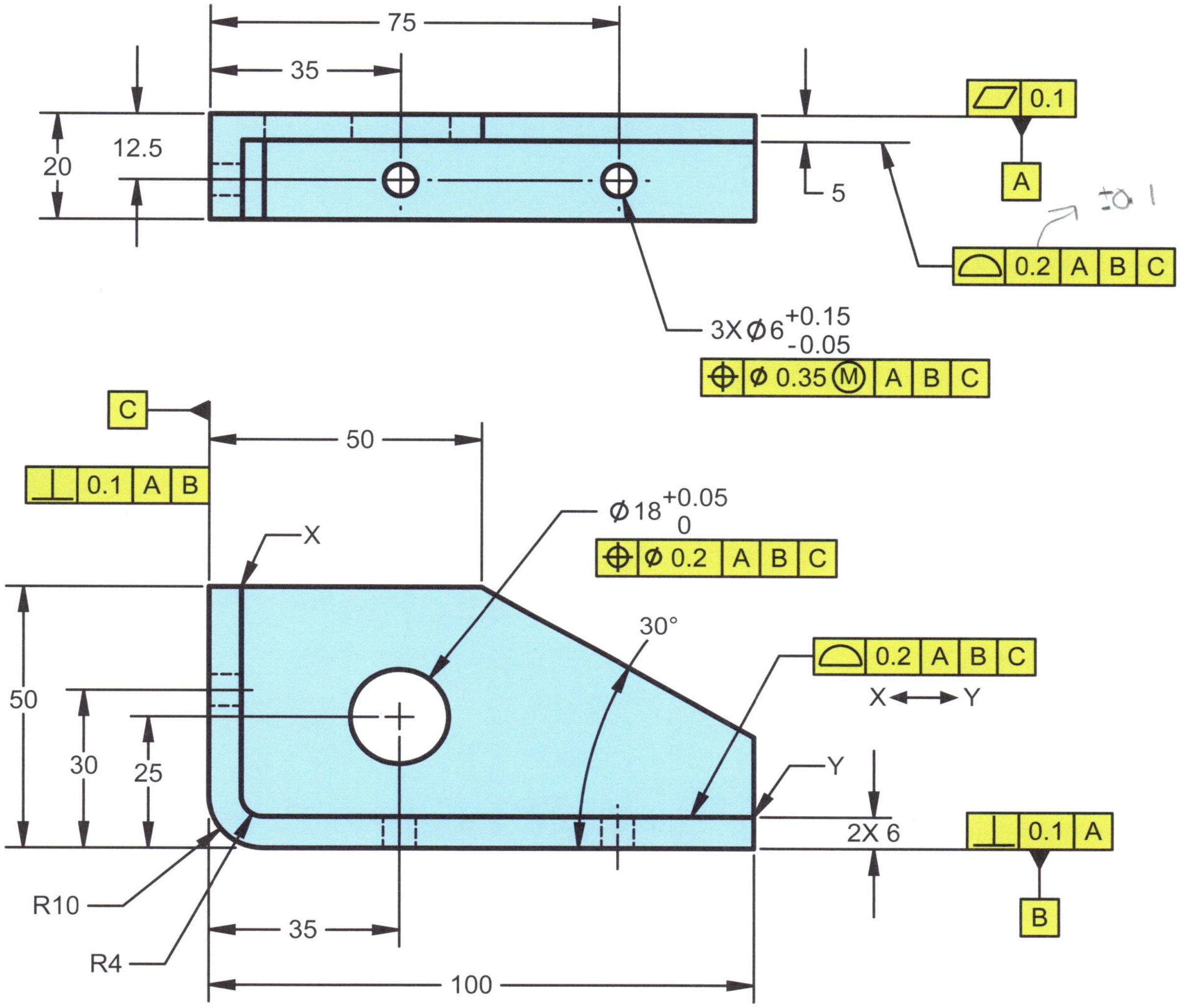

REINFORCEMENT BRACKET

INTERPRET TOLERANCING PER:
ASME Y14.5 - 2018

DIMENSIONS ARE IN MM

UNLESS OTHERWISE SPECIFIED:

DIMENSIONS ARE BASIC

ALL SURFACES:

⌓ | 0.5 | A | B | C

~~UOS TOLERANCES:~~
~~DIMENSIONS ± 0.25~~
~~ANGLES ±1°~~

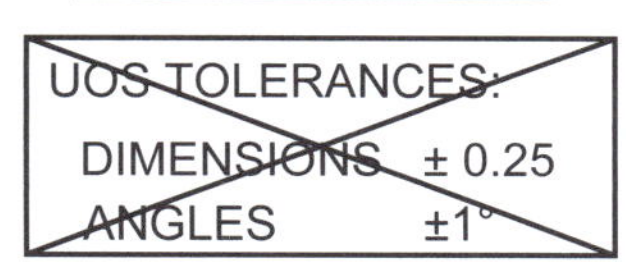

All dimensions without a direct plus/minus size tolerance are made basic with this note.

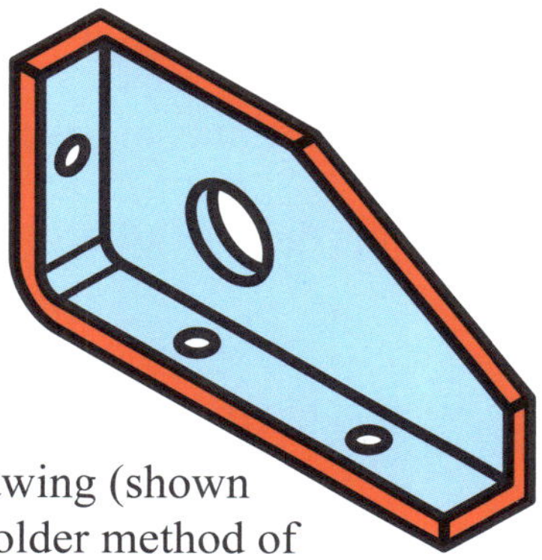

The profile in the UOS note applies to surfaces not directly toleranced in the body of the drawing (shown in red above). This replaces the older method of title block plus/minus tolerancing on dimensions. The drawing cannot have both UOS tolerancing methods.

Workshop Exercise 3.3

Use the dimensions and tolerances defined on the drawing on the previous page to answer the following questions.

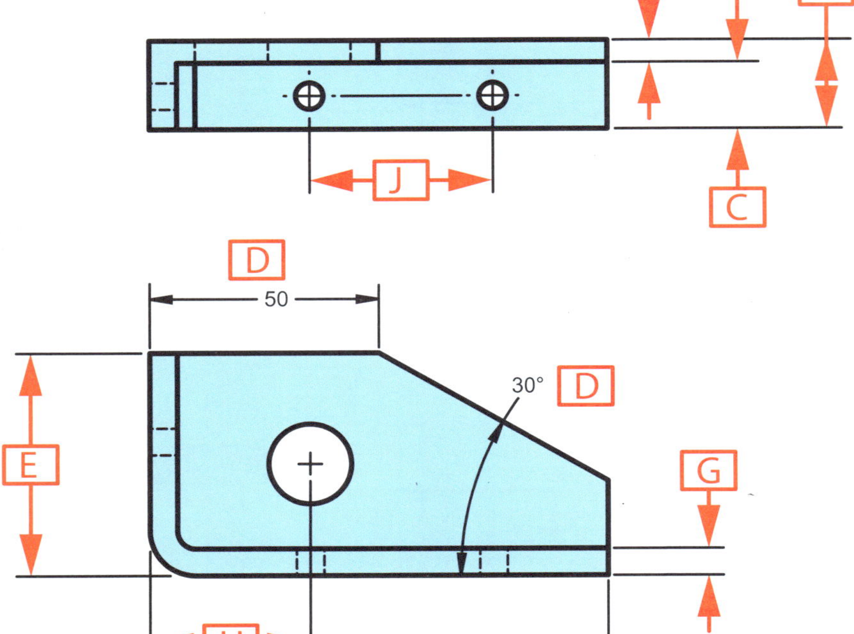

1. What is the max of distance A? a: 5.1 b: 5.15 c: 5.2 d: 5.25
2. What is the max of distance B? a: 20.05 b: 20.1 c: 20.25 d: 20.35
3. What is the max of distance C? a: 15 b: 15.1 c: 15.25 d: 15.35
4. What is the tolerance on the dimension and angle labeled D?
   a: no tolerance, they are basic dimensions b: ± 0.25 and ± 1° from the title block
5. What is the max of distance E? a: 50.05 b: 50.1 c: 50.25 d: 50.35
6. What is the max of distance F? a: 100.05 b: 100.1 c: 100.25 d: 100.35
7. What is the max of distance G? a: 6.05 b: 6.1 c: 6.25 d: 6.35
8. What is the max of distance H assuming the hole is produced at 18 mm?
   a: 35 b: 35.05 c: 35.1 d: 35.2
9. What is the max of distance J assuming the holes are produced at MMC?
   a: 40 b: 40.175 c: 40.35 d: 40.7
10. What is the max of distance J assuming the holes are produced at LMC?
   a: 40.275 b: 40.5 c: 40.55 d: 41

Conversion: Plus/Minus to GeoTol

Study the assembly at the lower right. Select datum features for the Hanger Bracket based on the mounting. Qualify the datum features with flatness and perpendicularity.
Apply position tolerance of diameter .005 to the large center hole.
Apply position tolerance of diameter .012 to the three clearance holes.
Apply position tolerance of diameter .020 to the two clearance holes.
Cross-out (eliminate) the title block plus/minus, and with a note apply profile tolerance of .020 to all surfaces. Make necessary dimensions basic.

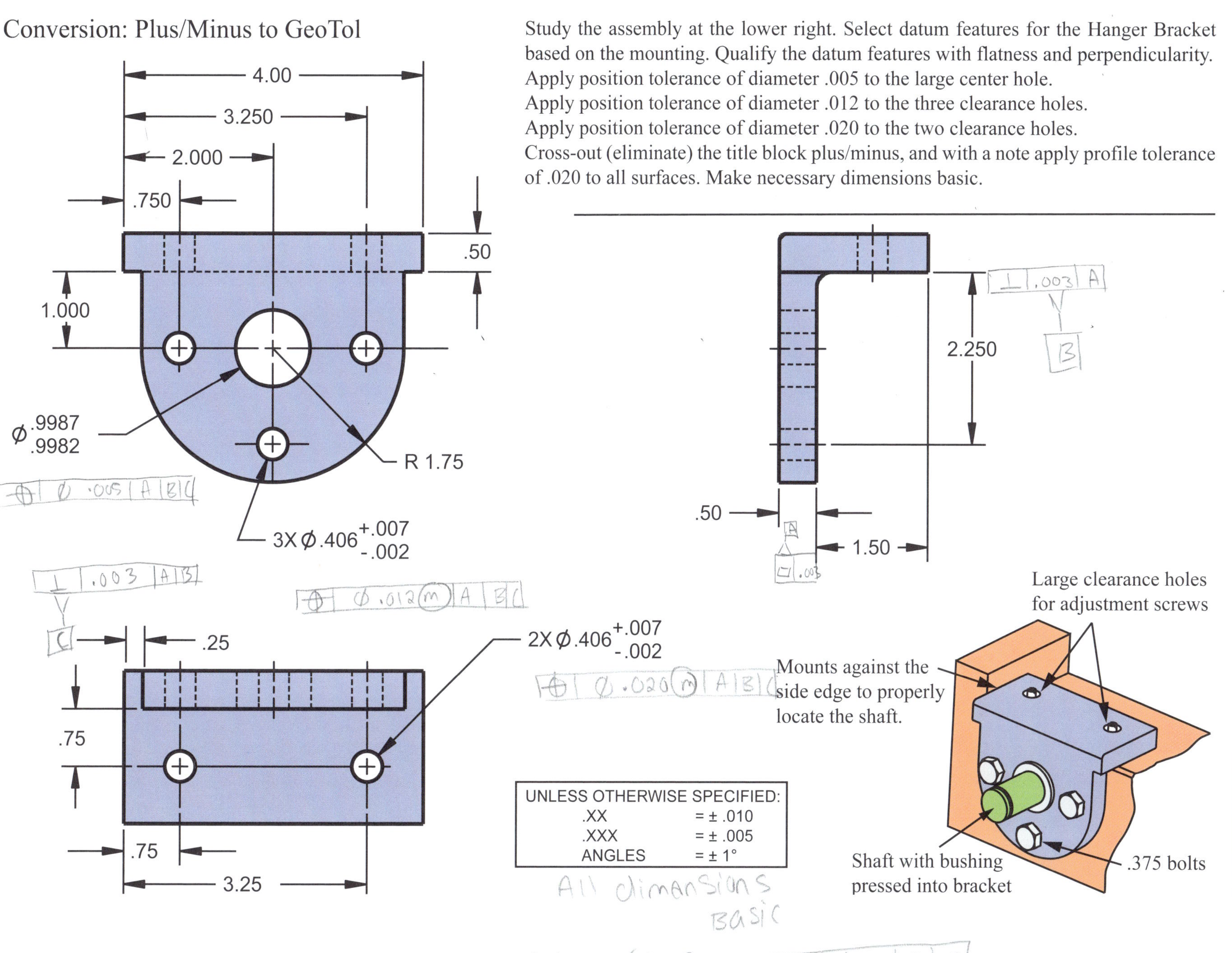

Unit 4

The Datum Reference Frame

Datum Reference Frame (DRF)

The Datum Reference Frame (DRF) is the most important concept in geometric tolerancing. In mathematics, it is called the Cartesian coordinate system, invented by a French mathematician, René Descartes in the 17th century. The DRF is the skeleton of the geometric system. It is the "frame of reference" to which all referenced geometric specifications are related and establish the constraints for the definition of the part. The DRF consists of three mutually perpendicular datum planes. Two intersecting planes create an axis, and all planes and axes intersect at an origin point. Therefore the DRF is composed of a point, axes and planes, called datums.

Design engineering, manufacturing and inspection all use a three plane DRF concept for constraint. Design engineers use a DRF to locate and orient features for product definition and boundary calculations. Manufacturing uses one to set the part up for processing, and quality uses one to set the part up for inspection. The DRF concept is imbedded in all our engineering, manufacturing and inspection equipment. The equipment is not perfect but is of such quality that it will adequately simulate the DRF. The equipment shown below are common datum reference frame simulators that use the 3 plane concept.

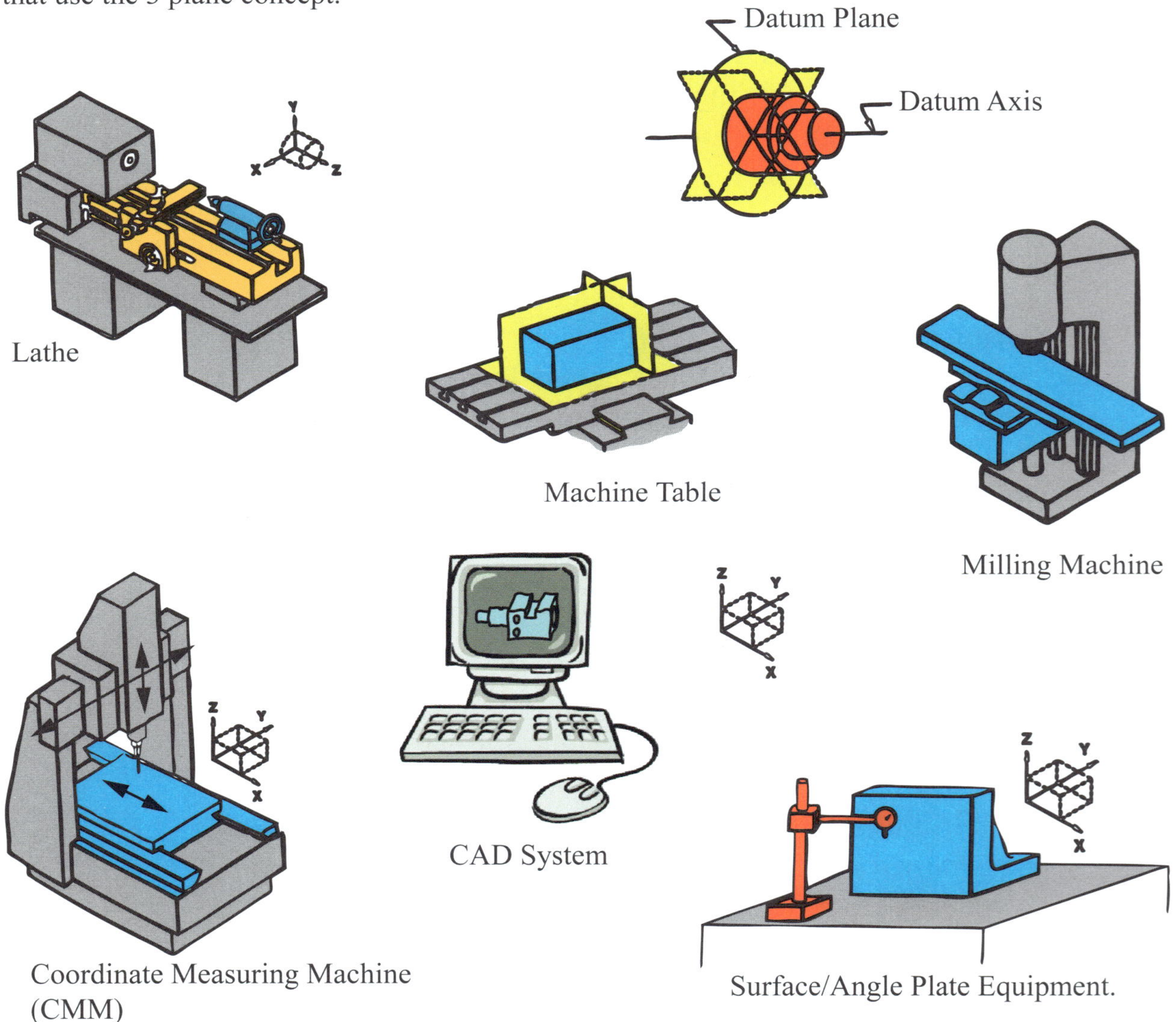

Note: Even though design and manufacturing both use a DRF, they may not necessarily use the same one. See unit 5 for more discussion.

Establishing a Datum Reference Frame

Establishing a datum reference frame on an imperfect part is done in a theoretical set of events: A design engineer will identify physical datum features that constrain the part in the assembly. These datum features are referenced in the rear compartments of a feature control frame, in an order of precedence. This order of precedence sets the sequence of how the perfect datum reference frame is related to the imperfect part. Since datum features have manufactured variations, perfect datums cannot be directly derived from these imperfect features. True geometric counterparts (TGC) are theoretically perfect inverse shapes of the datum features, and contact the datum features at their high points. These true geometric counterparts constrain the part's degrees of freedom, derive datums, and create a datum reference frame. The details and examples of establishing a DRF on a part are shown on the following pages of this unit. Below are important definitions to understand.

The **Datum Reference Frame (DRF)** is a three dimensional, Cartesian coordinate system. The engineers work in this theoretically perfect coordinate system to define their product and make necessary calculations. This DRF locates and orients part features. Basic dimensions and geometric tolerance zones are related to this DRF.

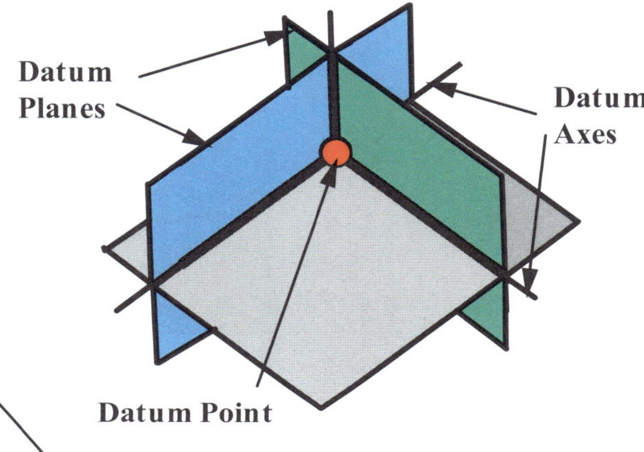

Datum Point

Datum Axis

Datum Plane

Datums are theoretically perfect points, axes, and planes that are components of the datum reference frame.

Datum features are the actual, physical features on the part (surface, hole, slot, shaft). They are not perfect and always have manufacturing variation.

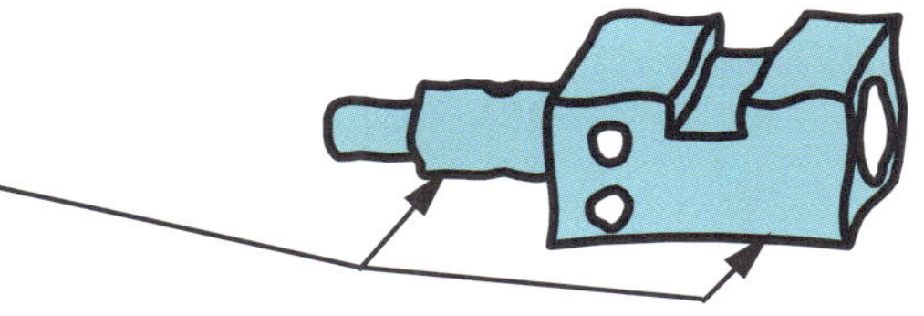

True geometric counterpart

True geometric counterparts (TGC) are the perfect inverse of a datum feature (smallest circumscribed cylinders, largest inscribed cylinders etc.) They engage with datum features and establish datums. Formerly called *theoretical datum feature simulator* in ASME Y14.5-2009.

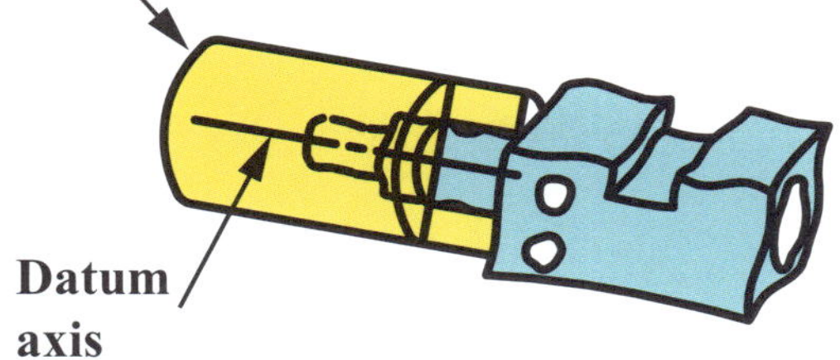

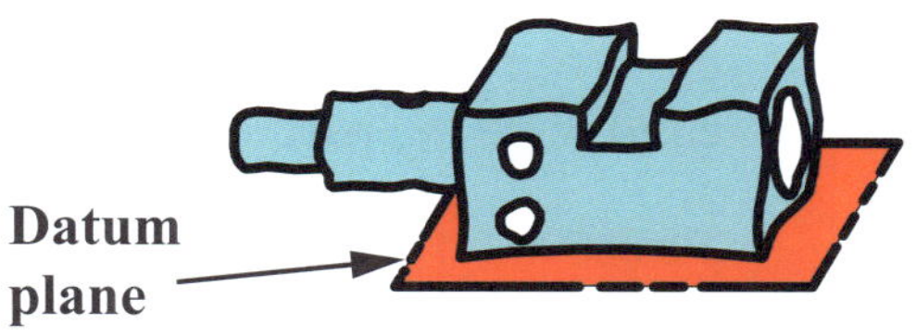

Implied Datums are not Clear

In the past before proper use of geometric tolerancing, implied datums were used. The part below has four holes with dimensions to the edges. We call this implied datums because it is assumed that the dimensions originate from the bottom edge and left edge. However, this is vague and does not specify the order to index the part to a perfect coordinate system.

Part shown with unclear definition and implied datums

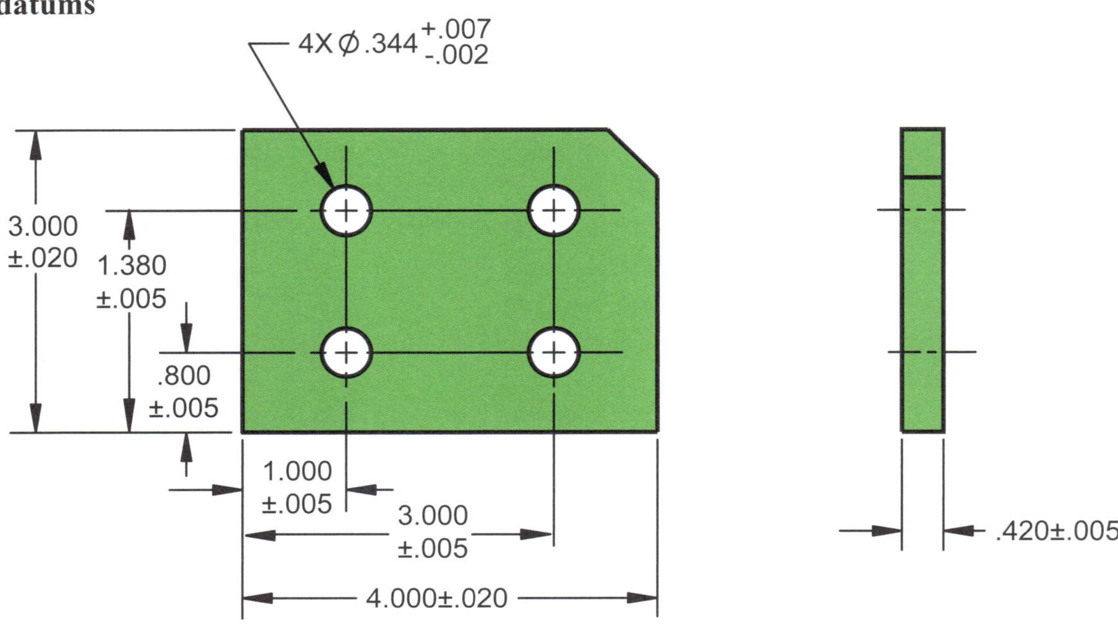

The actual produced part shown below (exaggerated for clarity) is not perfect and has inherent manufacturing error. (It will never be perfect, as we cannot manufacture perfect parts). Notice the surfaces are not flat or square, but still within the accepted limits for size and squareness.

Produced part

The imperfect part must be indexed to a perfect datum reference frame to define geometry boundaries and make measurements. However, the part does not fit exactly and will rock back and forth because of error in the implied datum surfaces. The implied datums do not have a specified order in which to mate the part to the datum reference frame.

The graphics below illustrate the problem of mating an imperfect, un-square part to a perfect datum reference frame. The are a number of combinations in which to mate the implied datum features to the datum reference frame.

Three possible DRF mating conditions with implied datums.

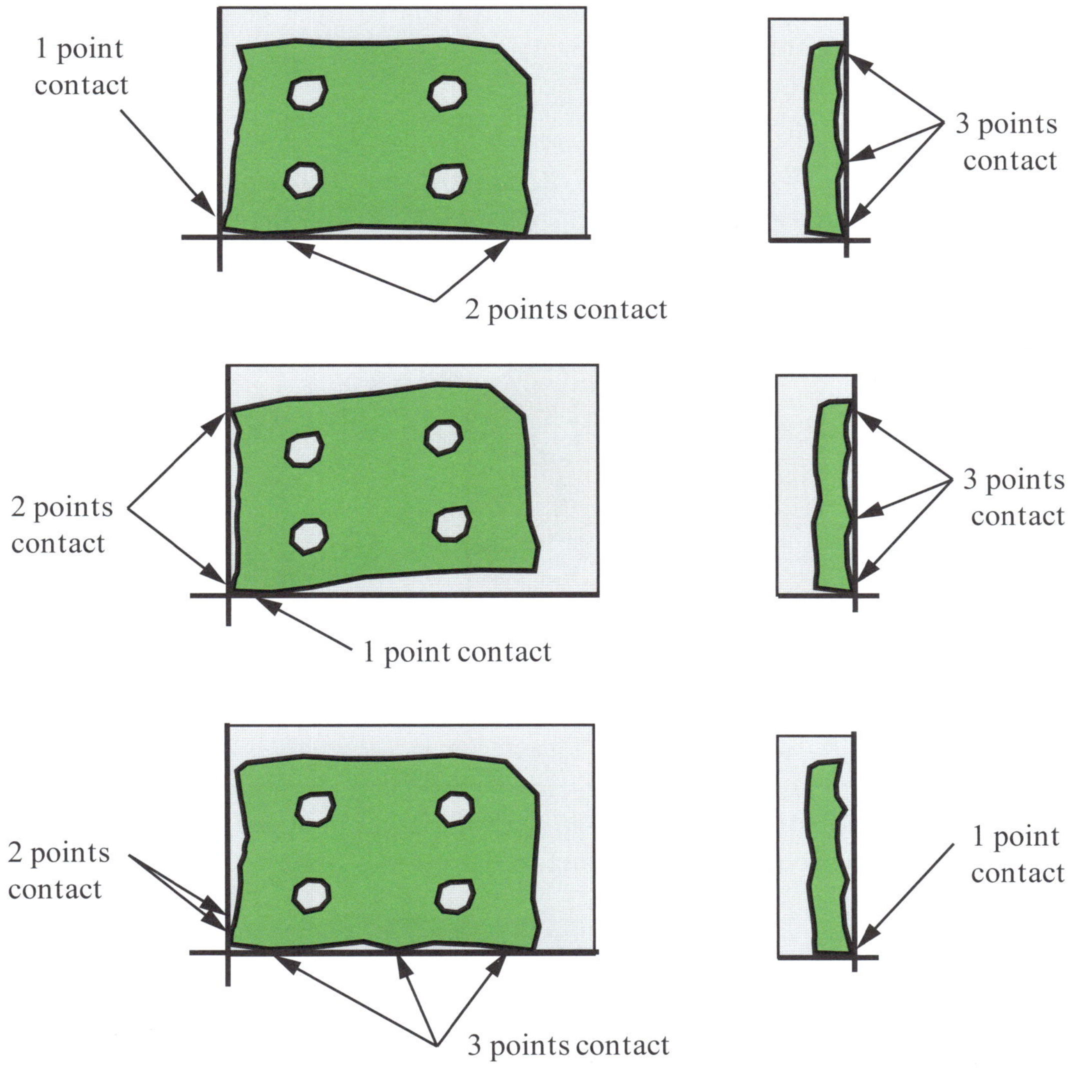

Implied datums are not clear enough to get a consistent interpretation of the alignment of the part. Engineering, manufacturing, and inspection may all have different ideas as to how the part is to be mated to the datum reference frame. This may result in confusion as to where the holes or other features must lie on the part, and will make the interchangeability between parts difficult.

This four hole part is a simple example. As the parts become more complex with more holes and surfaces, the order of the datum features becomes even more important. Engineering, manufacturing, and quality control must agree on a single definition of the tolerance specifications. Creating a proper DRF by labeling datum features in a specific order and using geometric tolerancing is mandatory to produce interchangeable parts.

Indexing Parts in a Datum Reference Frame

The part shown below has four holes that are located relative to a datum reference frame (DRF). The datum features referenced in the rear compartments of the feature control frame specify the order of how the part is mated to the DRF.

The primary datum feature is shown in the first compartment. In this example, it mates with the DRF on the highest 3 points of the surface. The secondary datum feature is shown in the second compartment and it mates with the highest 2 points. The tertiary datum feature is shown in the third compartment and it mates with one point of contact.

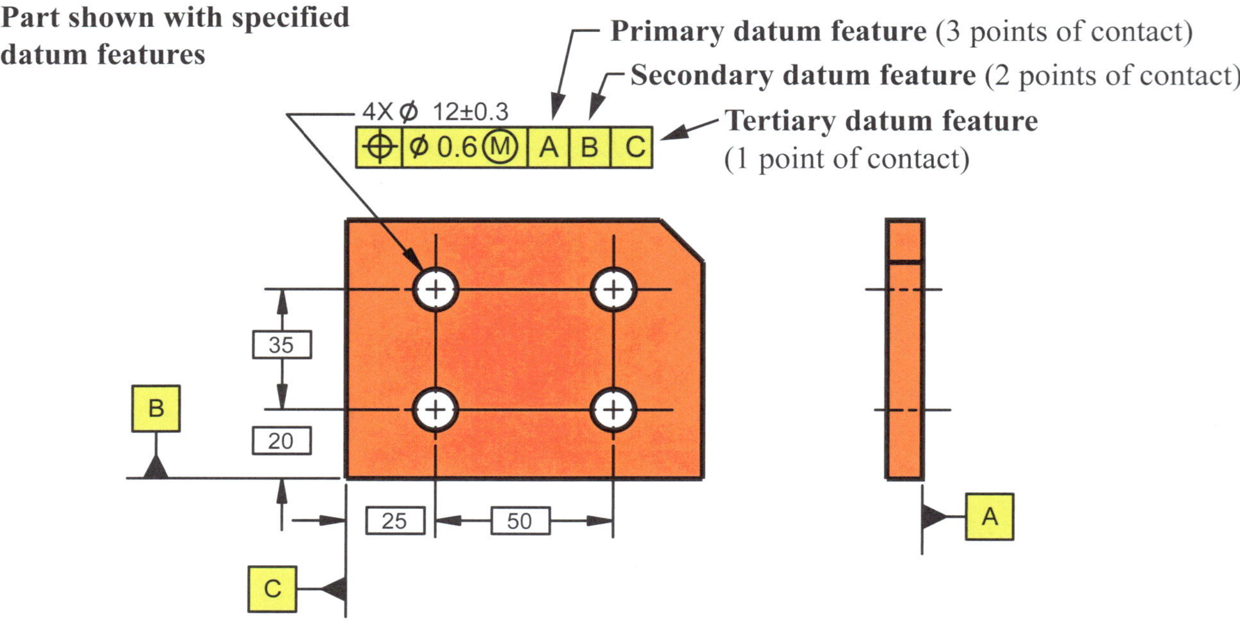

The order of the datum feature references in the rear compartment of the feature control frame define the indexing sequence of the part to the perfect DRF.

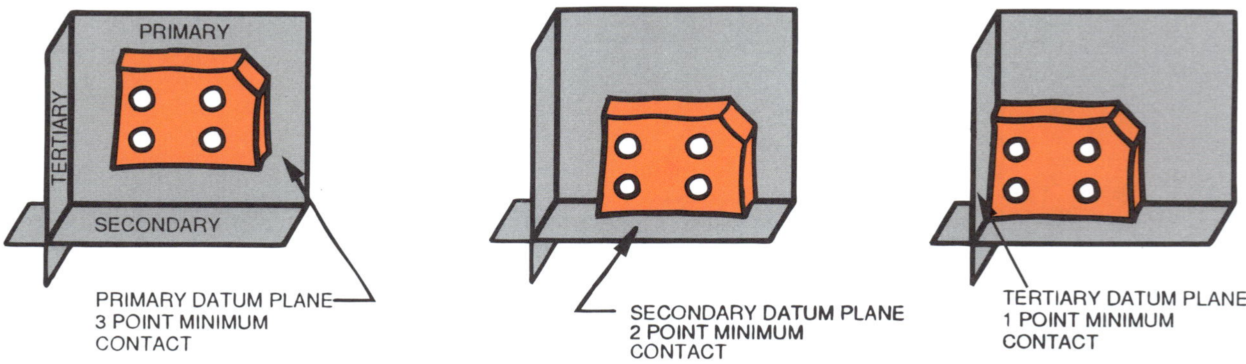

Interchangeable parts require a DRF established from specified datum features. We all must have the same understanding of the "frame of reference" for all tolerance definition and measurements.

Note: Not all parts mate to the DRF with the 3, 2, 1 points of contact. A better way to express the indexing sequence is with *degrees of freedom* constraints explained later in this unit.

The produced part shown below (exaggerated for clarity) is not perfect. None of the surfaces are exactly flat or square but are still within acceptable limits for size, flatness and perpendicularity.

The imperfect part is mated to the perfect DRF according to the order of the datum features referenced in the feature control frame. The order of the letters in the compartments is important rather than the alphabetical order. All dimensions and measurements originate from the DRF. If the order of the datum features in the feature control frame is rearranged, it changes the sequence the part is mated to the DRF.

Design usually selects the order of these datum features based on how the part mates in an assembly. Quality should set up the part the same way to collect meaningful inspection data.

The datum feature order sets the sequence.

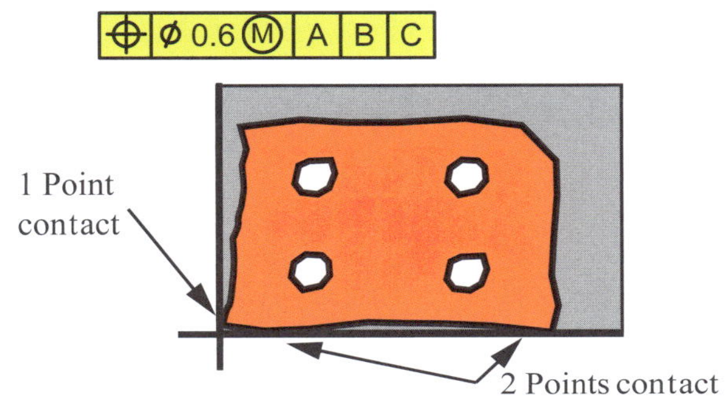

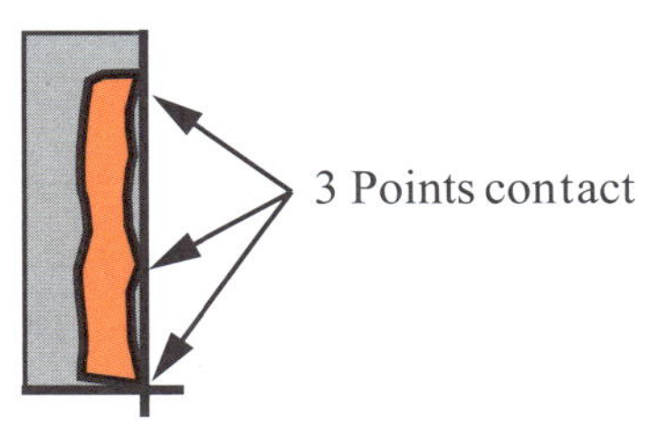

The datum feature order sets the sequence.

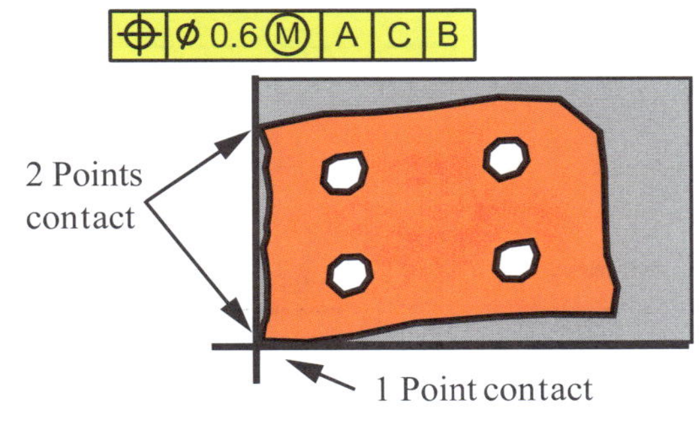

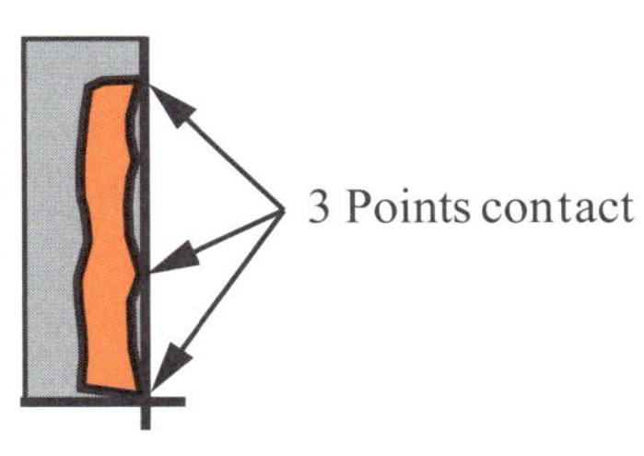

The datum feature order sets the sequence.

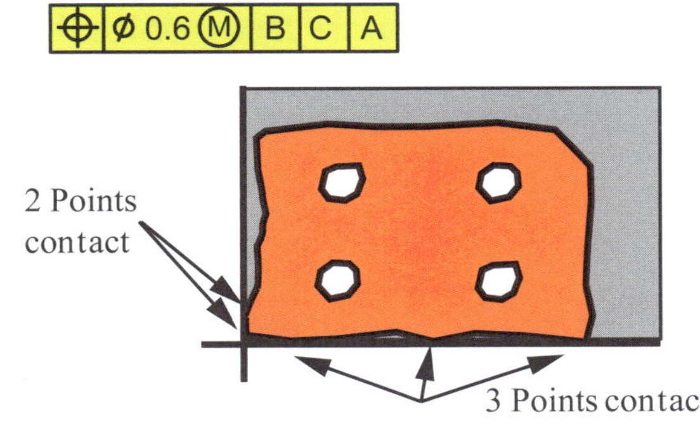

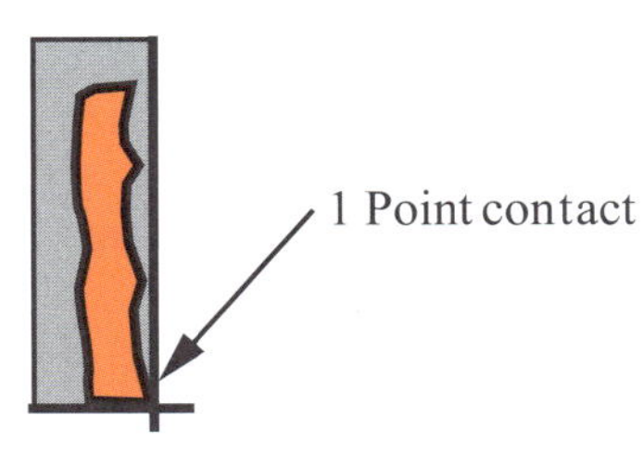

Planar Surfaces as Primary Datum Features

The drawing below shows examples of the datum feature symbol applied to a planar surface. The datum feature establishes a datum plane which contacts the high points of the surface(s).

The datum feature symbol may be attached to the surface or to an extension line of a surface (datum feature P, L, M, K below). The datum feature symbol may be placed on a feature control frame that is attached to the extension line (datum feature L). The datum feature symbol may be placed on a leader line that is directed to the surface or extension line (datum feature N). If a datum feature is multiple surfaces, the number of surfaces should be noted next to the symbol with nX (datum feature K).

Planar surface datum features

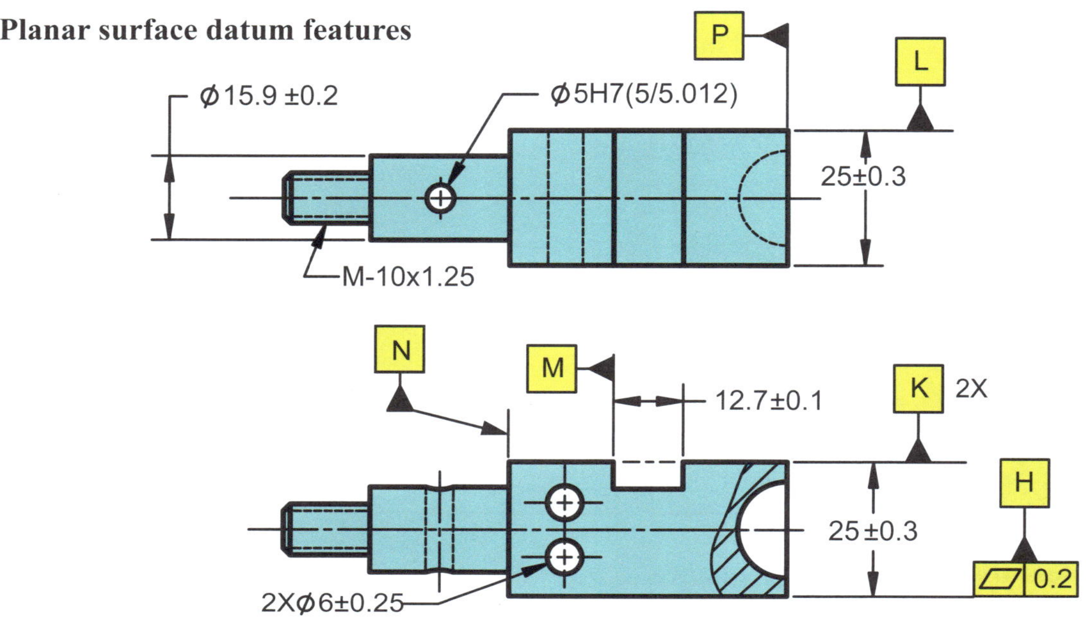

Datum planes established from planar datum features

Datum feature N is the left surface and establishes a datum plane on the high points.

Datum feature H is the bottom surface and establishes a datum plane on the high points.

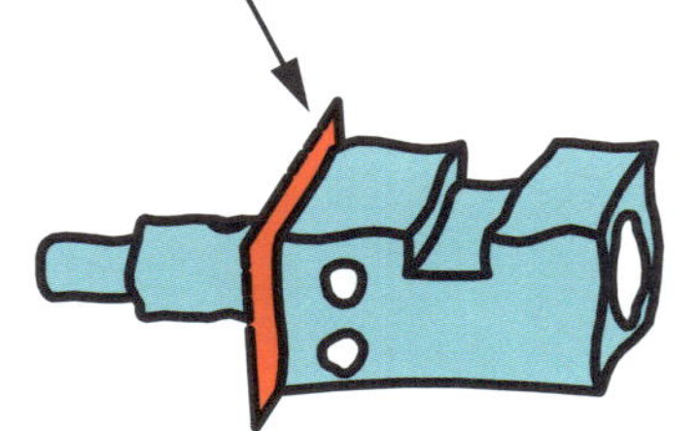

Datum feature L is the rear surface and establishes a datum plane on the high points.

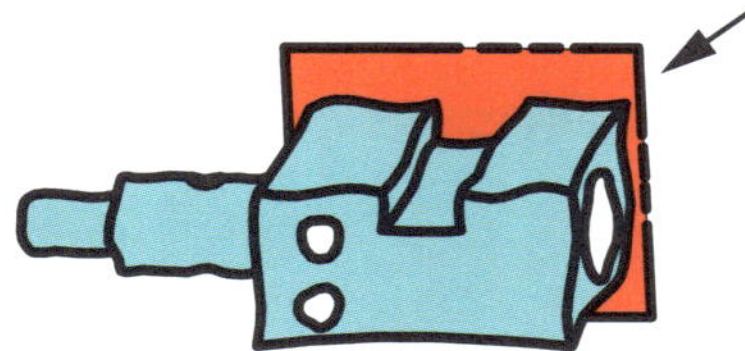

Datum feature M is the left side of the slot and establishes a datum plane on the high points.

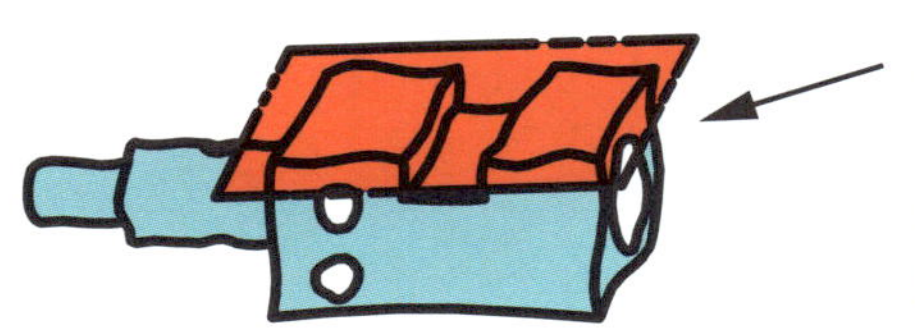

Datum feature K is two surfaces and establishes a datum plane on the high points.

Establishing Datums from Primary Planar Surfaces

Planar surfaces as datum features

When a planar surface is identified as a datum feature, it creates a theoretical datum plane on the high points.

In practice, a physical datum feature simulator is mated with the datum feature to derive a simulated datum plane.

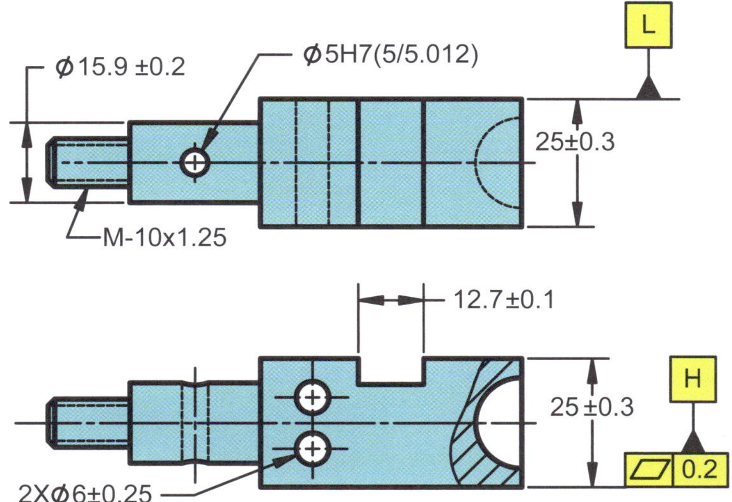

Theory

Datum features H and L are mated with a theoretical perfect datum plane contacting the high points.

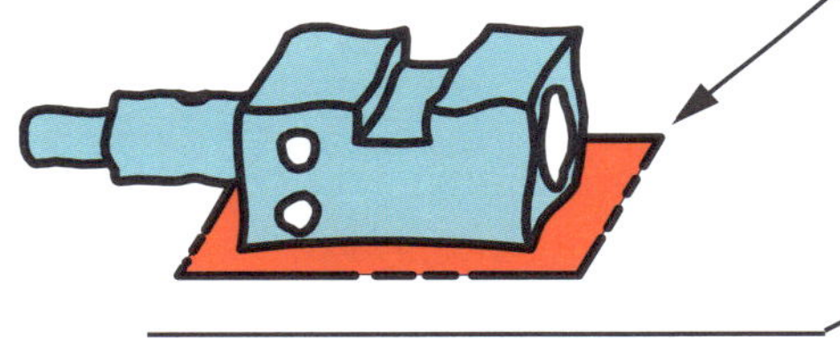

Physical

Since a "perfect" plane does not exist in the real world, a physical datum feature simulator, such as a surface plate, angle plate, bed on a machine, CMM etc., is used to establish the simulated datum. The simulated datum plane is established from the high points of the simulator.

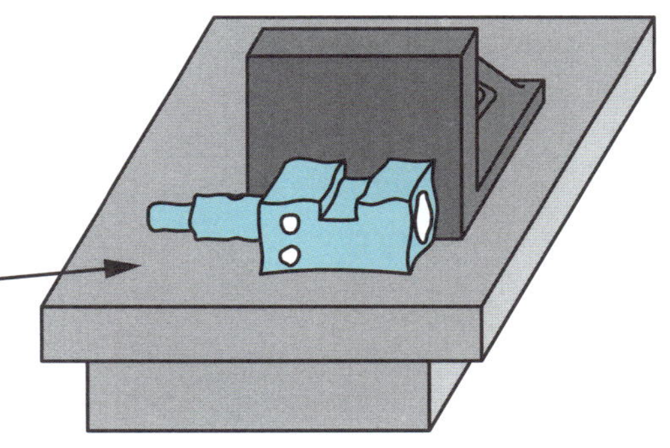

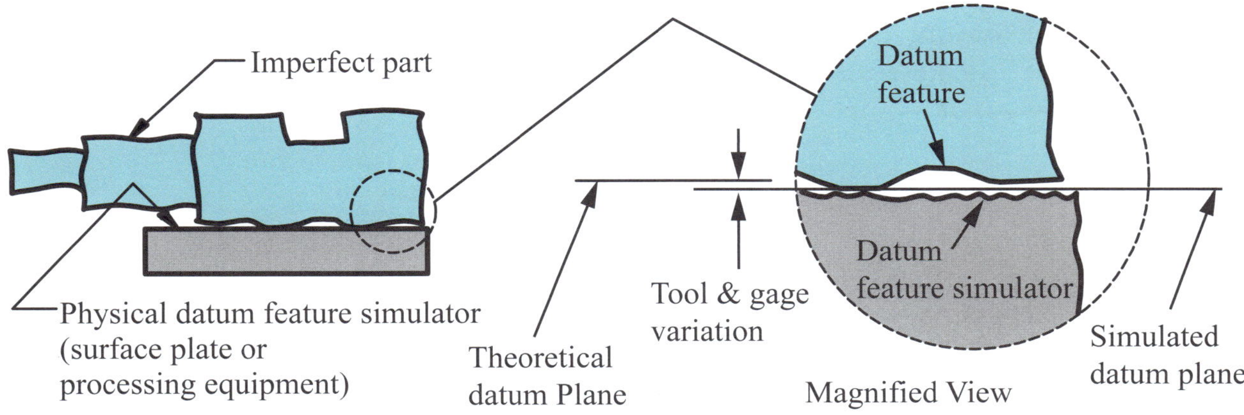

Default Stabilization for "Rocking" Datum Features

How is the datum established when the datum feature does not make unique contact with its true geometric counterpart? (A convex surface on a surface plate or a tapered shaft in a collet.) The default solution has changed from Y14.5-2009 to Y14.5-2018.

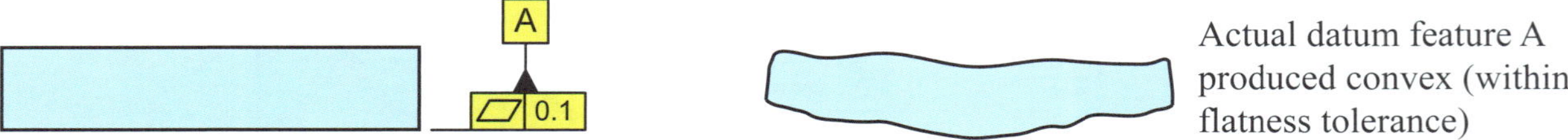

The default in ASME Y14.5-**2009** and 1994 is the *candidate datum set* defined by ASME Y14.5.1M-1994. This allows multiple possible datum planes because the part may be "rocked" to make all other features fit their tolerance zones. The datum plane is valid provided all contact points are not on the outer 1/3 regions.

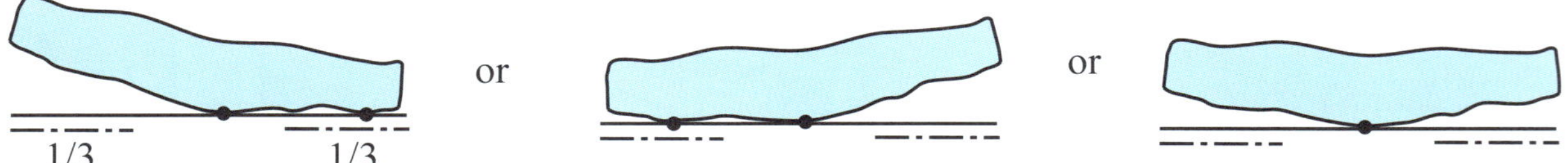

Multiple (actually infinite) permissible candidate datums may be created from the part above. Note that the planar surface may not make 3 point contact with the datum plane.

The default for establishing a datum in ASME Y14.5-**2018** is "*a single solution that minimizes the separation between the feature and the true geometric counterpart per ASME Y14.5.1.*" This could be accomplished by shimming the part on a surface plate or with a CMM algorithm. The theoretical algorithm defined in ASME Y14.5.1-2019 is *the constrained least squares (constrained L2) applied to the external envelope.*

Least squares (L2) is a common minimization algorithm used to establish a perfect plane from a imperfect surface point cloud. The L2 plane is one that minimizes the sum (integral) of the squared distances to the datum feature. However, L2 will create a plane in the middle of these points (therefore internal to the material) and is not the functional datum plane the part will contact in the assembly. Therefore, a constraint is added to the algorithm: to always make the plane external to the material. A *constrained L2* is a minimization algorithm that maintains high point contact.

One last issue is that the voids in the feature surface (low points) contribute to the constrained L2 minimization. A deeper void in the material will be a larger distance to the plane and contribute more to the "pulling" of the plane. However when the part mounts, these voids should not affect the location of other features. This has created an idea called "void-filling." The external-facing convex hull of the surface can be named the "external envelope". True geometric counterparts can then be applied to the external envelope surface and improve the functionality of the datum plane. All of this has led to the official algorithm again as: *constrained L2 applied to the external envelope.* See the Y14.5.1-2019 for more explanation and official math algorithms.

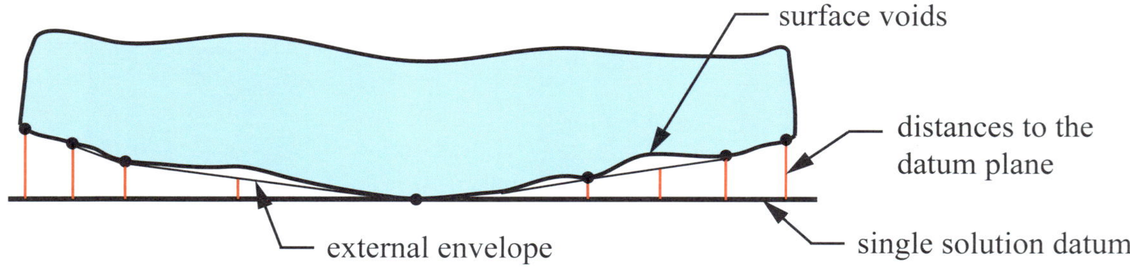

Workshop Exercise 4.1

1. The datum reference frame (DRF) consists of a point, axes, and planes. Label these components on the illustration to the right.

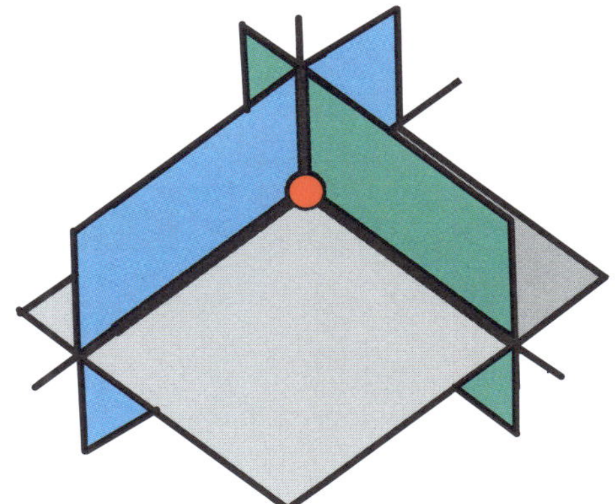

2. What is the name of this symbol?
   a. datum symbol
   b. datum feature symbol
   c. feature control frame
   d. datum feature simulator

3. On the illustration below, label the following terms:
   Physical datum feature simulator
   Datum feature
   Datum
   Simulated datum

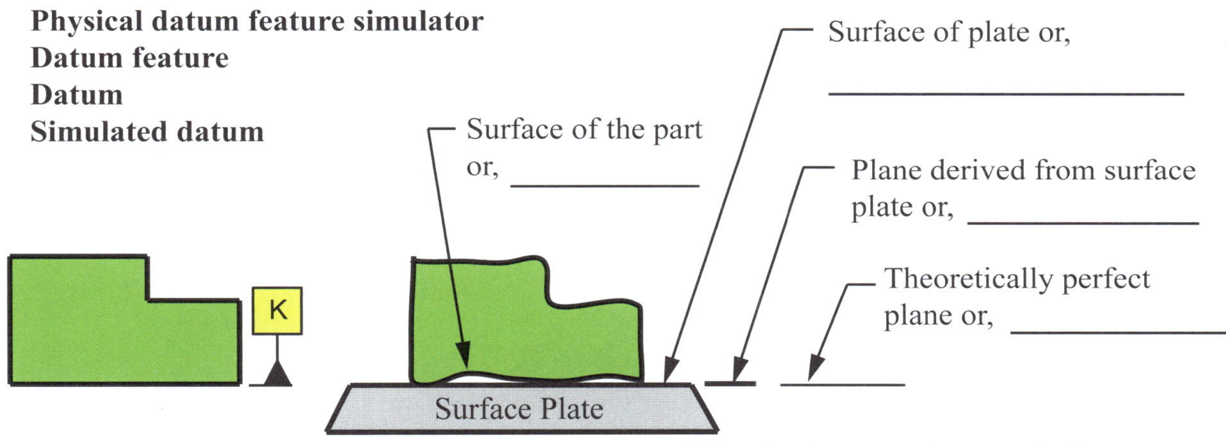

4. On the drawing below, which symbol is applied **incorrectly?**
   a. datum feature D
   b. datum feature K
   c. datum feature P
   d. datum feature T

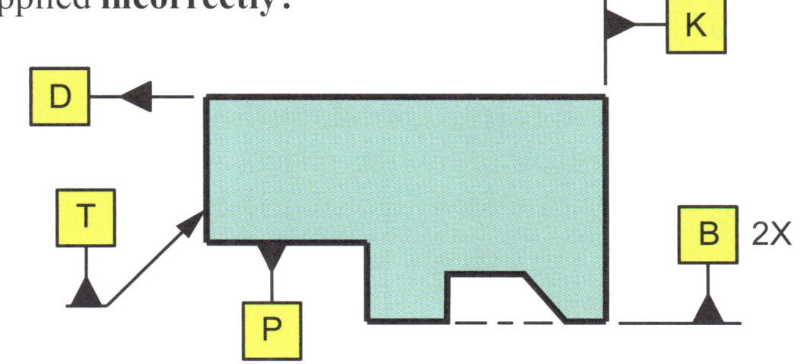

5. On the drawing above, what does the 2X mean next to datum feature B?
   a. there are two datum Bs established on the part
   b. two separate planes are established on the two surfaces
   c. the symbol will be displayed two times on the drawing
   d. two surfaces are the datum feature creating one datum plane

Datums vs. Datum Features

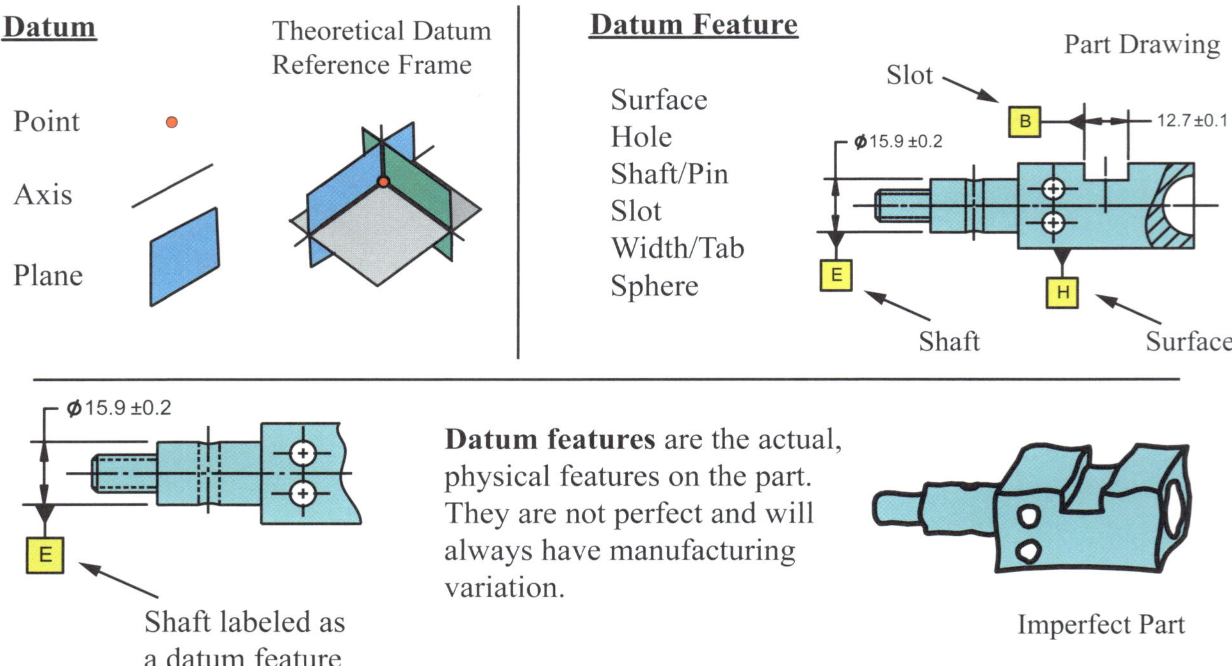

How is a theoretical perfect **datum** established from a physical imperfect **datum feature**? The answer is through a **true geometric counterpart (TGC)**. This TGC is a perfect inverse shape and contacts the highest points of the datum feature. The perfect datum is derived from the TGC. The TGC is the connection between the theoretical datum reference frame and physical part.

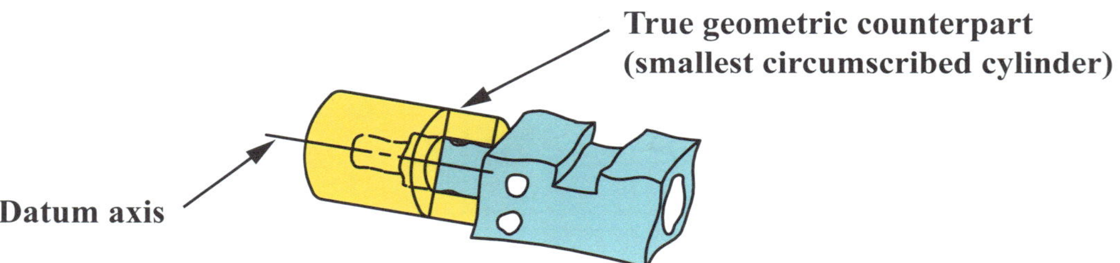

The drawing specification defines the theoretical **true geometric counterpart** to establish the datum (no measurement uncertainty). In real inspections, using a TGC is not possible. Instead, a **physical datum feature simulator** is used to establish a **simulated datum**. This could be either a piece of hard tooling (collet, chuck, surface plate, angle plate) that engages the feature or soft tooling (CMM or OMM algorithms) used on the measurement points.

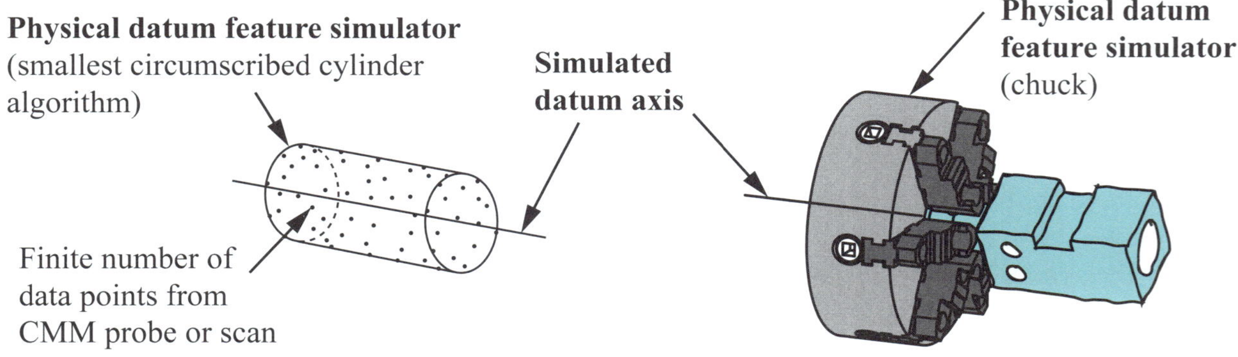

True Geometric Counterparts and Physical Datum Feature Simulators

A True Geometric Counterpart (TGC) is a theoretical boundary that establishes a datum from a datum feature. By default, the TGC is the perfect inverse geometry of the datum feature and expands/contracts to make maximum contact. Examples of this would be an unrelated or related actual mating envelope (AME).
Note: True geometric counterpart was a term first used in the ASME Y14.5-1994 standard but was changed to "datum feature simulator (theoretical)" in the 2009 standard. It was changed back to TGC in 2018.

A Datum Feature Simulator is a physical boundary, such as a surface plate, collet, gage block, CMM algorithm, that is used to establish a simulated datum from a datum feature. These simulators are not perfect, but they are of such quality that their surfaces, center planes, and axes are used for measurement in inspection.

In practice, it is impossible to measure from a theoretical datum reference frame. Datum features, physical simulators, and inspection systems are never perfect. The physical datum feature simulator mimics the TGC as close as possible within reasonable gage and tool tolerances. Gage tolerances are part of measurement uncertainty and are usually 10% to 15% of part tolerances. There is additional information on tool and gage tolerances in ASME Y14.43-2003.

Error in the hard gage, inspection equipment, or software must be accounted for in the measurement uncertainty to insure parts still lie within design tolerance limits. Measurement uncertainty is the bridge from the engineering theoretical world to the practical world of manufacturing and quality control. Inspection often uses guard banding techniques which artificially reduce the feature tolerance limits by the measurement uncertainty value. This insures the feature does not violate the hard tolerance limits even with measurement error.

The design engineer works in the theoretical CAD world, where everything is perfect. The datum reference frame, TGCs and basic dimensions are all perfect. This "perfect concept" allows the design engineer to make necessary calculations based on a mathematical foundation and convey ideal design intent with maximum allowable geometric tolerances. Also, by defining requirements in the ideal world, the designer does not force an inspection method. The experts in inspection (quality engineers and inspectors) have flexibility in their process to choose the best inspection method while balancing the time, cost, and accuracy needed.

This is important to note with all geometric specifications. Inspection will never be able to do what the engineering drawing states because the specifications are theoretical. The quality plan or inspection document dictates the actual measurement plan. Especially with larger tolerance specifications, inspection takes short cuts to save time and money. See unit 5 for more information on the quality plan.

Establishing Datums from Primary Datum Features of Size

The drawing shows datum feature symbols applied to features of size. The datum feature symbol is never attached to drawing center lines. Instead, the datum feature symbol is attached to the horizontal portion of the size dimension leader (datum feature C and F), placed in-line with the size dimension (datum feature B, E, and R), or attached to the feature control frame (datum feature D and G).

Identifying datum features of size

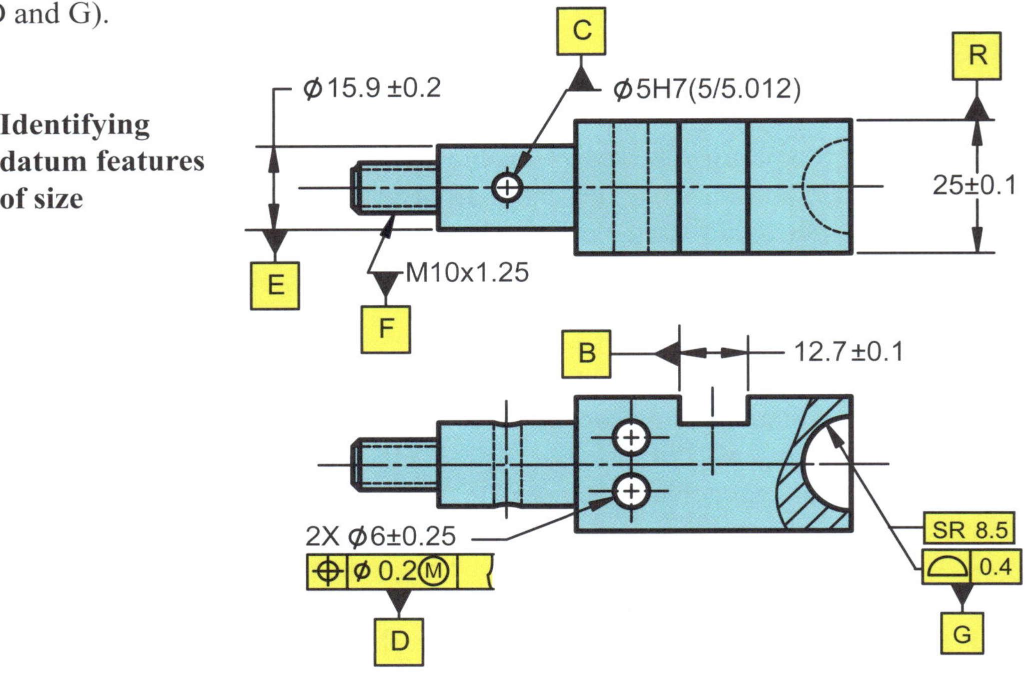

To establish the datum, a true geometric counterpart (TGC) is mated to the high points of the imperfect feature. The datum axis, center plane or point is then derived from the TGC. The examples in the next pages show the TGC to extract each of the above datums in theory and the datum feature simulator to extract the simulated datum in practice.

Establishing a datum axis from a shaft (datum feature E)

Theory

Datum E is the axis of the smallest circumscribed cylinder.

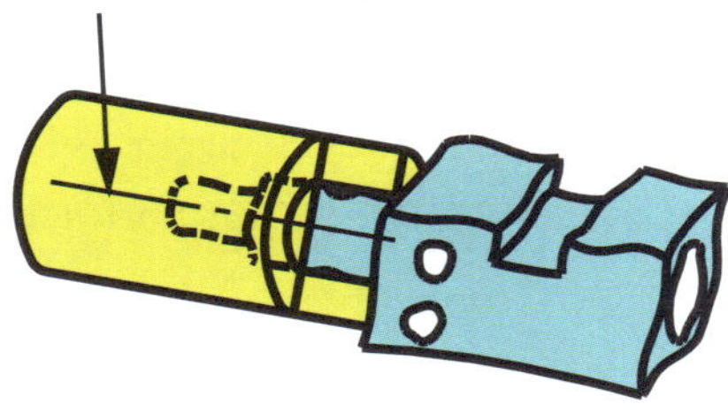

The shaft is mated with a TGC that is a circumscribed cylinder collapsing on the high points of the feature. The datum is the axis of the TGC.

Physical

Simulated datum E is the axis of a collet, chuck, or CMM algorithm.

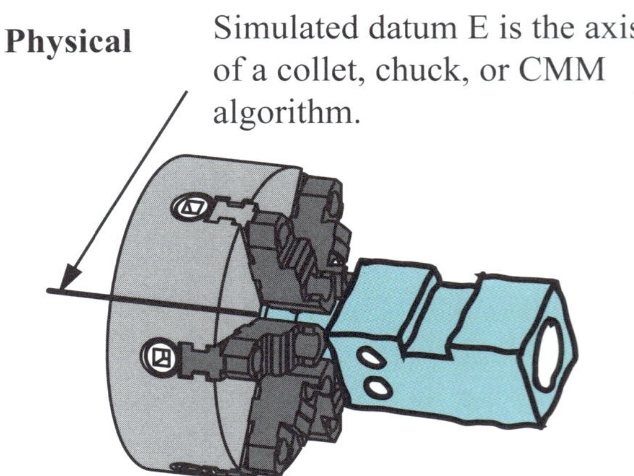

The shaft is mated with a datum feature simulator, like a collapsing chuck. The simulated datum is the axis of the datum feature simulator.

Establishing a datum center plane from an external width (datum feature R)

Theory

Datum R is the center plane of two parallel planes at minimum separation.

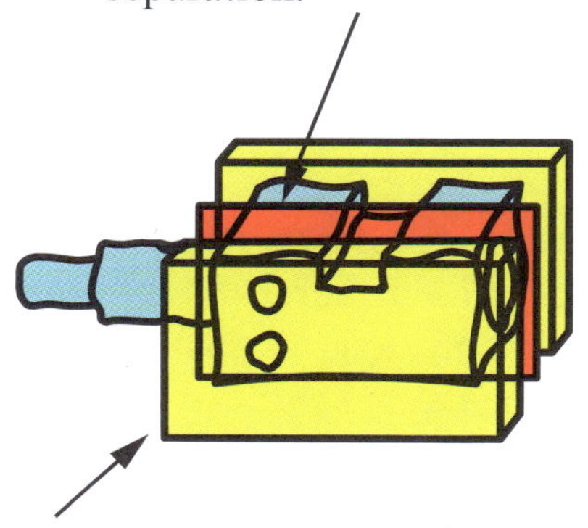

The width is mated with a TGC, that is two parallel planes at minimum separation contacting the high points of the feature. The datum is the center plane of the TGC.

Physical

Simulated datum R is the center plane of the vice jaws.

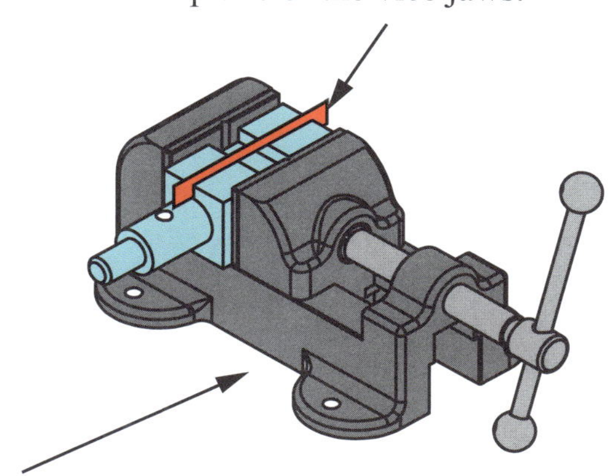

The width is mated with a datum feature simulator, such as the jaws on a machinist vice or CMM algorithm. The simulated datum is the center plane of this inspection or processing equipment.

Establishing a datum center plane from a slot (datum feature B)

Theory

Datum B is the center plane of two parallel planes at maximum separation.

The slot is mated with a TGC, that is two parallel planes at maximum separation contacting the high points of the feature. The datum is the center plane of the TGC.

Physical

Simulated datum B is the center plane of the gage block.

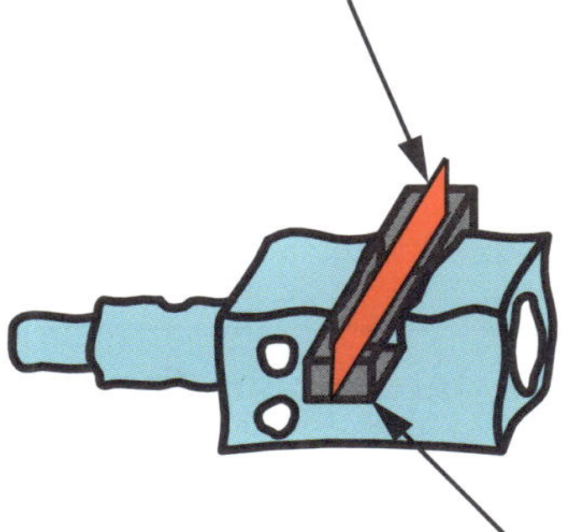

The slot is mated with a datum feature simulator, such as a gage block, CMM, etc., contacting the high points of the feature. The simulated datum is the center plane of this inspection or processing equipment.

Establishing a datum axis from a hole (datum feature C)

Theory

Datum axis C is the axis of the largest inscribed cylinder.

The hole is mated with a TGC that is an expanding inscribing cylinder contacting the high points of the feature. The datum is the axis of the TGC.

Physical

Simulated datum axis C is the axis of a gage pin.

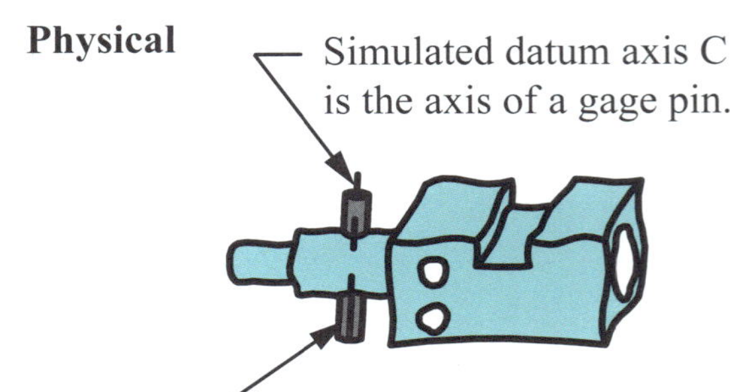

The hole is mated with a datum feature simulator, such as a gage pin, mandrel, CMM etc. The simulated datum is the axis of this inspection or processing equipment.

Establishing two datum planes from a pattern of two holes (datum feature D)

Theory

Datum D is two perpendicular planes established from two inscribed cylinders.

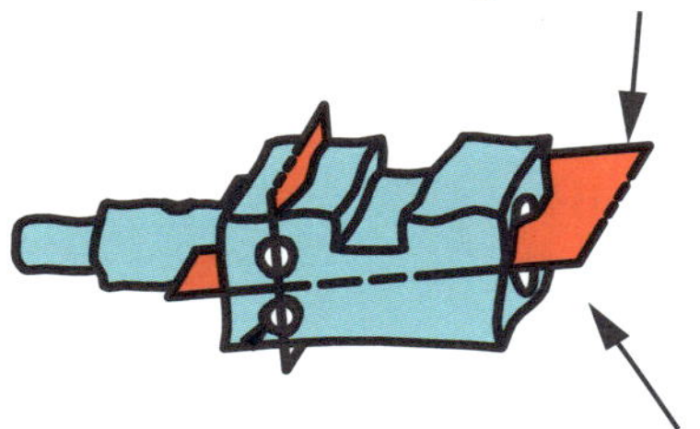

The two holes are mated with a TGC that is two inscribed cylinders fixed at basic location (expanded simultaneously) and making contact with the high points of the features. The datum planes are established from the TGC.

Physical

Simulated datum D is two planes established from the gage pins.

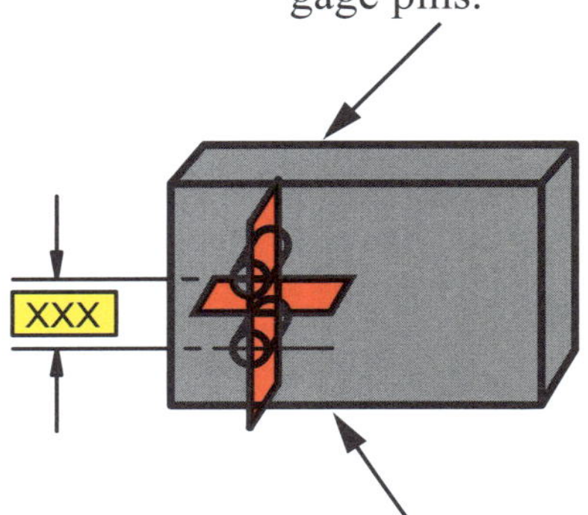

The two holes are mated with a datum feature simulator, like a hard or soft gage, CMM etc. The axis and two planes are established from this inspection or processing equipment.

Establishing a datum point from a sphere (datum feature G)

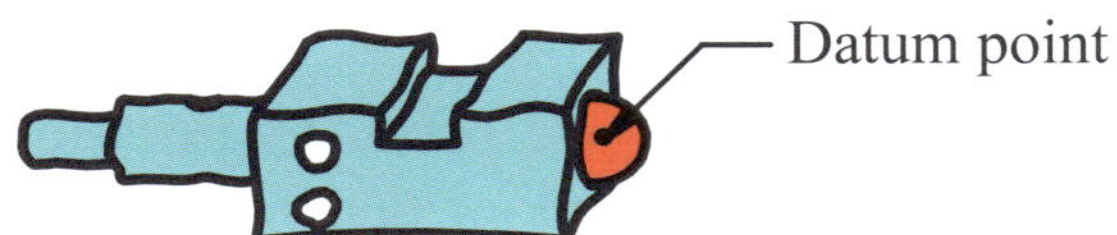

Datum point

Theory- TGC is an expanding sphere
Physical- CMM, gage ball, etc.

Note: This SR is not technically a feature of size, but does establish a boundary

Establishing a datum axis from the pitch dia of the threads (datum feature F)

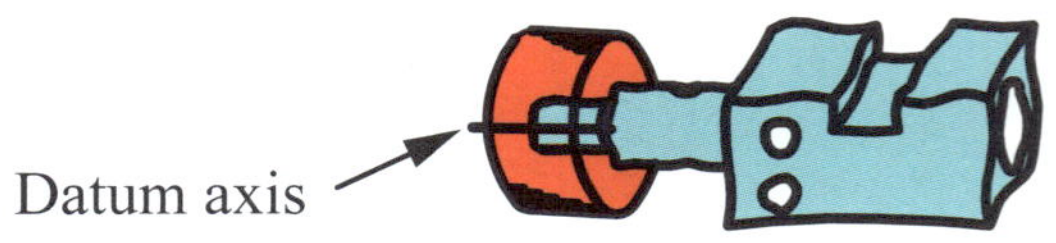

Datum axis

Theory- TGC is a collapsing pitch cylinder
Physical- Thread gage, thread wires etc.

Datum Feature Symbol Placement is Important

The datum feature symbol identifies physical features, and its placement is very important.

Datum features M and K are datum features without size and each establish a datum plane on the high points of the planar surface. The datum feature symbol is placed on the extension line of the feature, clearly removed from the size dimension line.

Datum features B and R are datum features of size (slot and width) and each establish a datum center plane. The datum feature symbol is placed in line with the size dimension line.

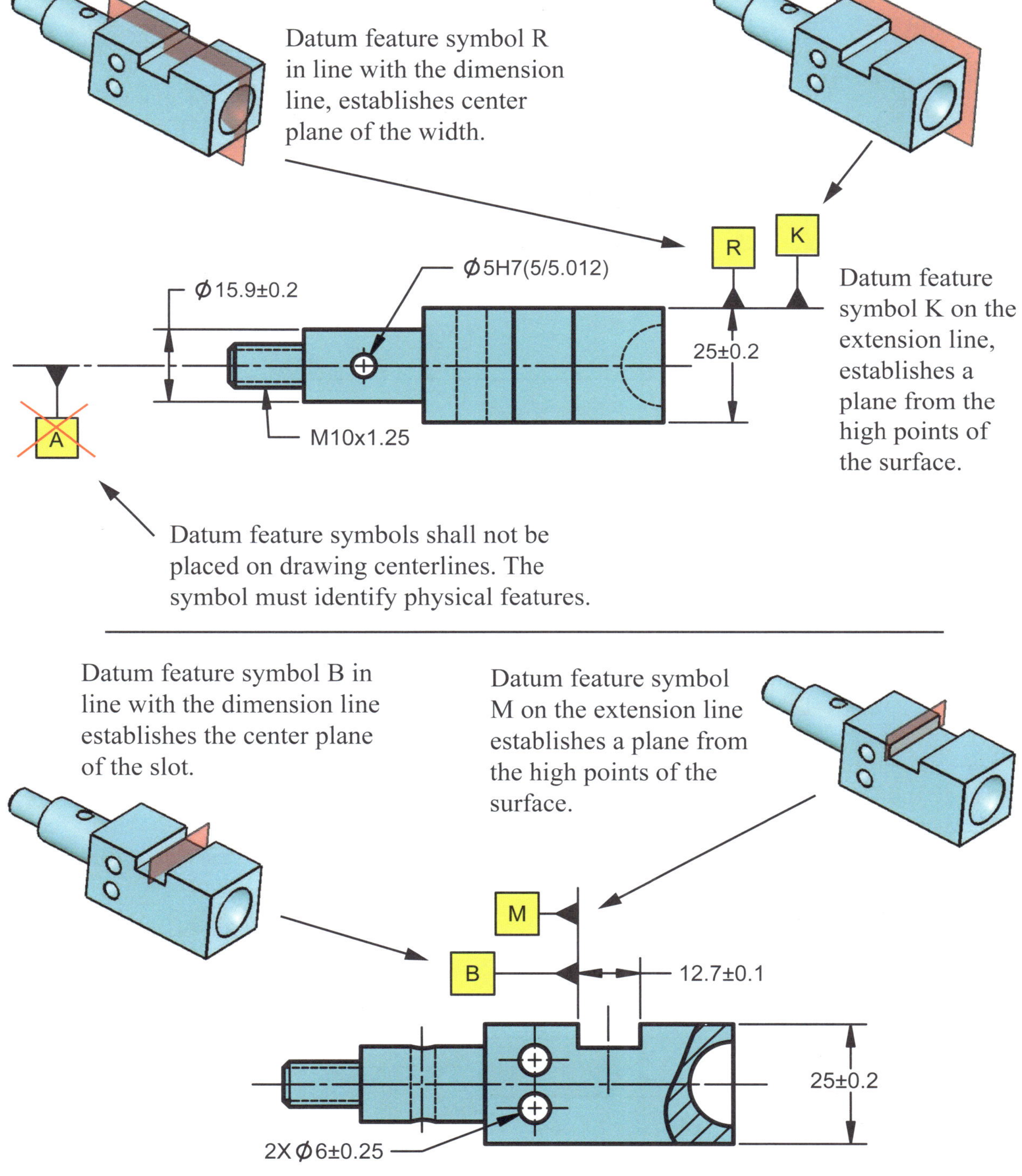

Partial Datum Features and Multiple Datum Features

By default, if a feature is identified as a datum feature, the entire surface shall be used to establish the datum. In some cases, a partial datum feature may be identified to make the measurement more functional or relax manufacturing tolerances.

Examples of partial datum features are shown below. The partial area is identified with basic dimensions. An offset chain line or cross-hatching may be used to identify the partial section. Datum targets and notes are another method to establish partial datum features. See datum target section in unit 8.

Partial datum features

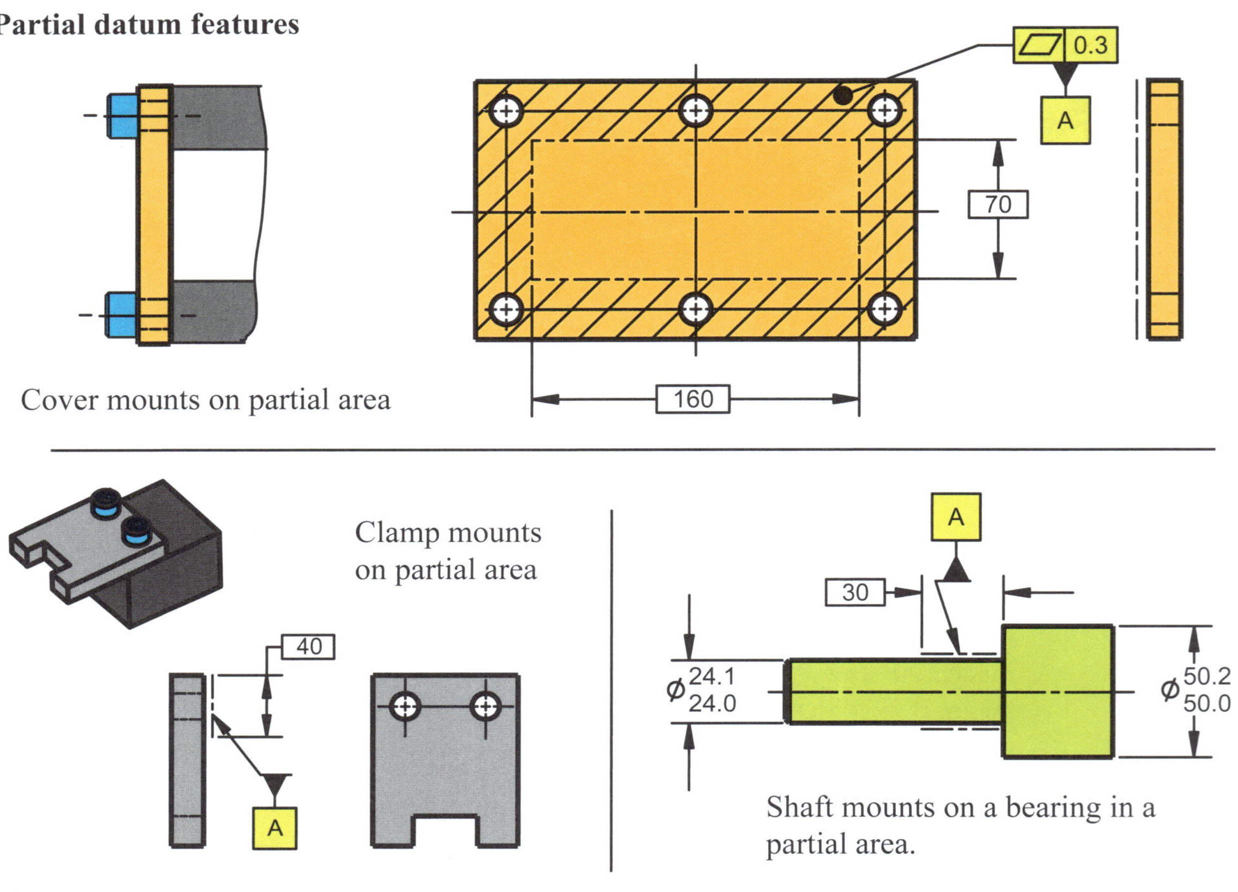

Cover mounts on partial area

Clamp mounts on partial area

Shaft mounts on a bearing in a partial area.

The shaft mounts on two bearing surfaces simultaneously. The datum feature letters are entered in the primary compartment of the feature control frame, separated by a dash. Both datum features together establish a single primary datum axis. See unit 9 for more explanation on A-B.

Common datum features

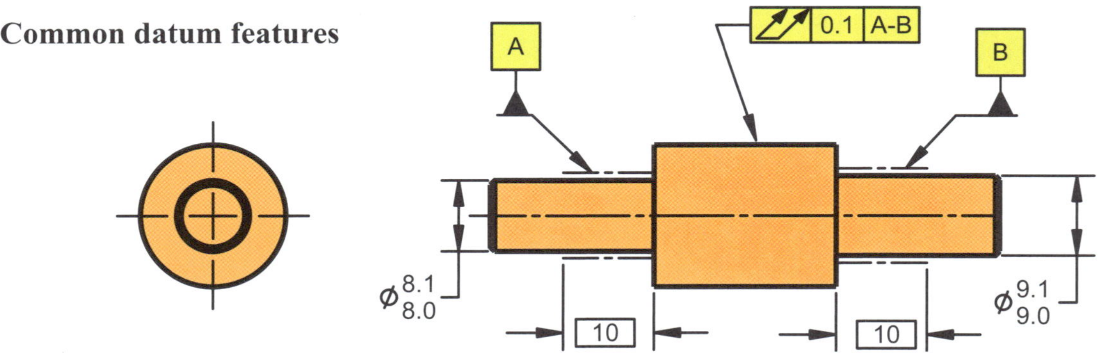

Datum Feature Symbols applied to 3D Model

The same part from previous examples is shown below in 3D to illustrate how to attach datum feature symbols in a CAD model per ASME Y14.41-2019.

Datum Features without Size

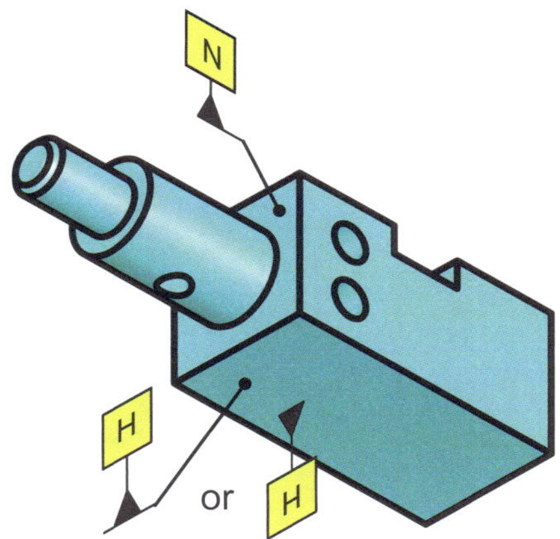

When the datum feature symbol is attached to the surface, it is placed in an annotation plane perpendicular to the surface. When the symbol is attached to a leader line directed to the surface with a dot, the symbol may be placed in any annotation plane.

When multiple features are identified as a datum feature, the 2X notation is placed next to the symbol and the feature associativity is also maintained.

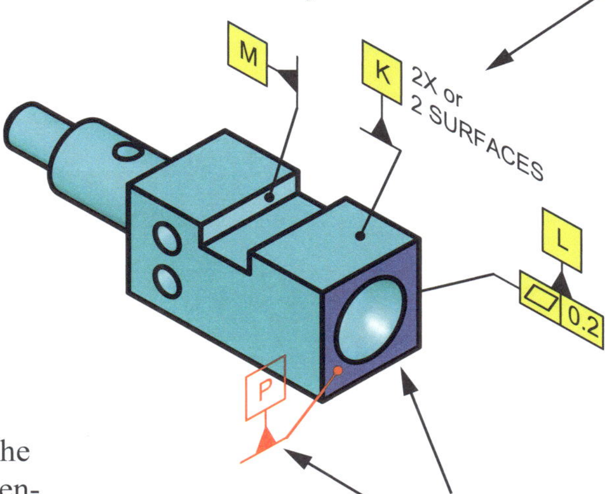

When a datum feature symbol is queried, the corresponding feature(s) shall highlight to show associativity.

Datum Features of Size

The annotation for a hole should be placed on the annotation plane perpendicular to the feature axis when the leader line terminates with an arrow.

The annotation for a slot or width shall be placed on an annotation plane perpendicular to the feature center plane.

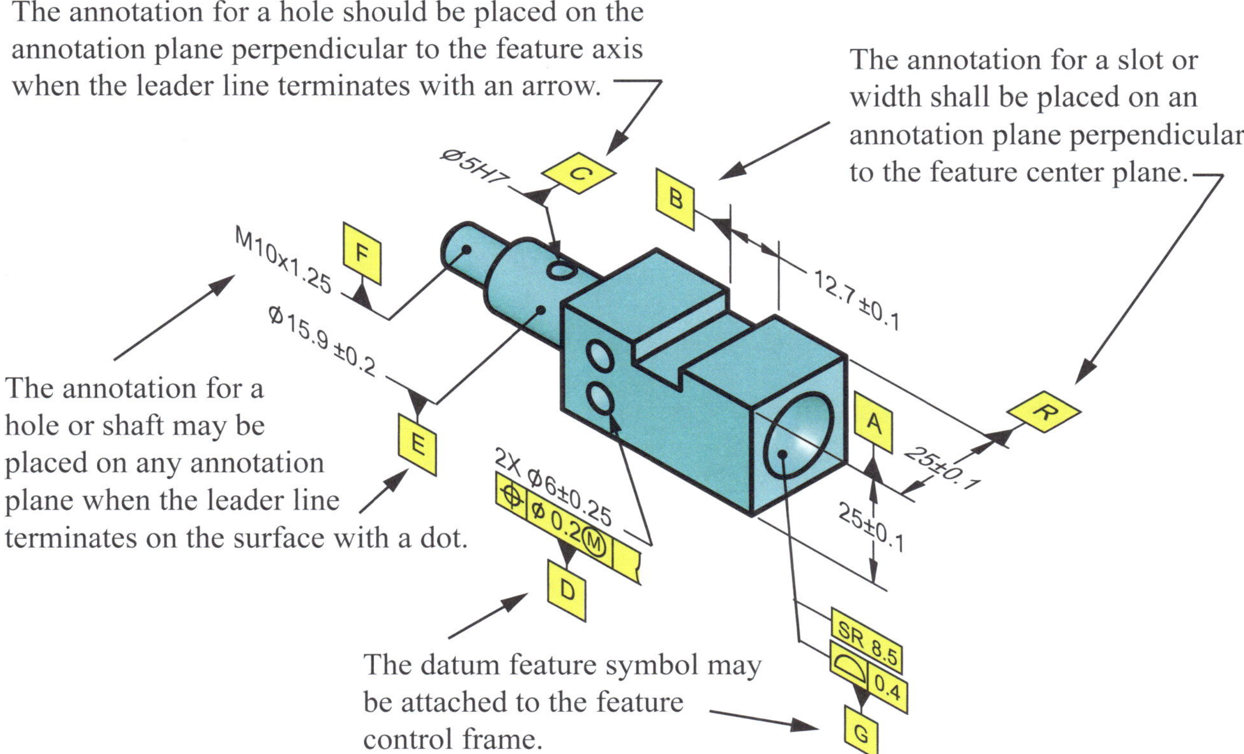

The annotation for a hole or shaft may be placed on any annotation plane when the leader line terminates on the surface with a dot.

The datum feature symbol may be attached to the feature control frame.

Workshop Exercise 4.2

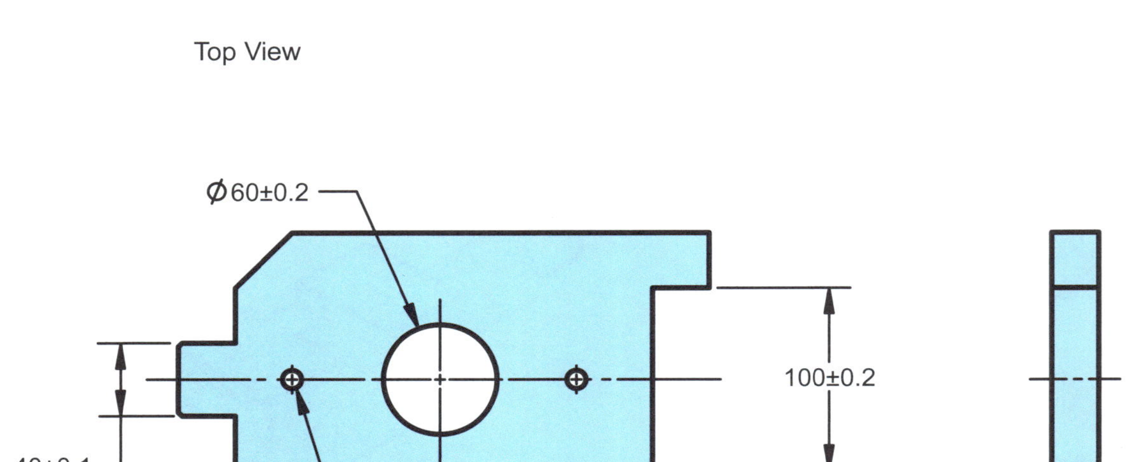

This exercise will provide practice to properly apply datum feature symbols. On the drawing above, draw datum feature symbols to create the following theoretical datums. If you need help, see application examples earlier in this unit.

1. Create datum plane A on the right hand face in the side view.

2. Create datum plane B on the bottom surface in the front view.

3. Create datum plane C on the top surface of the 40 mm tab.

4. Create datum center plane D in the center of the tab.

5. Create datum center plane E in the center of the 100 mm slot.

6. Create datum plane F on the left side of the slot.

7. Create a partial datum plane G on the top of the part in the front view. The length is 120 mm from the right side.

8. Create datum H, axis and two planes, through the two 10 mm holes.

9. Create datum axis J from the 60 mm hole.

10. Datum features can be placed in two categories - datum features of size and datum features without size. Place an "X" next to all the datum features of size.

The Six Degrees of Freedom

The datum reference frame constrains 6 degrees of freedom

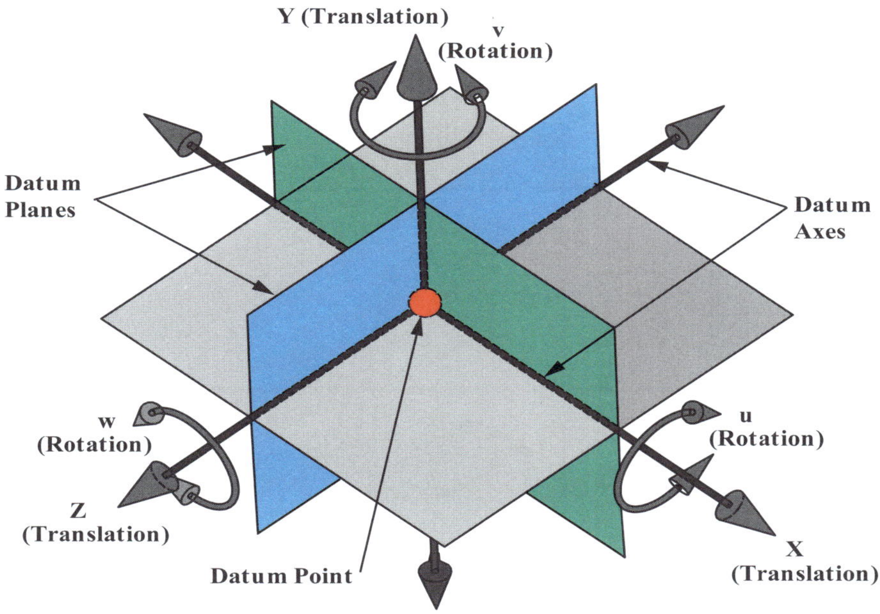

Three Translation Controls	**Three Rotation Controls**
X = Translation in "X" direction	u = Rotation around "X" axis
Y = Translation in "Y" direction	v = Rotation around "Y" axis
Z = Translation in "Z" direction	w = Rotation around "Z" axis

All parts have six degrees of freedom (DOF), three translations and three rotations, shown above. The part's degrees of freedom are constrained by contacting the datum features to the true geometric counterparts in the specified order of precedence. This establishes the relationship between the part and the datum reference frame. Ideally, these datum features should represent the part's mating relationship in the assembly as well.

In the earlier section of this unit, it was shown how datums, such as a plane or axis, are established from simpler shaped datum features, such as a surface, shaft, or slot though the true geometric counterpart. More complicated features may also be identified as a datum features, such as a conical surface, linear extrusion shape or complex shape. Examples of all possible types of primary datum features, their corresponding datum and constrained degrees of freedom are shown in the table on the next page.

Collections of features may also be used to establish a single datum, but for simplicity the table illustrates only single datum features.

The DOF table illustrates primary datum features only. The degrees of freedom constrained for a lower precedence datum feature depends on its geometry and order of precedence as a secondary or tertiary datum feature. This will be covered in the next section.

Degrees of Freedom Table - Primary Datum Feature

Feature Type	On the Drawing	Datum Feature	Datum	Datum and Constraining DOF
Planar Surface (a)	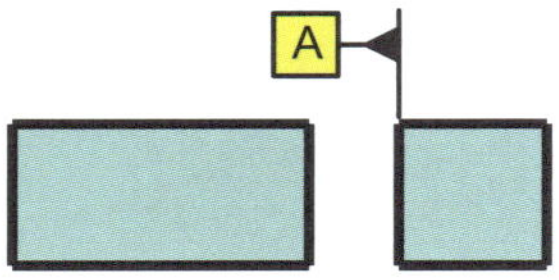 A	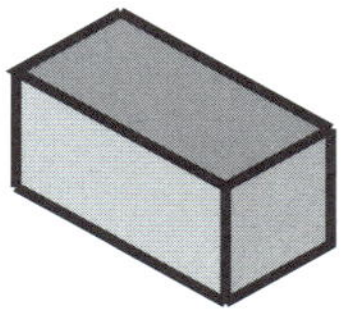	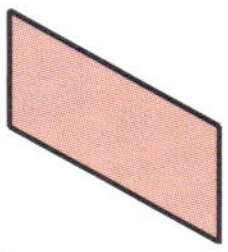 Plane	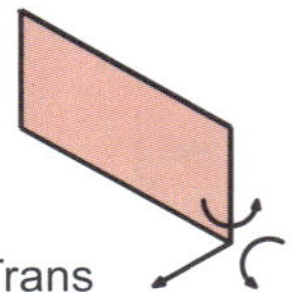 1 Trans 2 Rotate
Width (b)	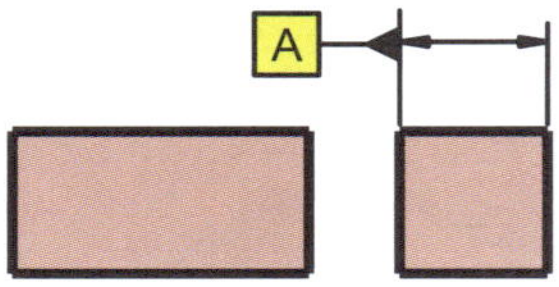 A	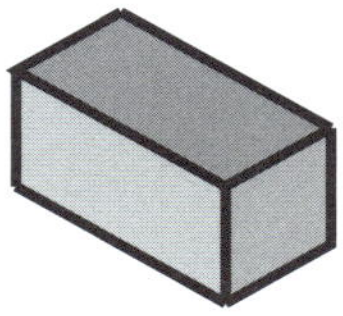	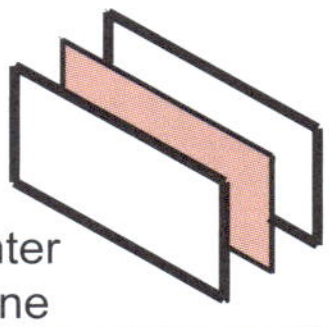 Center Plane	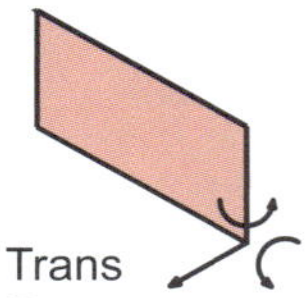 1 Trans 2 Rotate
Cylindrical (c)	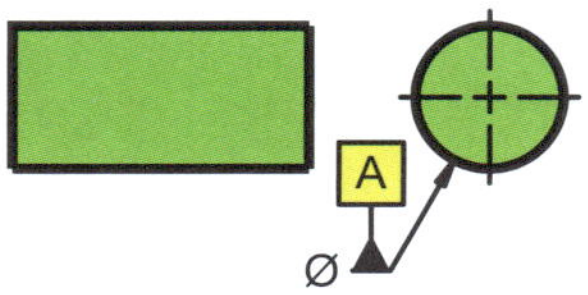 A Ø	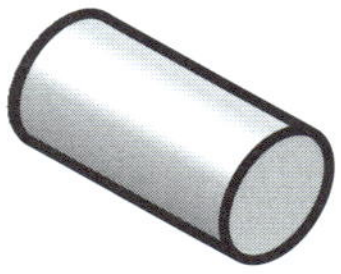	 Axis	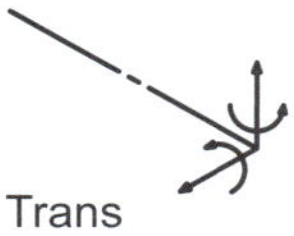 2 Trans 2 Rotate
Spherical (d)	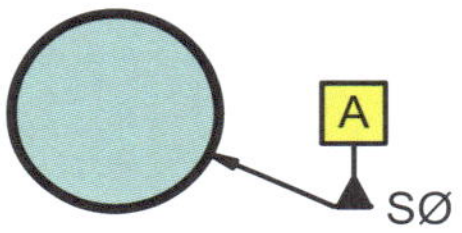 A SØ		Point	 3 Trans 0 Rotate
Conical (e)	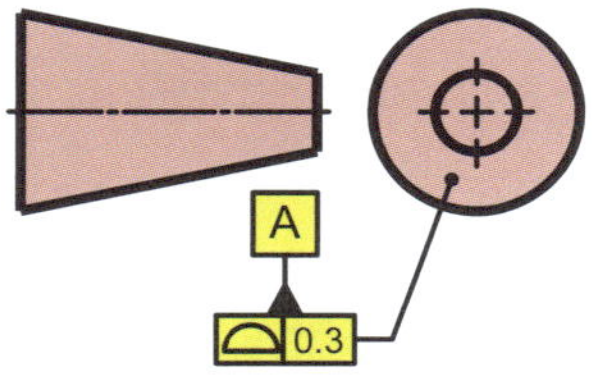 A 0.3		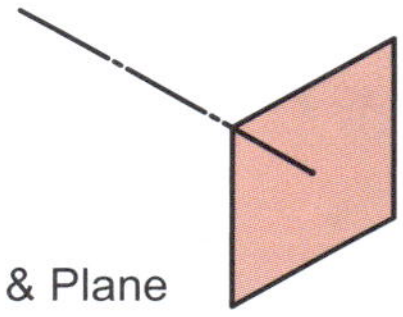 Axis & Plane	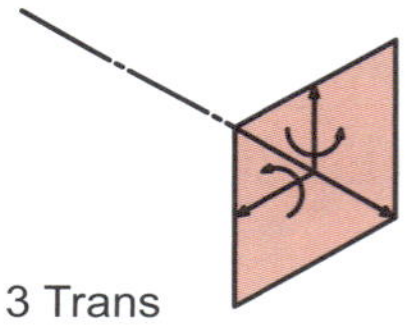 3 Trans 2 Rotate
Linear Extrusion (f)	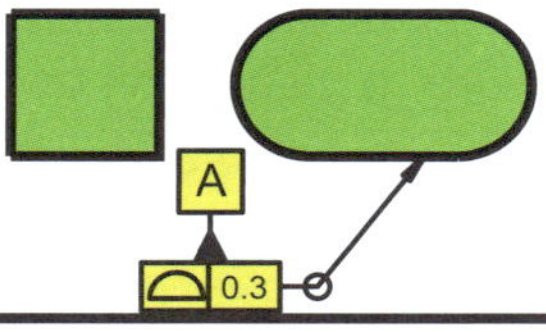 A 0.3	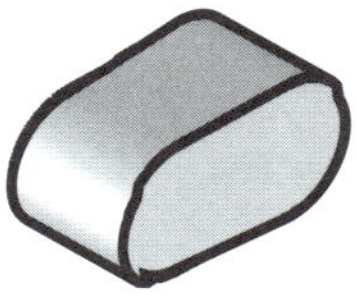	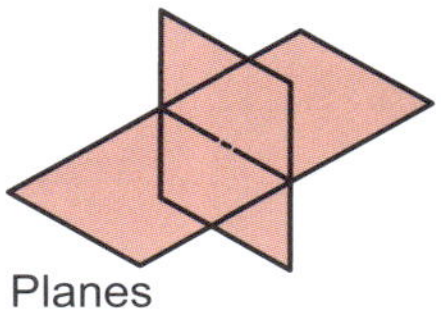 2 Planes	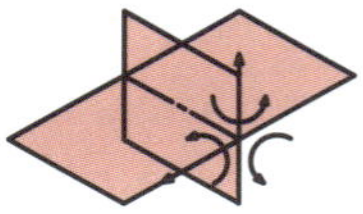 2 Trans 3 Rotate
Complex (g)	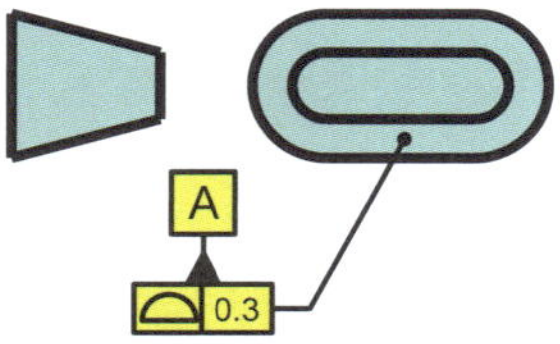 A 0.3	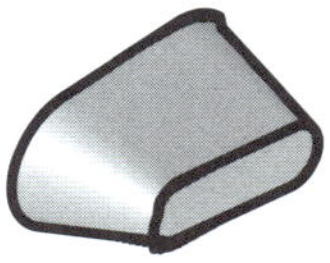	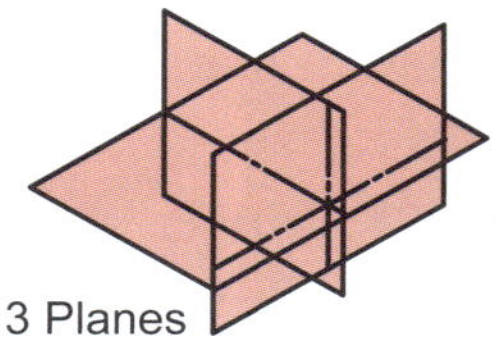 3 Planes	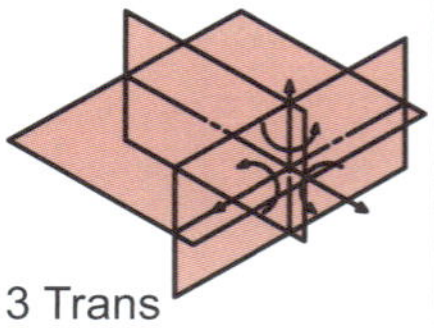 3 Trans 3 Rotate

Workshop Exercise 4.3 - Datum Feature Exercise

The part below has a variety of features that are labeled as datum features. Assume all are primary datum features for this exercise.

Next to the datum feature in the table below, identify if it establishes a point, axis, plane, or some combination of these datums. Also list the names of translational (x,y,z) and rotational (u,v,w) degrees of freedom constrained by the datum feature. See the isometric view to the right for the labeled degrees of freedom.

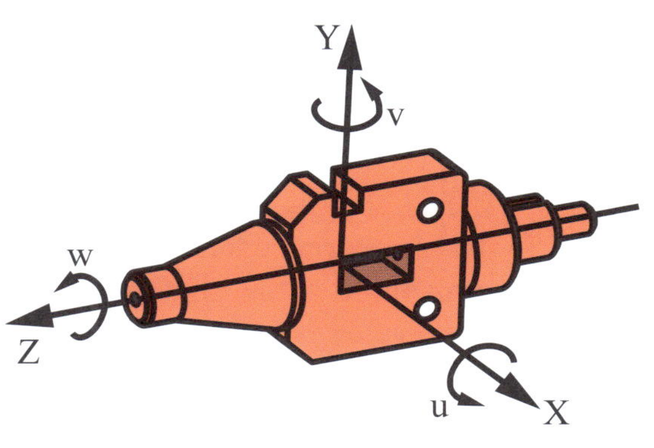

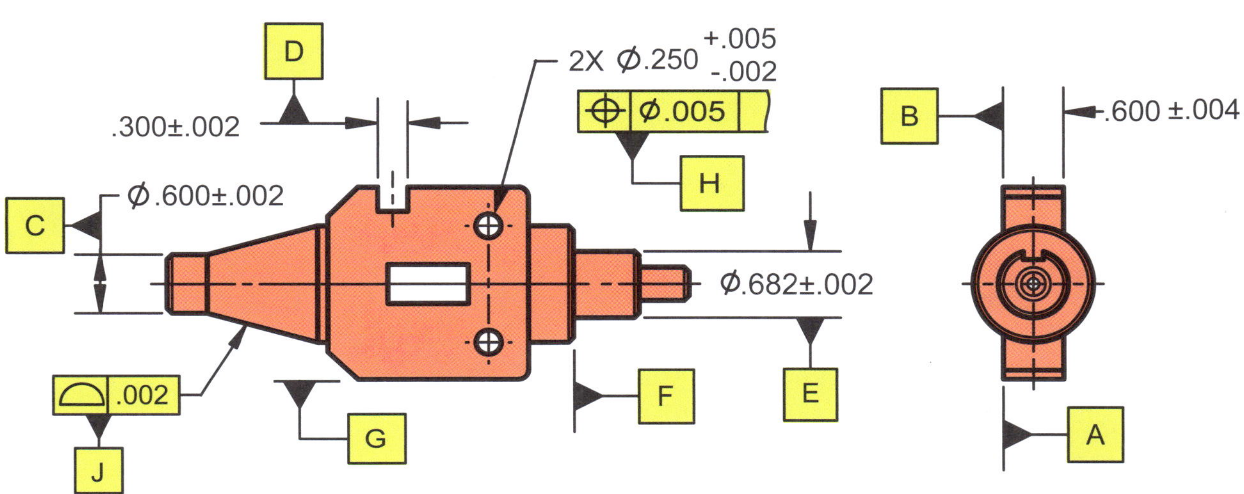

1. Point **2.** Axis **3.** Plane **4.** Center Plane **5.** Two Planes **6.** Axis & Plane

	Primary Datum Feature	Established Datum	Constrained Degrees of Freedom: Translations (x,y,z)	Constrained Degrees of Freedom: Rotations (u,v,w)
1.	A	Plane	x	v, w
2.	B			
3.	C-E			
4.	D			
5.	F			
6.	G			
7.	H			
8.	J			

Discussion: Some of the above datum features may be too unstable (short in length) to be a primary datum feature and constrain all of the listed degrees of freedom. Which ones are they?

Datum Feature Precedence

The explanations in this unit so far have only shown primary datum features and the corresponding true geometric counterpart (TGC). Often, secondary and tertiary datum features must also be referenced to adequetely constrain the part. The order of the datum features in a feature control frame is called the *order of precedence* and establishes the relationship of the primary, secondary, and tertiary TGCs. The lower precedence TGC must be perfectly oriented and if applicable, located to the higher precedence TGC. For example, if a shaft is the **primary** datum feature, the TGC is an **unrelated** actual mating envelope. If the shaft is a **secondary**, the TGC is a **related** actual mating envelope. Alphabetical order does not matter; do not always assume "A" will be the primary. In the two examples below, notice how the part will be set up differently if the order of precedence is changed in the feature control frame.

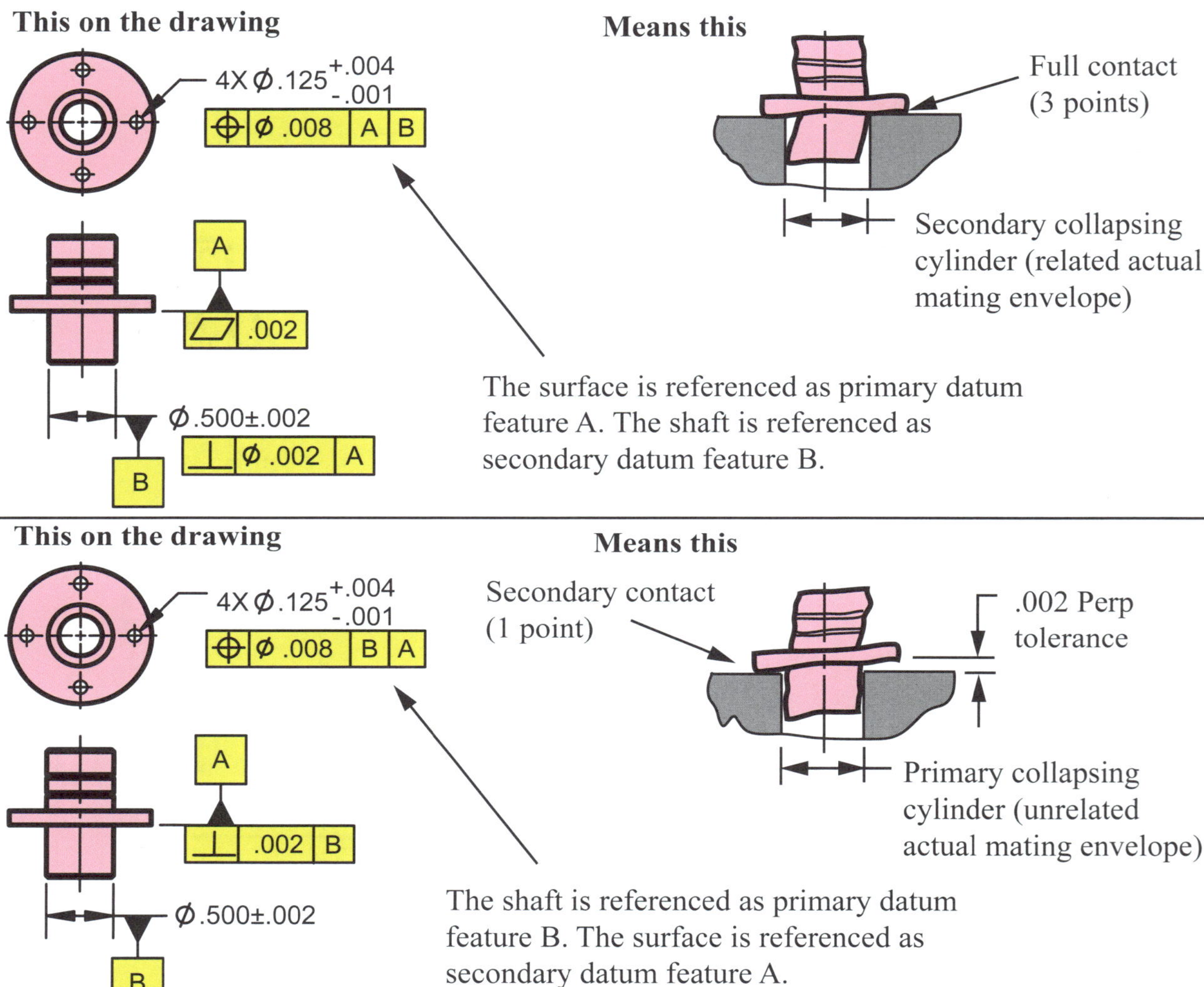

A lower precedence datum feature can not override any degrees of freedom already constrained by a higher precedence datum feature(s). Each subsequent referenced datum feature in the feature control frame will constrain all degrees of freedom possible within its ability. The datum feature order of precedence is selected based on function. Both of the above examples are valid, but measuring the part in its functional assembly state is the goal. The primary datum feature is usually a long/large feature that is a stable set of initial reference. It should establish a long axis or large plane that adequately constrains the initial 2 of 3 rotational degrees of freedom for the part.

Establishing a DRF - Planar Surfaces

The H, L, P - DRF on the drawing

The figures below illustrate the sequence of events to establish the H, L, P datum reference frame to constrain the 6 degrees of freedom on the part.

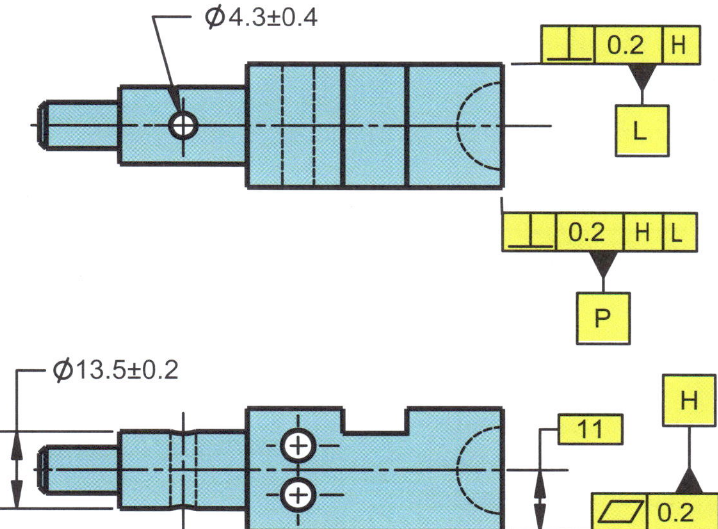

A lower precedence datum feature can not override the degrees of freedom already established by a higher precedence datum feature.

Establishing the H, L, P - DRF on the part

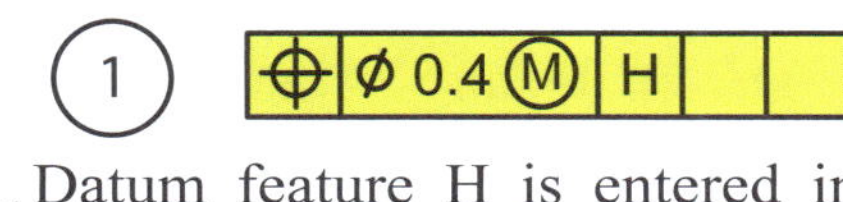

Datum feature H is entered in the first compartment as the primary datum feature. It establishes a plane and constrains 1 translation and 2 rotations. The surface is qualified with a flatness tolerance.

3 point min contact to establish primary plane

2 point min contact to establish secondary datum plane

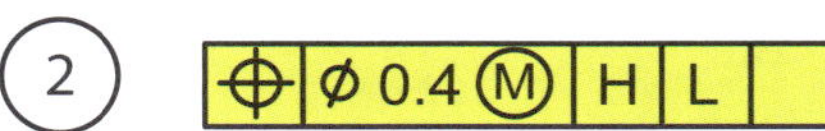

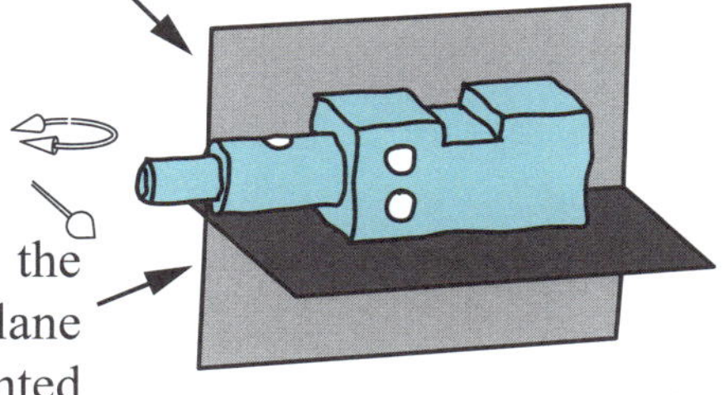

Datum feature L is entered in the second compartment as the secondary datum feature. The feature surface establishes a plane and constrains 1 translation and 1 rotation. The feature is oriented with a perpendicularity tolerance.

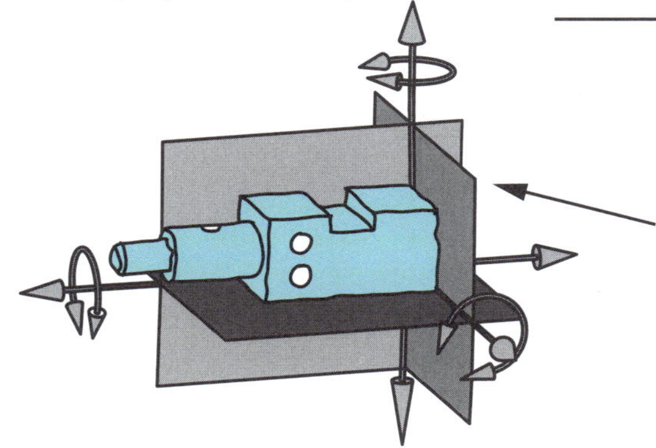

3 ⌖ Ø 0.4 Ⓜ | H | L | P

Datum feature P is entered in the third compartment as the tertiary datum feature. It establishes a plane and constrains 1 translation. The datum feature is oriented relative to datums H and L with a perpendicularity tolerance. The DRF is complete, and all 6 degrees of freedom are constrained on the part.

Establishing a DRF - Surface, Shaft, Surface

The N, E, H - DRF on the drawing

The figures below illustrate the sequence of events to establish the N, E, H datum reference frame to constrain the 6 degrees of freedom on the part.

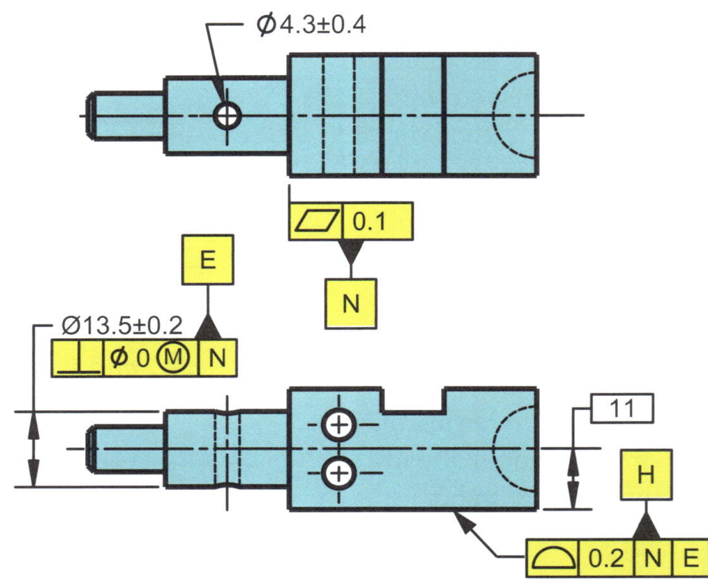

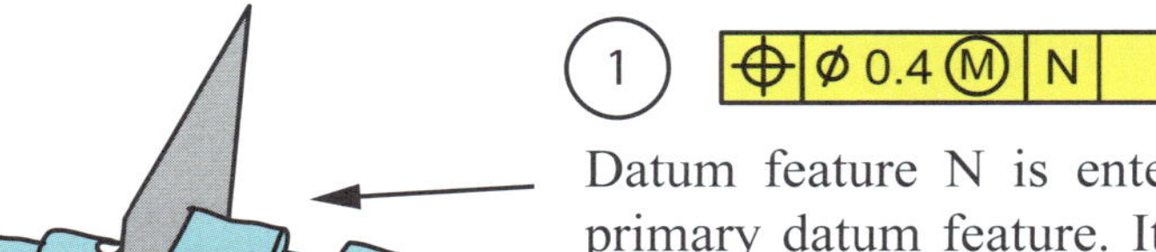

A lower precedence datum feature can not override the degrees of freedom already established by a higher precedence datum feature.

Establishing the N, E, H - DRF on the part

1 Ø 0.4 Ⓜ N

Datum feature N is entered in the first compartment as the primary datum feature. It establishes a plane and constrains 1 translation and 2 rotations. The surface is qualified with a flatness tolerance.

3 point contact to establish primary plane

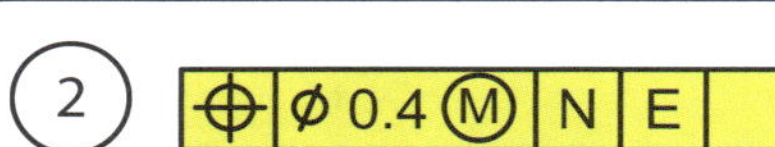

Datum feature E is entered in the second compartment as the secondary datum feature. The feature establishes an axis and constrains 2 translations. The intersection of the axis and plane establish the origin point. The feature is oriented with a perpendicularity tolerance.

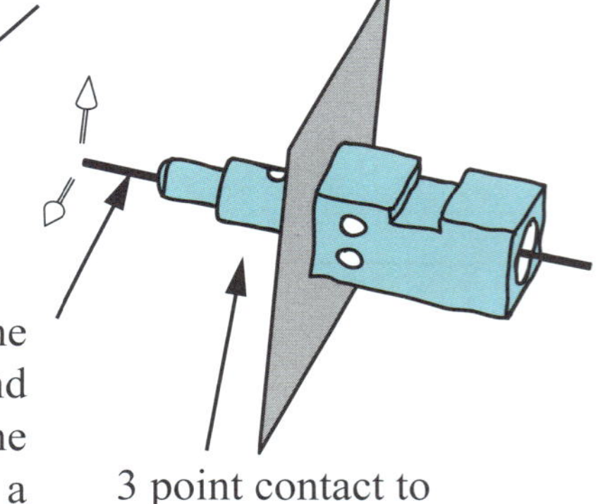

3 point contact to establish secondary datum axis

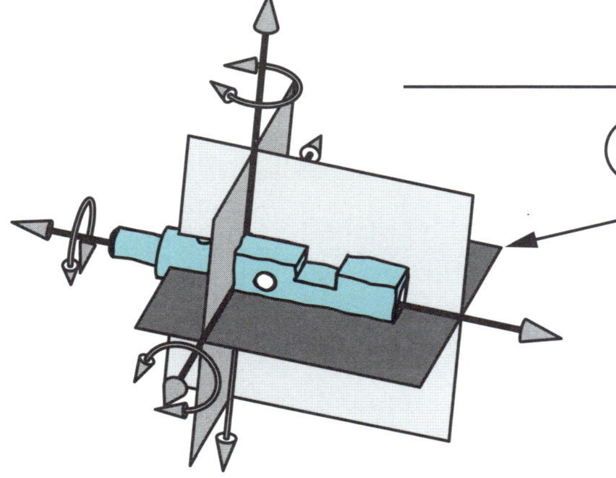

3 Ø 0.4 Ⓜ N E H

Datum feature H is entered in the third compartment as the tertiary datum feature. It constrains 1 rotation. The datum feature is located relative to the origin point with a profile tolerance. The DRF is complete, and all 6 degrees of freedom are constrained on the part.

Establishing a DRF - Shaft, Surface, Width

The E, N, R - DRF on the drawing

The figures below illustrate the sequence of events to establish the E, N, R datum reference frame to constrain the 6 degrees of freedom on the part.

⊕ | Ø 0.4 Ⓜ | E | N | R

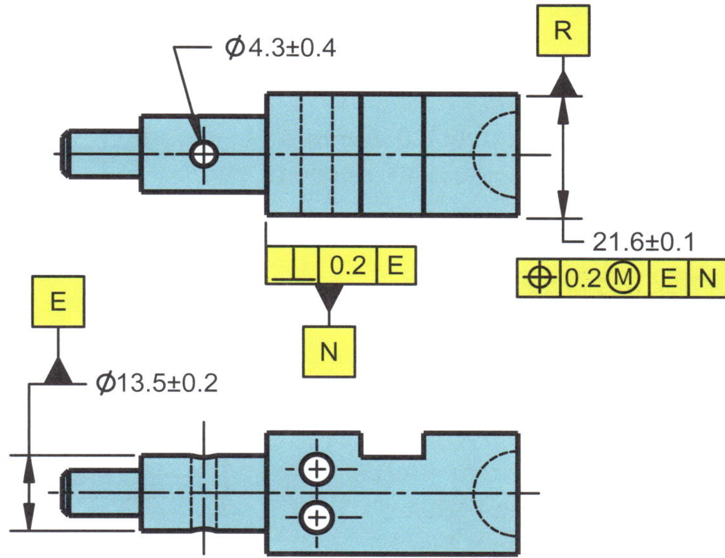

A lower precedence datum feature can not override the degrees of freedom already established by a higher precedence datum feature.

Establishing the E, N, R - DRF on the part

1 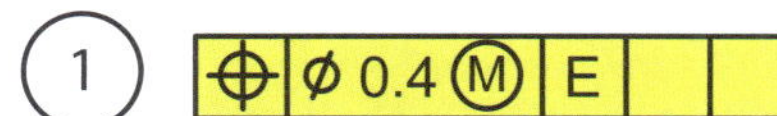

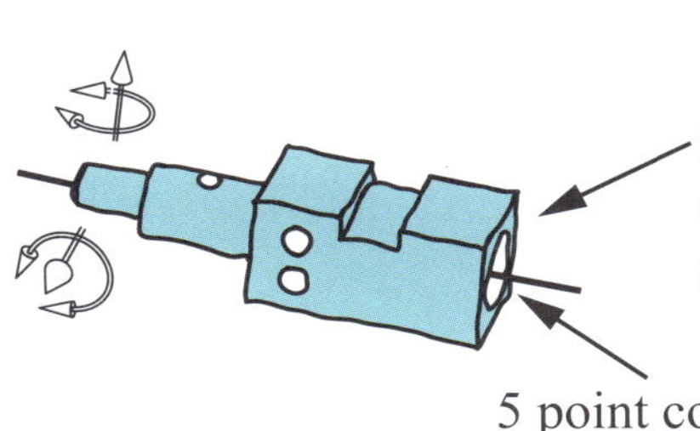

Datum feature E is entered in the first compartment as the primary datum feature. It establishes an axis and constrains 2 translations and 2 rotations. The diameter is qualified with a size tolerance.

5 point contact to establish a primary axis

2 ⊕ | Ø 0.4 Ⓜ | E | N |

Datum feature N is entered in the second compartment as the secondary datum feature. It establishes a plane and constrains 1 translation. The intersection of the axis and plane establish the origin point. The feature is oriented with a perpendicularity tolerance.

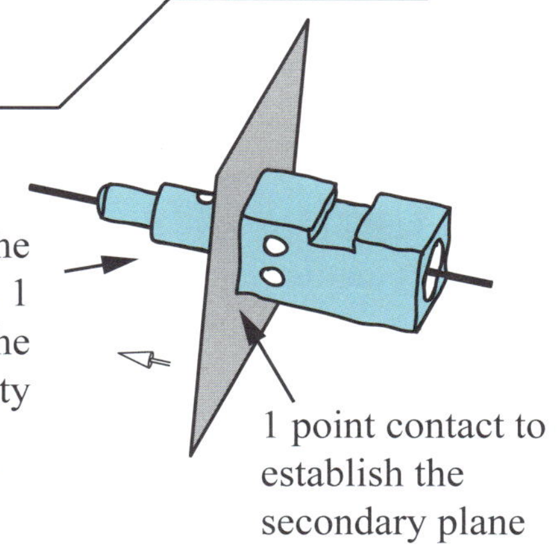

1 point contact to establish the secondary plane

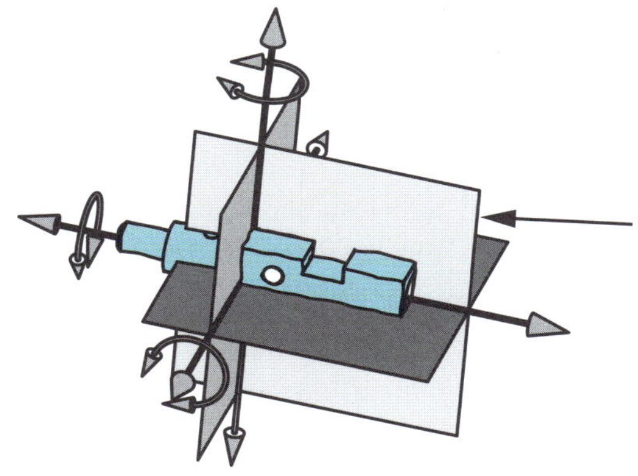

3 ⊕ | Ø 0.4 Ⓜ | E | N | R

Datum feature R is entered in the third compartment as the tertiary datum feature. The feature establishes a center plane and constrains 1 rotation. The datum feature is located relative to the origin point with a position tolerance. The DRF is complete, and all 6 degrees of freedom are constrained on the part.

Establishing a DRF - Surface, Surface, Shaft

The H, N, E - DRF on the drawing

The figures below illustrate the sequence of events to establish the H, N, E datum reference frame to constrain the 6 degrees of freedom on the part.

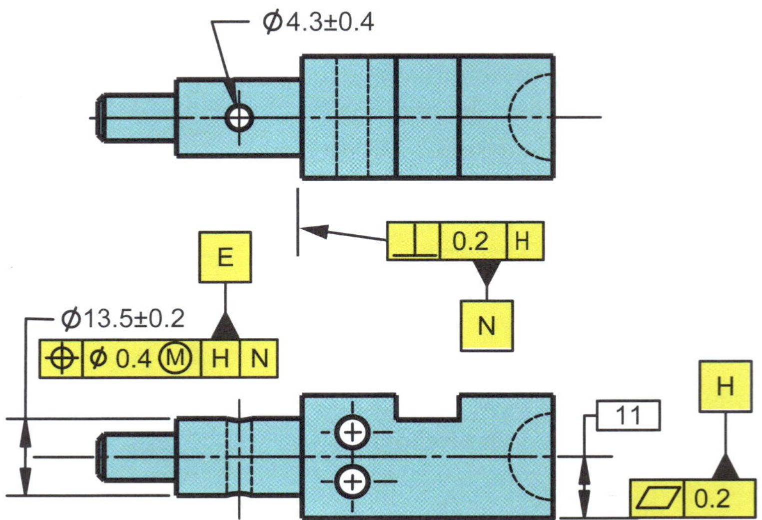

⌖ Ø 0.4 Ⓜ | H | N | E

A lower precedence datum feature can not override the degrees of freedom already established by a higher precedence datum feature.

Establishing the H, N, E datum reference frame on the part

1 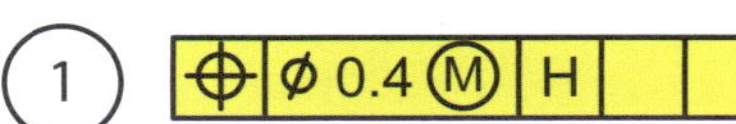

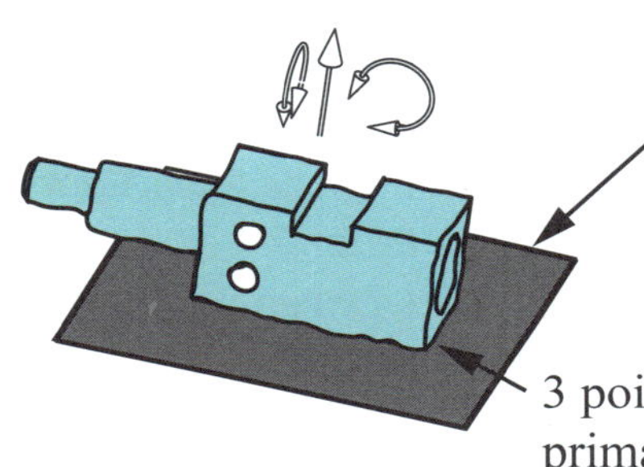

Datum feature H is entered in the first compartment as the primary datum feature. It establishes a plane and constrains 1 translation and 2 rotations. The surface is qualified with a flatness tolerance.

3 point contact to establish primary plane

2 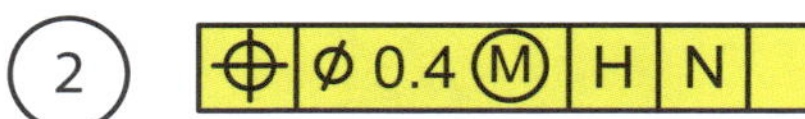

Datum feature N is entered in the second compartment as the secondary datum feature. The feature surface establishes a plane and constrains 1 translation and 1 rotation. The feature is oriented with a perpendicularity tolerance.

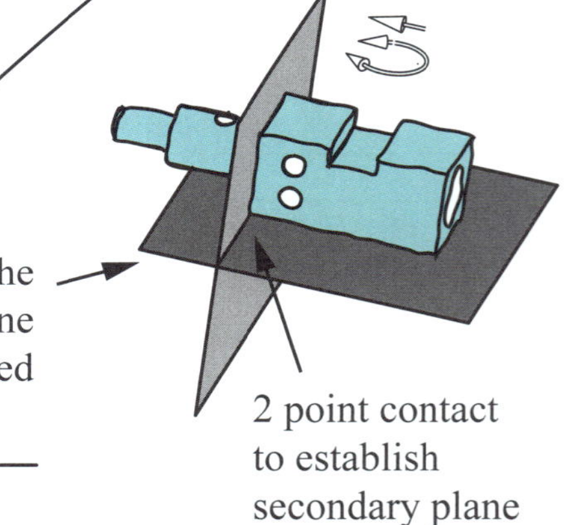

2 point contact to establish secondary plane

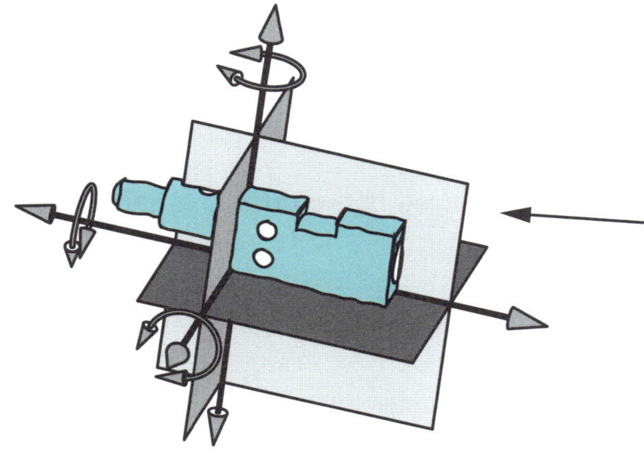

3 ⌖ Ø 0.4 Ⓜ | H | N | E

Datum feature E is entered in the third compartment as the tertiary datum feature. The feature axis constrains 1 translation. The datum feature is located to H and N with a position tolerance. The DRF is complete, and all 6 degrees of freedom are constrained on the part.

Constrained Degrees of Freedom Example

Datum features referenced in a feature control frame establish a datum reference frame based on an order of precedence. In the examples at the beginning of this unit, the order of precedence was explained with surface points of contact (3,2,1). A more mathematical way to explain the order is with degrees of freedom. The DRF constrains the 6 degrees of freedom on a part.

Remember, "A lower precedence datum feature can not override any degrees of freedom already established by a higher precedence datum feature. Each subsequent referenced datum feature in the feature control frame constrains all degrees of freedom possible within its ability."

The default constraints of the standard feature control frame below are expressed mathematically in brackets of the lower feature control frame. (for explanation purposes only)

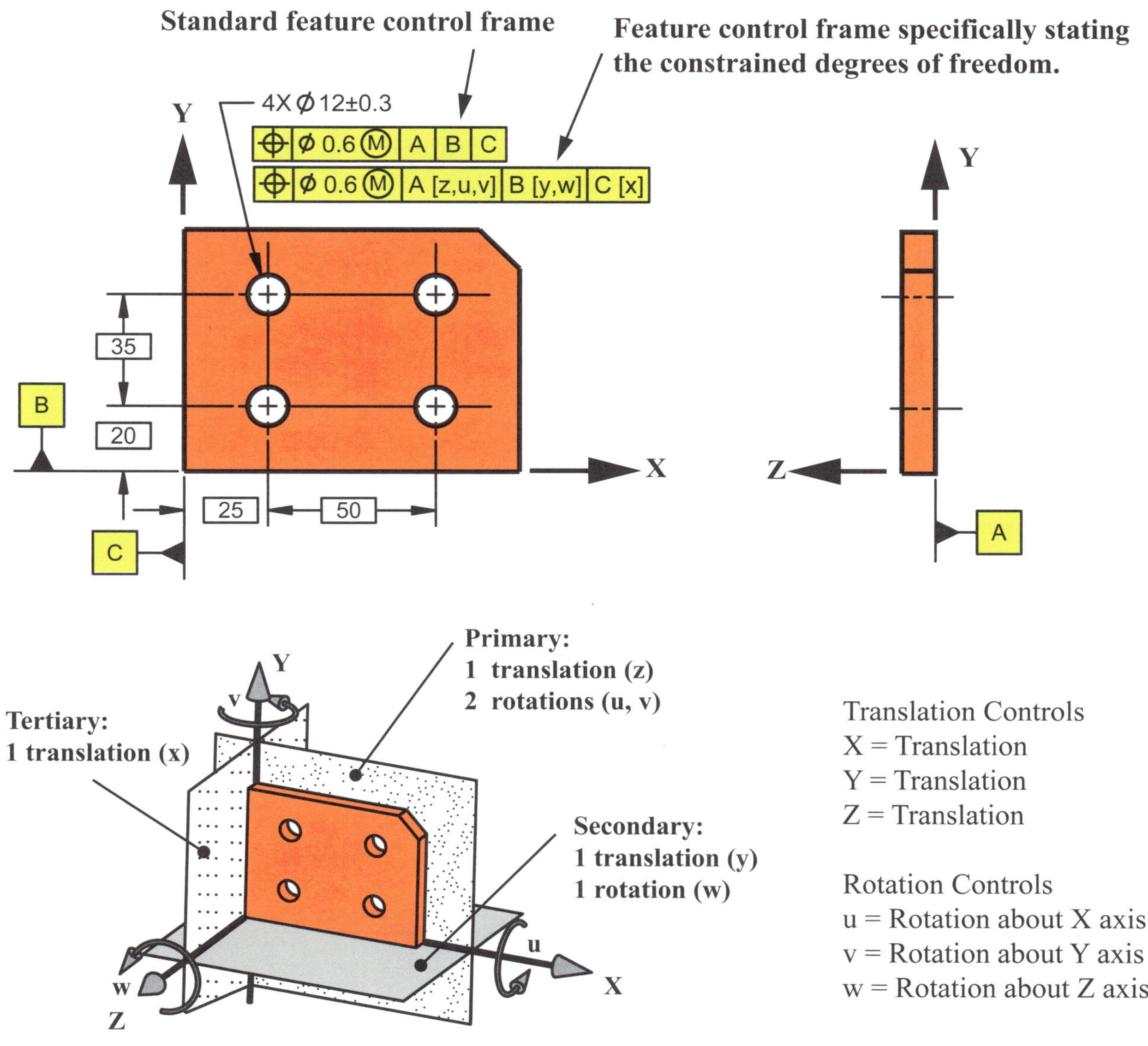

It is not necessary to state the default degrees of freedom constrained in a standard feature control frame. This figure is only used to show the principles of the default condition. Unit 9 will explore options to customize the degrees of freedom in more complicated requirements.

Workshop Exercise 4.4 - Datum Reference Frame Exercise

The table below has a variety of feature control frames that create different datum reference frames. Next to each feature control frame, identify the degrees of freedom (x,y,z,u,v,w) constrained by each referenced datum feature.

Remember, a lower precedence datum feature can not constrain any degrees of freedom that a higher precedence datum feature has already constrained. See the isometric view to the right for the labeled degrees of freedom.

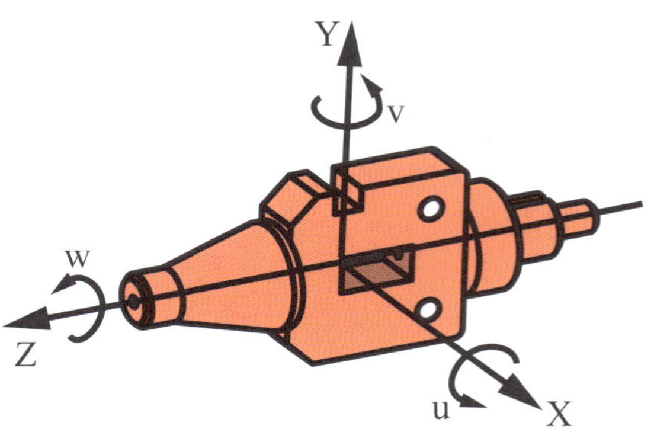

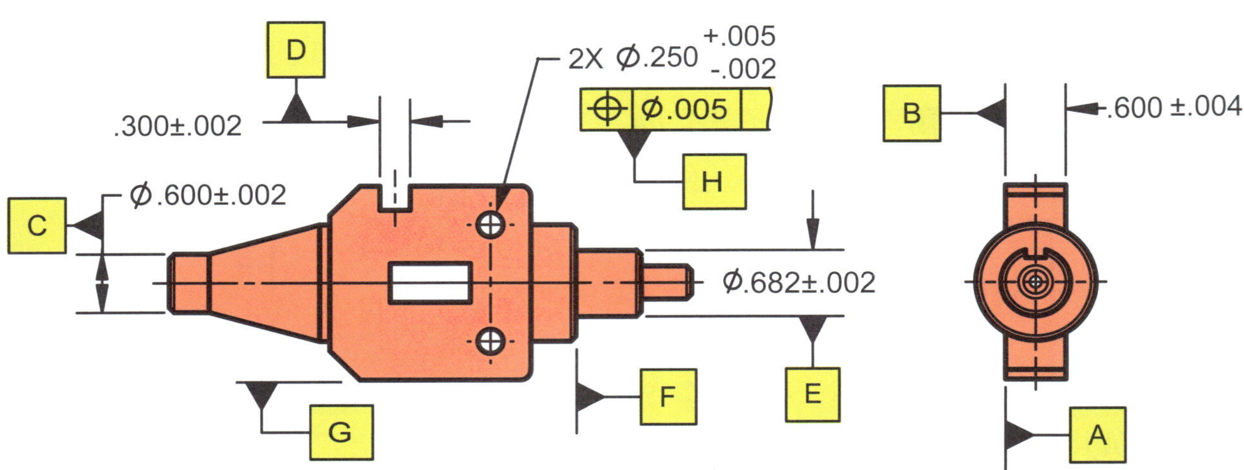

This datum reference frame		Constrained Degrees of Freedom (x,y,z,u,v,w)		
		Primary	Secondary	Tertiary
⌖ Ø.005 A G D	1.			
⌖ Ø.005 E F B	2.			
⌖ Ø.005 F E B	3.			
⌖ Ø.005 C-E D A	4.			
⌖ Ø.005 A H	5.			

Qualifying the Datum Features

Geometric tolerances are related to the perfect DRF. However, the datum features that establish the DRF are not perfect. Datum features shall be qualified by applying size and geometric tolerances as necessary. Relationships between datum features to be considered:

1. The primary datum feature's qualification to itself or the location between features in a pattern.
2. The secondary datum feature(s) orientation and/or location as applicable, to the primary.
3. The tertiary datum feature(s) orientation and/or location as applicable, to the primary and secondary. There are four types of tolerances that may be needed to qualify the datum features:

Size tolerance: controls how large and small a feature may be to itself, also controls form.
Symbol: **plus/minus**

Form: controls shape of an individual feature to itself.
Symbol: **flatness**

Orientation: controls angle of an individual feature to a DRF
Symbol: **perpendicularity, angularity**

Location: controls distance to a DRF, also controls distance between features in a pattern.
Symbol: **position** for features of size, **profile** for surfaces

---

⌖ | ⌀ 0.4 Ⓜ | N | E | H

Datum feature N is flat to itself. Datum feature E is 90 degrees to N, so a perpendicularity relationship is added to N. The origin has been set by NE. With a distance of 11 mm away, H must be located. Since H is a surface, profile tolerance is used.

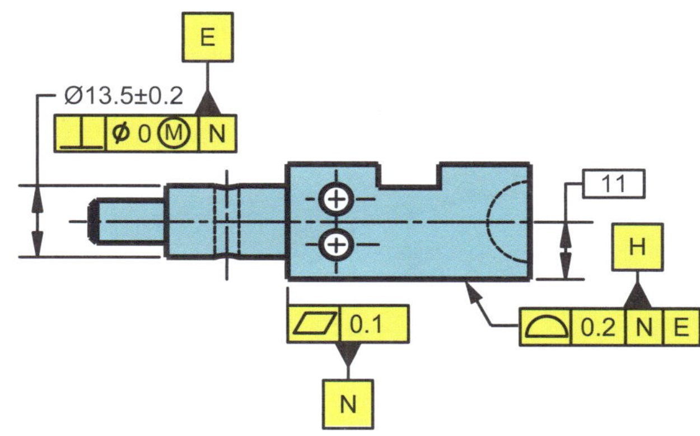

⌖ | ⌀ 0.4 Ⓜ | H | N | E

Datum feature H is flat to itself. Datum feature N is 90 degrees to N, so a perpendicularity relationship is added to N. The origin has been set by HN. With a distance of 11 mm away, E must be located. Since E is a feature of size, position tolerance is used.

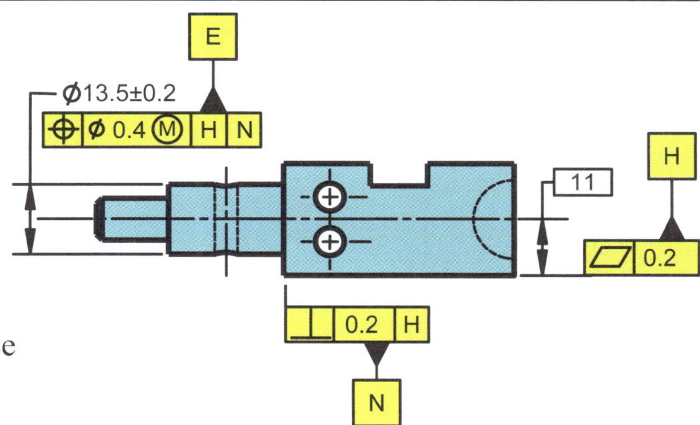

⌖ | ⌀ 0.4 Ⓜ | E | N | R

Datum feature E has a size tolerance to itself. Datum feature N is 90 degrees to E, so a perpendicularity relationship is added to N. The origin has been set by EN. With a distance of 0 mm away, R must be located. Since R is a feature of size, position tolerance is used.

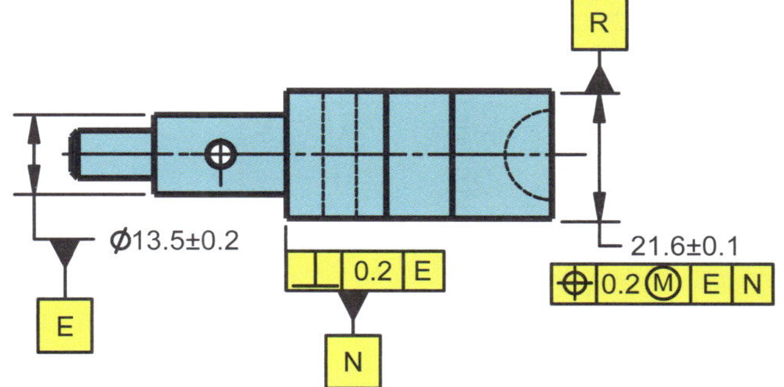

Workshop Exercise 4.5 - Qualify the Datum Features

The datum reference frame established by the datum features is theoretical and perfect. However, the physical datum features are never perfect. In the table below, draw the symbol that would properly qualify the datum feature to itself and the higher precedence datum feature.

- The primary datum feature must be qualified to itself. If there are multiple primary datum features, they must be qualified to each other.
- The secondary datum feature must be qualified relative to the primary. If there are multiple secondary datum features, they must also be qualified to each other.
- The tertiary datum feature must be qualified relative to the primary and secondary. If there are multiple tertiary datum features, they must also be qualified to each other.

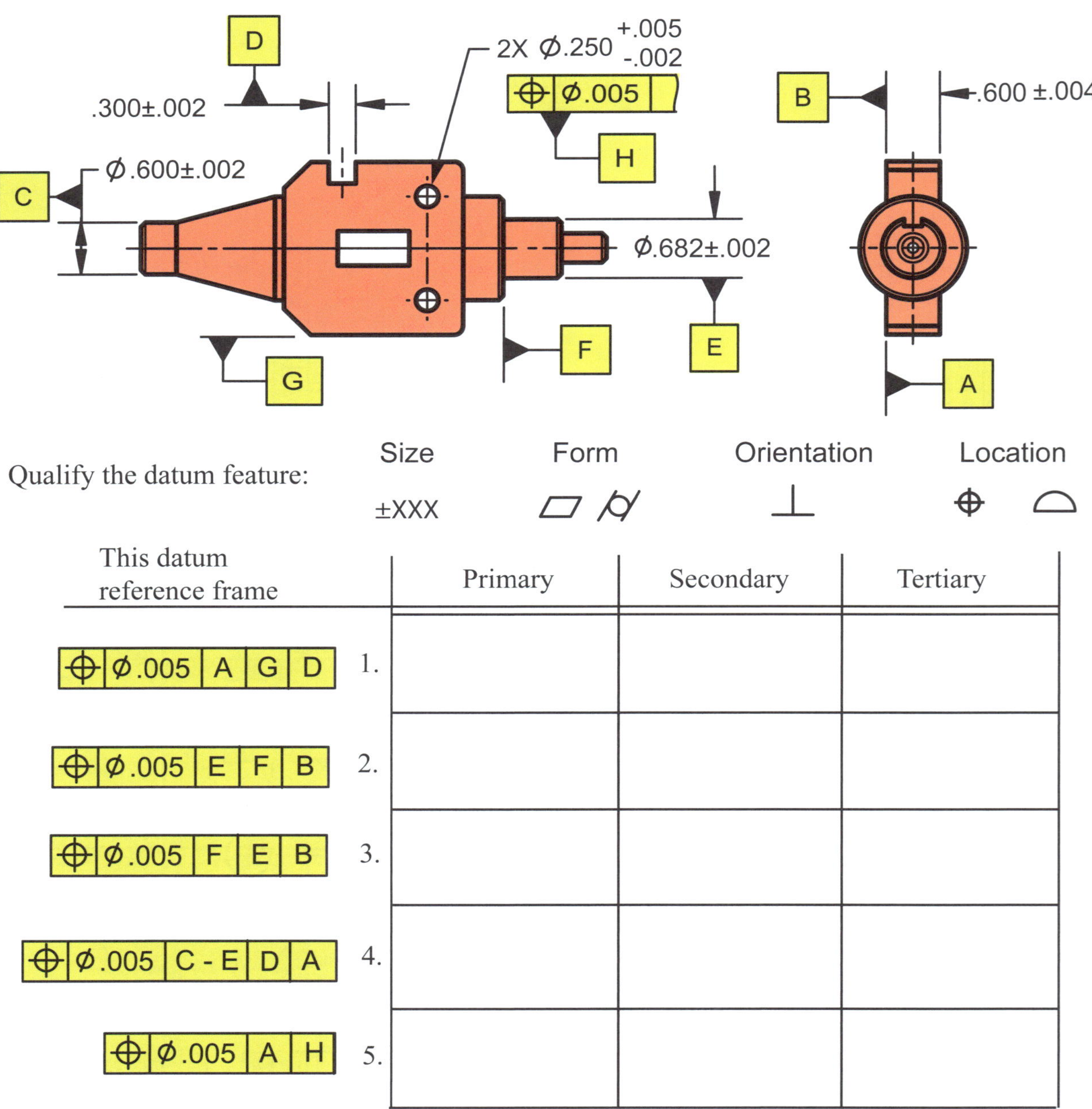

This datum reference frame		Primary	Secondary	Tertiary
⊕ Ø.005 A G D	1.			
⊕ Ø.005 E F B	2.			
⊕ Ø.005 F E B	3.			
⊕ Ø.005 C - E D A	4.			
⊕ Ø.005 A H	5.			

Workshop Exercise 4.6

The drawings to the left show datum feature symbols, dimensions, and tolerances. The sketches to the right represent the imperfect manufactured part. On the next two pages, draw the datum reference frame on the imperfect parts 1-3. Use a straight edge to make sure the DRF is straight and perpendicular.

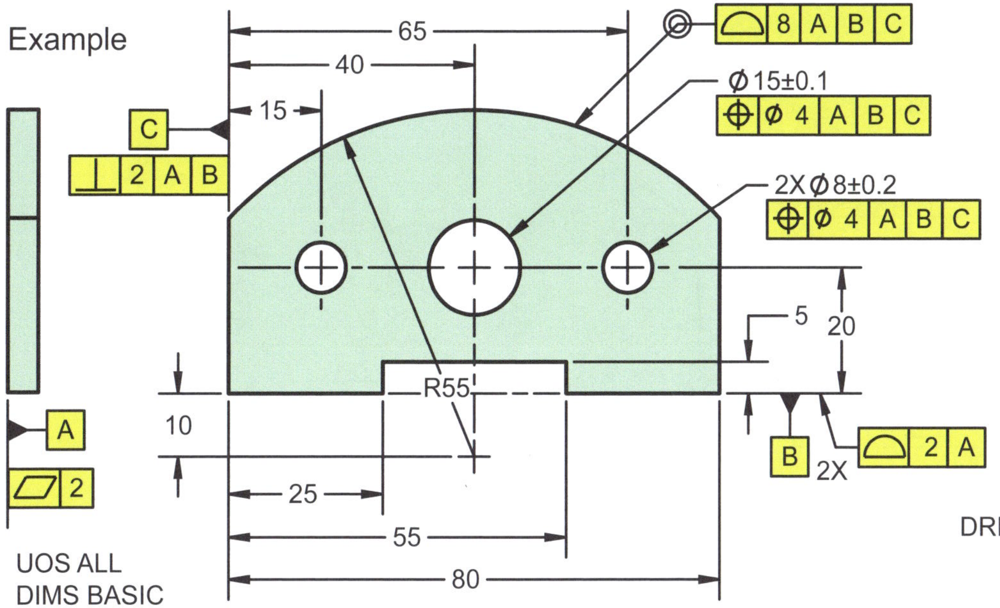

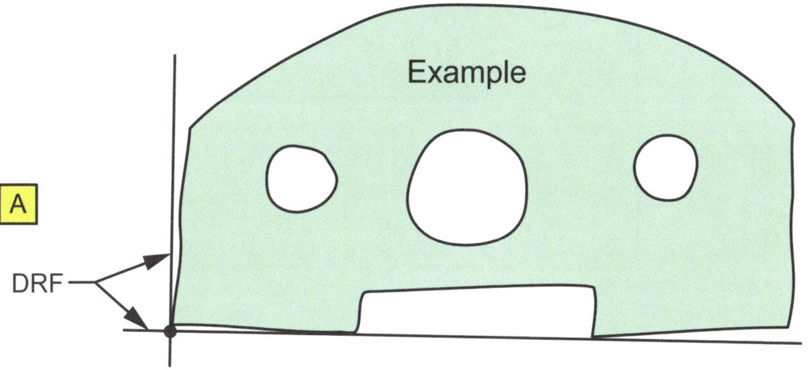

Example

UOS ALL
DIMS BASIC

Example

DRF

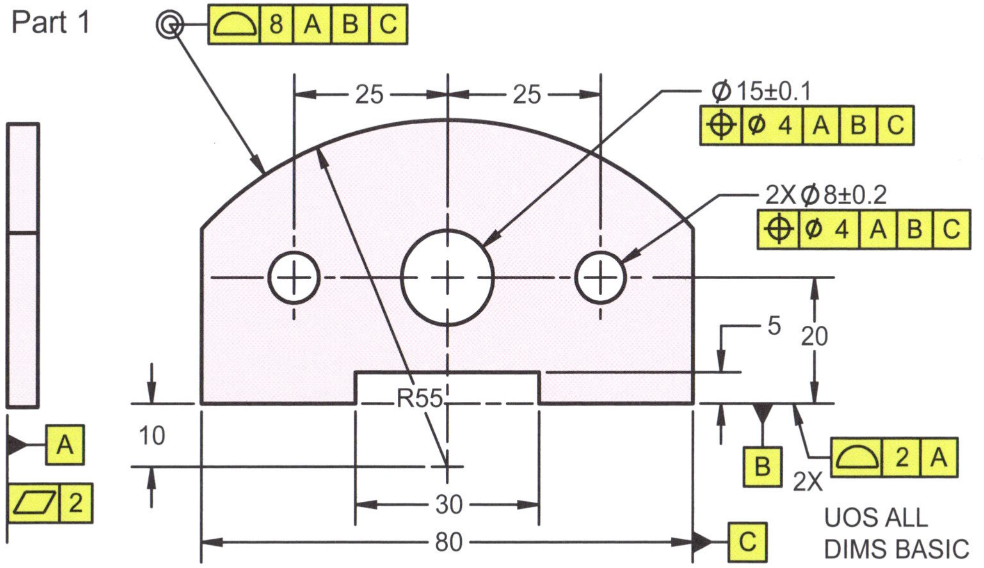

Part 1

UOS ALL
DIMS BASIC

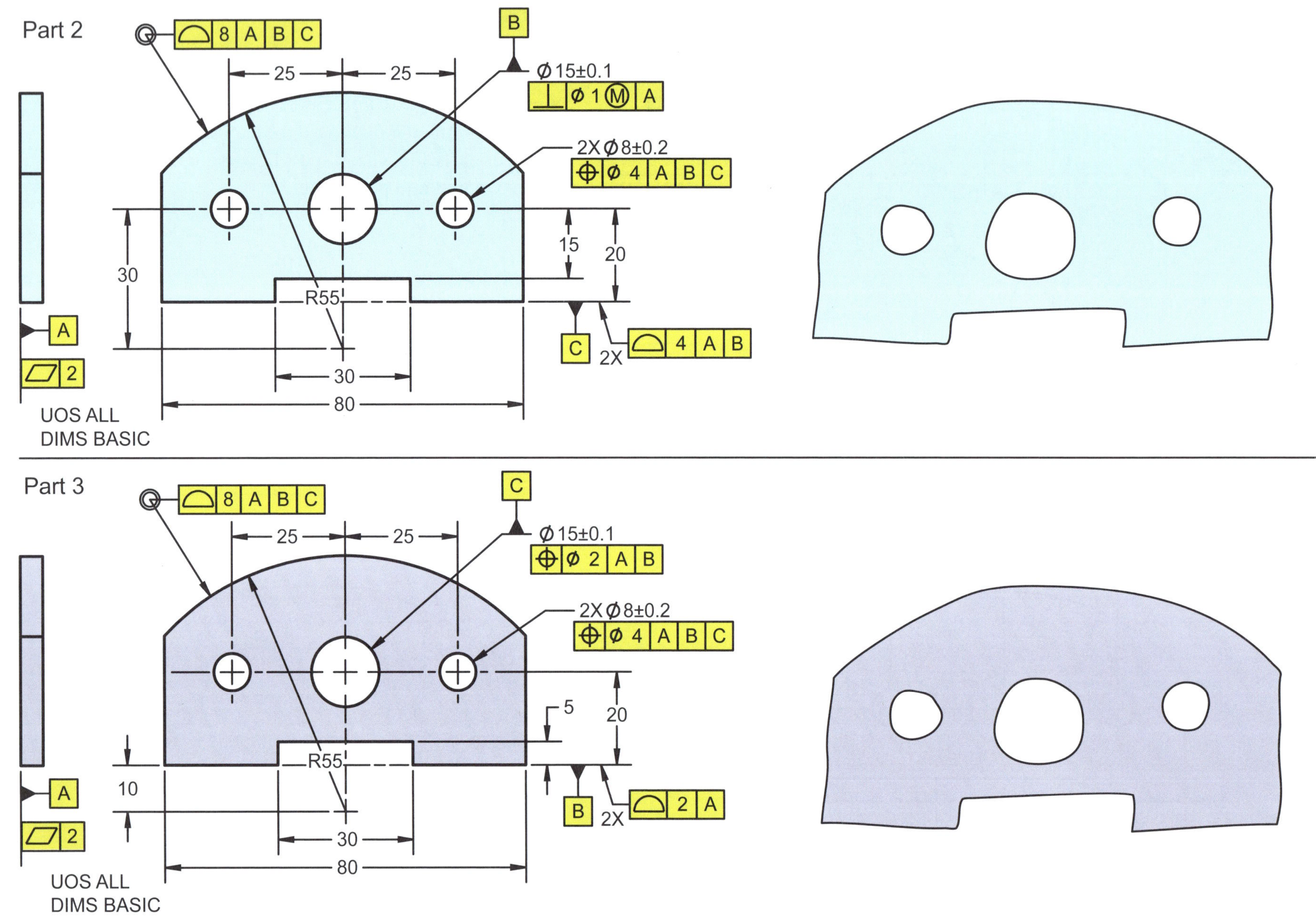

Part 2
8 A B C
25
25
B
Ø15±0.1
Ø 1 Ⓜ A
2X Ø8±0.2
Ø 4 A B C
15
20
30
R55
A
2
C
2X
4 A B
30
80
UOS ALL
DIMS BASIC
Part 3
8 A B C
25
25
C
Ø15±0.1
Ø 2 A B
2X Ø8±0.2
Ø 4 A B C
5
20
R55
A
10
2
B
2X
2 A
30
80
UOS ALL
DIMS BASIC

Unit 5

The Three Product Plans and Position Inspection

The Hub - Design Product Drawing

The design product drawing below has geometric tolerancing applied to document the engineering requirements. The datum features are selected based on functional fit with the mating part. Tight position and profile tolerances are applied to control the important features.

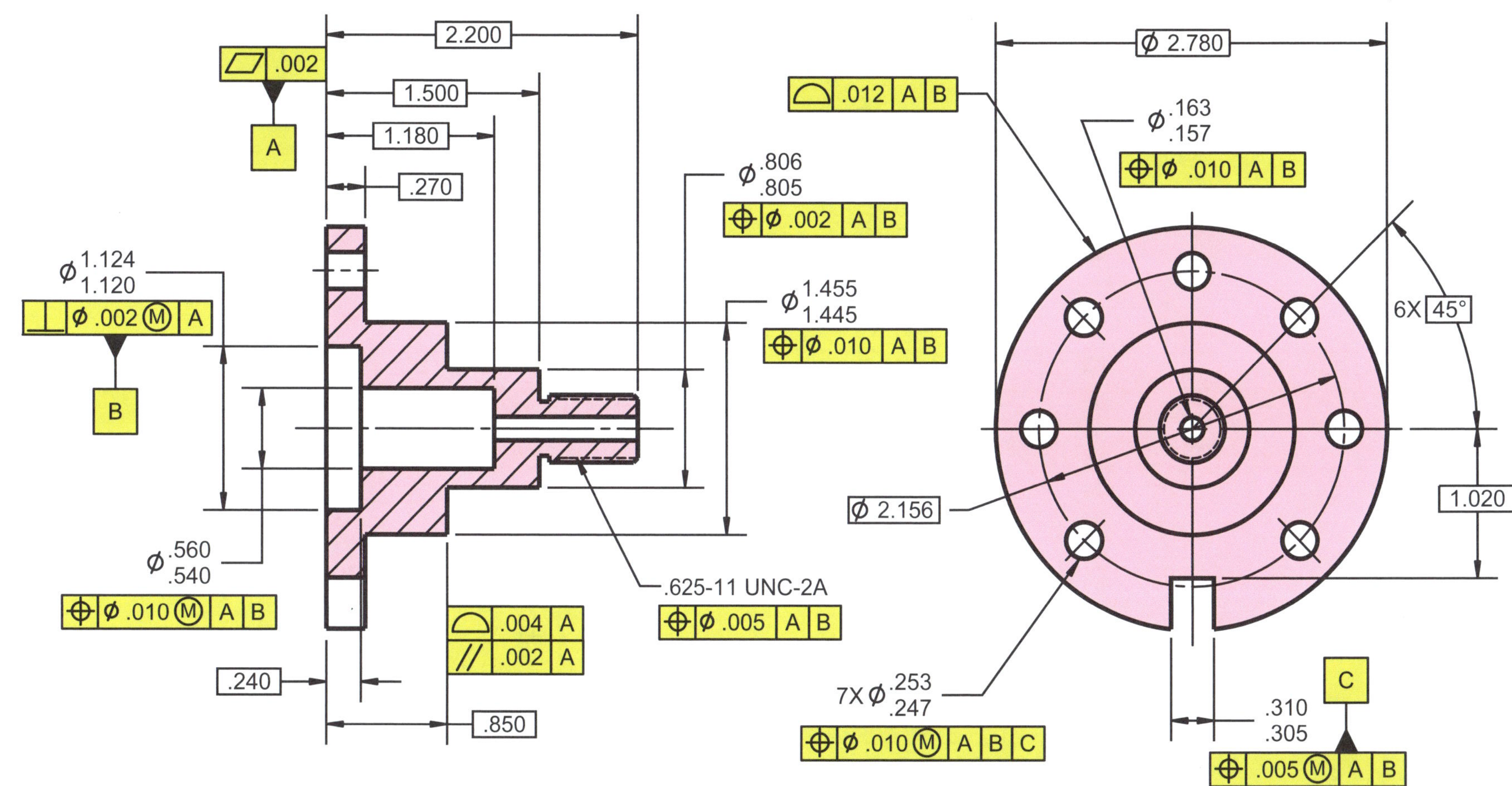

INTERPRET THIS DRAWING PER ASME Y14.5-2018

UOS, ALL DIMENSIONS ARE IN INCHES

UOS, ALL SURFACES: .030 A B C

Geometric tolerancing may be applied to the 3D model per ASME Y14.41-2019 and Y14.47-2019. Notice the associativity when querying the specifications.

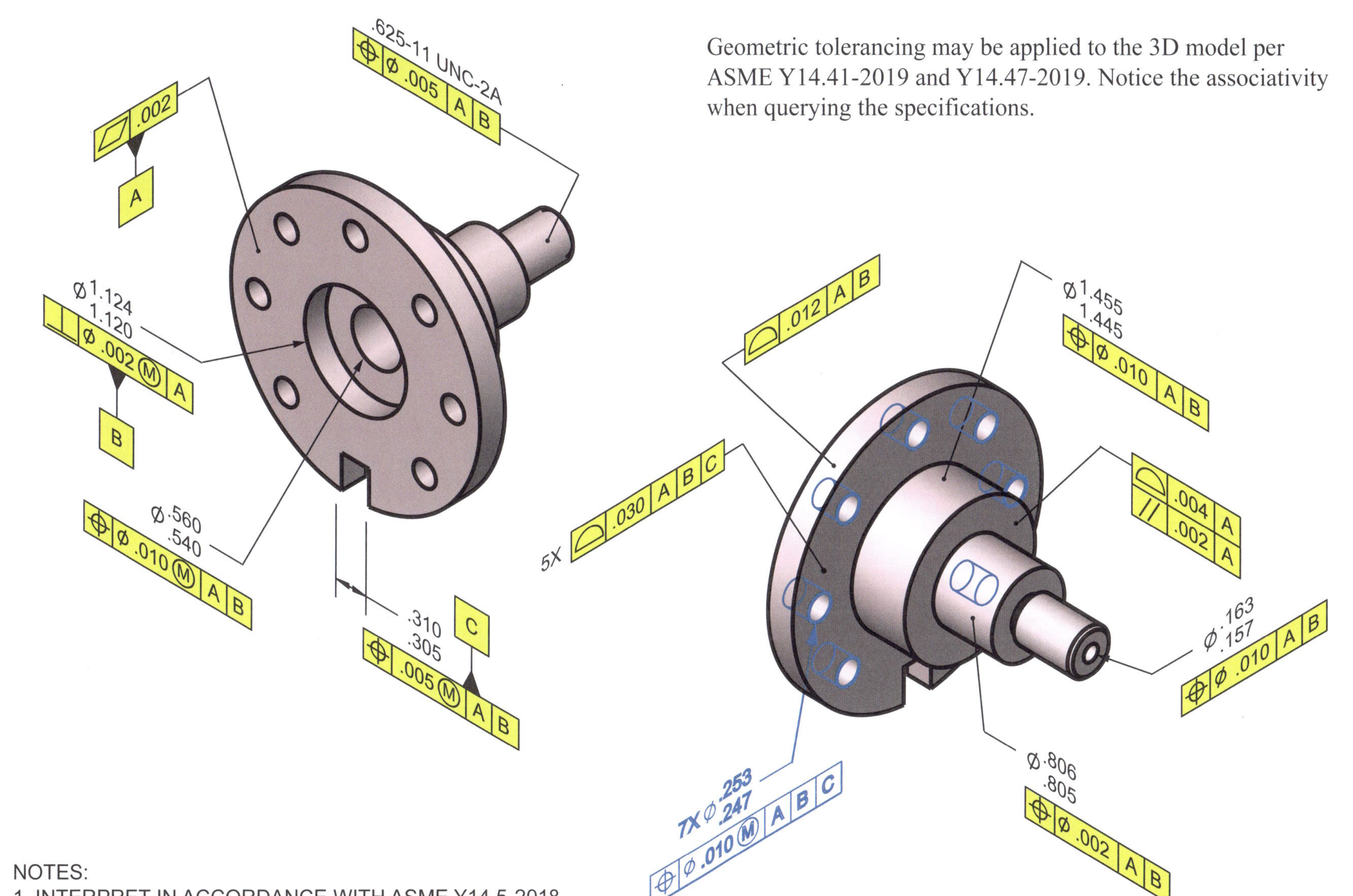

NOTES:
1. INTERPRET IN ACCORDANCE WITH ASME Y14.5-2018, ASME Y14.41-2019 AND ASME Y14.47-2019.
2. UOS, DIMENSIONS ARE IN INCHES.
3. UOS, DIMENSIONS OBTAINED FROM THE MODEL ARE BASIC

Three Plans for Proper Documentation

In the past, the engineering drawing was thought of as the one place to get all design, manufacturing and inspection requirements. However, this can cause conflict because of everyone's own agendas and goals. Design, manufacturing, and inspection may all want to influence how datum features are selected, how much geometric vs. plus/minus tolerancing is used, and how many points should be inspected. For example, manufacturing may prefer the datum feature as an edge because it is easy to manufacture from, but design prefers an alignment hole as a datum feature because it is more functional. As another example, design may identify a profile tolerance on a complicated geometry for function. Inspection may push back because they cannot measure every point due to the limitations in their current inspection equipment. This drawing cannot document everything.

Each area of engineering has their own goals:

Design

- Fit and function of the part
- Define worst case geometry
- Minimize tolerance stacks

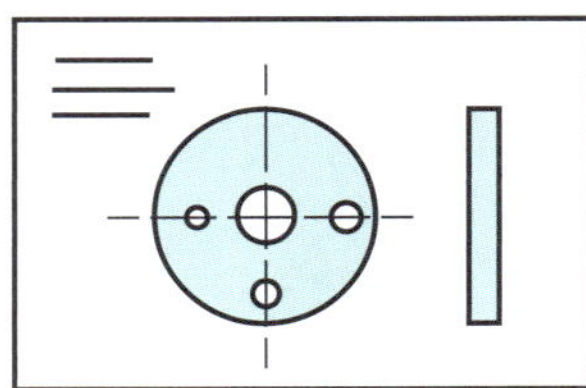

Manufacturing

- Document tooling setups
- In-process checks for process control data
- Minimize time and cost

Quality

- Document inspection equipment and methods
- Number of measurement points and locations
- Minimize time and cost

The engineering drawing will be in conflict if it tries to meet each one of these engineering area's goals.

The solution to this conflict is to separate into 3 different drawings/plans. Design applies the tolerancing scheme as a documentation of functional theoretical requirements only. A separate manufacturing plan may be created to document the manufacturing setups and requirements. A separate quality plan is created to go into details on the inspection methods.

The three documents or plans are:

1. **The Design Product Drawing**
   -Defines the functional requirements of the product.
2. **The Manufacturing Process Plan**
   -Defines how to make the product.
3. **The Quality Dimensional Measurement Plan**
   -Defines how to verify the product.

These other two documents can vary in complexity. In some cases, these steps can be very detailed written documents. In other cases, these steps can be informal verbal instructions. The formality of these documents depends on the complexity of the part, the amount of parts to be produced, and the particular organization.

Three Plans for Proper Documentation

Design Product Drawing: This drawing of a part is created by the design engineer and is considered the most valuable document for the company. This document provides the nominal geometry with a tolerancing scheme that clearly defines the worst-case variations allowed for function. This document is usually kept locked in a vault or master database where no changes can be made without the approval of design engineering.

On this drawing, datum features are selected by how the part mounts or how it is fixtured for function. The tolerances define the functional requirements of the features. It explains what the part is supposed to look like before it is assembled to the next level or delivered to the customer. The datum reference frame established on the product drawing may not reflect the manufacturing setup. Manufacturing information is not to be included on the design drawing. For example, a hole diameter requirement lists the size tolerance of a hole but does not list whether it is drilled, reamed or punched, unless that information is critical to the function. The manufacturing plan will define the details of the manufacturing process. Inspection information is also not on this drawing, the quality plan will define details of the inspection process.

Manufacturing Process Plan: This plan defines how to produce the part and is usually created by a manufacturing engineer or high level machinist. Every manufacturing organization has process plans; they may be formal or informal. For a complicated part such as an engine housing, a series of documents called operation sheets (also called process sheets) define the steps, tools, setups and general workflow for the part to get manufactured from start to finish. This level of documentation is not necessary for a simpler part or an initial prototype. The process plan may be as simple as a CAM program file or a drawing of a fixture that holds the part. In some cases, the manufacturing plan may be in the machinist's head and not even written down.

More detailed manufacturing process plans may also contain manufacturing process drawings. These drawings contain tolerances and requirements critical to manufacturing. In these drawings, datum features are selected based on tooling setups to document the fixturing routines. The datum reference frames created by manufacturing are often different than those for the design drawing. The tolerances on the process drawings are usually tighter to account for subsequent operations. For example, a sheet metal part is built in two operations: a flat pattern created with a CNC laser and a bending process to create the 90 degree flanges. A process drawing could be created for the flat pattern to check the laser cutting process. The datums would be the fixturing locations during the next bending operation. Another example of a process drawing is a casting with datum targets showing the fixturing points for the next level machining operation.

These manufacturing process plans are often flexible and can be tweaked by the manufacturing engineer to achieve a better or cheaper end product. Keeping the manufacturing information on a separate document from the design drawing allows process changes to be made without affecting the end part function. Sometimes, a single part from a design product drawing may be made by different processes in different locations. In this case, the part has multiple process plans to reflect the operations of the different facilities.

Quality Dimensional Measurement Plan: This plan establishes the details of the inspection process and represents the strategy for catching non-conforming parts before assembly or delivery. It is created by a quality engineer or high level inspector sometimes with the influence from a design engineer. As with the manufacturing process plan, this dimensional measurement plan can be a formal written document or it can be informal, and left up to the individual inspectors discretion. If the part is produced by an outside supplier, either the supplier or design company may create the quality plan.

The engineering requirements outlined in the design drawing define the functional limits for the features with theoretical boundaries. These limits also assume all points on the features are gathered. Since gathering "all the points" is impossible, this inspection plan must balance the allowable risk of passing a non-conforming part with the time/money spent on the inspection. The plan is sometimes developed after an evaluation of the manufacturing process. Usually the plan focuses on tighter tolerances and difficult manufacturing areas to catch the most problems with minimal time and cost. For example, a sheet metal part is produced in two steps, cutting a flat pattern and a bending process. The CNC laser cutting the flat pattern is a well controlled process and we expect minimal variations. However, the bending process is subject to more variation so the quality plan focuses on tolerances affected by the looser bending process and minimal inspections are done on the laser cut holes.

Different inspection methods or devices yield different results during the verification of the products. This is evident by the different results obtained from a CMM vs. open setup surface plate techniques. This is often referred to as "methods divergence". The dimensional measurement plan should define the acceptable measurement method and the associated uncertainty of results. More detailed plans define the quantity and location of measurement points or number of cross sections to be measured. In a large quantity production run, measuring 100% of the parts is not necessary and the number of parts to be inspected is also defined.

The new ASME standard: Y14.45 Measurement Data Reporting, also recommends the quality plan to document the reporting method required to help shape the inspection report. These reporting methods are called A, B, and C in the standard:

Method A: Attribute data (pass/fail)

Method B: A single reported value for the tolerance representing the zone (measured flatness zone, measured profile zone, measured position zone)

Method C: Variable data for each sampled location or measured feature (plus/minus material values for profile or x,y location values for position)

These quality plans are often flexible and can be tweaked by the quality engineer for less risk or a more economical product. Keeping the inspection methods on a separate document from the design drawing allows inspection changes to be made without affecting the end part function. Sometimes, a single part may be measured by different methods in different locations. In this case, the part has multiple quality plans to reflect the operations of the different facilities. This quality plan could also contain different inspections for first article versus a well-controlled production run.

As you can see, it is important to separate the design requirements from the manufacturing and inspection methods. Throughout a product life cycle, manufacturing and inspection methods improve, and new equipment may be purchased, but this should not affect the definition of the original design. We need to be confident that new measurement or manufacturing techniques are still providing a quality product. The geometric tolerancing on the engineering drawing clearly documents the boundaries of variation. This is especially important as our supplier base expands for cheaper parts while maintaining the same level of quality. The expansion of the engineering drawing to the three plan system allows us to identify and solve any problems or differences we may have along the way. In order to have quality parts, you must have communication and documentation throughout the design, manufacturing and verification process.

Separating the functional tolerancing requirements in the design drawing from the manufactuing and inspection methods allows better documentation and communication between the areas of engineering. Each area has their own document to record their strategy. Below is a diagram for documentation and communication between the three areas. The bigger arrows represent a direct responsibility while the smaller arrows represent avenues of influence.

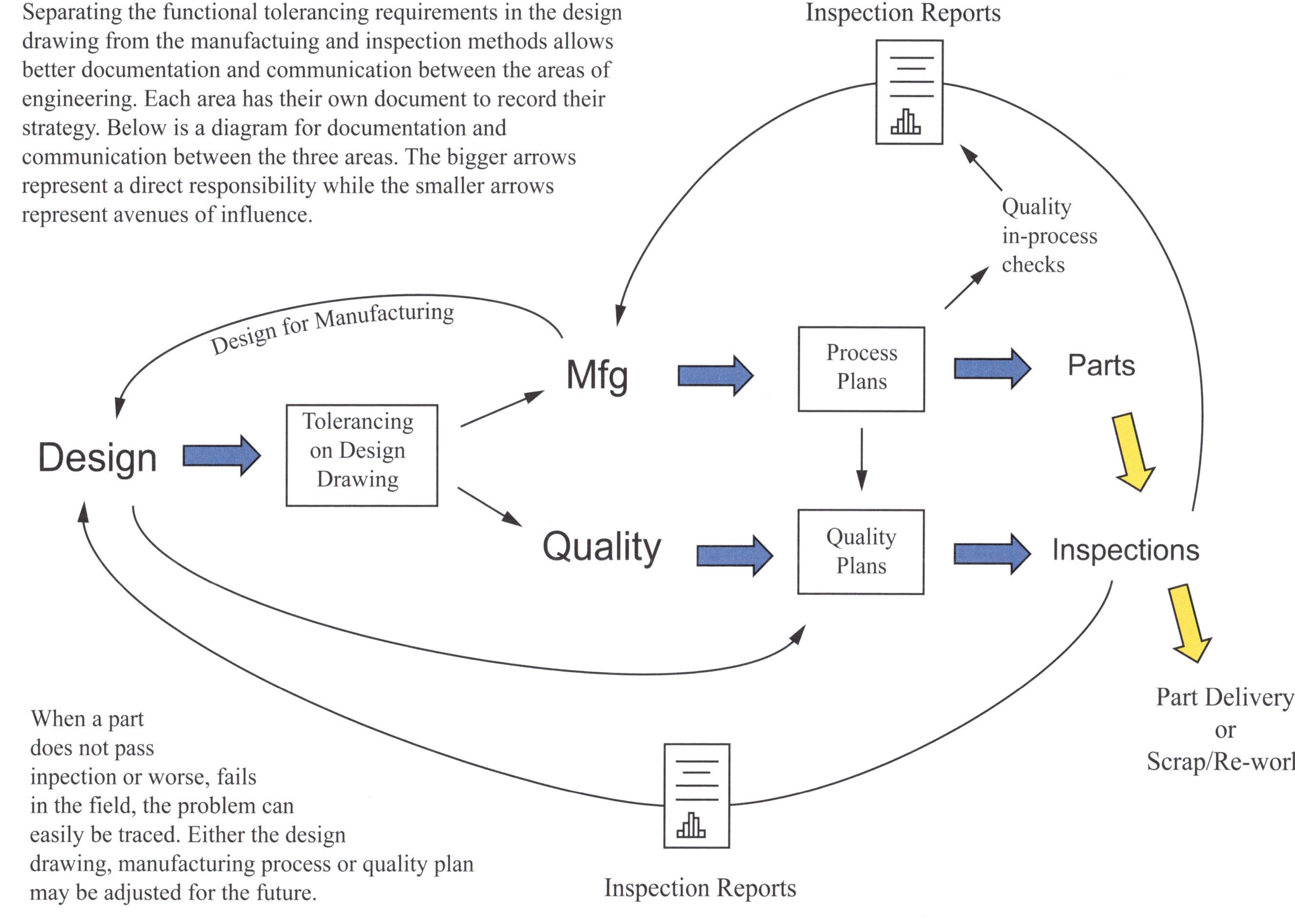

When a part
does not pass
inpection or worse, fails
in the field, the problem can
easily be traced. Either the design
drawing, manufacturing process or quality plan
may be adjusted for the future.

Sample Portion of Manufacturing Process Plan

Operation Sheet
Sequences 1,2 of 4

Part Name : Hub	**Machine Type** : CNC Lathe
Part Number: 0034228	**Machine Number**: 28L

Seq 1 Instructions:
Load blank to turn down datum feature A and B also cut 2.780 OD and internal diameters.

Seq 2 Instructions:
Clamp datum feature X surface as primary and datum feature Y diameter 2.780 shown. Watch for chips in the jaws, they must be spotless. Turn .805 and 1.455 diameters. Verification chart required.

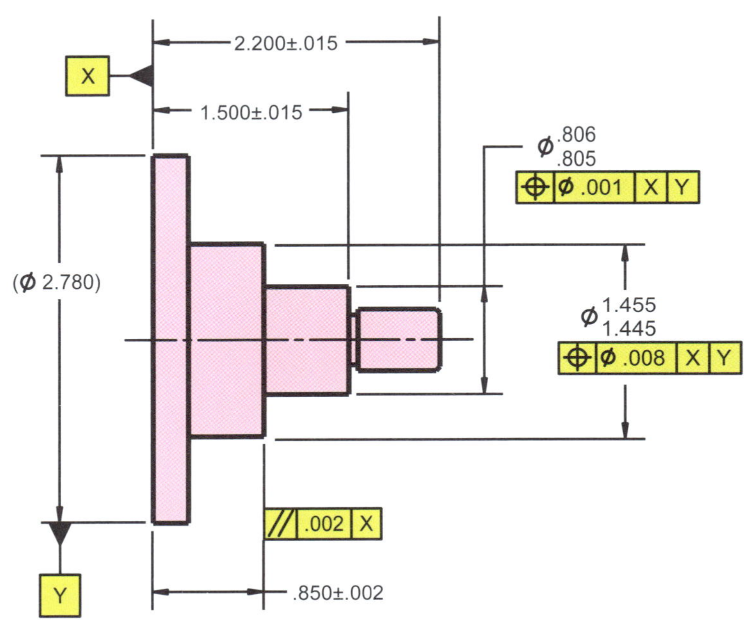

Tools Required	Tool Number
Gage ring .806	GL806
Gage ring .805	GL805
Height gage w/ .0001 indicator	6987
Calipers	---
CNC Program	34228.2A
Turn Tool	TL1532
Roughing Tool	TL 1280

Sample Quality Dimensional Measurement Plan

Dimensional Measurement Plan for Open Set-up

Part Name : Hub

Part Number: 0034228

Special Instructions:
Watch for Burrs
3 parts per shift

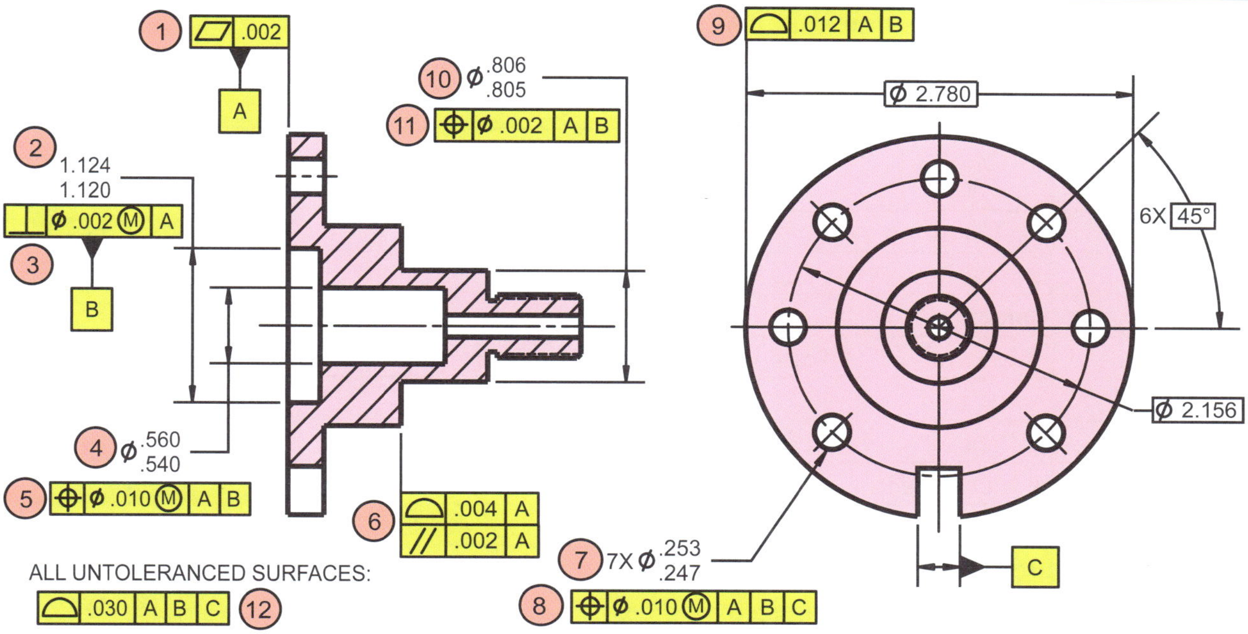

Item Number	Inspection Requirement	Reporting Method	Equipment or gage
1	Check with indicator min 6 locations	B	height gage
2	go/ no-go	A	gage pin
3	not measured, process well controlled	-	-
4	two point check, min 2 locations	A	calipers
5	not measured, process well controlled	-	-
6	Check with height gage min 10 locations	B	height gage
7	gage pins	B	.250 gage pin set
8	Height gage to find X, Y locations	C	height gage
9	Set up in vee block. Check with height gage, measure 7 locations above holes	C	height gage, gage pin, 90° vee block
10	two point check, min 4 locations	B	calipers
11	Check with indicator, set up in vee block using gage pin, rotate 360 degrees	B	height gage, gage pin, 90° vee block
12	Check min 5 locations, must be within total 60% of tolerance range. If any outside 60%, check additional 10 locations.	A	height gage

Reporting Methods from ASME Y14.45:
A: Attribute data (pass/fail)
B: A single reported value or zone (actual profile zone, actual position zone)
C: Variable data for each sampled location or measured feature (plus/minus material values for profile or x,y location values for position)

Sample Quality Dimensional Measurement Plan

Dimensional Measurement Plan for CMM

Part Name: Hub	Part Number: 0034228
Machine: CMM trigger probe	Machine number: 04 C
Stylus: 2mm ruby, 265-2R	Program: Hub34228.2

Datum Establishment: Datum feature A, 16 locations randomized, use L2 constrained algorithm for datum A. Datum feature B, 8 locations top and bottom, use least squares algorithm for datum axis B. Datum feature C, two opposing points at mid length of slot to constrain rotation.

Item Number	Inspection Requirement	Reporting Method
1	16 locations, randomized sample	B
2	8 locations at top and bottom, MIC	B
3	same as 2	B
4	4 locations at top and bottom, least squares circle	B
5	same as 4	B
6	8 locations, see table for specified points 6.1-6.8	C
7	6 locations min, randomized cylinder, MIC	B
8	5 locations, top and bottom, record X and Y deviations	C
9	15 locations equally spaced, 9.1-9.15 shown	C
10	12 locations randomized cylinder, MCC	B
11	same as 10	B
12	20 locations minimum total, must touch each feature	B

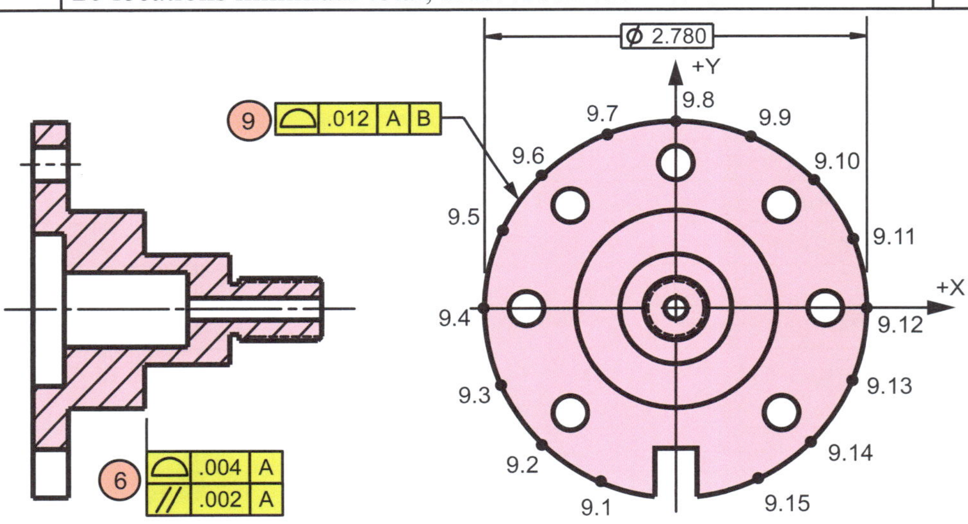

Point #	X	Y
6.1	-.700	0
6.2	-.470	0
6.3	+.700	0
6.4	+.470	0
6.5	0	-.700
6.6	0	-.470
6.7	0	+.700
6.8	0	+.470

The quality dimensional measurement plan documents the inspection methods for the part. Characteristic IDs (numbered circles) are placed next to the requirements that correlate with the methods in the plan. When the deviation of specific points is to be recorded, they may be shown on a drawing view or included in an X,Y chart on the inspection plan.

Introduction to Position Verification

This section covers the verification of position tolerances and the reporting of the variations. These exercises ensure understanding of the position concepts covered in unit 3 including the effect of the MMC, LMC, and RFS modifiers. The exercises contain both metric and inch values and allow the reader to choose example problems in their native units.

There are many ways to record position data in an inspection report. The ASME Y14.45, Measurement Data Reporting standard, gives some guidelines but still allows many options. The following pages show our preferred method for inspection reporting.

If you have been working with plus/minus tolerances in the past, there are some significant changes in verifying position tolerances. In plus/minus tolerancing, the dimension has a nominal with tolerance, and the actual measured dimension is recorded on the inspection sheet. However, this recording of data is too simplistic to accurately represent the location of a feature, the capability of a machine, or to find solutions for the repair of a part. It is unclear the origin of the measurement, how the part is indexed, whether the measurement includes orientation effects, etc.

In position tolerancing, a datum reference frame is established with basic dimensions locating the true position of a theoretical tolerance zone. The size of the zone is defined by the value in the feature control frame and the applicable material condition modifier, MMC, LMC, RFS. This position tolerance zone determines the feature's allowed locational variation from true position. It is important to note, the basic dimensions have no tolerance and may be chained without causing accumulations. The basic dimensions could also be defined in a CAD model data set.

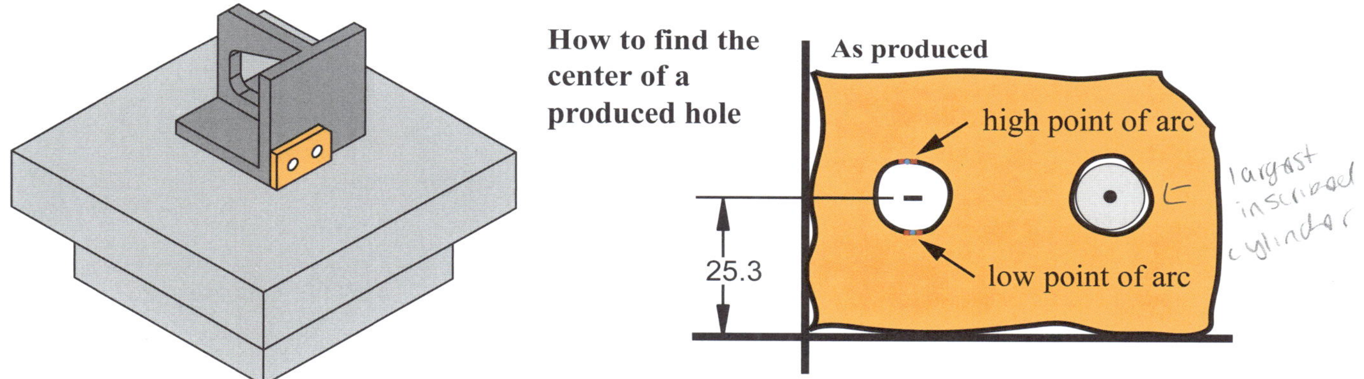

A coordinate measuring machine (CMM) may be used to digitally align to the datum features and probe the holes to report size as well as X and Y locations for the axis.

The location measurements may also be made with an angle plate setup and height gage with a spherical tip. First the datum features ABC are aligned in order to the surface plate and angle plate. The inspector uses the height gage to find the highest and lowest points on the arc. Halfway between these is the hole center in the Y direction. A digital height gage with a live tip makes this easy. Rotate angle plate 90° with part clamped for the X direction and repeat.

Note: The axis should be established using the unrelated actual mating envelope. Unsymmetrical form variation on the hole may throw off the measured center. Probing the the best fit gage pin with the height gage could be a more precise but time intensive method. Similarly, a CMM should be using a largest inscribed cylinder algorithm with an adequate number of probe points to find the axis, but a least squares algorithm is often used to save time.

Note: the following examples are simplifiying the 3D cylindrical holes to 2D circles in the first exercises. Later we will talk about evaluating and reporting both ends of the hole axis.

Position - Hole Verification at MMC

The example below illustrates the reporting procedure for a hole position tolerance at MMC.

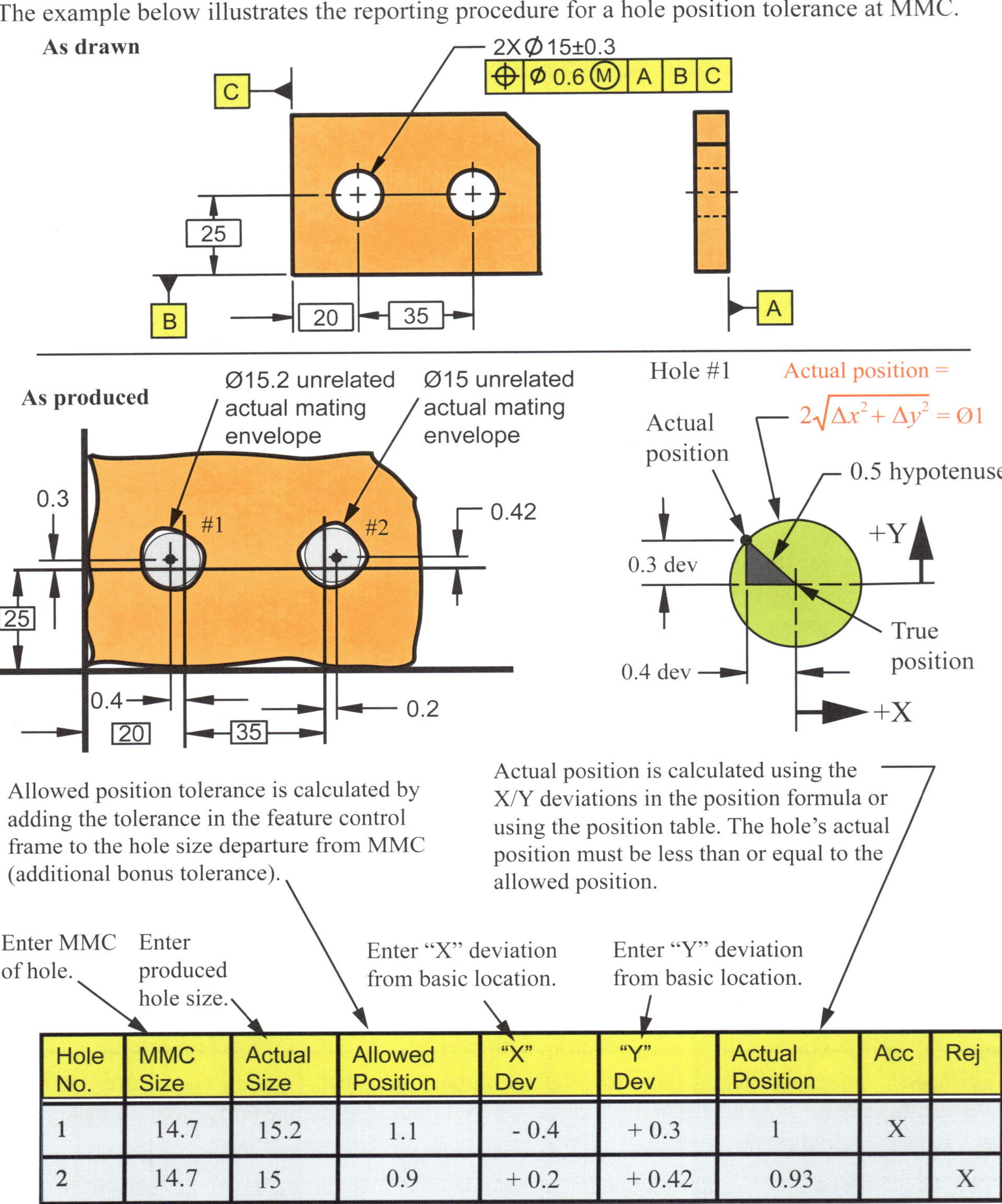

Hole No.	MMC Size	Actual Size	Allowed Position	"X" Dev	"Y" Dev	Actual Position	Acc	Rej
1	14.7	15.2	1.1	- 0.4	+ 0.3	1	X	
2	14.7	15	0.9	+ 0.2	+ 0.42	0.93		X

The actual locations are reported as deviations relative to true position in the view in which the holes are specified on the drawing. This also must be stated on the inspection report. If a feature falls to the right of true position, it will have a plus X value, and if it falls to the left, a minus X value. The feature above its basic address is a plus Y value, below is a minus Y value. There is also a section at the end of this unit on the paper gage concept. This graphing procedure allows a visual picture of multiple hole deviations.

Class Exercise - Position Verification at MMC, Metric

The top drawing has a position tolerance applied. The lower illustration is the imperfect produced part indexed to the datum reference frame (DRF). Evaluate the measured distances on the produced part to verify conformance to the specification. Use the table below to record your calculations.

As drawn

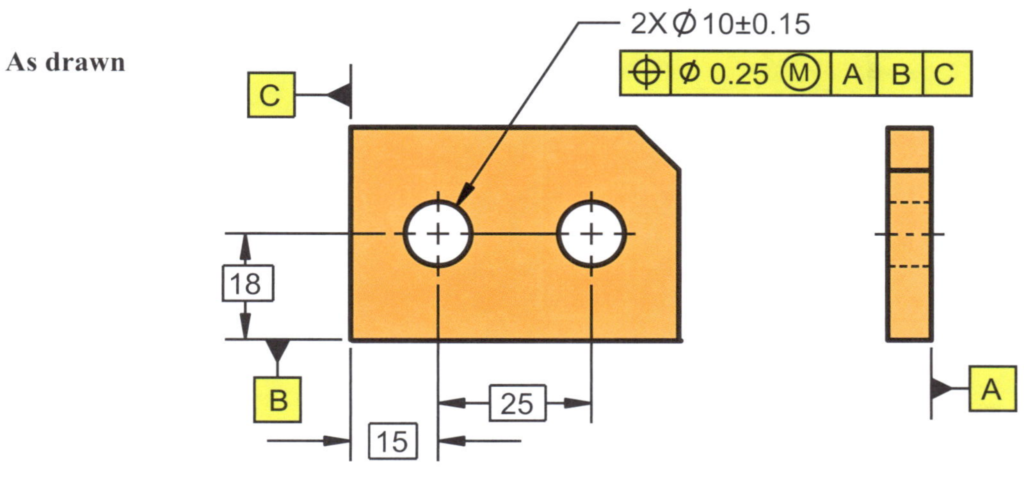

As produced

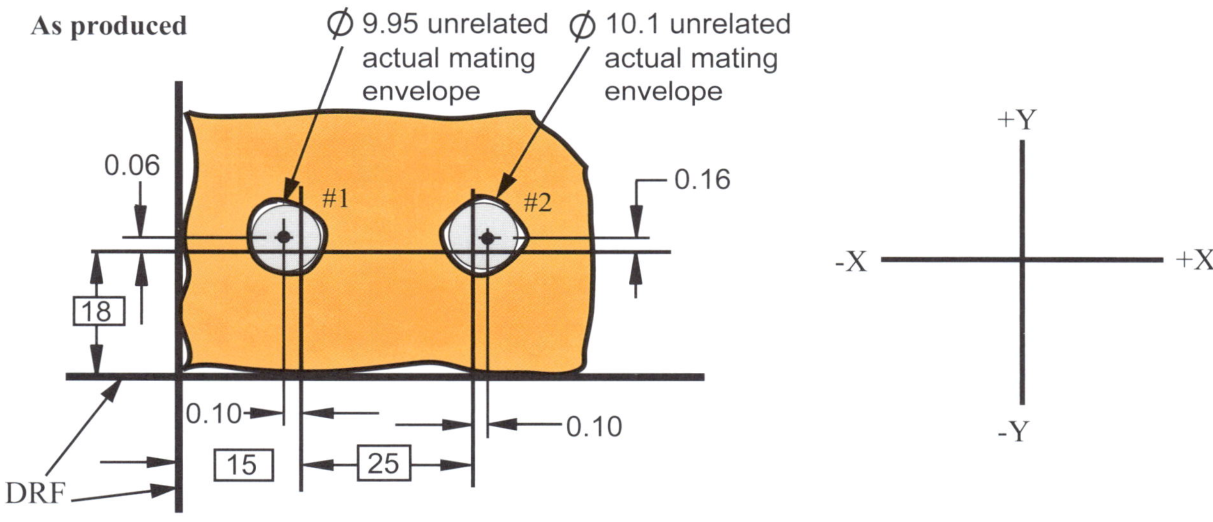

Hole No.	MMC Size	Actual Size	Allowed Position	"X" Dev	"Y" Dev	Actual Position	Acc	Rej
1								
2								

Class Exercise - Position Verification at MMC, Inch

The top drawing has a position tolerance applied. The lower illustration is the imperfect produced part indexed to the datum reference frame (DRF). Evaluate the measured distances on the produced part to verify conformance to the specification. Use the table below to record your calculations.

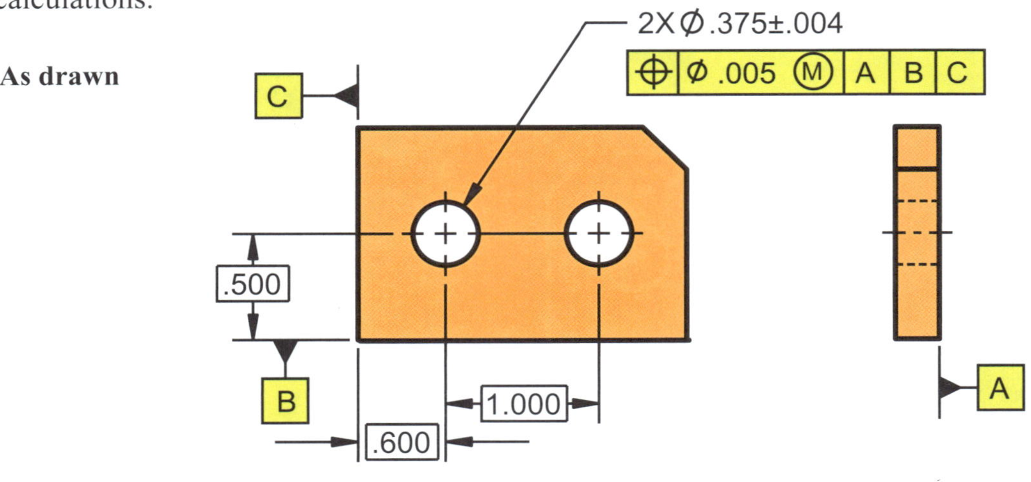

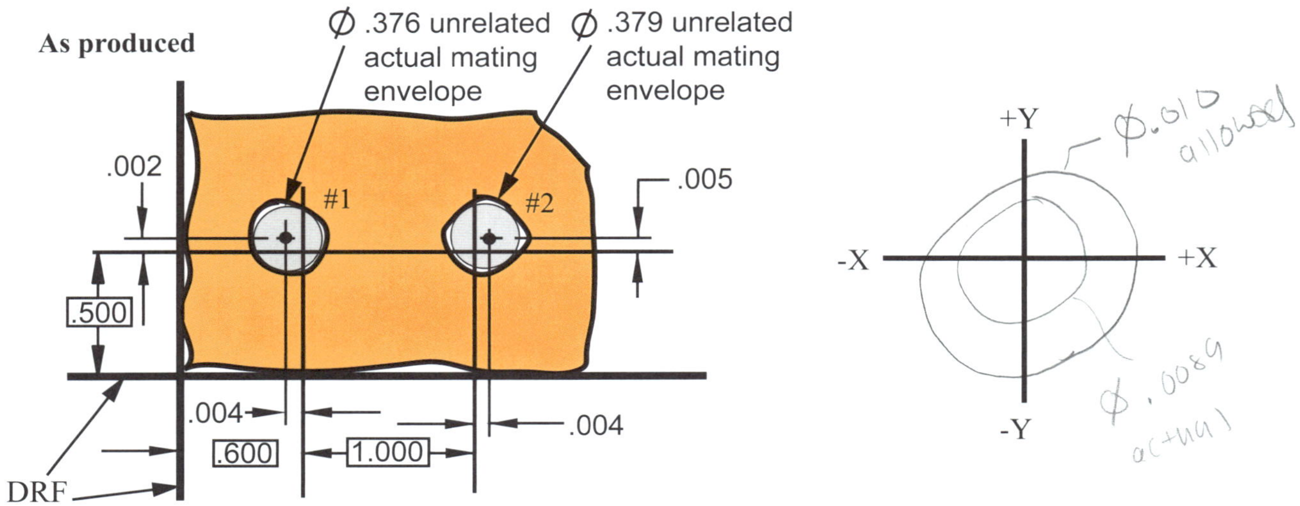

Hole No.	MMC Size	Actual Size	Allowed Position	"X" Dev	"Y" Dev	Actual Position	Acc	Rej
1	.371	.376	.010	-.004	+.002	.0089	X	
2	.371	.379	.013	+.004	+.005	.0128	X	

Conversion of Coordinate Measurement to Position Tolerance Zones - Inch

The chart below will convert coordinate (x and y) inch measurements to position diameter tolerance zones. It is simply, double the Pythagorean Theorem. The formula is shown below.

Y (DEV)	Position Zone (Diameter)																			
.025	.0500	.0502	.0504	.0506	.0510	.0514	.0519	.0525	.0531	.0539	.0546	.0555	.0564	.0573	.0583	.0594	.0605	.0616	.0628	.0640
.024	.0480	.0482	.0484	.0487	.0490	.0495	.0500	.0506	.0513	.0520	.0528	.0537	.0546	.0556	.0566	.0577	.0588	.0600	.0612	.0625
.023	.0460	.0462	.0464	.0467	.0471	.0475	.0481	.0487	.0494	.0502	.0510	.0519	.0528	.0539	.0549	.0560	.0572	.0584	.0597	.0610
.022	.0440	.0442	.0444	.0447	.0451	.0456	.0462	.0468	.0475	.0483	.0492	.0501	.0511	.0522	.0533	.0544	.0556	.0569	.0581	.0595
.021	.0420	.0422	.0424	.0428	.0432	.0437	.0443	.0449	.0457	.0465	.0474	.0484	.0494	.0505	.0516	.0528	.0540	.0553	.0566	.0580
.020	.0400	.0402	.0404	.0408	.0412	.0418	.0424	.0431	.0439	.0447	.0457	.0466	.0477	.0488	.0500	.0512	.0525	.0538	.0552	.0566
.019	.0381	.0382	.0385	.0388	.0393	.0398	.0405	.0412	.0420	.0429	.0439	.0449	.0460	.0472	.0484	.0497	.0510	.0523	.0537	.0552
.018	.0361	.0362	.0365	.0369	.0374	.0379	.0386	.0394	.0402	.0412	.0422	.0433	.0444	.0456	.0469	.0482	.0495	.0509	.0523	.0538
.017	.0341	.0342	.0345	.0349	.0354	.0361	.0368	.0376	.0385	.0394	.0405	.0416	.0428	.0440	.0453	.0467	.0481	.0495	.0510	.0525
.016	.0321	.0322	.0326	.0330	.0335	.0342	.0349	.0358	.0367	.0377	.0388	.0400	.0412	.0425	.0439	.0453	.0467	.0482	.0497	.0512
.015	.0301	.0303	.0306	.0310	.0316	.0323	.0331	.0340	.0350	.0361	.0372	.0384	.0397	.0410	.0424	.0439	.0453	.0469	.0484	.0500
.014	.0281	.0283	.0286	.0291	.0297	.0305	.0313	.0322	.0333	.0344	.0356	.0369	.0382	.0396	.0410	.0425	.0440	.0456	.0472	.0488
.013	.0261	.0263	.0267	.0272	.0279	.0286	.0295	.0305	.0316	.0328	.0341	.0354	.0368	.0382	.0397	.0412	.0428	.0444	.0460	.0477
.012	.0241	.0243	.0247	.0253	.0260	.0268	.0278	.0288	.0300	.0312	.0326	.0339	.0354	.0369	.0384	.0400	.0416	.0433	.0449	.0466
.011	.0221	.0224	.0228	.0234	.0242	.0251	.0261	.0272	.0284	.0297	.0311	.0326	.0341	.0356	.0372	.0388	.0405	.0422	.0439	.0457
.010	.0201	.0204	.0209	.0215	.0224	.0233	.0244	.0256	.0269	.0283	.0297	.0312	.0328	.0344	.0361	.0377	.0394	.0412	.0429	.0447
.009	.0181	.0184	.0190	.0197	.0206	.0216	.0228	.0241	.0255	.0269	.0284	.0300	.0316	.0333	.0350	.0367	.0385	.0402	.0420	.0439
.008	.0161	.0165	.0171	.0179	.0189	.0200	.0213	.0226	.0241	.0256	.0272	.0288	.0305	.0322	.0340	.0358	.0376	.0394	.0412	.0431
.007	.0141	.0146	.0152	.0161	.0172	.0184	.0198	.0213	.0228	.0244	.0261	.0278	.0295	.0313	.0331	.0349	.0368	.0386	.0405	.0424
.006	.0122	.0126	.0134	.0144	.0156	.0170	.0184	.0200	.0216	.0233	.0251	.0268	.0286	.0305	.0323	.0342	.0361	.0379	.0398	.0418
.005	.0102	.0108	.0117	.0128	.0141	.0156	.0172	.0189	.0206	.0224	.0242	.0260	.0279	.0297	.0316	.0335	.0354	.0374	.0393	.0412
.004	.0082	.0089	.0100	.0113	.0128	.0144	.0161	.0179	.0197	.0215	.0234	.0253	.0272	.0291	.0310	.0330	.0349	.0369	.0388	.0408
.003	.0063	.0072	.0085	.0100	.0117	.0134	.0152	.0171	.0190	.0209	.0228	.0247	.0267	.0286	.0306	.0326	.0345	.0365	.0385	.0404
.002	.0045	.0057	.0072	.0089	.0108	.0126	.0146	.0165	.0184	.0204	.0224	.0243	.0263	.0283	.0303	.0322	.0342	.0362	.0382	.0402
.001	.0028	.0045	.0063	.0082	.0102	.0122	.0141	.0161	.0181	.0201	.0221	.0241	.0261	.0281	.0301	.0321	.0341	.0361	.0381	.0400
X (DEV)	**.001**	**.002**	**.003**	**.004**	**.005**	**.006**	**.007**	**.008**	**.009**	**.010**	**.011**	**.012**	**.013**	**.014**	**.015**	**.016**	**.017**	**.018**	**.019**	**.020**

Actual position = $2\sqrt{x^2 + y^2}$

Conversion of Coordinate Measurement to Position Tolerance Zones - Metric

The chart below will convert coordinate (x and y) metric measurements to position diameter tolerance zones. It is simply, double the Pythagorean Theorem. The formula is shown below.

Y (DEV)	Position Zone (Diameter)																								
0.60	1.201	1.203	1.206	1.211	1.217	1.224	1.232	1.242	1.253	1.265	1.278	1.292	1.308	1.324	1.342	1.360	1.379	1.399	1.420	1.442	1.465	1.488	1.512	1.537	1.562
0.58	1.161	1.163	1.166	1.171	1.177	1.185	1.193	1.203	1.215	1.227	1.241	1.255	1.271	1.288	1.306	1.325	1.345	1.365	1.387	1.409	1.432	1.456	1.481	1.506	1.532
0.56	1.121	1.123	1.126	1.131	1.138	1.145	1.154	1.165	1.176	1.189	1.203	1.219	1.235	1.252	1.271	1.290	1.310	1.331	1.354	1.376	1.400	1.424	1.449	1.475	1.501
0.54	1.081	1.083	1.087	1.092	1.098	1.106	1.116	1.126	1.138	1.152	1.166	1.182	1.199	1.217	1.235	1.255	1.276	1.298	1.321	1.344	1.368	1.393	1.419	1.445	1.472
0.52	1.041	1.043	1.047	1.052	1.059	1.067	1.077	1.088	1.101	1.114	1.129	1.145	1.163	1.181	1.201	1.221	1.243	1.265	1.288	1.312	1.337	1.362	1.389	1.415	1.443
0.50	1.001	1.003	1.007	1.013	1.020	1.028	1.038	1.050	1.063	1.077	1.093	1.109	1.127	1.146	1.166	1.187	1.209	1.232	1.256	1.281	1.306	1.332	1.359	1.386	1.414
0.48	0.961	0.963	0.967	0.973	0.981	0.990	1.000	1.012	1.025	1.040	1.056	1.073	1.092	1.111	1.132	1.154	1.176	1.200	1.224	1.250	1.276	1.302	1.330	1.358	1.386
0.46	0.921	0.923	0.928	0.934	0.941	0.951	0.962	0.974	0.988	1.003	1.020	1.038	1.057	1.077	1.098	1.121	1.144	1.168	1.193	1.219	1.246	1.273	1.301	1.330	1.359
0.44	0.881	0.884	0.888	0.894	0.902	0.912	0.923	0.936	0.951	0.967	0.984	1.002	1.022	1.043	1.065	1.088	1.112	1.137	1.163	1.189	1.217	1.245	1.273	1.302	1.332
0.42	0.841	0.844	0.849	0.855	0.863	0.874	0.885	0.899	0.914	0.930	0.948	0.967	0.988	1.010	1.032	1.056	1.081	1.106	1.133	1.160	1.188	1.217	1.246	1.276	1.306
0.40	0.801	0.804	0.809	0.816	0.825	0.835	0.848	0.862	0.877	0.894	0.913	0.933	0.954	0.977	1.000	1.024	1.050	1.076	1.103	1.131	1.160	1.189	1.219	1.250	1.281
0.38	0.761	0.764	0.769	0.777	0.786	0.797	0.810	0.825	0.841	0.859	0.878	0.899	0.921	0.944	0.968	0.994	1.020	1.047	1.075	1.103	1.133	1.163	1.193	1.224	1.256
0.36	0.721	0.724	0.730	0.738	0.747	0.759	0.773	0.788	0.805	0.824	0.844	0.865	0.888	0.912	0.937	0.963	0.990	1.018	1.047	1.076	1.106	1.137	1.168	1.200	1.232
0.34	0.681	0.685	0.691	0.699	0.709	0.721	0.735	0.752	0.769	0.789	0.810	0.832	0.856	0.881	0.907	0.934	0.962	0.990	1.020	1.050	1.081	1.112	1.144	1.176	1.209
0.32	0.641	0.645	0.651	0.660	0.671	0.684	0.699	0.716	0.734	0.755	0.777	0.800	0.825	0.850	0.877	0.905	0.934	0.963	0.994	1.024	1.056	1.088	1.121	1.154	1.187
0.30	0.601	0.605	0.612	0.621	0.632	0.646	0.662	0.680	0.700	0.721	0.744	0.768	0.794	0.821	0.849	0.877	0.907	0.937	0.968	1.000	1.032	1.065	1.098	1.132	1.166
0.28	0.561	0.566	0.573	0.582	0.595	0.609	0.626	0.645	0.666	0.688	0.712	0.738	0.764	0.792	0.821	0.850	0.881	0.912	0.944	0.977	1.010	1.043	1.077	1.111	1.146
0.26	0.522	0.526	0.534	0.544	0.557	0.573	0.591	0.611	0.632	0.656	0.681	0.708	0.735	0.764	0.794	0.825	0.856	0.888	0.921	0.954	0.988	1.022	1.057	1.092	1.127
0.24	0.482	0.487	0.495	0.506	0.520	0.537	0.556	0.577	0.600	0.625	0.651	0.679	0.708	0.738	0.768	0.800	0.832	0.865	0.899	0.933	0.967	1.002	1.038	1.073	1.109
0.22	0.442	0.447	0.456	0.468	0.483	0.501	0.522	0.544	0.569	0.595	0.622	0.651	0.681	0.712	0.744	0.777	0.810	0.844	0.878	0.913	0.948	0.984	1.020	1.056	1.093
0.20	0.402	0.408	0.418	0.431	0.447	0.466	0.488	0.512	0.538	0.566	0.595	0.625	0.656	0.688	0.721	0.755	0.789	0.824	0.859	0.894	0.930	0.967	1.003	1.040	1.077
0.18	0.362	0.369	0.379	0.394	0.412	0.433	0.456	0.482	0.509	0.538	0.569	0.600	0.632	0.666	0.700	0.734	0.769	0.805	0.841	0.877	0.914	0.951	0.988	1.025	1.063
0.16	0.322	0.330	0.342	0.358	0.377	0.400	0.425	0.453	0.482	0.512	0.544	0.577	0.611	0.645	0.680	0.716	0.752	0.788	0.825	0.862	0.899	0.936	0.974	1.012	1.050
0.14	0.283	0.291	0.305	0.322	0.344	0.369	0.396	0.425	0.456	0.488	0.522	0.556	0.591	0.626	0.662	0.699	0.735	0.773	0.810	0.848	0.885	0.923	0.962	1.000	1.038
0.12	0.243	0.253	0.268	0.288	0.312	0.339	0.369	0.400	0.433	0.466	0.501	0.537	0.573	0.609	0.646	0.684	0.721	0.759	0.797	0.835	0.874	0.912	0.951	0.990	1.028
0.10	0.204	0.215	0.233	0.256	0.283	0.312	0.344	0.377	0.412	0.447	0.483	0.520	0.557	0.595	0.632	0.671	0.709	0.747	0.786	0.825	0.863	0.902	0.941	0.981	1.020
0.08	0.165	0.179	0.200	0.226	0.256	0.288	0.322	0.358	0.394	0.431	0.468	0.506	0.544	0.582	0.621	0.660	0.699	0.738	0.777	0.816	0.855	0.894	0.934	0.973	1.013
0.06	0.126	0.144	0.170	0.200	0.233	0.268	0.305	0.342	0.379	0.418	0.456	0.495	0.534	0.573	0.612	0.651	0.691	0.730	0.769	0.809	0.849	0.888	0.928	0.967	1.007
0.04	0.089	0.113	0.144	0.179	0.215	0.253	0.291	0.330	0.369	0.408	0.447	0.487	0.526	0.566	0.605	0.645	0.685	0.724	0.764	0.804	0.844	0.884	0.923	0.963	1.003
0.02	0.057	0.089	0.126	0.165	0.204	0.243	0.283	0.322	0.362	0.402	0.442	0.482	0.522	0.561	0.601	0.641	0.681	0.721	0.761	0.801	0.841	0.881	0.921	0.961	1.001
X (DEV)	**0.02**	**0.04**	**0.06**	**0.08**	**0.10**	**0.12**	**0.14**	**0.16**	**0.18**	**0.20**	**0.22**	**0.24**	**0.26**	**0.28**	**0.30**	**0.32**	**0.34**	**0.36**	**0.38**	**0.40**	**0.42**	**0.44**	**0.46**	**0.48**	**0.50**

Actual position = $2\sqrt{x^2 + y^2}$

Workshop Exercise 5.1 - Metric

The top drawing has a position tolerance applied. The lower illustration is the imperfect produced part indexed to the datum reference frame (DRF). Evaluate the measured distances on the produced part to verify conformance to the specification. Use the table below to record your calculations.

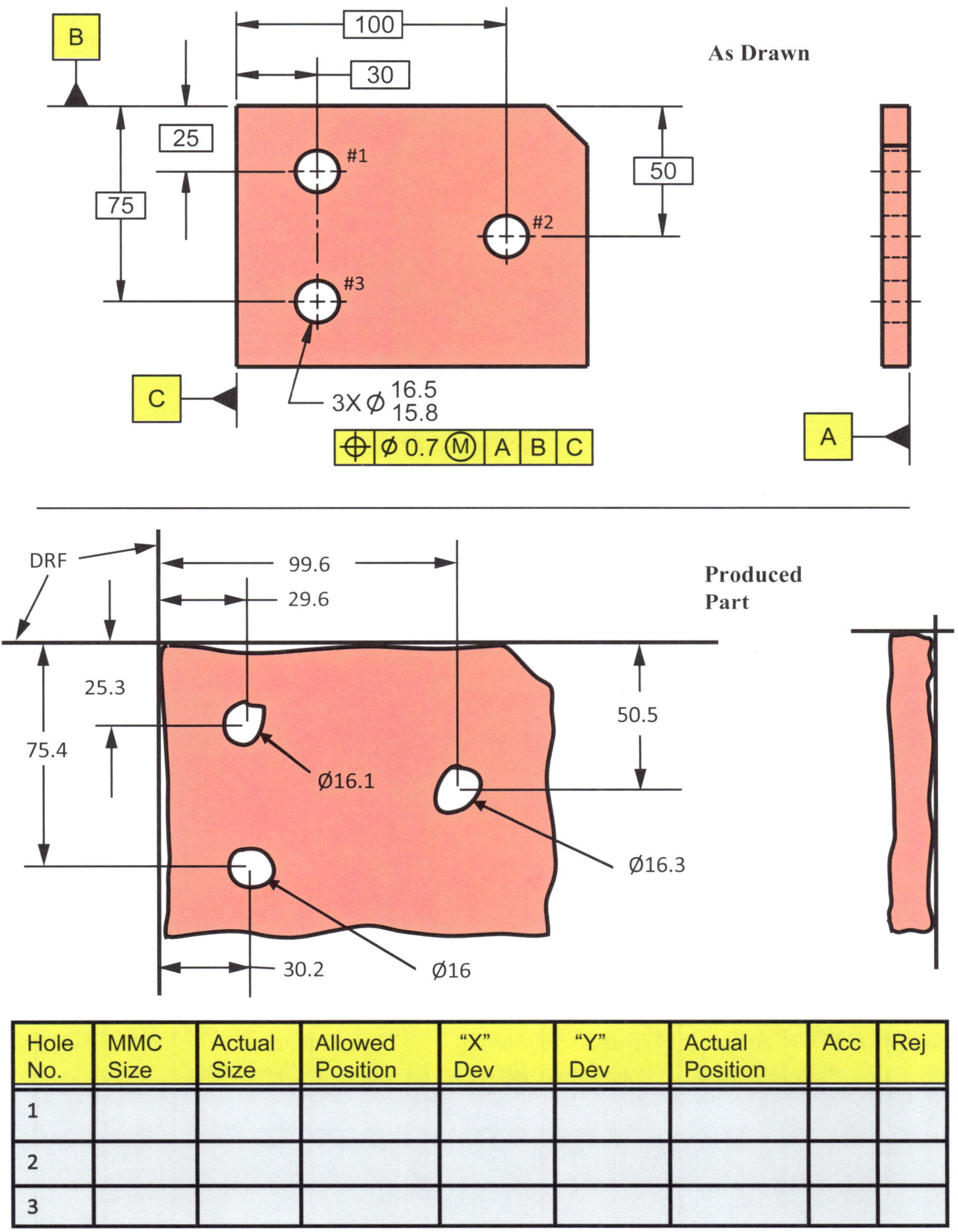

Hole No.	MMC Size	Actual Size	Allowed Position	"X" Dev	"Y" Dev	Actual Position	Acc	Rej
1								
2								
3								

Workshop Exercise 5.2 - Metric

The top drawing has a position tolerance applied. The lower illustration is the imperfect produced part indexed to the datum reference frame (DRF). Evaluate the measured distances on the produced part to verify conformance to the specification. Use the table below to record your calculations.

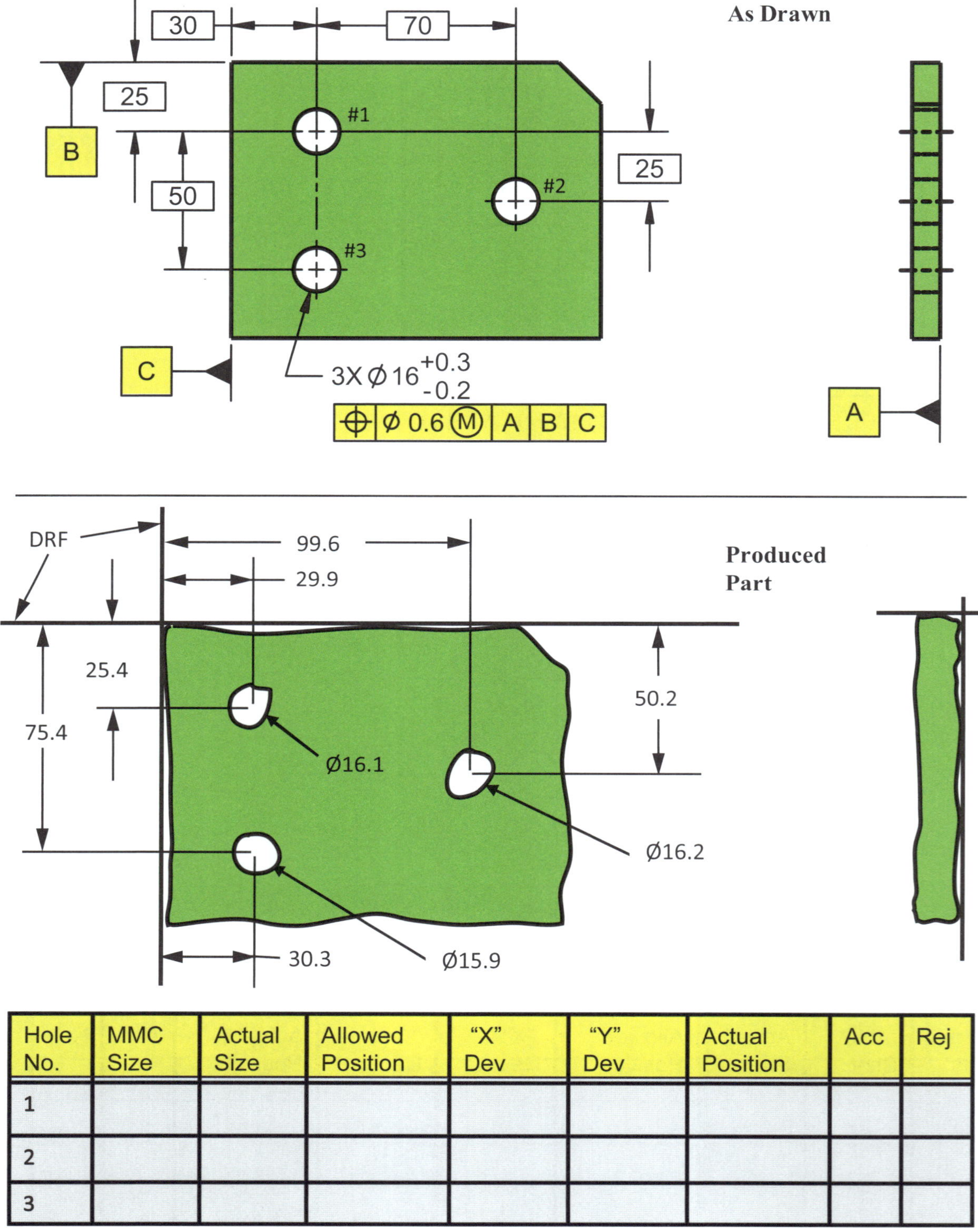

Hole No.	MMC Size	Actual Size	Allowed Position	"X" Dev	"Y" Dev	Actual Position	Acc	Rej
1								
2								
3								

Workshop Exercise 5.3 - Metric

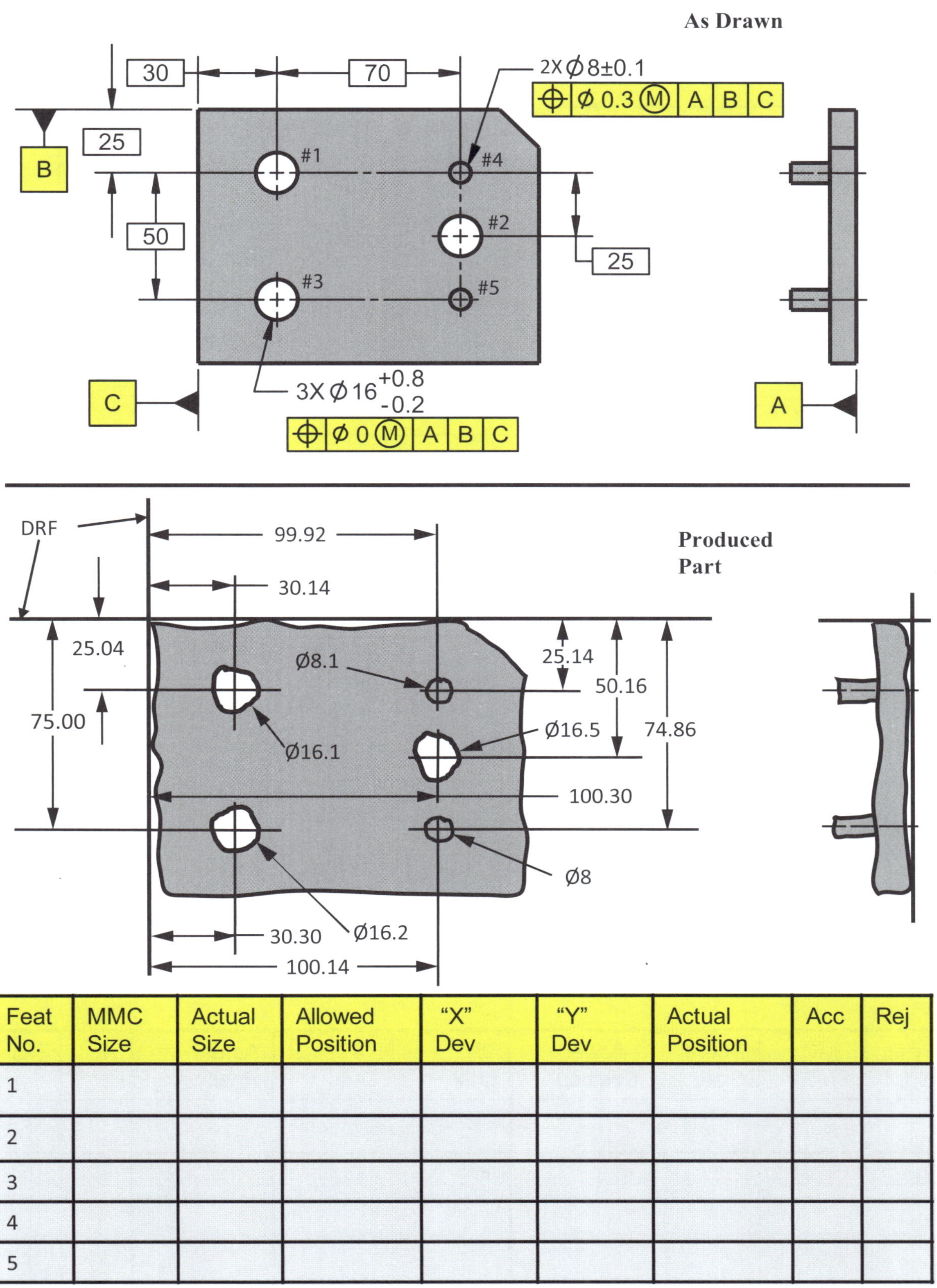

Feat No.	MMC Size	Actual Size	Allowed Position	"X" Dev	"Y" Dev	Actual Position	Acc	Rej
1								
2								
3								
4								
5								

Workshop Exercise 5.4 - Metric

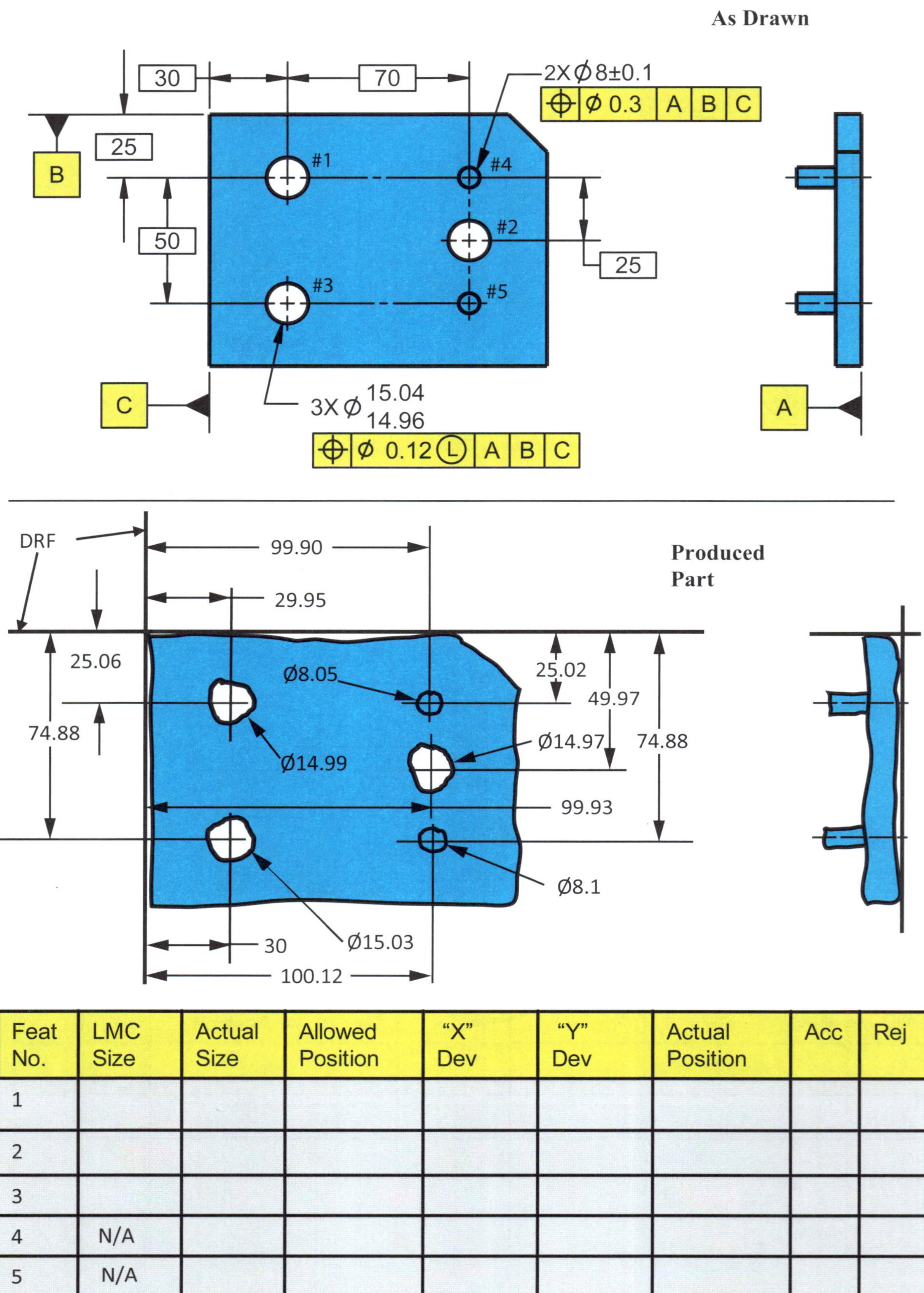

Feat No.	LMC Size	Actual Size	Allowed Position	"X" Dev	"Y" Dev	Actual Position	Acc	Rej
1								
2								
3								
4	N/A							
5	N/A							

Workshop Exercise 5.5 - Metric

The top drawing has a position tolerance applied. The lower illustration is the imperfect produced part indexed to the datum reference frame (DRF). Evaluate the measured distances on the produced part to verify conformance to the specification. Use the table below to record your calculations. This part will be evaluated again in unit 7 with the datum features at MMB.

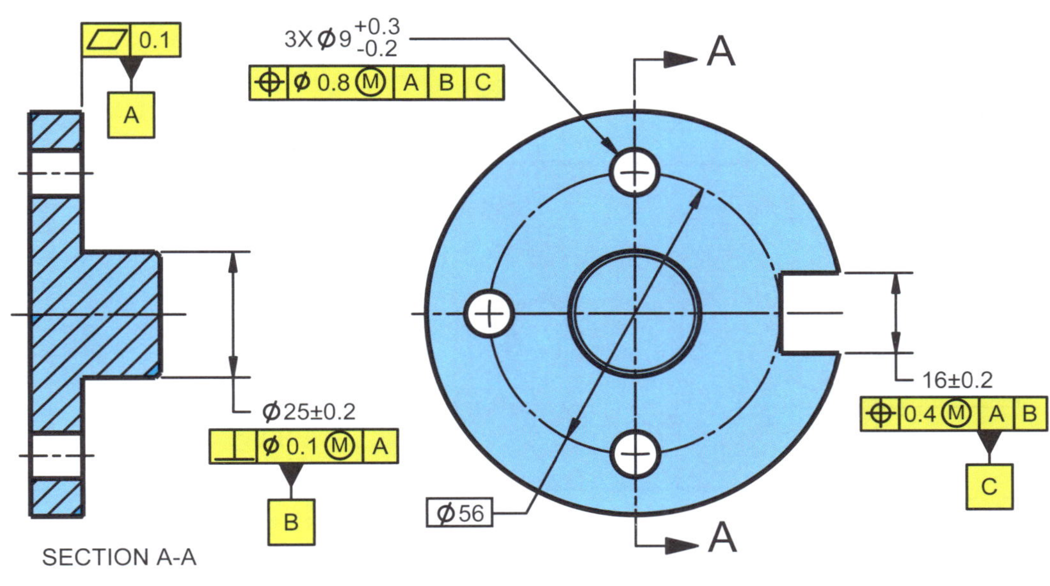

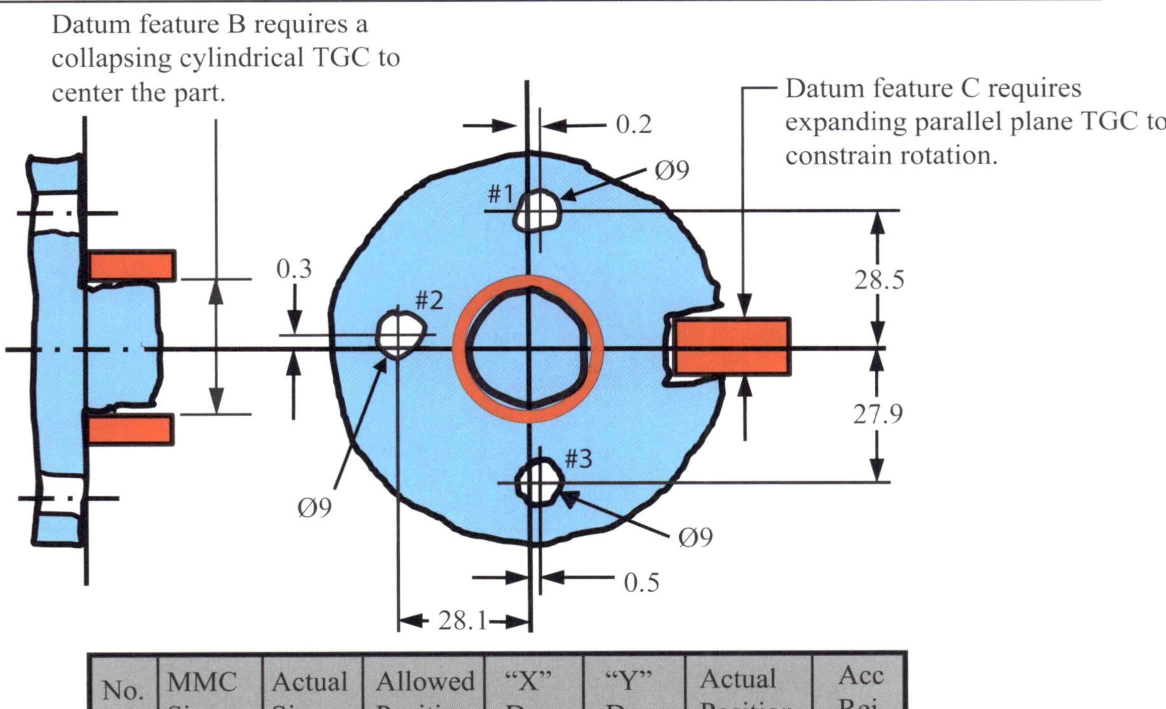

No.	MMC Size	Actual Size	Allowed Position	"X" Dev	"Y" Dev	Actual Position	Acc Rej
1							
2							
3							

Workshop Exercise 5.6 - Inch

The top drawing has a position tolerance applied. The lower illustration is the imperfect produced part indexed to the datum reference frame (DRF). Evaluate the measured distances on the produced part to verify conformance to the specification. Use the table below to record your calculations.

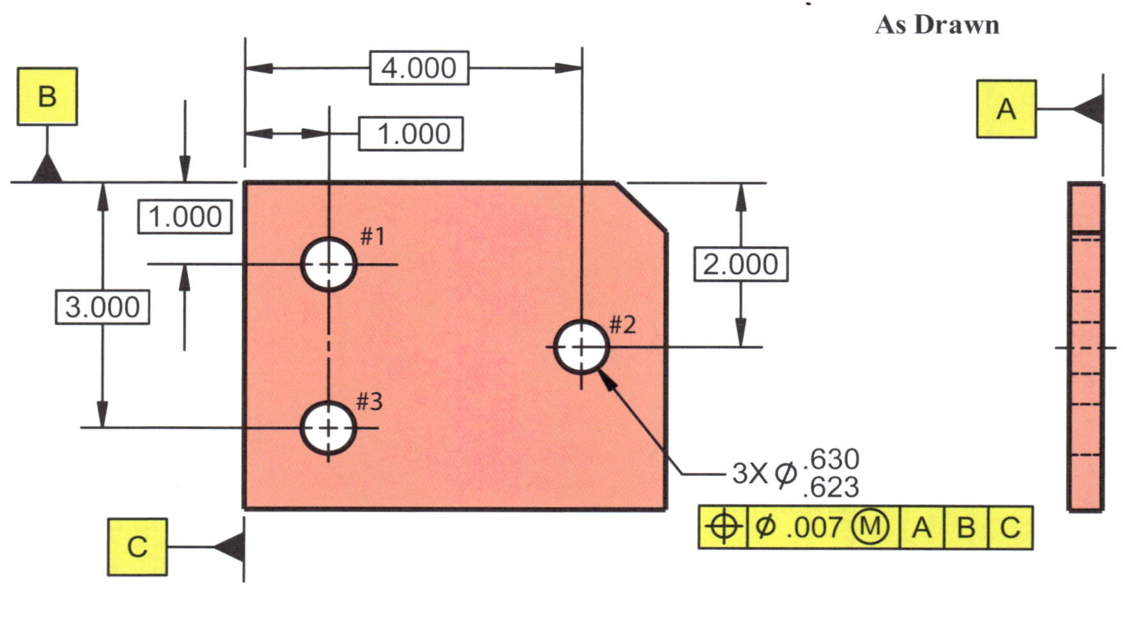

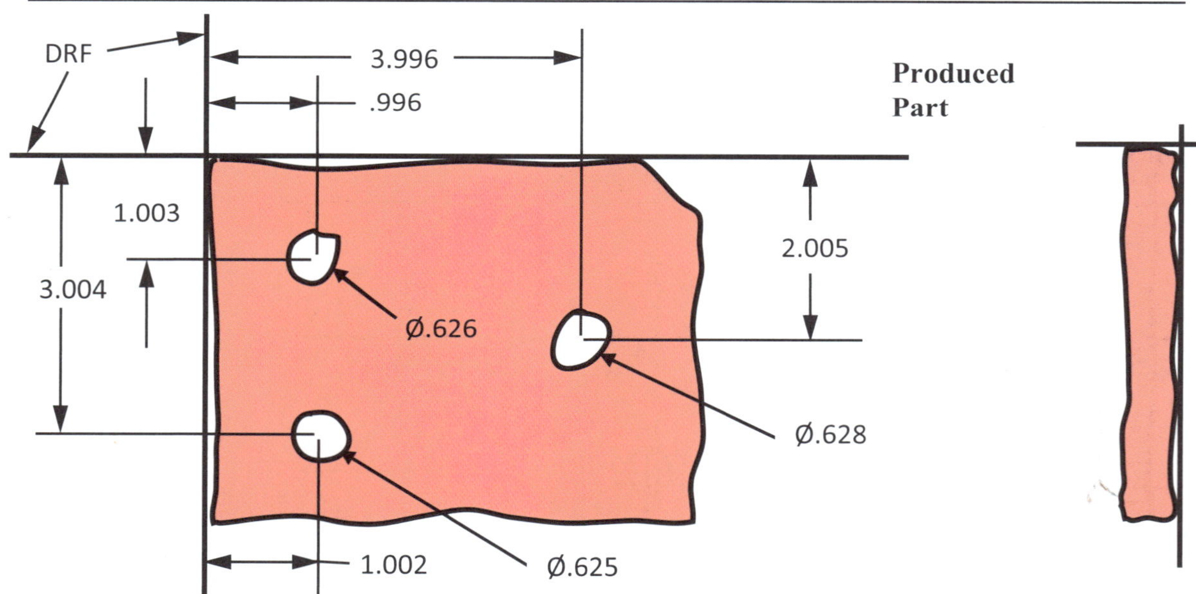

Hole No.	MMC Size	Actual Size	Allowed Position	"X" Dev	"Y" Dev	Actual Position	Acc	Rej
1	.623	.626	.010	-.004	-.003	.010	X	
2	.623	.628	.012	-.004	-.005	.0128		X
3	.623	.625	.009	+.002	-.004	.0089	X	

Workshop Exercise 5.7 - Inch

The top drawing has a position tolerance applied. The lower illustration is the imperfect produced part indexed to the datum reference frame (DRF). Evaluate the measured distances on the produced part to verify conformance to the specification. Use the table below to record your calculations.

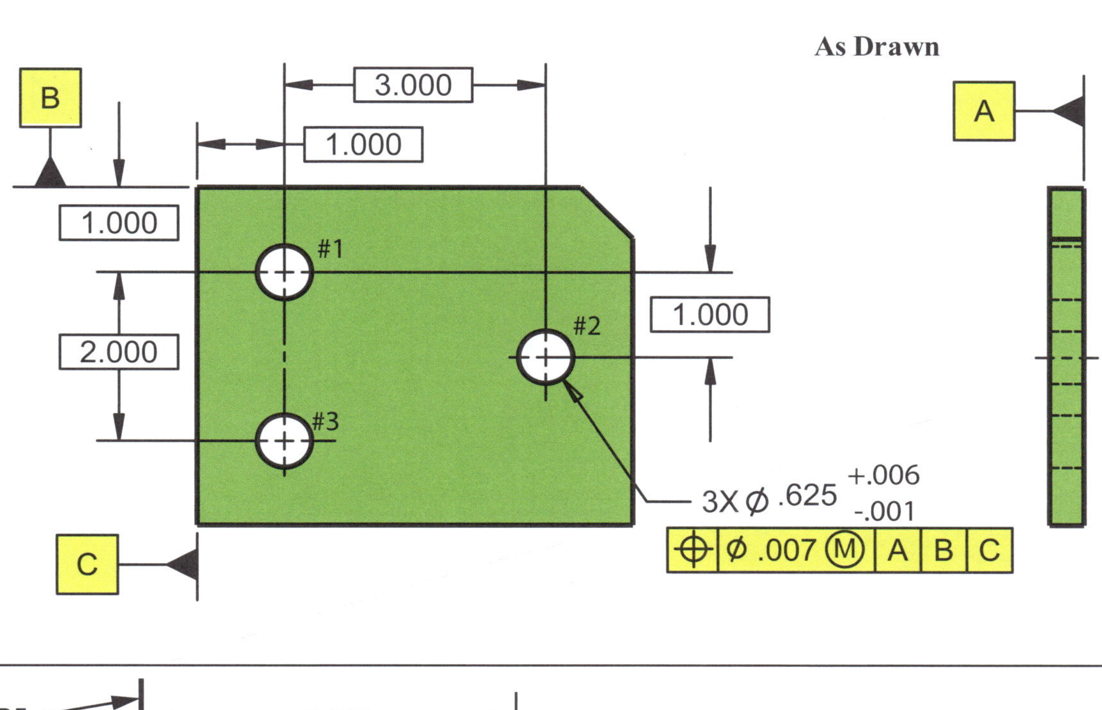

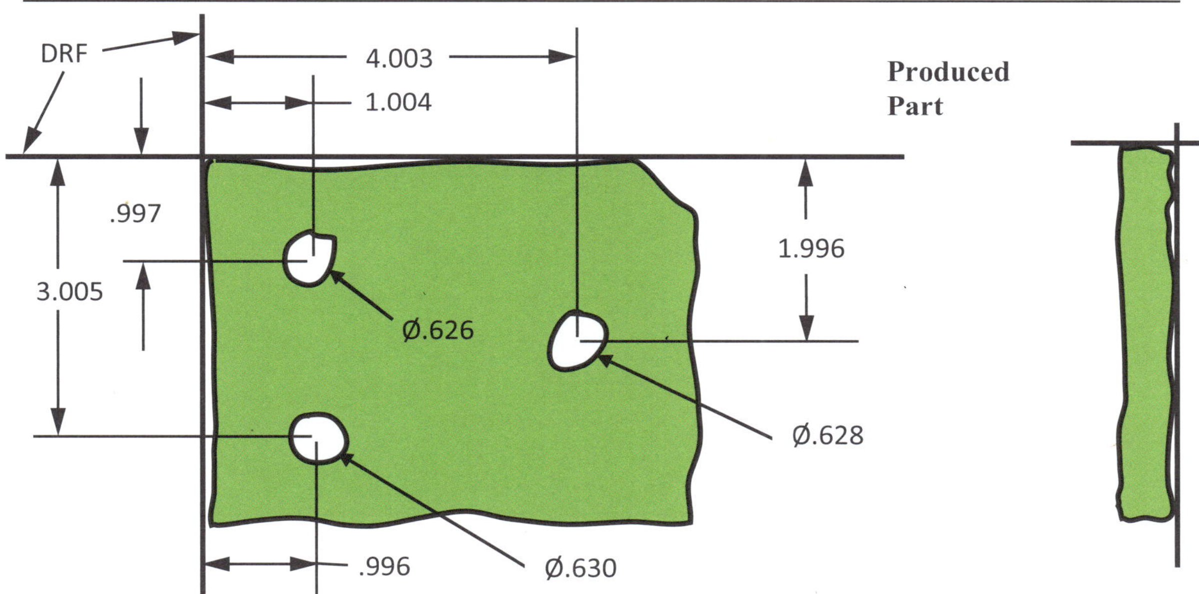

Hole No.	MMC Size	Actual Size	Allowed Position	"X" Dev	"Y" Dev	Actual Position	Acc	Rej
1	.624	.626	.009	+.004	+.003			
2	.624	.628	.011	+.003	+.004			
3	.624	.630	.013	-.004	+.005			

Workshop Exercise 5.8 - Inch

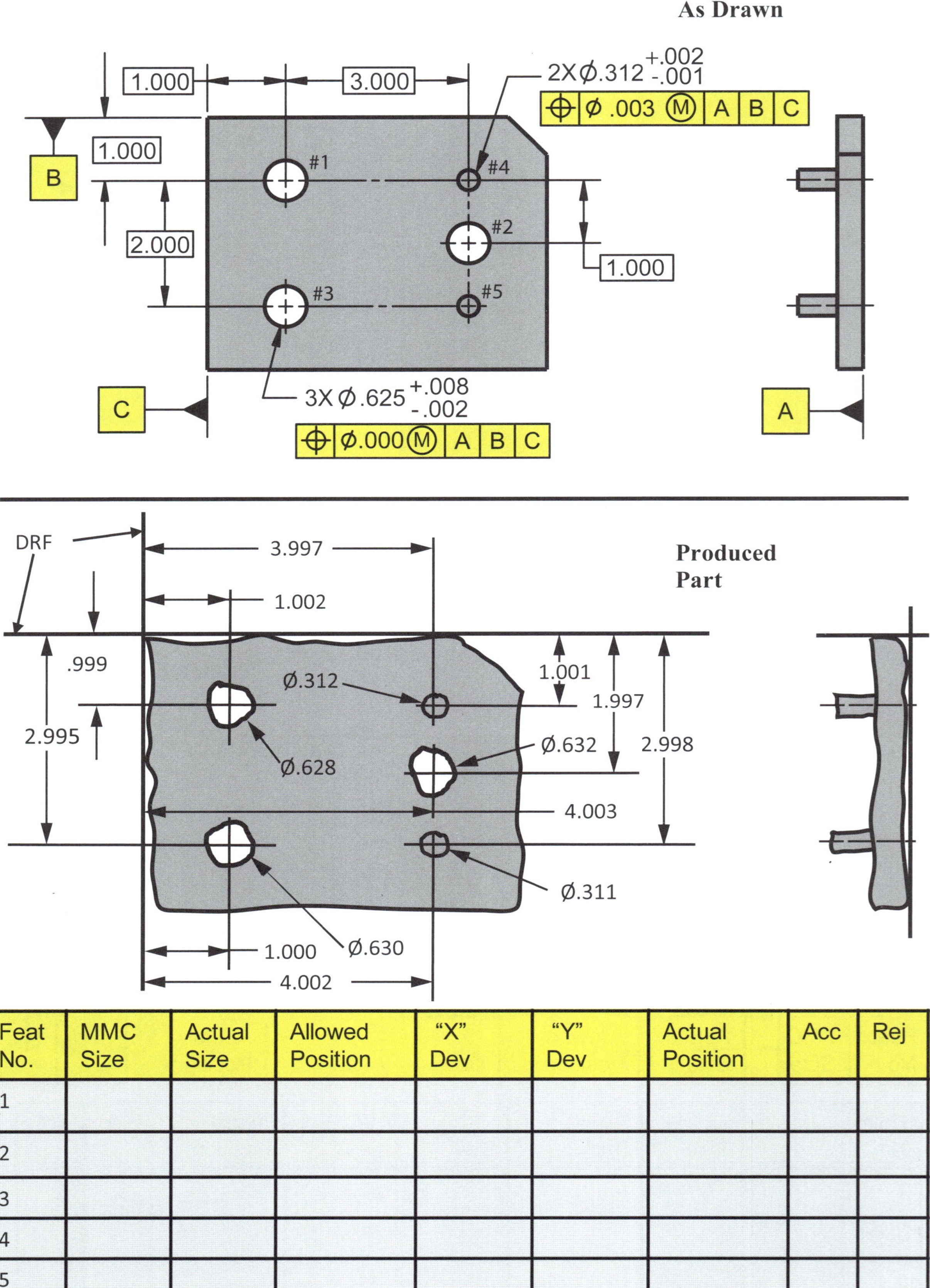

Feat No.	MMC Size	Actual Size	Allowed Position	"X" Dev	"Y" Dev	Actual Position	Acc	Rej
1								
2								
3								
4								
5								

Workshop Exercise 5.9 - Inch

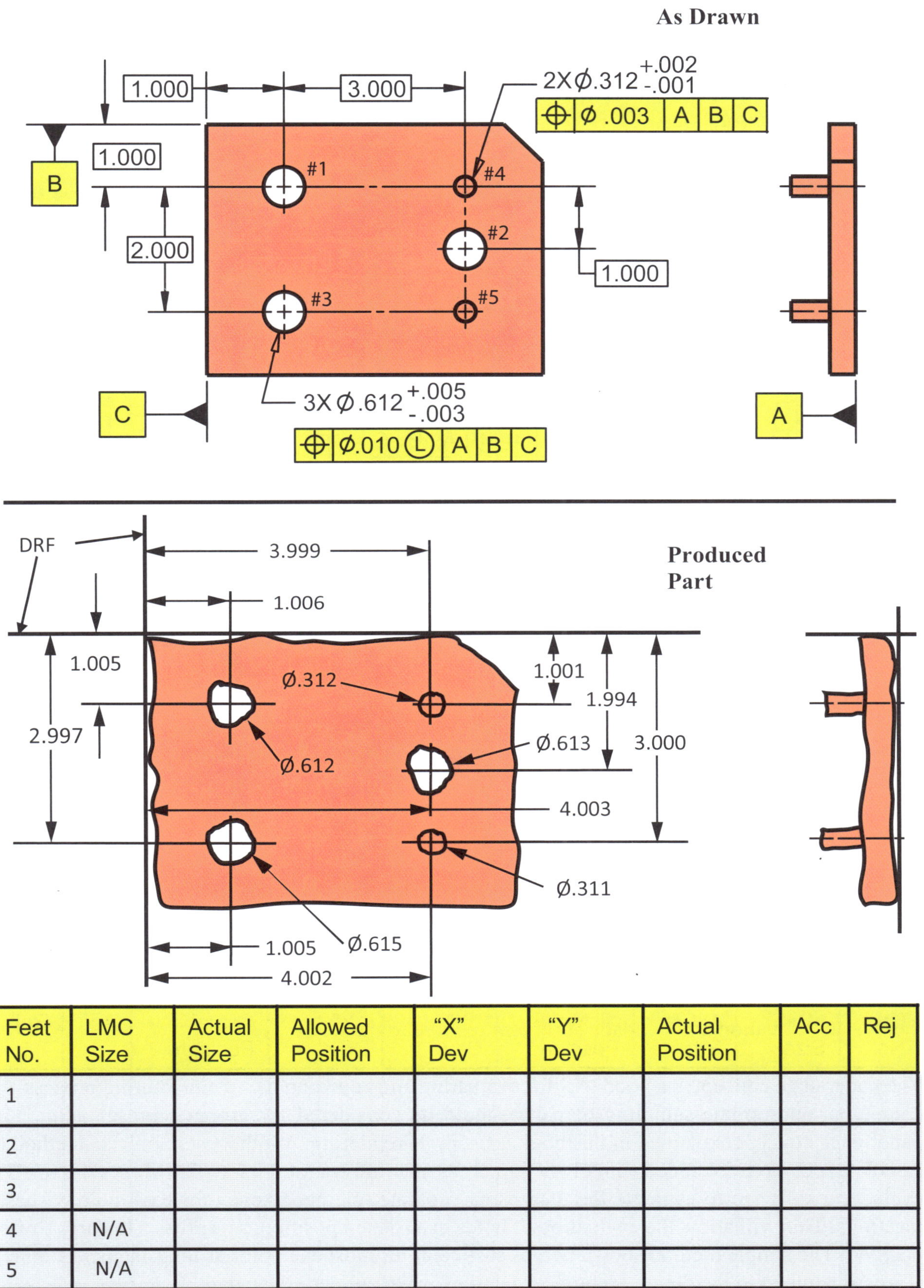

Feat No.	LMC Size	Actual Size	Allowed Position	"X" Dev	"Y" Dev	Actual Position	Acc	Rej
1								
2								
3								
4	N/A							
5	N/A							

Paper Gage Concept

The paper gage concept is a good tool for understanding and evaluating geometric tolerancing. Paper gage concepts are used throughout this book to help illustrate many of the geometric concepts. The part below was evaluated in exercise 5.1-Metric. Hole 2 was found to be out of position. The paper gage plotting technique below highlights the manufacturing problem and suggests possible solutions.

Inspection report from exercise 5.1

Hole No.	MMC Size	Actual Size	Allowed Position	"X" Dev	"Y" Dev	Actual Position	Acc	Rej
1	15.8	16.1	1	-0.4	-0.3	1	X	
2	15.8	16.3	1.2	-0.4	-0.5	1.281		X
3	15.8	16	0.9	+0.2	-0.4	0.894	X	

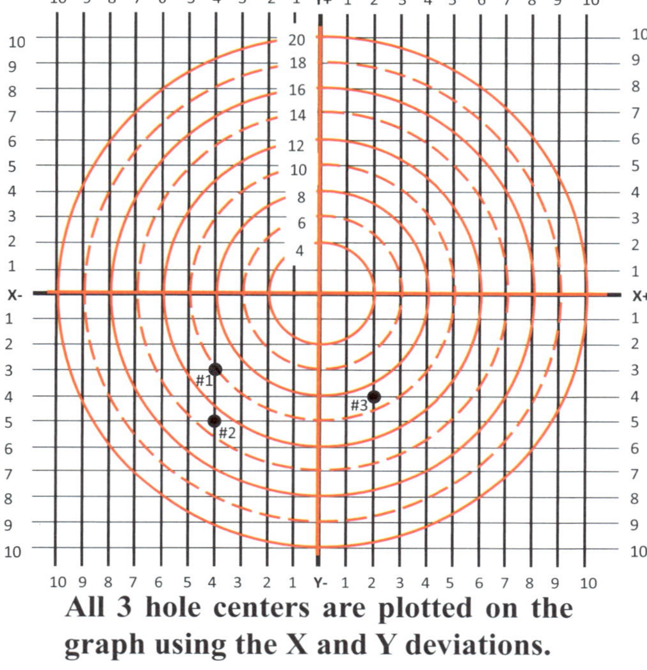

All 3 hole centers are plotted on the graph using the X and Y deviations.

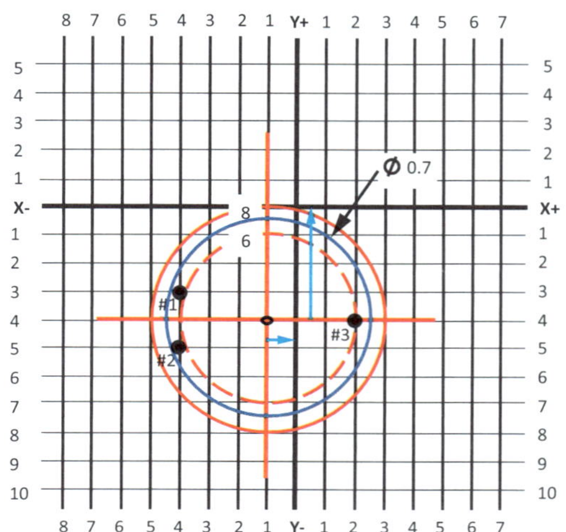

The grouping of the 3 holes to each other is within dia 0.7. The center of the group is dispaced -0.1 in X and -0.4 in Y.

At first glance, it appears only hole #2 must be relocated in the manufacturing process. However, the paper gage evaluation shows the location between the 3 holes is tight, but the group is displaced to the DRF.

The 3 holes are positioned to each other within a 0.7 diameter zone. In order to center the process, the origin of the holes as a group (0.7 ring) must be relocated by +0.1 in X and +0.4 in Y. It seems there is an "elevation and windage" problem relative to the DRF.

The paper gage concept is a good tool for evaluating and adjusting the manufacturing process. Of course, an appropriate sampling of parts should be considered for proper representation. The paper gage concept explained in this book is a simple rendering. Another more precise method to calculate position tolerances involves inputting the information in a CMM system or 3D evaluation software to evaluate the data using separate tolerance zones for each hole on basic locations. This will allow the evaluation of holes in a rotated position, as well as a linearly shifted position. The simple method shown here is sufficient for most examples as long as inspection has correctly aligned to the datum features or features when collecting the data.

Other Reporting Methods for Position

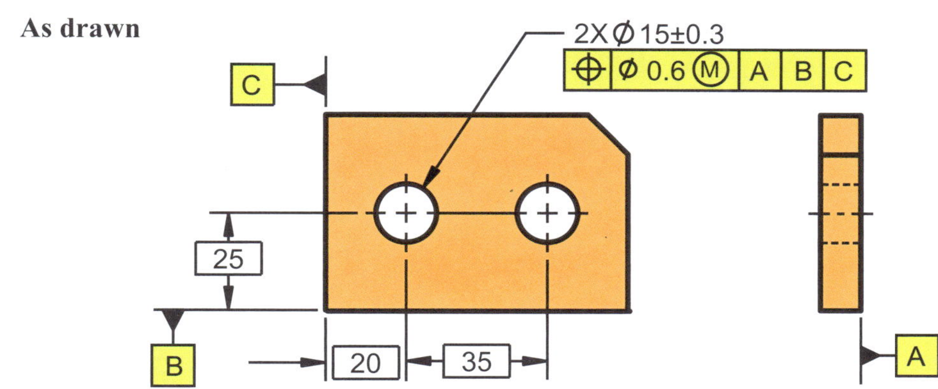

Reporting both ends of the axis

Hole No.	MMC Size	Actual Size	Allowed Position	X Dev Bottom	Y Dev Bottom	X Dev Top	Y Dev Top	Actual Position	Pass/ Fail
1	14.7	14.9	0.8	0.10	0.24	0.12	0.24	0.537	Pass
2	14.7	14.9	0.8	-0.40	0.10	0.32	0.16	0.825	Fail

Bottom of hole

Top of hole

When a feature has significant depth, the quality plan may require the inspection location of the bottom and top of the axis. This will show if the feature is shifted or tilted in the tolerance zone. The end of the axis with the worst deviation determines the actual position. From the data above, the first hole is perpendicular but shifted, while the second hole is significantly tilted in the X direction. The plan may not require reporting of both ends of the axis. The worst end may be the only one reported as seen in the other examples in this unit.

Other Reporting Options

Hole No.	MMC Size	Actual Size	Allowed Position	X	Y	X Dev	Y Dev	Actual Position	% of Tol Used	Pass/ Fail
1	14.7	15.0	0.9	20.3	25.3	0.30	0.30	0.849	94.3	Pass
2	14.7	14.9	0.8	54.6	25.12	-0.40	0.12	0.835	104.4	Fail

The X and Y distances from the datum reference frame may be recorded. However, the numbers may be deceiving as they will not always match the basic dimensions given. The X/Y deviations are needed for the actual position calculation.

The percent of tolerance used is a helpful column to quickly see if the feature is well within its tolerance or barley making it. The pass/fail can be color coded for a quick look at the capabilities. Green is well within, red is outside, yellow is barely within tolerance.

Also see the surface method using virtual condition in unit 7 for another way of evaluating a position tolerance at MMC,

Unit 6

Orientation and the Hierarchy of Tolerances

Orientation Tolerances Overview

Symbol	Orientation Tolerance	Common Shape of Tolerance Zone	2D / 3D	Application of Feature Modifier
∠	Angularity	2 Parallel Lines 2 Parallel Planes Cylindrical	3D or 2D*	Yes, if feature has size No, if feature is a surface
⊥	Perpendicularity			
//	Parallelism			

Overview: The orientation tolerances of perpendicularity, parallelism, and angularity control the orientation (tilt/angle) of individual features and must have at least one datum feature reference.

According to the past ASME Y14.5 standards (1994 and earlier), if the feature is 90 degrees from the primary datum, use the perpendicularity symbol. If the feature is 0/180 degrees from the primary datum, use the parallelism symbol. For all other angles, use angularity. However, the 2009 standard changed this to allow the angularity symbol to be used in place of the others to simply mean orientation. The math behind the three orientation tolerances is nearly identical with the only difference being the numerical angle relative to the primary datum. In many places in this text, the word orientation is used in place of parallelism, angularity and perpendicularity to help you think generically about orientation tolerances. In some complex examples, it is difficult to determine which symbol should be used. An angularity tolerance will control the orientation of an individual feature at the implied or specified angle(s) to the datum reference frame.

Orientation tolerances may control planar surfaces as well as features of size (holes, pins, slots, tabs). An orientation tolerance applied to a surface also controls the form, and the feature control frame must be directly attached or have a leader line attached to the surface or extension line. When an orientation tolerance controls a feature of size, the feature control frame is placed under the size tolerance (no leader line, and not attached). This will control the axis or center plane of the feature, and therefore does not control the form of the feature. The size requirements of rule #1 will control the form and size. The axis or center plane is determined by the unrelated actual mating envelope. Material condition modifiers (MMC, LMC, RFS) are only applicable on orientation tolerances controlling features of size.

Orientation tolerances do not locate features. They only constrain the rotational degrees of freedom to the datum reference frame. A profile or position tolerance is used to control location. The orientation tolerances refine the orientation and therefore must have a smaller value than the location tolerance.

*The orientation tolerances are 3D by default. The note “EACH ELEMENT” placed under the feature control frame changes the specification to a series of cross-sectional 2D requirements. ASME Y14.5-2018 no longer supports orientation with “EACH RADIAL ELEMENT” because it invokes a translational degree of freedom that cannot be controlled by orientation tolerances. When control of radial elements is required, profile shall be used. See Y14.5-2018, sec 9.3.3.

Parallelism on a Surface

Parallelism is the condition of a surface, axis, or center plane, oriented at 0°/180° to the datum reference frame.

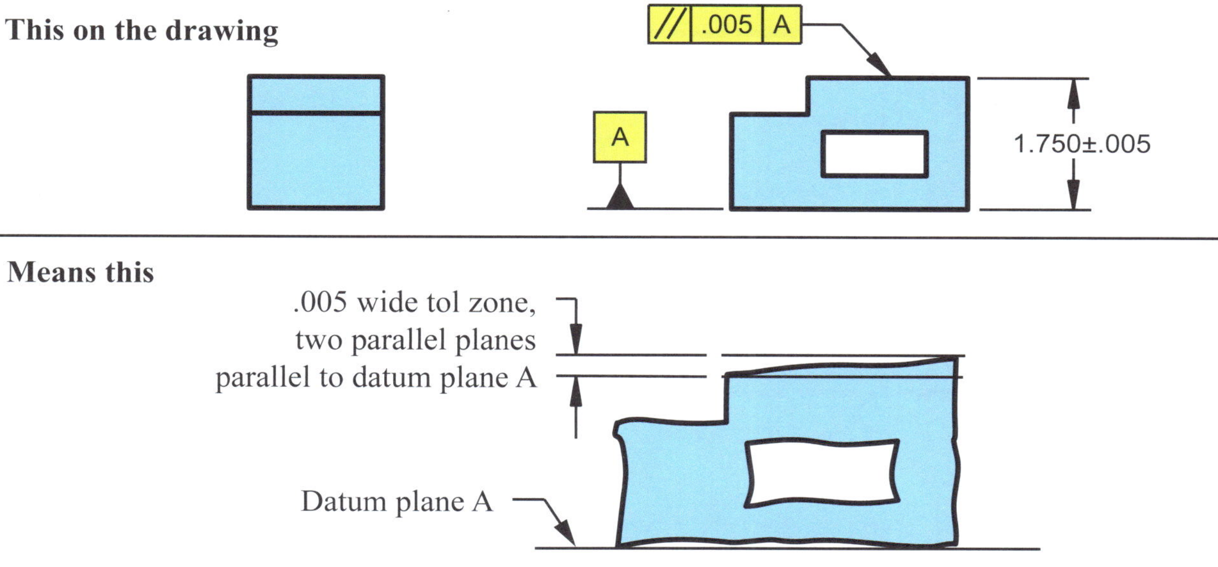

All points of the surface must lie within two parallel planes .005 apart which are parallel to datum plane A. In addition, the surface must be within the limits of size or profile tolerance. Since parallelism is a refinement of the size or location, the value must be tighter in order to be effective. **Note that parallelism on a planar surface also controls the flatness.**

Since the above parallelism specification is a surface control, the material condition modifiers MMC, LMC, and RFS are not applicable.

Sample Inspection for Parallelism

Both the datum feature and indicator stand are mounted on the surface plate and the dial indicator is placed on the surface. As the indicator traverses the feature, the full indicator movement (FIM) or total indicator reading (TIR) can be no more than .005 (max-min).

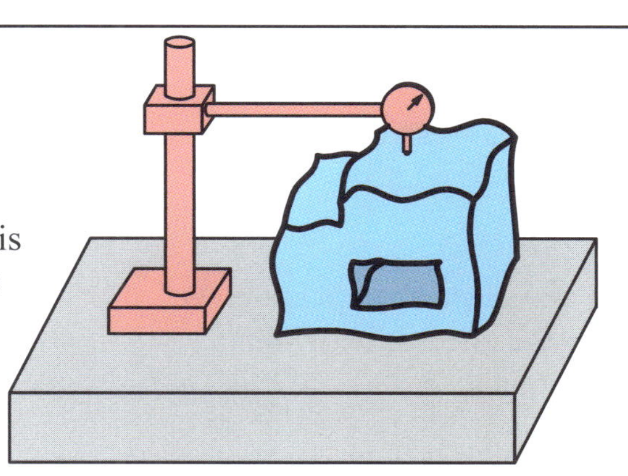

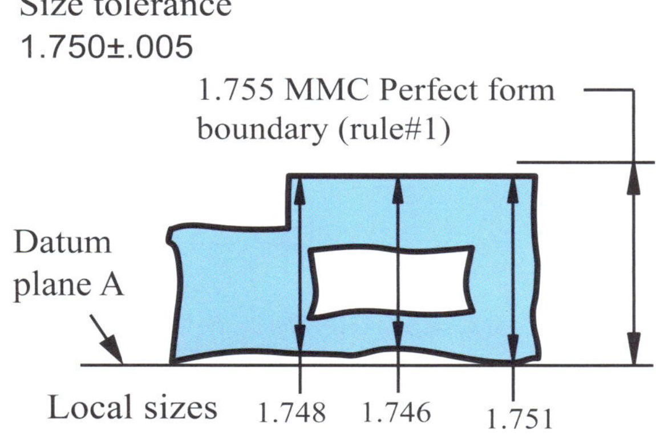

Note: Local sizes are defined as point-to-point distances and not relative to the datum plane. The local sizes and parallelism do not directly correlate. The local sizes may be changing because of the imperfections on the datum feature, and the top surface may still be perfectly parallel.

If the height should be also be evaluated to the datum, use profile tolerance instead of plus/minus (see next example).

Parallelism Application - Bearing Spacer

This bearing spacer is a good application for a loose location tolerance with a tighter parallelism requirement.

The first bearing seats on the shaft. The spacer mounts on top of the first bearing. The second bearing seats on the top surface of the spacer.

The distance between the two bearings is relatively unimportant, but the second bearing must seat parallel to the first.

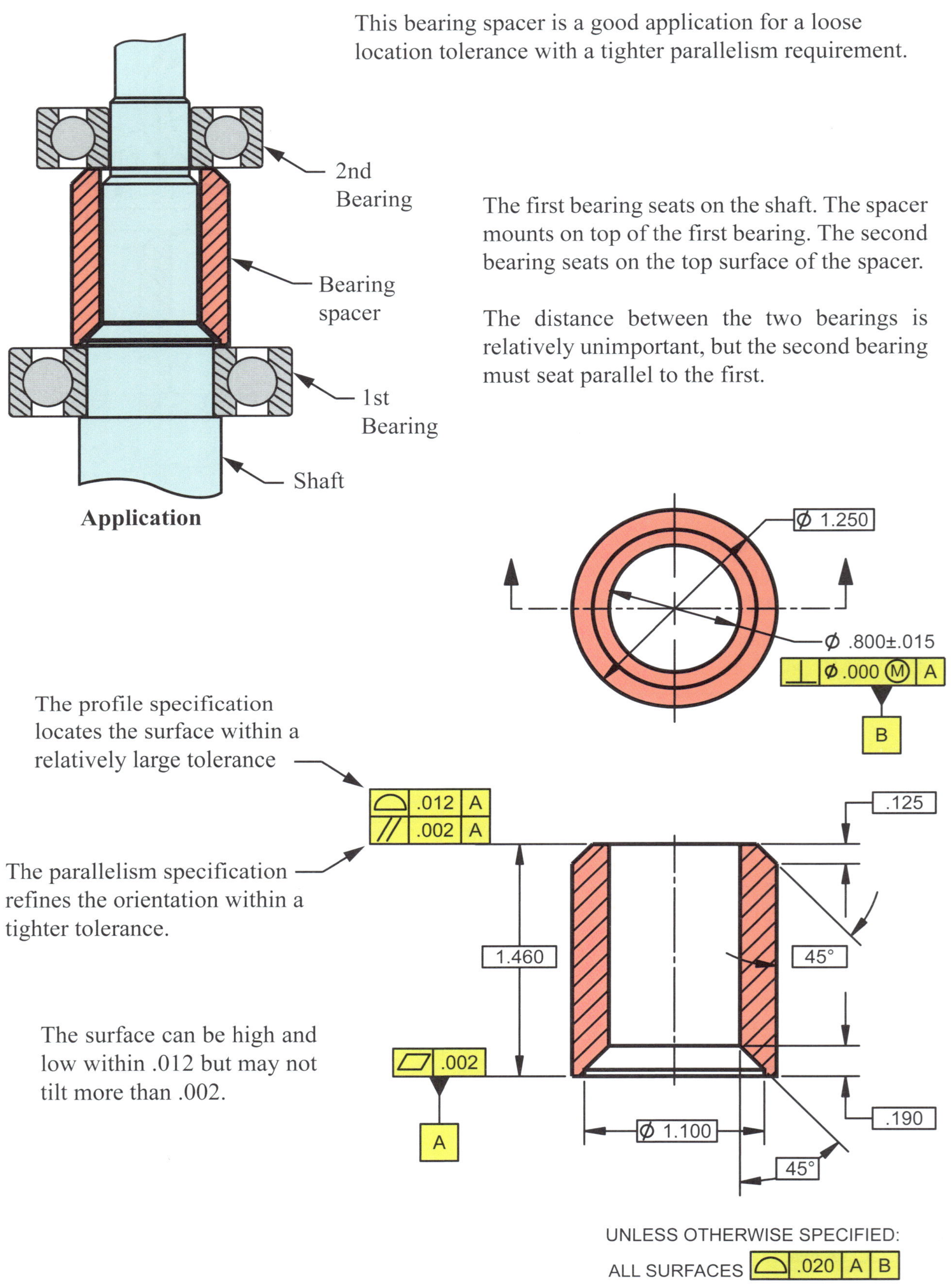

Parallelism Inspection and Reporting - Bearing Spacer

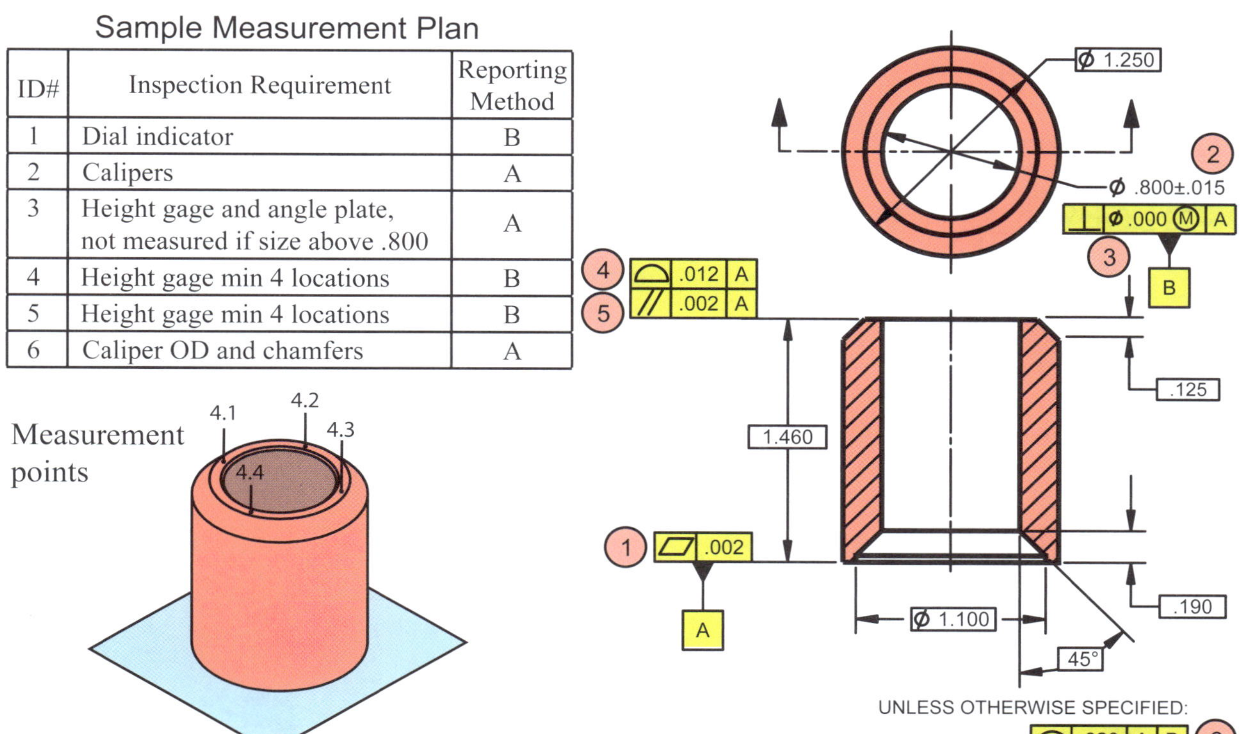

Sample Measurement Plan

ID#	Inspection Requirement	Reporting Method
1	Dial indicator	B
2	Calipers	A
3	Height gage and angle plate, not measured if size above .800	A
4	Height gage min 4 locations	B
5	Height gage min 4 locations	B
6	Caliper OD and chamfers	A

Tolerance Zones and Actual Part

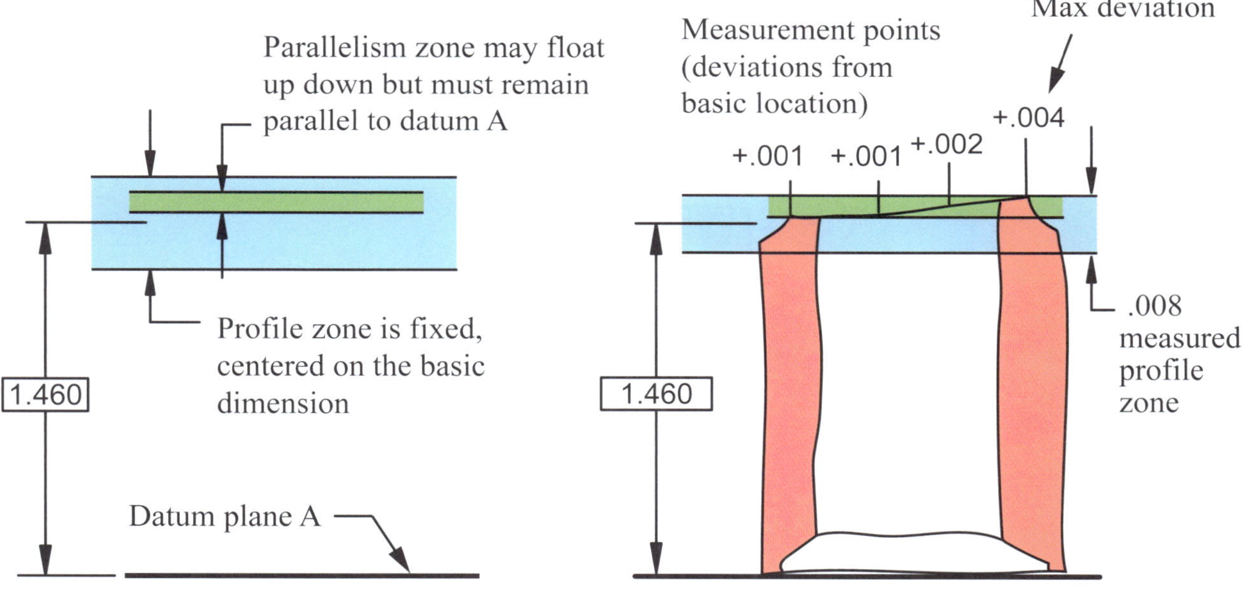

Sample Inspection Report

ID#	Tolerance Type	Allowed Tolerance	Measured Value	Accept Reject
4	Profile	.012	.008	A
5	Parallelism	.002	.003	R

Measured profile value = 2*(max deviation) = .008

Measured parallelism value = max - min = .003

Angularity on a Surface

Angularity is the condition of a surface oriented at a specified angle to the DRF. This example shows a surface with an angularity tolerance as a refinement of the profile tolerance.

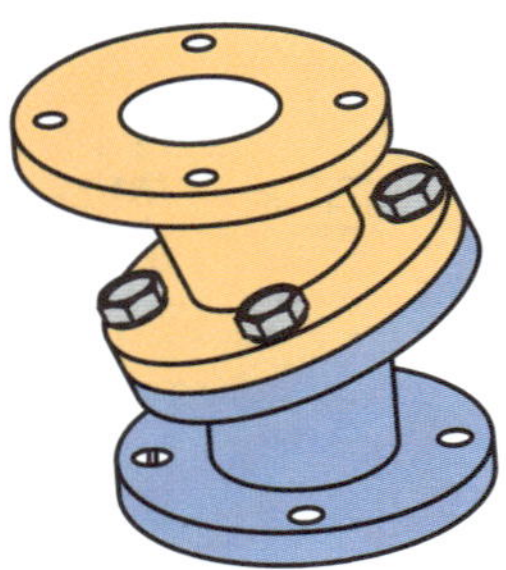

The assembly shows two angled fittings. The lower fitting is mounted to a main structure on the bottom surface and located by the center hole. The slot on the lower left rotationally aligns the part. The height of the top surface is not as important as the orientation (tilt/angle).

The top surface is located within a 1 mm profile tolerance and orientation refined with a 0.2 angularity tolerance. The 20° angle and 30 mm dimension must be basic.

This on the drawing

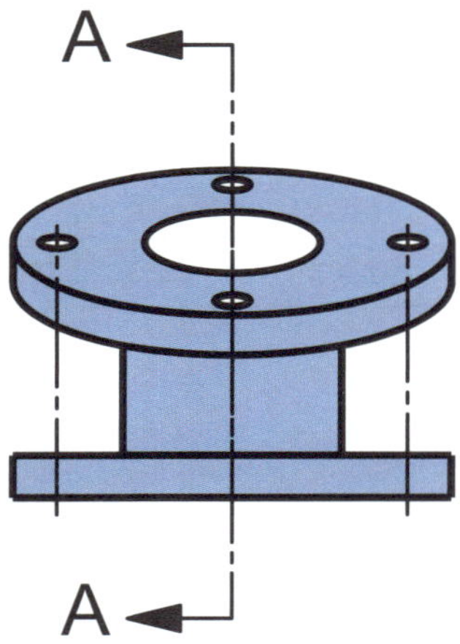

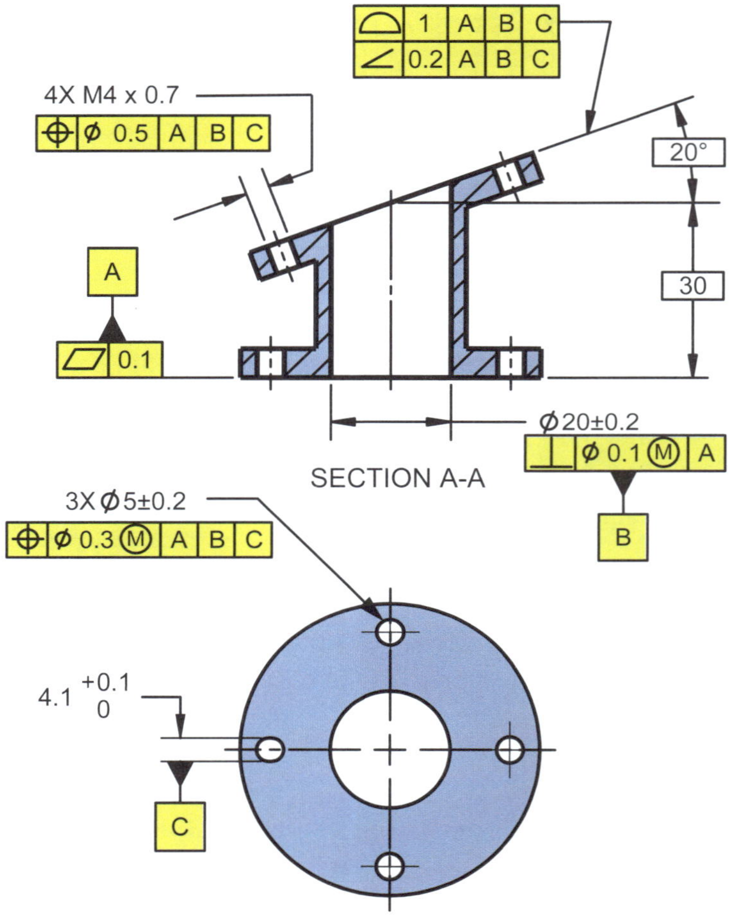

SECTION A-A

Datum reference frame established by datum features A, B, C.

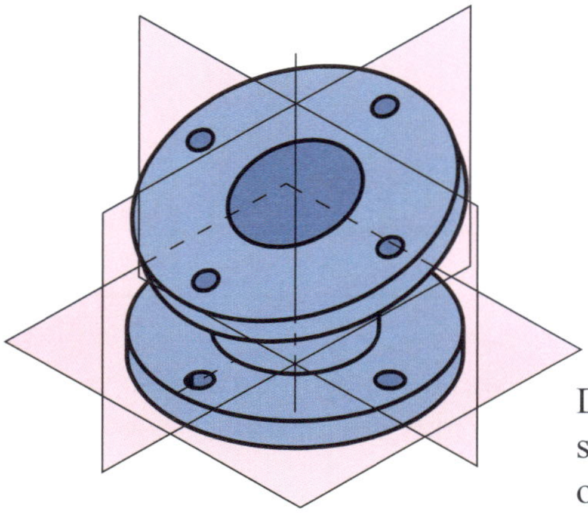

Datum feature A establishes a datum plane on the bottom surface. Datum features B and C create an axis and two orientation planes. The angularity tolerance zone is defined at basic 20 degrees to datum plane A and implied 90

Means this

1 mm profile zone basically **located** and **oriented** to the DRF established by datum features A, B, & C

⌓	1	A	B	C
∠	0.2	A	B	C

20°

30

0.2 angularity zone basically **oriented** to the DRF. The zone may translate back/forth and up/down, but the zone must remain at the basic angles (oriented) to the DRF.

Angularity is a 3D control; the tolerance zone is two parallel planes. Angularity tolerance applied to a plane surface also controls the flatness on the surface.

Sample Inspection

To verify the angularity requirement, the part is mounted on datum feature A, centered on datum feature B, and rotated to datum feature C. The part is then inclined at 20 degrees using a sine plate. The surface to be measured should now be near parallel to the surface plate. The full indicator movement on the surface should be no more than 0.2 (max-min).

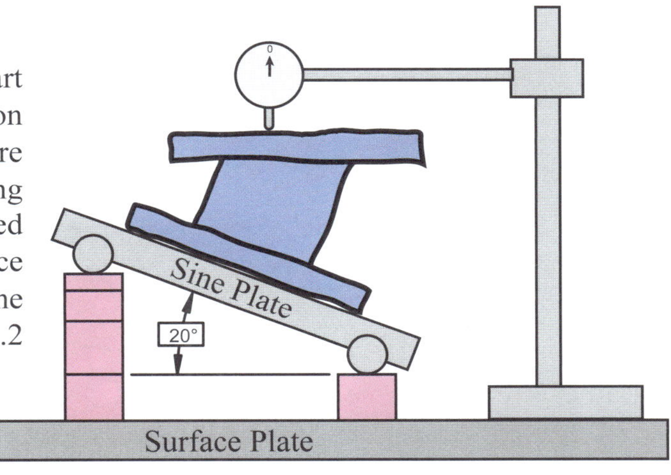

A CMM may be used to measure both the profile and angularity of the surface. The CMM first probes the datum features to establish the DRF. The basic dimensions or CAD data is imported to define the true profile. The CMM then measures and reports the surface deviations from true profile. These deviations are used to calculate the measured tolerance zones.

The CMM head may or may not rotate but probe must move normal to true profile (to avoid cosine error).

Measured profile value =
2*(max deviation) = 0.48 PASS

Measured angularity value =
max - min = 0.32 FAIL

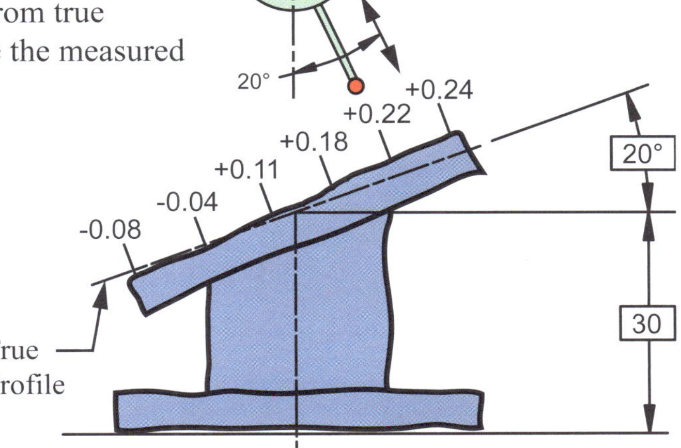

Perpendicularity on a Surface

Perpendicularity is the condition of a surface, median plane, or axis oriented at 90° to the datum reference frame.

This on the drawing

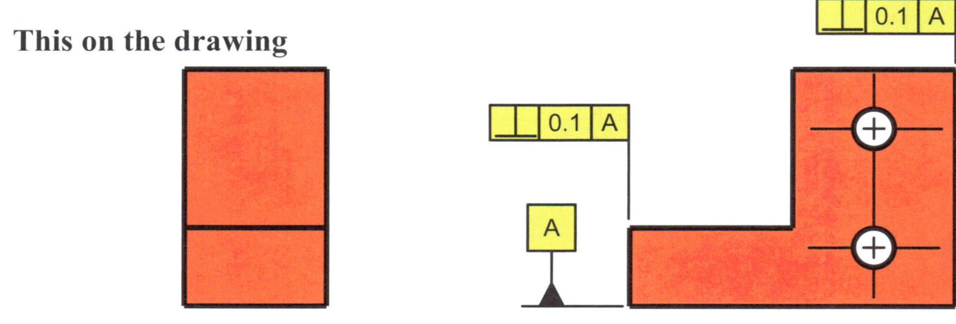

Application

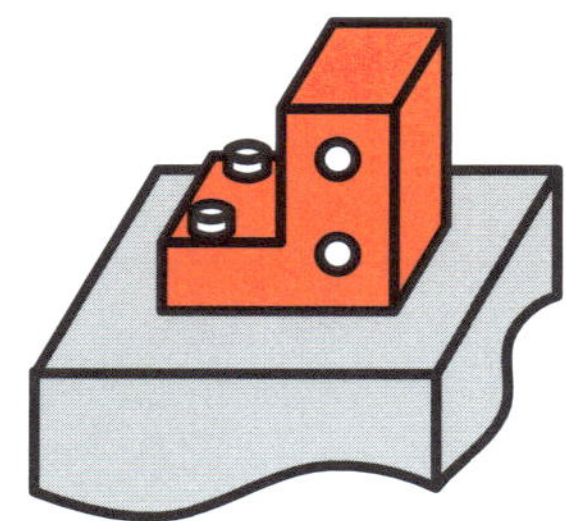

Two surfaces must be perpendicular when part is mounted on bottom surface.

Means this

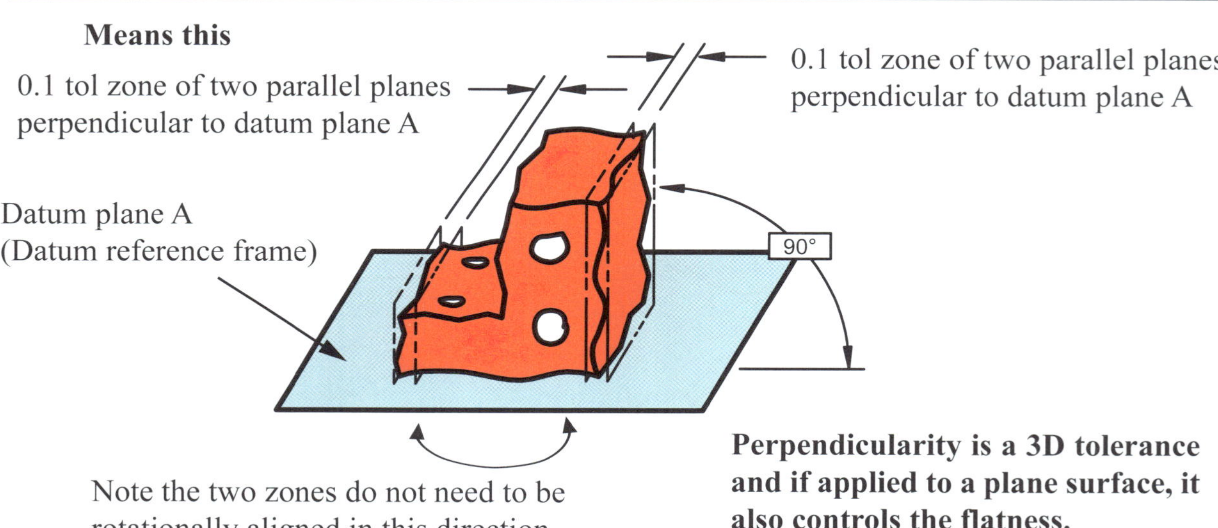

Perpendicularity is a 3D tolerance and if applied to a plane surface, it also controls the flatness.

Sample inspection

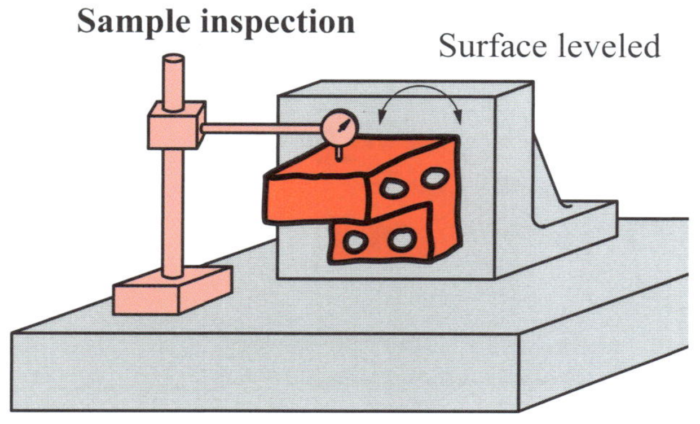

The part is mounted on datum feature A and the surface to be verified is leveled. The full indicator movement must not exceed 0.1 (max-min).

Perpendicularity Line Elements (2D)

By default, orientation tolerances are 3D. The note "EACH ELEMENT" placed under the feature control frame changes the orientation tolerance to a series of 2D tolerance zones. The direction of the tolerance zone applies normal to the surface and in the view where it is specified.

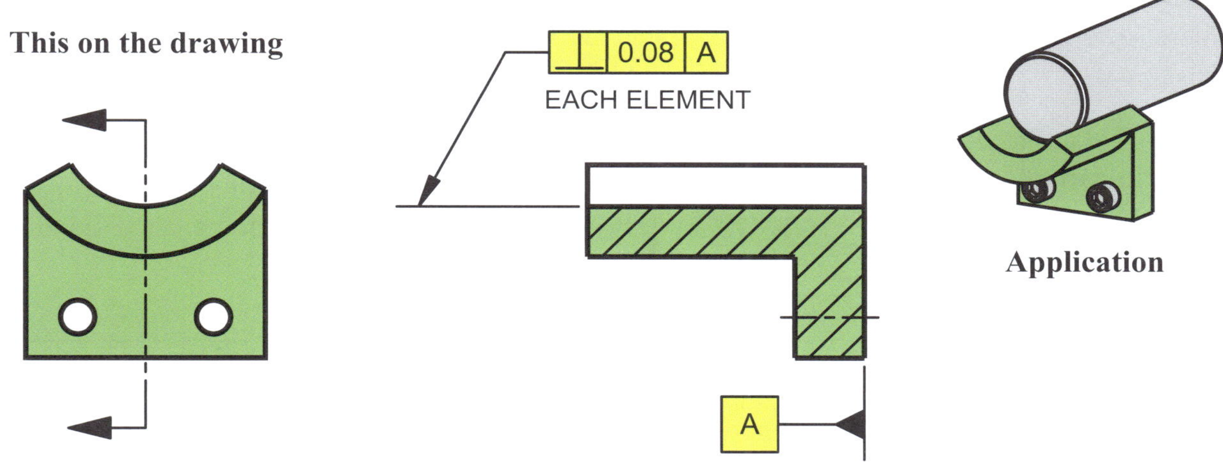

Each line element of the surface must lie between two parallel lines 0.08 apart which are oriented perpendicular to datum A. The cutting planes are normal to the true surface. In addition, the surface must lie within the applicable profile tolerance.

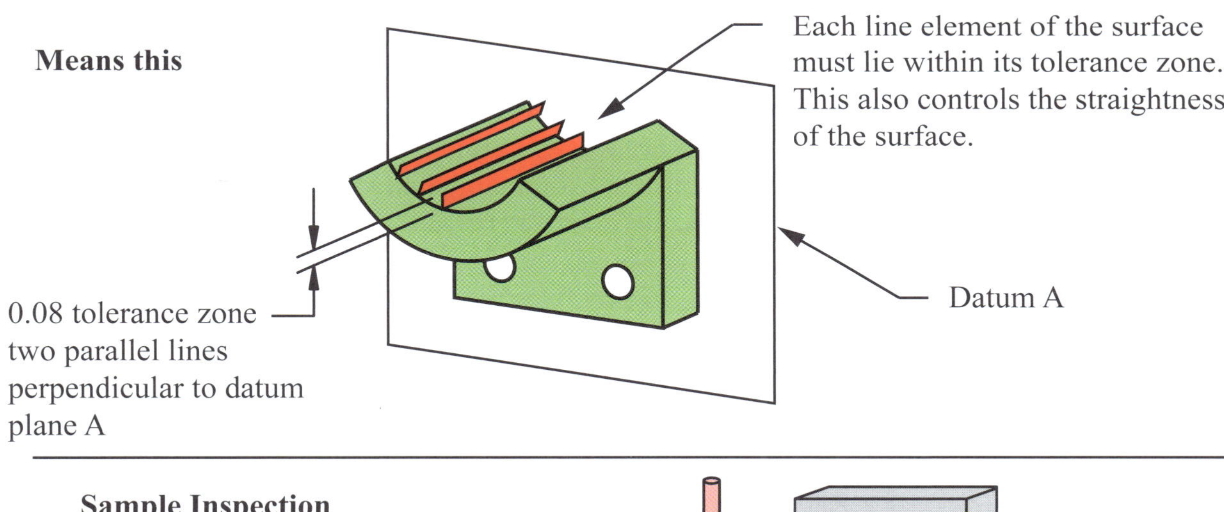

Sample Inspection

Part is mounted on datum feature A and the indicator is placed normal to the true surface. The FIM may be no more than 0.08 while evaluating each line element separately.

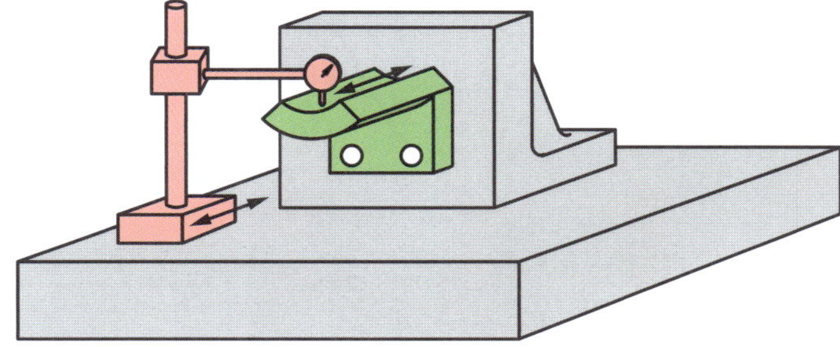

Note: Earlier versions of ASME Y14.5 expanded the 2D orientation control to each radial element around a datum axis. ASME Y14.5-2018 now recommends not to use orientation with "EACH RADIAL ELEMENT" because it invokes a translational degree of freedom that cannot be controlled by orientation tolerances. When control of radial elements is required, profile shall be used. See Y14.5-2018, sec 9.3.3.

Orientation with two Datum Feature References

Often multiple datum features need to be referenced to fully orient a feature. Orientation tolerance zones are constrained only in rotational degrees of freedom (not translational) relative to the datum reference frame. Thus, even where datum features may constrain all degrees of freedom, the tolerance zone only orients to that datum reference frame. On the part below, the angularity tolerance is refining the orientation set by the larger location tolerance (profile).

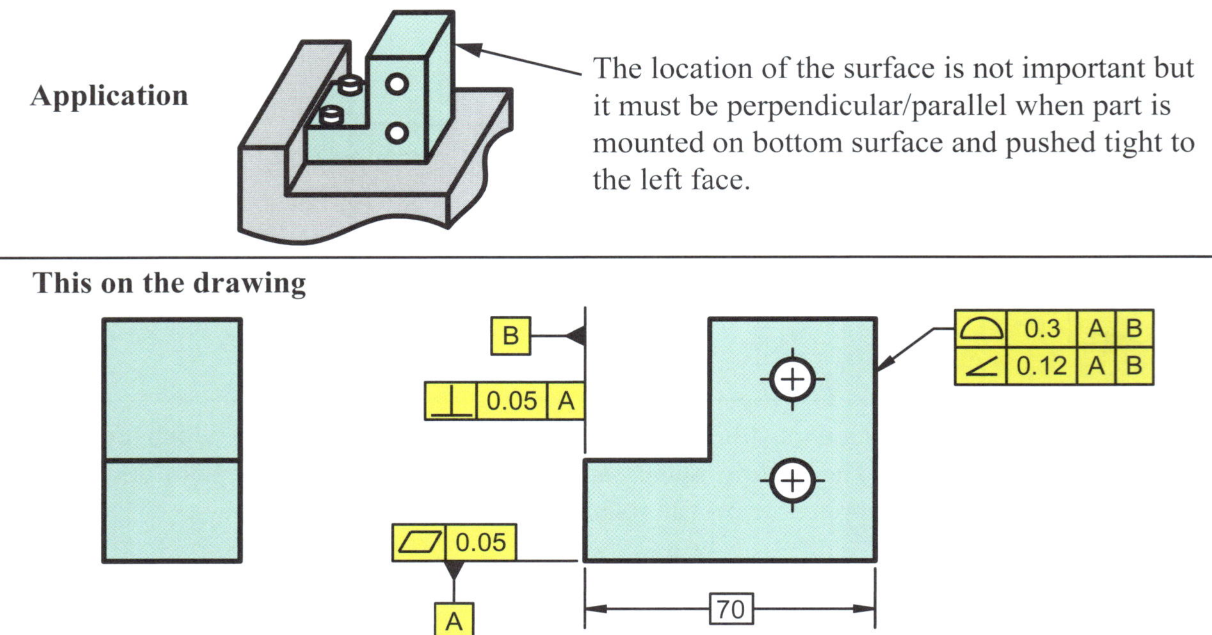

The ASME Y14.5 standard allows the use of the angularity symbol for all orientation tolerances. This practice sometimes makes the specification easier to understand. The right surface must be oriented to the datum reference frame established by datum features A primary and B secondary. The tolerance zone is oriented at the basic angle indicated (in this case implied 90° basic to A and implied 180° basic to B).

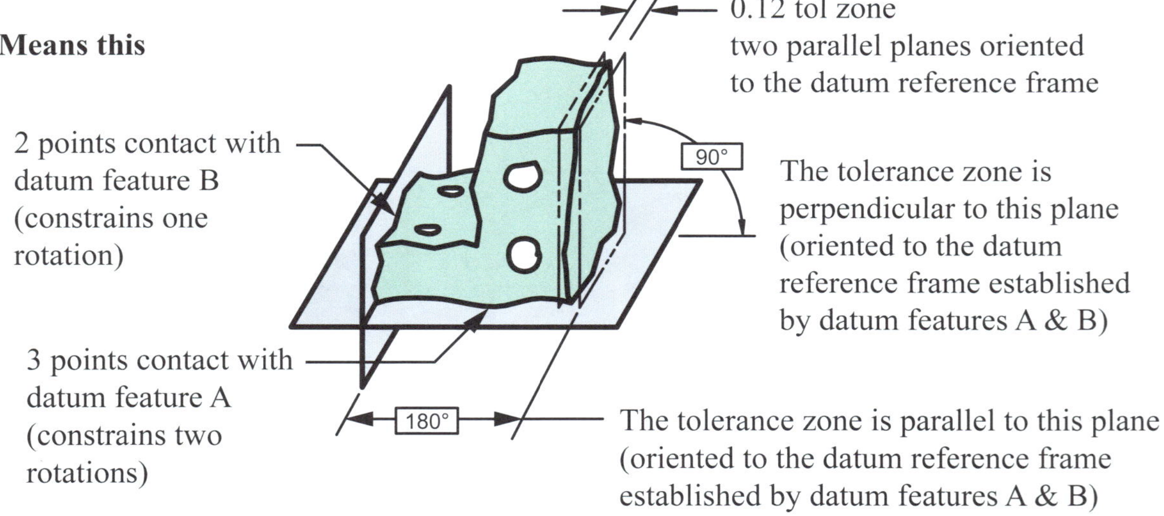

Note: Separate feature control frames on the drawing with a perpendicularity to A and a parallelism to B will yield different results. This will create two different primary datums and as a result have different inspection setups. This will not match the mounting conditions shown.

Orientation Inspection

Location tolerances are constrained in translational and rotational degrees of freedom. Therefore, the profile tolerance is fixed at the basic dimensions. Orientation tolerances are only constrained in rotational degrees of freedom and are free to translate (float). Since the high points of the left surface establish the datum B, this surface does not need a location tolerance.

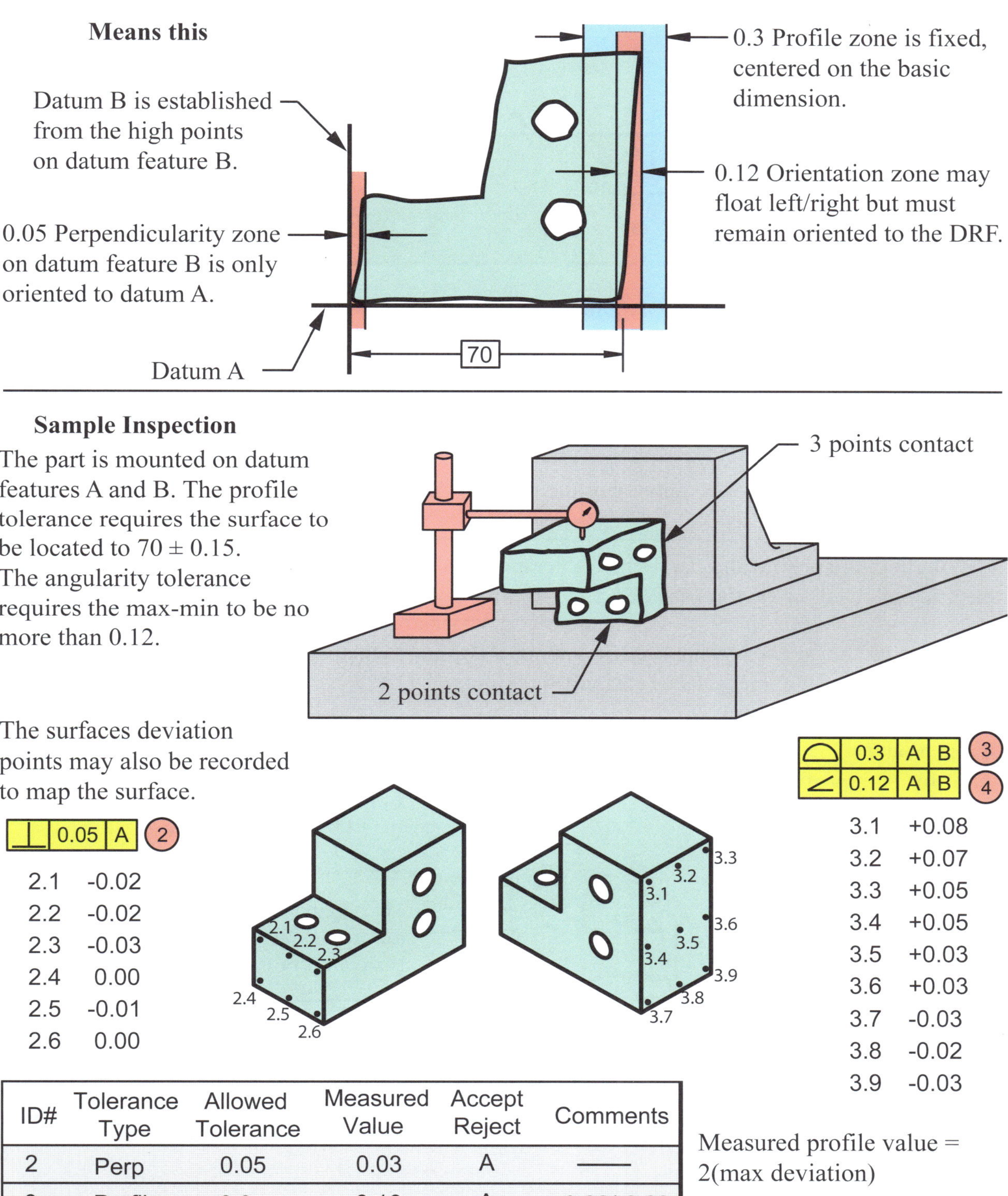

Sample Inspection

The part is mounted on datum features A and B. The profile tolerance requires the surface to be located to 70 ± 0.15. The angularity tolerance requires the max-min to be no more than 0.12.

The surfaces deviation points may also be recorded to map the surface.

Point	Deviation
2.1	-0.02
2.2	-0.02
2.3	-0.03
2.4	0.00
2.5	-0.01
2.6	0.00

Point	Deviation
3.1	+0.08
3.2	+0.07
3.3	+0.05
3.4	+0.05
3.5	+0.03
3.6	+0.03
3.7	-0.03
3.8	-0.02
3.9	-0.03

ID#	Tolerance Type	Allowed Tolerance	Measured Value	Accept Reject	Comments
2	Perp	0.05	0.03	A	——
3	Profile	0.3	0.16	A	+0.08/-0.03
4	Ang	0.12	0.11	A	——

Measured profile value = 2(max deviation)

Measured orientation value = max - min

Workshop Exercise 6.1

1. Name the three orientation tolerances. ______________________

2. Are datum feature references always required with orientation tolerances? ________

3. Which of the orientation symbols may be used in place of the other two symbols? ______

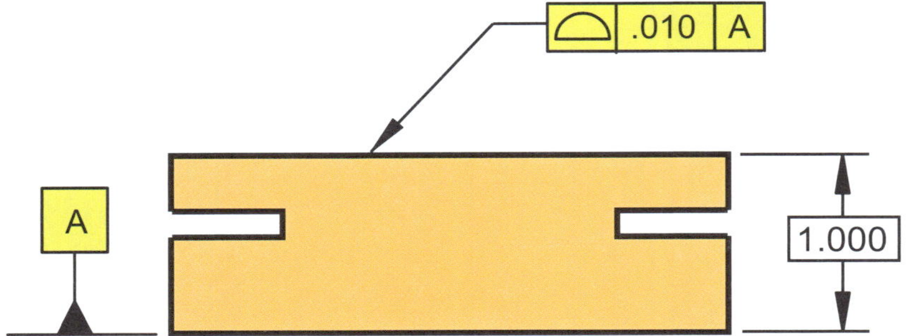

4. On the part above, what is the maximum variation in parallelism with only the profile applied? ______________

5. On the part above, specify a parallelism tolerance to make the top surface parallel to datum A within a total of .002. (draw a feature control frame above)

6. Can the MMC modifier be applied to the feature tolerance? Why or why not?

____

7. With both the profile and parallelism tolerance applied to the part above. What is the flatness tolerance allowed on the top surface? ______________

8. With both the profile and parallelism tolerance applied to the part above, what is the maximum height allowed of the top surface to datum A.

____

9. The produced part is below and measurement data points shown. What is the reported measured zones for both profile and parallelism?

Measured profile zone = ________

Measured parallelism zone = ________

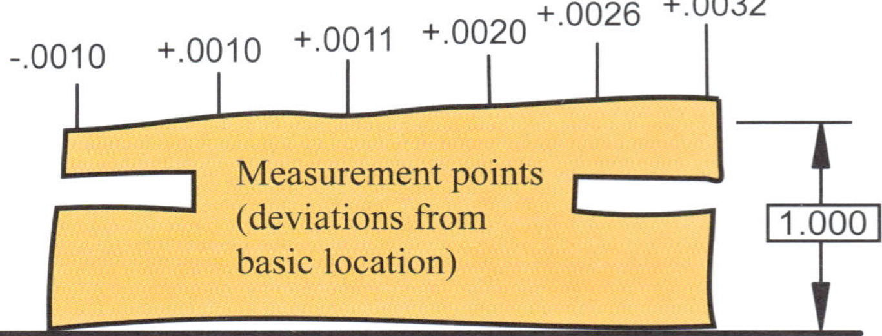

10. On the produced part above with the measurement points shown, the flatness value is difficult to calculate without best fitting. But, what can you expect the measured flatness to be?

a. Less than the profile and parallelism measured values

b. Less than the profile but greater than the parallelism measured values

c. Greater than the profile and parallelism measured values

d. Nothing can be inferred about the measured flatness

Workshop Exercise 6.2

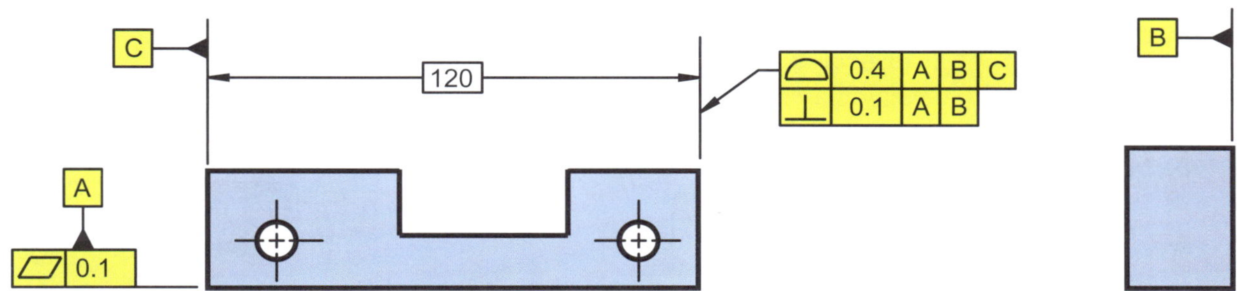

1. On the drawing above, draw a feature control frame to qualify datum feature B to relate it to higher precedence datum features. Use a tolerance value of 0.1.

2. On the drawing above, draw a feature control frame to qualify datum feature C to relate it to higher precedence datum features. Use a tolerance value of 0.1.

3. Can material condition modifiers (MMC or LMC) be applied to these feature control frames?

4. On the part above, what is the flatness requirement on the right surface? ______________

5. On the part above, what is the max length? ______________

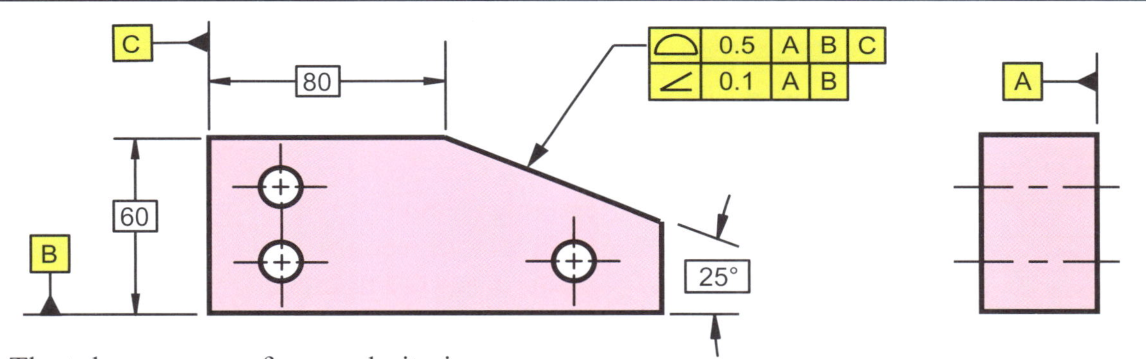

6. The tolerance zone for angularity is:

   a. two parallel planes fixed at the basic angle but allowed to translate

   b. two parallel planes fixed at the basic location and angle

   c. wedge shaped ± degrees and fixed at the basic angle but allowed to translate

   d. wedge shaped ± degrees and fixed at the basic location and angle

7. Below is the produced part and measurement points shown as deviations from true profile. What are the reported measured zones for both profile and angularity?

Measured profile zone = __________

Measured angularity zone = __________

Workshop Exercise 6.3

A partially completed drawing is shown below with an accompanying measurement plan. The specifications have been inspected and surface deviation points have been reported. Fill out the inspection report with the calculated measured value and Accept/Reject for each specification.

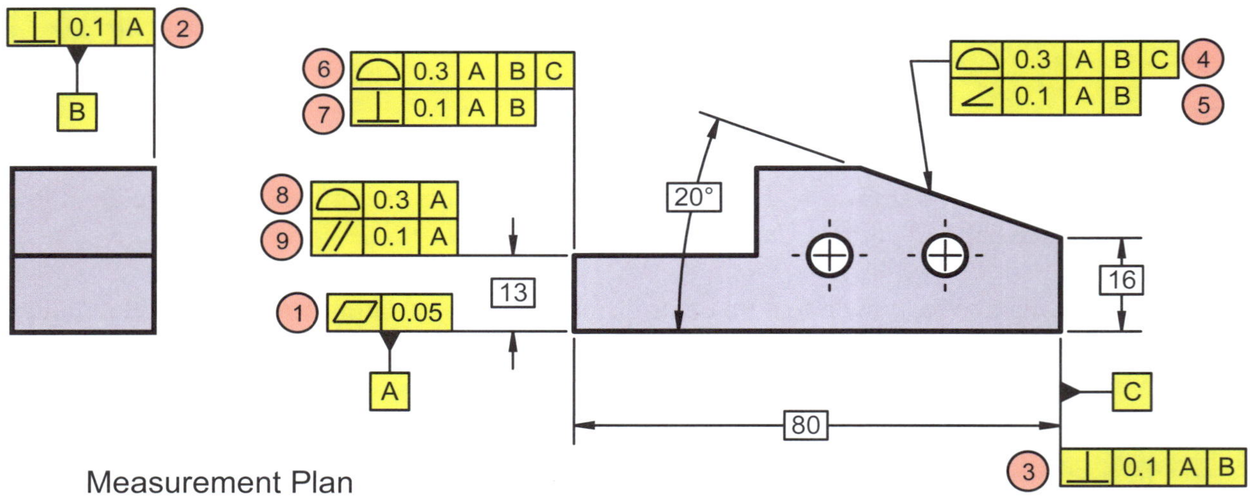

Measurement Plan

Use angle plate and surface plate to set up part against datum features. Use electronic height gage to measure all surface deviations.

ID#	Inspection Requirement	Reporting Method
3	4 locations shown	C
4	6 locations, rotate with sine bar	C
5	6 locations	B
6	4 locations shown	C
7	4 locations	B
8	4 locations shown	C
9	4 locations	B

Reporting method C from ASME Y14.45 requires variable data to be recorded.

Measured profile value = 2(max deviation)

Measured orientation value = max - min

Use the surface deviation points to calculate the measured values and Accept/Reject for each specification.

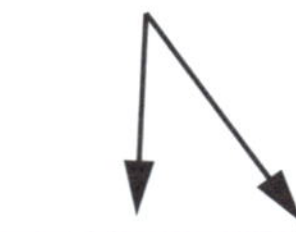

Surface deviation points

3.1 -0.02
3.2 -0.01
3.3 -0.01
3.4 0.0

4.1 -0.02
4.2 -0.01
4.3 -0.02
4.4 +0.06
4.5 +0.08
4.6 +0.10

6.1 -0.12
6.2 -0.11
6.3 -0.10
6.4 -0.12

8.1 +0.14
8.2 +0.12
8.3 +0.08
8.4 +0.06

Inspection Report

ID#	Tolerance Type	Allowed Tolerance	Measured Value	Accept Reject
3	Perp	0.1		
4	Prof	0.3		
5	Ang	0.1		
6	Prof	0.3		
7	Perp	0.1		
8	Prof	0.3		
9	Paral	0.1		

Orientation of a Hole

The part below is mounted by aligning the three surfaces shown and fastened with the two screws. This example shows a hole with an orientation tolerance as a refinement of the position tolerance. All locating dimensions are basic and defined in the CAD model.

Application

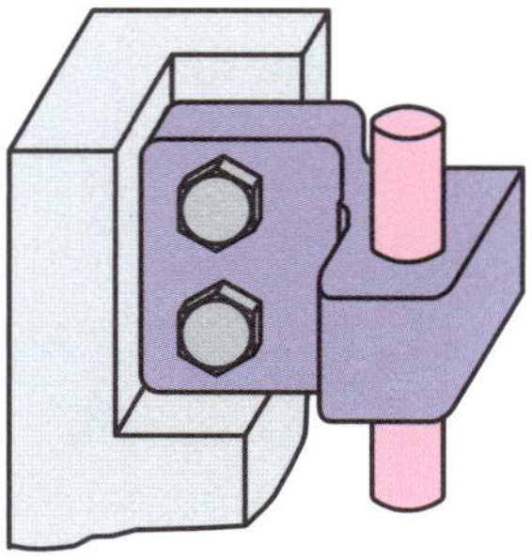

The three aligned mounting surfaces are selected as the datum features. The location of the .313 hole is not important and is given a relatively large .010 position tolerance. The position tolerance also controls the orientation (tilt) of the hole. Because the orientation of the hole is more important, a tighter parallelism tolerance is added.

This on the drawing

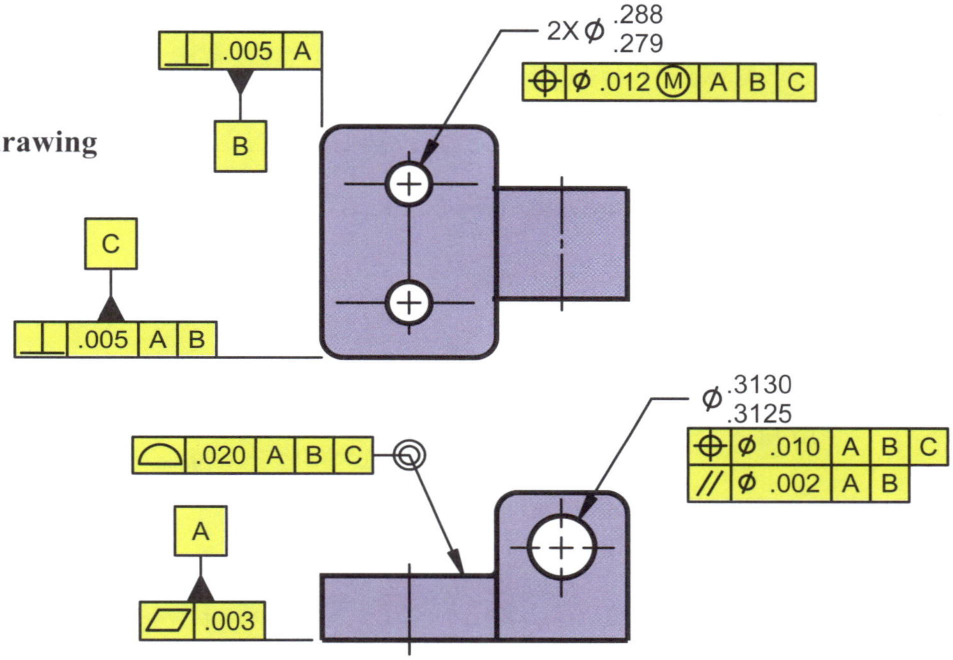

2X ⌀ .288 .279

⌖ | ⌀ .012 Ⓜ | A | B | C

⊥ | .005 | A

B

C

⊥ | .005 | A | B

⌀ .3130 .3125

⌖ | ⌀ .010 | A | B | C

// | ⌀ .002 | A | B

⌓ | .020 | A | B | C

A

⏥ | .003

SEE CAD FILE FOR
BASIC DIMENSIONS

Means this

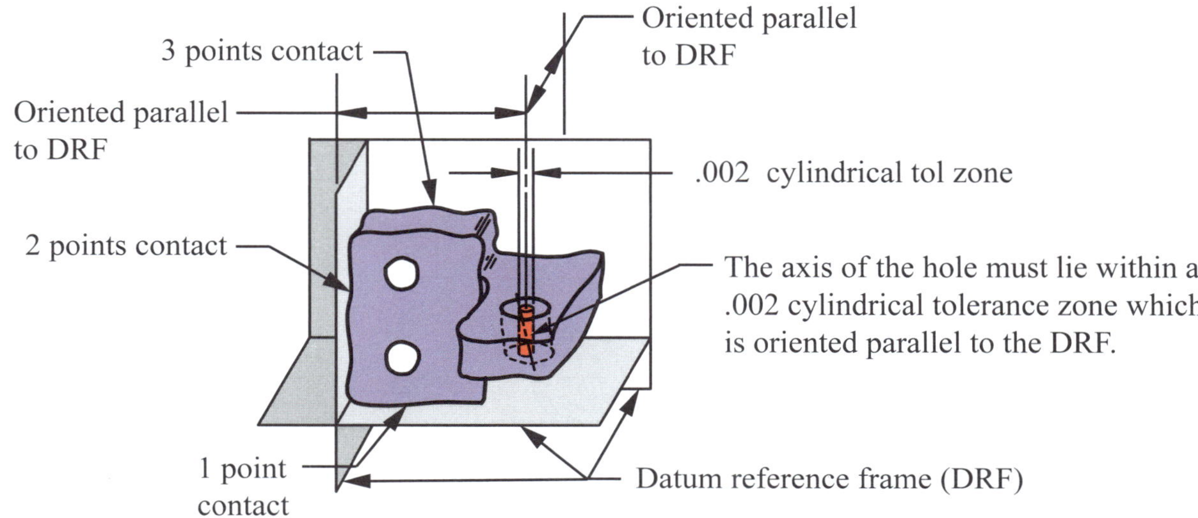

Orientation of a Hole - Tolerance Zones and Inspection Reports

Shown below are tolerance zones created by the location and refined orientation specifications.

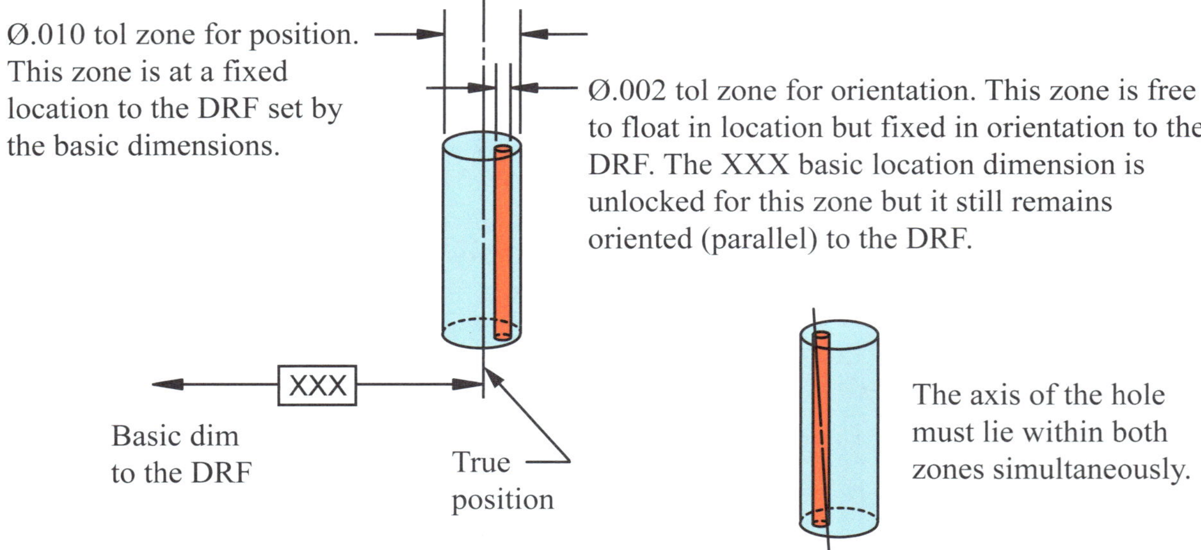

For inspection, the part is first aligned to the datum reference frame A,B,C. The axis of the hole is found at both the front and back of the hole. These X,Y locations are recorded as deviations from true position.

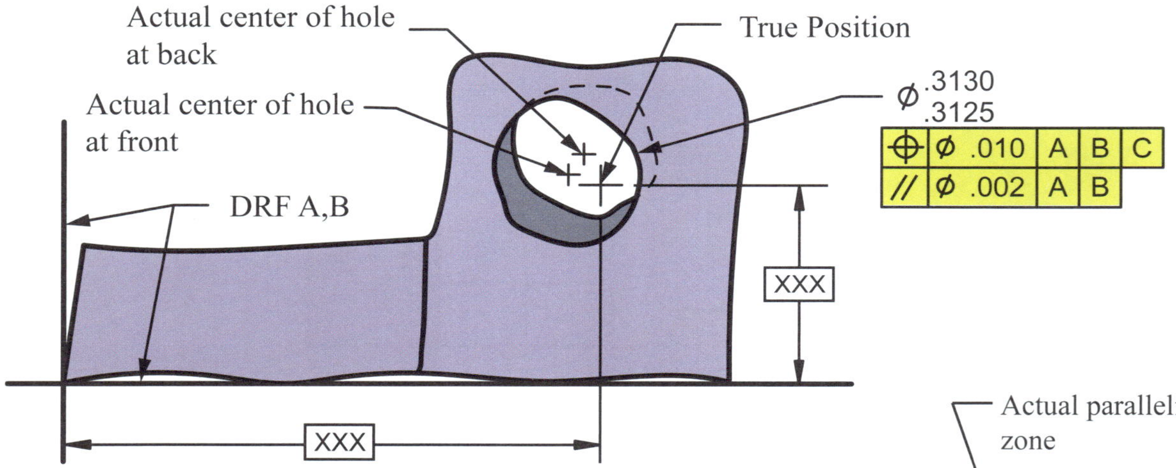

Actual center of hole at back

Actual center of hole at front

True Position

DRF A,B

Ø .3130 .3125

⌖	Ø .010	A	B	C
//	Ø .002	A	B	

XXX

XXX

Actual parallelism zone

X_B, Y_B

X_F, Y_F

5 4 3 2 1 Y+ 1 2 3 4 5

X- X+

Y-

Actual position zone

See unit 5 for how X,Y deviations are calculated

	Allowed ⌖	XDev	YDev	Actual ⌖	Pass/Fail
X_F, Y_F (Axis Front)	.010	-.003	+.002	.0072	Pass
X_B, Y_B (Axis Back)	.010	-.002	+.004	.0089	Pass

Actual position = $2\sqrt{x^2 + y^2}$

$\Delta X = X_{Max} - X_{Min}$

$\Delta Y = Y_{Max} - Y_{Min}$

Allowed //	ΔX	ΔY	Actual //	Pass/Fail
.002	.001	.002	.0022	Fail

Actual parallelism = $\sqrt{\Delta x^2 + \Delta y^2}$

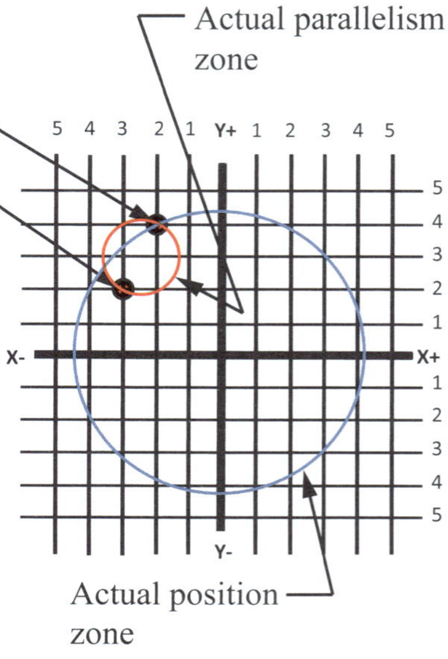

Orientation to a Datum Reference Frame

This example is to reinforce the idea that tolerances are related to the datum reference frame established by the datum features, not the datum features themselves. Datum features are selected based on the functional requirements. For this example, the mounting face is selected as datum feature A and the two mounting holes are selected as datum feature B. For the .313 hole, an angularity is used to refine the position instead of a parallelism.

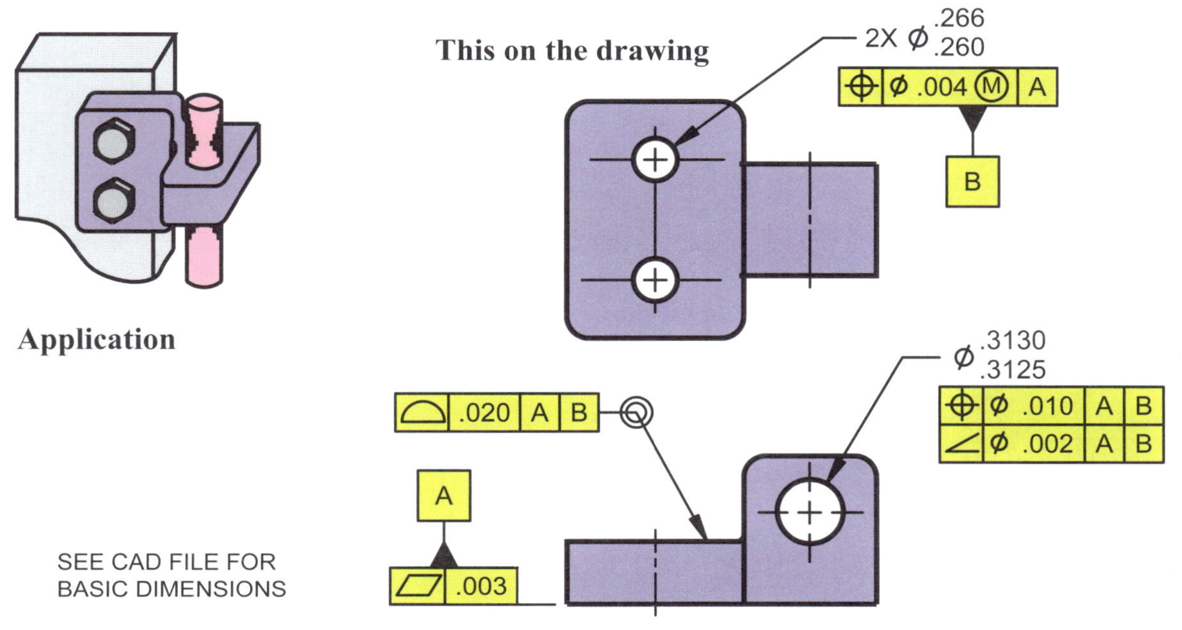

The back face establishes a primary datum plane. The two mounting holes constrain the remaining three degrees of freedom to create the DRF.

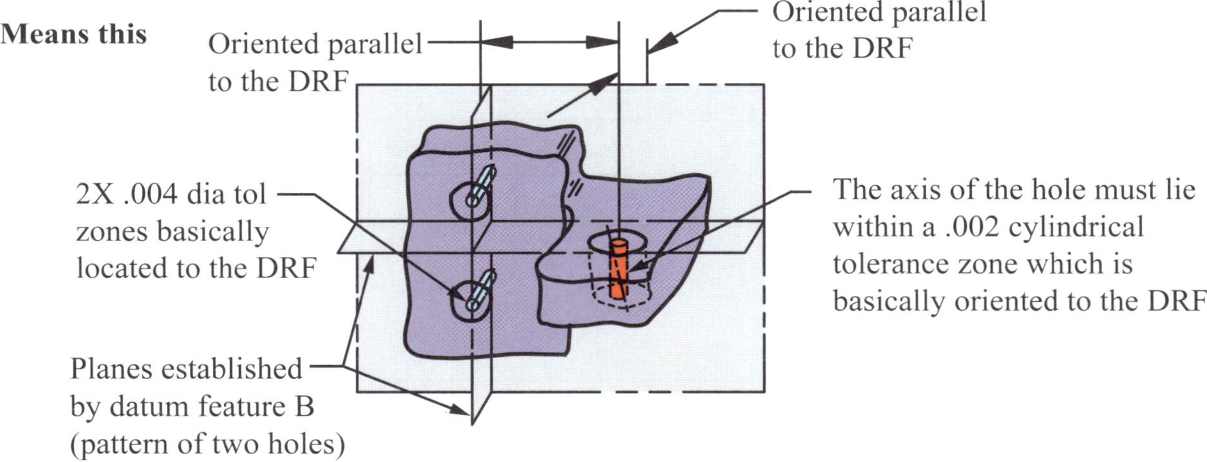

This orientation specification also reinforces the discussion in the overview in the beginning of this unit. As the orientation requirements on the part becomes more complex and is related to more than one datum feature, it is difficult to decide whether to use a parallelism, perpendicularity, or angularity. In the final analysis, it probably does not matter which symbol is used. This is why in the ASME Y14.5 standard, the angularity symbol may be used to control the orientation of a feature at any angle specified.

Workshop Exercise 6.4

The two pins below have both a position and refined orientation (perpendicularity) specification. During inspection, the part is first aligned to the datum reference frame A,B,C. The location of the axis is found at both the top (Z=.500) and bottom (Z=.000). These X,Y locations are recorded as deviations from true position in the report.

1. Use the measurement data given to determine the actual values and pass/fail.

2. Plot the axis center points on the paper gages on the right. Draw and label the resulting position and perpendicularity tolerance zones on the graph.

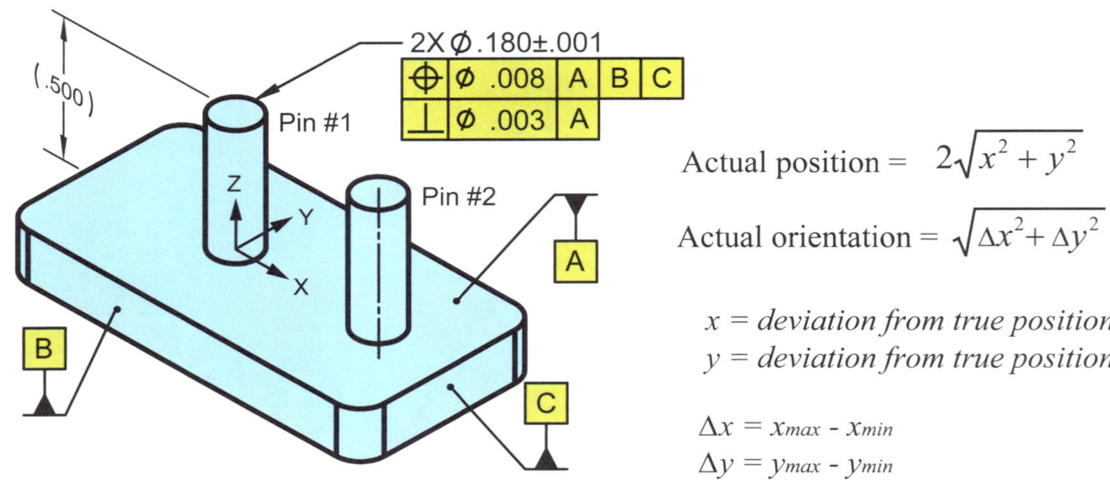

$$\text{Actual position} = 2\sqrt{x^2 + y^2}$$

$$\text{Actual orientation} = \sqrt{\Delta x^2 + \Delta y^2}$$

x = deviation from true position
y = deviation from true position

$\Delta x = x_{max} - x_{min}$
$\Delta y = y_{max} - y_{min}$

Pin #1

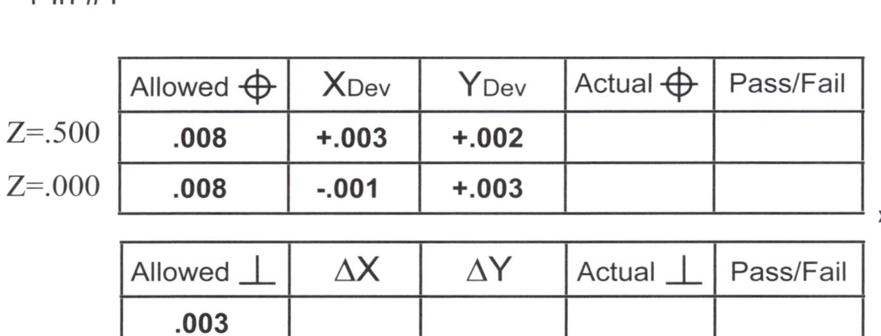

	Allowed ⌖	XDev	YDev	Actual ⌖	Pass/Fail
Z=.500	**.008**	**+.003**	**+.002**		
Z=.000	**.008**	**-.001**	**+.003**		

Allowed ⊥	ΔX	ΔY	Actual ⊥	Pass/Fail
.003				

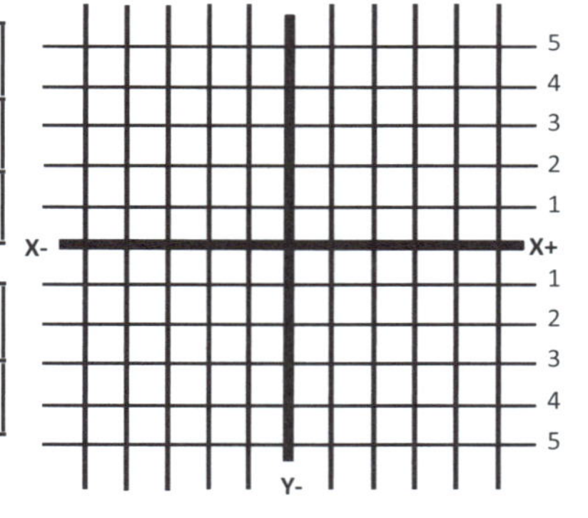

Pin #2

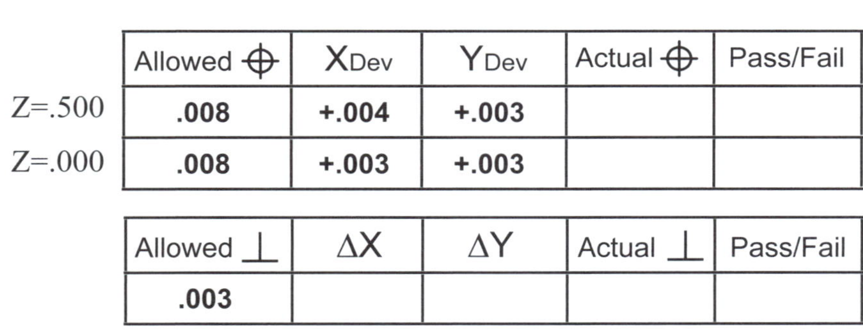

	Allowed ⌖	XDev	YDev	Actual ⌖	Pass/Fail
Z=.500	**.008**	**+.004**	**+.003**		
Z=.000	**.008**	**+.003**	**+.003**		

Allowed ⊥	ΔX	ΔY	Actual ⊥	Pass/Fail
.003				

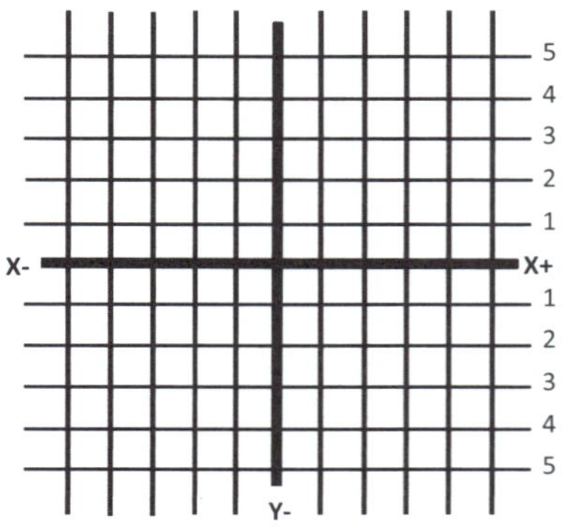

GeoTol Summary and Hierarchy of Tolerances

Geometric tolerancing is a feature-based tolerancing system. There are two types of features: features without size (surface) and features of size (hole, slot, tab, pin). The size, form, orientation, and location of these features must be controlled relative to a datum reference frame. Position and profile tolerances are the most powerful geometric tolerances. Other tolerances may be added to refine but are not always necessary.

A surface (feature without size) can vary in three ways:

⌓ **Location -** distance to a DRF
// **Orientation -** tilt/angle to a DRF
⏥ **Form -** shape to itself

A profile tolerance controls all types of variation.
An orientation tolerance may be added to refine.
A flatness tolerance may be added to refine.

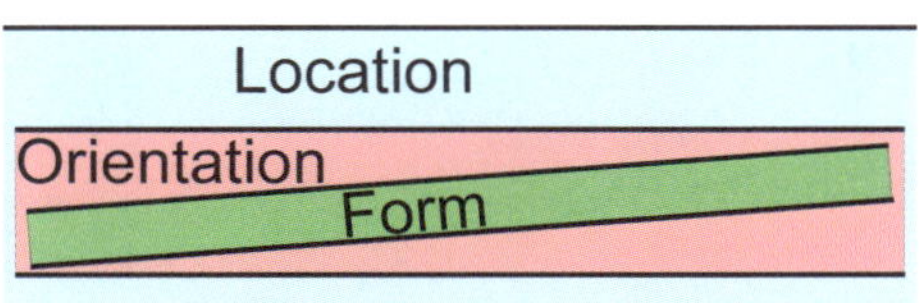

Datum features are unique features because they establish the location and orientation constraints for the DRF. Therefore, they do not always need location or orientation tolerances.

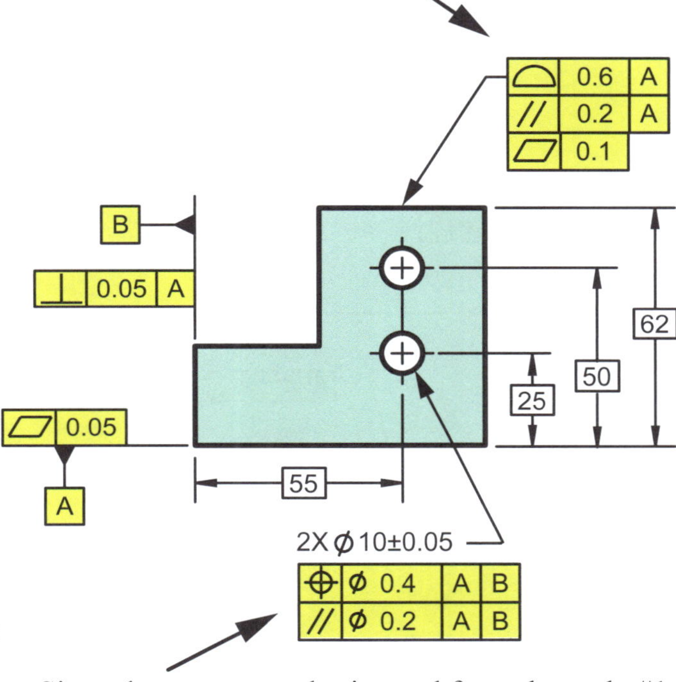

A feature of size can vary in four ways:

±0.05 **Size -** big/small to itself
Form - shape to itself

⌖ **Location -** distance to a DRF
// **Orientation -** tilt/angle to a DRF

Size tolerance controls size and form thru rule #1.
A form tolerance may be added to refine.

Position controls location and orientation to the DRF.
An orientation tolerance may be added to refine.

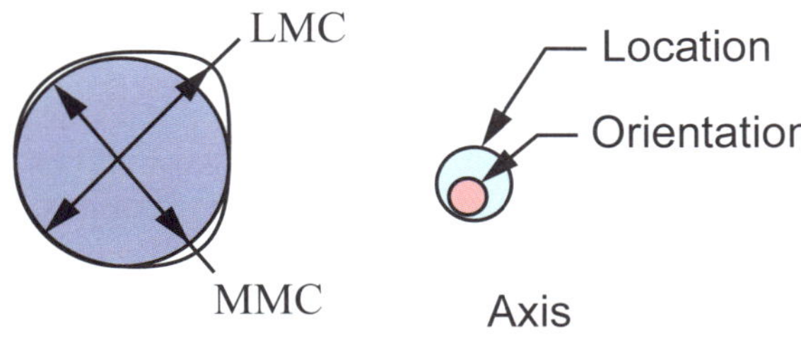

ϕ10

Note: a feature of size may have a basic dimension for the size, and profile controls all variation: size, form, orientation and location to the DRF. See unit 13 for examples.

Geometric Tolerancing Practical Application

These two drawings of a gear box housing and lid are used as examples to practice reading geometric tolerancing. The parts fit together by mating to the front and back surface and align using two alignment pins into the hole and slot. The larger center holes locate bushings and mating gears. A good tolerancing scheme should communicate the function of how the parts fit and identify important features to manufacturing and inspection.

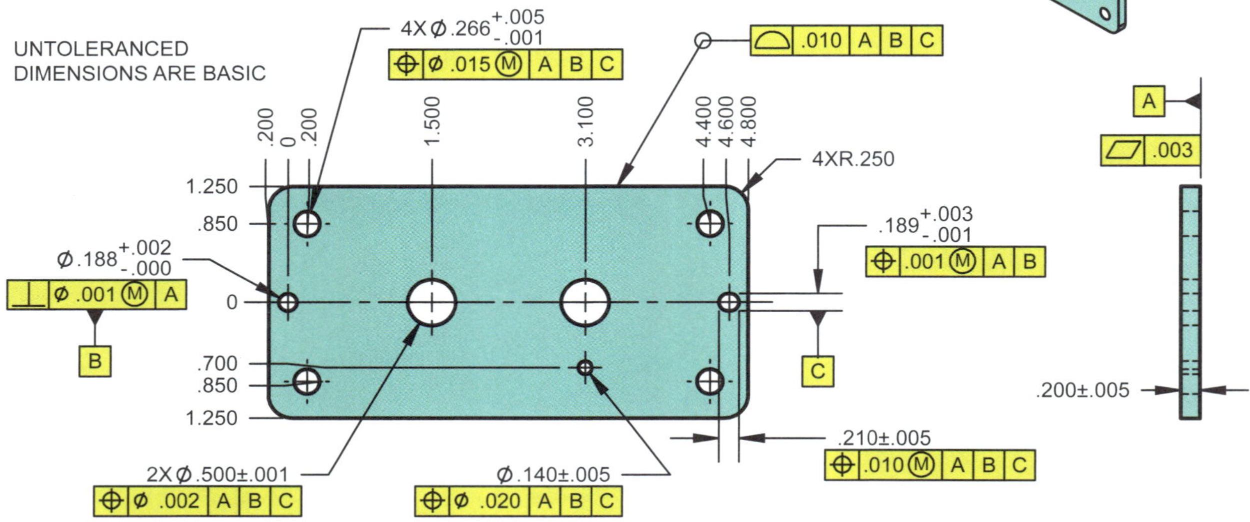

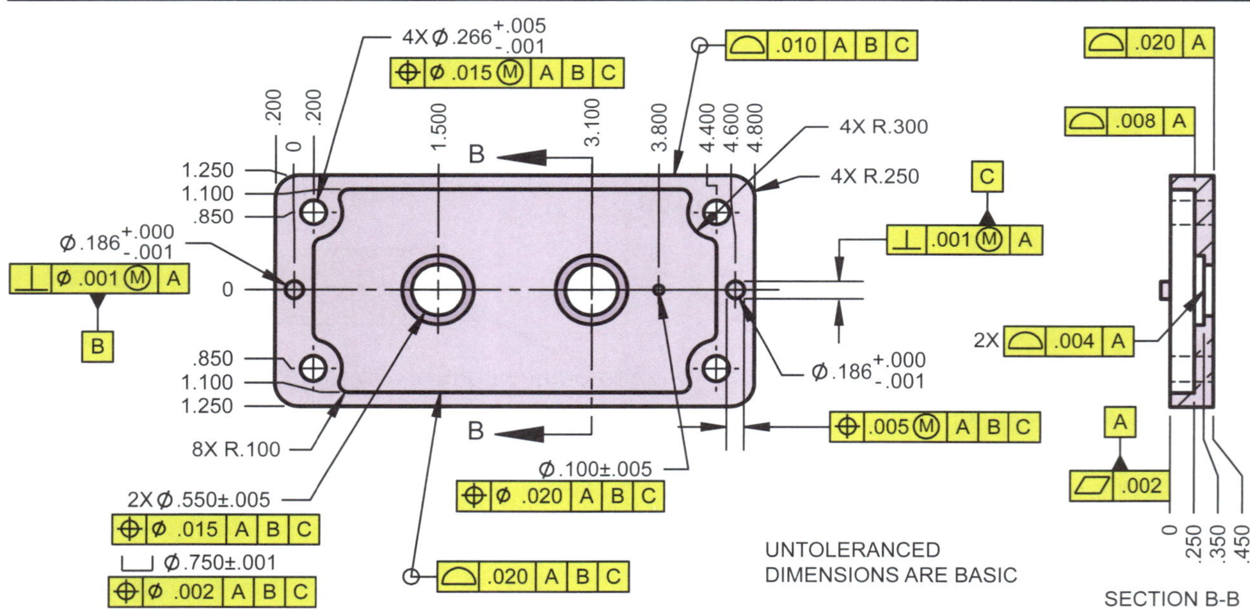

Notice the datum reference frame ABC on the two parts match. The datum features are qualified to each other and the virtual conditions of the pins and holes allow proper fits. The location tolerances of position and profile are applied to the remaining features to insure functionality. Tight tolerances (.001-.004) are applied to critical features, medium tolerances (.005-.010) are applied to moderately important features, and loose tolerances (.015-.020) are applied to unimportant features. Geometric tolerancing is applied to a design drawing to communicate the functional engineering requirements. This should influence manufacturing and inspection and allow them to produce and inspect a better part.

Unit 7

Virtual Condition and Material Boundary Modifiers

Virtual Condition

The Hub drawing from unit 5 is shown again below along with the mating part. The features are controlled using a size tolerance and geometric tolerance with an MMC modifier. The collective effect of both of these tolerances create a worst case boundary called the virtual condition (VC). The virtual conditions can be calculated to insure a proper fit with the mating part. See the next page for explanations and formulas for the calculations.

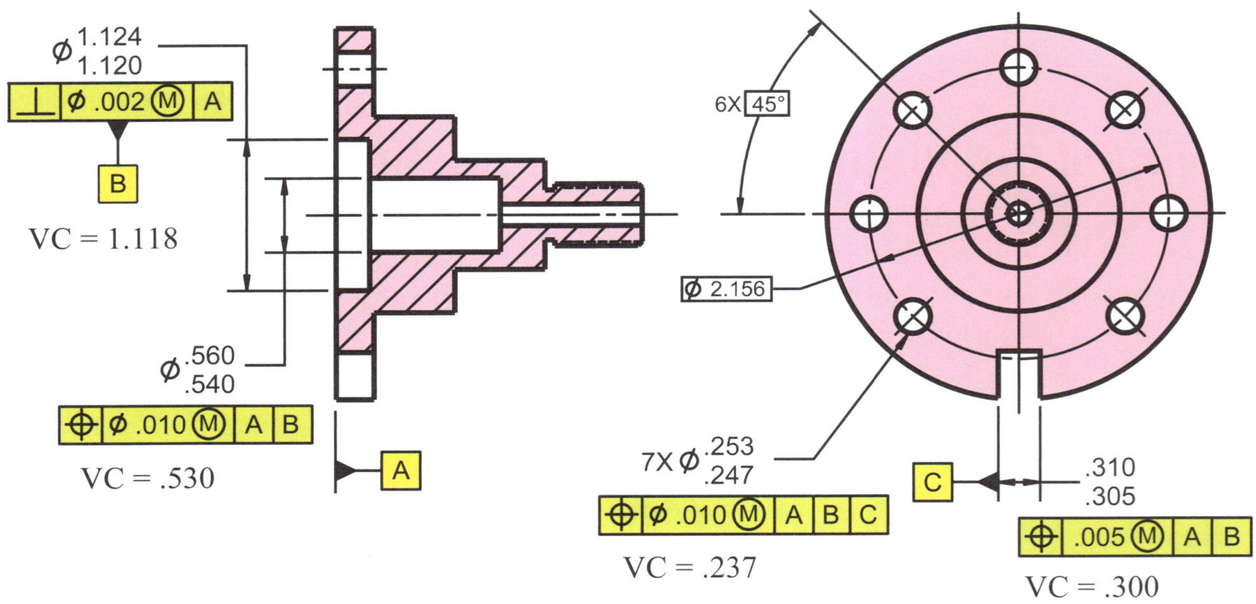

The virtual conditions for the internal features on the Hub match the virtual conditions for the external features on the mating part. The calculations are shown at line-to-line worst case. Sometimes clearances are also designed between these virtual conditions to allow ease of assembly and disassembly.

Hub Mating Part

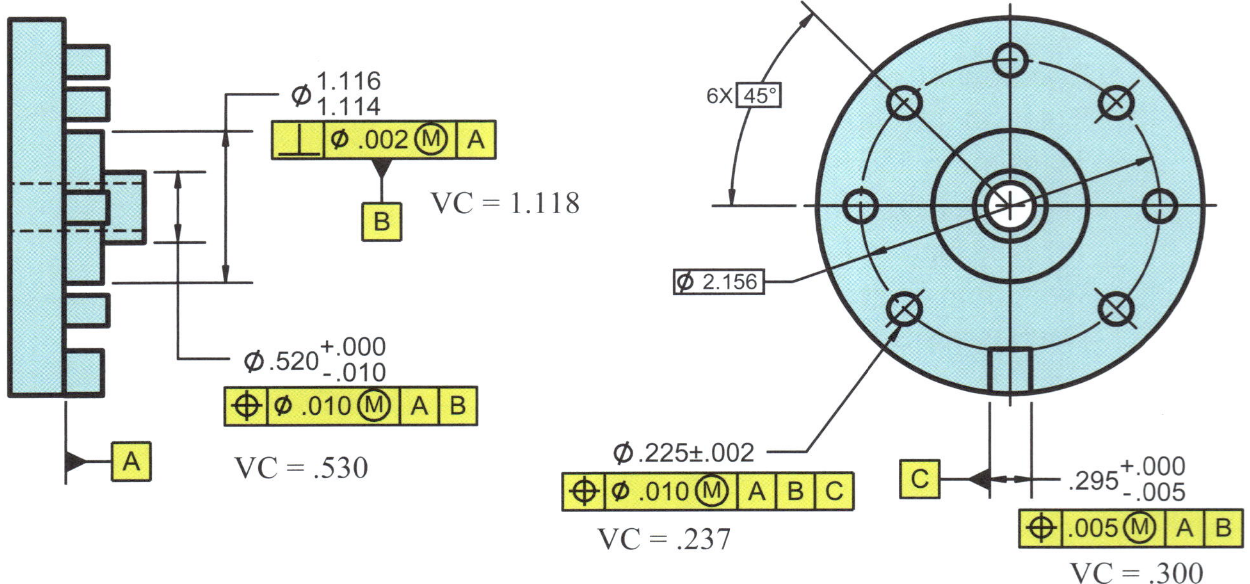

The smallest possible hole is MMC Ø .247, but when this hole is off position by Ø .010 in all possible locations, the worst case boundary created is the virtual condition, Ø .237. This calculation can be used to guarantee interchangeability with a mating part or design a functional gage element or CMM inspection.

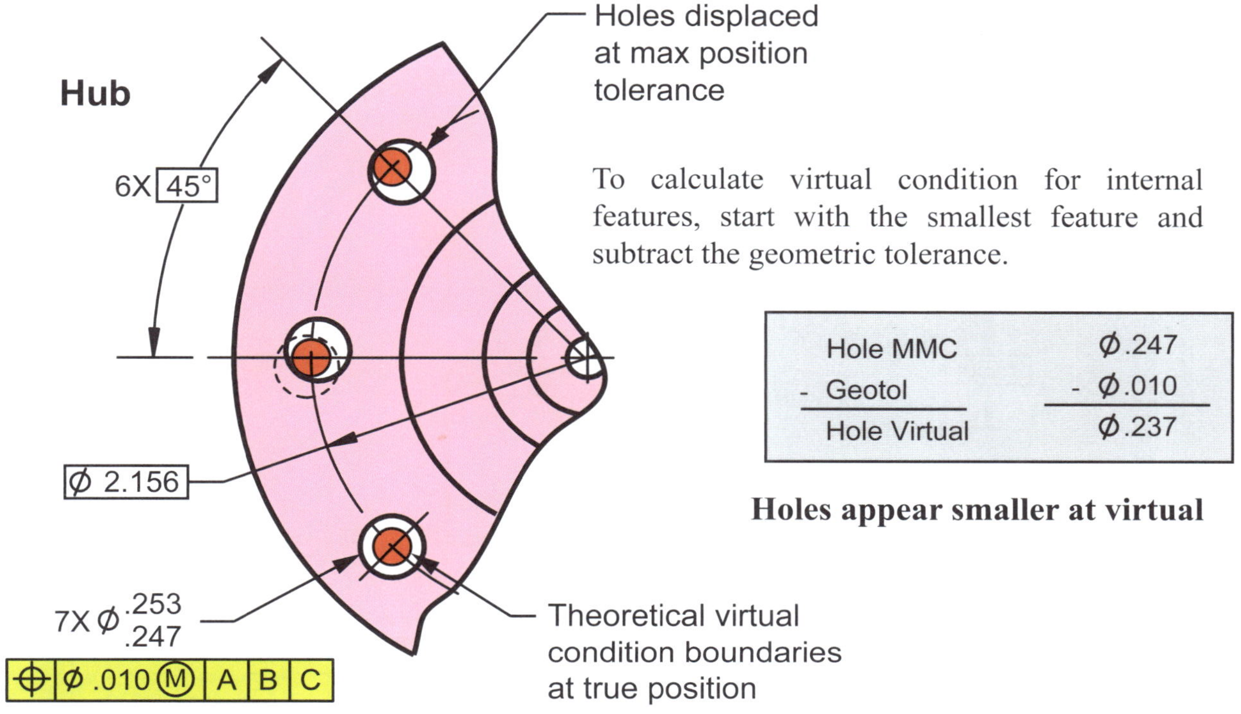

To calculate virtual condition for internal features, start with the smallest feature and subtract the geometric tolerance.

Hole MMC	Ø.247
- Geotol	- Ø.010
Hole Virtual	Ø.237

Holes appear smaller at virtual

The biggest possible pin is MMC Ø .227, but when this pin is off position by Ø .010 in all possible locations, the worst case boundary created is the virtual condition, Ø .237. This calculation can be used to guarantee interchangeability with a mating part or design a functional gage element or CMM inspection.

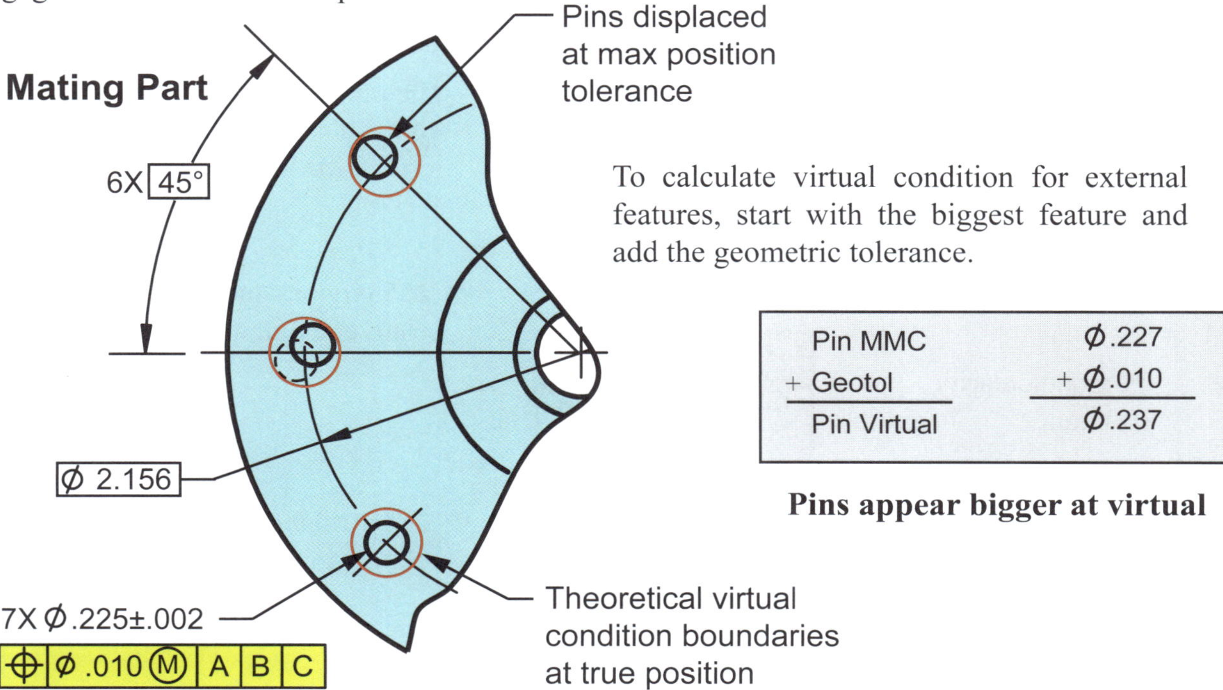

To calculate virtual condition for external features, start with the biggest feature and add the geometric tolerance.

Pin MMC	Ø.227
+ Geotol	+ Ø.010
Pin Virtual	Ø.237

Pins appear bigger at virtual

Virtual Condition - Multiple Feature Control Frames

Virtual condition is a constant boundary generated by the collective effects of size and the geometric tolerance applied. Sometimes, features may have multiple geometric controls. This will create multiple virtual conditions.

The pin below has a size tolerance and two feature control frames applied, and therefore two virtual condition boundaries exist. The .255 diameter virtual condition relative to datum A is a result of the perpendicularity tolerance. The .265 diameter virtual condition relative to datums A, B, and C is a result of the position tolerance.

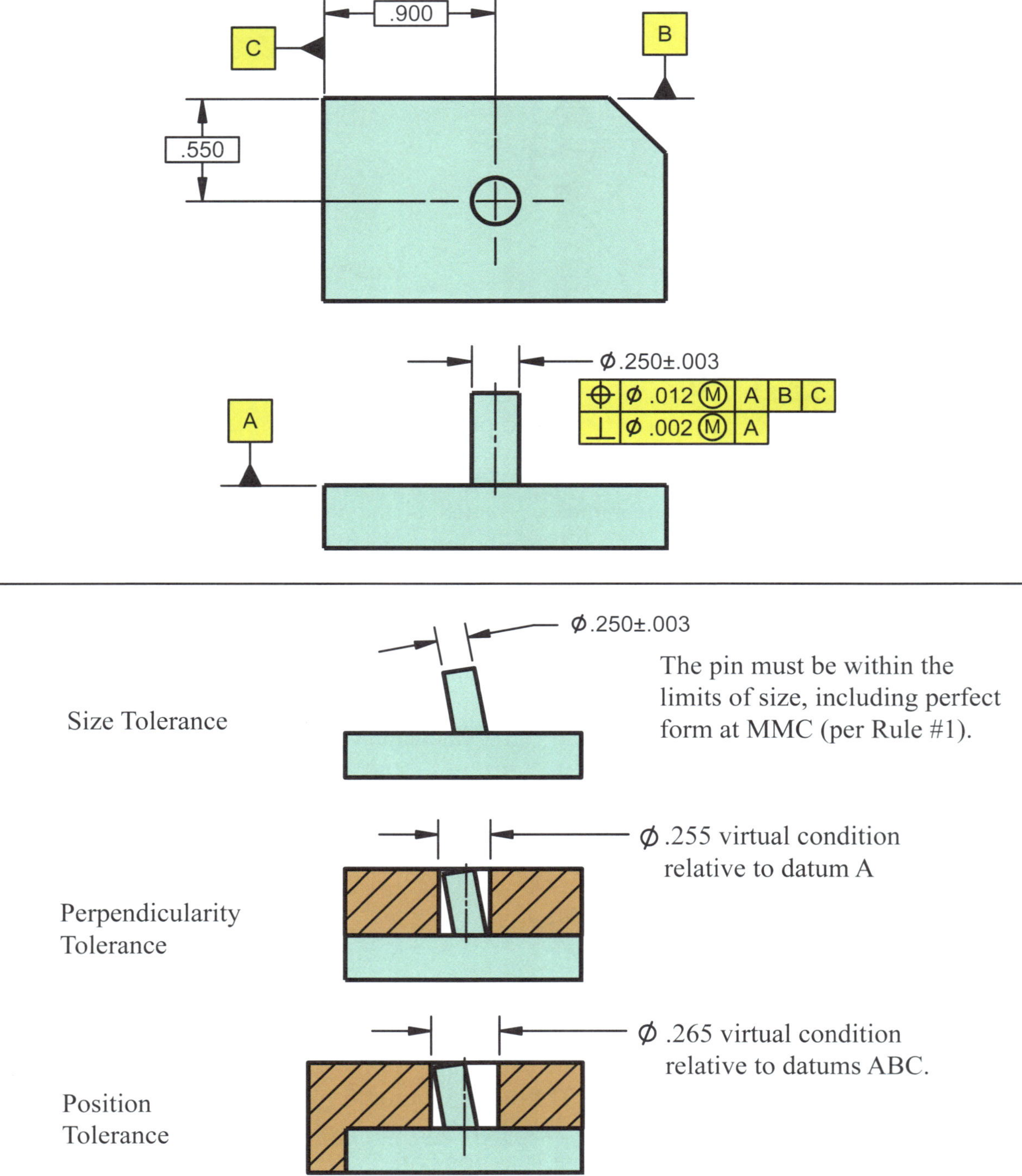

Workshop Exercise 7.1

The two parts below are produced by two different suppliers and must always fit together. Calculate the virtual conditions for the pins and holes. Then evaluate if they are guaranteed to assemble.

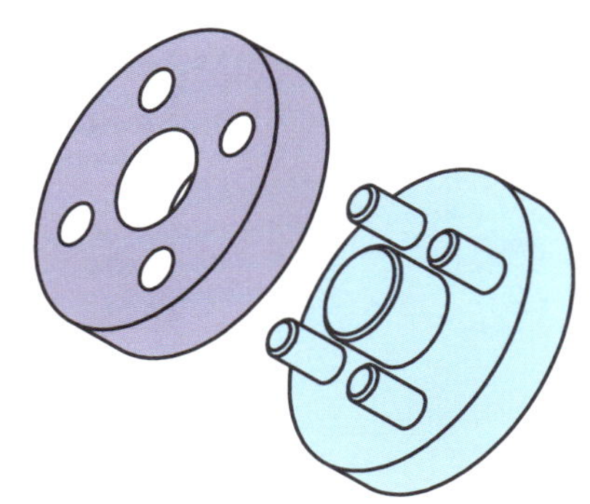

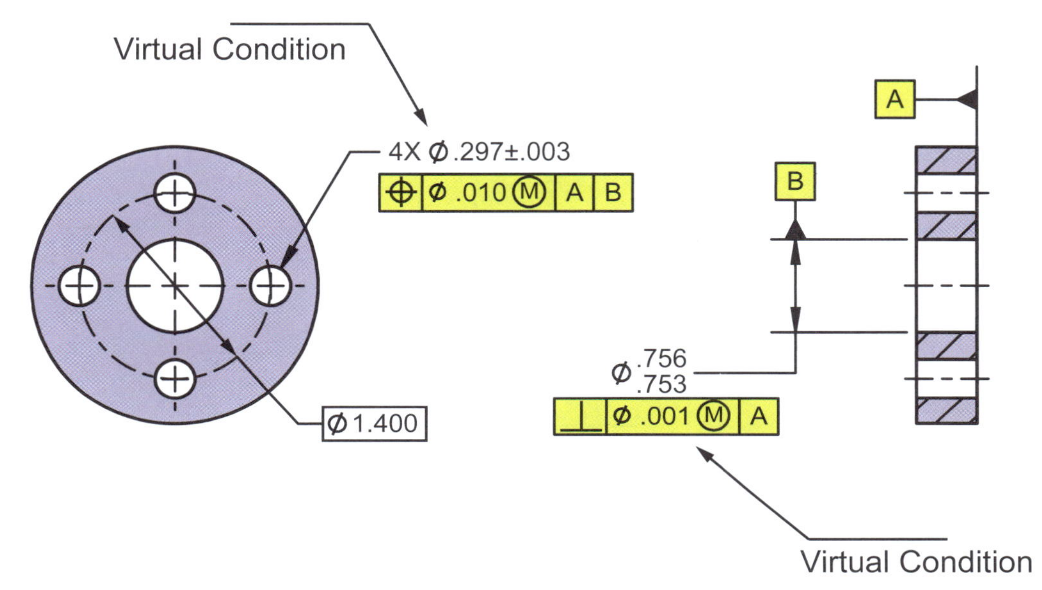

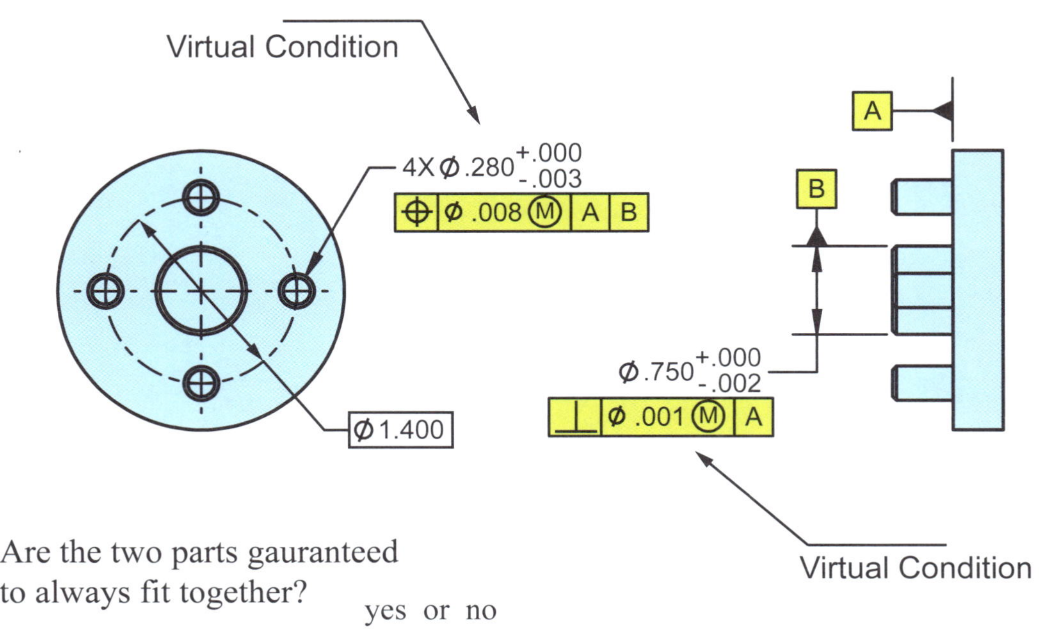

Are the two parts gauranteed to always fit together? yes or no

Workshop Exercise 7.2

Multiple geometric controls for a feature of size create multiple virtual conditions. On the drawing below, calculate the virtual condition for each of the geometric tolerance specifications.

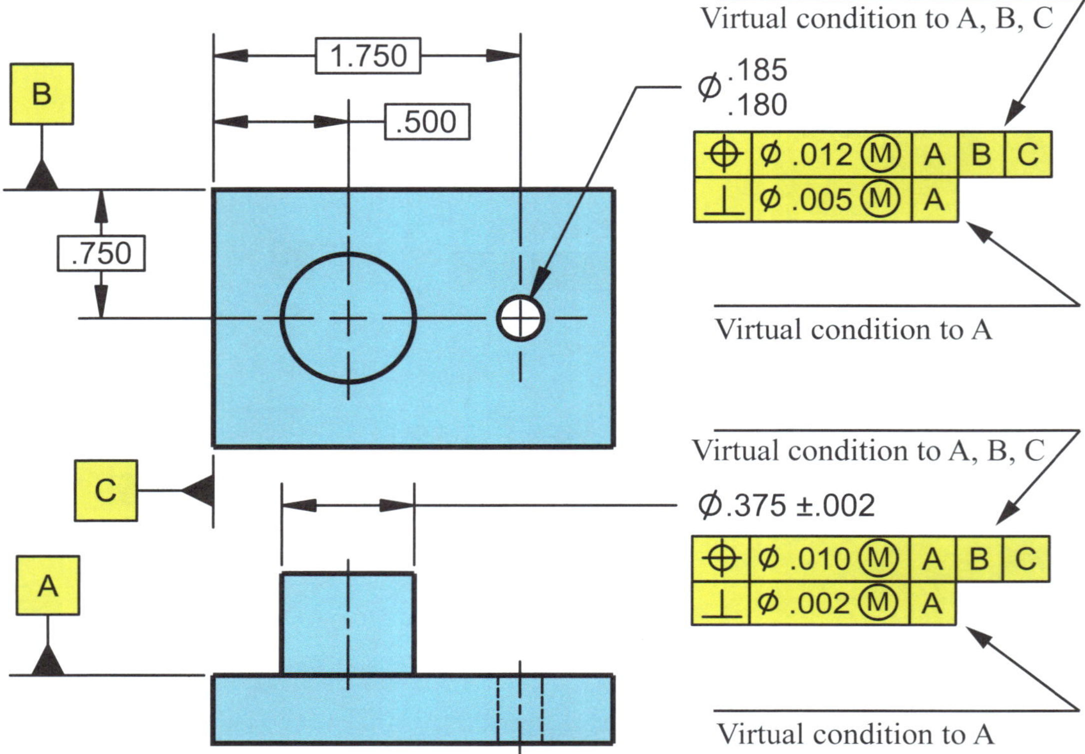

Workshop Exercise 7.2

Below are three assemblies for the part on the previous page. Use the drawing on the previous page to calculate the smallest virtual condition or mating hole size possible on the three rings. Pay close attention to how the rings mount in the assemblies.

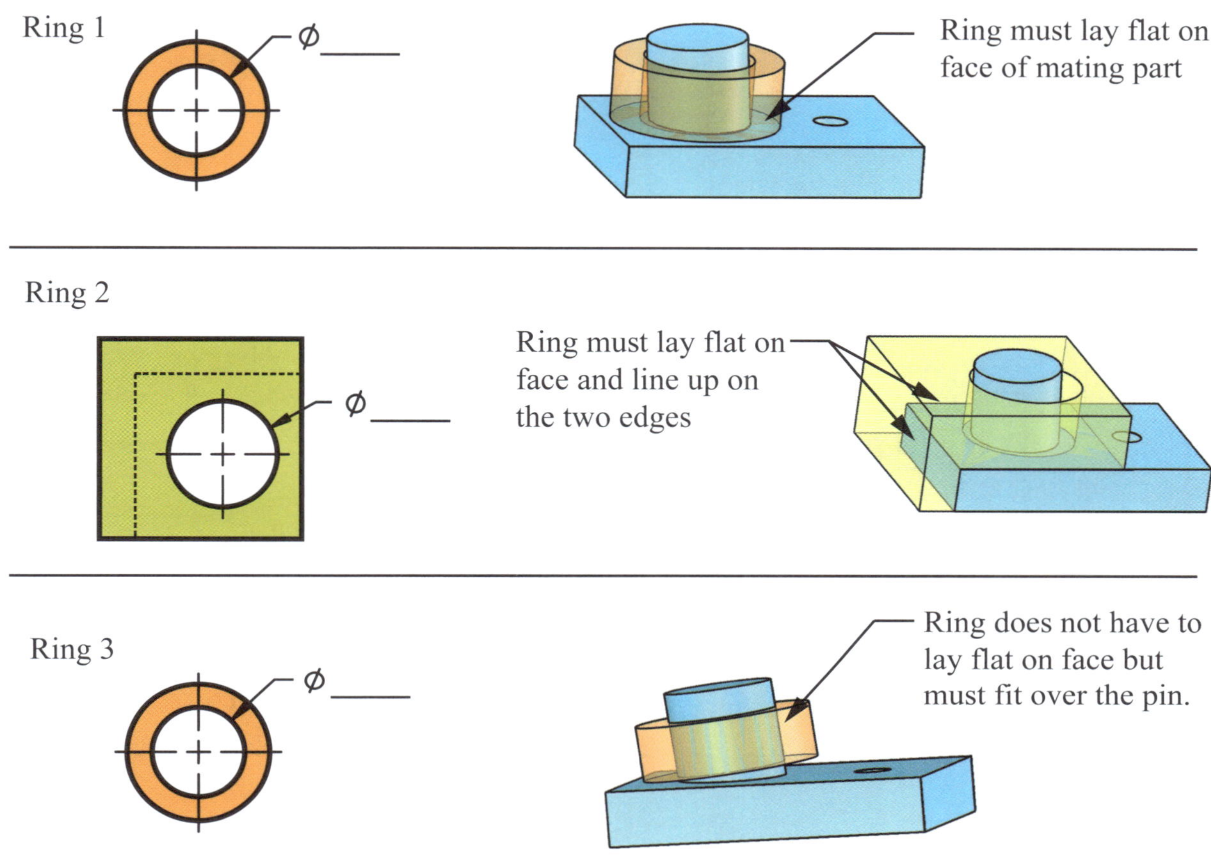

Fill in the two feature control frames below for rings 1 and 2. Use the virtual condition sizes from above, and size tolerance below, to calculate the position or perpendicularity tolerances. Make sure to include the correct material condition modifier.

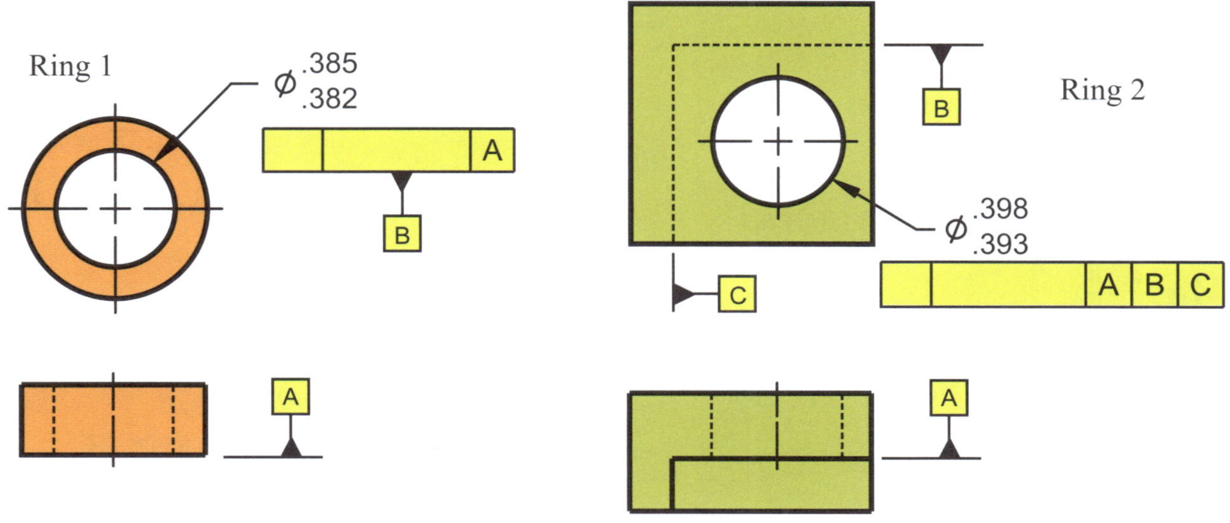

Perpendicularity of Zero at MMC

The two examples shown each represent a mating assembly. Example 1 specifies a .002 at MMC perpendicularity requirement. Example 2 specifies a .000 at MMC requirement. Notice example 2 provides a greater variation on size tolerane while still maintaining the same virtual condition as example 1. The zero tolerancing at MMC or LMC may be applied to position tolerance as well.

Example 1

Use this method if it is necessary to control the size and orientation with separate specs.

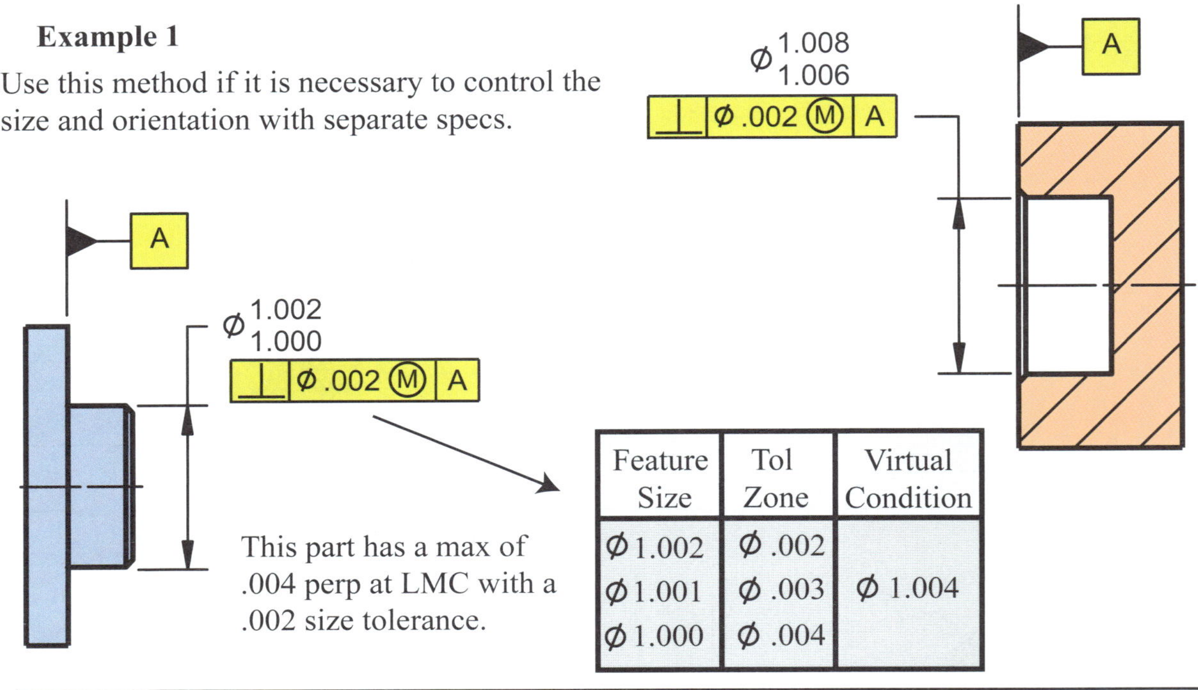

This part has a max of .004 perp at LMC with a .002 size tolerance.

Feature Size	Tol Zone	Virtual Condition
Ø 1.002	Ø .002	
Ø 1.001	Ø .003	Ø 1.004
Ø 1.000	Ø .004	

Example 2

Use this method if it is not necessary to control the size and perpendicularity with two values. This method combines the size and orientation and simply states the virtual condition of the feature. It is a common specification on pilots. It maintains the same perpendicularity but provides more size tolerance than example 1.

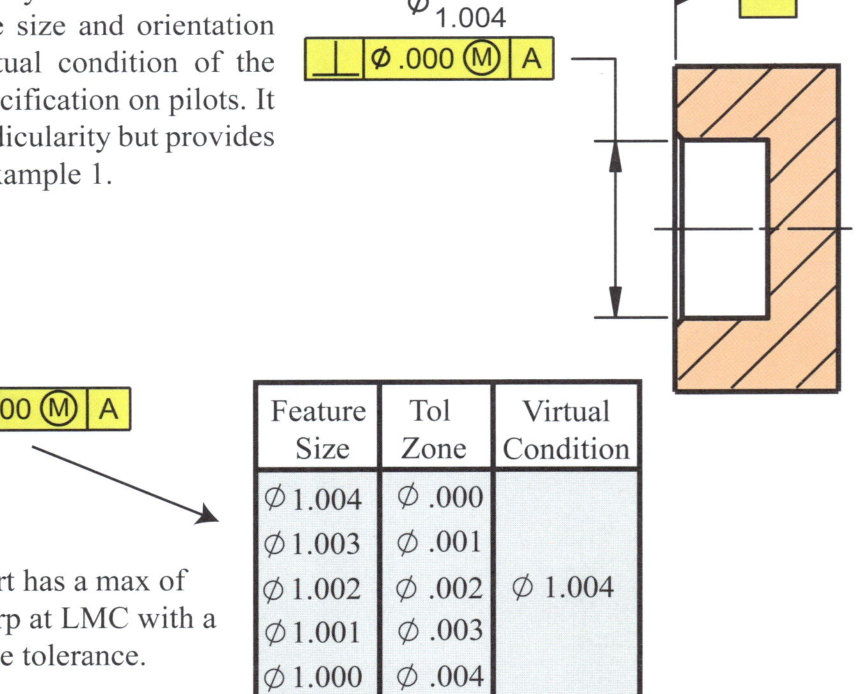

This part has a max of .004 perp at LMC with a .004 size tolerance.

Feature Size	Tol Zone	Virtual Condition
Ø 1.004	Ø .000	
Ø 1.003	Ø .001	
Ø 1.002	Ø .002	Ø 1.004
Ø 1.001	Ø .003	
Ø 1.000	Ø .004	

Workshop Exercise 7.3

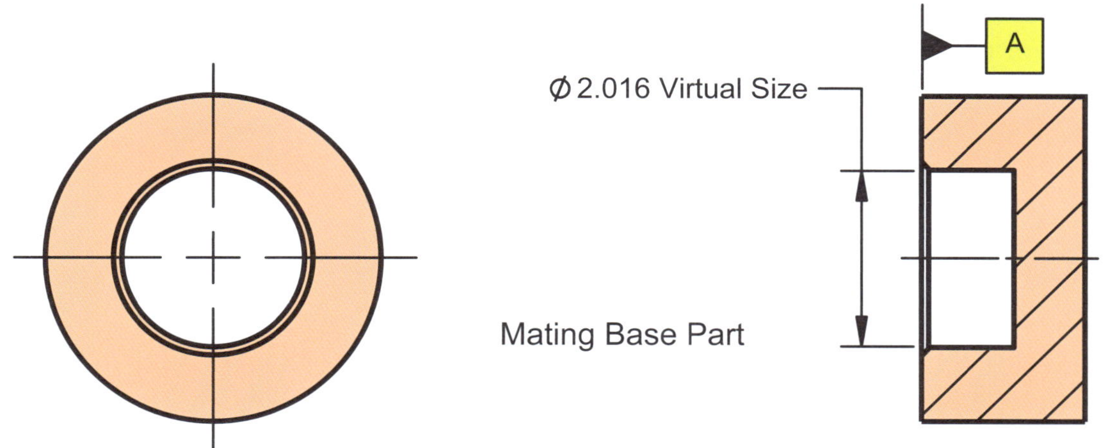

The two pilot parts below mate with the part above. There is a design clearance of .002 between the virtual fit of the two parts. Complete the two charts below showing the perpendicularity for the different pilot sizes and virtual condition values.

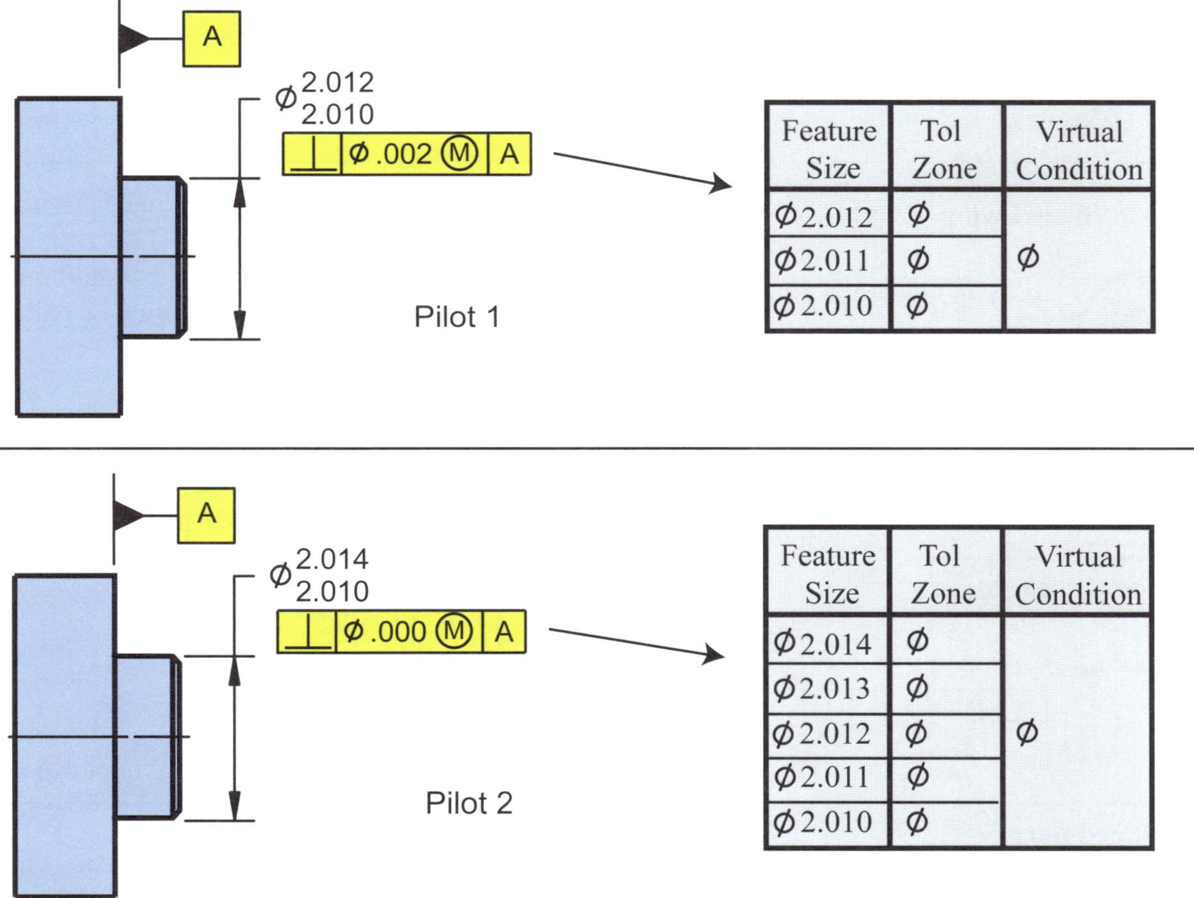

Feature Size	Tol Zone	Virtual Condition
Ø2.012	Ø	Ø
Ø2.011	Ø	
Ø2.010	Ø	

Feature Size	Tol Zone	Virtual Condition
Ø2.014	Ø	Ø
Ø2.013	Ø	
Ø2.012	Ø	
Ø2.011	Ø	
Ø2.010	Ø	

Which part provides the most manufacturing tolerance and is easiest to work with, part 1 or 2? Explain why.

____

____

Virtual Condition - MMB - Related AME

Virtual condition is the single worst-case boundary that incorporates the collective effects of size, geometric tolerance, and the bonus tolerance from the MMC modifier. Other boundary terms called *maximum material boundary* (MMB) and *related actual mating envelope* (related AME) are explained and illustrated below.

This on the drawing

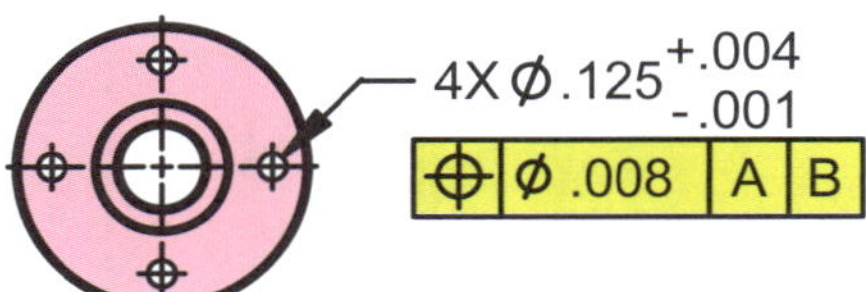

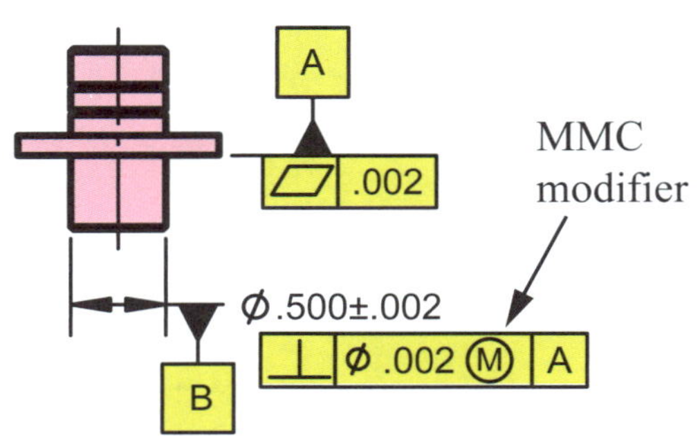

The MMC modifier allows bonus tolerance for the feature as it departs from MMC while **maintaining a constant worst-case boundary through the range of size**. This Ø.504 boundary is known as virtual condition, but it may also be called the maximum material boundary (MMB).

Feature Size	Tol Zone	Virtual Condition	
⌀.502	⌀.002		
⌀.501	⌀.003		
⌀.500	⌀.004	⌀.504	← MMB
⌀.499	⌀.005		
⌀.498	⌀.006		

This on the drawing

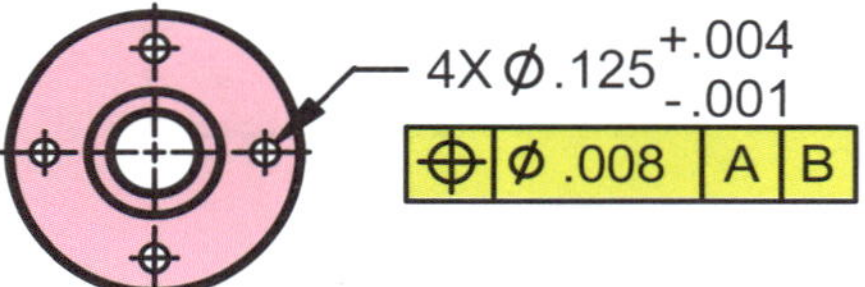

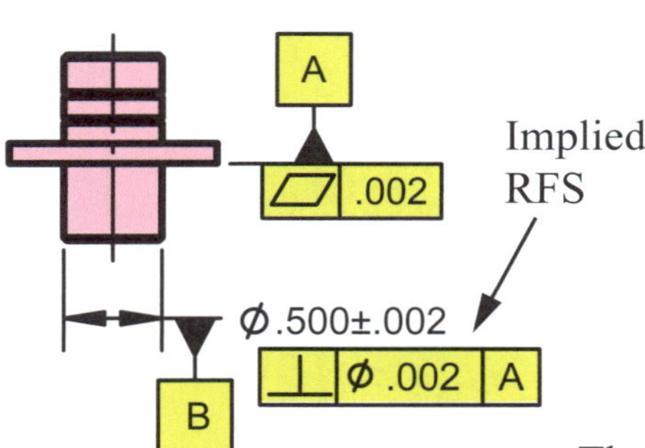

Without the MMC modifier, the perp tolerance remains constant at .002 through the range in size. This still creates a worst case boundary of Ø.504 but should not be called the virtual condition. Instead it must be called the maximum material boundary (MMB).

Feature Size	Tol Zone	Worst Case Related AME	
⌀.502	⌀.002	⌀.504	← MMB
⌀.501	⌀.002	⌀.503	
⌀.500	⌀.002	⌀.502	
⌀.499	⌀.002	⌀.501	
⌀.498	⌀.002	⌀.500	

The feature does not have a virtual condition if referenced RFS

Produced part

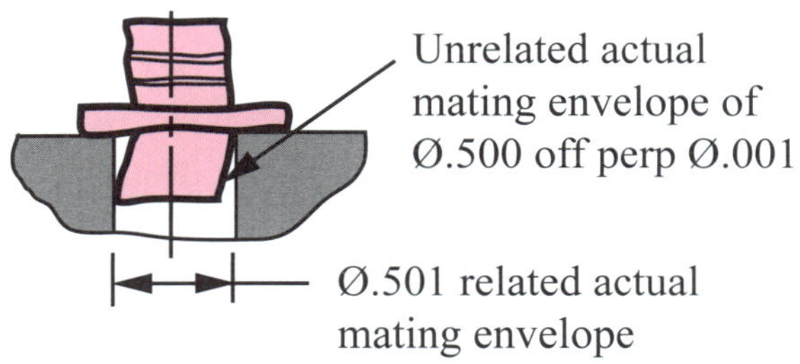

While MMB is the worst case boundary, the actual produced feature will create a different boundary. The collective effect of its actual size and actual geometric tolerance creates a boundary called the *related actual mating envelope* (related AME).

Position Verification Using the Boundary Method

The part below is from Unit 5, position verification. Unit 5 showed how to evaluate a hole's actual position by measuring the X and Y deviations from true position and using a formula to calculate the tolerance zone. This is called the axis interpretation/method in Y14.5. The method below uses boundaries to evaluate the hole's actual position and is called the surface interpretation/method in ASME Y14.5.

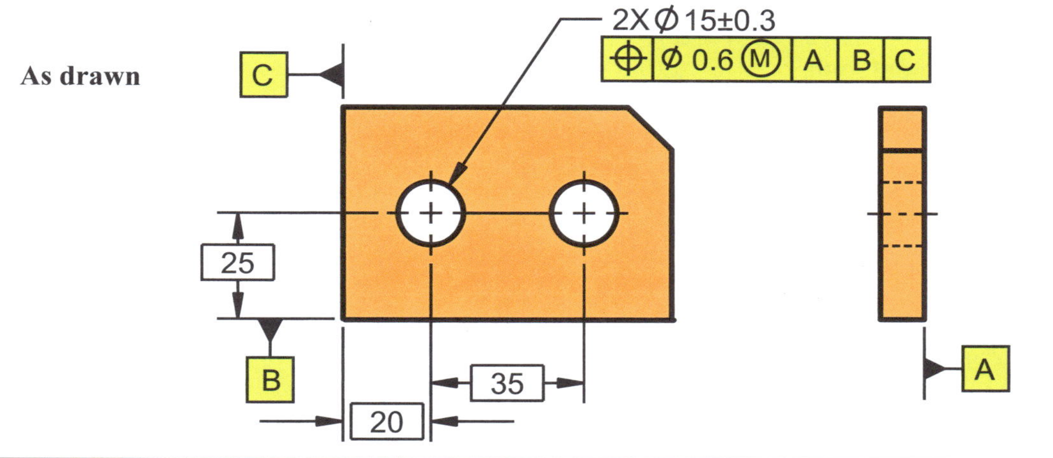

A functional gage could be a tool for evaluating a position requirement modified at MMC. The gage pins represent the 3D virtual condition boundaries at basic location that the holes must fit over. A separate check is done to evaluate the feature's size.

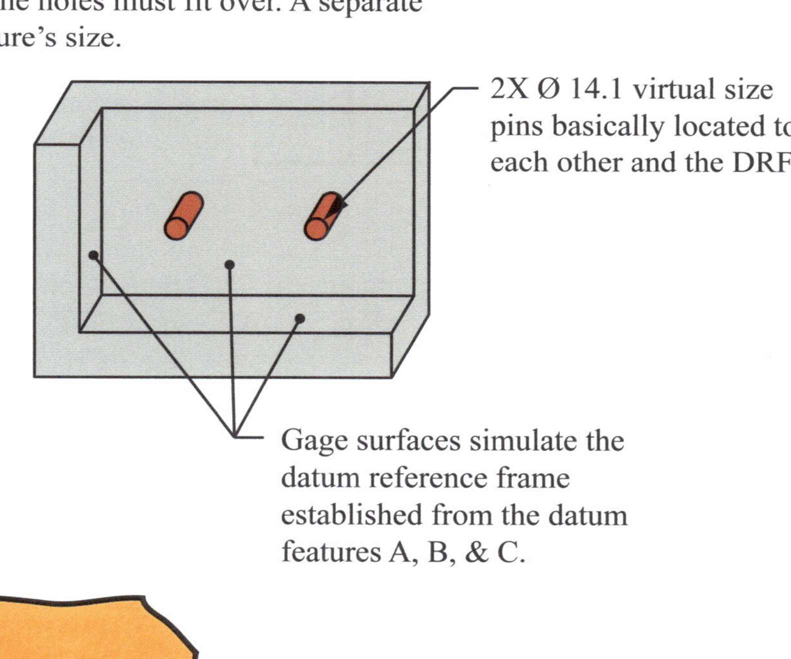

The holes pass the position tolerance if they clear the Ø14.1 virtual boundaries while indexed on the datum features.

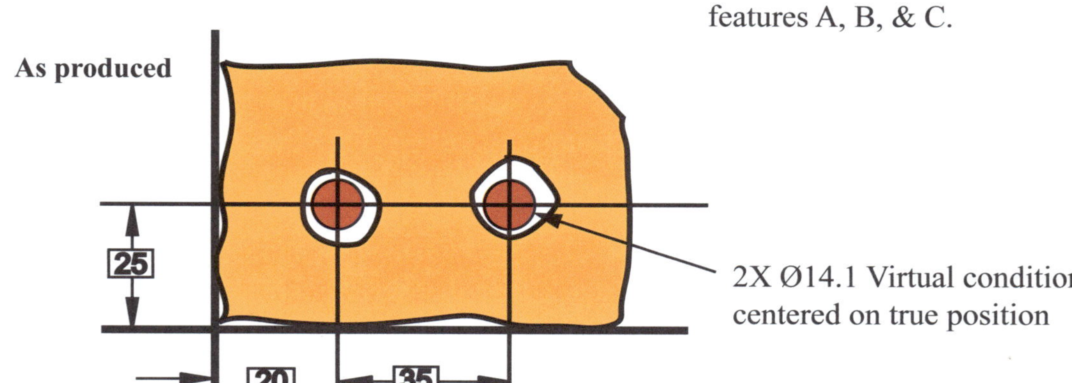

A functional gage can be a valid way to evaluate a position tolerance at MMC and can check a large quantity of parts quickly. However, this inspection only gives you attribute data (pass/fail). You may know a part is bad but cannot quantify how bad or which feature in the group is failing. The boundary method can also be used in CMM measurement to gather more than attribute data. Below is the same produced part from Unit 5, but the evaluation will be done using the boundary method instead of the axis method.

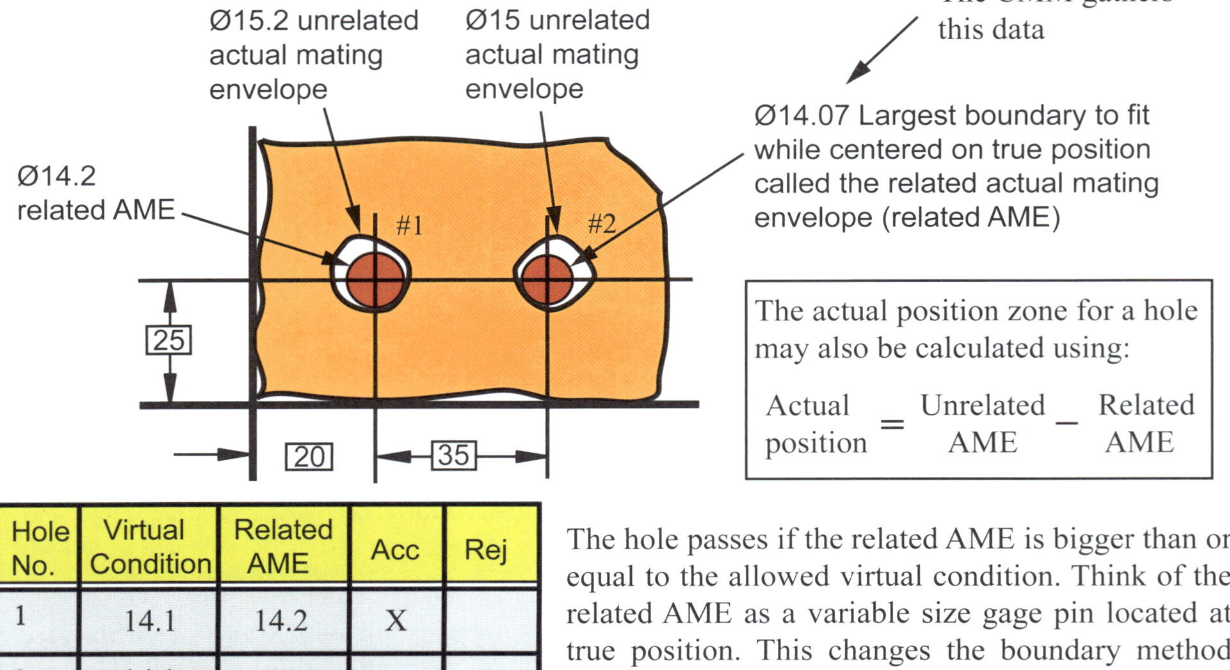

The actual position zone for a hole may also be calculated using:

Actual position = Unrelated AME − Related AME

Hole No.	Virtual Condition	Related AME	Acc	Rej
1	14.1	14.2	X	
2	14.1	14.07		X

The hole passes if the related AME is bigger than or equal to the allowed virtual condition. Think of the related AME as a variable size gage pin located at true position. This changes the boundary method into more than just a pass/fail inspection.

Feature Size	Position Tolerance	Virtual Condition
15.3	1.2	14.1
15.2	1.1	
15.1	1.0	
15.0	0.9	
14.9	0.8	
14.8	0.7	
14.7	0.6	

The boundary method can be a better way to evaluate the manufacturing process for a geometric tolerance modified at MMC or LMC. Statistical CPK values are based on how well a process stays within its spec limits. The problem with an MMC modifier is it keep changes these spec limits as the hole changes size. Notice what does stay constant is the virtual condition boundary. The process can be evaluated statistically by using a one sided spec limit at virtual condition and evaluating how close the related AME comes to this one sided specification.

Note: The axis method evaluates the axis of the unrelated actual mating envelope, while the boundary method evaluates the surface of the feature relative to the virtual boundary. In most cases, the two methods will give you similar enough results. However, unsymmetrical form deviations on the feature will not make them identical (the form deviations must be quite extreme to give meaningful differences, think keyhole shape). The axis method is always a more conservative evaluation. The Y14.5 standard states that the surface interpretation shall take precedence when a geometric control is defined at MMC or LMC, however, the axis interpretation is more commonly used in industry. The axis interpretation takes precedence when defined RFS. See unit 12, axis versus surface method for more information.

Workshop Exercise 7.4

This part was evaluated in Unit 5 using the axis method. The same part will now be evaluated using the boundary method.

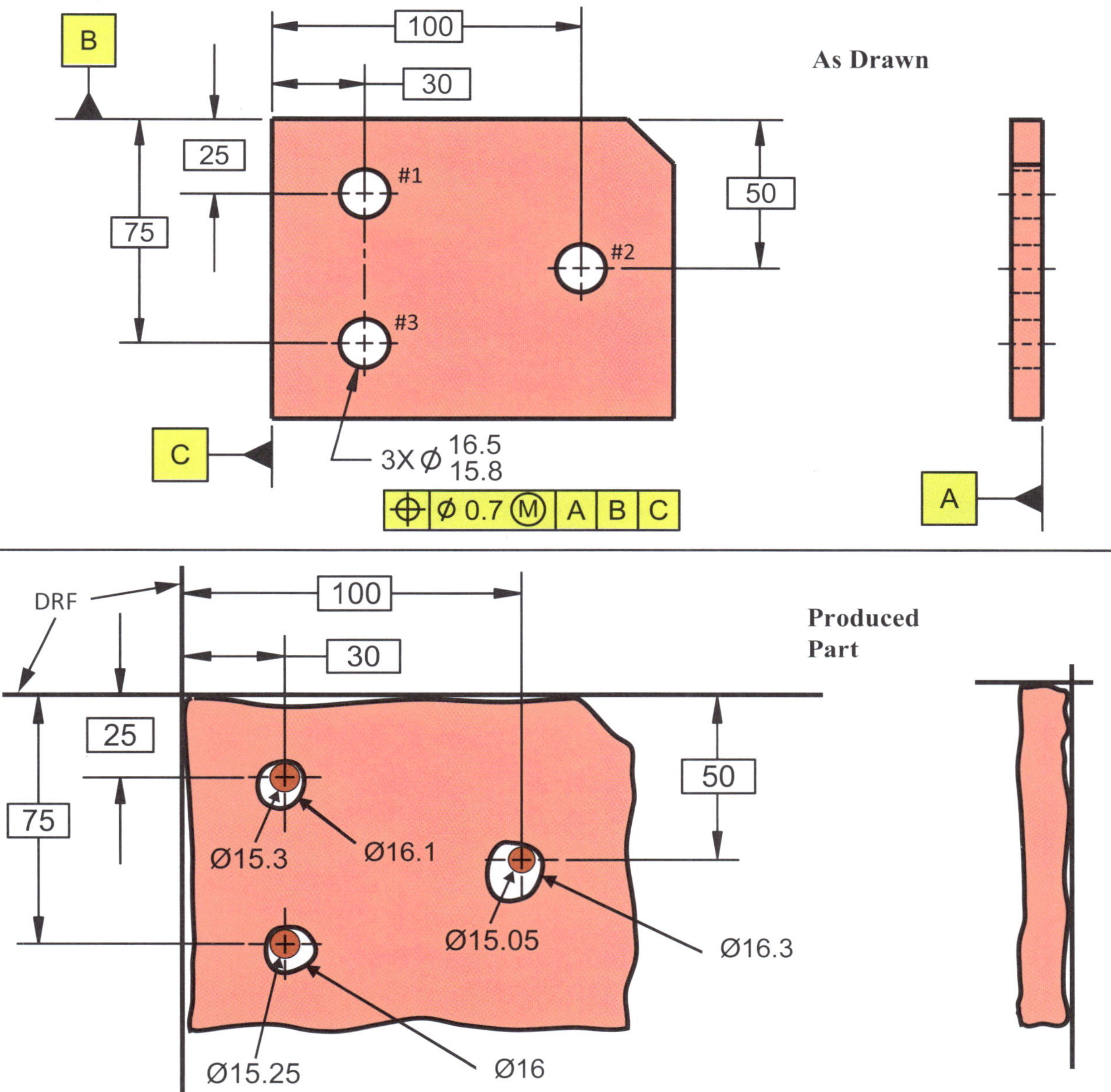

Fill out this chart to see if the holes pass inspection.

Hole No.	Virtual Condition	Related AME	Acc	Rej
1				
2				
3				

Material Boundary Modifiers - MMB, LMB and RMB

This next section will explain the definition of material boundary modifiers, (sometimes called datum feature modifiers) MMB, LMB, and RMB, applied to datum features and their role in the establishment of a datum reference frame. These modifiers only apply to datum features of size and surfaces that establish a boundary.

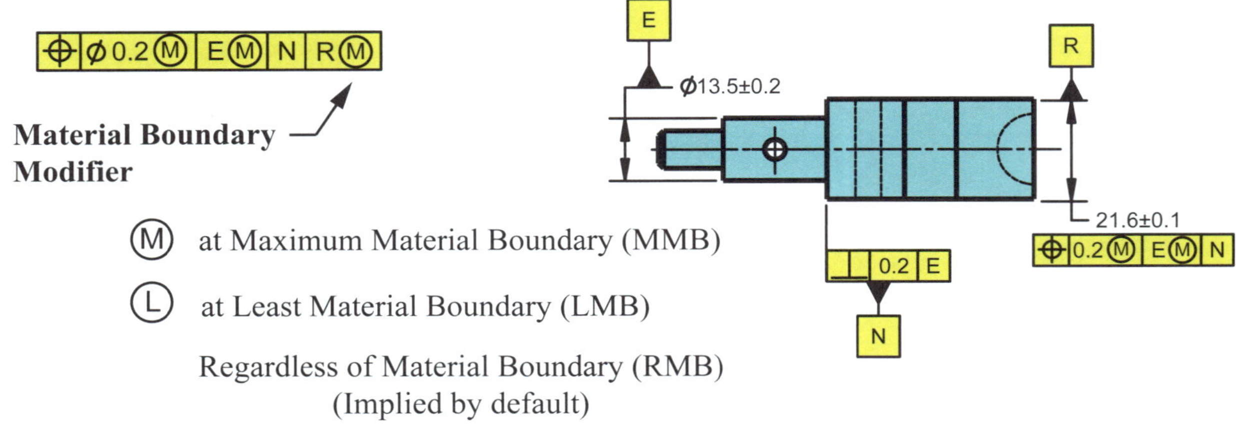

A True Geometric Counterpart (TGC) is a theoretically perfect inverse shape of the datum feature that is used to establish a datum. The drawing above shows a feature control frame referencing two datum features of size: E and R. The material boundary modifier defines how the TGC shall engage the size-variable datum feature. Note that datum feature N is a surface and material boundary modifiers do not apply. The following rules set the requirements for TGCs:

TGCs have the following requirements:

(a) perfect form.

(b) basic orientation relative to one another.

(c) basic location relative to one another unless otherwise specified.

(d) movable location when the translation modifier or the movable datum target symbol is specified.

(e) fixed at the designated size, when the MMB or LMB modifier is specified.

(f) adjustable in size, when the datum feature applies RMB. (The TGC shall expand, compress, or progress to make maximum contact with the datum feature.)

Referencing datum features in an order of precedence in a feature control frame establishes a set of TGCs (primary, secondary, and tertiary). The size, shape, and relationship of the TGC is based on the geometry of the datum feature, order in the feature control frame, and the material boundary modifier specified. The requirements of the TGCs are the foundation principles for establishing a DRF from imperfect datum features. These rules were first introduced in the Y14.5-2009 standard and removed the ambiguity in the earlier versions of Y14.5 and other related standards.

Note: The terms MMB, LMB, and RMB were new to ASME Y14.5-2009 and replaced the RFS, MMC, and LMC datum feature modifiers used in previous editions of the standard. These terms were replaced because their meaning did not clearly represent the boundaries established by the collective effects of size, geometric tolerances, and order of precedence.

Material Boundary Modifiers: MMB, LMB and RMB

This discussion will focus on TGC requirements (e) and (f) shown on the previous page. These requirements are set by how the datum feature is referenced in the feature control frame.

Datum Features at RMB (the default): The TGC geometry originates at the MMB and expands/contracts/progresses to make maximum contact with the extremities of the datum feature. If another fitting routine is required (such as a least squares algorithm), it shall be stated on the drawing. A practical example of this TGC would be a datum feature simulator that is variable, such as a collet or chuck, that engages a shaft and establishes the simulated datum axis.

Specifying Datum Features at MMB: The size of the TGC is fixed at the MMB size boundary. A practical example of this TGC would be a datum feature simulator that remains constant, such as a fixed size gage pin, that engages a hole and establishes the simulated datum axis.

Specifying Datum Features at LMB: The size of the TGC is fixed at the LMB size boundary. A practical example of this TGC is difficult with a physical datum feature simulator because the LMB boundary is within the material. CMM software is necessary to simulate the LMB boundary of a TGC that is used to establish the simulated datum. This will not be explained in this text.

In cases where the datum feature boundary needs clarification, or another boundary is desired, the size of the boundary may be included inside the feature control frame in brackets following the modifier. The symbol [BSC] sets the TGC at the basic location.

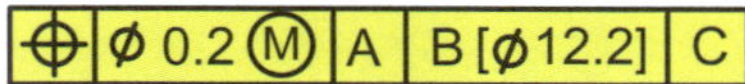

Defines the size of the boundary at Ø12.2

⌖	Ø 0.2 Ⓜ	A	B [BSC]	C

Defines the boundary to be fixed at basic

Geometric tolerances are related to the perfect DRF established by the TGCs. However, the datum features are not perfect. Datum features shall be qualified to each other by applying size and geometric tolerances as necessary. On the drawing below, datum feature E is qualified with a size tolerance. Datum feature N is qualified with a perpendicularity and datum feature R with a position tolerance. This makes it possible to calculate the TGC boundaries:

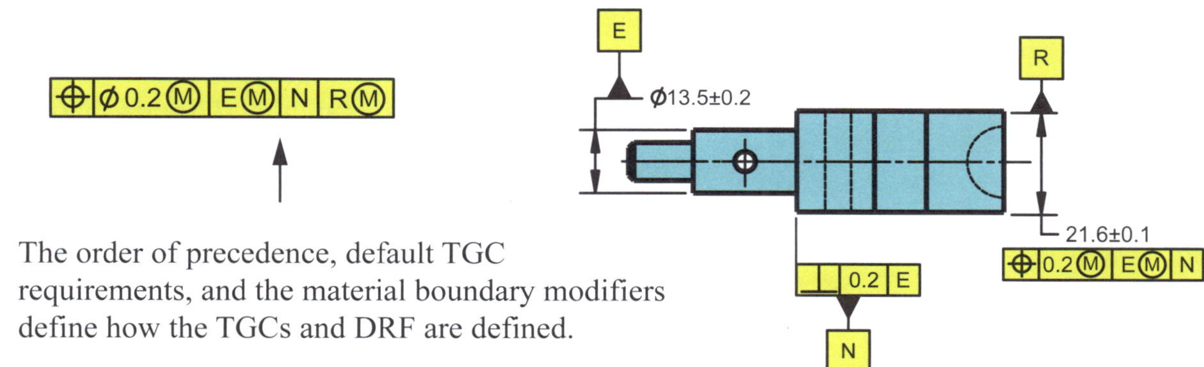

The order of precedence, default TGC requirements, and the material boundary modifiers define how the TGCs and DRF are defined.

- •The TGC for datum feature E is an MMB hole of Ø13.7 (MMC).
- •Datum feature N is a surface that does not establish a boundary and material boundary modifiers do not apply. The TGC is a plane perpendicular to E.
- •The TGC for datum feature R is an MMB slot of 21.9 (21.7 MMC + 0.2 position) located (centered) on the E axis.

Development of a Datum Reference Frame at RMB

The next pages will use a practical example to explain the TGC requirements as well as the difference between referencing datum features of size at the default RMB versus at MMB.

Selecting a datum reference frame for a part

The design engineer examines the assembly and determines the functional relationships between the parts. The major mounting features of the part are established as the datum features. They are selected in an order of precedence in a feature control frame to establish a datum reference frame. This constrains the six degrees of freedom on the part.

There are leader features, and follower features on a part. The leaders are selected as the datum features to establish the DRF. The planar surface, hole, and slot locate the alignment plate in the assembly. The features that follow are the two clearance holes and the grooved top surface.

Notice how the part mates in the assembly.

Primary: The part is bolted down to the back face. This planar face establishes the initial orientation of the part and is identified as the primary datum feature A. It constrains one translation and two rotations. It is qualified with a flatness tolerance.

Secondary: The large alignment hole fits over the red pin. (The bolt holes are too sloppy to locate the part). This hole is identified as datum feature B, and it constrains two translations. It is qualified with a perpendicularity tolerance to A.

Tertiary: The slot fits over the red key and is identified as datum feature C. It constrains the final rotation of the part. It is qualified with a position tolerance to A and B.

All other features are located to the DRF established by datum features A, B and C.

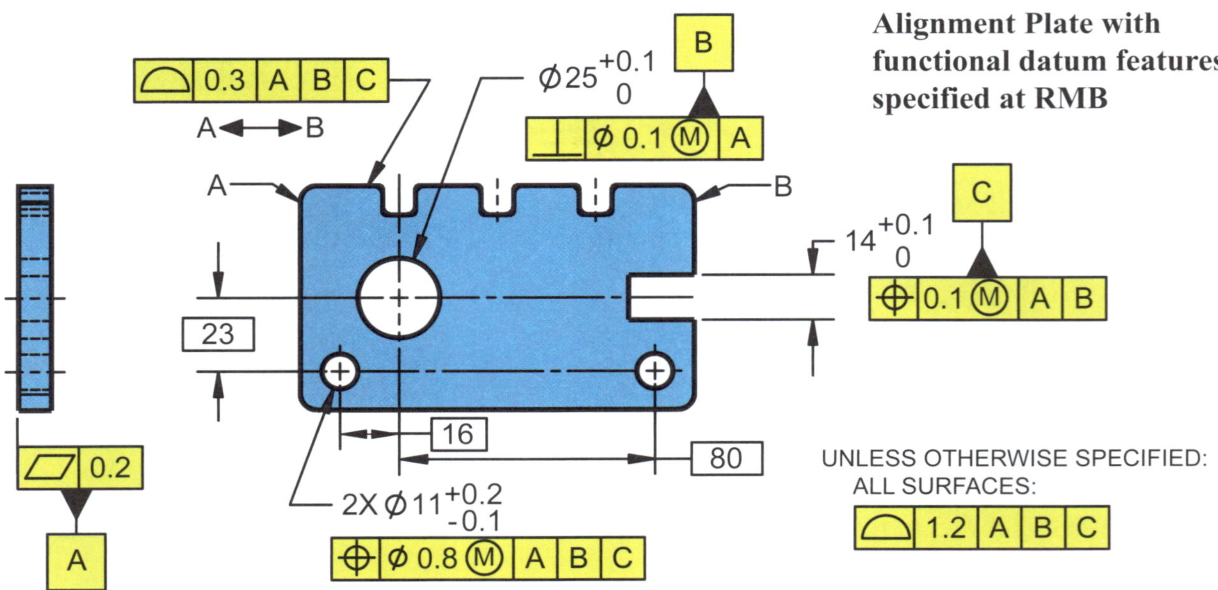

Alignment Plate with functional datum features specified at RMB

Development of a Datum Reference Frame at RMB

The true geometric counterparts (TGCs) are used to create the DRF and are established in accordance with the TGC requirements shown earlier in this section. Notice the feature control frame references the datum features of size (B and C) at the default *regardless of material boundary* (RMB).

Theoretical sequence of events in the development of a DRF with datum features referenced RMB.

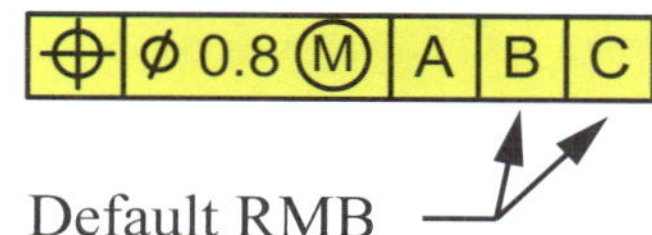

1. The TGC for primary datum feature A establishes a datum plane that contacts the high points of the feature. This plane sets the initial orientation; it constrains 1 translation and 2 rotations.

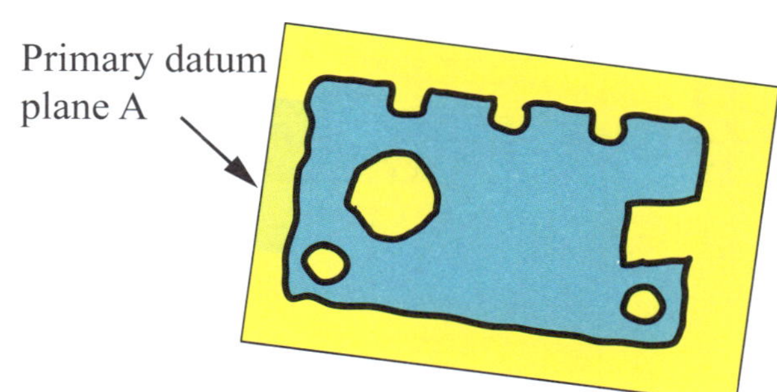

2. The TGC for datum feature B is a cylinder that expands to make maximum contact with the hole. Since B is secondary, the TGC is oriented 90° basic to datum plane A. An axis is established from the center of the TGC. This constrains 2 translations.

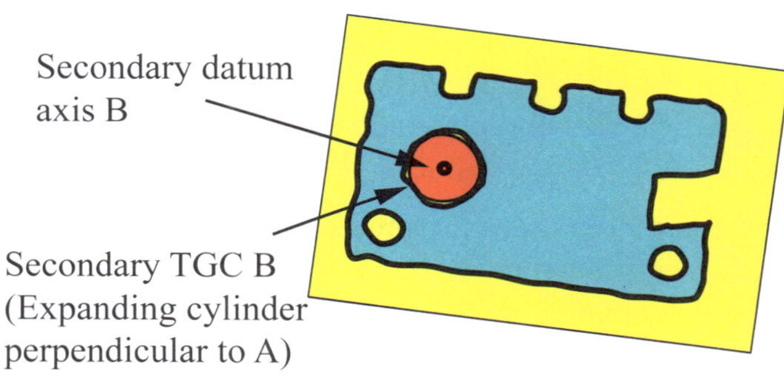

3. The TGC for datum feature C is a width that expands about basic, to make maximum possible contact with slot. Since C is tertiary, the TGC is oriented 90° basic to datum plane A and located (on center) to datum axis B. A center plane is established by the TGC. This constrains the final rotation.

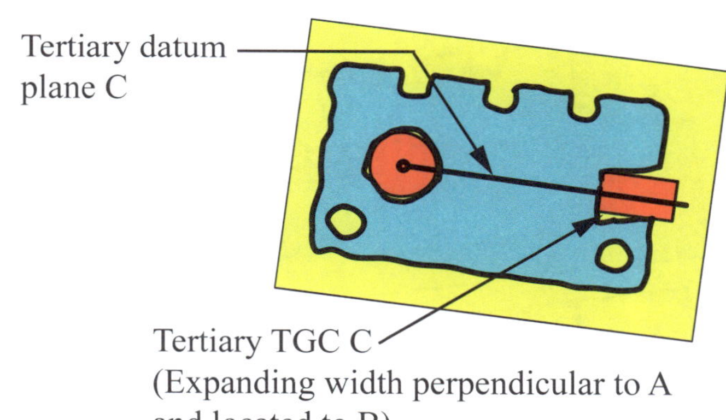

4. The datum reference frame constrains the part's six degrees of freedom and is used as the origin for all geometric tolerances.

Datum reference frame established by datum features A, B and C.

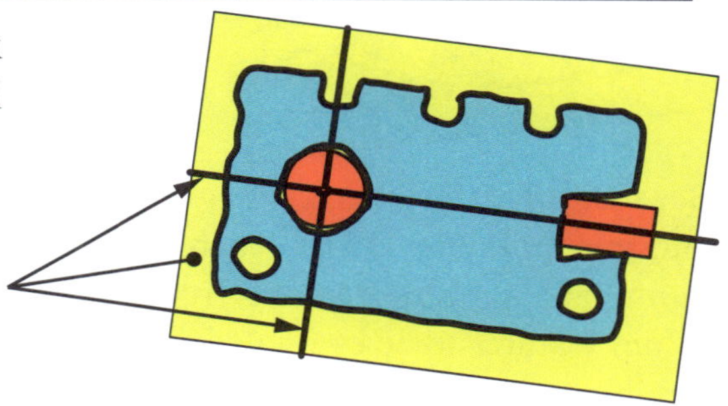

Development of a Datum Reference Frame at MMB

In the preceding example, a DRF was established on the alignment plate with the datum features at default RMB. In this example, the datum features are modified at MMB for comparison.

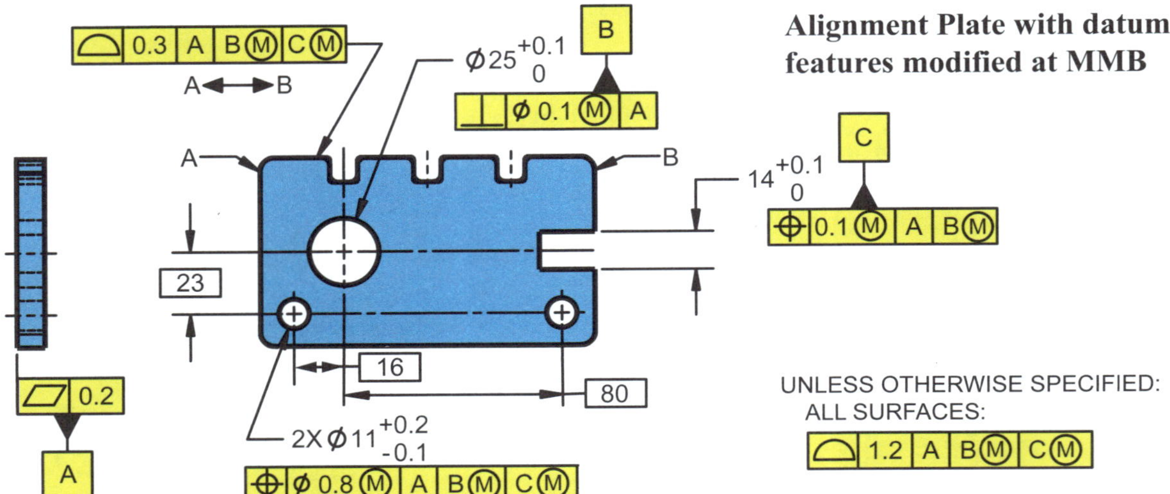

The DRF establishments at RMB and MMB are identical except for the size of the true geometric counterparts (TGCs). Instead of variable size TGCs, MMB modifiers require them to be fixed in size at their MMB. The MMB for datum feature B is 24.9 (25 MMC - 0.1 perp) considering the worst-case size and perpendicularity relative to datum feature A. The MMB for datum feature C is 13.9 (14 - 0.1), considering the worst case size and position to datum features A and B.

If the datum features are produced at their MMB, they will be centered by their respective TGC. However, if the datum features depart from their MMB (get larger in this case), they could "rattle around" and be allowed to shift/displace within the confines of the TGCs. This is called "datum feature shift". The datum features are allowed to shift for other features to meet their tolerances.

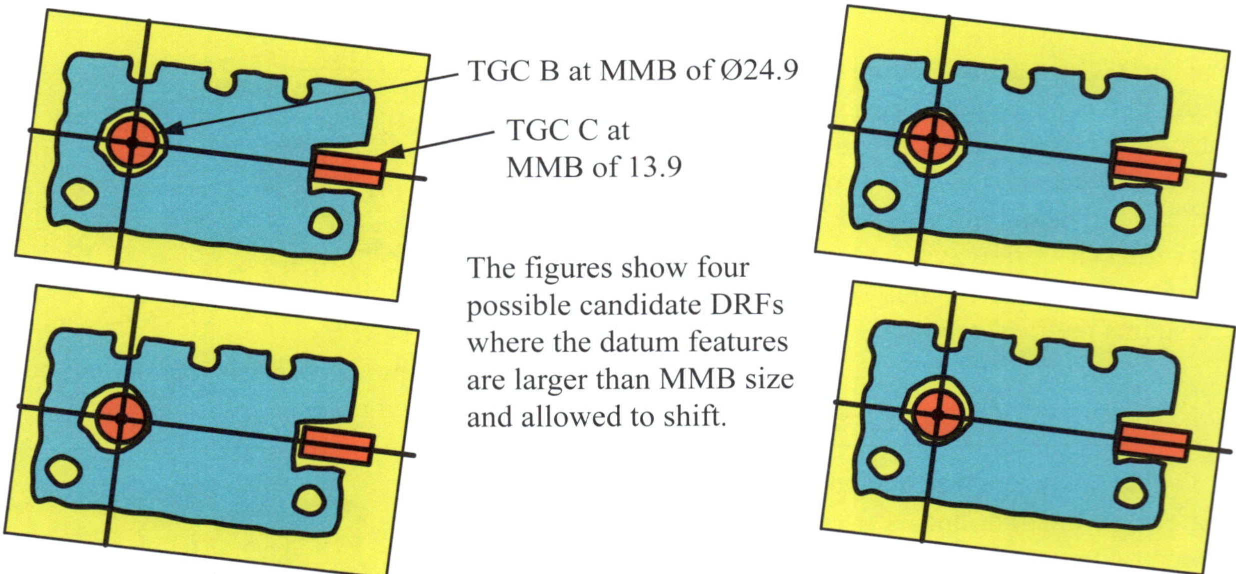

The figures show four possible candidate DRFs where the datum features are larger than MMB size and allowed to shift.

Because of the clearance between the produced datum features and their TGCs, the part has multiple possible DRFs, each called a "candidate DRF" in the Y14.5.1 standard. A default "simultaneous requirement" requires all position and profile tolerances referencing the same datum features to be evaluated simultaneously to the same candidate DRF. The correct DRF is the candidate DRF that produces the smallest actual values for the feature tolerances.

Comparison Between Modifiers RMB and MMB

The material boundary modifiers MMB and RMB affect the engagement of the true geometric counterparts (TGCs) with the imperfect datum features.

Regardless of Material Boundary (RMB) requires the TGC to expand/collapse to make maximum contact with the datum feature. The DRF is established from the theoretical TGCs.

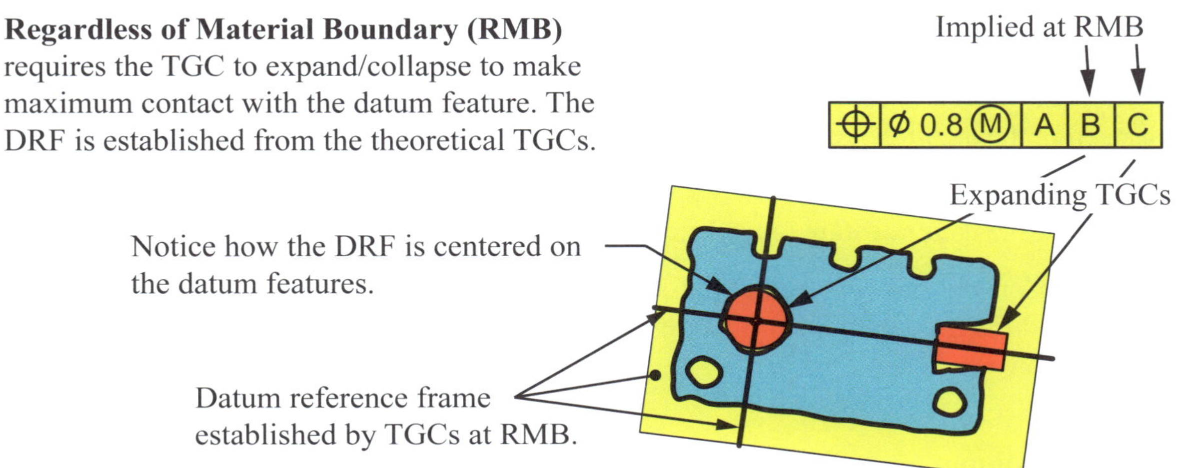

This centering of the datum reference frame is done easily with an open-set-up inspection using a height gage probe tip touching the feature and centering regardless of its produced condition. This centering is also easily done using CMM probe tips and preprogrammed algorithms.

The default RMB is used on a drawing when a part needs to be precise and aligned/centered with little adjustment possible; assembly stack ups are important (think of a part mounting on bearings, precision journals, pilots, dowels, alignment pins/holes, etc.)

Maximum Material Boundary (MMB) modifier requires the TGC to be fixed at the MMB size. As the datum feature departs from MMB, it is allowed to shift/displace within the confines of the TGC (datum feature shift).

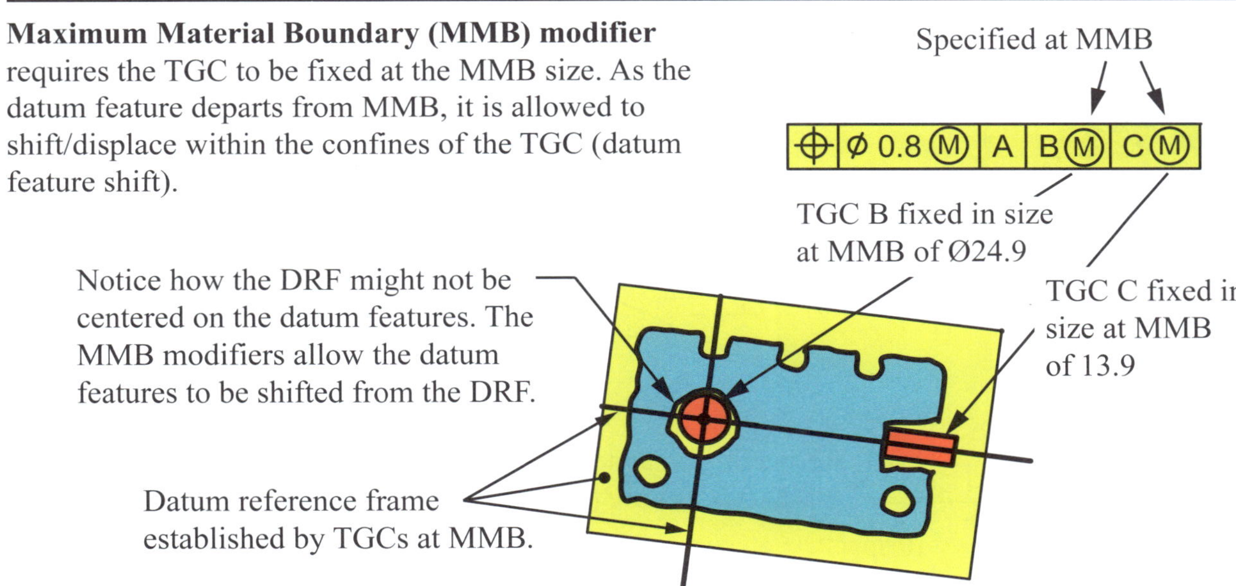

If the part were checked with a functional gage, the datum feature shift would be factored in automatically by adjusting the part on the simulators to meet the position and profile tolerances. All tolerances must be met simultaneously (simultaneous requirement). However, factoring in the datum feature shift in an open-set-up inspection or CMM is more difficult. Paper gaging, holding fixtures or more sophisticated CMM software may assist in the evaluation.

The MMB modifier is typically used on a drawing in clearance conditions and when the part can be adjusted in the assembly to an optimum location (think of a part mounting on sloppy clearance holes). The alignment of features is not that important because of the adjustable design.

Calculating Boundaries for Datum Features at MMB

The datum feature's MMB and corresponding TGC are determined by both its size and relationship to higher precendence datum features. A datum feature can have multiple geometric tolerances which create multiple MMB. Below are rules and examples to calculate the correct MMB (and TGC) for the establishment of the DRF.

For an internal datum feature of size, use the largest MMB that the datum feature will contain while respecting the datum feature precedence. (MMC minus relationship to higher datums)

For an external datum feature of size, use the smallest MMB that will contain the datum feature while respecting the datum feature precedence. (MMC plus relationship to higher datums)

The three holes on the drawing below are shown with 4 different options for feature control frames, all with different datum feature references. The MMB calculation for the datum feature is shown for each DRF.

Calculating Maximum Material Boundary (MMB)

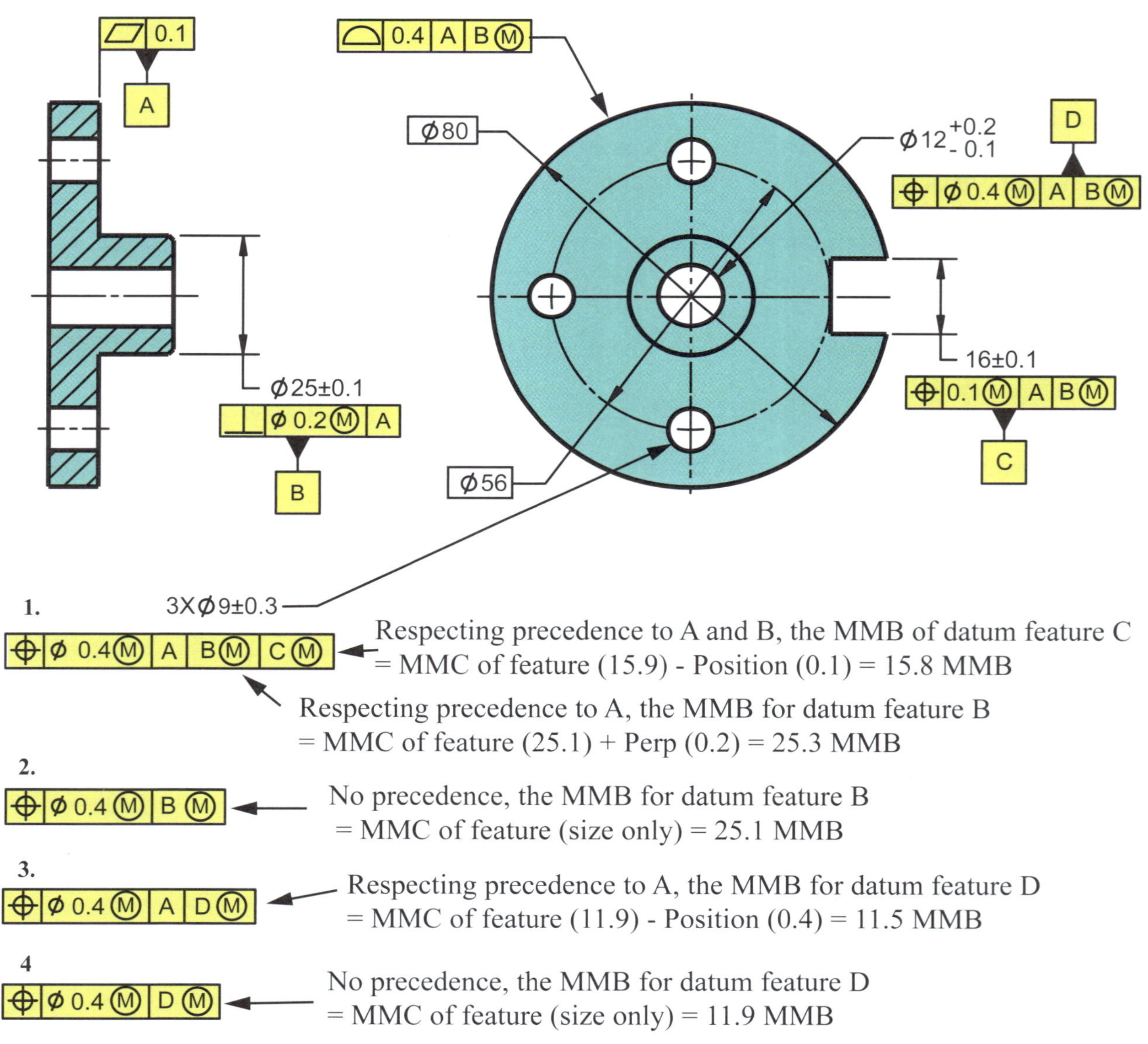

Workshop Exercise 7.5 - Calculating Datum Feature Boundaries

On the drawing below, there are four options for feature control frames on the three holes. Each feature contol frame has a different set of datum feature references. Calculate the MMB for each of the datum feature's TGC, and enter it in the spaces below. Show your work.

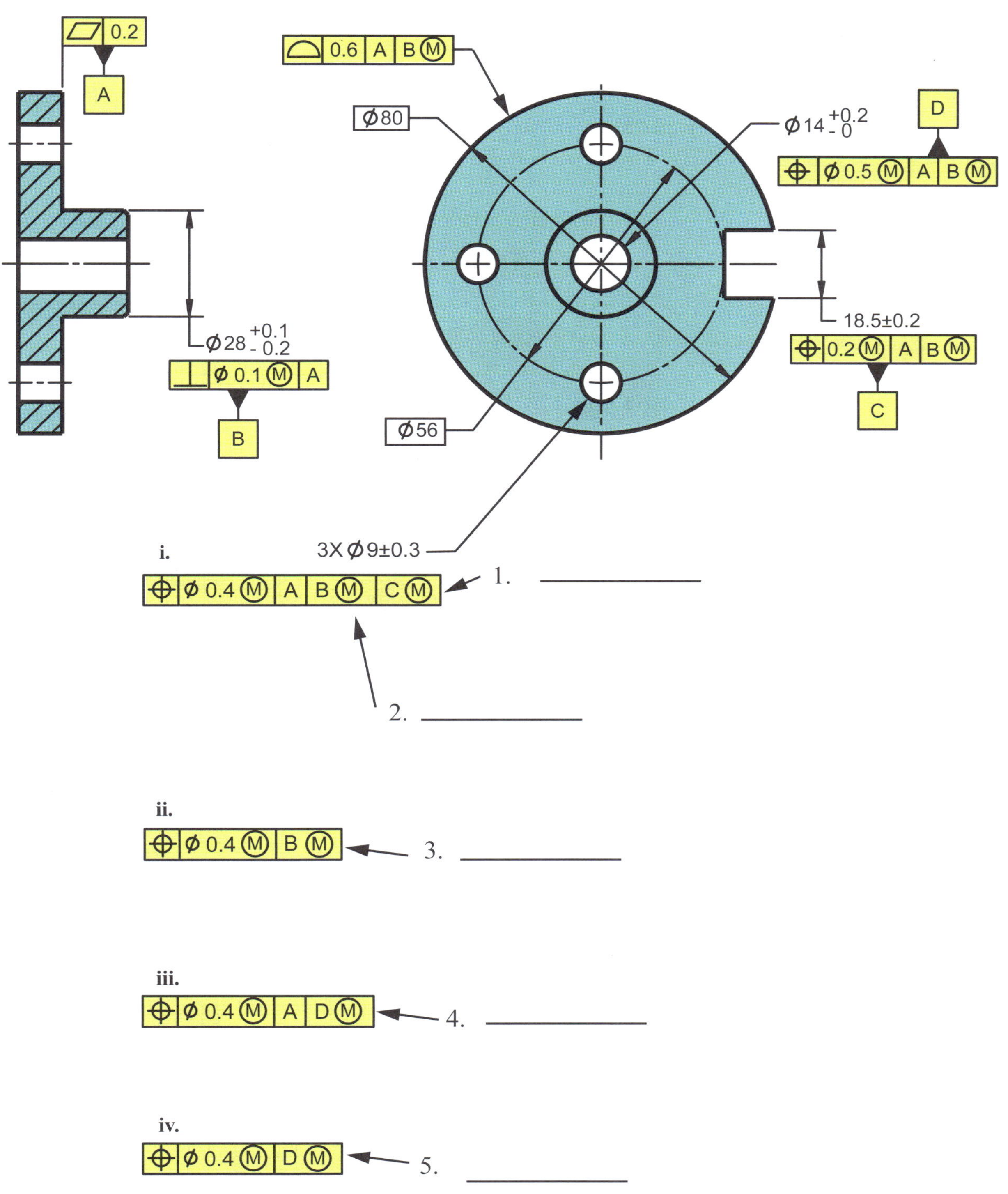

Simultaneous Requirement is Implied as Default

A simultaneous requirement applies to position and profile tolerances that are related to common datum features referenced in the same order of precedence at the same boundary conditions. In a simultaneous requirement, there is no translation or rotation between the datum reference frames of the included geometric tolerances, thus creating a single pattern.

In the part below, the two sets of hole positions and outside profile are all related to A and B at MMB. This constitutes a single pattern and all the features must meet their respective tolerances simultaneously. Since all features are considered a single pattern, another datum feature to constrain the rotation is not necessary. Best fit rotation of the part as well as datum feature shift create multiple candidate DRFs. All position and profile tolerances must use the same candidate datum reference frame.

Simultaneous requirement is implied by default

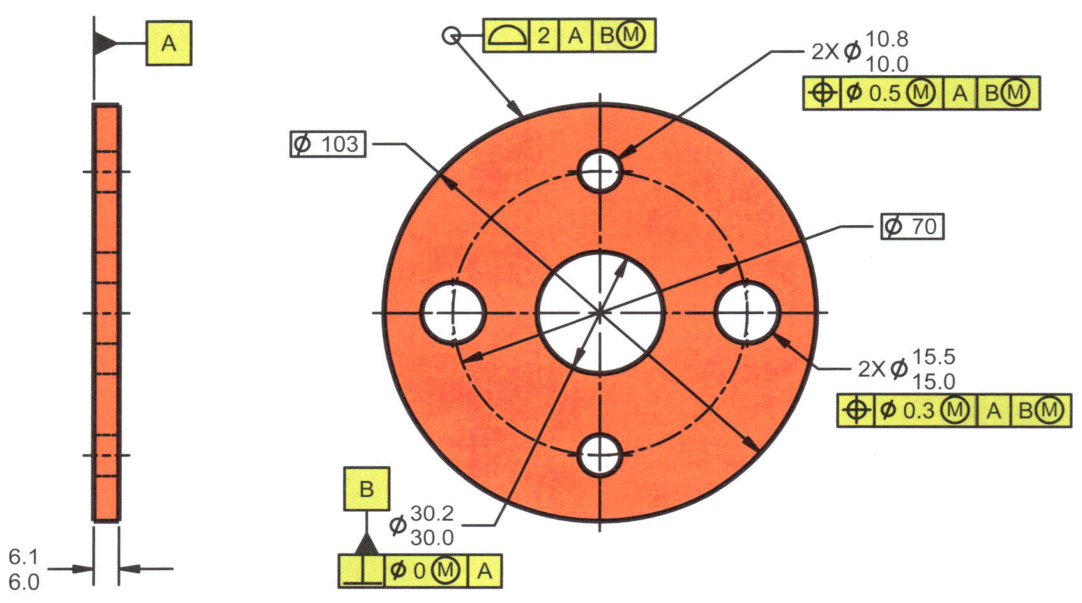

This sample functional gage is shown to illustrate the concept of the implied simultaneous requirement. It checks all the features at once and will not allow the two groups of holes and the profile specification to rotate or shift relative to one another more than the allowable position and profile tolerances.

In a surface plate set-up or CMM check, all features must be rotationally balanced to each other and checked in one set-up as if they were a single pattern.

Hole location and profile specifications are implied simultaneous and may not rotate or shift to each other.

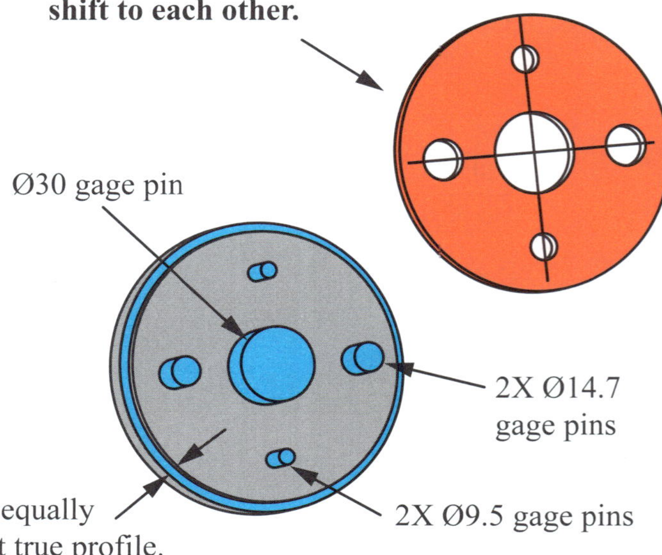

Separate Requirement Must be Specified

To override a default simultaneous requirement, the notation SEP REQT (Separate Requirement) is placed under each feature control frame. On the part below, the notes constitute three separate patterns and the sets of the features may rotate or shift to each other as datum feature B departs from MMB. The grouping of holes is still held within the pattern but each pattern may be evaluated to different candidate DRFs.

Separate requirement must be stated

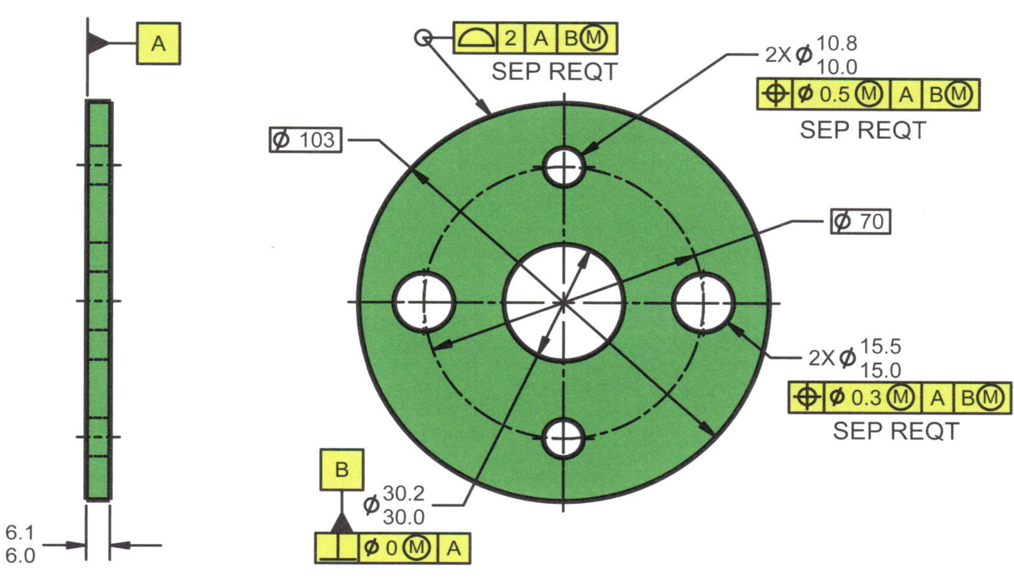

These sample functional gages are shown to illustrate the concept of the specified separate requirement. There are three separate gages to check each individual requirement. This allows the two groups of holes and the profile specification to rotate or shift to one another as they are now separate requirements.

In a rotational surface plate set-up or CMM check, all the features may be checked individually for conformance without regard to the other features labeled SEP REQT.

Hole location and profile specifications are not related and may rotate or shift to each other.

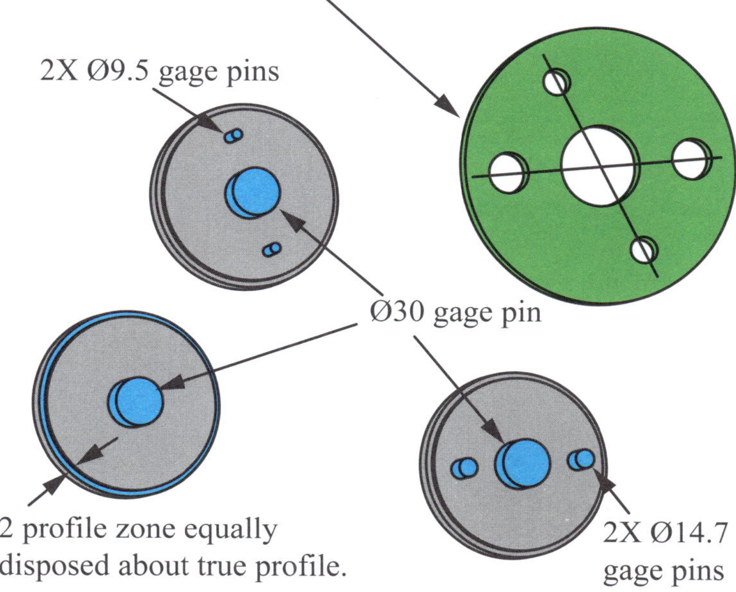

Rotational Control - Opposed Planar Surface

This page illustrates a surface as a tertiary datum feature constraining rotation and the difference between modifying at MMB and RMB. Usually material boundary modifiers do not apply to surfaces, but this is a special case of constraining rotation around an axis or point that was first clarified in the Y14.5-2009 standard. On both drawings below, the back face is defined as datum feature A and the center hole as B at RMB. The periphery of the part is located with a 2 mm all around profile tolerance. On both parts, the true geometric counterpart (TGC) for datum feature A is a plane and for B is an expanding cylinder.

The bottom surface is identified as datum feature C to stop rotation. On the upper part, the four holes are positioned to A, B, C **at MMB**. On the lower, they are positioned to A, B, C **at RMB**.

Datum feature C at MMB

The TGC for datum feature C is a **plane fixed at 66 MMB** (65 from the center of datum B plus ½ profile tolerance). Datum feature C may rotate and is free to move within the confines established by the MMB boundary. This constrains/limits the rotation of the part.

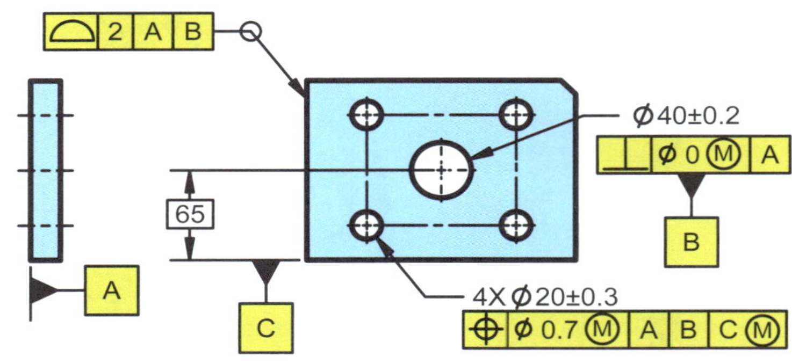

Datum feature C, modified at MMB, establishes a fixed TGC at 66 to orient the DRF to the part

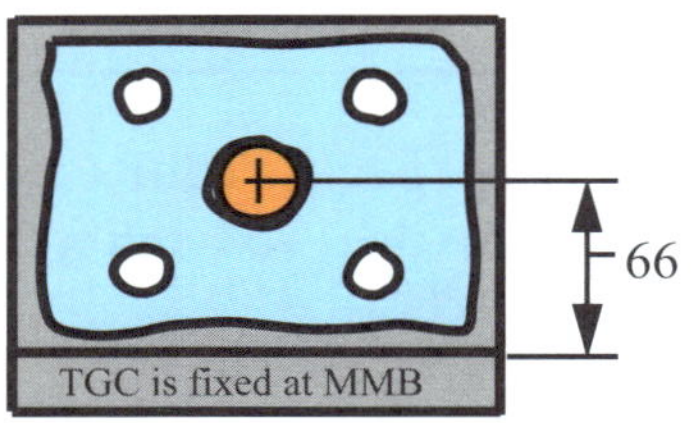

Datum feature C at RMB

The TGC for datum feature C is a **plane that moves/progresses** from MMB to make maximum contact with the datum feature. This constrains the rotation of the part.

RMB TGC moves to make maximum contact, and level the datum feature.

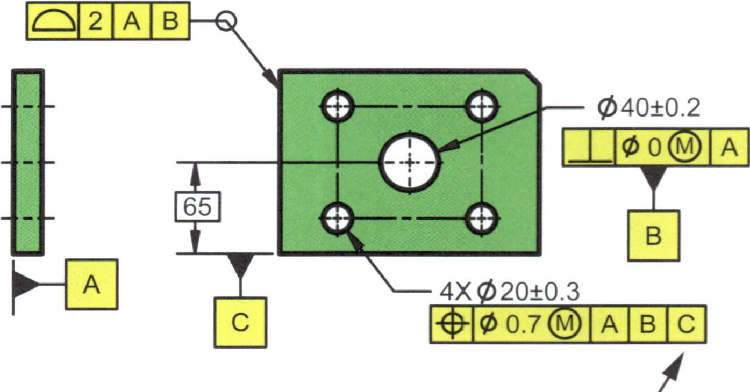

Datum feature C at RMB, establishes a TGC that moves/progresses to make maximum contact with the datum feature and constrains rotation.

Rotational Control - Unopposed Planar Surface

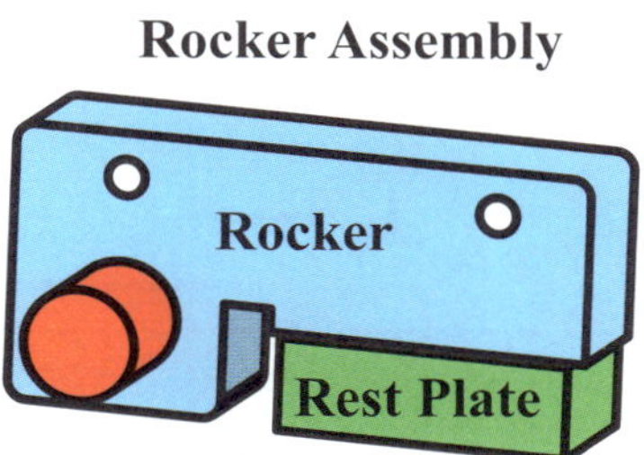

This assembly contains a rocker that mounts through the large hole with a press fit on the shaft. The rotation of the rocker is based on the engagement with the rest plate. Based on these mating requirements, the AB DRF is established on the drawing below. The large hole is defined as datum feature A, at RMB. The bottom plane surface is defined as datum feature B to stop rotation.

Modifying a surface datum feature at MMB, RMB, and Basic

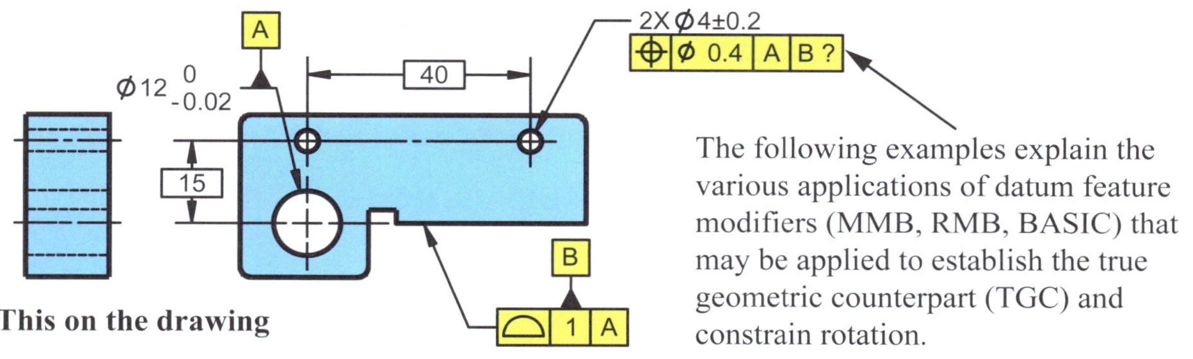

The following examples explain the various applications of datum feature modifiers (MMB, RMB, BASIC) that may be applied to establish the true geometric counterpart (TGC) and constrain rotation.

Profile requirement

The large hole is primary datum feature A, implied at RMB. This requires an expanding TGC to establish datum axis A.

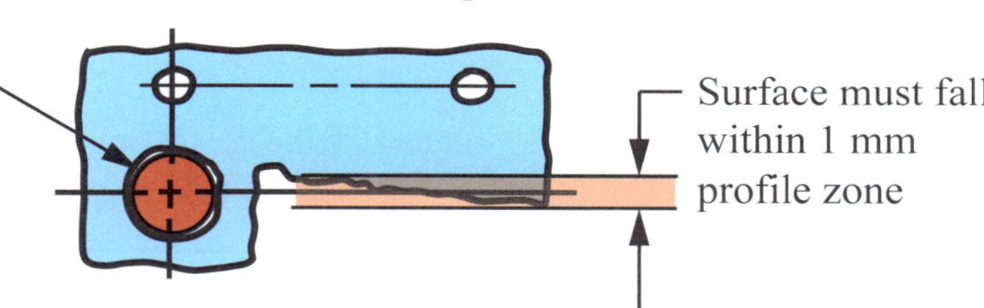

Surface must fall within 1 mm profile zone

Datum feature B referenced at RMB

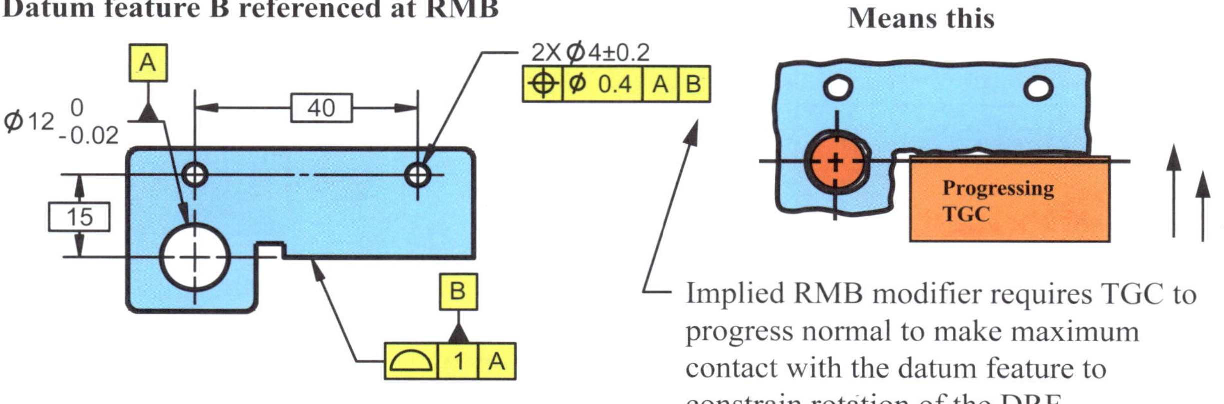

Implied RMB modifier requires TGC to progress normal to make maximum contact with the datum feature to constrain rotation of the DRF.

Datum feature B implied at RMB requires the TGC to expand/progress from the MMB, within the allowable profile tolerance, to make maximum contact with the datum feature. This will result in the datum feature rotating level (parallel). The established DRF is centered on the A axis and rotated to the TGC for B.

Implied RMB might be selected if the corresponding mating feature to datum feature B were adjustable to make it level or parallel in the assembly.

Rotational Control - Unopposed Planar Surface at MMB and Basic

Datum feature B referenced at MMB

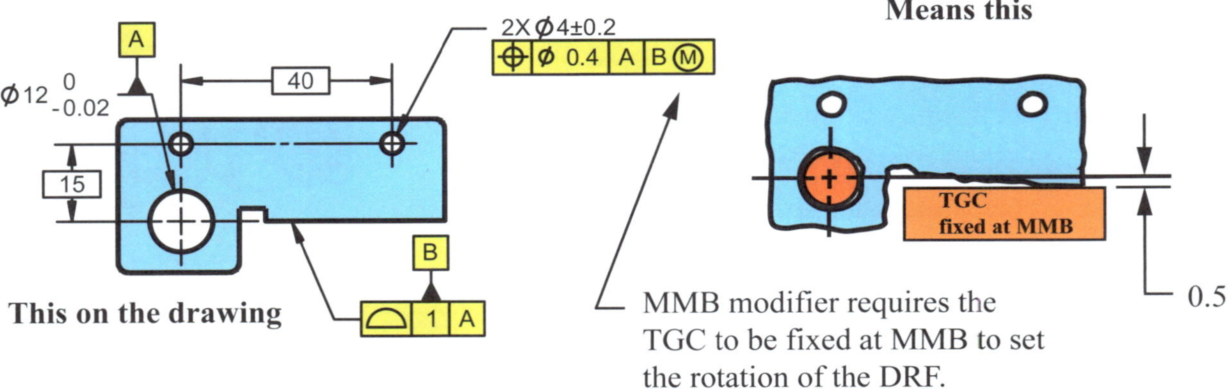

Datum feature B referenced at MMB requires the TGC to be fixed at the MMB, 0.5 below basic (1/2 the profile tol). If the surface is produced high or low, within the profile tolerance, it may rotate to a fixed stop at the MMB to establish the DRF. Where datum feature B departs from MMB, relative movement (rotation) can occur between datum feature B and the TGC. Datum feature B may rotate within the profile boundaries and the confines created by its departure from MMB. The datum feature might not remain in contact with the true geometric counterpart.
(Note this is a change in Y14.5-2018. The 2009 standard required the unopposed surface datum feature at MMB to always make contact with the TGC.)

The MMB modifier might be selected if the corresponding mating feature to datum feature B were adjustable in the assembly within the profile tolerance.

Datum feature B referenced at basic

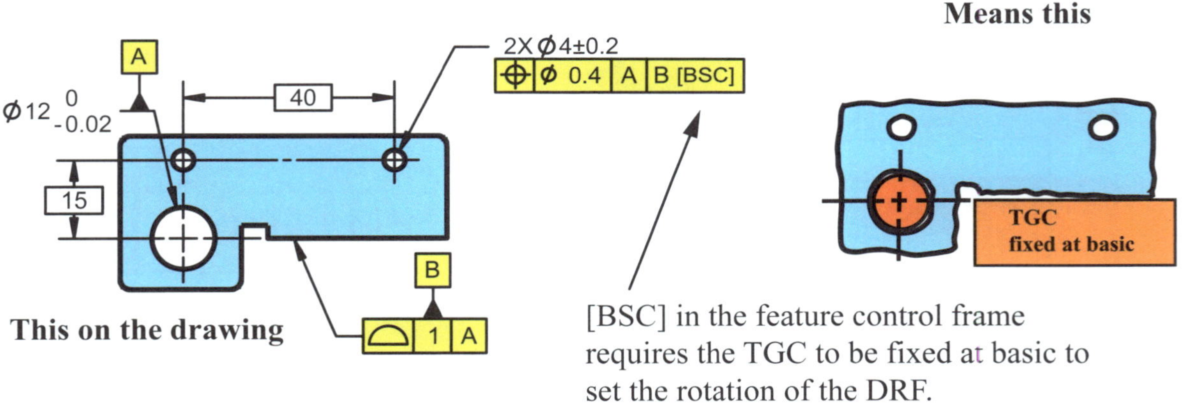

Datum feature B referenced in brackets at [BSC], establishes the TGC at the basic location of zero from datum axis A. The feature must always stay in contact with the TGC. If the surface is manufactured high or low, within the profile tolerance, it must always rotate to a fixed stop at basic to establish the DRF.

Datum feature B, referenced at [BSC], might be selected if the corresponding mating feature to datum feature B were fixed in the assembly at basic. This is the most common reference for unopposed surfaces controlling rotation of a DRF.

Translation Modifier

The true geometric counterpart (TGC) requirements state that for datum reference frame construction, all TGCs are fixed at basic unless otherwise specified. The translation modifier applied to a datum feature reference instead allows the TGC to translate. Translation modifiers are usually not necessary for datum features modified at MMB or LMB because the boundary for the datum feature includes the location error.

In the example below, datum feature A is the back surface, datum feature B is the center hole at RMB, and datum feature C is the width of the bar at RMB. Two scenarios are shown for the DRF: with and without the translation modifier on the datum feature C reference.

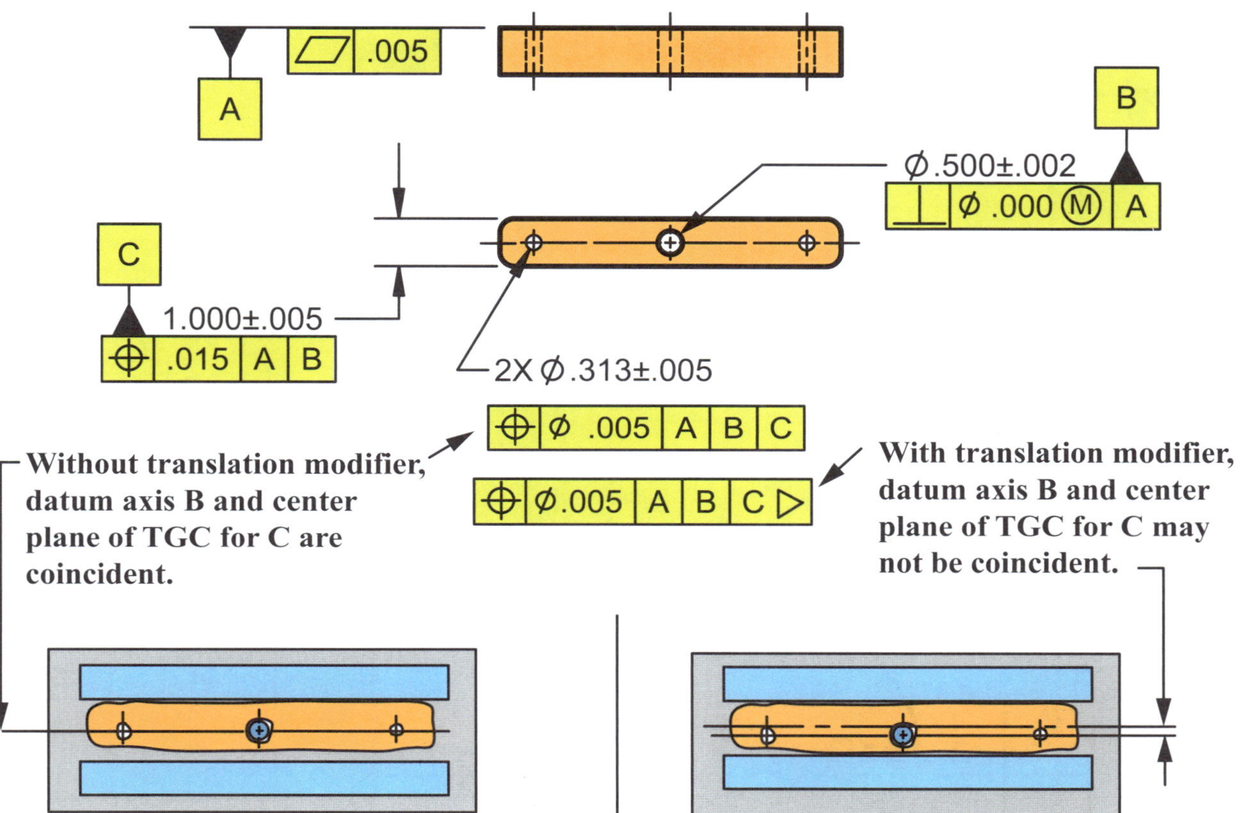

In the upper feature control frame, datum feature C applies at default RMB. **This requires the TGC to collapse** on the datum feature while perpendicular to datum plane A **and centered about datum axis B.**

When the produced datum feature C is off center to datum axis B, the TGC will only contact one side of the datum feature. The center plane of the TGC establishes the rotation of the DRF.

In the lower feature control frame, a translation modifier follows the tertiary datum feature C at RMB. **The translation modifier allows the TGC to translate while collapsing to fully engage the datum feature C.**

Datum feature C TGC will collapse while remaining perpendicular to datum A and be able translate relative to datum axis B in an amount equal to the .015 position tolerance. The center plane of the TGC establishes the rotation of the DRF.

Secondary Datum Feature at MMB - Paper Gage Calculations

This problem was shown earlier on page 5-21 with the datum features at RMB. The example is now shown again but with MMB modifiers to illustrate the calculations to factor in additional tolerance from the allowable datum feature shift. The produced part has been set up in inspection by "zeroing" on datum features A, B, and C. Inspection data has been collected and the results shown in the table below. The data shows the location of the 3 holes are out of position, but notice the datum features B and C are modified at MMB. Additional tolerance may be available from the allowable datum feature shift.

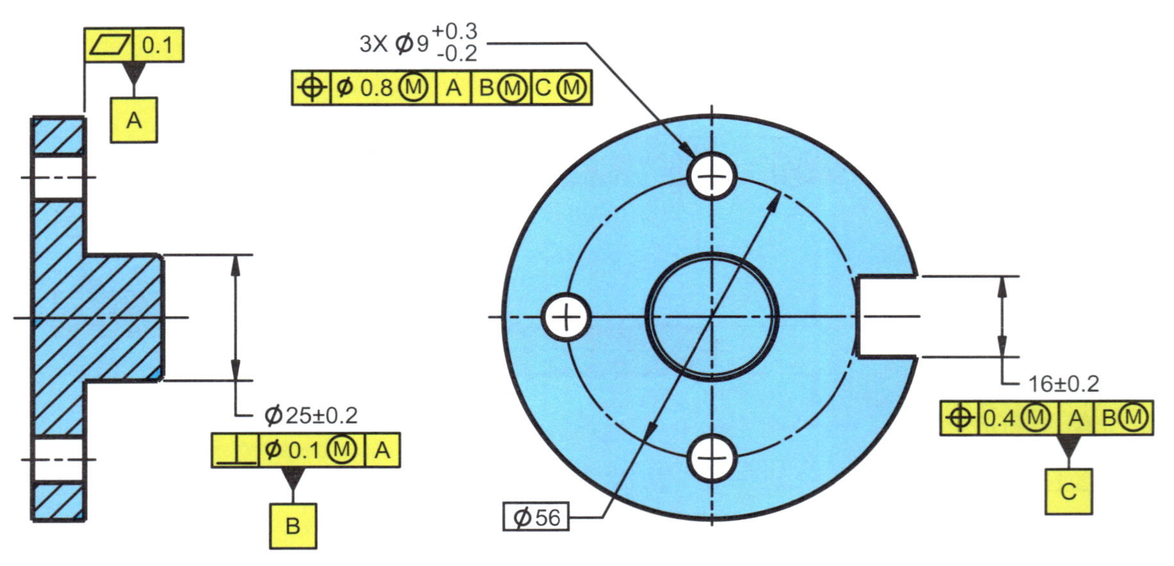

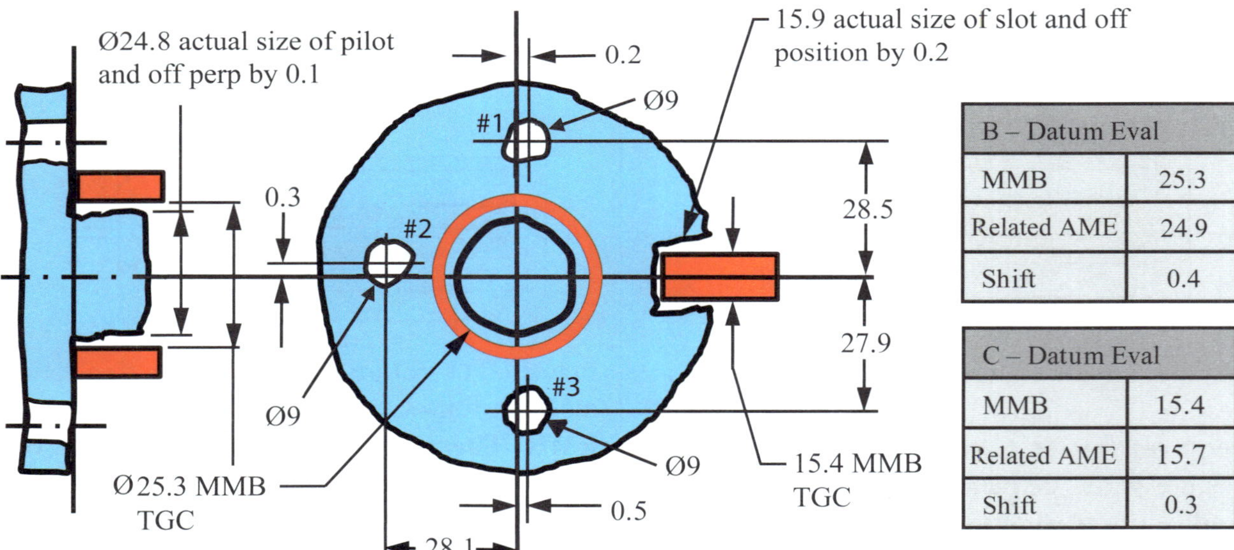

B – Datum Eval	
MMB	25.3
Related AME	24.9
Shift	0.4

C – Datum Eval	
MMB	15.4
Related AME	15.7
Shift	0.3

No.	MMC Size	Act Size	Allow Pos	"X" Dev	"Y" Dev	Act Pos	Acc Rej	Datum Feature Evaluation	Acc Rej
1	8.8	9	1	+0.2	+0.5	1.077	R	Datum feature B - Ø0.4 departure from MMB allows Ø0.4 shift of the datum feature. Paper gage evaluation accepts location of 3 holes.	A
2	8.8	9	1	-0.1	+0.3	0.632	A		A
3	8.8	9	1	+0.5	+0.1	1.020	R		A

The drawing on the previous page shows both datum features B and C with the MMB modifier. This allows the datum feature to shift as it departs from the MMB to allow other features to meet position and profile tolerances. The produced datum feature B pilot was produced smaller than the MMB of 25.3. Since its related actual mating envelope was produced at 24.9, additional shift allowance of 0.4 is available from the pilot. Inspection is allowed to shift the axis of datum feature B within a 0.4 cylinder to obtain conformance on the three hole position tolerance. This datum feature departure tolerance CANNOT be just added to the position tolerance for the holes. It must be plotted and factored in as shown below.

This bonus tolerance from the pilot is accommodated automatically if verified with a functional hard gage. A good CMM operator can also manipulate the software to factor in this additional tolerance by figuring it as a pattern of 4 holes, rather than just 3 holes. The paper gage concept is another way to show this effect.

The 3 holes are plotted on the paper gage using the XY deviation data in the inspection report. Squares on the graph are in increments of 0.1 mm and circles are in 0.2 mm. The XY locations are shown labeled with numbers corresponding to their numbering on the produced part. The paper gage before shifting shows two of the holes outside their allowed position tolerance of 1 mm.

Since the related actual mating envelope of the produced pilot is 0.4 smaller than the MMB, the datum feature B axis could shift off the datum B axis by a dia of 0.4. Looking at the graph, after shifting the datum feature off center by 0.4 dia (0.2 radius), the 3 holes are well within the 1 mm position tolerance. To prove the results obtained by the paper gage, the part could be reset in the inspection procedure and the origin of the pilot could be offset the center by 0.4 dia (R 0.2).

Datum feature C also departed from MMB. This datum feature shift was not used, as the datum feature B shift was enough to accept the part. See next page for an evaluation of a tertiary datum feature modified at MMB.

The paper gage calculations are an approximate evaluation of the hole pattern. Other factors, such as form variation and number of datum points, will affect the outcome. The example is intended to illustrate the general concepts. Data may also be evaluated by appropriate CMM software or on a CAD system.

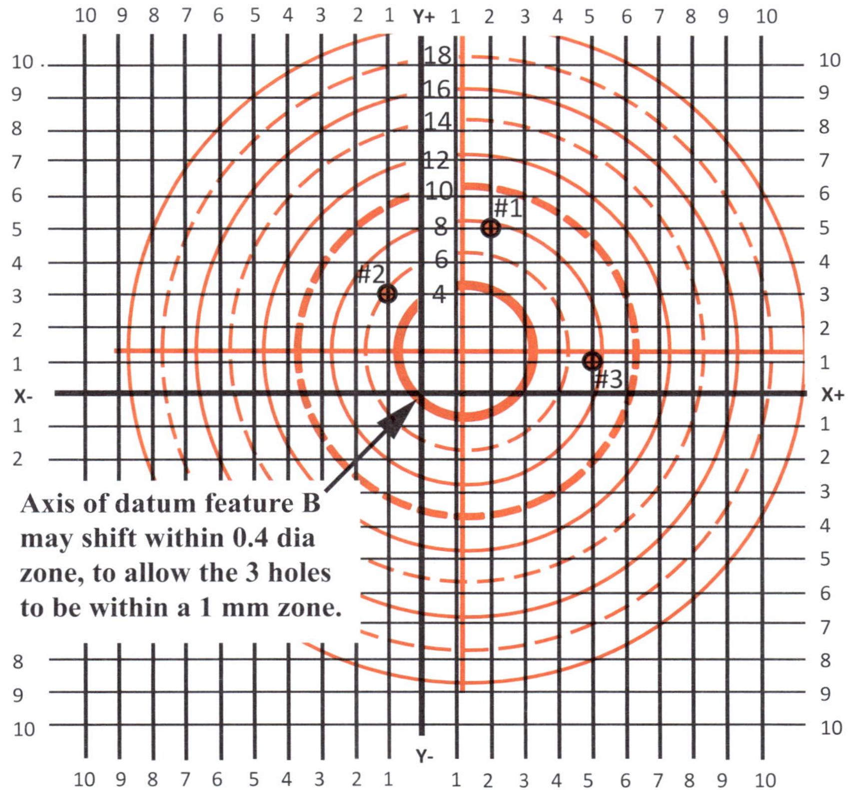

The paper gage evaluation shows the position tolerance of the 3 holes passes when datum feature B shifts from the axis of the TGC by Ø0.4.

Tertiary Datum Feature at MMB - Paper Gage Calculations

This problem was shown earlier on page 5.20 with the datum features at RMB. The example is now shown again but with MMB modifiers to illustrate the calculations to factor in additional tolerance from the allowable datum feature shift. The produced part has been set up in inspection by "zeroing" on datum features A, B and C. Inspection data has been collected and the results shown in the table below. The data shows the location of the 3 holes are out of position, but notice the datum features B and C are modified at MMB. Additional tolerance may be available from the allowable datum feature shift.

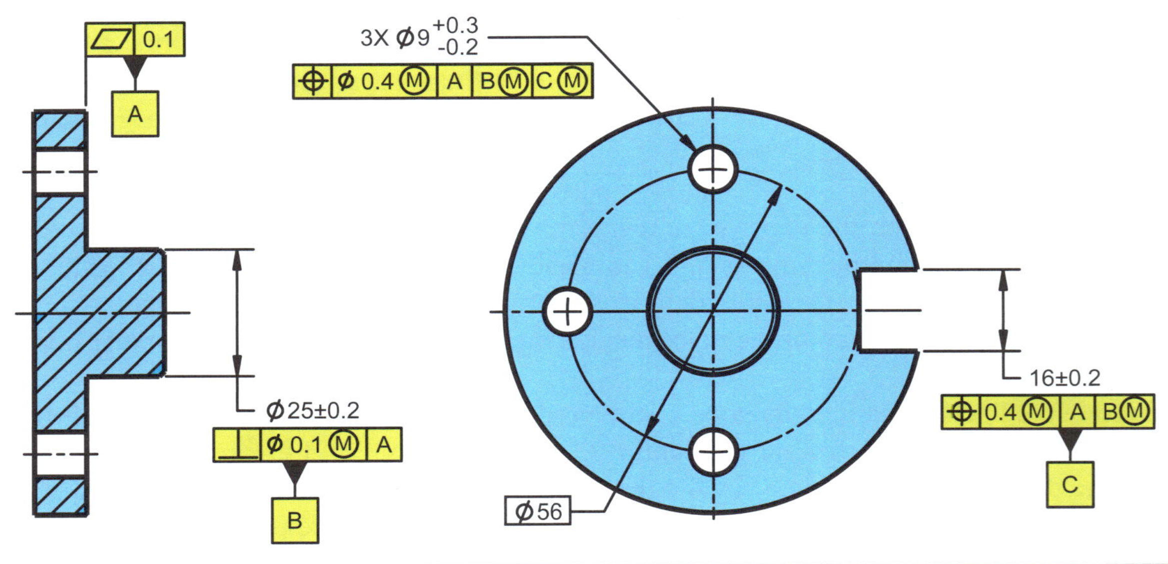

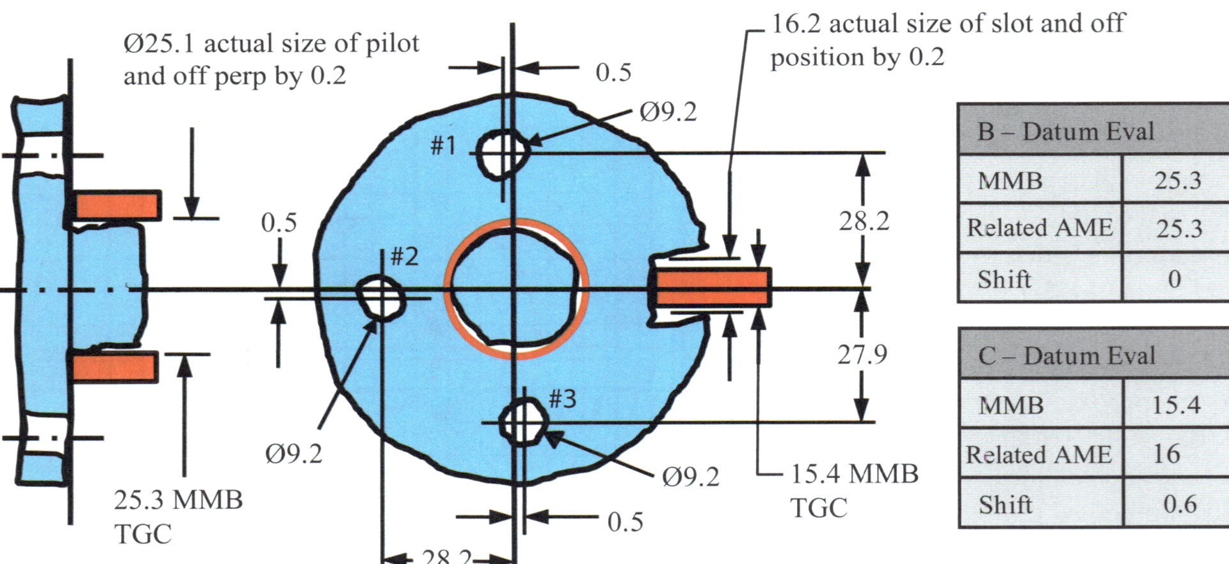

B – Datum Eval	
MMB	25.3
Related AME	25.3
Shift	0

C – Datum Eval	
MMB	15.4
Related AME	16
Shift	0.6

No.	MMC Size	Act Size	Allow Pos	"X" Dev	"Y" Dev	Act Pos	Acc Rej	Datum Feature Evaluation	Acc Rej
1	8.8	9.2	0.8	-0.5	+0.2	1.077	R	Datum feature C- 0.6 departure from MMB allows 0.6 rotation at slot. Paper gage evaluation accepts location of 3 holes.	A
2	8.8	9.2	0.8	-0.2	-0.5	1.077	R		A
3	8.8	9.2	0.8	+0.5	+0.1	1.020	R		A

The drawing on the previous page shows both datum features B and C with the MMB modifier. Since the produced datum feature B did not depart from its MMB, there is no additional tolerance available from this datum feature. However, datum feature C did depart from the MMB of 15.4. Additional shift tolerance of 0.6 is available from the slot since its related actual mating envelope was produced at 16. Inspection may rotate the part about the axis of datum B back and forth a total of 0.6 (±0.3) to obtain conformance on the position tolerance for the 3 holes. The datum feature shift tolerance CANNOT be just added to the position tolerance for the 3 holes, it must be plotted and factored in as shown below.

This departure tolerance from the slot is accommodated automatically if verified with a functional hard gage. It is difficult however, for a open set up or CMM software to factor in this bonus tolerance. The paper gage concept is another way to show the effect of the MMB modifier on datum feature C.

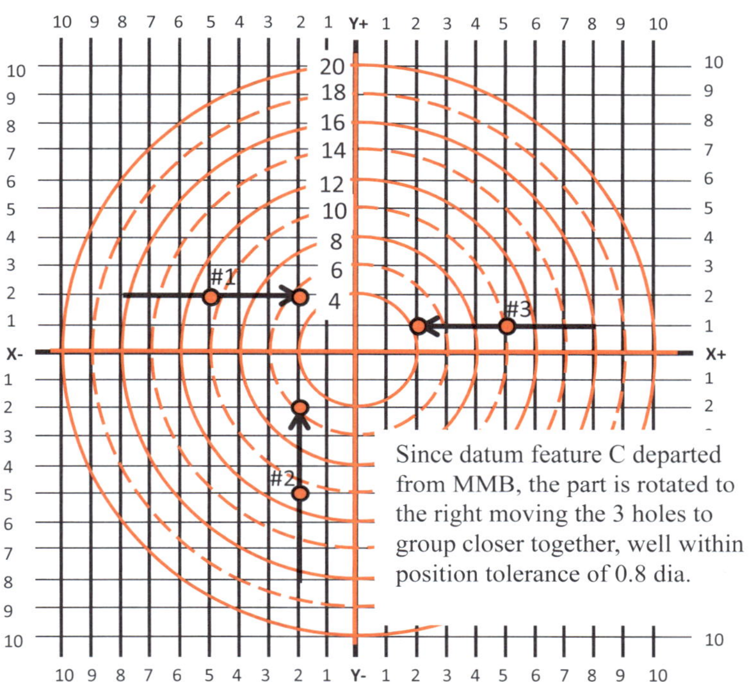

The paper gage evaluation shows 3 holes can be rotated 0.6 (0.3 each way) to an acceptable position tolerance because datum feature C departed from MMB.

The 3 holes are plotted on the paper gage coordinate using the XY deviation data shown on the inspection report. The hole locations are shown labeled with numbers corresponding to their numbering on the produced part. The paper gage before shifting shows all holes outside their allowed position tolerance of 1 mm.

Since the produced slot's related actual mating envelope is 0.6 larger than the MMB size TGC, this will allow the 3 holes to rotate together back and forth about the datum B axis approximately 0.6. This is because the distance of the slot from the datum axis is approximately the same as the distance of the 3 holes from the datum axis. (If the distance were not the same, then a sensitivity/ ratio factor needs to be in the calculations.)

If the part is rotated clockwise 0.3 (1/2 datum feature departure), hole #1 moves to the right by 0.3, hole #2 moves up, hole #3 moves to the left. After the rotation shown by the arrows on the graph, the 3 holes are well within the 1 mm position tolerance. To prove the results obtained by the paper gage, the part could be reset in the inspection procedure with the new datum feature alignment.

The paper gage calculations above are an approximate evaluation of the hole pattern. Other factors, such as the form variation and number of datum points will affect the outcome. The example is intended to illustrate the general concepts. Data may also be evaluated by appropriate CMM software or on a CAD system.

Workshop Exercise 7.6 - Calculating Allowable Datum Feature Shift

Shown below are two separate parts produced from the drawing shown earlier on page 7-28. Evaluate the departure from MMB for the datum features on these two produced parts. Calculate the related AME and determine the amount of datum feature shift that is allowed for each datum feature. Record your answers for each datum feature in the tables below to the right.

Part 1

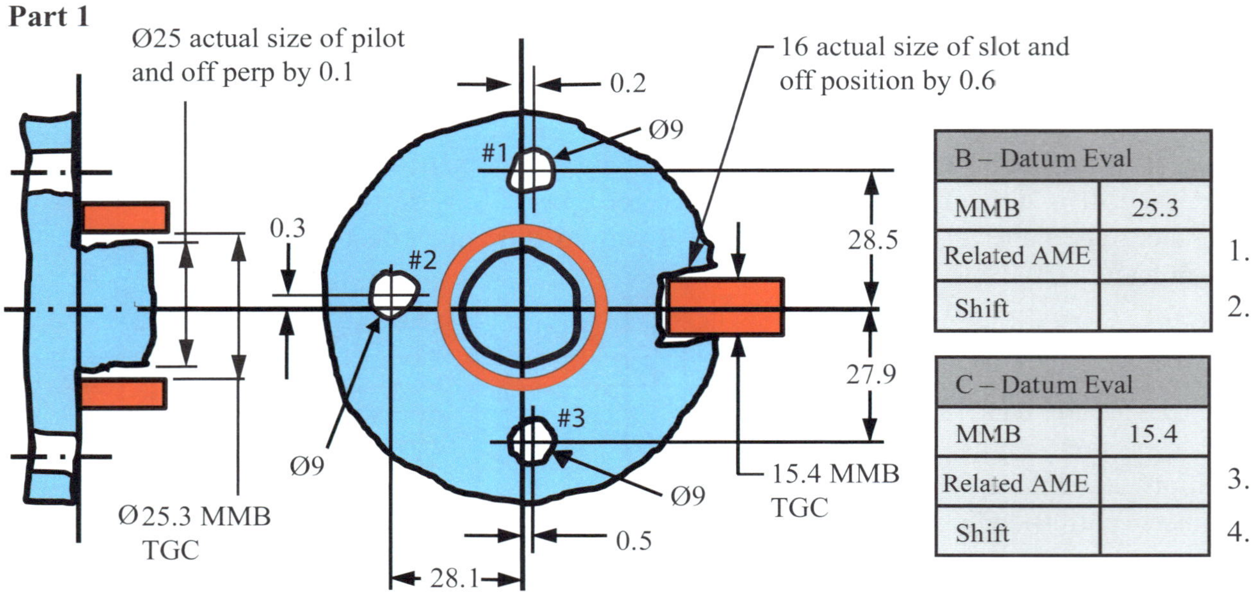

B – Datum Eval		
MMB	25.3	
Related AME		1.
Shift		2.

C – Datum Eval		
MMB	15.4	
Related AME		3.
Shift		4.

Part 2

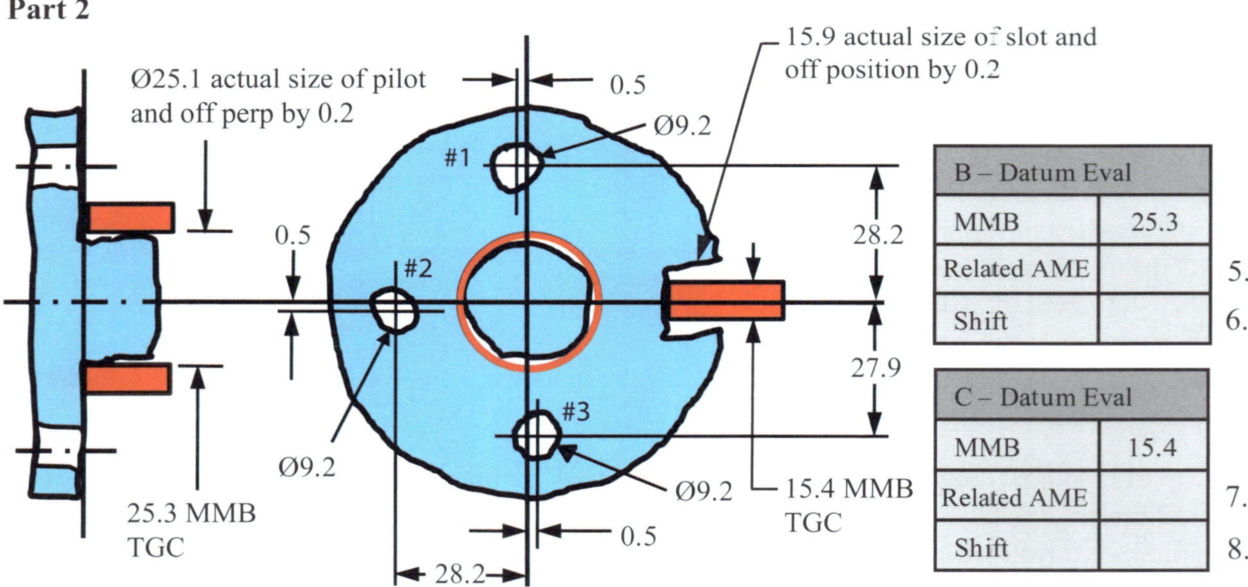

B – Datum Eval		
MMB	25.3	
Related AME		5.
Shift		6.

C – Datum Eval		
MMB	15.4	
Related AME		7.
Shift		8.

9. Features related with basic dimensions using the same datum feature reference, in the same order of precedence, with the same material boundary modifiers, constitute a simultaneous requirement for position and profile tolerances. True or False

Boundaries Summary

Worst-case boundaries of a feature are created from the collective effects of a size tolerance and geometric tolerance. Below is a collection of the terms used in Y14.5-2018.

Maximum Material Boundary (MMB): the worst-case boundary that exists on or outside the material of a feature(s) and is defined by the combined effects of size and geometric tolerances.

Least Material Boundary (LMB): the worst-case boundary that exists on or inside the material of a feature(s) and is defined by the combined effects of size and geometric tolerances.

Inner Boundary (IB): a worst-case boundary generated by the collective effects of the smallest feature of size (MMC for an internal feature of size, LMC for an external feature of size) and the applicable geometric tolerance.

Outer Boundary (OB): a worst-case boundary generated by the collective effects of the largest feature of size (LMC for an internal feature of size, MMC for an external feature of size) and the applicable geometric tolerance.

Virtual Condition (VC): a constant boundary generated by the collective effects of a considered feature of size's specified MMC or LMC and the geometric tolerance for that material condition.

Resultant Condition: the single worst-case boundary generated by the collective effects of a feature of size's specified MMC or LMC, the geometric tolerance for that material condition, the size tolerance, and the additional geometric tolerance derived from the feature's departure from its specified material condition.

MMB and LMB are the most versatile terms and match with the MMC and LMC size boundaries. They can be used in place of the IB and OB. The terms VC and resultant condition are only applicable for geometric tolerances with MMC or LMC modifiers. Graphical descriptions and other quick formulas are shown on the following pages.

For an Internal Feature (**Hole**) with a geotol at **RFS**
MMB = MMC – gtol = IB
LMB = LMC + gtol = OB

For an External Feature (**Pin**) with a geotol at **RFS**
MMB = MMC + gtol = OB
LMB = LMC – gtol = IB

*gtol = value in feature control frame
*bonus = max departure from stated material condition

For an Internal Feature (**Hole**) with a geotol at **MMC**
MMB = MMC – gtol = IB = Virtual Condition
LMB = LMC + gtol + bonus = OB = Resultant Condition

For an External Feature (**Pin**) with a geotol at **MMC**
MMB = MMC + gtol = OB = Virtual Condition
LMB = LMC – gtol – bonus = IB = Resultant Condition

For an Internal Feature (**Hole**) with a geotol at **LMC**
MMB = MMC – gtol – bonus = IB = Resultant Condition
LMB = LMC + gtol = OB = Virtual Condition

For an External Feature (**Pin**) with a geotol at **LMC**
MMB = MMC + gtol + bonus = OB = Resultant Condition
LMB = LMC – gtol = IB = Virtual Condition

Boundaries - Position with MMC Modifier Pin/Hole

The graphical representation and names of the boundaries created by the collective effects of size and position tolerance at MMC.

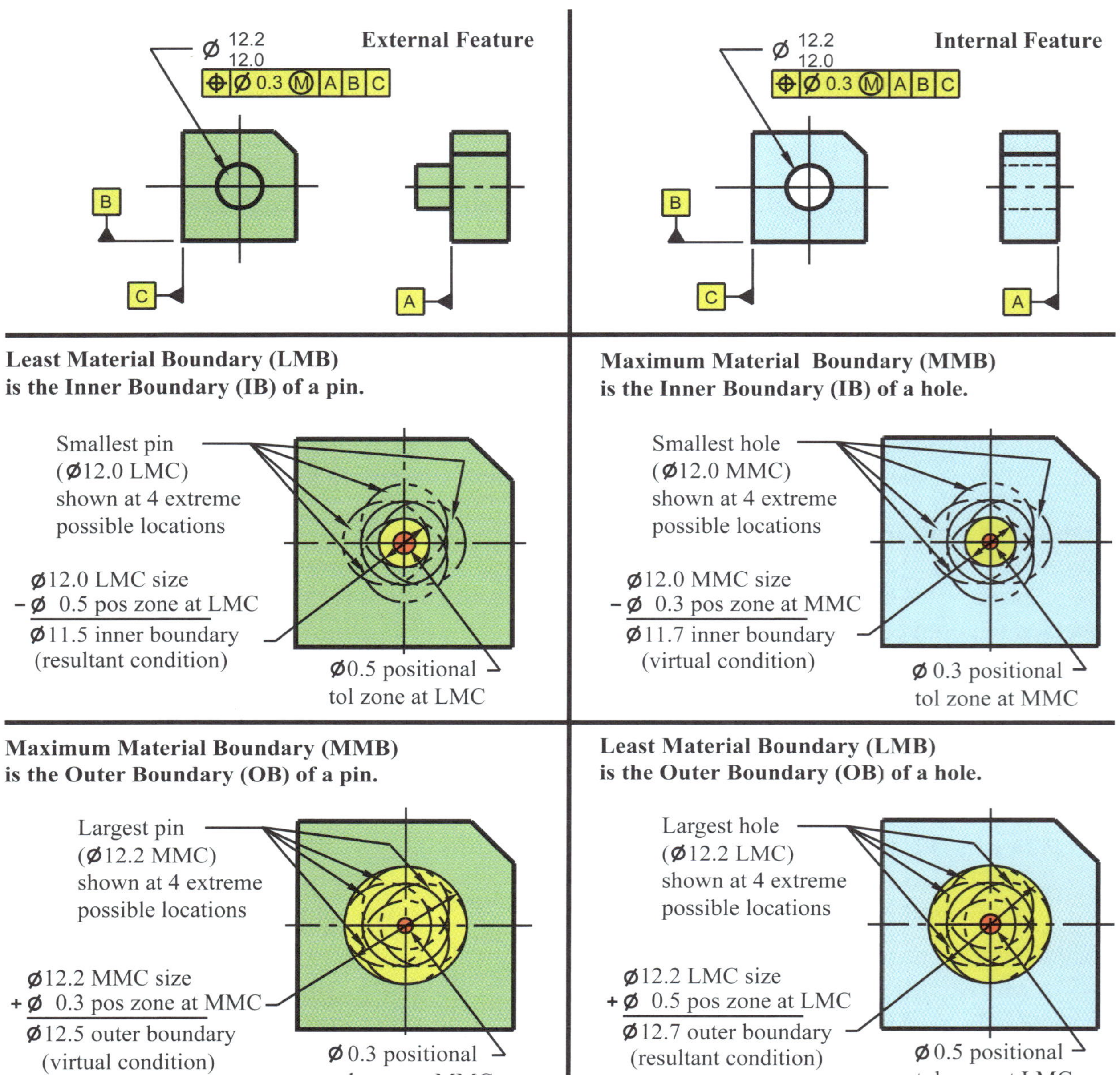

Quick formulas to calculate the MMB and LMB:

If MMC modifier is applied:	MMB/LMB = LMC ± (Tst + Gtol)
If LMC modifier is applied:	MMB/LMB = MMC ± (Tst + Gtol)
If RFS default applies:	MMB/LMB = Mean Size ± (0.5Tst + Gtol)

Tst = total size tolerance
GTol = value in feature control frame.

See the advanced book: **GeoTol Applications and Tolerance Stacks** for more on boundaries and their use in tolerance stacks.

Unit 8
The Datum Reference Frame II
Datum Targets and Irregular Surfaces

Inclined Datum Features

The datum reference frame (DRF) is three mutually perpendicular planes that represent a coordinate system. Datum features creating the DRF do not necessarily have to be nominally perpendicular to each other.

This assembly shows the wear plate mounts on the back surface, the bottom surface and pushes to the left to make contact on the inclined 45° surface. (The three holes do not locate the part, but provide clearance for bolts to clamp the plate in position.) Based on functional requirements, a datum reference frame is developed using the non-orthogonal mounting surfaces.

Wear Plate Assembly

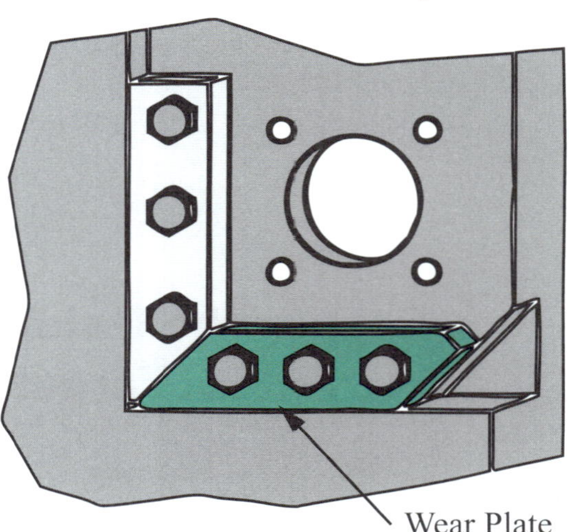

On the drawing below, the angles between the datum features are either implied 90° basic or specified 45° basic. The primary datum feature A is qualified with a flatness specification. The secondary datum feature B is qualified with a perpendicularity tolerance. The tertiary datum feature C is qualified to the primary and secondary datum features with an angularity tolerance.

Note: The ASME Y14.5 standard allows the angularity symbol to be used for features at all basic angles (0, 90, or 45) to control the orientation.

Wear plate drawing with an inclined datum feature

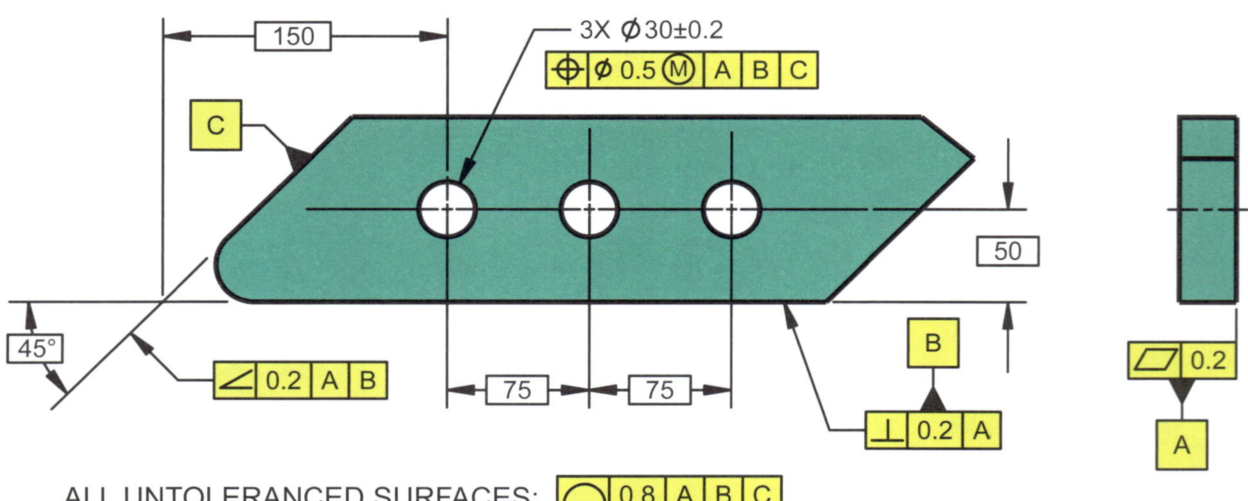

The planes in the datum reference frame (DRF) are always 90° to each other. The datum features may be at other basic angles than 90, including compound angles. The DRF is created using true geometric counterparts that are oriented relative to each other at the defined basic angle(s).

3D illustration of DRF established from inclined datum feature

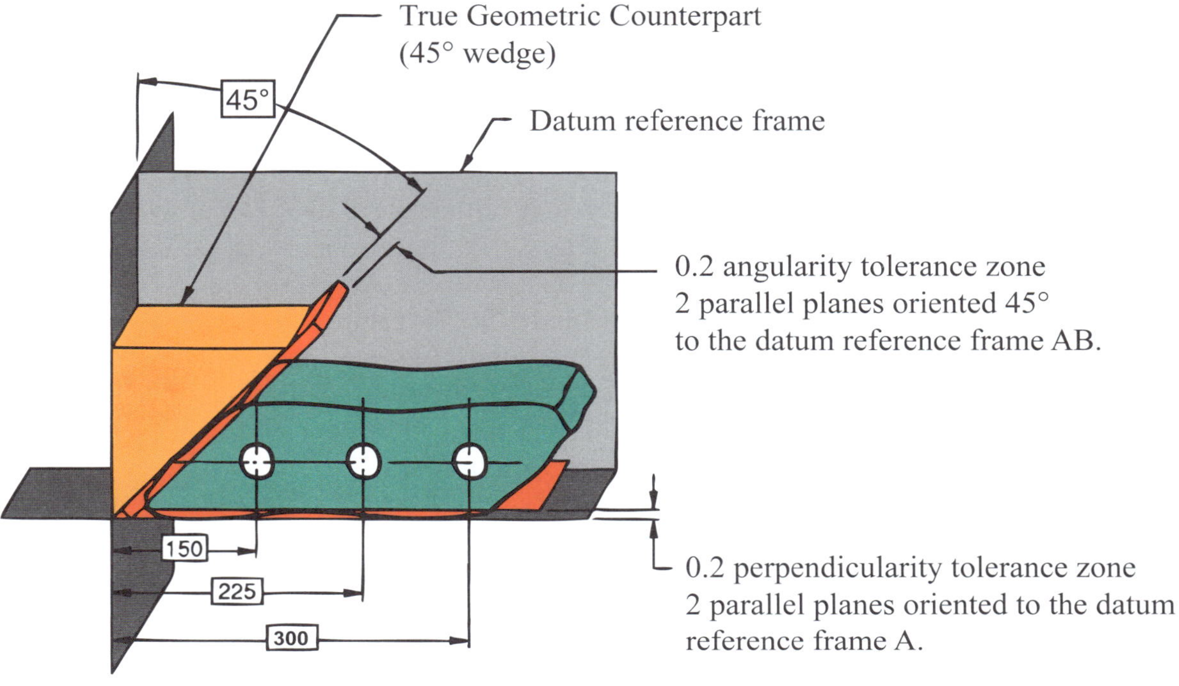

Since the datum features are 3 planar surfaces, the part will make contact with the primary datum at 3 points, the secondary at 2 points, and the tertiary at 1 point. All measurements originate from the datum reference frame and not the part. The part may be verified in a functional gage, coordinate measuring machine (CMM) or rotated on a sine plate in an open set-up.

2D illustration of DRF established from inclined datum feature

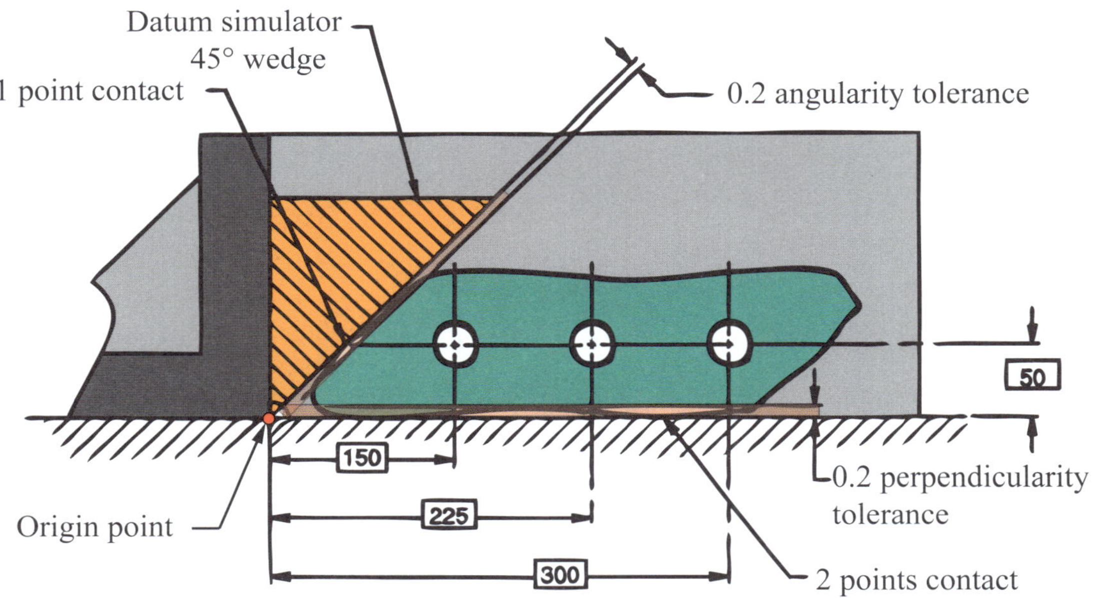

Contoured Datum Feature - Access Door

Access Door Application

The access door mounts on a partial contoured surface as shown. The door is fastened down with 12 screws. The contoured surface geometry, the hole locations, and other product definition are defined in a CAD file.

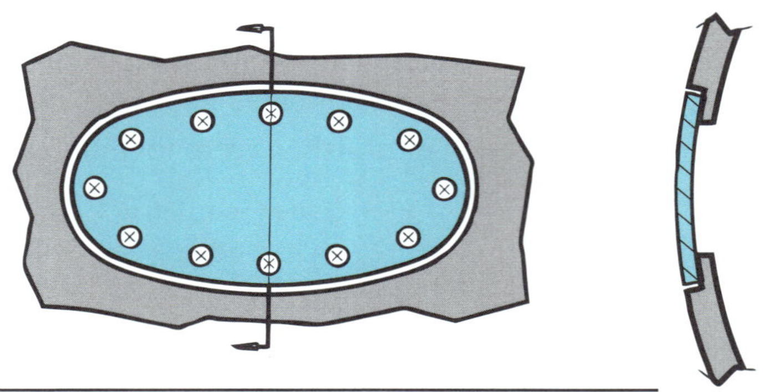

The drawing below reflects the functional requirements of the access door assembly. The partial area of the contoured surface is the main mounting surface and primary datum feature A. By default, a non-planar datum feature requires the true geometric counterpart to expand to make full contact. However, the modifier [BSC] is placed behind A in the feature control frame and instead requires the TGC set at basic defined in the CAD file. Datum feature A is controlled with a profile tolerance to itself. (If the curve were more aggressive, a unilateral profile tolerance would be used.) The two smaller alignment holes on the ends are selected as the datum features B and C. The 10 holes are positioned and other surfaces are profiled to ABC.

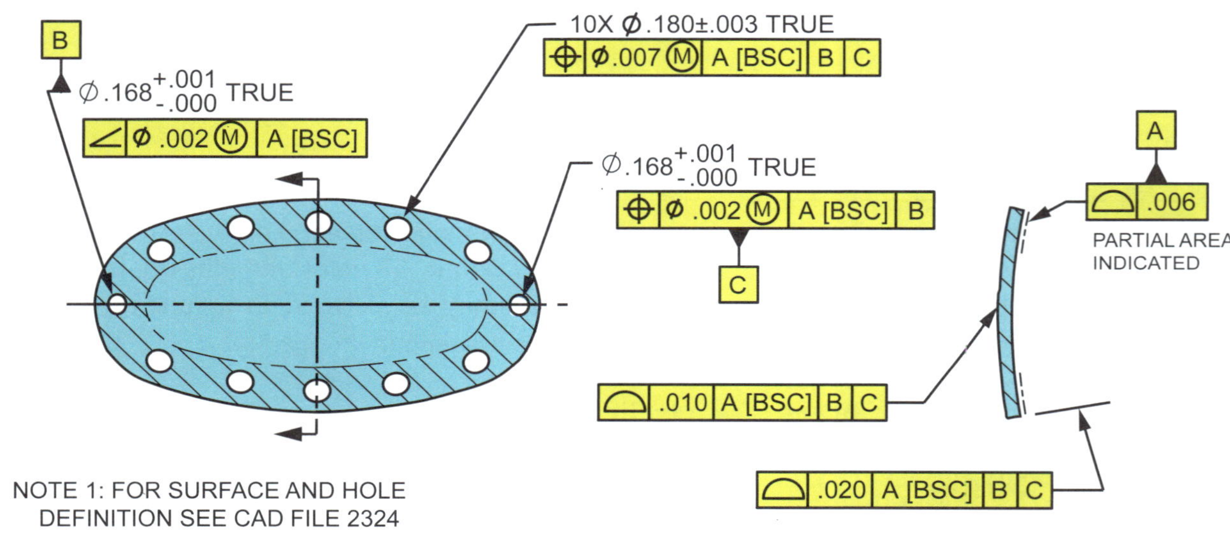

Sample check/holding fixture

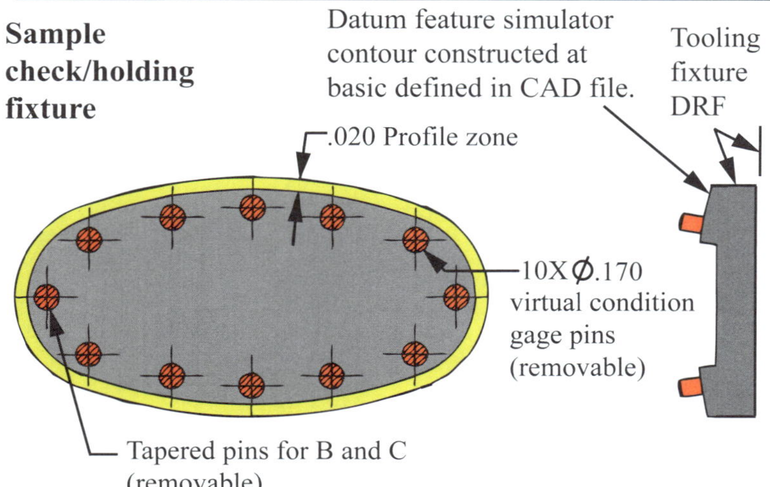

The geometry on the holding fixture is constructed from the basic CAD data using a DRF established from the bottom surface and sides of the fixture. This fixture DRF can be used in inspection to measure the other surfaces and holes of the part.

Datum Target Definition

To establish a datum reference frame, the designer may select specific points of contact on a feature rather than use an entire surface. This may occur to document a manufacturing fixture and/or because surface irregularities make the use of the entire surface impractical. Examples of these type of applications might be on castings, forgings, sheet metal, plastic parts and weldments.

In the past, these areas of contact were sometimes called "set up points", "tooling points", "fixture points", "principle locating points". The correct Y14.5 term is "datum targets". The datum target is not a spot on the part, rather it defines the true geometric counterpart or datum feature simulator. Datum targets can be areas, lines, or points of contact.

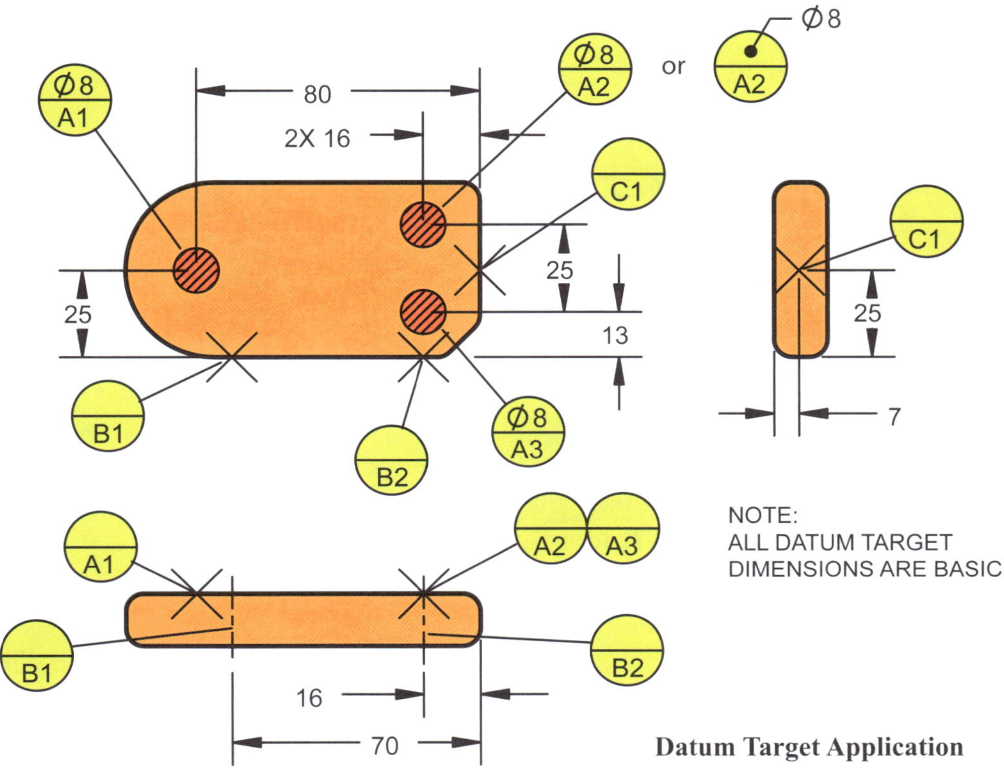

Datum Target Application

Area Contact: If the target is an area contact, the area is indicated by section lines inside a phantom outline with size dimensions. If the definition of the target area is clear, the section lines may be omitted. If the target shape is a circle or square, the shape and size may be designated in the upper half of the datum target symbol. The size may also be indicated with a leader directed to the upper half of the symbol defined or in a note. In other views, the target area is shown as an "X". See datum targets A on the part above.

Line Contact: If the target is a line contact, it is shown as a phantom line in its true view. On other views, it is shown as an "X". See datum targets B on the part above. Where the length of the line contact is important, the length shall be dimensioned.

Point Contact: If the target is a point contact, the point is shown as an "X" in its true view. It is also shown as an "X" in subsequent views. See datum target C on the part above.

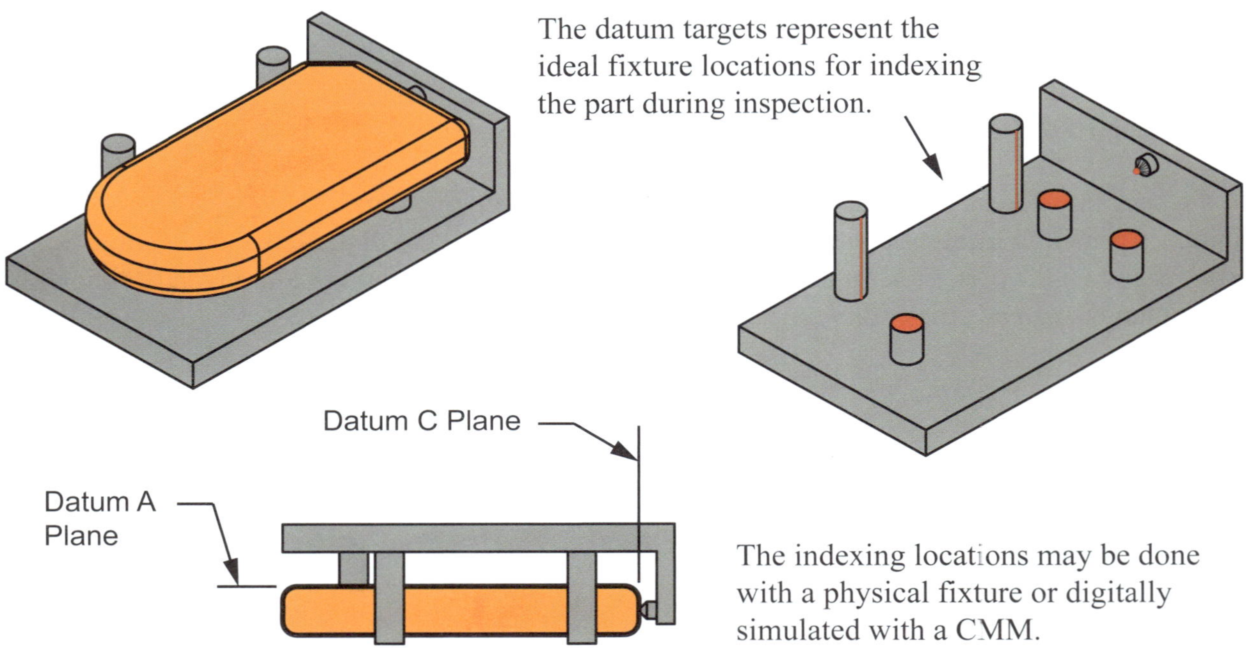

Other Notes About Datum Targets:

The datum target symbol is placed outside of the part outline and directed with a leader line. If the target area is on the near visible side of the part, a solid leader line is used. **If the target area is on the far (hidden) side of the part, the leader line is dashed.**

The location and size of the datum targets are usually defined with basic dimensions. If targets are defined with basic dimensions, tooling and gaging tolerances are assumed to apply adding to measurement uncertainty. If necessary, the targets may also be defined with toleranced dimensions.

Datum target symbols can be used alone to establish a DRF or in combination with datum feature symbols. Targets can be any size or shape as long as they are clearly defined on the drawing.

Datum targets are labeled with letters of the alphabet. In some company practices, datum features are labeled A, B and C on the machining drawings and X, Y and Z on casting drawings. This is done to differentiate the DRF labeling from the machining to the casting.

Where the datum target simulator is required to move, and the movement is not normal to the true profile, the movable datum target symbol should be used with the movement direction clearly defined. See movable datum target later in this unit.

Datum Targets at RMB and MMB

Where datum targets establish a center point, axis, or center plane, the material boundary modifiers apply at RMB by default. This requires the true geometric counterpart to expand/collapse or progresses normal to the theoretical surface. A movable datum target symbol may be used for clarification. When MMB is applied to the datum features, the material boundary modifiers are fixed at their designated size/location.

Datum Targets - Turbine Blade

Datum targets are useful for establishing a DRF on parts with irregular surfaces. The turbine blade casting is a good example of an application with datum targets because none of the surfaces are flat or square.

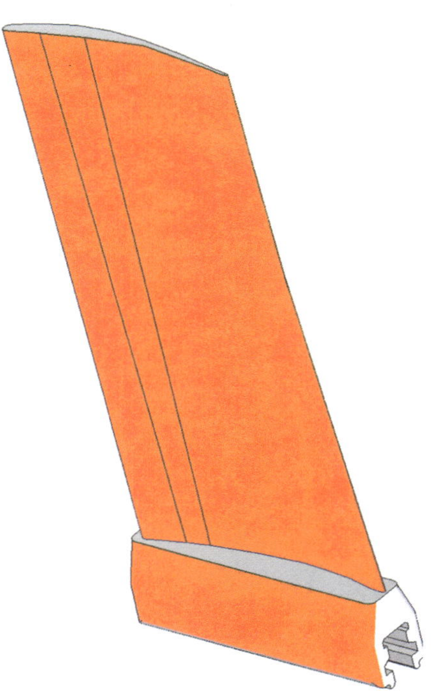

Turbine blade model

The turbine blade is produced with inherent variations due to the casting process. A datum reference frame must be established on the part in order to define design requirements. Datum target lines and points are established on the blade surface to create the datum reference frame.

The targets were selected based on the holding fixture for machining the casting. The leading edge and trailing edge on the casting are aligned to the ideal air flow and the dovetail feature is machined (broached). The check fixture below simulates the datum targets and is a replica of the machining fixture. This DRF is necessary for product definition, verification, and manufacturing.

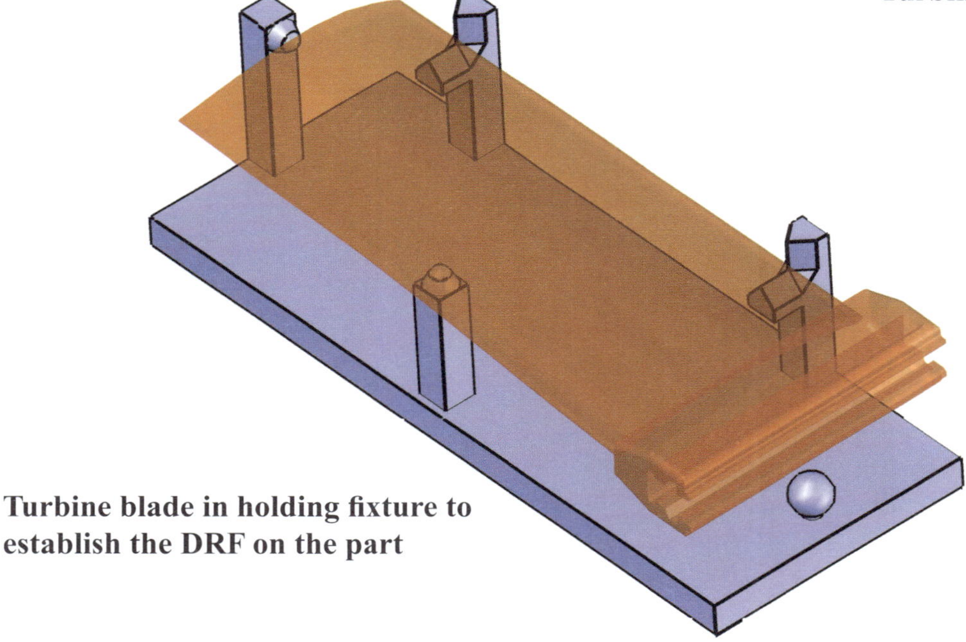

Turbine blade in holding fixture to establish the DRF on the part

The figure above represents a fixture to contain the turbine blade as defined by the datum target symbols specified on the drawing. The size, shape and location of the datum target locators are practically represented in this fixture. Measurements can be made from the tooling ball (and rotating to the planar faces) on the fixture because of the known relationship between the locators and the tooling ball. In some cases, it may be necessary to define a restraint requirement.

Turbine Blade Drawing

Datum target symbols are applied to the turbine blade drawing below to match the holding fixture on the previous page. Datum targets X1 and X2 define line contacts. Datum target X3 defines a point contact. Datum targets Y1 and Y2 define line contacts. Datum target Z is a point contact. The basic definition of the blade can be found in the math data of the CAD model.

Drawing of turbine blade casting with datum targets

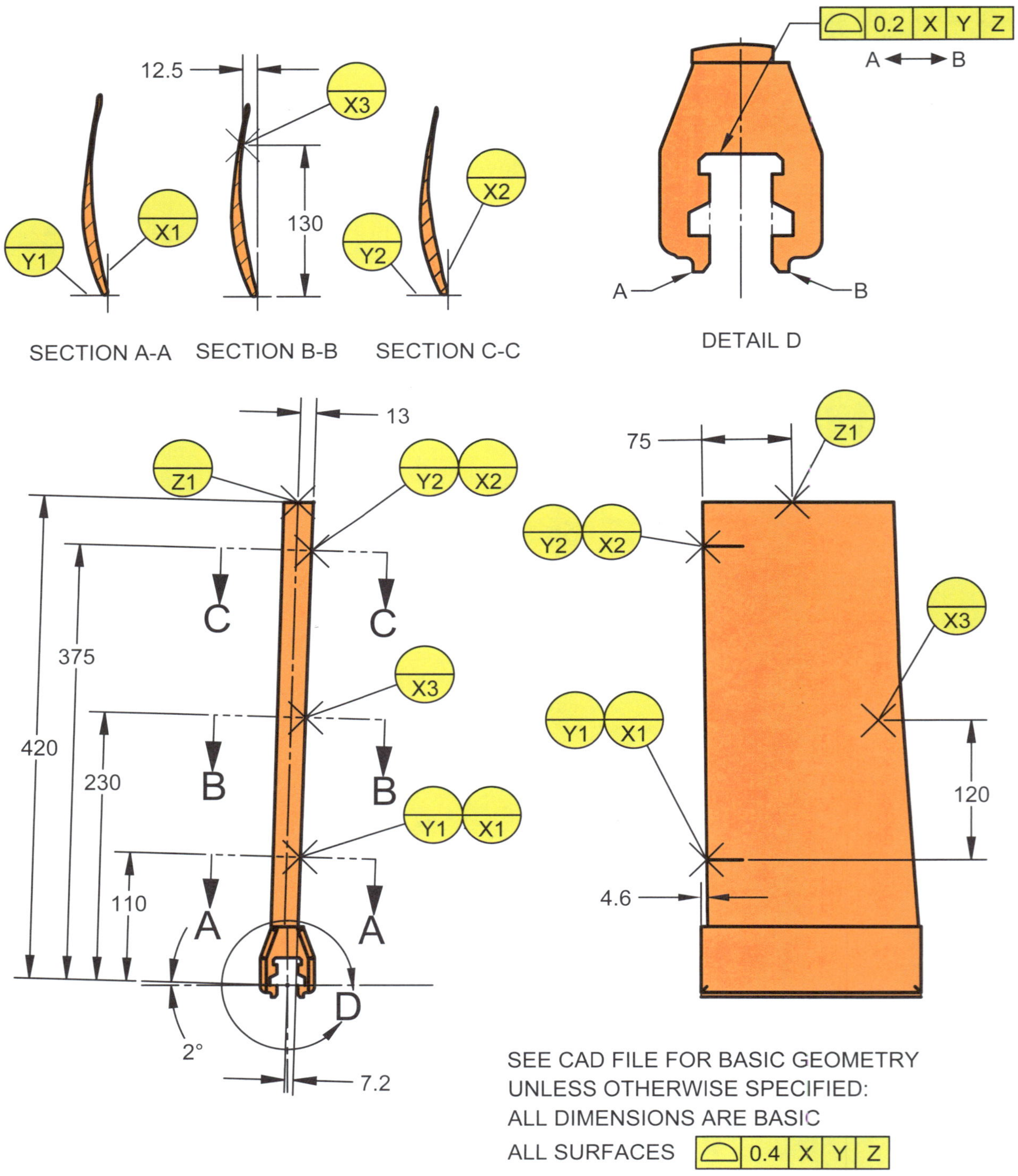

Datum Targets - Offset Datum Plane

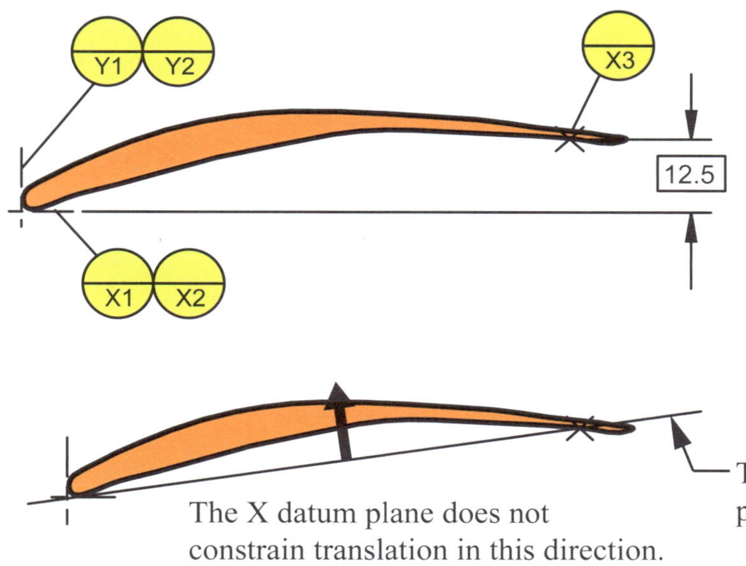

Datum targets defining a datum plane do not have to be coplanar. They may be offset by basic dimensions.

The datum targets X1 and X3 are offset by 12.5 mm. A common question is: "If the targets are offset, then where is the X datum plane?"

The X datum plane is not a plane passing thru all three target points.

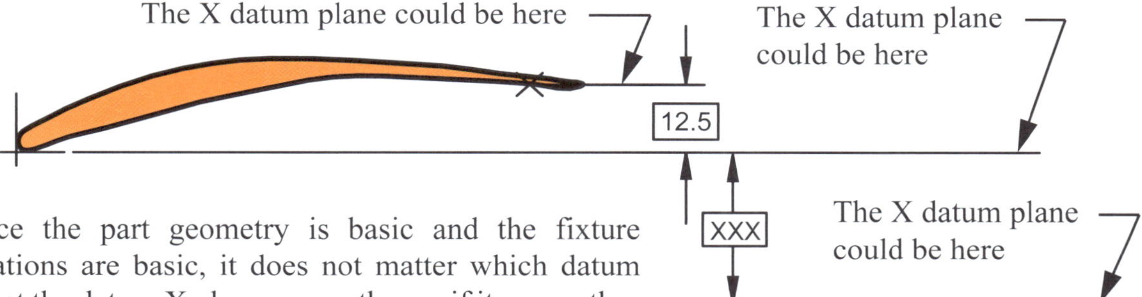

Since the part geometry is basic and the fixture locations are basic, it does not matter which datum target the datum X plane passes thru or if it passes thru any of them. The important thing is these targets constrain the degrees of freedom in the up/down direction. The datum plane X is a horizontal plane wherever is most convenient to define and dimension the part's features. In automotive and aerospace, it is common to dimension the part in the vehicle body position with dimensions defined from the assembly coordinate system. This is fine as long as datum targets or datum features are labeled on the part to constrain the six degrees of freedom.

The dimensioning scheme and the datum features do not always have to be coincident. However, there must be a connection of basic dimensions from the datum features or datum targets and the part features.

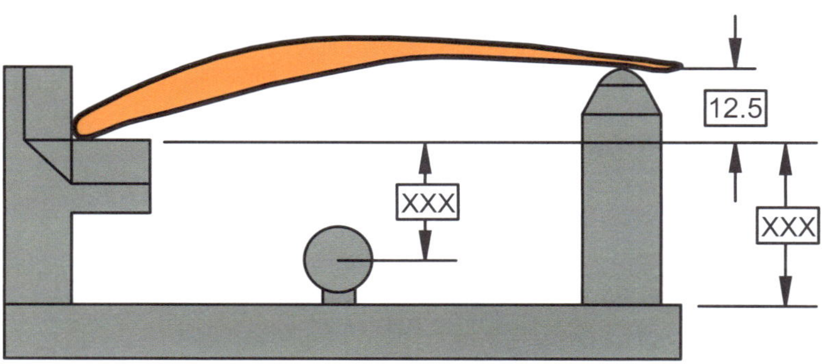

The X datum targets represent theoretical fixture locations that constrain the part up/down. The measurement could come from the horizontal plane thru the X3 location or the X1 location because there is a basic distance between them. Often, the measurement is made off tooling balls or the base of the fixture for both convenience and accuracy.

Datum Targets on a Cylindrical Feature

Datum targets may establish a datum axis or center plane. By default, datum targets on features of size apply at RMB which requires a centering procedure. The targets may also be modified at MMB where the targets will be fixed at the MMB radial distance/size.

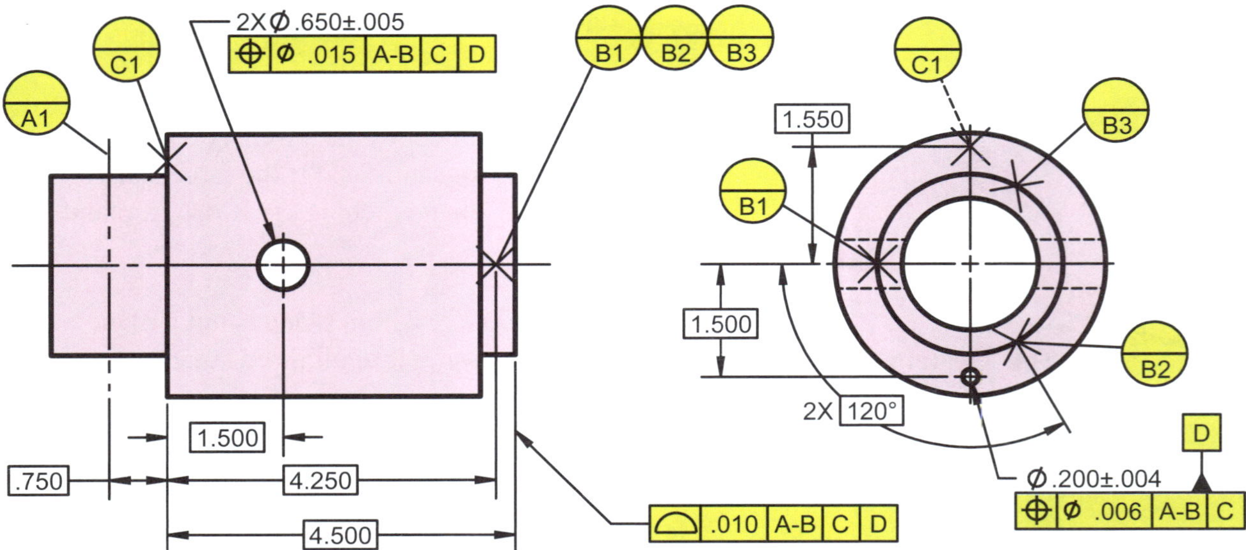

In the above example, target A1 is a contracting circular element creating a center point. B1,B2,B3 are three equally spaced contacting datum target simulators moving radially also creating a center point. Together, A-B is a single axis created from these A and B targets. The C1 point constrains the last translational degree of freedom. Tertiary datum feature D constrains the last rotation.

To ensure repeatability of the location of the three B datum target points, a tertiary datum feature is necessary. The profile tolerance of .010 does not require the datum reference D to define the location of the surface. However, the tertiary datum is neccessary to define the rotational location of the B datum targets.

The dashed line for C1 in the right view indicates the datum target is on the far (hidden) surface.

Datum Target Clarifications

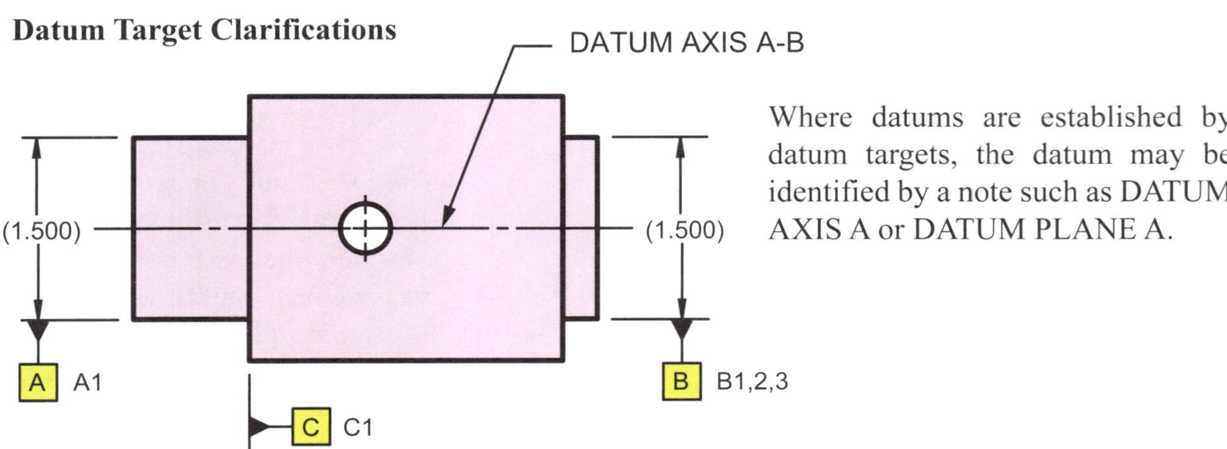

Where datums are established by datum targets, the datum may be identified by a note such as DATUM AXIS A or DATUM PLANE A.

The datum feature symbol may also be added to the above drawing to clarify the datum targets. The letter and numbers (separated by commas) identifying the associated datum targets shall be shown near the datum feature symbol. This is new for ASME Y14.5-2018 and ISO 1101-2017.

Plastic Part with Draft

Below is a plastic part with drafted surfaces to allow it to disengage from the molding tool. Datum targets can be helpful on drafted surfaces to get a more repeatable set-up. The DRF is established by datum A plane, datum B center point (creating an perpendicular axis) and another center point to stop rotation. The Y14.8-2009 Castings, Forgings and Molded Parts standard has more symbols and tolerance clarifications for these types of parts.

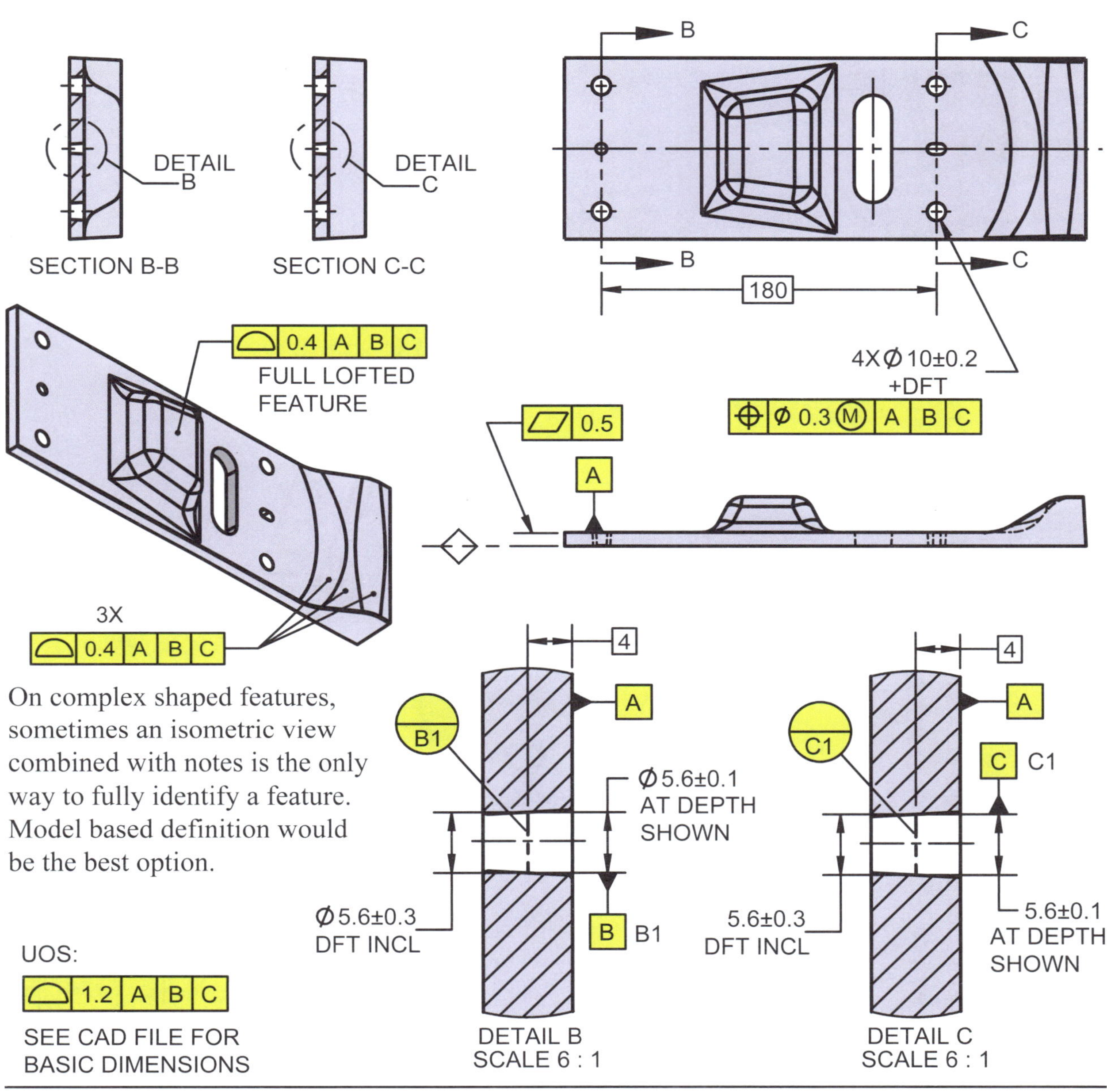

On complex shaped features, sometimes an isometric view combined with notes is the only way to fully identify a feature. Model based definition would be the best option.

Ø5.6±0.1 AT DEPTH SHOWN	This means only the circular cross section of the hole at the depth of 4 must lie within the 5.5-5.7 size boundaries
Ø5.6±0.3 DFT INCL	This means the entire hole must lie within the 5.3-5.9 size boundaries
Ø10±0.2 +DFT	This means the smallest end of the hole must lie within the 9.8-10.2 size boundaries

◇– — Parting line symbol

See ASME Y14.8-2009 for more draft symbols and explanations

The datum reference frame for this outer hood panel is created using datum targets based on how the part loads in the assembly fixture with the hood panel inner reinforcement. The targets are located relative to the body grid system. Since more than 3 targets are selected for the primary datum, a restraint requirement is added. The section views show the part mounting in the check/assembly fixture. When a datum target area is shown on a nonplanar surface, the shape of the datum target is the same as the basic shape of the surface. See the next page for the tolerances.

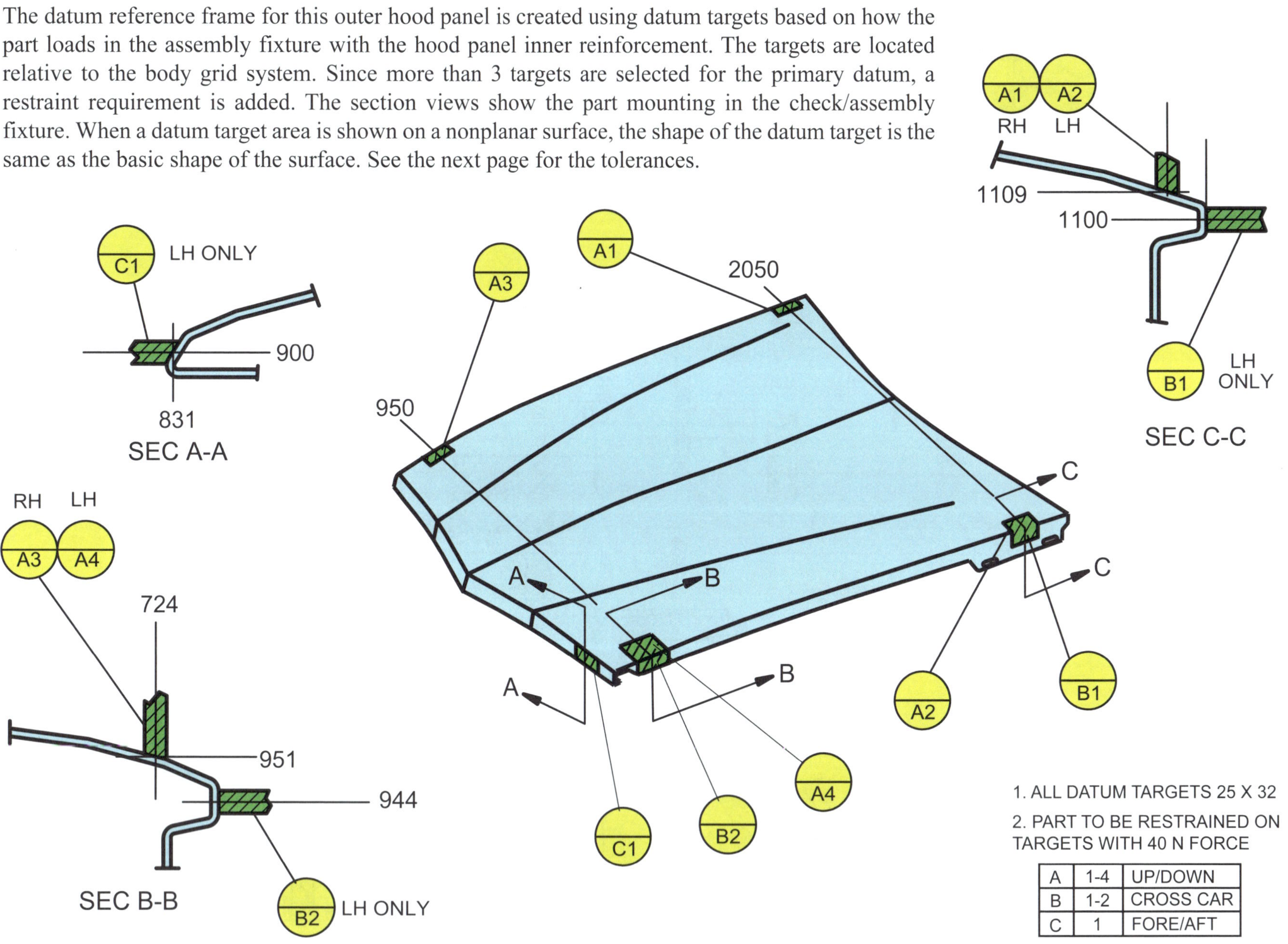

A	1-4	UP/DOWN
B	1-2	CROSS CAR
C	1	FORE/AFT

This flexible sheet metal part is mathematically defined in a CAD model. The dimensions and math data are defined as basic. This page defines the tolerances applied to the surfaces, and the datum targets defines the datum reference frame. The profile controls apply in the restrained condition. These tolerances will help control the “gap” and “flush” requirements for the assembly with other body panels.

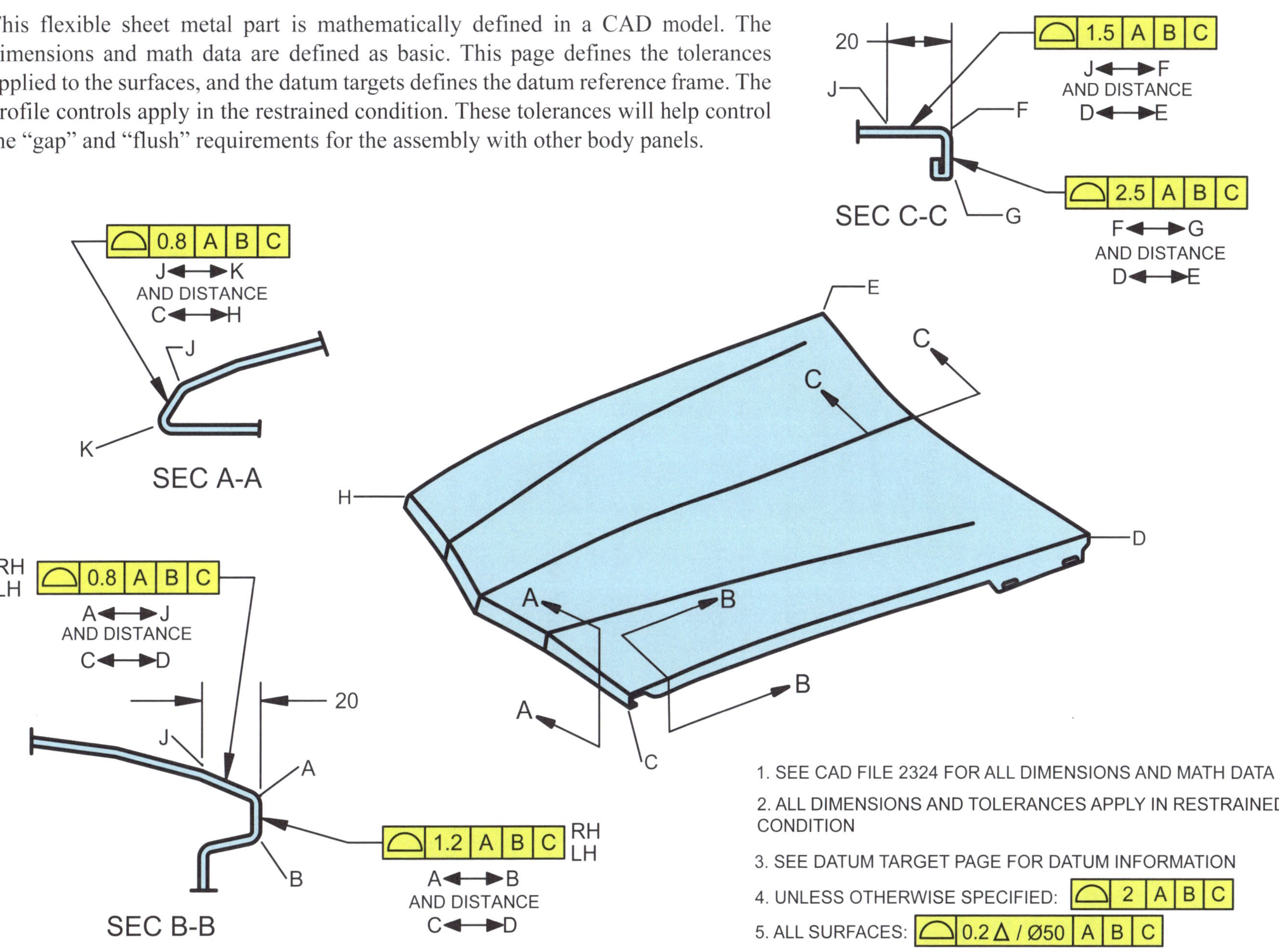

Nonrigid Parts - Restrained Condition

Unless otherwise specified, Y14.5-2018 states all dimensions and tolerances apply in a free state condition with no restraint (outside force applied). Some parts, such as thin metal, plastics and rubber, are nonrigid in nature and it may be necessary to specify design requirements in a restrained condition. This instead requires the part to be verified with a restraint (force) to evaluate the tolerances. The restraint is usually applied to resemble the functional mating fit.

Example: A thin sheet-metal stamping may have surfaces with spring-back due to the stamping operation. The part is inspected in the default free state and the part is out of tolerance. However, the part functions fine when the datum feature surface is bolted down in the assembly. The designer may instead specify the tolerances apply while the datum features are restrained (with a specified force) to resemble the bolted assembly condition.

Nonrigid parts have been built for a long time without such detailed restraint notes. In the past, the designer might have allowed "standard shop procedures" or "common sense" to apply, but technically these outside forces may not be applied until the restraint note is added. Before applying restraint notes, a designer may consult with manufacturing and quality to mimic any procedures already in place. If all company parts are similar or there is a standard restraint procedure, this information may be specified in a company standard and referenced on the drawing. There should not be any assumptions about required forces in the design requirements.

To invoke a restrained condition, a general note, a flag, or a local note shall be specified on the drawing defining the restraint requirements. Here are some guidelines for the restraint note to consider:

Magnitude of Restraint:

The allowed or required magnitude of force (clamp load, torque, etc.) or condition used to restrain a part on the physical datum feature simulators.

Location, Direction, Sequence, and Area of Restraint

Parameters such as the location, direction, sequence, and area of restraint may be shown on the drawing. There are two default requirements set by Y14.5-2018:

(a) When datum targets are specified, the restraint load shall be applied over each datum target, normal to the surface at that location and the same size and shape as the datum target UOS.

(b) When the entire surface is specified as the datum feature, the restraint load shall be applied over the entire datum feature, normal to the true geometric counterpart and the same size and shape as the datum feature UOS.

Gravity

The direction of gravity may be indicated on parts that install in a certain orientation and sag of the part may affect specifications. Examples would be a car hood or dash board panel.

The note for restraining the part can vary widely depending on the application and can be very detailed or kept purposefully vague for flexibility. There is no standard note or symbol that will cover all the possible restraint conditions. The ASME Y14.5-2018 standard expanded this restraint note section from 2009. A new standard is in the works: ASME Y14.48: Universal Load and Direction Indicators that will help standardize and mathemetize the written notes. ISO standards users also see ISO 10579:2010 Dimensioning and Tolerancing - Non-Rigid Parts.

Restrained Condition and Free State Symbol

Thin walled and flexible parts like the one below need a note to restrain the part during inspection. This note should explain how the part is restrained and the force required. A sample note is shown on the drawing below.

In addition to the tolerances in the restrained condition, it may be necessary to specify some tolerances with the part in the free state condition. This is done with the free state symbol (circle F). Before restraint, the part should be checked to make sure it is not bent beyond its elastic limit and too much force is needed to assemble and insert screws. In another case, a part may be bent so much that the forces required to restrain it will deform the mating part during assembly. The free state symbol is applied by placing it next to the size tolerance or in a feature control frame following the feature tolerance and any modifiers. The free state modifier is shown on the circularity specification below.

Also see the Hat Bracket in unit 11 for an example of a sheet metal bracket in which some tolerances apply in the restrained condition and others in the free state.

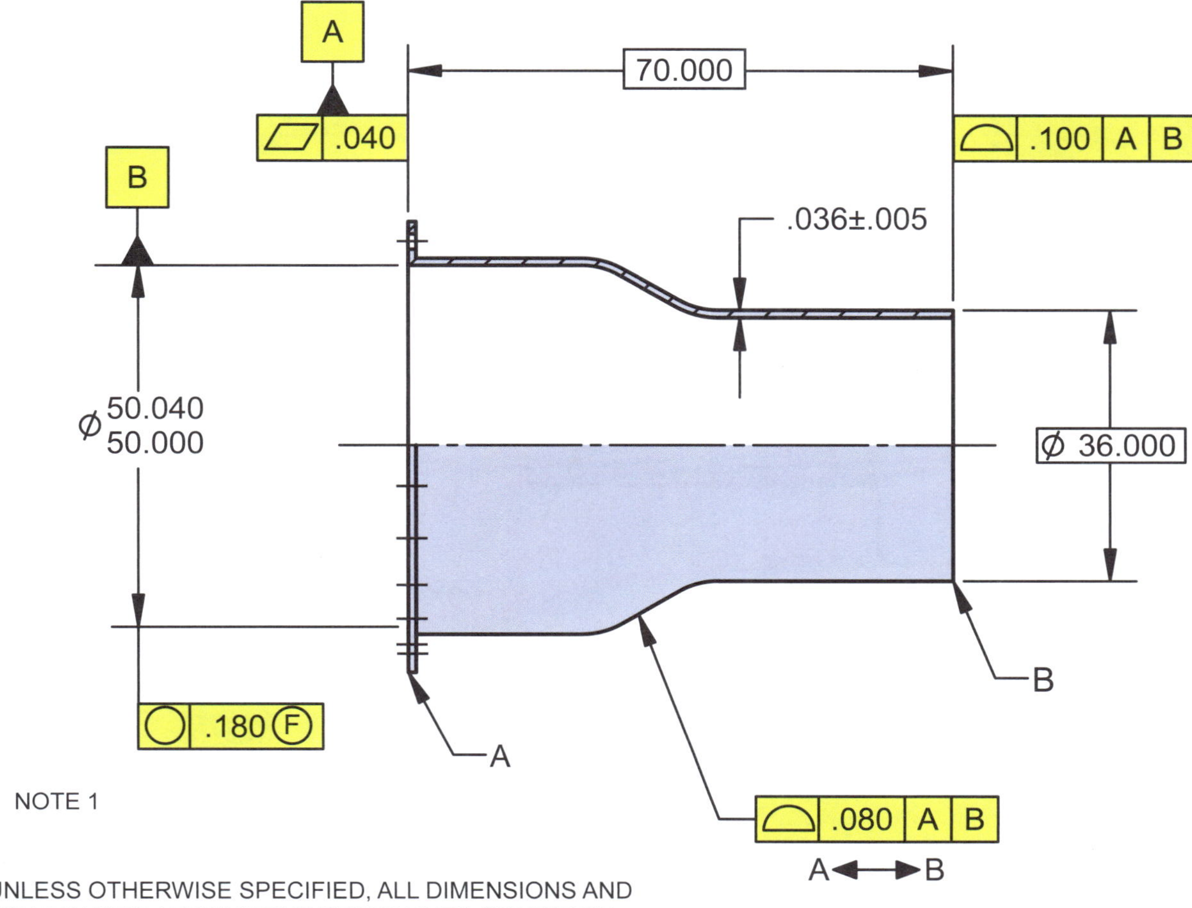

NOTE 1

UNLESS OTHERWISE SPECIFIED, ALL DIMENSIONS AND TOLERANCES APPLY IN THE RESTRAINED CONDITION.

MOUNT THE PART ON DATUM FEATURE A USING 24 .500-13 UNC BOLTS TORQUED TO 120 INCH POUNDS, WHILE RESTRAINING DATUM FEATURE B AT ITS SPECIFIED LIMIT.

Pillow Block Machining

The following pages will show how to create two separate drawings for a machined part that begins as a casting. Controlling both drawings is important to keep track of multiple processes and troubleshoot the design and manufacturing issues.

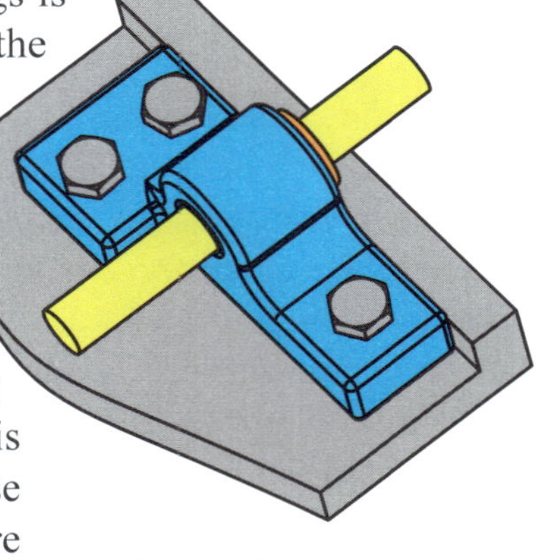

Pillow block assembly

Start with the machined part: The pillow block mounts on the bottom face, aligns to the side face and is centered in the assembly by the large hole. The three clearance holes allow bolts to fix the part in the assembly.

The datum features are selected based on these functional mating conditions. The bottom face is datum feature A, the side face is datum feature B and the 13.2 mm hole is datum feature C. These features, in order, establish the DRF. The datum features are qualified with a flatness, perpendicularity and position tolerance respectively. All remaining machined features are located to this DRF. The pillow block will be made from a casting, which is shown on the next pages. We will come back to this drawing to link the machining and casting.

Machining Drawing

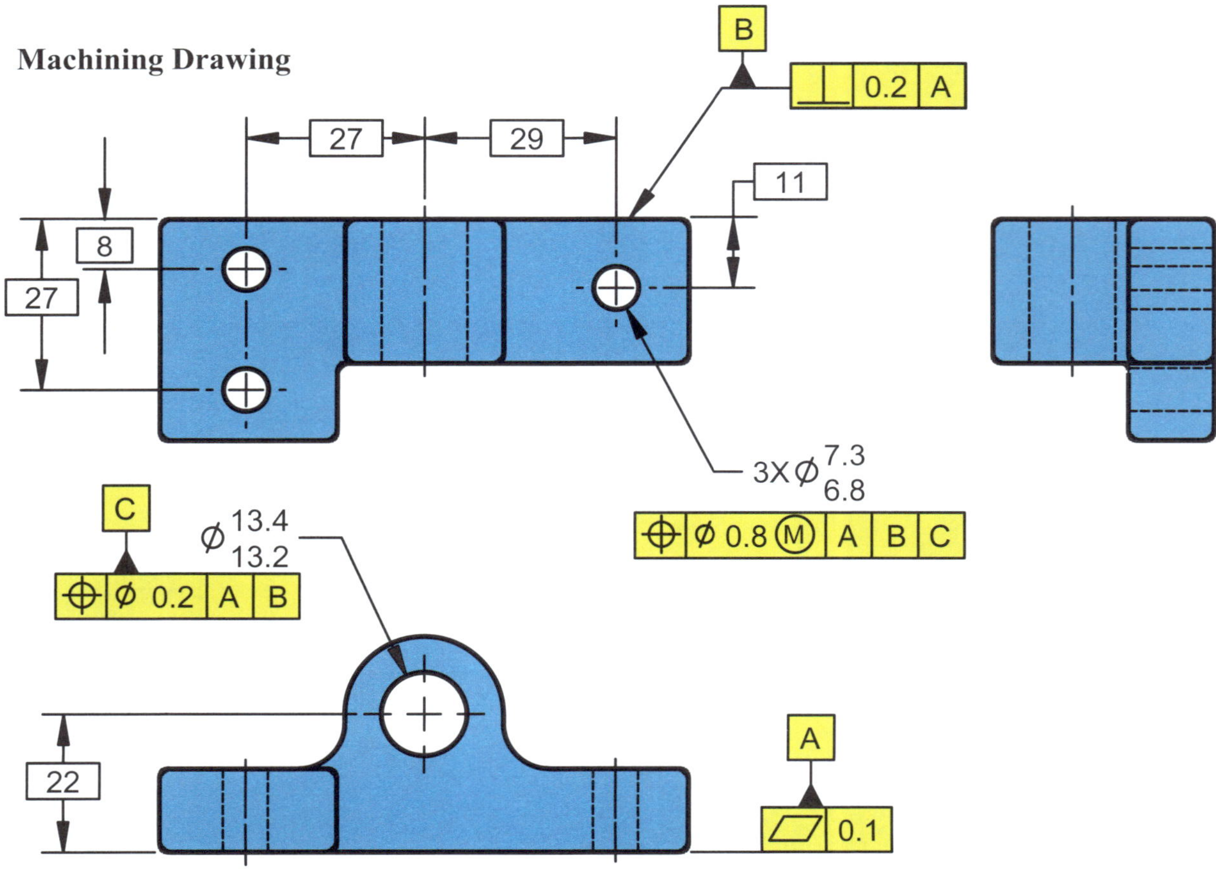

Pillow Block Casting

The casting has been defined on the drawing below. Manufacturing, in consultation with design, determines the manufacturing process and fixturing necessary to machine the pillow block. It has been decided to use one fixture and perform all machine operations in one set-up. The XYZ datum targets on the drawing correspond to the locating points on the fixture (3,2,1).

The X datum targets have their centers removed to accommodate the 3 hole drilling operation.

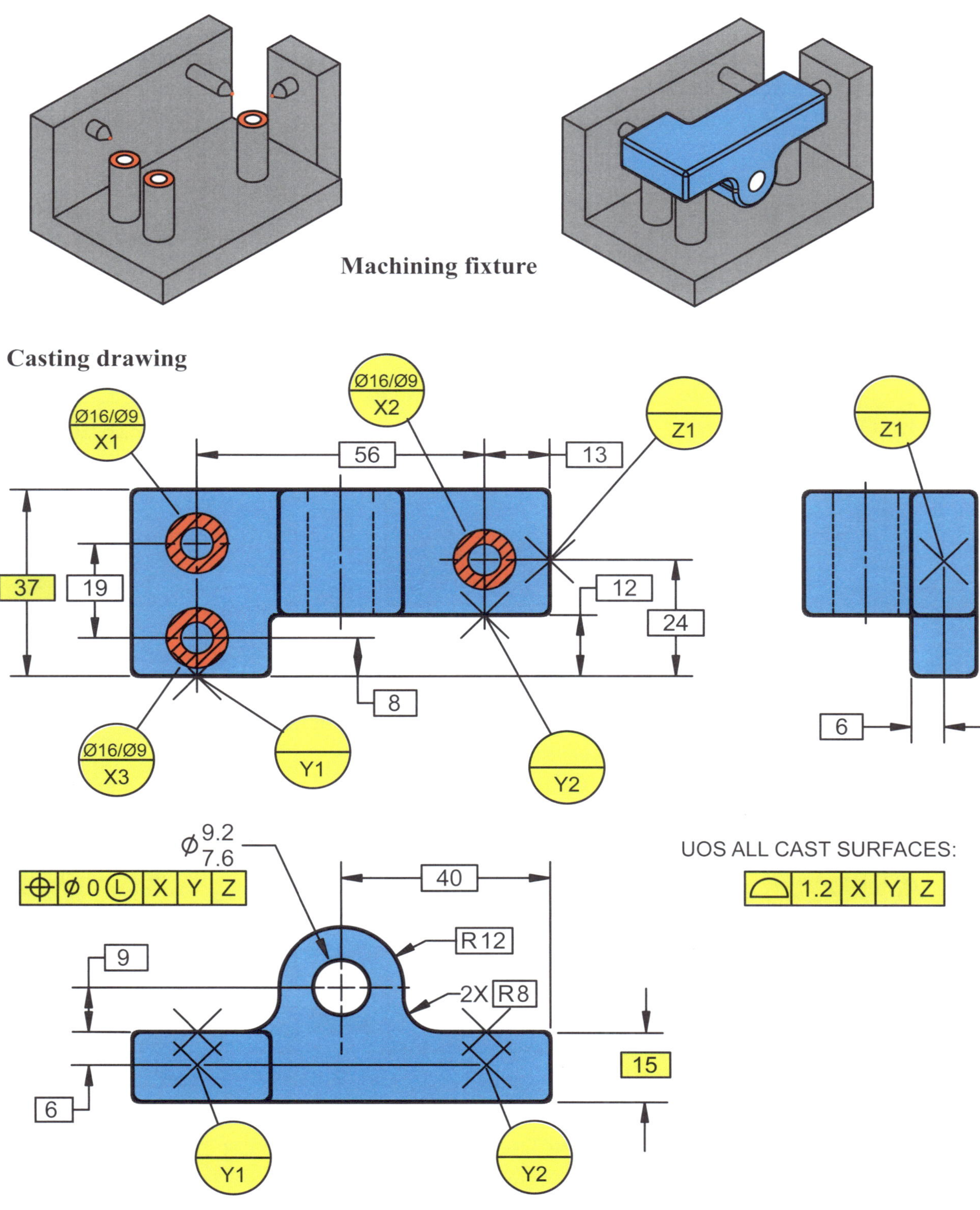

Option 1: Linking the Machining to the Casting

The machined part has an ABC datum reference frame established, and all machined features are located to this DRF. The cast part has an XYZ datum reference frame, and all cast features are located to this DRF.

To figure the cast part dimensions and resulting wall thickness calculations, the machined datum features must be located to the cast DRF. The bottom surface labeled as primary datum feature A on the machined part has a profile tolerance to locate it to the cast XYZ DRF. The rear surface labeled as the secondary datum feature B has a profile tolerance to locate it to the cast DRF. The 13.2 mm hole is the tertiary datum feature on the machined part and it is positioned to the cast DRF. These profile and position tolerances (indicated by note 2) locate the machine DRF to the cast DRF. This is what we formerly called the "first machine cuts."

XYZ - casting DRF
All cast features located to this

ABC - machining DRF
All machined features located to this

ABC ⟶ XYZ

Machining DRF must be located to the casting DRF

Machining drawing showing location from casting

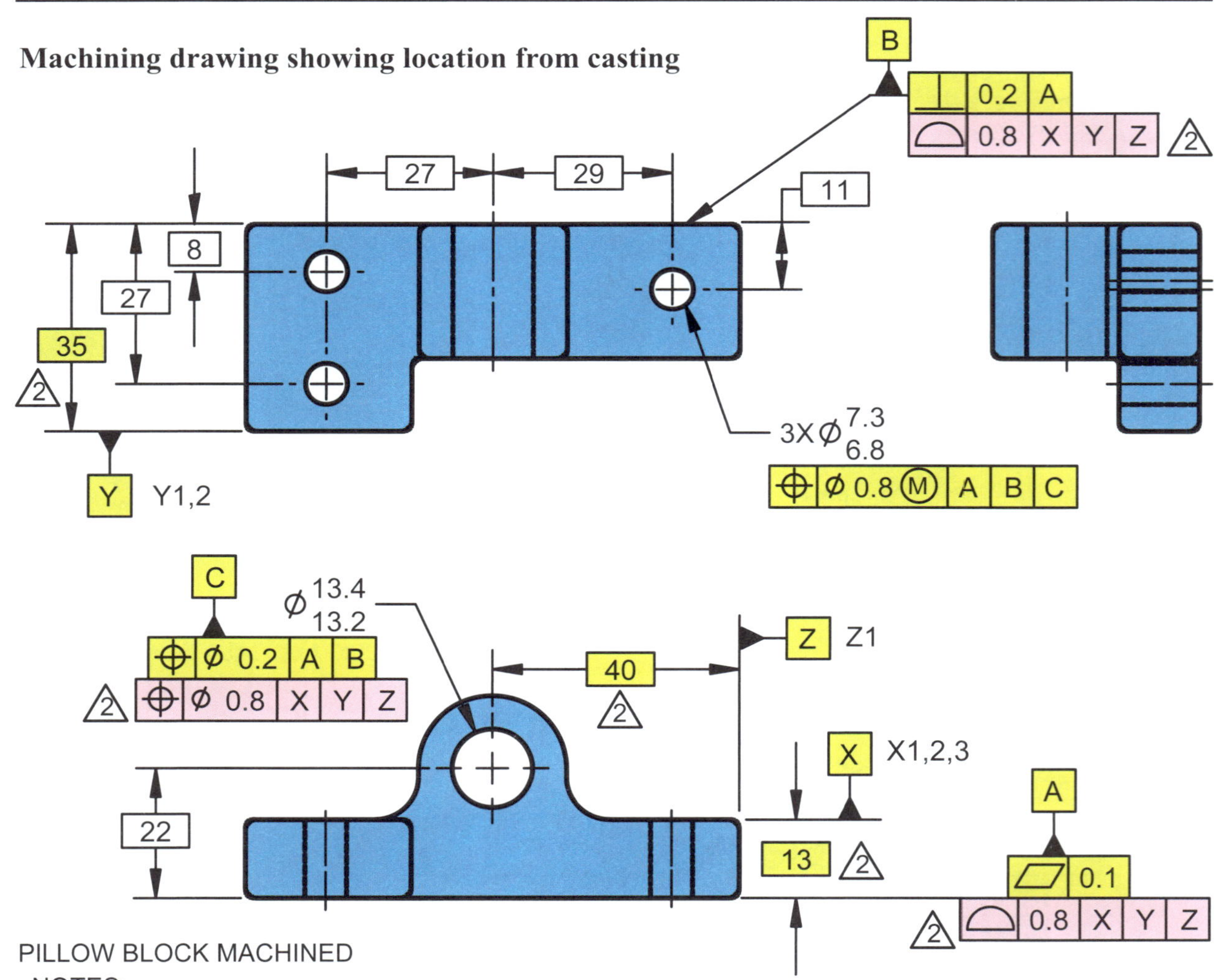

NOTES:

1. MAKE FROM PILLOW BLOCK CASTING. SEE CASTING DRAWING FOR DATUM TARGETS

△2 DESIGNATES THE LOCATION OF THE MACHINING TO CASTING

Calculations for Proper Clean-up

Some engineers try to "lean out the casting" as much as possible. An extra big casting costs money for two reasons: Extra material in the casting, and more machining time to remove it. Here are the calculations for the most efficient casting while guaranteeing the clean up from stack up issues:

Calculations for casting dimensions for proper clean-up:
The surface on the machined part is defined with a 13 mm basic dimension and a profile tolerance of 0.8 from the datum targets XYZ. This tolerance is to account for multiple manufacturing issues:

1. Tolerance on the machining fixture (datum targets not located correctly, fixture wear).
2. Improper loading into the machining fixture - part not clamped against targets (dirt/chips present)
3. Tolerance for the milling machine movements

A profile tolerance of 1.2 mm is applied to the casting surface before it is machined. This is tolerance for the casting process alone. This is usually set by the casting vendor.

A minimum of 1 mm clean-up is required on the casting. A certain amount of cast material must be removed to get down to a good clean machined surface. This value can be trial and error.

Machine basic dimension	13
+ ½ machine location tol	+0.4
+ ½ cast profile tol	+0.6
+ 1 cast stock removal	+1.0
Cast basic dimension	15

Expanded view showing casting mounted on datum targets, with calculations for casting dimensions

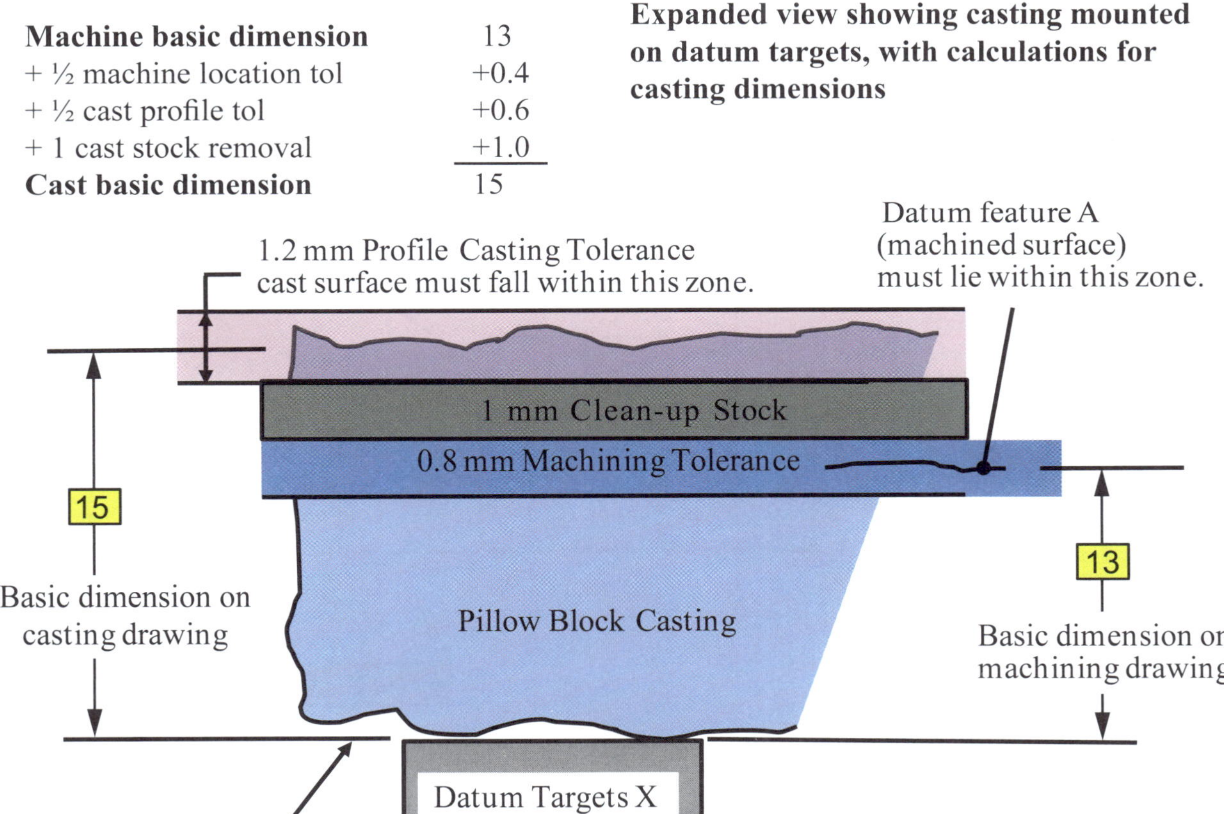

This is an expanded view of the part mounted on the datum targets which establish the XYZ DRF. The casting is defined and the first machining operations are located from this DRF. The datum targets represent the size and location of the datum locators on both the machining fixture and the inspection fixture. The locators on the machining fixture and the inspection fixture should be identical to troubleshoot problems.

Option 2: Locating all Features to the Machining

In the previous example, the machined datum features ABC are located to the cast XYZ. In the separate cast drawing, the cast features are located to the same XYZ. Relating these sets of features to the same DRF ties all casting and machined features together. Both drawings are needed to do resulting wall thickness calculations and other relationships.

The drawing below shows another method to relate cast and machined features. All features, machined and cast, are controlled to the functional and machined ABC. Machined features are directly toleranced, and a note is added with all cast features profiled within a large tolerance. All final dimensions for cast and machined are shown on one drawing. This method only specifies the end functional need without going thru the process of how to index the casting or how much extra stock to add. The casting drawing may be created separately with input from in-house manufacturing or by a supplier who knows the details of tooling locations and stock additions.

The benefit of this method is to separate functional needs from how we get there. The final machined drawing shows the functional end result, while the casting drawing documents the tooling locations and casting sizes. These tooling locations and cast dimensions may be changed as needed to get a more efficient process or better end result without changing the documentation of functional final limits.

Both the cast and machined drawing have all over profile tolerances for cast surfaces. The profile tolerance value on the machined drawing (2) must be larger than on the cast drawing (1.2). The difference between these numbers (0.8) is the allowance needed for placing the machined features on the casting.

Final machining drawing showing location of all features

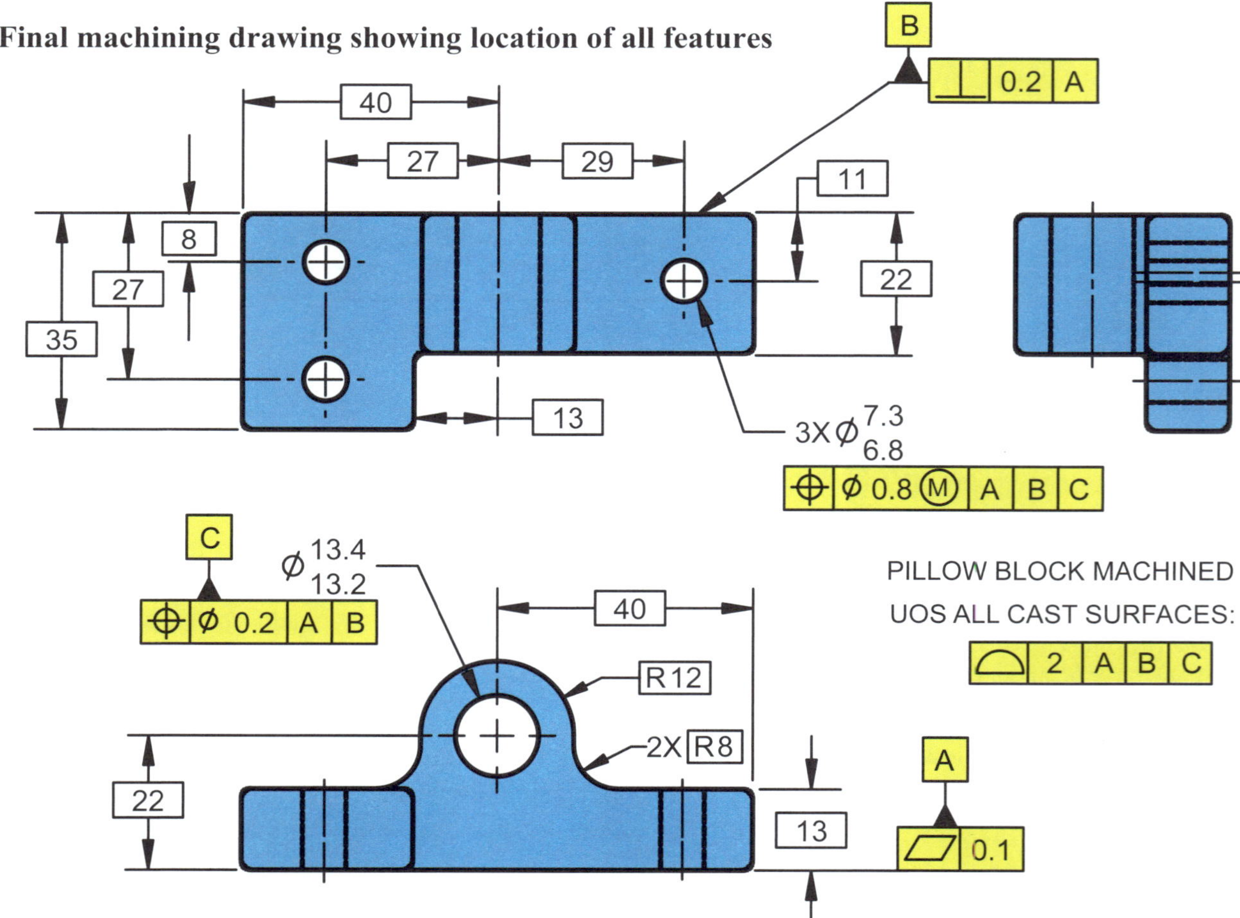

Movable Datum Target with Vee Locator

The true geometric counterpart (TGC) requirements in unit 7 state that all TGC are fixed at basic. To designate or clarify that a TGC should move to engage the datum feature, a movable datum target may be used. The movable datum target symbol, shown below on C1 and C2 on the left view, is differentiated from the datum target symbol with a triangle attached to the side. (Looks like a bird beak).

The movable datum target designates that the datum target moves to fully engage the part. By default, the movement is normal to the true surface. If another movement is desired, it must be shown on the drawing. This may be shown with a line element drawn touching the surface with basic angles defining the direction of movement. Another option is XYZ labeled on the drawing and defining a unit vector with component values [i,j,k] placed next to the movable datum target symbol. The movable datum target symbol was first introduced in the ASME Y14.5-2009 standard.

In the example below, datum targets B1 and B2 establish two 90 degree planar simulators (like a vee-block). Datum targets C1 and C2 in the front view are point contact and are required to move perpendicular to the surface and stop rotation.

This on the drawing

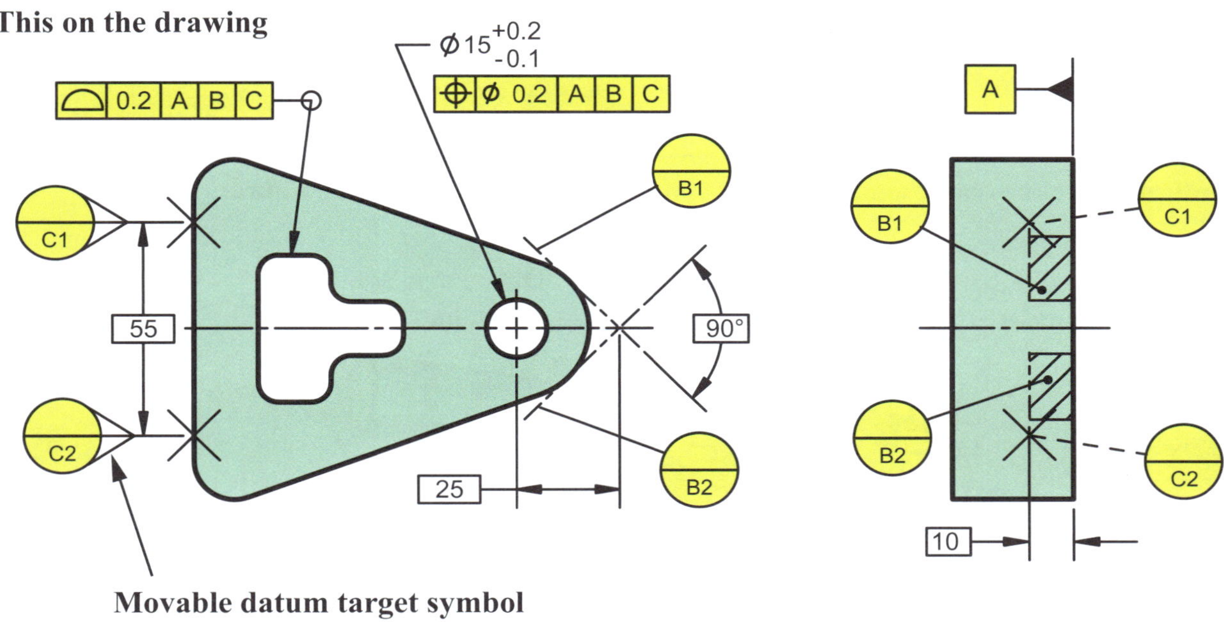

Movable datum target symbol

Defines this holding/checking fixture

Holding/checking fixture with a fixed vee-block and movable rail. The two C datum target point locators move to make contact with the surface to fully constrain the part.

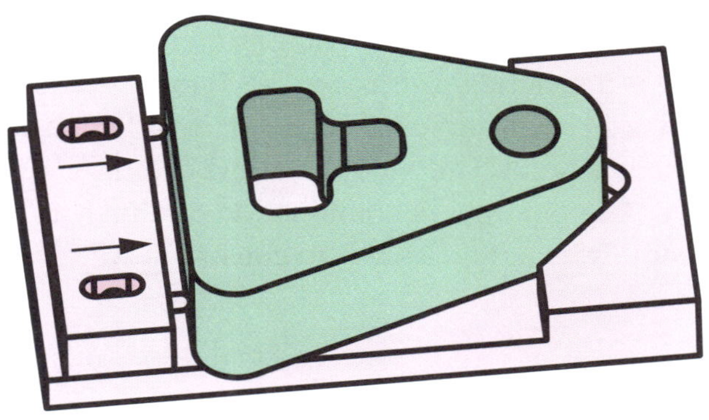

Movable Datum Target with Spherical Locator

Below is another example of a moveable datum target symbol. Datum target A is defined as a spherical diameter of 2.200. Datum target B is defined as a spherical diameter of 1.750 and is movable. The direction of movement is clear, so no angular dimensions showing movement are necessary.

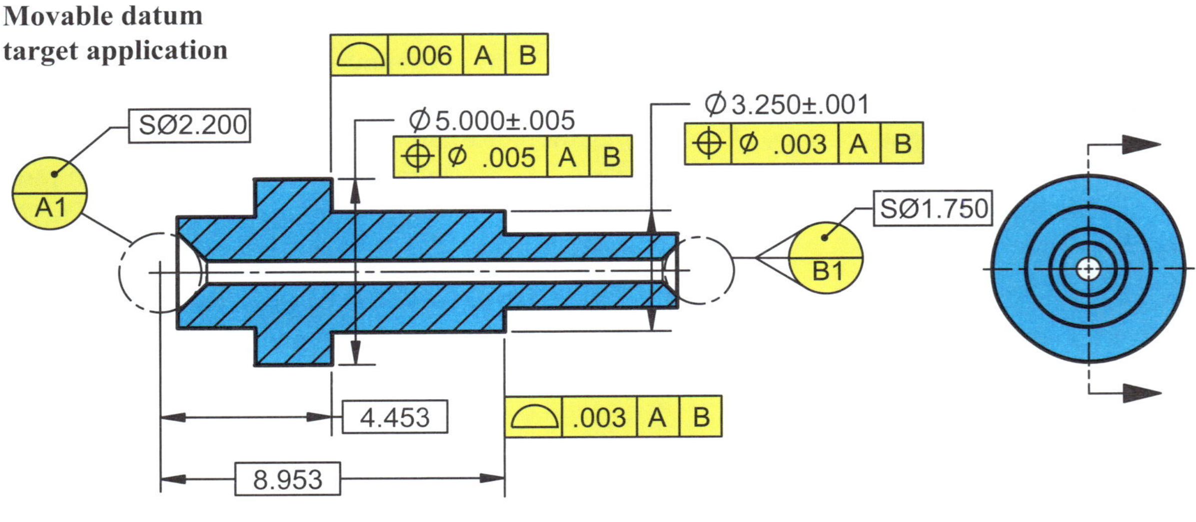

Datum reference frame established by datum target A and movable datum target B

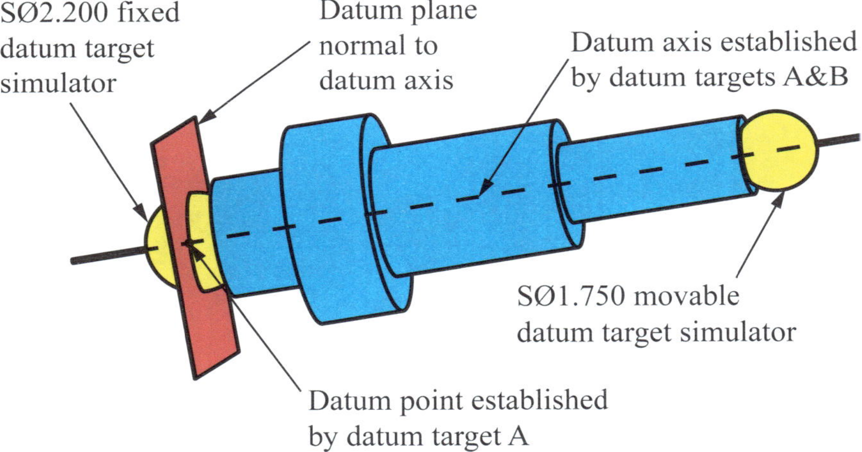

The graphic illustrates the datum reference frame established by datum targets A and B. Datum target A is a spherical simulator 2.200 in diameter and establishes a datum point and origin. This constrains 3 translational degrees of freedom. Datum target B is a spherical simulator 1.750, establishes a point, and moves toward datum A. This constrains 2 rotational degrees of freedom. The two datum points in combination establish an axis and plane DRF. The last rotational degree of freedom was not necessary to constrain. All measurements originate from this DRF.

Workshop Exercise 8.1

1. True or False? Datum planes in a datum reference frame are always 90 degrees apart, but datum features may be at angles other than 90 degrees to each other.

True or False

2. Which of the following is a correct way to show a datum target symbol X1 that creates a square target of .250? (There may be more than one correct answer.)

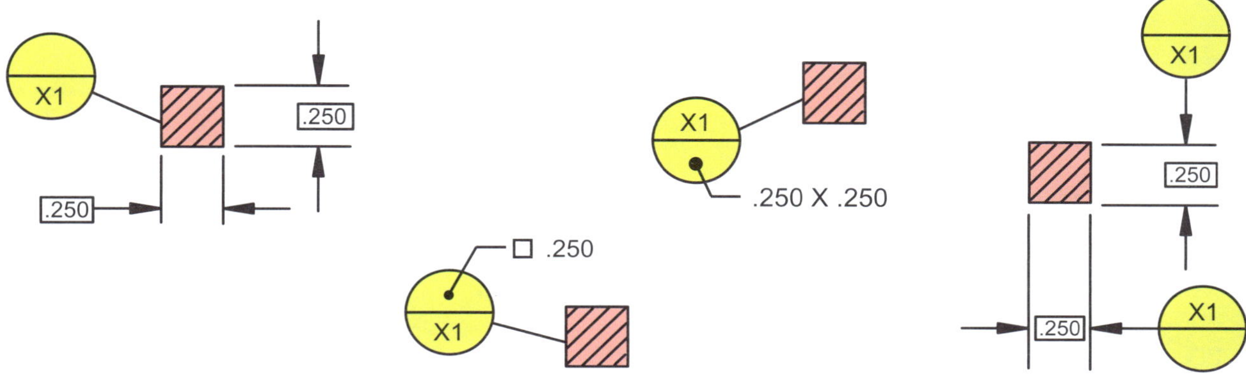

3. What is the minimum amount of datum target points required to establish a primary datum plane?

____

4. What does it mean when the leader line to a datum target is dashed (shown as a hidden line) as sketched above?

____

5. Which of the following is a movable datum target symbol.

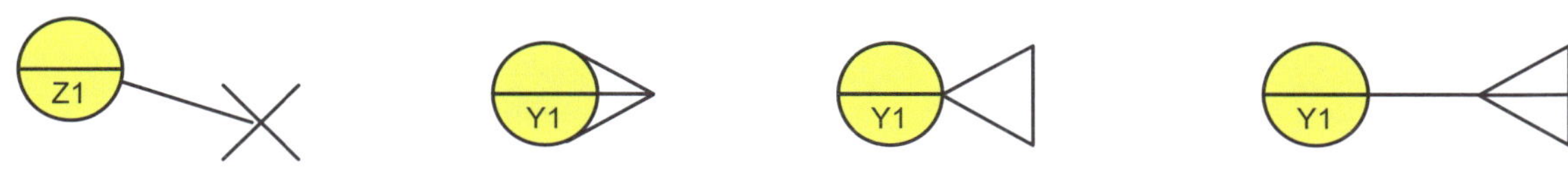

6. Match the sketches below with the following types of datum targets.

datum target point   datum target area   datum target line

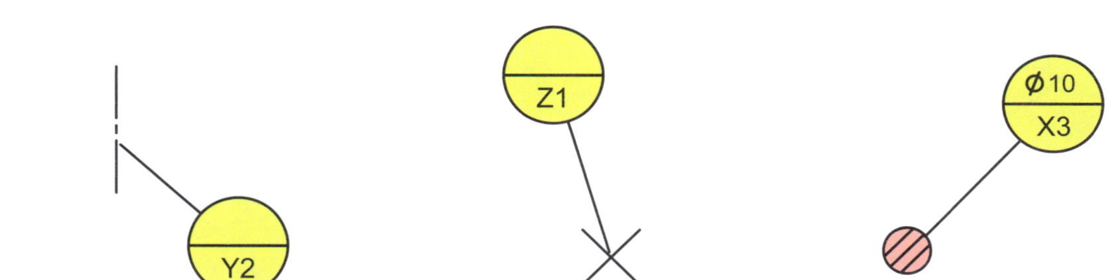

Workshop Exercise 8.2

Study the fixture and setup for the Horse Shoe Casting below. Apply datum target symbols to the drawing views to document the fixture setup shown. Use letters other than ABC (those are reserved for the machined DRF). Make sure to dimension the targets to each other by simply estimating the distances. Assume all round pads are 10 mm in diameter. Then apply an all over profile in reference to the datum features within 1.5 mm.

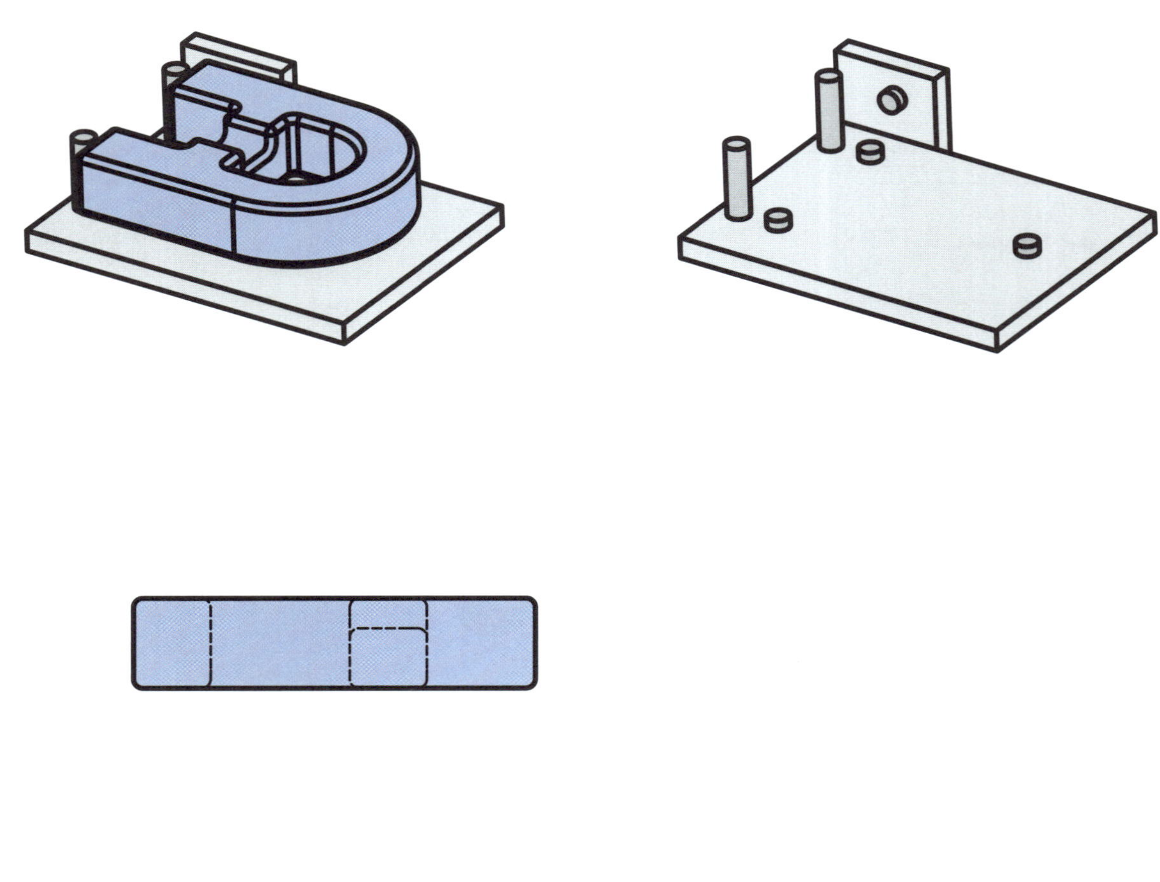

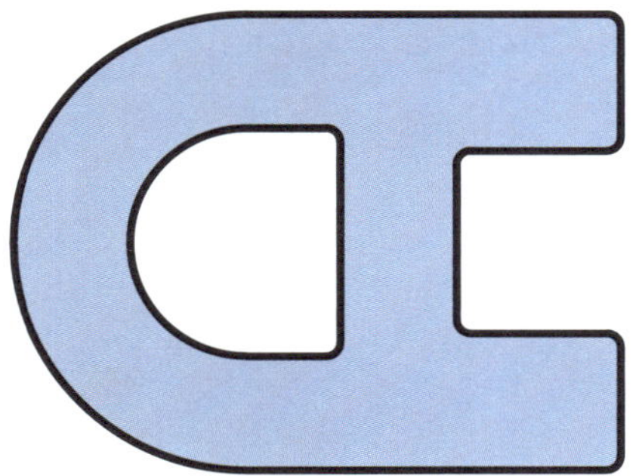

Workshop Exercise 8.3

This is the machined part made from the Horse Shoe Casting on the previous page. The datum features ABC must be located to the datum reference frame from the casting drawing.

Label the cast surfaces with datum feature symbols and place target letters and numbers next to them (X1,2,3).

Apply basic dimensions, and location feature control frames to each of the machined datum features. Use a tolerance of 0.8.

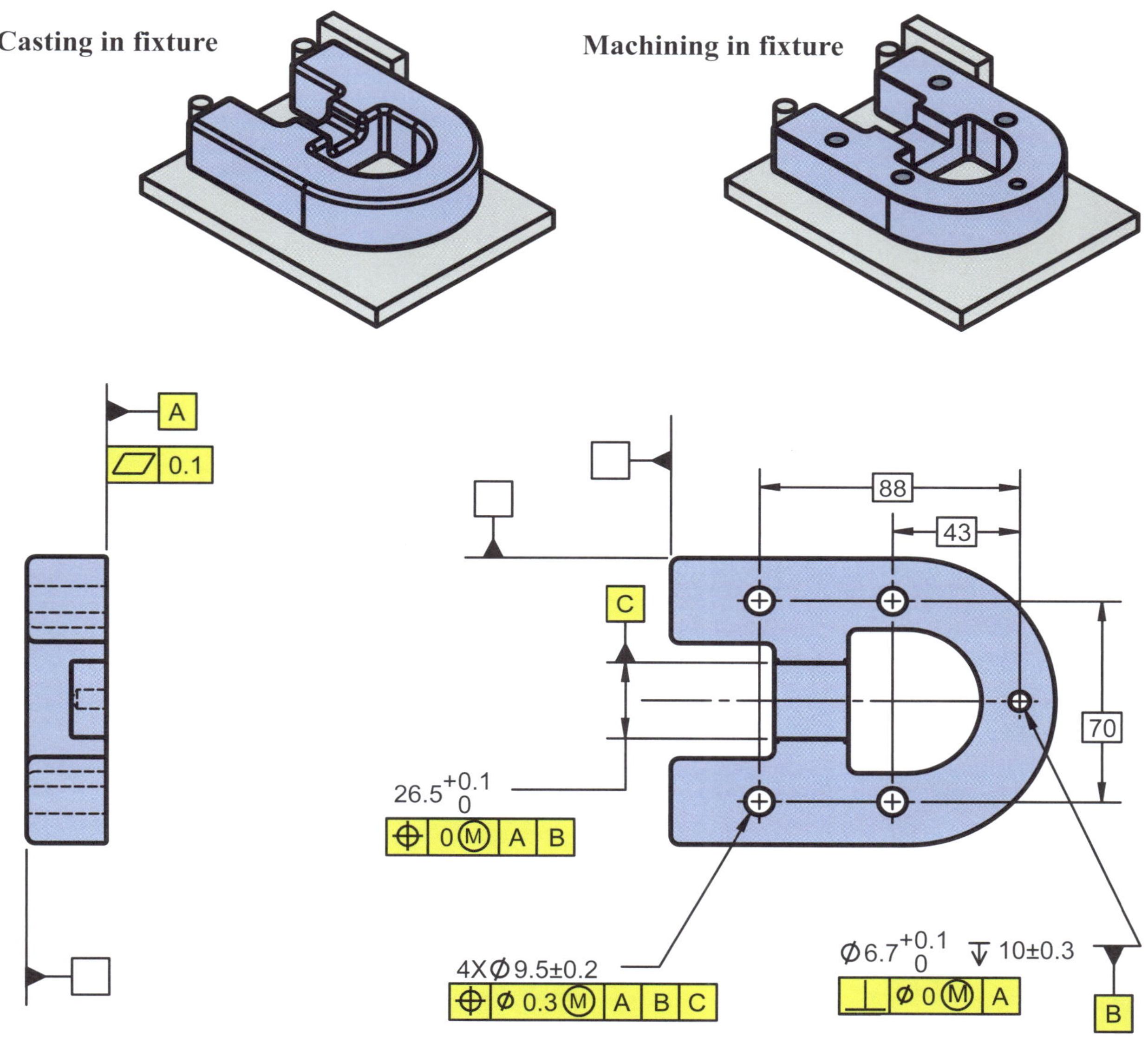

HORSE SHOE MACHINED

NOTES:

1. MAKE FROM HORSE SHOE CASTING
2. SEE CASTING DRAWING FOR DATUM TARGETS

Unit 9

The Datum Reference Frame III
Advanced Concepts

Common Datum Features A-B
Coaxial Holes as a Datum Feature
Workshop Exercise 9.1
Irregular Feature of Size as a Datum Feature
Two Holes as a Datum Feature
Hole and Slot as Datum Features
Workshop Exercise 9.2
Pattern of Holes as a Datum Feature
    Paper Gage Evaluation
Datum Center Planes
Establishing a Relationship Between Two DRF
Multiple DRF Example
Global and Local DRF
Multiple DRF Done Wrong
Datum Features Referenced Individually
Workshop Exercise 9.3
Inseparable Assemblies - All Tolerances at Assembly Level
Inseparable Assemblies - Tolerances at Assembly and Detail Level
Workshop Exercise 9.4- Inseparable Assemblies
Customized Datum Reference Frame - Square Hole and Slot
Workshop Exercise 9.5 - Customized Datum Reference Frame

Common Datum Features A-B

The shaft mounts in the assembly on two journals. Both journals share the same mounting importance. The A-B is common for establishing a single datum axis from two coaxial datum features.

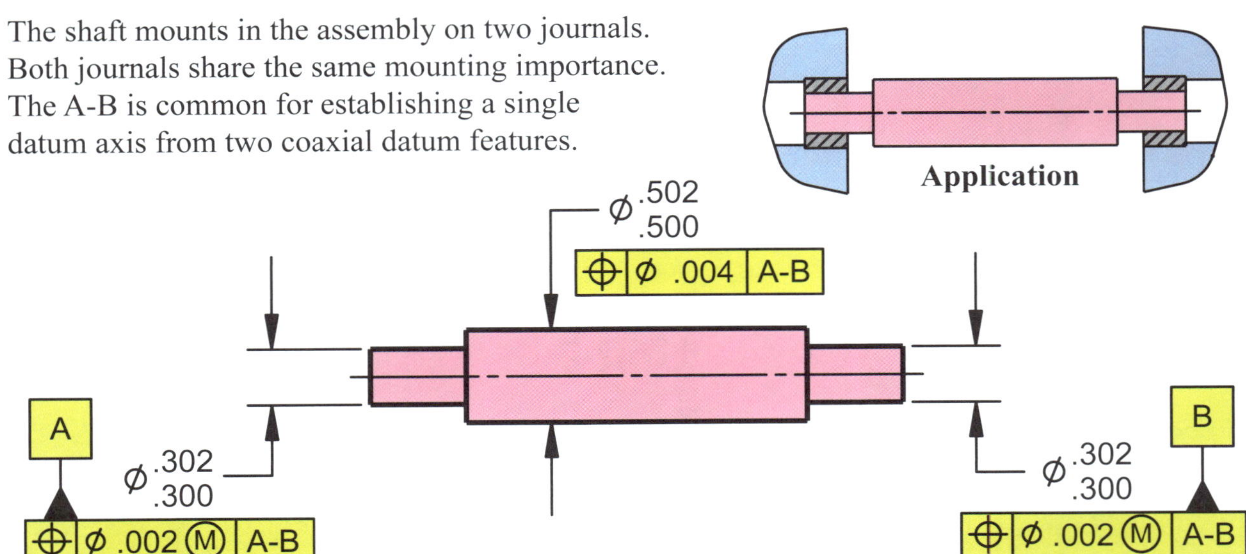

A-B notation is called common datum features in Y14.5-2018. This uses multiple datum features to create an average datum. To establish the average axis between these two shaft features, two coaxial true geometric counterparts (TGC) collapse at the same rate to make maximum contact. Neither shaft will engage fully with its counterpart but will balance between them creating the average A-B axis.

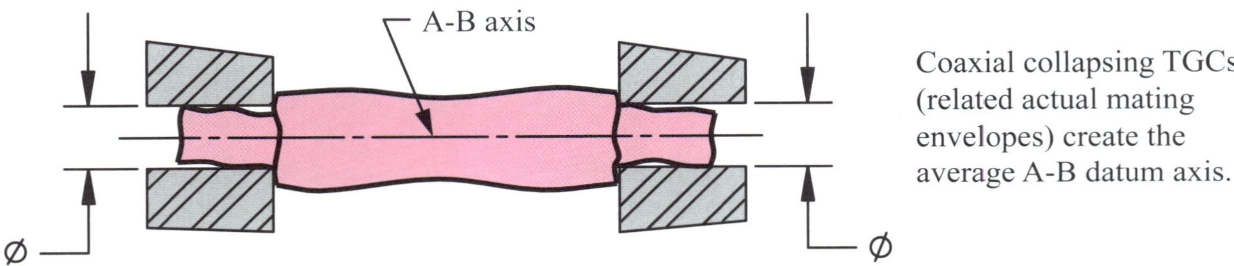

Coaxial collapsing TGCs (related actual mating envelopes) create the average A-B datum axis.

Since A and B are separate features, a position tolerance is applied to each to keep the features coaxial to the average A-B datum axis (controlling them to each other). When designing the size openings on the mating part, the virtual conditions of the features must be considered (Ø.304). The position error means the shaft axes are cocked (tilted) relative to each other and creates a larger related actual mating envelope. An MMC modifier may be used if it is clearance fit into the mating part. If bearings are pressed on the journals, they should be at RFS. If the size and the tilt/coaxiality of the journals could be combined in one value, consider the use of zero position tolerancing at MMC.

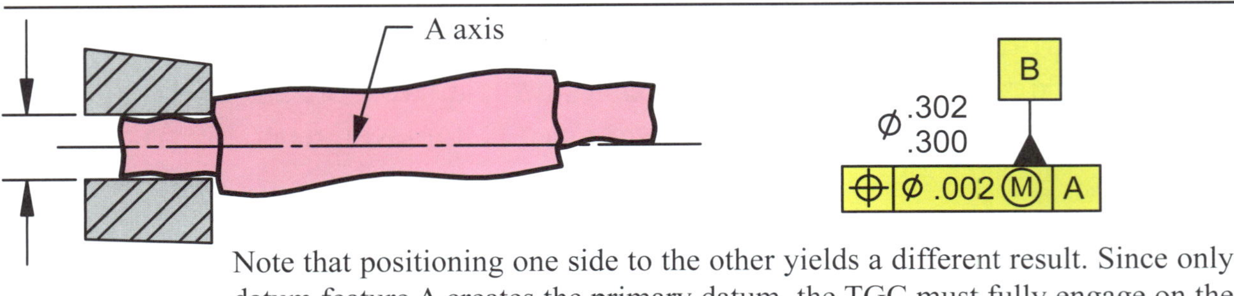

Note that positioning one side to the other yields a different result. Since only datum feature A creates the primary datum, the TGC must fully engage on the short imperfect feature and makes the other journal's coaxiality much worse.

The A-B average datum may be estimated using unrelated envelopes. First establish the simulated datum axes A and B separately.

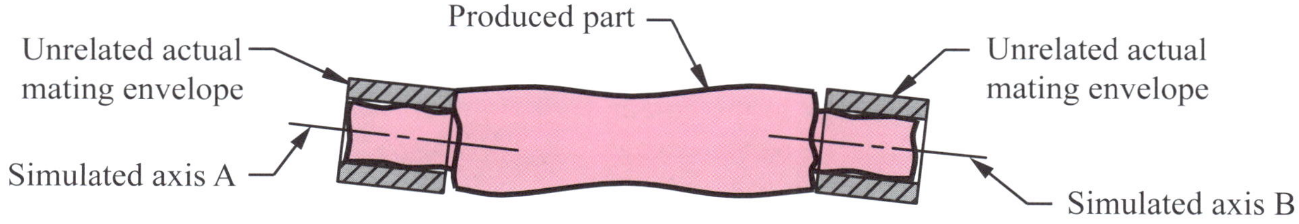

Then, collapse the smallest cylinder around both axes A and B. The axis of this cylinder is the A-B axis. The A-B axis is the average of the two axes.

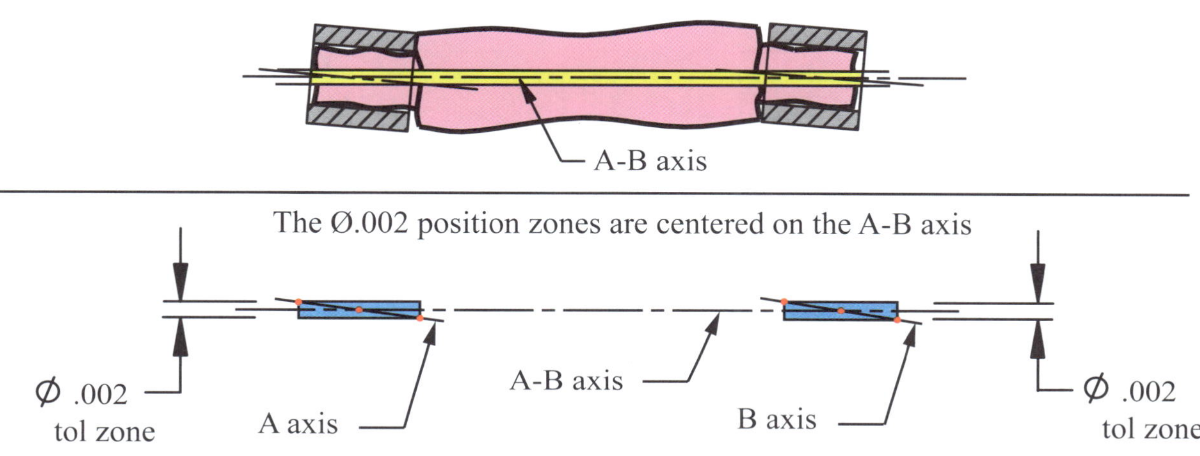

The drawing below is another way to control the relationship between two coaxial diameters of the same size. The end result is identical to the A-B call out on the previous page. If the diameters are a different size, the A-B specification may be more appropriate. See the seat latch part for another similar example with two coaxial holes creating a single datum axis.

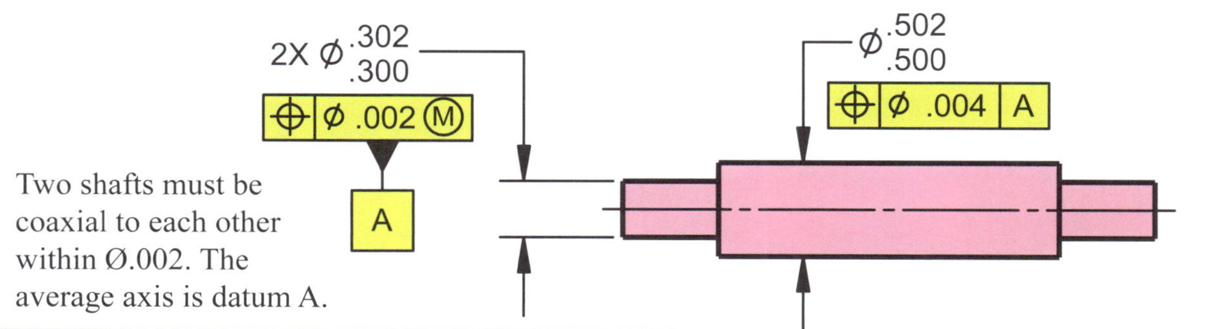

The part may be set up in two vee blocks to simulate the two mating journals. An indicator is used to check the position requirements. A CMM could also be used by setting a cylinder alignment on both journals simultaneously to establish the A-B axis. The individual journals are then verified for position conformance to the A-B axis.

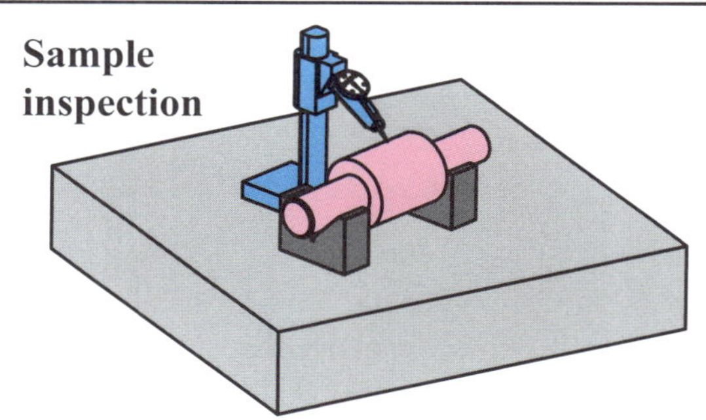

Coaxial Holes as a Datum Feature

Application

The seat latch bracket mounts on a single pin through the two coaxial holes and fits inside the frame. The three square slots engage in the seat rack. The adjustment lever attaches to the hole in the seat latch bracket and rotates the part to engage and disengage for various locked seat positions.

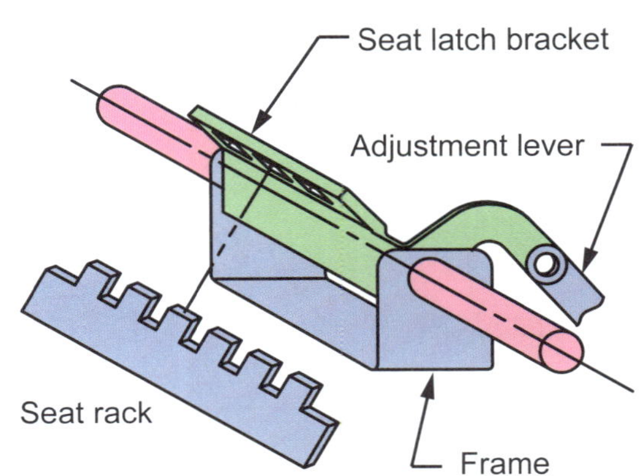

This on the drawing

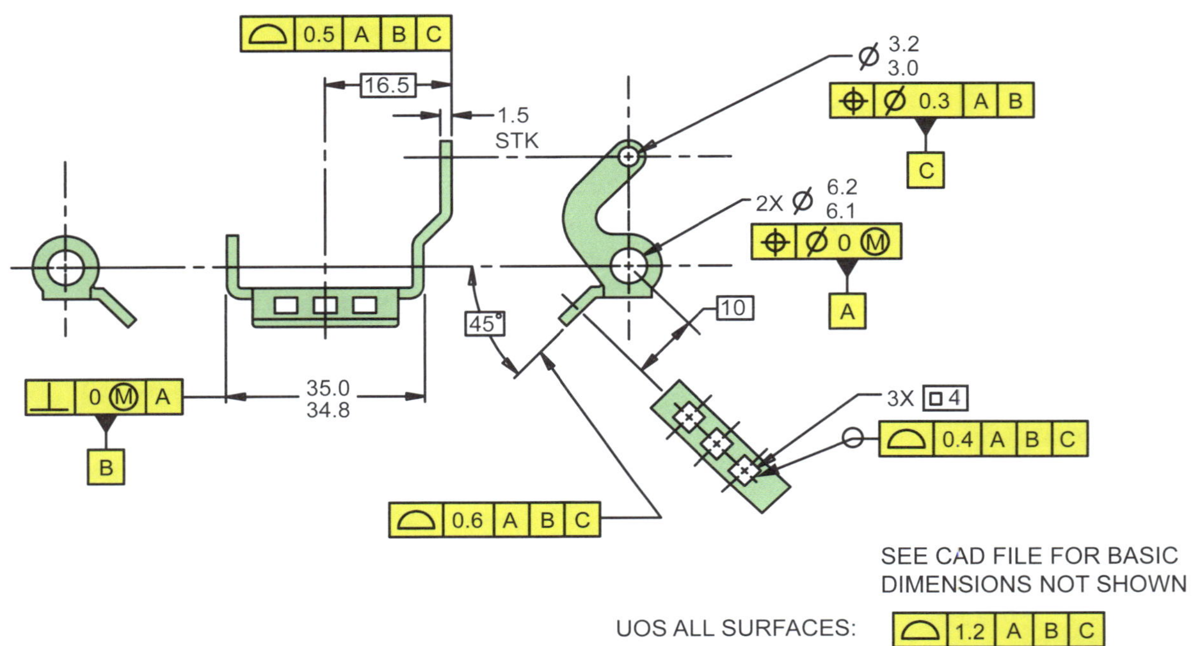

Means this

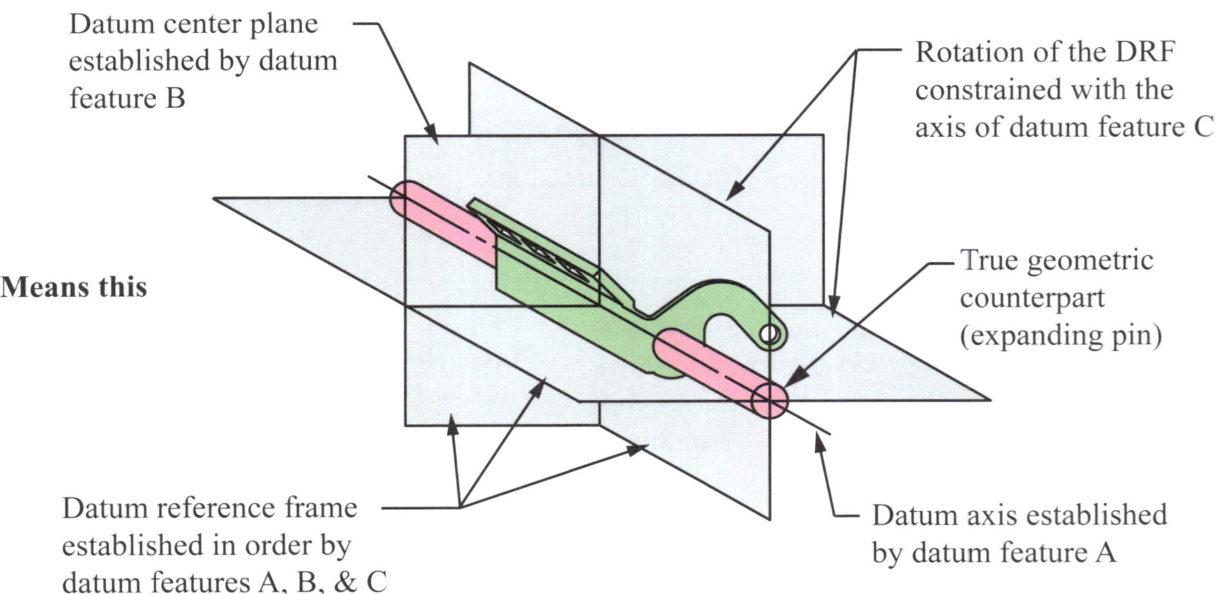

Workshop Exercise 9.1

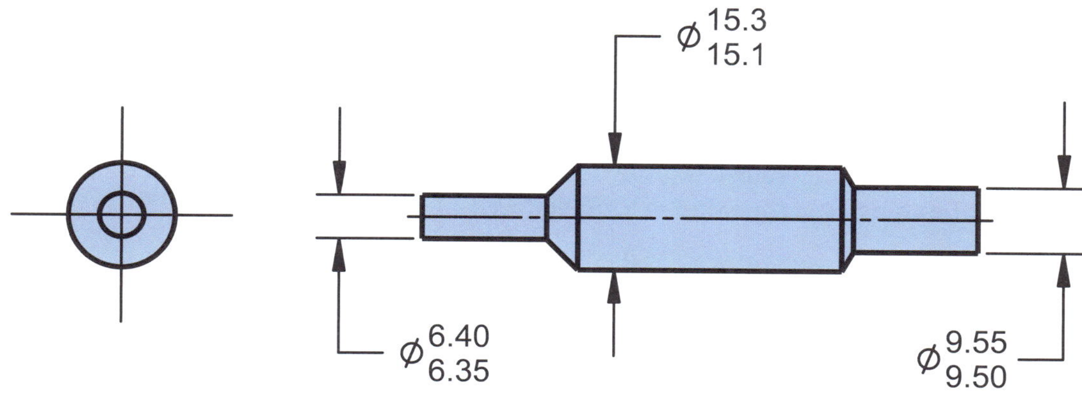

1. On the drawing above, before any geometric controls are applied, what is the coaxiality tolerance implied between the diameters?

____

2. On the part above, apply datum feature symbols to create a datum axis A-B by using the right and left diameters.

3. Apply a position coaxiality between the right and left diameter of 0.1 at MMC.

4. Apply a position tolerance to the large center diameter within a diameter of 0.3 in relation to the single datum axis established by both datum features A and B.

5. Calculate the virtual conditions for the right and left diameters and label them on the virtual gage below.

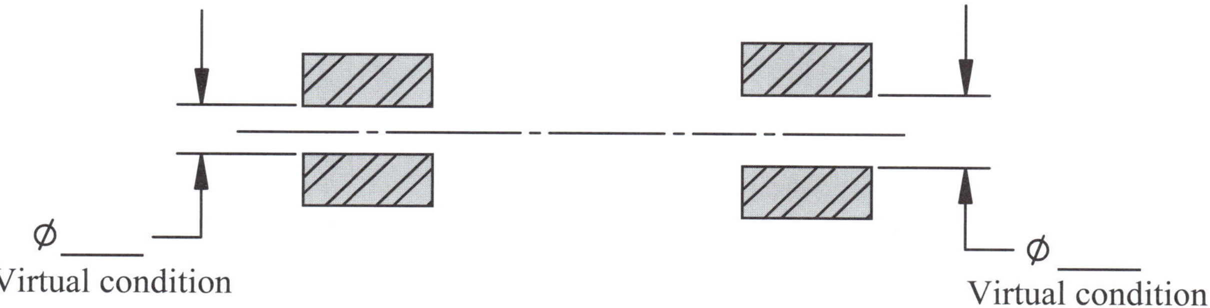

6. To define the A-B datum axis, do the true geometric counterparts collapse to make contact with the datum features or are the TGCs fixed at the MMB (virtual) size?

____

____

Irregular Feature of Size as a Datum Feature

Feature of Size - There are two types of features of size: regular and irregular. A *regular feature of size* is a hole, pin, slot, tab, or sphere with a plus/minus tolerance explained in unit 2.

Irregular Feature of Size - There are two types of irregular features of size:

1. A directly toleranced feature or collection of features that may contain or be contained by an actual mating envelope that is a sphere, cylinder or pair of parallel planes.

2. A directly toleranced feature or collection of features that may contain or be contained by an actual mating envelope other than a sphere, cylinder or pair of parallel planes.

The term *irregular feature of size* was first introduced in Y14.5-2009. The prior definition for *feature of size* was too narrow to encompass more complicated functional features. This expanded the definition to allow an irregular closed shape and collections of surfaces to act like a feature of size. They should be toleranced for size with profile tolerance, but may be located with position tolerance with material condition modifiers. They may also be labeled as a datum feature with material boundary modifiers.

The compartment lid below shows an irregular feature of size (type 1) as datum feature A.

Compartment Lid Assembly

The compartment lid mounts on the pivot pin on the three radii in the tabs. The geometry of the radii are enough to contain the pin.

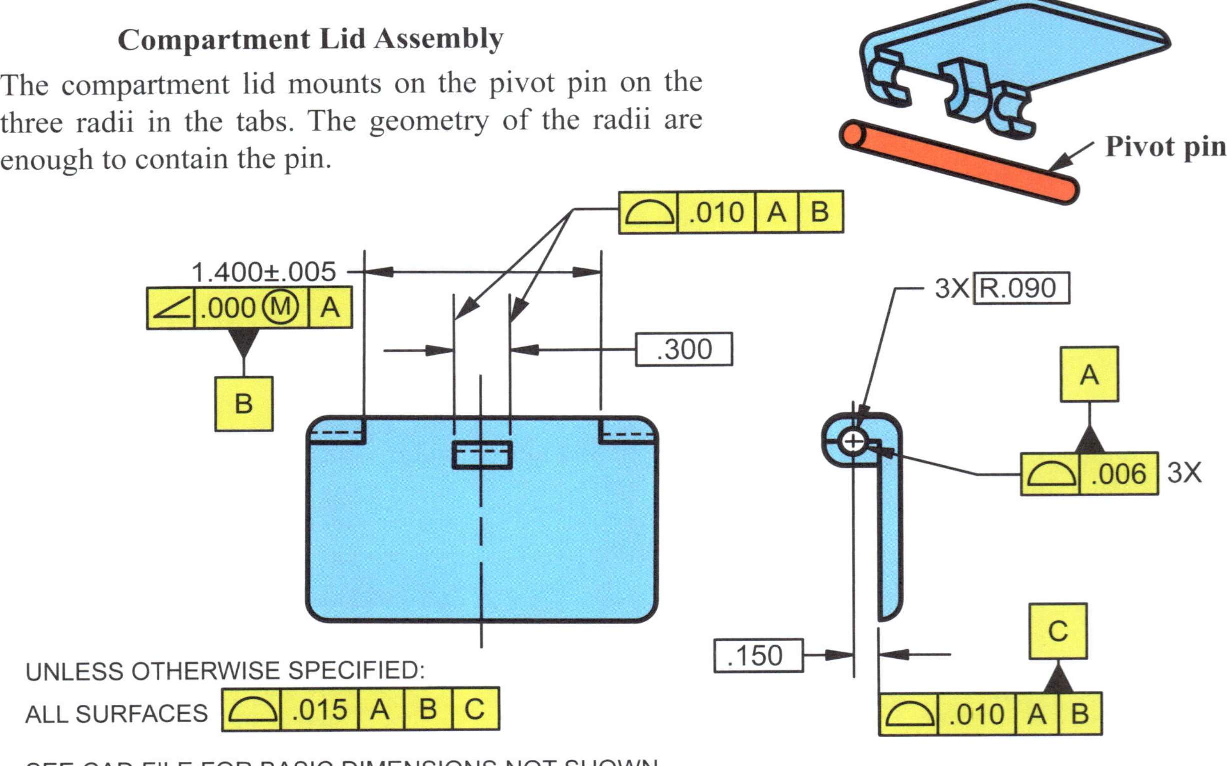

Examples of Irregular Features of Size (type 2)

The type 2 irregular feature of size should be controlled for size with profile tolerance but may be located with either a position tolerance at MMC/LMC (see unit 12) or profile tolerance (see unit 11). They may also be labeled as a datum feature and material boundary modifiers apply. They are classified as a linear extruded shape datum feature in the degrees of freedom table (see unit 4).

Two Holes as a Datum Feature

The example shows a pattern of holes (two) as a datum feature. In the assembly of the base and sheet metal cover plate, it is important that the three 4 mm holes in the base are lined up with the three holes in the cover plate. Two alignment pins and holes are used to index the parts together.

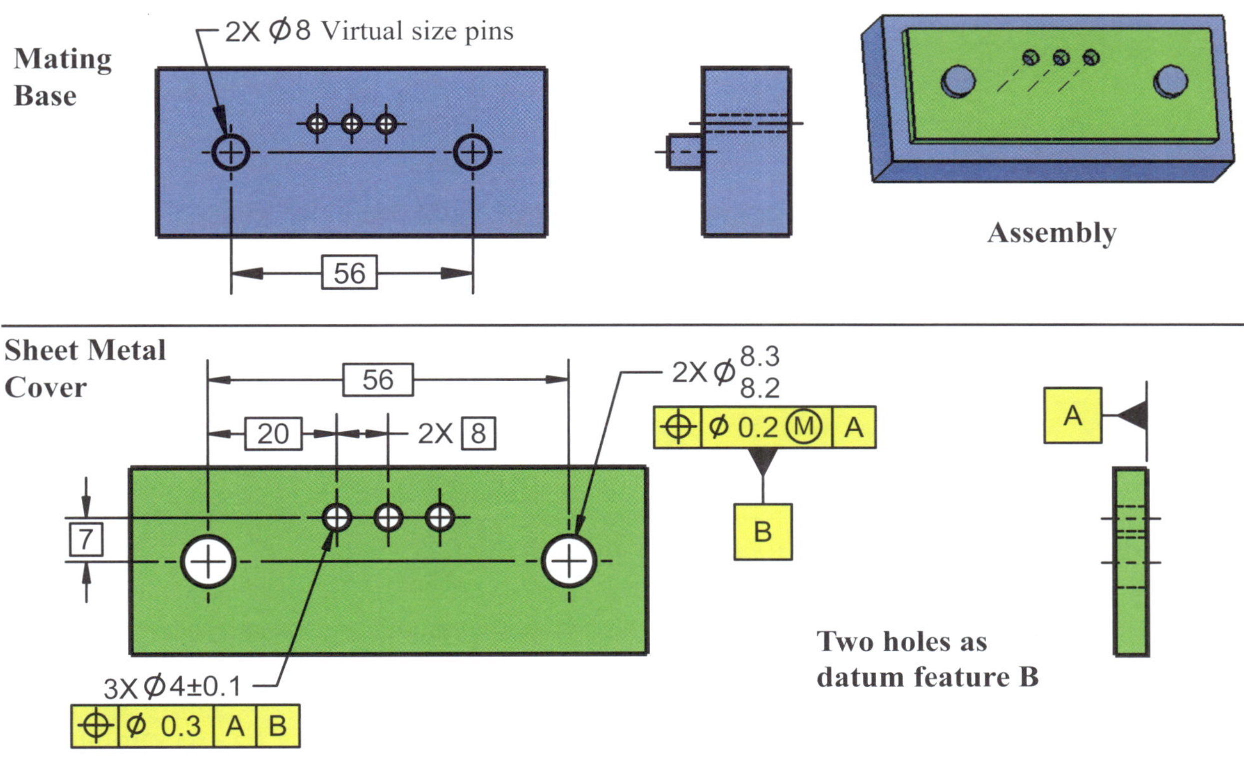

Both holes as datum feature B balances the DRF between the features

Datum feature B is both holes and constrains two translations and one rotation of the DRF. This creates two perpendicular planes and sets the origin of the DRF as the average of the holes. The position tolerance controls the holes to each other and perpendicular to datum A. The tolerance is calculated as 8.2-8.0=0.2 (Hole MMC - Pin Virtual).

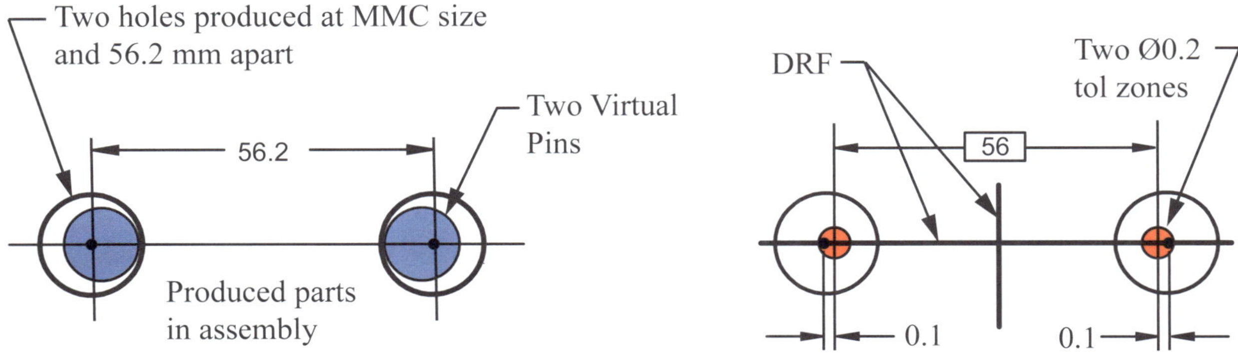

When two imperfect holes match to the mating pins, neither hole will be centered on the mating pin. The assembly will balance between them.

When the distance between the two holes varies, the error is balanced between them. Each hole has a Ø0.2 tolerance zone and the DRF is established in the middle.

Hole and Slot as Datum Features

Below is an alternative design to the cover in the assembly on the previous page. The two alignment holes are changed to a hole and slot instead. A hole and slot design is the best way to precisely align parts together. Because of the slotted geometry of the second hole, the distance between the holes is now unimportant. This also allows smaller hole sizes for a more precise fit.

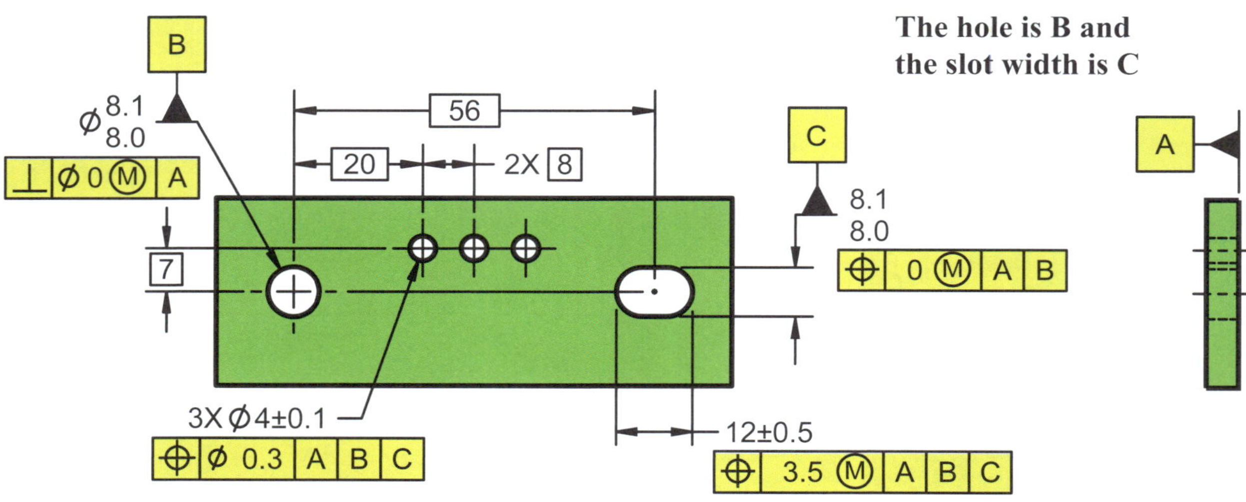

Hole and slot datum features centers the DRF in the hole

Datum feature B is the left hole and constrains two translations of the DRF. Datum feature C is the slot width and constrains one rotation. This creates two perpendicular planes and sets the origin of the DRF in the center of the left hole and rotationally aligned to the slot. The left hole is made perpendicular to datum A (this is probably unnecessary because of the thin sheet metal). The slot is positioned in two directions. The position in the up/down direction is only controlling the rotation of the slot because the slot establishes the DRF.

When assembled, the hole will be centered on the left mating pin. The slot width will engage on the mating pin and only constrain rotation despite its large center distance variation.

The DRF is centered in the hole and aligned rotationally thru the slot. Since the slot establishes the DRF, the position in the up/down direction is only controlling rotation of the slot (this is very easy to meet because of the short slot length to distance ratio.)

The slotted geometry allows for a large position tolerance on the length of the slot. This can be calculated as 11.5-8.0=3.5 (MMC hole-virtual pin). This slot also allows hole sizes closer to the mating pin size for tighter fitting assembly.

Hole and slot designs work well on sheet metal and plastic, but slots can be difficult to produce on machined parts. Another option to achieve the same result is using two round holes with a pin and diamond pin. The pin locates in two directions and the diamond pin stops rotation.

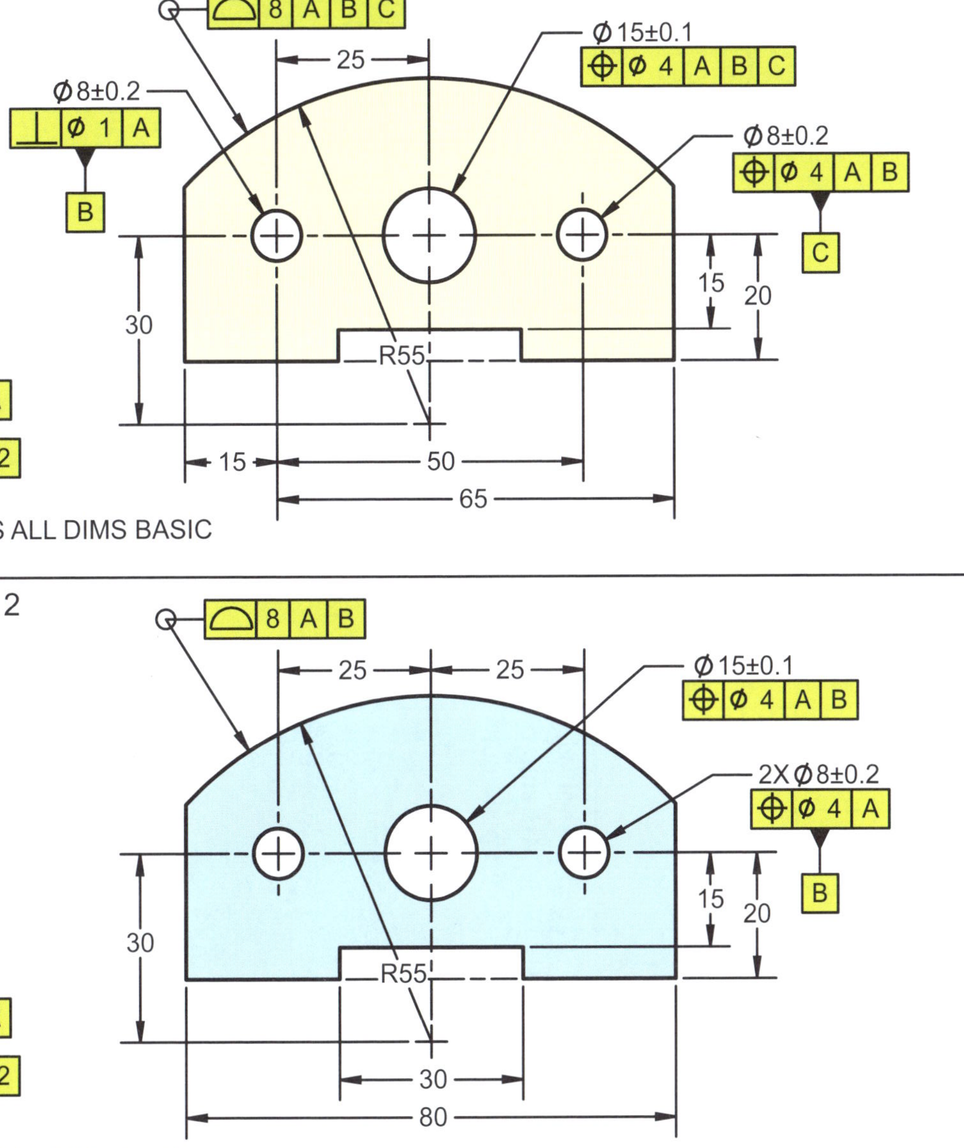

Workshope Exercise 9.2

Draw the datum reference frame on the imperfect parts. Use a straight edge to make sure the DRF is straight and perpendicular.

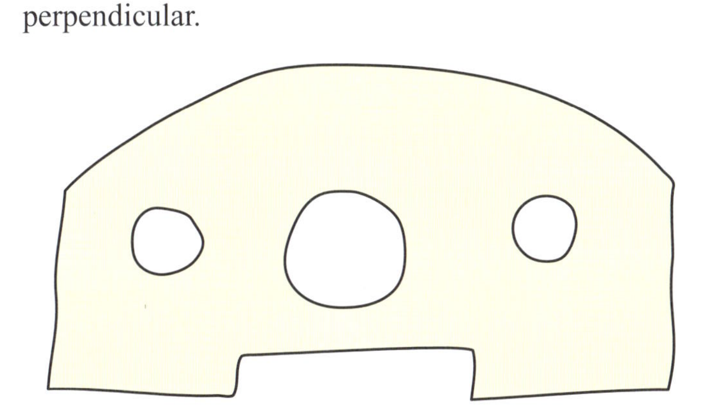

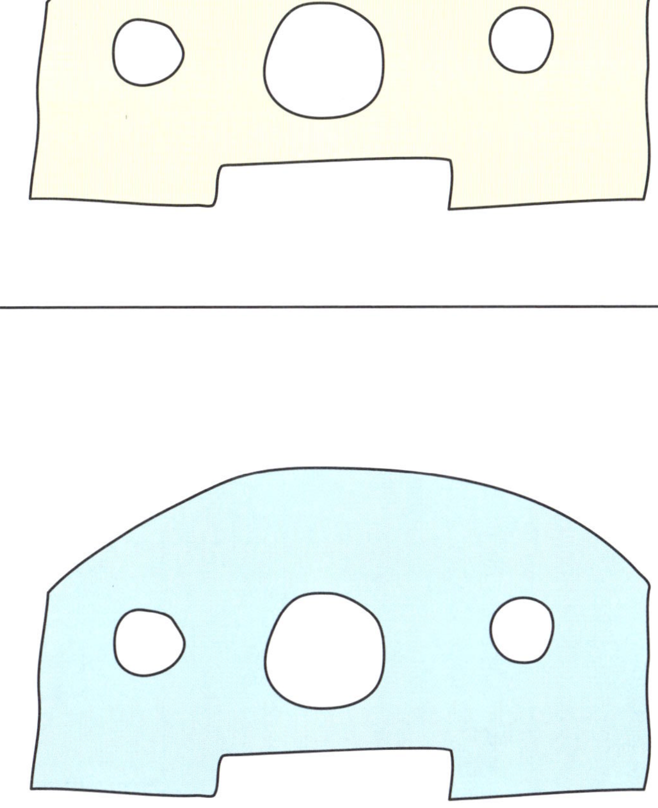

Pattern of Holes as a Datum Feature

A pattern of holes may be used as a datum feature. On the part below, the back surface is datum feature A and constrains one translation and two rotations. The four holes are positioned to each other with respect to datum A and are the secondary datum feature B. These four holes make contact with their true geometric counterpart (TGC) of four fixed-location MMB cylinders. This contact with the TGC constrains the final two translations and one rotation. The theoretical DRF is derived from the perfect TGCs.

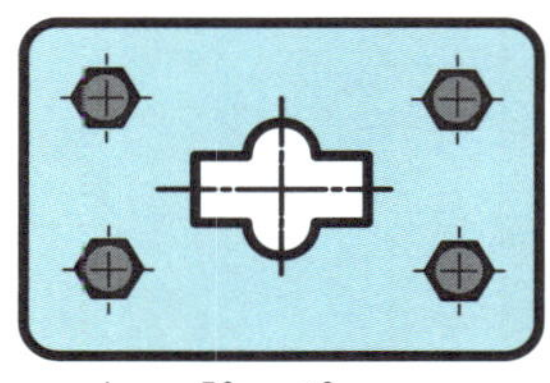

Application

The light switch cover mounts on the four holes and must clear the switch. The outside edges are not important.

This on the drawing

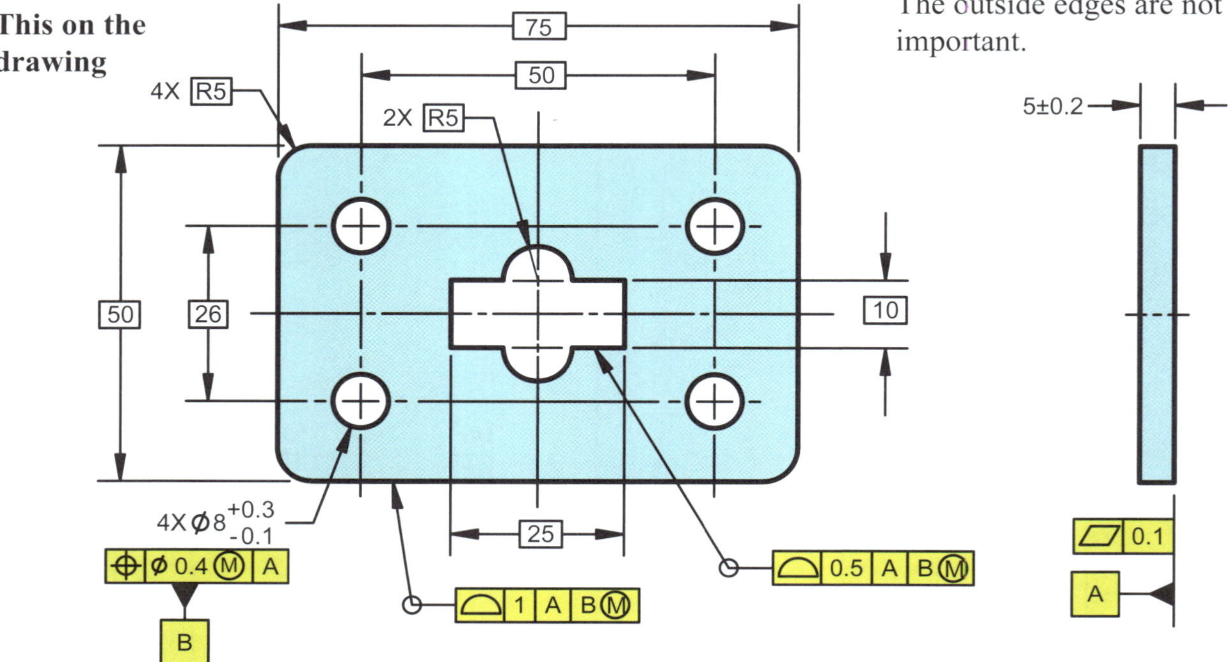

Means this

The four holes as datum feature B modified at MMB creates a TGC of four 7.5 MMB size pins at true position. These theoretical TGCs establish the two perpendicular planes of the datum refence frame.

Primary plane established by datum feature A.

2 Planes and axis established by the TGC of datum feature B.

13 13 25 25

Basic dimensions may originate from any of the holes or the drawing centerlines because all features are connected with basic dimensions. The basic dimensions originate from the axis of the theoretical TGCs not the individual produced holes. The engagement of the actual holes with these TGC's constrain the degrees of freedom for the part.

The pattern of holes restrict the movement of the part in translation and rotation. Function dictates that the entire "best fit" pattern establishes the DRF. This can be illustrated with a gage below.

Functional gage for hole and profile specifications

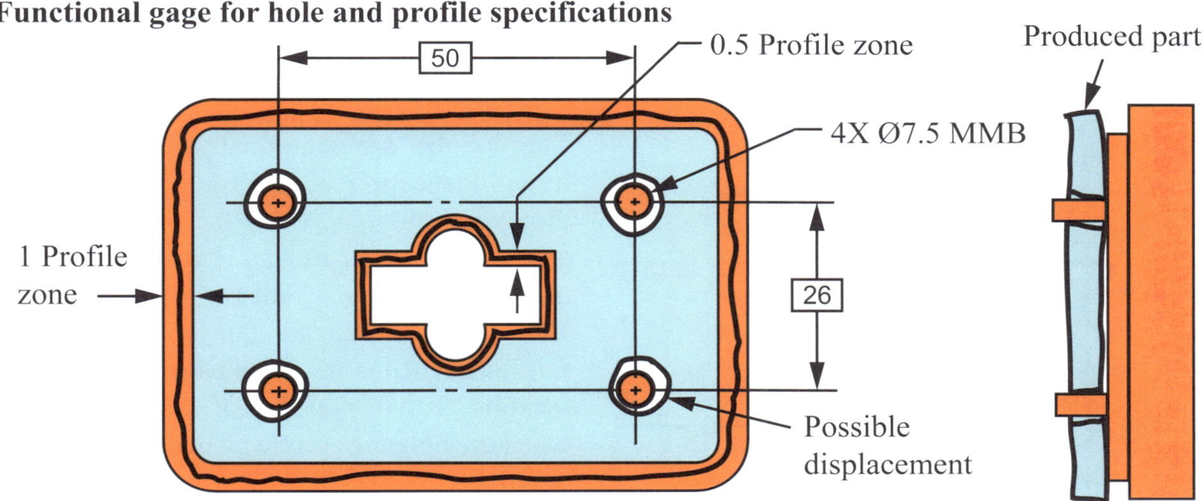

A theoretical gage is shown with the TGCs and the tolerance zones all located at basic. This creates a theoretical relationship between the boundaries. The produced part is then connected to the perfect gage. Since the TGCs were set at MMB and the actual holes were produced larger with good location, the part may shift to allow the surfaces to pass the profile tolerances (datum feature shift). Notice how none of the holes are centered on their respective TGC. The "best fit" of the pattern is locating the part. In a best fit alignment, the produced holes with the smallest related actual mating envelope (smallest size and furthest from true position) will locate the part.

The above example shows the datum feature modified at MMB and the TGC pins are fixed at the MMB size. If the datum feature instead applies at RMB, the TGCs expand simultaneously to make maximum contact with the datum features to establish the DRF. The graphics below represent the 4 fixed-location TGCs and the 4 actual displaced holes superimposed upon one another.

Datum feature B modified at MMB

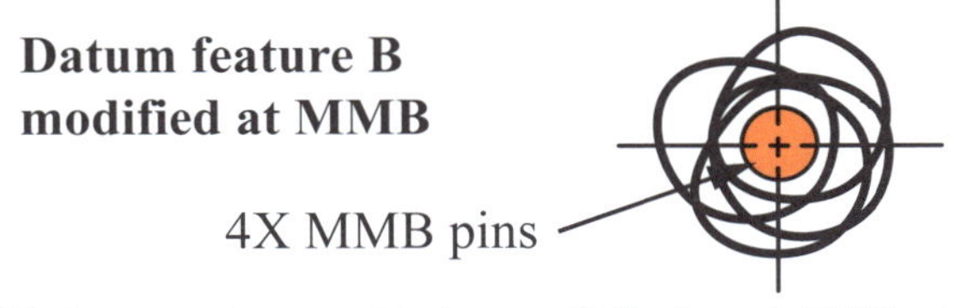

If datum feature B is modified at MMB, it requires the 4 TGCs to be fixed at basic and **fixed in size** at the MMB of 7.5. Clearance between the TGC and datum features will allow datum feature shift in inspection.

Datum feature B implied at RMB

If datum feature B is implied RMB, it requires the 4 TGCs to be fixed at basic and **expand simultaneously** from the MMB to make maximum contact with the datum features. Datum feature shift is nonexistent.

A pattern of holes as a datum feature may also maximize tolerance, since a pattern of holes is "best fit" during the manufacturing process. Good parts may show bad if inspection aligns on only two holes. If inspection chooses only two holes to set-up the part and the part checks good, it is good. If the part checks bad while set up to the 2 holes, it may be "best fit" similar to a functional gage to insure acceptance. This balancing method of "squeezing out the last bit of tolerance" may be accomplished by CMM's with appropriate software or by the paper gage method. See next page.

Pattern of Holes as a Datum Feature - Paper Gage Evaluation

To establish a DRF from a pattern of holes on a CMM or open set-up inspection, the pattern of holes should first be "best fit" to insure conformance to the position tolerance. Without reorienting the part, the remaining features are checked relative to this set-up. The DRF origin may be basically relocated since all tolerance zones are related with basic dimensions.

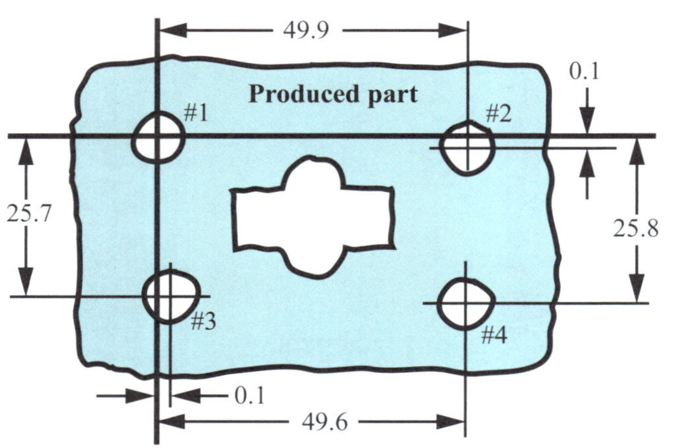

The 4 holes are rotationally aligned in the initial inspection set-up by leveling the Y direction center between the two left holes and the two right holes. Then, hole #1 was used as the origin to measure distances and X/Y deviation data for the report below. In this initial evaluation, hole #4 is shown out of location with a position of 0.89. However, when the holes are plotted and evaluated with the paper gage, all holes are within their acceptable 0.8 tol zone. See graphs below.

Hole No.	MMC Size	Actual Size	Allowed Position	"X" Dev	"Y" Dev	Actual Position	Acc Rej	Paper Gage Evaluation	Acc Rej
1	7.9	8.3	0.8	0	0	0	A	The pattern of holes fall within 0.6 tol zone to each other after paper gage evaluation.	A
2	7.9	8.3	0.8	-0.1	-0.1	0.28	A		A
3	7.9	8.3	0.8	+0.1	+0.3	0.63	A		A
4	7.9	8.3	0.8	-0.4	+0.2	0.89	R		A

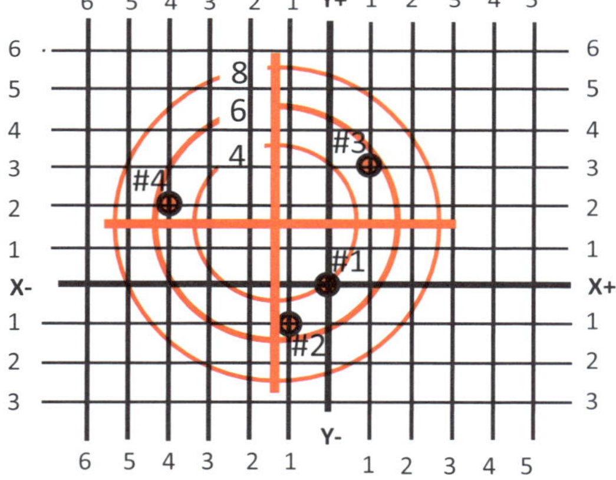

The paper gage evaluation shows the four holes are within a 0.6 actual zone to each other (well within their tolerance). The best-fit origin of the DRF (established by the pattern of holes) is the center of the 0.6 tolerance ring. The center is approximately -0.13 in the x direction and +0.16 in the y direction from the #1 hole (initial origin). Inspection may reset the origin of measurement to this new point from any of the actual hole locations.

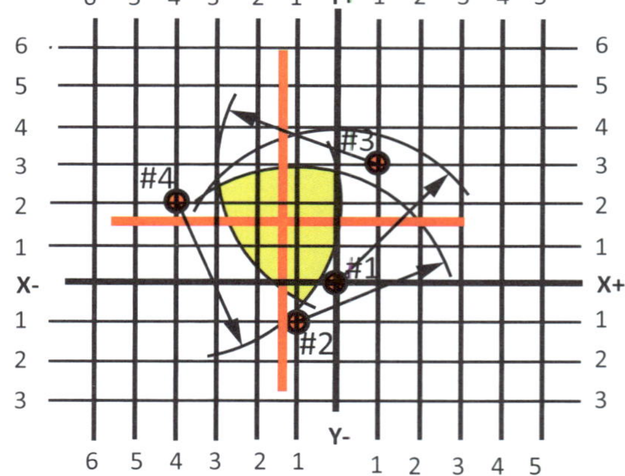

The MMB modifier allows datum feature shift in an amount equal to the difference between the datum feature's MMB and the related actual mating envelope. The yellow area above is created by striking a 0.8 dia position tolerance zone from the actual location of each hole. The area within the arcs is the boundary within which the origin of the DRF may displace. The paper gage mathematically reflects the mechanics of a part fitting in a functional gage. Notice hole #1 falls well within the 0.6 zone and does not contribute to the location of the part.

Datum Center Planes

The part below has a datum reference frame established from its mating features, the back face and the two outside widths. These two outside widths create datum center planes. The profile and position tolerance zones located with the basic dimensions are implied centered about the centerlines. Datum center planes keep the tolerance zones symmetrical about the outside shape, and is also consistent with the way the part fits in its mating pocket.

Application

This on the drawing

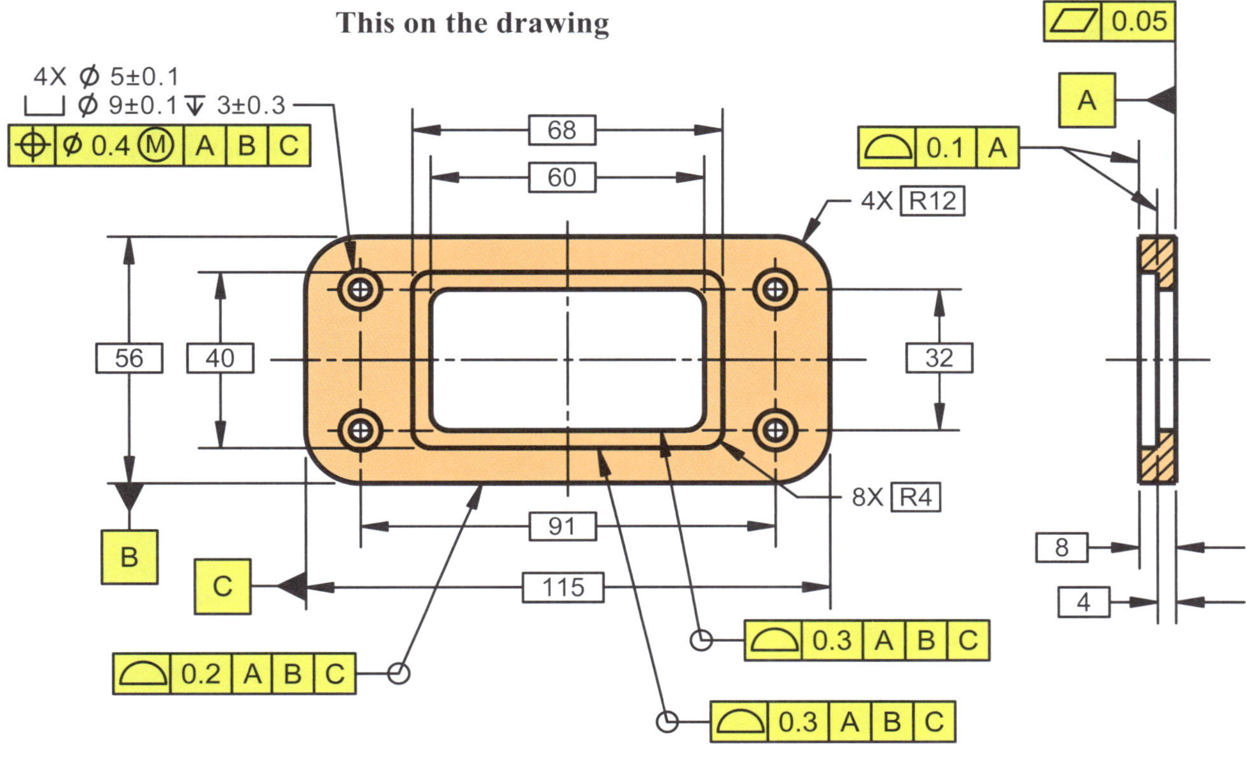

Datum center planes with position and profile tolerance zones

Means this

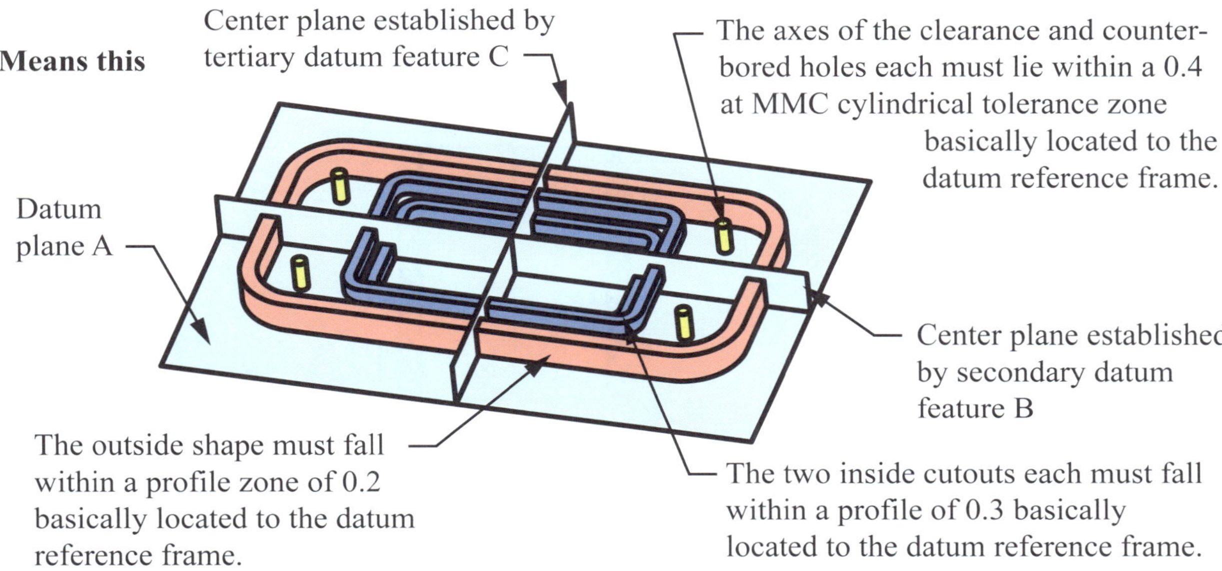

Establishing a Relationship Between Two DRF

Datum reference frames (DRF) are selected based on functional fits to mating parts. Usually, one global DRF on a part is sufficient and keeps tight relationships between all features. However, parts with multiple mating requirements, such as a gearbox housing or engine block may require additional local DRFs. For example, on an engine block, the location of the tapped holes for the mating cylinder head is not important to the main DRF set up on the crankshaft. Therfore, a local DRF may be used to locate these tapped holes instead to the cylinder head alignment pins. This keeps the design intent functional and helps manufacturing meet requirements on features that are separated in different processing set-ups. In other cases, even though the part could have multiple DRFs, design decides to stay with only one when tolerances are already relatively large and to keep definition and inspection set-ups simple. This is a design choice between keeping the tolerance scheme simple and maximizing the manufacturing tolerances.

The drawing below shows an adapter that has multiple DRFs. The adapter mounts to the main housing on the bottom surface, aligned with the lower pilot, and fastened with four bolts (this establishes the global DRF). An electric motor mounts to the upper surface, aligned with the upper pilot, and fastened with four bolts (this establishes the local DRF). The relationship of the features on the bottom of the adaptor are important to each other. The relationship of the features on the top are also important to each other. However, the relationship between the two groups is less important. The drawing below and next pages will show how to establish multiple DRFs to tolerance local features while keeping the relationship between the groups.

This drawing for the adaptor has two datum reference frames: [A/B] and [C/D]. The global DRF AB, has been established by the bottom surface and the lower pilot. A local DRF CD, is established from the top surface and upper pilot. The next page illustrates the two DRFs and how the local CD is related to the global AB.

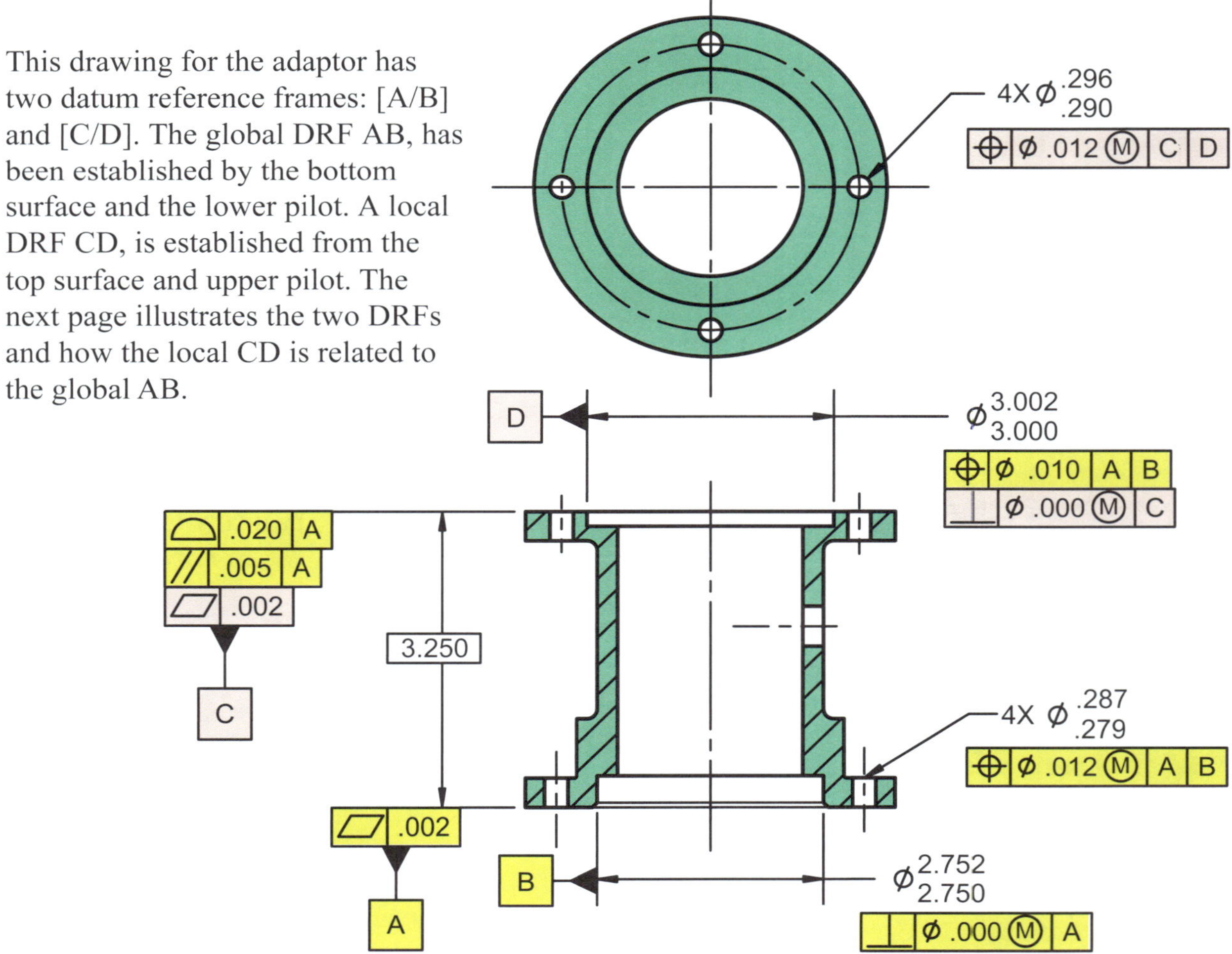

1. The upper face and pilot are located to the global AB DRF by the profile and position tolerances. The upper face orientation is further refined by the parallelism tolerance zone.

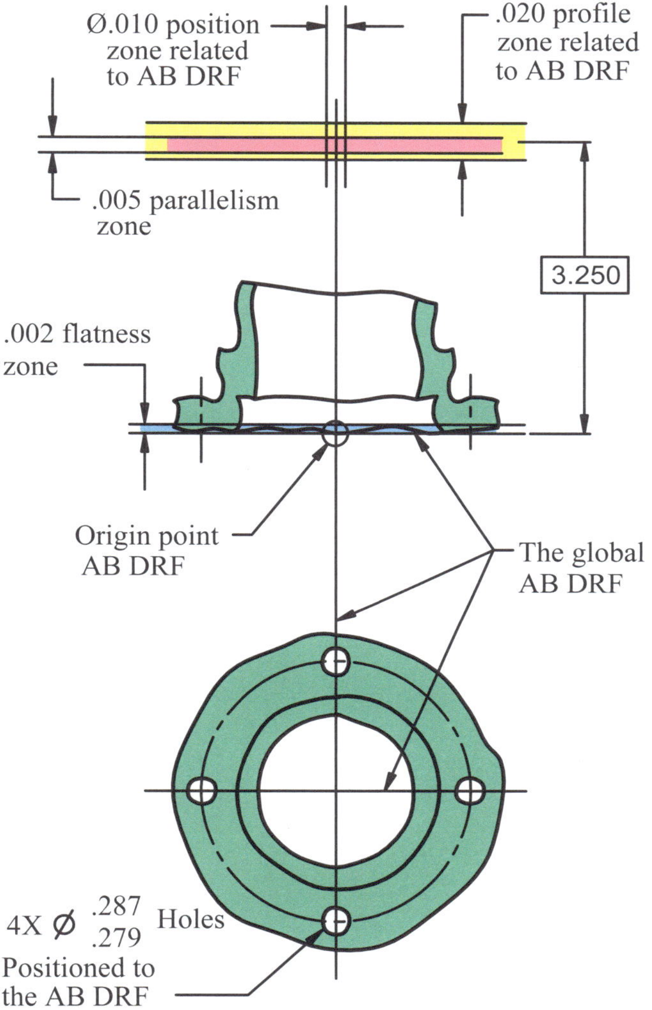

2. The upper face and pilot establish the local CD DRF. This DRF may move up and down within the profile zone, move diametrically within the position zone, and tilt within the parallelism zone all relative to the global AB DRF.

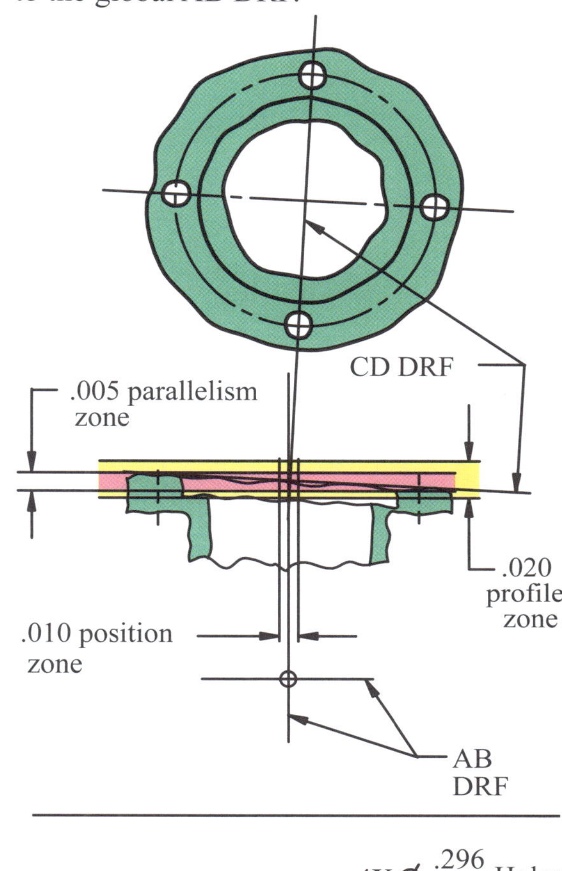

3. The local datum features C and D are qualified to each other. Surface C is controlled with a flatness. The pilot D is related to C with a perpendicularity tolerance. The four holes are then related to the local CD DRF.

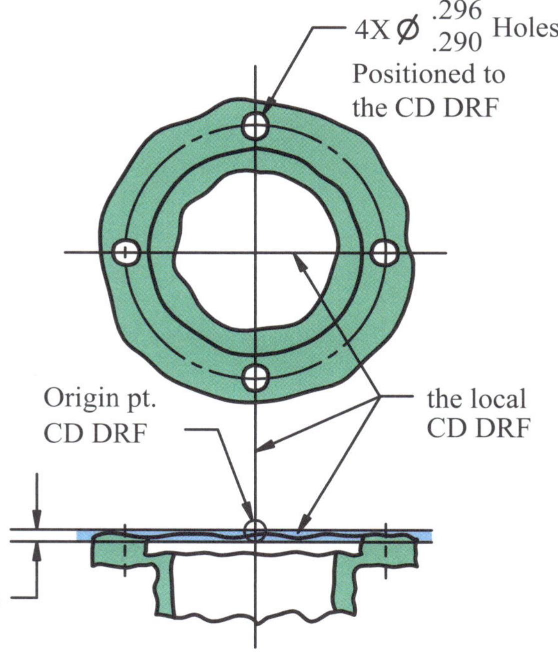

Multiple DRF Example

The following pages show another example of multiple datum reference frames (DRF). The DRFs are linked for proper relationships using a global and local set-up. The assembly below locates a lens under a light source that must move up and down to adjust the height of the focal point. The Lens Mount mates to the main Carrier through the two alignment pins into the hole and slot. The Lens Bracket locates on to the Lens Mount with a similar set up using a hole and slot into alignment pins.

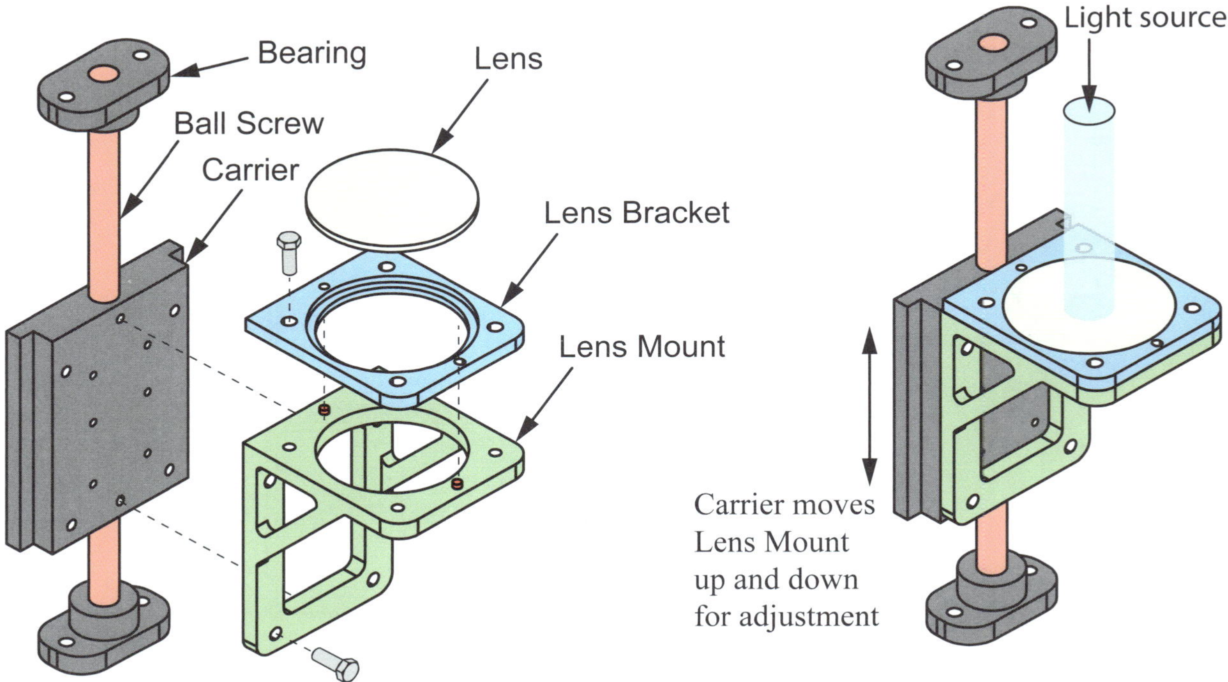

This discussion will focus on the mating of the Lens Mount to two parts: the Carrier and Lens Bracket. They are each aligned using two pins into a hole and slot. The hole constrains the part in two translations and the slot constrains rotation.

Slot
Hole
Hole
Alignment pins
Slot
Alignment pins

Global and Local DRF

The Lens Mount has two DRFs, [A/B/C] and [D/E/F] to represent the two different mount conditions. The part mounts to the main Carrier on ABC. This is chosen as the global DRF and most features will be related to it. The DEF is a local DRF and only some specific features are related to it. The local DEF must be linked to the global ABC to control relationships and make stack calculations possible. This is done by locating the datum features D, E, and F with position and profile tolerances to ABC.

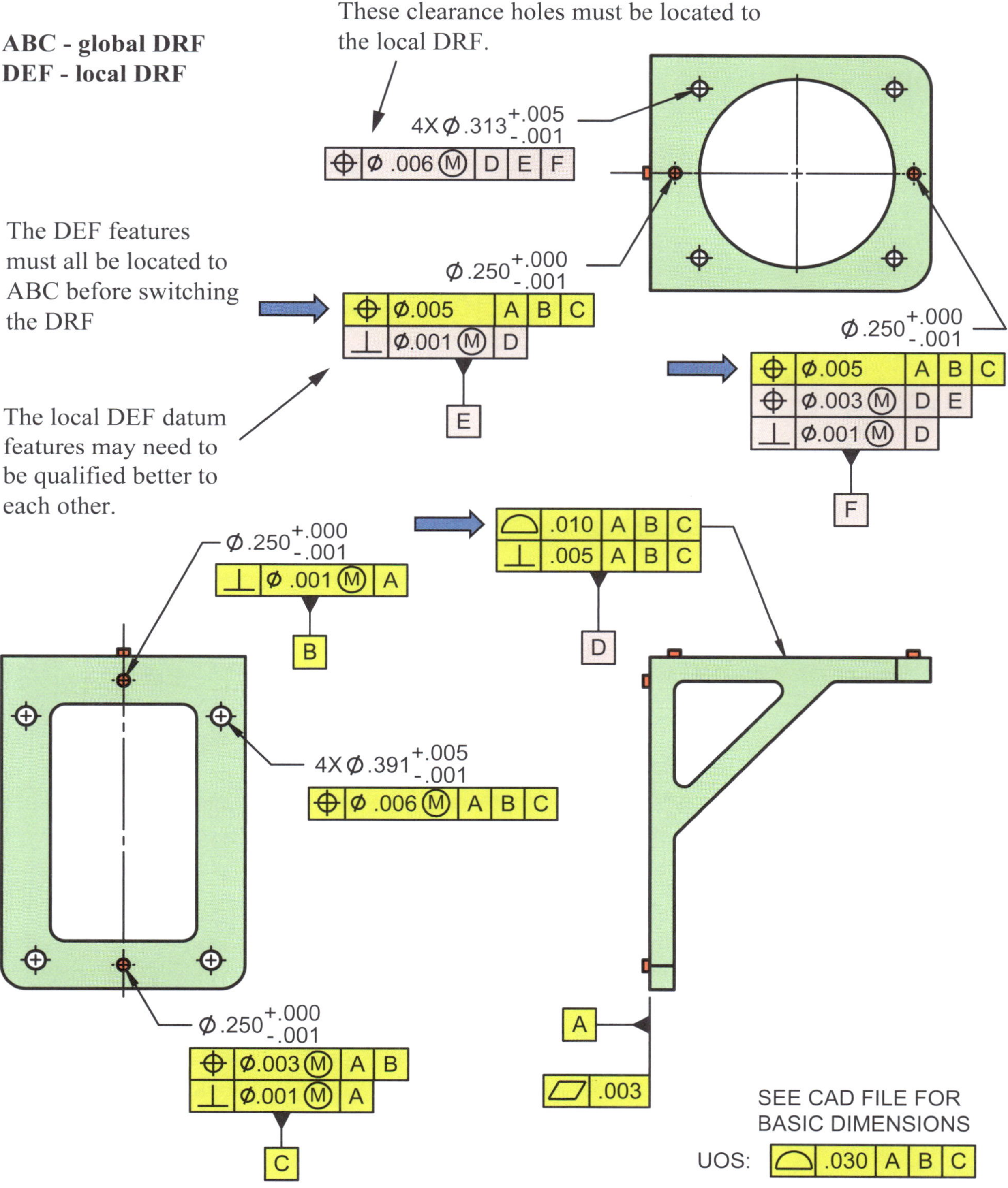

Multiple DRF Done Wrong

The tolerancing scheme below shows a disastrous mistake for a part with multiple DRFs. All datum features in the new DEF are not located to the original ABC. The secondary and tertiary are located to DRFs with datum features from both the original and new coordinate systems (DAB, DEA). This creates more set-ups for inspection that make the part more complicated to measure, create tolerance stack issues, and give false (non functional) measurement data.

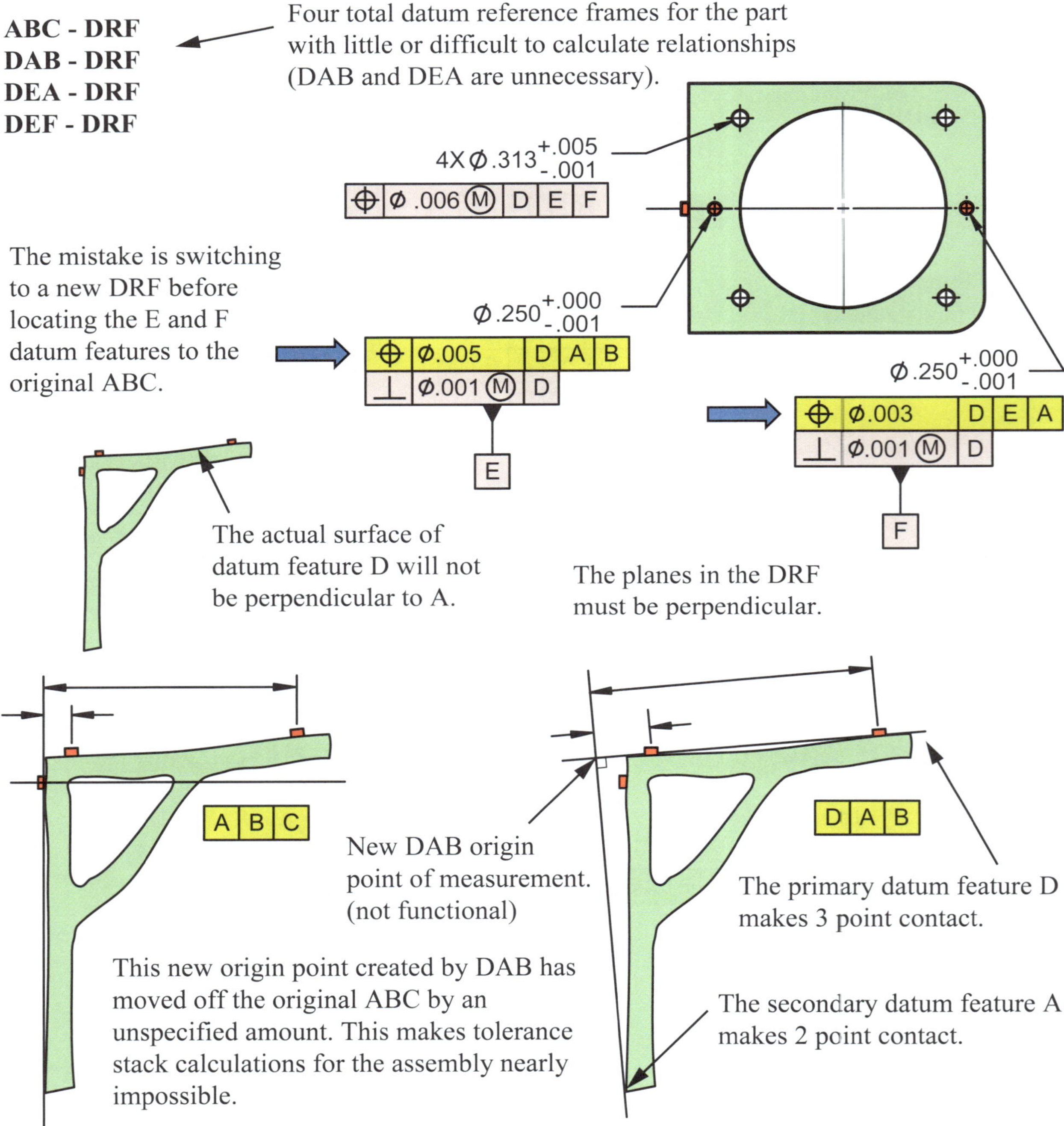

This is a relatively simple part and two DRFs turned to four. If this mistake is done on a more complicated housing or frame, it can cause many more DRFs (often exhausting the alphabet). The stacks become impossible and we loose trust in our measurement data. Instead, use the method of a **global DRF** and related **local DRFs** shown earlier to decrease the number of inspection set-ups and hold better relationships between features.

Datum Features Referenced Individually

This assembly includes a plate with three separate connectors. Each connector pilots on the large center hole, clocks to the slot, and is fastened through the holes. Each set of screw holes must follow its respective pilot hole and slot but is not important to the edges.

This on the drawing

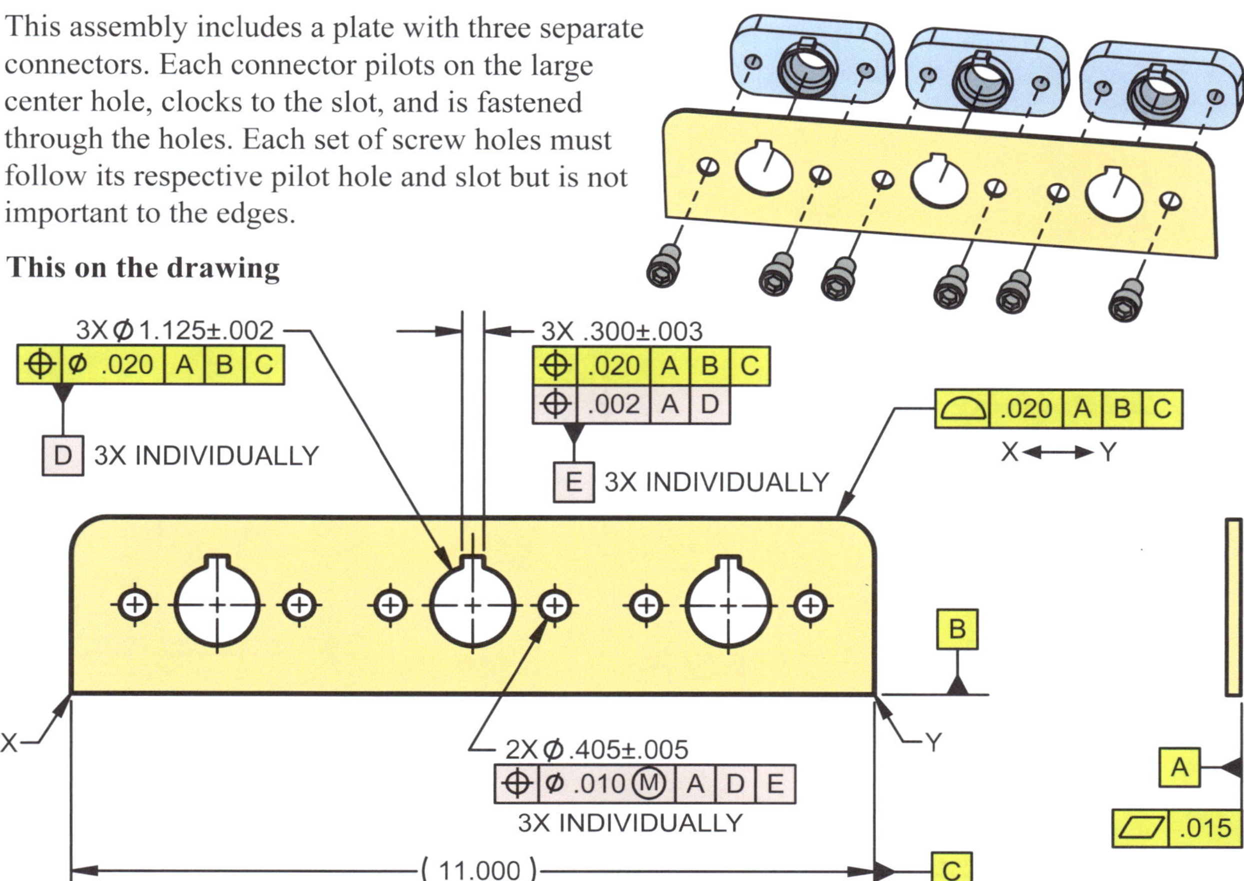

A global ABC DRF is established from the back face, bottom edge and outside width. The positions of .020 on the three pilot holes and three slots locate the mating connectors to ABC.

A local ADE DRF is created from the pilot hole and slot. The position of .002 and position of .010 insure the slot and screw holes follow their respective pilot hole.

The notation INDIVIDUALLY is applied to the datum feature D and E to identify the three pilot holes as individual datum features (not as a pattern). The INDIVIDUALLY notation is also applied to the position tolerance for the screw holes. Individually is used to create multiple local DRFs without the need to label each with a separate datum feature symbol.

Or this on the drawing

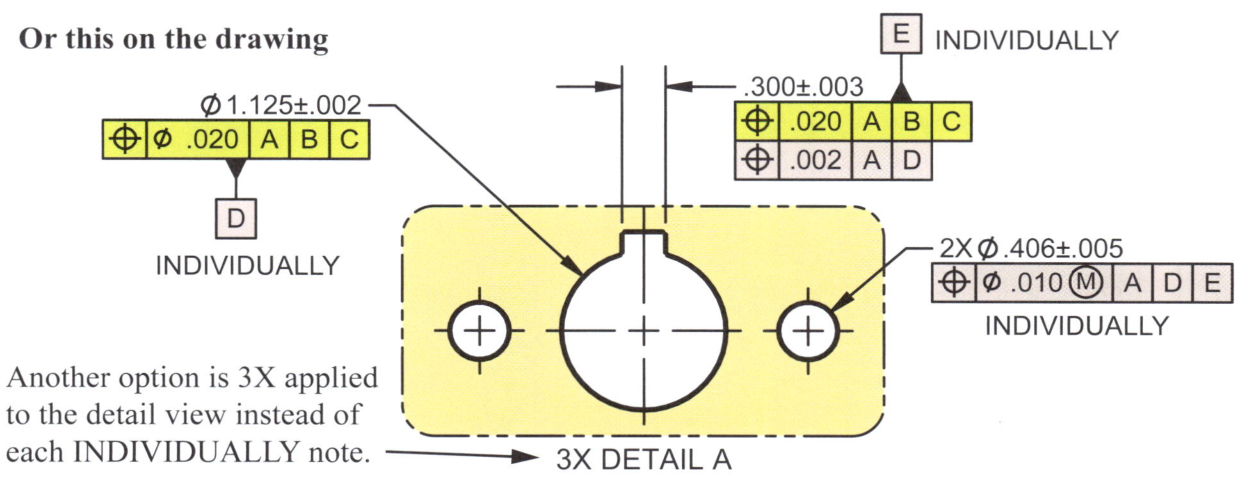

Another option is 3X applied to the detail view instead of each INDIVIDUALLY note.

Workshop Exercise 9.3

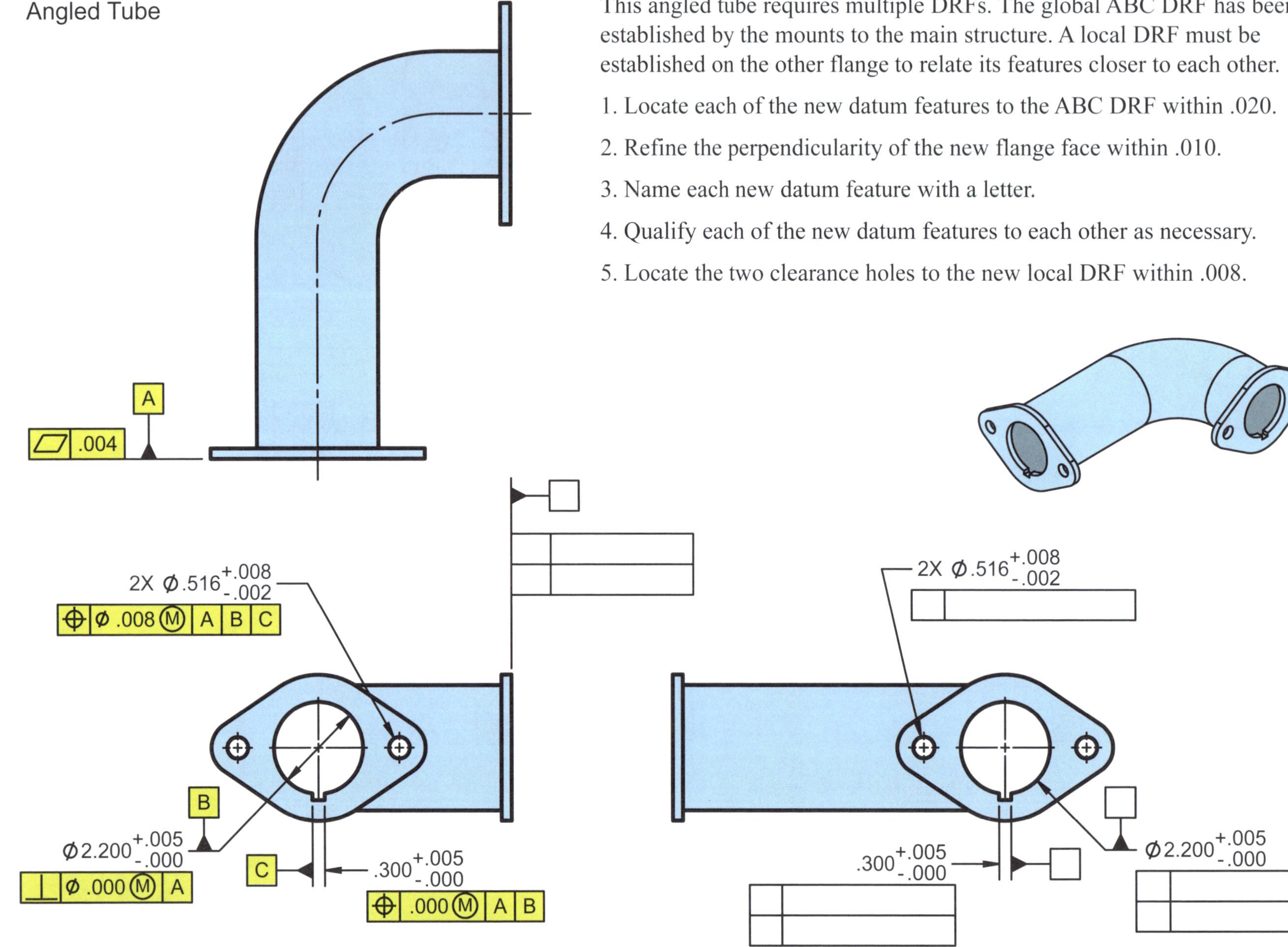

This angled tube requires multiple DRFs. The global ABC DRF has been established by the mounts to the main structure. A local DRF must be established on the other flange to relate its features closer to each other.

1. Locate each of the new datum features to the ABC DRF within .020.
2. Refine the perpendicularity of the new flange face within .010.
3. Name each new datum feature with a letter.
4. Qualify each of the new datum features to each other as necessary.
5. Locate the two clearance holes to the new local DRF within .008.

Inseparable Assemblies - All Tolerances at Assembly Level

The Support Lift Bracket below is an inseparable weldment that is fully toleranced at the assembly level. The datum reference frame and tolerances are selected based on the functional mating requirements for the next upper level. Although separate drawings could be created for the three individual piece parts in the lower level, it is not necessary.

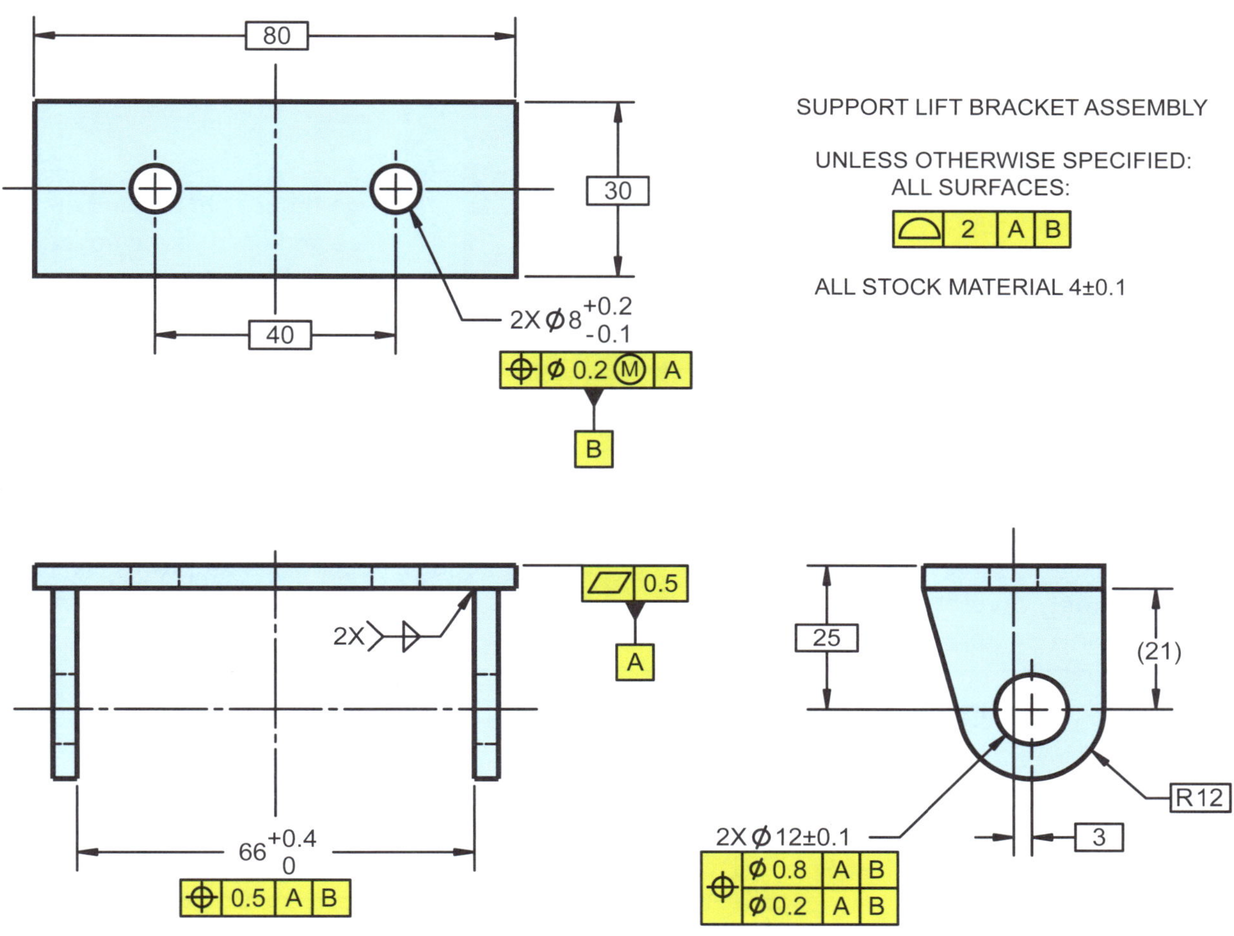

Functional relationships are documented at this assembly level for design to do necessary calculations for the next level assembly. This also benefits manufacturing by giving them flexibility in production. This assembly will have multiple manufacturing steps: cutting the individual parts and then welding them together. Piece parts may be made by a flame cutter, laser cutter, or water-jet machine. The manufacturer may choose to produce the holes in the piece parts before welding or post machine the holes after welding. The manufacturer may choose to build a welding fixture to hold tighter requirements. This manufacturing order or process is not important to the design and therefore is not necessary for design to dictate piece part tolerances with individual detail drawings. The manufacturer must work out the details of the manufacturing process to meet the final requirements at the assembly level shown.

Inseparable Assemblies - Tolerances at Assembly and Detail Level

Below is another example of an inseparable assembly. In this scenario, some tolerances apply at the assembly level and other requirements apply at the lower detail levels. Design shows requirements in the assembly level to match to the next level assembly and also works with manufacturing or possible multiple suppliers to show fixturing and tolerances for the individual component drawings.

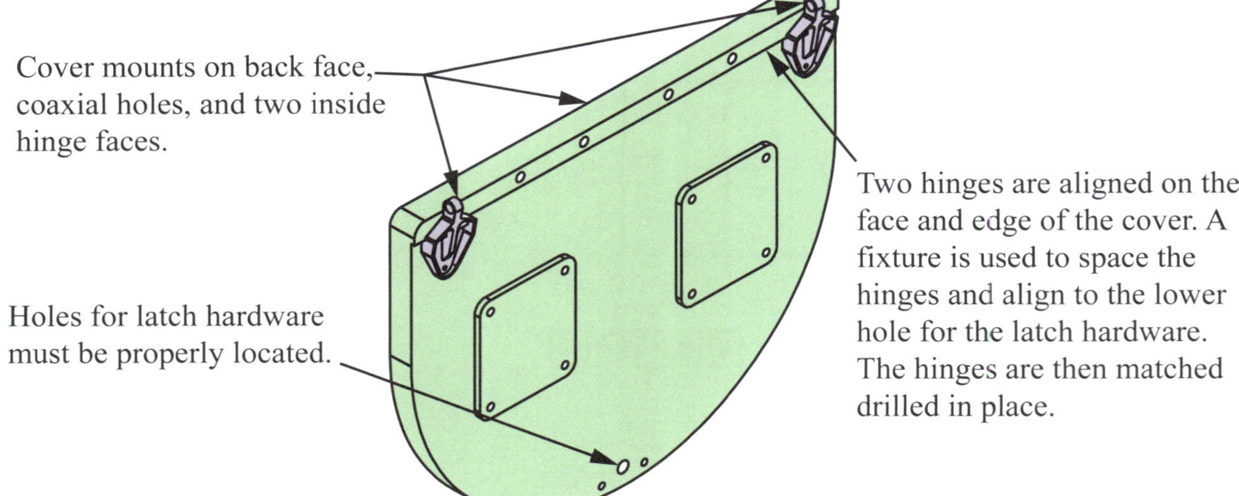

The Hatch Cover Assembly drawing shows the important requirements when all pieces are fixed at the assembly level. Detail drawings (shown on the next page) are made for the piece parts for other tolerance requirements at the lower levels.

Assembly Drawing for Hatch Cover Assembly

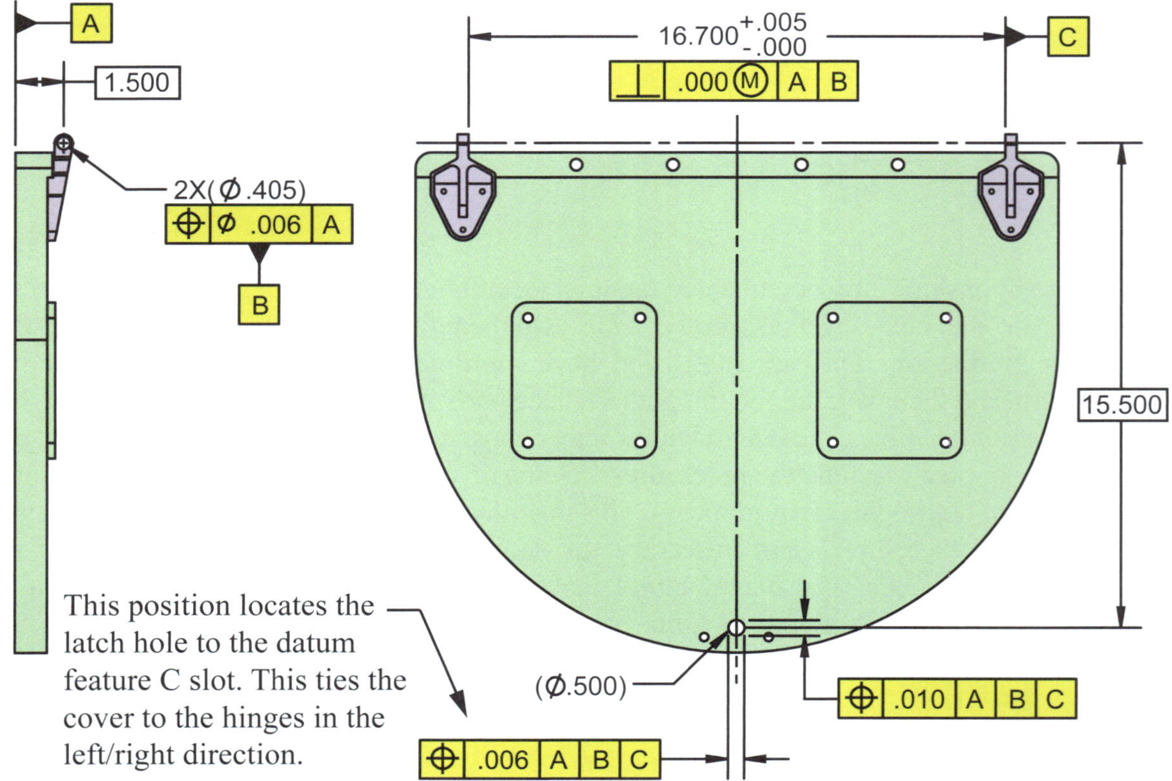

Inseparable Assemblies - Tolerances at Assembly and Detail Level

On the cover detail, the primary datum feature remains the same as the assembly. Datum features E and F are selected because they are used to fixture the cover to the hinges.

Detail drawing for hatch cover

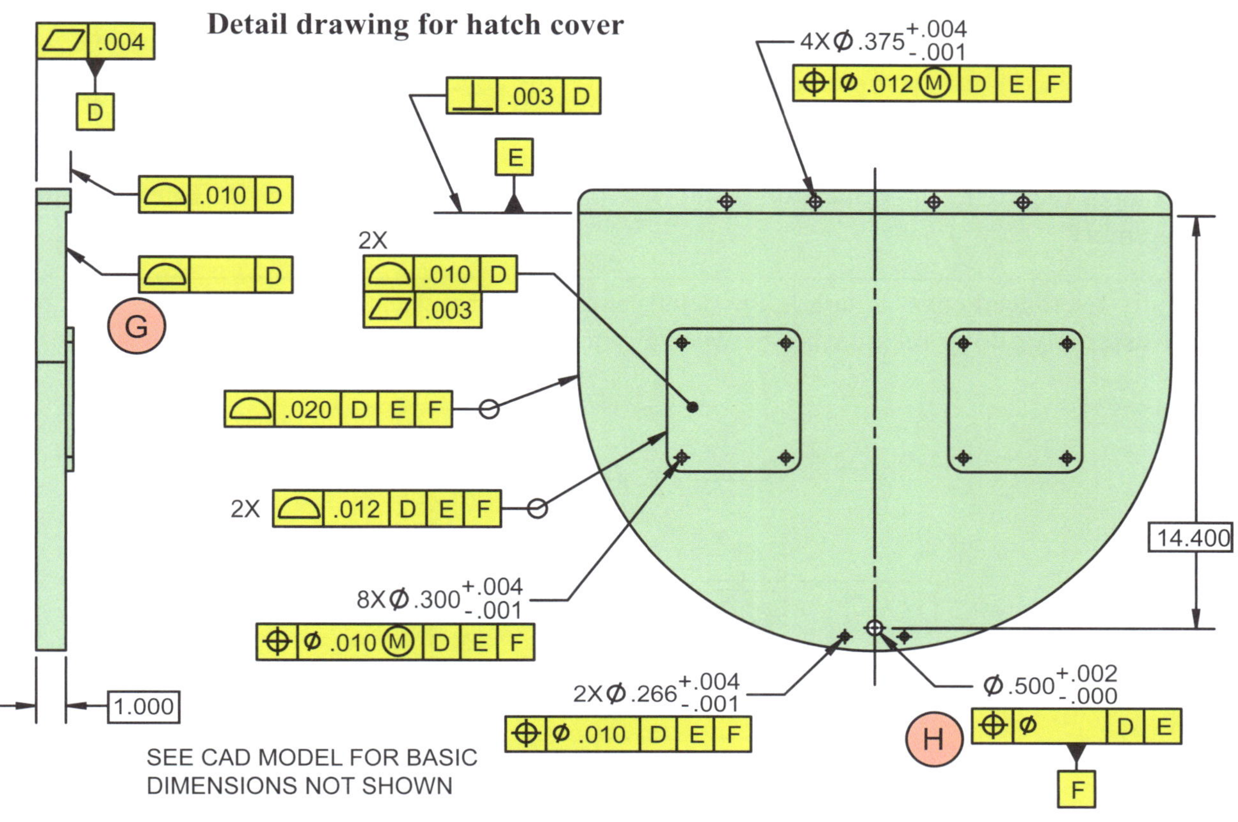

On the Hinge detail, datum features are selected based on how it fits to the cover and fixtured in place. Since both sides of the .350 width are important, the center is chosen as datum C.

Detail drawing for hinge

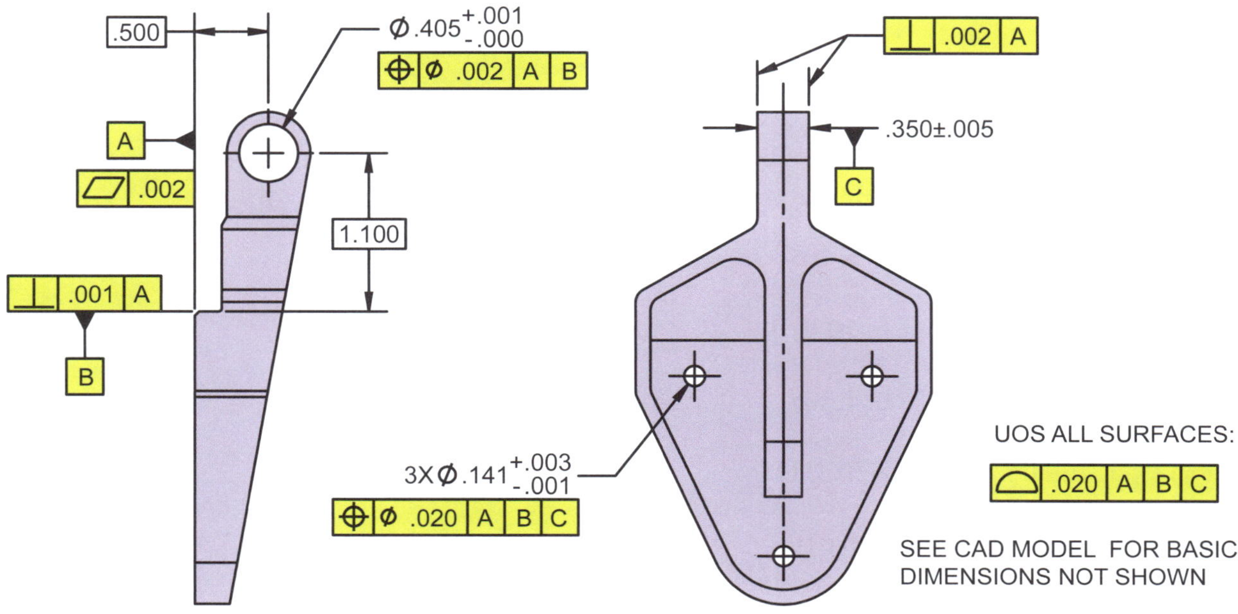

Workshop Exercise 9.4- Inseparable Assemblies

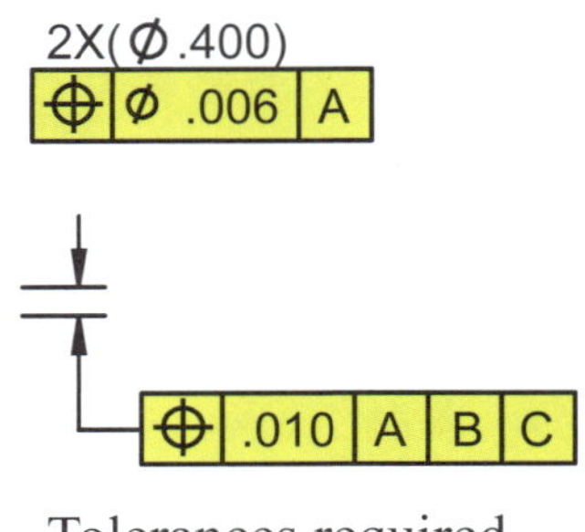

Tolerances required at assembly

The addition of all piece part tolerances may not exceed the tolerance limit on the assembly without possible post assembly machining. A simple stack must be completed for the max tolerances for G and H on the cover. Use the final tolerances for the assembly and the given tolerances on the hinge to calculate tolerance values for G and H.

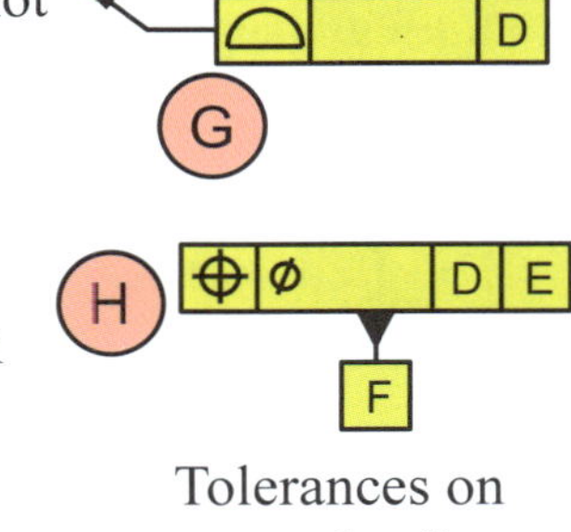

Tolerances on cover detail

The fully toleranced cover detail, hinge detail, and tolerancing relationship of the datum features on the assembly allows relationship between any features to be calculated.

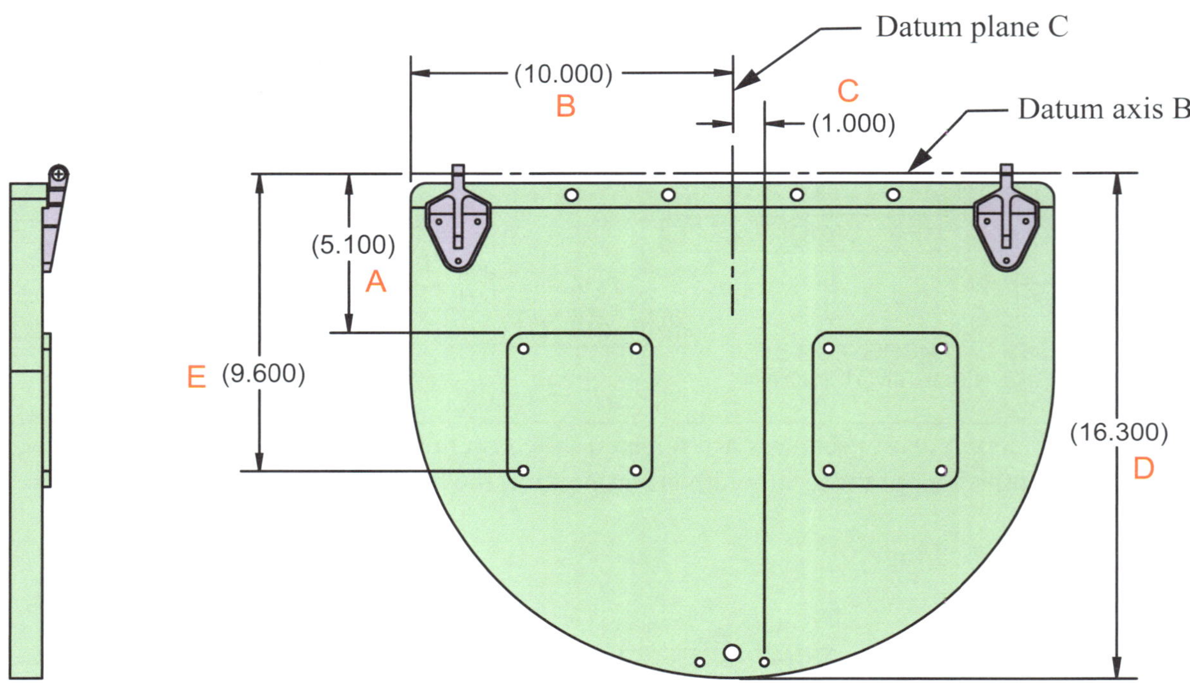

Use the detail drawings and assembly drawing to calculate the max possible of the distances labeled above. Assume all holes are produced at MMC (no bonus tolerance).

A	a. 5.106	b. 5.107	c. 5.108	d. 5.112
B	a. 10.006	b. 10.010	c. 10.013	d. 10.020
C	a. 1.005	b. 1.008	c. 1.010	d. 1.018
D	a. 16.306	b. 16.311	c. 16.312	d. 16.318
E	a. 9.606	b. 9.610	c. 9.612	d. 9.618

Customized Datum Reference Frame - Square Hole and Slot

The drawing below illustrates a customized DRF applied to the Leveling Bar. The back face on the bar is datum feature A and constrains translation z and rotations u and v. The square hole is datum feature B and by default constrains translations x and y and rotation w. In a standard DRF, all degrees of freedom would be constrained with only datum features A and B.

In the assembly however, the square hole locates the part, but the slot at the end constrains rotation rather than the shorter square hole. Therefore, the feature control frames state the constraints in brackets behind each datum feature reference to define a customized DRF. Customized DRFs require the datum axes (X,Y, and Z) to be labeling on the drawing.

The Leveling Bar drawing with a customized DRF.

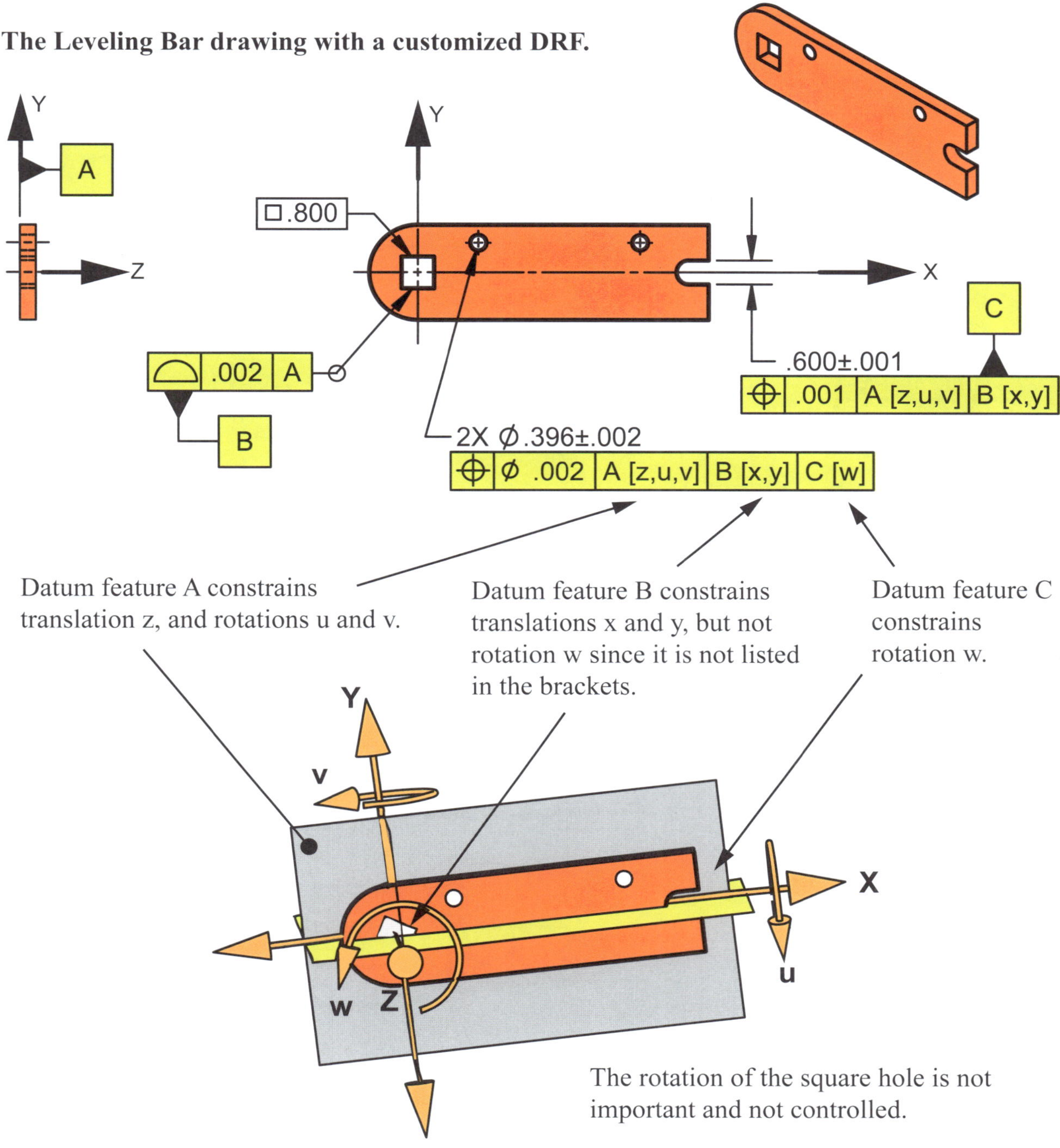

Workshop Exercise 9.5 - Customized Datum Reference Frame

The two drawings below represents the same part with different options for a DRF. The upper drawing has a standard DRF with primary datum feature A at RMB. This conical shape constrains 3 translations and 2 rotations and no other datum features are needed. The design engineer feels the taper on the cone is too shallow to adaquetly constrain the translation along the axis and instead wants to use the large back face for this translation.

On the lower drawing create a customized DRF in the feature control frame and use datum feature A as the primary and the large shoulder face as datum feature B. Release the translational degree of freedom along the axis from A, and instead use datum feature B to constrain this translation. Make sure to create and label axes on the drawing to clearly identify your X, Y and Z directions.

Standard Datum Reference Frame

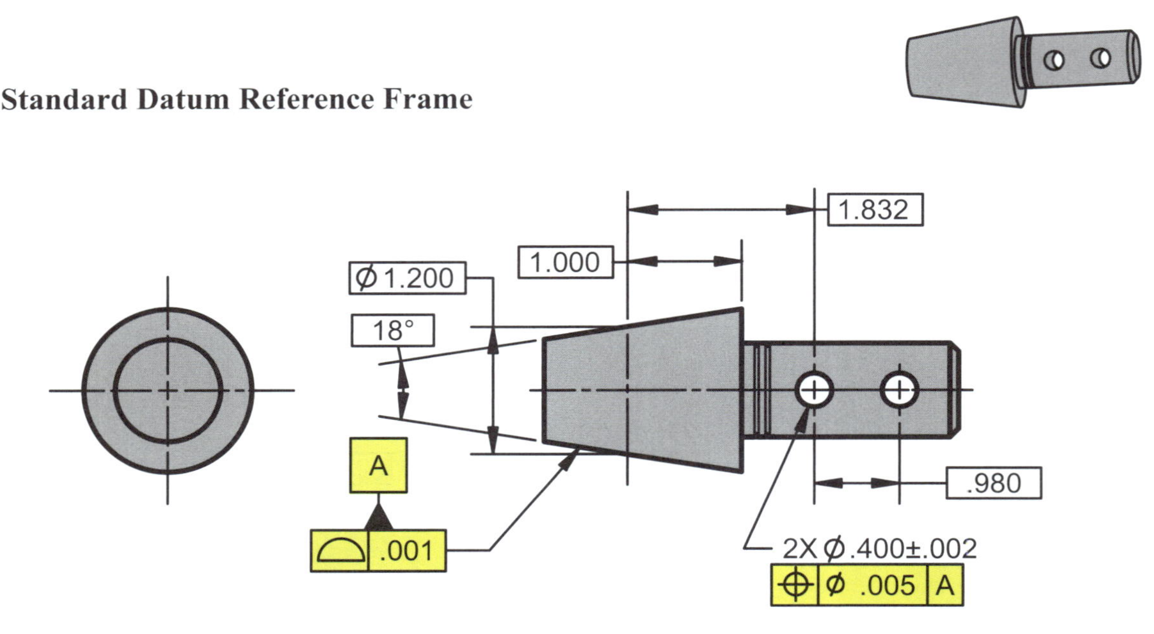

Customized Datum Reference Frame

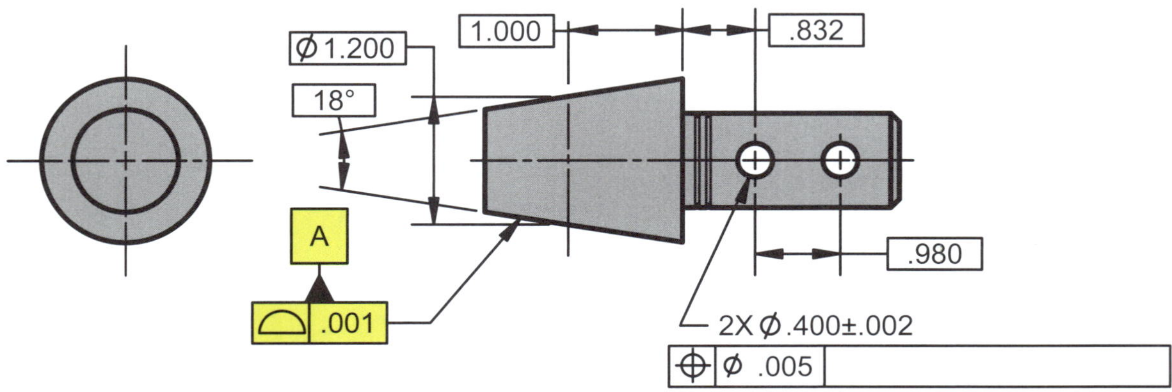

Unit 10

Form Tolerances

Form Tolerances

Symbol	Form Tolerance	Common Shape of Tolerance Zone	2D / 3D	Application of Feature Modifier
—	Straightness-Line Elements	2 Parallel Lines	2D	No Controls Surface
⏥	Flatness - Surface	2 Parallel Planes	3D	
○	Circularity (Roundness)	2 Concentric Circles	2D	
⌭	Cylindricity	2 Concentric Cylinders	3D	
—	Straightness - Median Line	Cylindrical	3D	Yes Controls Median Line or Plane
⏥	Flatness - Median Plane	2 Parallel Planes	3D	

Overview:

Form tolerances control the shape of an individual feature to itself, and therefore no datum feature references are allowed.

There are six form tolerances (only 4 different symbols) shown in the chart above. Flatness and straightness are split into two concepts, one for controlling the surface (or line elements of the surface) and another for controlling the median plane or line.

Material condition modifiers (MMC, LMC, and RFS) are applicable only to straightness-median line and flatness-median plane. All other form tolerances control the surface of the feature and material condition modifiers do not apply.

As we know, the default *limits of size* (rule #1) in ASME Y14.5 also control the form (perfect form at MMC required). Therefore, any form tolerance applied to a feature of size will either refine or relax the form defined by the standard size tolerance. The first four form tolerances in the table above refine the form defined by rule #1. The last two form tolerances relax the form of rule #1.

Note that in ISO standards, perfect form at MMC is not required by default for features of size. This will have an effect on the rules for applying form tolerances to features of size.

The tolerances of straightness-line elements and circularity are 2D versions of 3D flatness and cylindricity respectively.

Flatness

Flatness is the condition of a surface having all elements in one plane. A flatness tolerance specifies a tolerance zone defined by two parallel planes within which the surface must lie. The most common applications of flatness are to qualify the primary datum feature (planar surface) and as a refinement of profile tolerance.

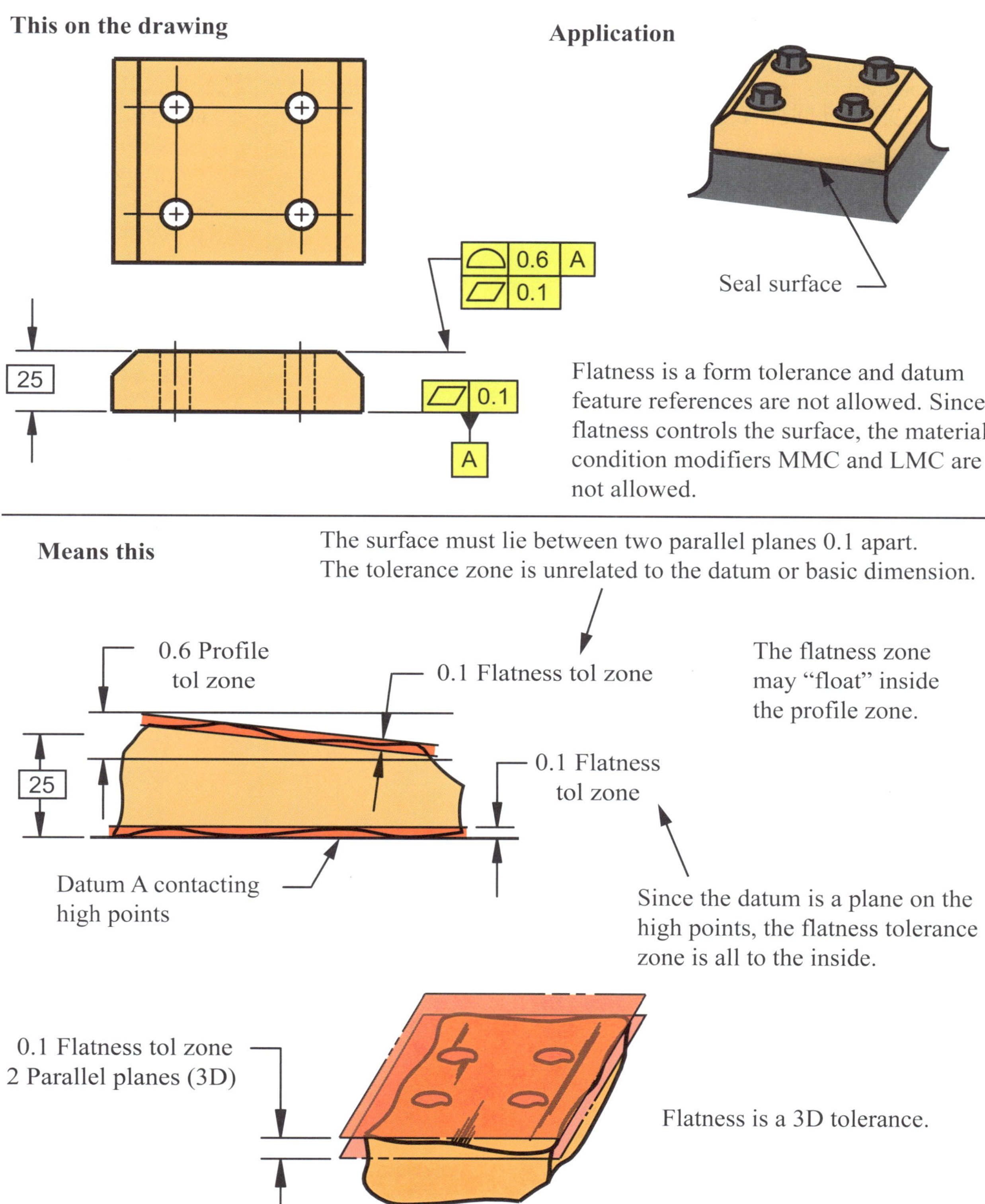

Flatness Verification

There are many ways to check a flatness specification, with some methods more precise (and time consuming) than others. As for any tolerance, the inspection method depends on many factors: How many parts are there to check? Is this the first part produced or the 1000th? Is the process capability well within the tolerance? Are statistical process controls being done? How tight is the tolerance? What kind of equipment is available? Is it an in-process check, or a final check? How much time/money are we willing to dedicate to this check? What are the consequences of a nonconforming part in the field? These factors and more may affect the inspection method. While the theoretical design requirements are documented on the drawing, the details of verification procedures should be documented in the dimensional measurement plan (see unit 5).

The measurement techniques shown below are only intended to assist the reader in understanding the concepts. There are many other ways to check flatness, including a coordinate measuring machine (CMM), laser scanners, and optical flats.

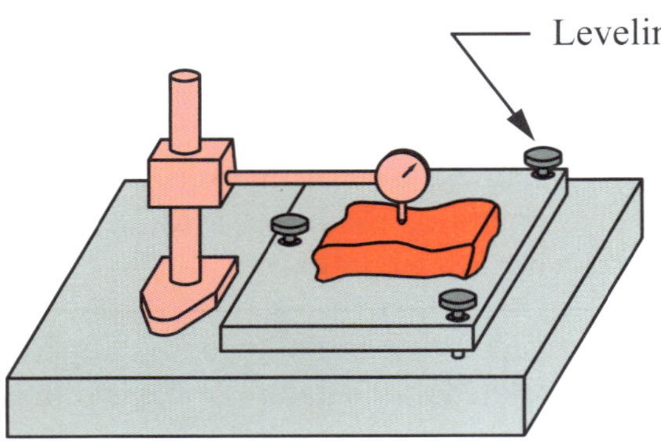

Level part on surface plate using the three adjusters and move indicator over surface. The readings must not exceed flatness tolerance. This is a good check but it may be time consuming.

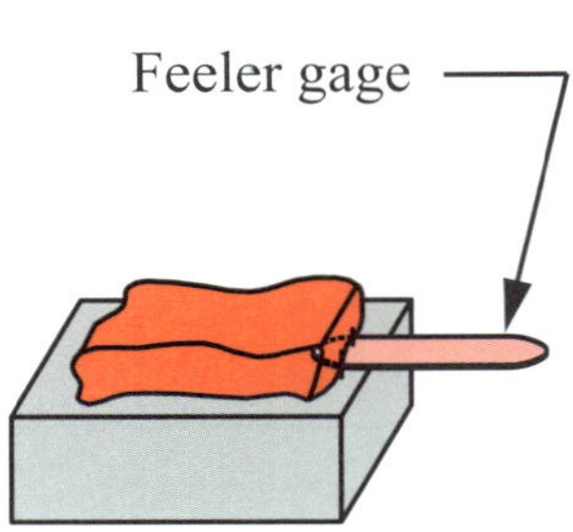

Set part on surface plate and use feeler gage. This is a quick check used for larger tolerances. It may miss concave variations.

Set part upside-down on gage blocks of equal height, then indicate underneath. This is also a precise check but cannot indicate on surface resting areas. Also subject to part “sag”.

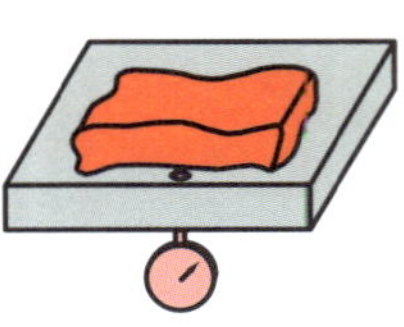

Indicate surface through a hole in the surface plate while sliding part. This is a good in-process check. It may misread on convex parts.

Flatness Design Considerations

The manufacturability of a surface with a flatness tolerance (or any geometric tolerance) is not just dependent on the width value of the tolerance zone, but also the relative size of the feature. A large flatness tolerance on a long feature can be more difficult to produce than a small tolerance on a short feature. To understand if a tolerance is "tight" and difficult to manufacture to, the designer should consider the length of the controlled feature as well as the size of the tolerance zone.

Flatness is often used to qualify datum features. Specifying a flatness control on a primary datum surface will limit the amount of rock (instability) of the surface relative to the datum plane. The instability cannot be eliminated, but only minimized through a flatness control. There is a general rule: "a datum feature should be qualified as well as the features that are related to it." If a datum feature is unstable (can rock), then the features related to it will also rock. However, if the datum feature has a flatness tolerance of .005, this does not mean that all the related features will rock .005. Also consider the relative size of the datum feature and relative distance to figure the amount of rock of the related features (a small surface rocking .005 has a greater effect elsewhere than a larger surface rocking .005).

Flatness is often applied to sheet metal, plastic, or flanged surfaces that will be bolted or welded together. The flatness tolerance may be limiting how much the parts deform or stress in the assembly process.

Flatness may also be applied as a refinement of a profile tolerance or size. The profile will define a tolerance zone locating all points on the surface. This also controls the flatness, but a smaller flatness tolerance may be applied to refine the form of the surface. This technique is used when the location of the surface does not matter, but it must make a good seal.

Flatness is used on gasket or seal surfaces. The flatness tolerance will control the size of the gap or crack when two parts are assembled. A flatness on two mating surfaces of .005 each could result in a maximum .010 total gap.

Other examples for a flatness control include surfaces for heat transfer or electrical contacts, thrust bearings, clutches, and optics.

There is sometimes a question of how flatness affects the surface finish. The surface finish must fall within the flatness tolerance zone and is usually on a much smaller scale. Surface finish is a localized check from an adjacent peak to valley to determine roughness on a surface, while flatness controls an entire surface at once. Surface finish is a localized check and is also specified on curved surfaces. However, flatness may only be specified on flat surfaces.

Flatness Per Unit Area

Flatness may be applied per unit area to prevent an abrupt surface variation within a small area. This can be thought of as a rate of change control. The per unit variation may be applied in combination with a total tolerance or alone. The feature units can be specified as a square or diameter.

Note: This type of unit basis control may be used with straightness, perpendicularity, profile, and other geometric controls to obtain similar effects.

This on the drawing

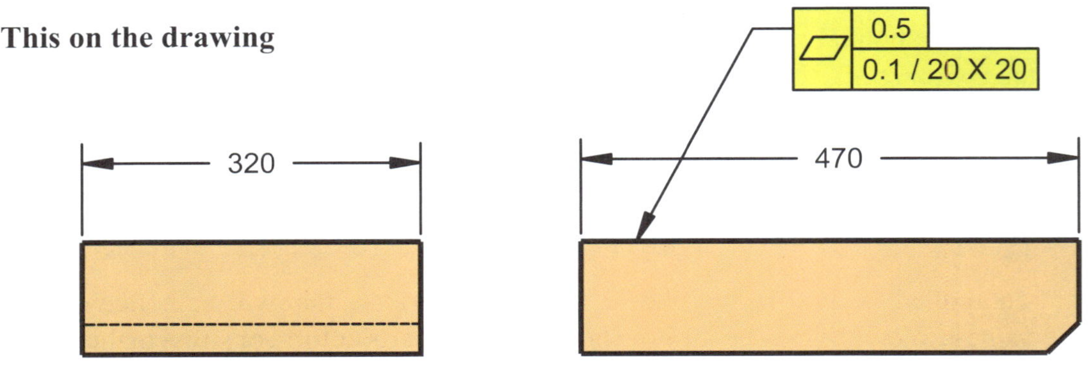

The entire surface must lie within two parallel planes 0.5 apart. In addition, each 20 X 20 unit of the feature (infinite overlapping units) must lie within two parallel planes 0.1 apart.

Means this

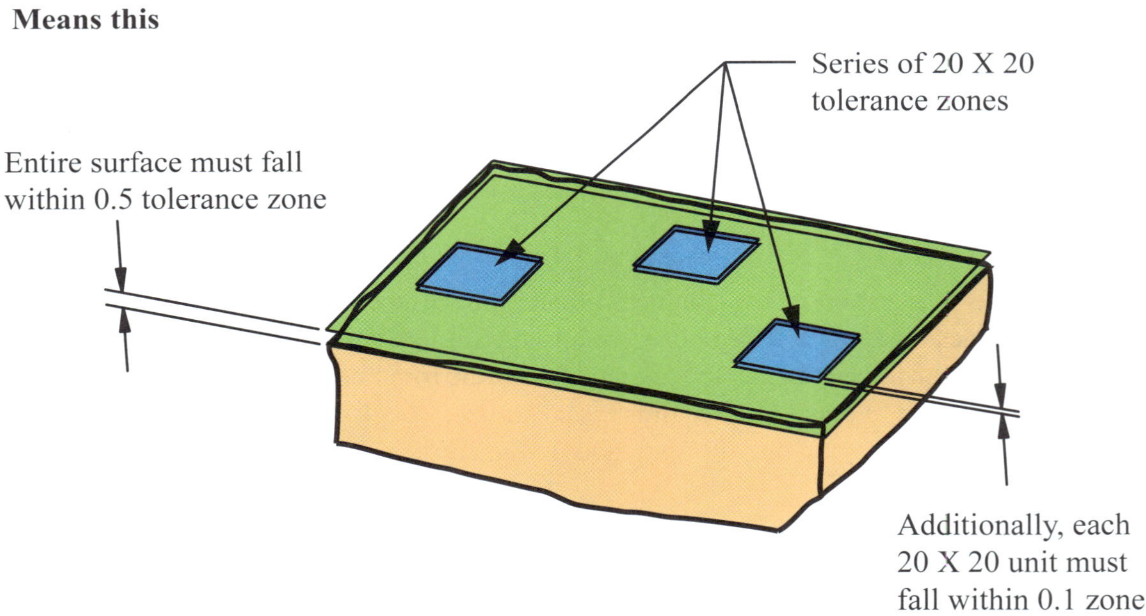

The 0.1 flatness per unit controls each section separately and can produce a cumulative effect if allowed to continue over the entire length of the feature. The overall flatness of 0.5 limits this cumulative effect.

Two Types of Straightness and Two Types of Flatness

Straightness:

There are two types of straightness controls that use the same geometric characteristic symbol. The placement of the feature control frame determines which control applies.

1. Straightness - line elements: The feature control frame is directed to the surface with an arrow or placed on the extension line for the surface. This is a 2D specification; creates a series of tolerance zones of two parallel lines to control line elements of surface. **This control refines the form provisions of the *limits of size* (rule#1)** if applicable. This control may also be applied to features without a size tolerance. Material condition modifiers are not allowed.

2. Straightness - median line: The feature control frame is placed under, or associated with, the size tolerance. This is a 3D specification; creates a cylindrical tolerance zone to control the derived median line of cylindrical features of size (hole/pin). **This control relaxes the form control provisions of the *limits of size* (rule#1)** and the perfect form boundary at MMC may be violated. Material condition modifiers are applicable and most commonly specified at MMC.

Flatness:

There are two types of flatness controls that use the same geometric characteristic symbol. The placement of the feature control frame determines which control applies.

1. Flatness - surface: The feature control frame is directed to the surface with an arrow or placed on the extension line for the surface. This is a 3D specification, creates a tolerance zone of two parallel planes and controls the entire surface unless a partial length is applied. **This control refines the form provisions of the *limits of size* (rule#1)** if applicable. This control may also be applied to features without a size tolerance. Material condition modifiers are not allowed. This flatness specification is the most common of the two.

2. Flatness - median plane: The feature control frame is placed under, or associated with, the size tolerance. This is a 3D specification, creates a tolerance zone of two parallel planes and controls the derived median plane of non-cylindrical features of size (usually slots, widths, or tabs). **This control relaxes the form control provisions of the *limits of size* (rule#1)** and the perfect form boundary at MMC may be violated. Material condition modifiers are applicable and most commonly specified at MMC.

Straightness Line Elements Applied on a Flat Surface

Straightness - line elements is a condition where an element of a surface is a straight line. Each line element of the surface shall lie between two parallel lines separated by the tolerance value. The tolerance zones are oriented by the orthographic view in which it applies or with supplemental geometry in the model. The feature control frame is directed to the surface or extension line.

Straightness in two directions is sometimes used instead of flatness on rectangular surfaces where the length is much greater than the width and different tolerances are needed for the two directions. It can be used on corrugated material where control in only one direction is needed. It can also be used as a refinement to geometric tolerances (flatness, parallelism, profile).

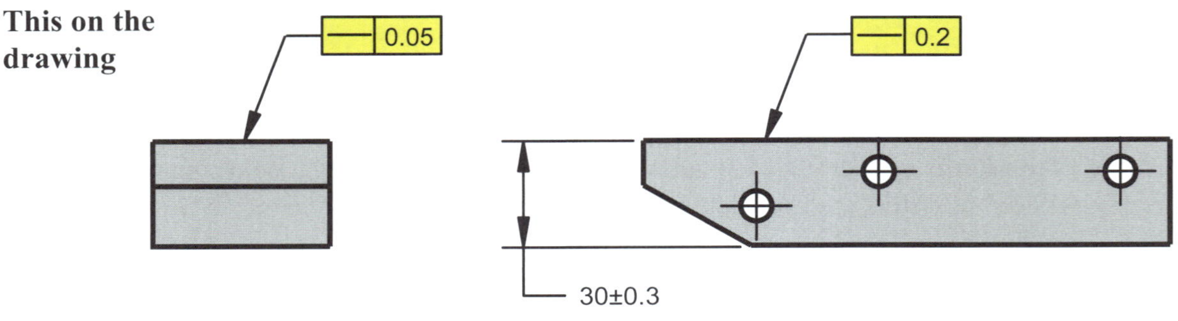

In the view shown, the surface elements must lie between a series of two parallel lines 0.2 apart. In addition, the feature must be within the limits of size. The straightness on the surface is a refinement on the form provisions defined by the size tolerance (rule #1).

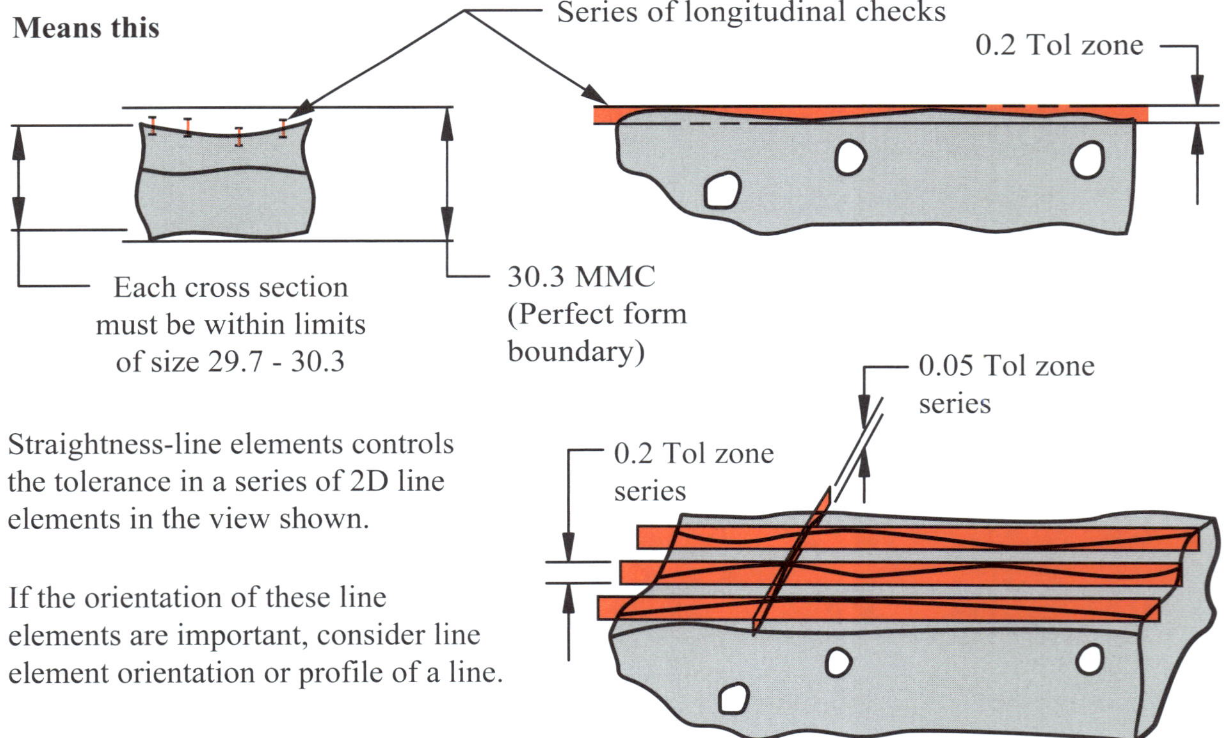

Straightness-line elements controls the tolerance in a series of 2D line elements in the view shown.

If the orientation of these line elements are important, consider line element orientation or profile of a line.

Caution: As we know, the line elements apply in the view in which shown. Manufactured parts are not perfect and in some instances, it may be unclear on how to orient the part in order to make the straightness line element checks.

Straightness Line Elements on a Pin

Straightness - line elements may be applied to the surface of a pin. The specification defines a tolerance zone in which the line elements on the surface must lie. The feature control frame is directed to the surface. MMC and LMC modifiers are not allowed.

This on the drawing

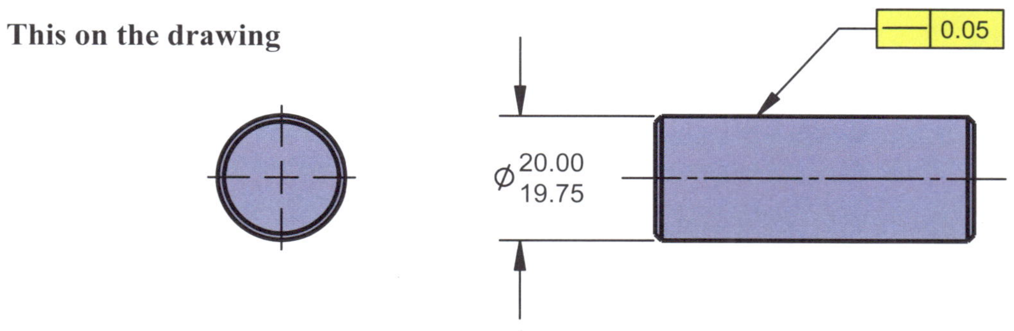

Each longitudinal element of the surface must lie between two parallel lines 0.05 apart where the two lines and axis of the unrelated actual mating envelope share a common plane. In addition, the feature must be within the limits of size, including perfect form at MMC. Straightness - line elements controls wasting, barrelling, and bending of the feature. It does not control taper or circularity.

Means this

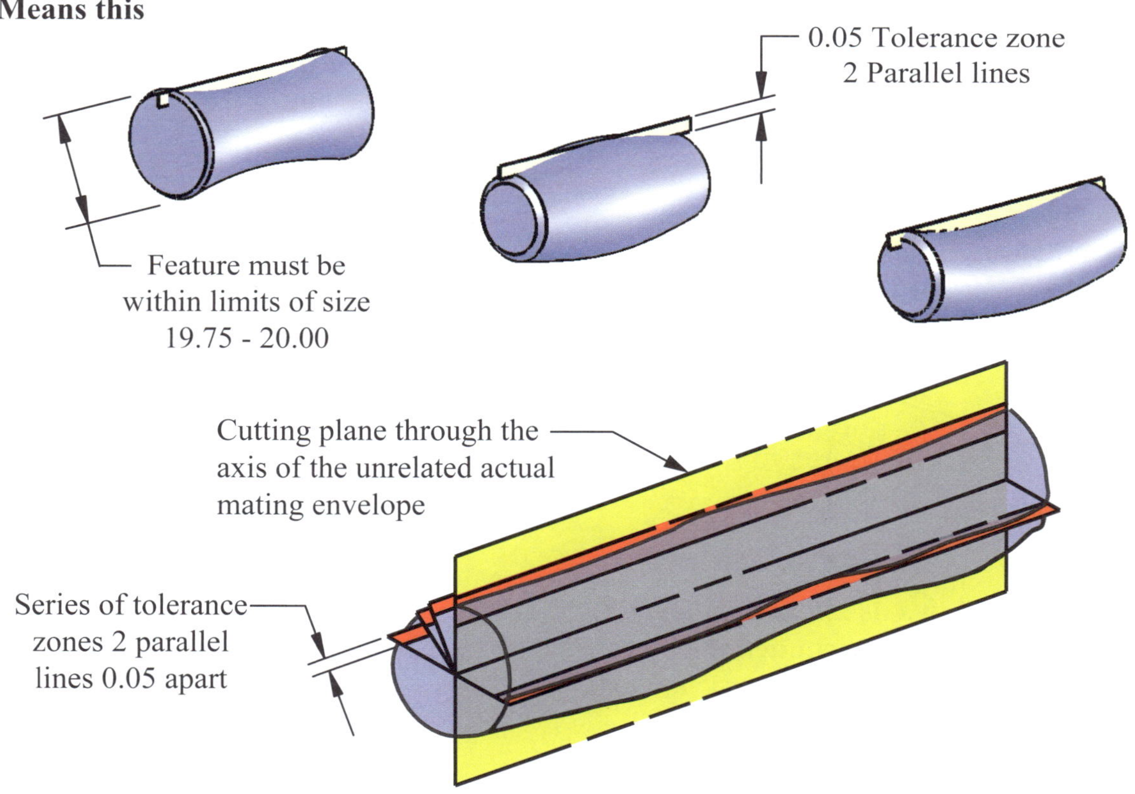

This type of control is used on dowel pins or shafts where the straightness must be better than provided with the size control (rule #1). It is sometimes used on heavy press fit shafts that must be hammered into place. The circularity is less important but must be straight in the direction of assembly.

Straightness of a Median Line

Straightness of a median line is a condition where the median line is a straight line. The specification defines a tolerance zone in which the derived median line must lie. When specifed at MMC, it also defines a virtual condition boundary which the surface must not violate. Note the feature control frame is associated with the size tolerance (placed below) to make it a median line control. Use with an MMC modifier is most common.

This type of control is used where the local size of the pin is important, but the pin can bend/bow beyond the perfect form at MMC requirement defined by Rule #1 (usually long shafts or rods and deep drilled holes).

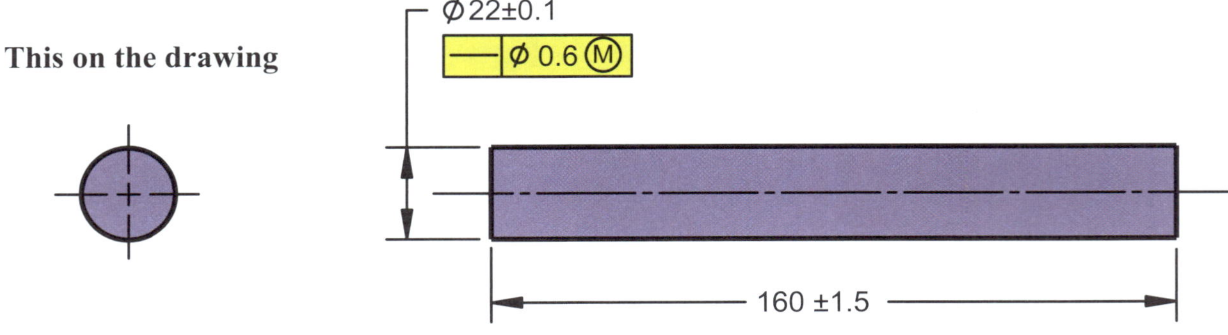

The derived median line of the feature's actual local sizes must be within a cylindrical tolerance zone of 0.6 at MMC. As the local size departs from MMC, an increase in the local diameter of the tolerance cylinder is allowed equal to the amount of such departure. In addition, each circular element must be within the limits of size.

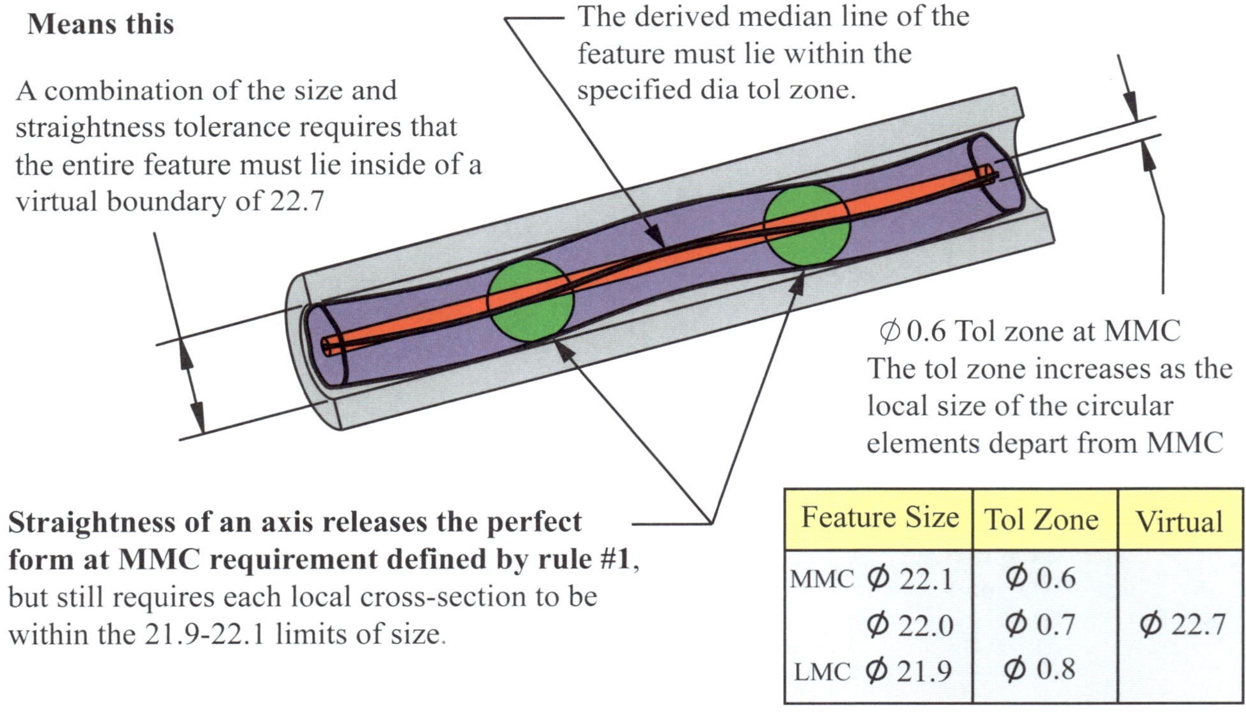

Straightness of an axis releases the perfect form at MMC requirement defined by rule #1, but still requires each local cross-section to be within the 21.9-22.1 limits of size.

Feature Size	Tol Zone	Virtual
MMC Ø 22.1	Ø 0.6	
Ø 22.0	Ø 0.7	Ø 22.7
LMC Ø 21.9	Ø 0.8	

Caution: The ASME standards do not clearly define how to find the derived median line. Due to form error, each local cross-section may have multiple center points. It is recommended to use this specification with an MMC modifier and instead evaluate the feature's unrelated actual mating envelope relative to the virtual condition boundary.

Flatness of a Median Plane

Flatness of a median plane is similar to straightness of a median line but for non-cylindrical features (slots, widths, and tabs). Flatness of a median plane is a condition where the median plane is a flat plane. The specification defines a tolerance zone in which the derived median plane must lie. When specified at MMC, it defines a vitual condition boundary which the surface must not violate. Note the feature control frame is associated with the size tolerance (placed below) to make it a median plane control. Use with an MMC modifier is most common.

This type of control is used on shims or large plates. The local size of the feature may be important but the part may bend or bow within a relatively large flatness-median plane tolerance.

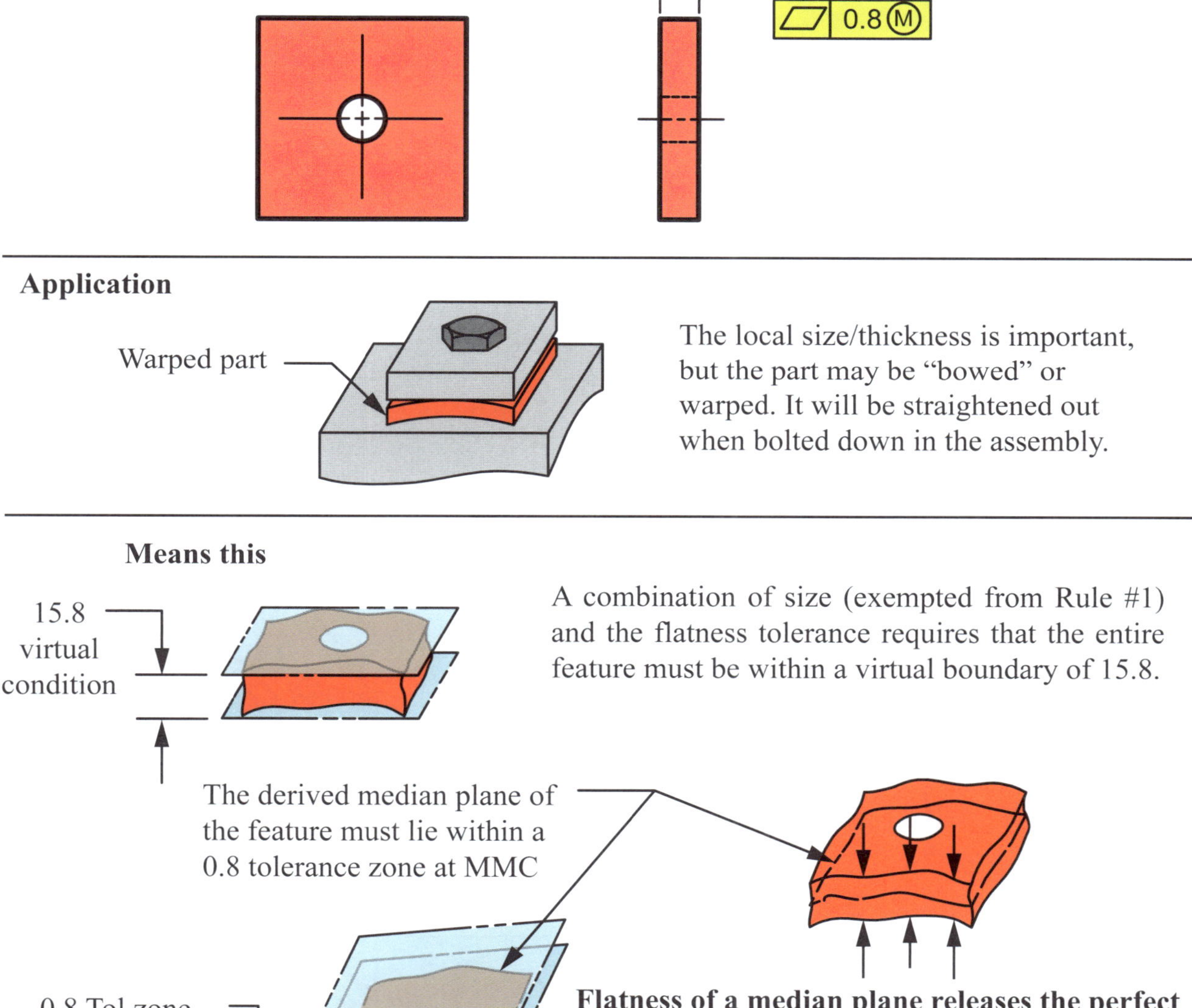

Flatness of a median plane releases the perfect form at MMC requirement defined by Rule #1, but still requires each local cross-section to be within the 14.9-15 limits of size.

Note: Another method with a similar result is using an independency symbol (circle I) next to the size tolerance (controlling thinkness only) and a flatness of a surface applied to one side.

Circularity (Roundness)

Circularity is a condition of a surface where:

a. for a feature other than a sphere, all points of the surface intersected by any plane perpendicular to an axis are equidistant to that axis.

b. for a sphere, all points of the surface intersected by any plane passing through a common center are equidistant from that center.

This on the drawing

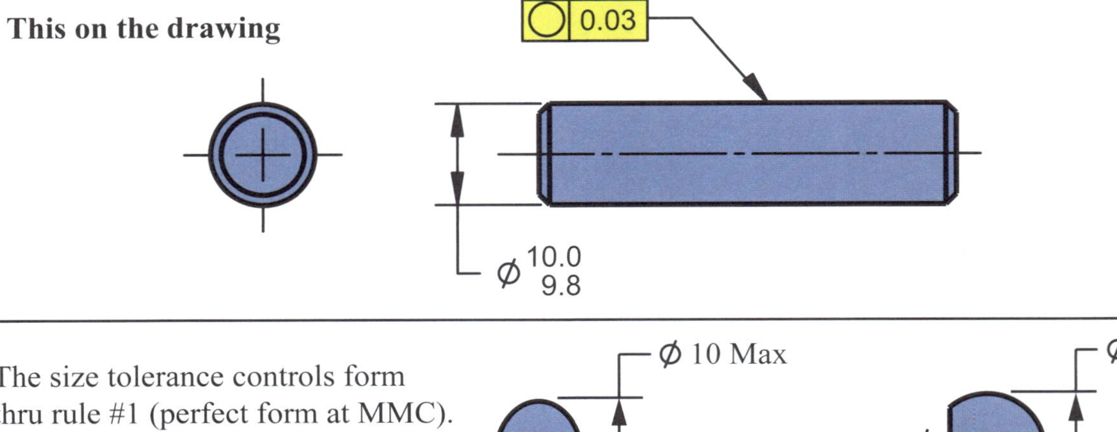

The size tolerance controls form thru rule #1 (perfect form at MMC). The max circularity variation is 0.2 before a circularity tolerance is applied.

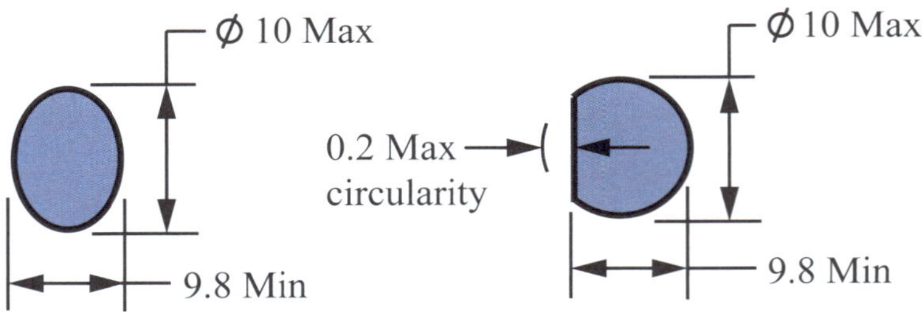

Circularity is a 2D tolerance. It controls circular elements, not longitudinal elements. Each circular element of the surface in a plane perpendicular to the axis must lie between two concentric circles, one having a radius 0.03 larger than the other. In addition, the feature must be within the limits of size, including perfect from at MMC.

Means this

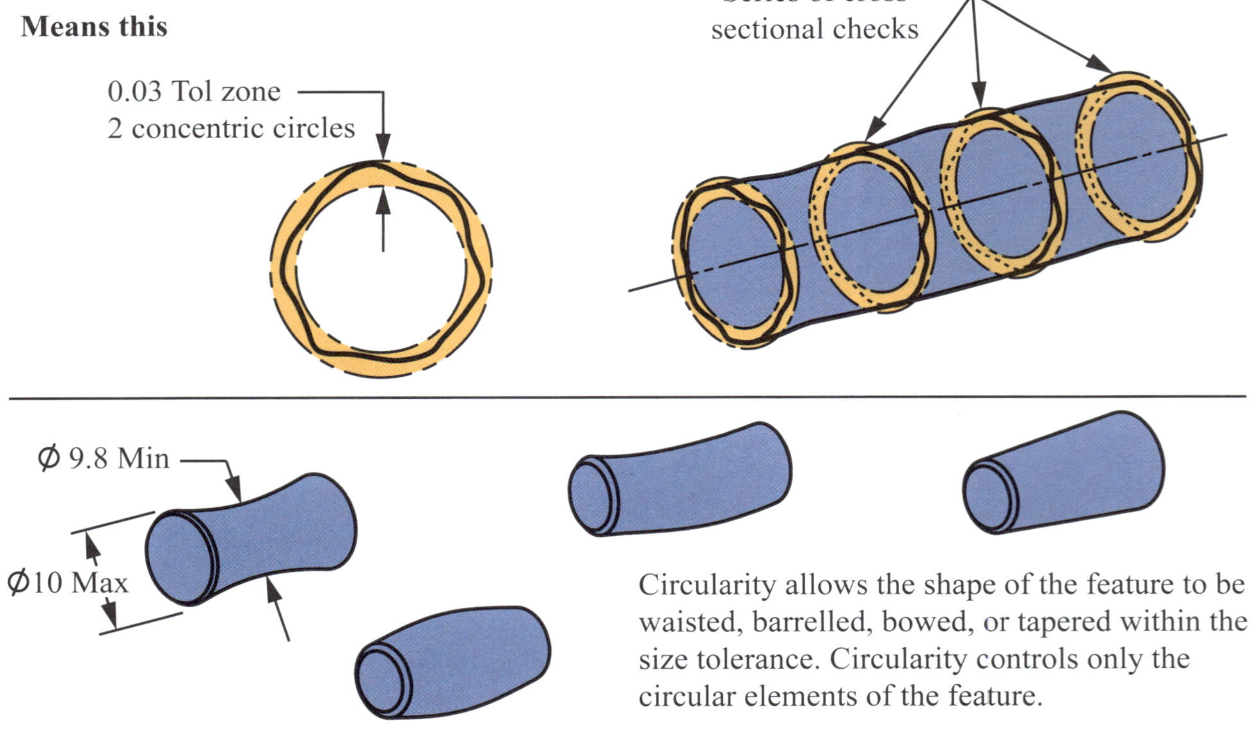

Circularity allows the shape of the feature to be waisted, barrelled, bowed, or tapered within the size tolerance. Circularity controls only the circular elements of the feature.

Cylindricity

Cylindricity is the condition of a surface of revolution within which all points of the surface are equidistant from a common axis. The tolerance zone is two concentric cylinders within which the surface must lie.

This on the drawing

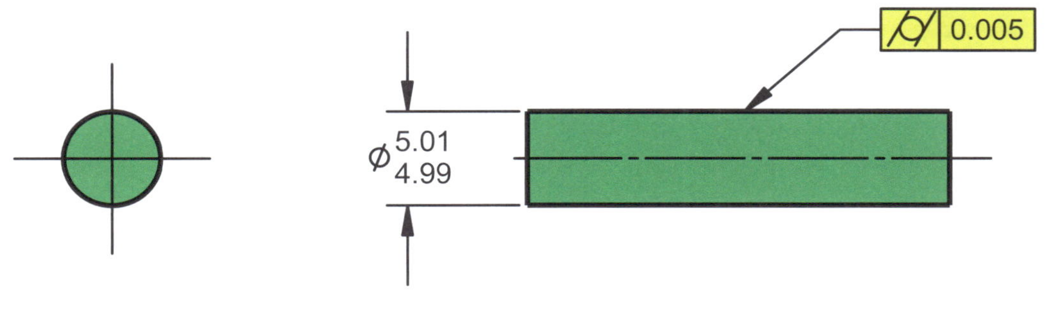

Application

The size of the bearings can vary within a greater tolerance relative to the cylindricity.

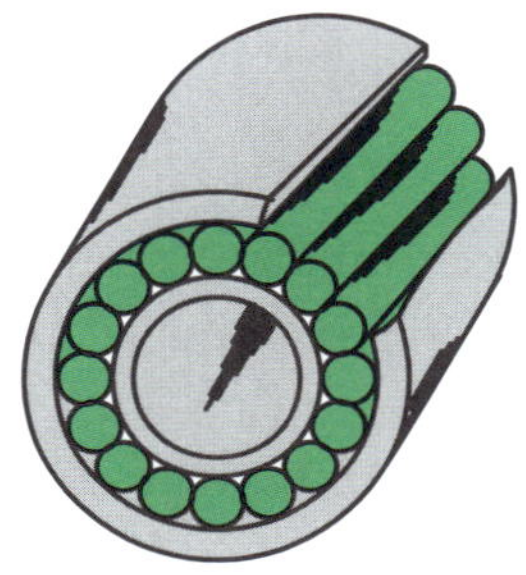

Cylindricity is a 3D tolerance. It controls both the circular and longitudinal elements of the feature. It includes circularity, straightness, and taper of the surface. The cylindrical surface of the feature must lie between two concentric cylinders, one having a radius of 0.005 larger than the other. In addition, the feature must be within the limits of size, including perfect from at MMC.

Means this

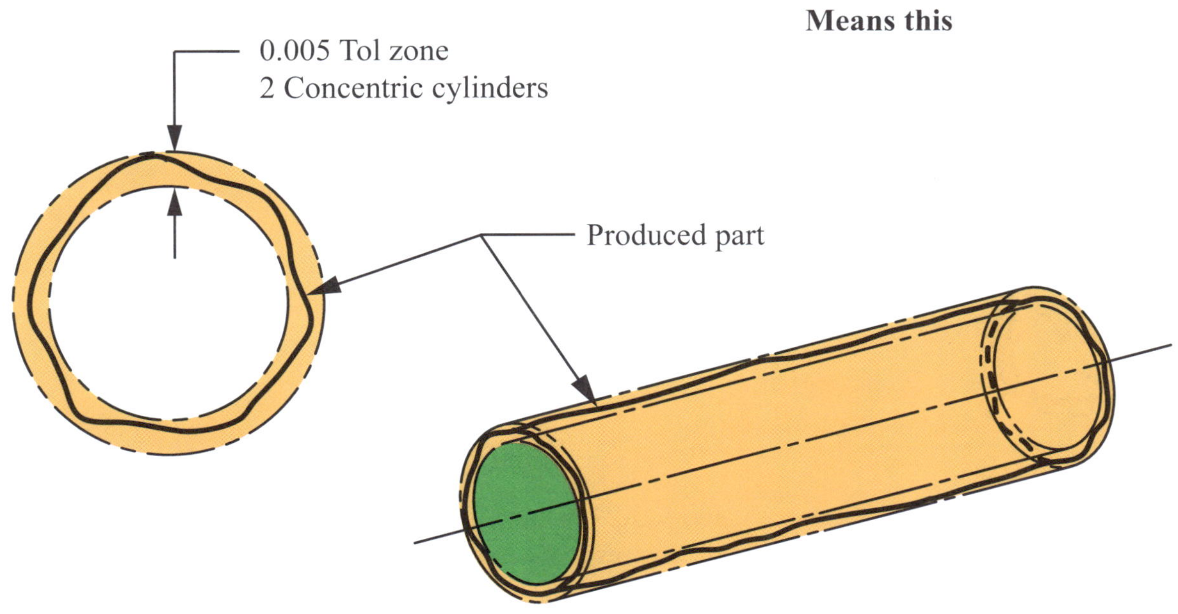

More on Circularity and Cylindricity, Average Diameter

Circularity and cylindricity are both form tolerances, therefore datum feature references are not allowed. They are also surface controls, therefore the modifiers MMC, LMC and RFS are not applicable. These controls refine the form requirements and the value must be less than the size tolerance, except with the use of average diameter (see below).

Examples of use for circularity: ball bearings, tubes, hoses, pipes, and circular elements of tapered, barreled or waisted parts such as nose cones, seals, valves, etc. It can also be used as a 2D refinement of cylindricity.

The verification of cylindricity and circularity are often difficult without a precision CMM. The surface periphery of the part must be verified relative to a reference axis. Often an external feature is rotated in a vee bock, and the surface is verified with an indicator. This is a rough check. Depending on the varying number and arrangement of lobes on the part, plus the angle of the vee bock, this verification method can give varying results. In some cases, it can show a good part bad and other times it can show a bad part good.

A more precise method of verification is through the use of a roundness machine where the part is rotated utilizing a precision spindle. A stylus reads the surface and transcribes an enlarged profile of the part periphery on a polar graph or strip chart. A precision CMM could also be used.

The method of describing circularity in the ASME Y14.5 standard is called minimum radial separation. In the ANSI B89.3.1 standard on roundness, there are other methods available for more specific needs. The method often used by CMMs is "mean least squares" which determines the circular form based on a mathematical formula. There are also methods such as minimum circumscribed circle (MCC) and maximum inscribed circle (MIC). Consult the ANSI B89.3.1 standard for more specifics.

Average Diameter - Free State Variation

Average diameter (abbreviation AVG) next to a size tolerance allows a feature to exceed the size and form requirements of rule #1. An example is a large flexible aircraft ring that goes "out of round" after fabrication, but during assembly they come back to shape.

The **average of several distances** (Y14.5 states at least four) across the feature must be within the size tolerance. Each individual distance may violate the size tolerance, therefore a circularity tolerance will limit the form to ensure the feature will not be deformed beyond its elastic limit. The size may also be evaluated with a CMM using a least squares algorithm or if the tolerance is large enough, with a circumference measurement using a pi tape.

This on the drawing

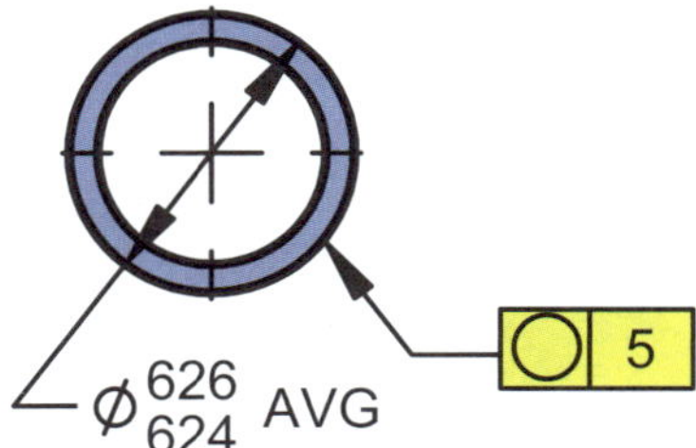

Means this

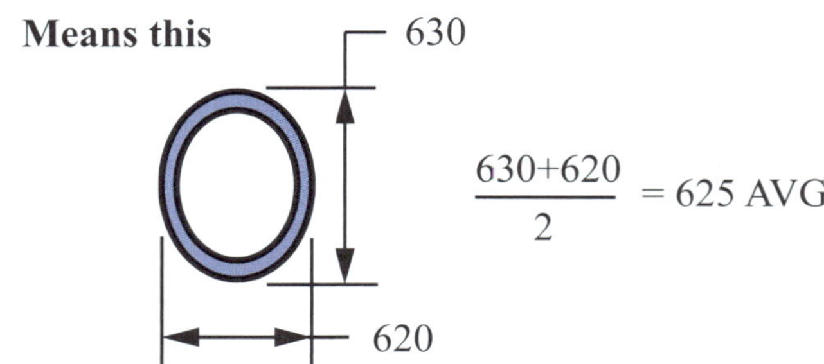

Individual distances may exceed the size tolerance but the average of all distances must be between 624-626. The circularity tol will limit the form error to 5 per side.

Workshop Exercise 10.1

1. Show the symbol and name for each of the four form tolerances.

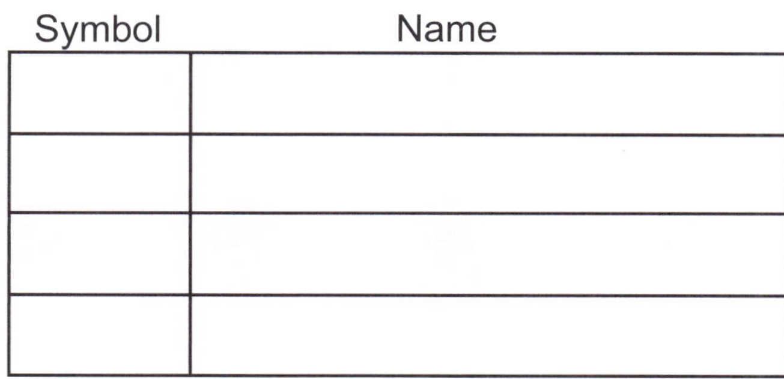

Symbol	Name

2. Can any of the form tolerances have datum feature references in the feature control frame?

___

3. Can any of the form tolerances have material condition modifiers? If so, which ones?

___

4. List the two dimensional (2D) form tolerances.

___

5. List the three dimensional (3D) form tolerances.

___

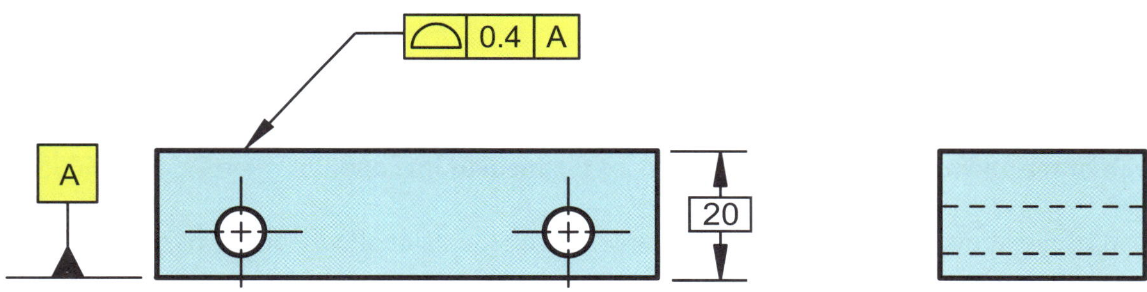

6. On the part above, what is the flatness on the top surface with only the profile applied?

___

7. Apply a 0.1 flatness control to the top surface.

8. On the part above, what is the flatness on the bottom surface labeled datum feature A?
   a. it must be perfectly flat
   b. not defined
   c. same as the top surface 0.1
   d. within the profile tolerance 0.4

Workshop Exercise 10.2

1. What implied rule in ASME Y14.5 controls the form of a feature within the limits of size?

____

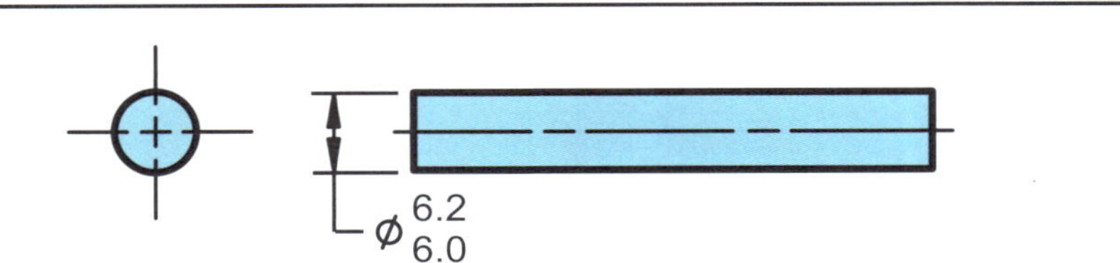

2. On the drawing above, what is the maximum **line element straightness** tolerance allowed before any geometric control is given? ________________

3. On the drawing above, what is the maximum **median line straightness** tolerance allowed before any geometric control is applied? ________________

4. Which of the straightness tolerances releases the size requirement of perfect form at MMC?

median line straightness or line element straightness

5. Which of the straightness tolerances must be smaller than the size tolerance?

median line straightness or line element straightness

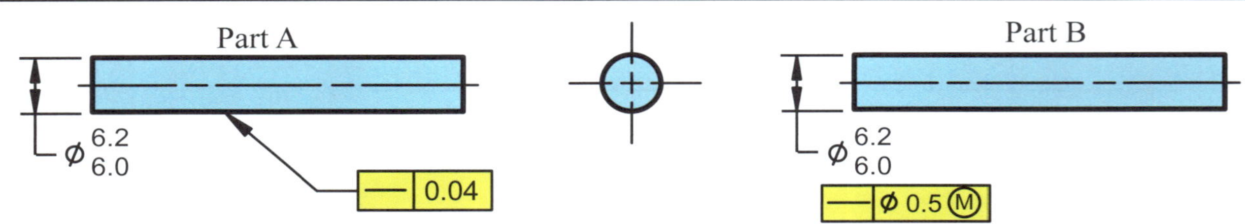

6. Which of the above parts has a straightness of the median line applied? part A or part B

7. Which of the above parts has a straightness of line elements applied? part A or part B

8. Match the "means this" below to the specification for part A and B above.

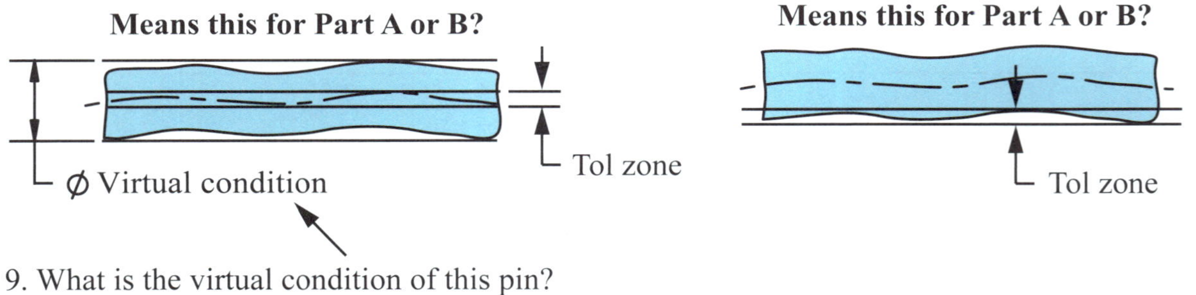

9. What is the virtual condition of this pin? ________________

10. True or false, line element straightness may also be applied to a planar surface?

Workshop Exercise 10.3

1. What is the max circularity and cylindricity variation allowed on the part below before a feature control frame is applied?

____

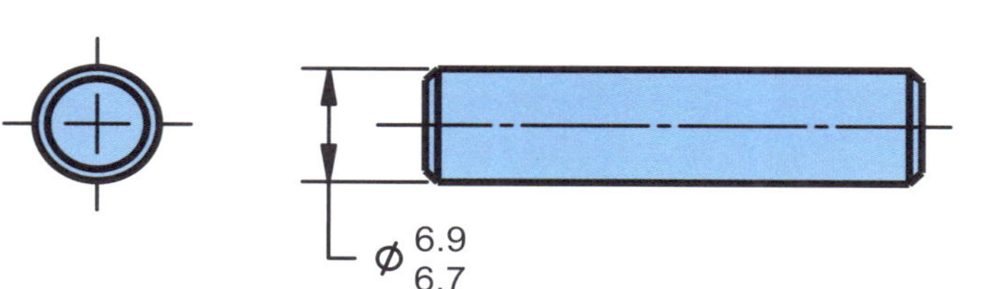

2. What is the difference between a cylindricity and circularity specification?

   a. Circularity applies to 2D cross sections while cylindricity applies to the entire 3D feature
   b. Circularity controls only one cross section while cylindricity controls all cross sections
   c. Circularity applies on a radius while cylindricity applies on a diameter
   d. Circularity controls taper while cylindricity does not

3. Which specification is tighter, cylindricity or circularity?

4. Do circularity and cylindricity require a diameter symbol in the feature control frame?

   a. yes with circularity but no with cylindricity
   b. no with circularity but yes with cylindricity
   c. yes with both
   d. no with either

5. Below is a chart showing the symbols of circularity and cylindricity. Mark the types of variation each symbol controls.

Symbol	Type of Variation			
	Circularity	Straightness	Taper	Size
○				
⌭				

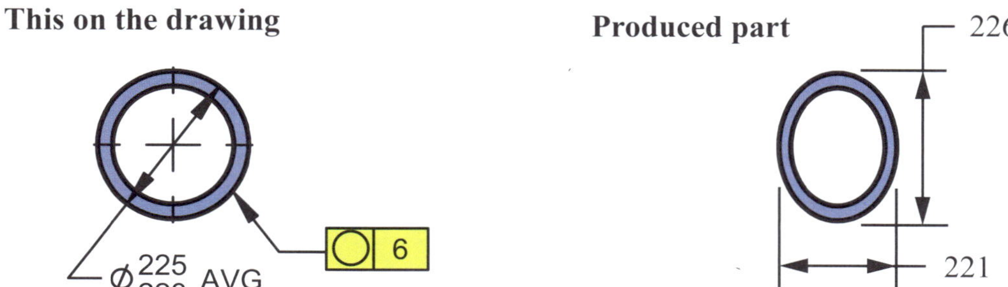

6. Does the produced part above meet all specifications shown on the drawing? yes or no

7. If the "AVG" were removed, would the produced part still meet all specifications? yes or no

Unit 11

Profile Tolerancing

Profile Tolerancing Overview
Profile of a Surface - Bilateral
Profile of a Surface - Unequal Modifier
Profile - Unequal ASME Past Practices and ISO UZ Modifier
Workshop Exercise 11.1 - Unilateral Profile
Profile of a Line
Profile of a Surface - Cam Wheel
Profile of a Surface - Inspection Reporting
Track Pad - Profile Measurement Data
Workshop Exercise 11.2 - Profile Measurement Data
Profile of a Surface - Application Armor Plate
Measurement Plan for Armor Plate
Inspection Report for Armor Plate
Profile of a Surface - Fuel Line Bracket
Fuel Line Bracket 2D with Rotational Offset
Profile of a Surface - Fuel Line Clamp
Workshop Exercise 11.3
Profile of a Surface - Hat Bracket
Workshop Exercise 11.4
Composite Profile Tolerancing
Composite Profile - One Datum Feature
Composite Profile - Two Datum Features
Composite Profile - Irregular Feature of Size
Profile - Coplanarity
Workshop Exercise 11.5 - Coplanarity
Tangent Plane Symbol
Profile Tolerance on Sharp Corners
Profile Tolerance - Non-Uniform Zone
Dynamic Profile Modifier - Form Only
Dynamic Profile Modifier - Form, Orientation, Location
Dynamic Profile Modifier - Measurement
Radius and Controlled Radius
Dynamic Profile Instead of Controlled Radius
Profile of a Surface - Per Unit Area
Workshop Exercise 11.6 - Composite Profile Stack

Profile Tolerancing

Symbol	Type of Tolerance	Common Shape of Tolerance Zone	2D / 3D	Application of Feature Modifier
⌒	Profile of a Line	2 Dimensional Uniform Boundary	2D	No
⌓	Profile of a Surface	3 Dimensional Uniform Boundary	3D	No

Overview:

There are two types of profile tolerances: Profile of a surface (3D) and profile of a line (2D). Profile of a surface is the most powerful tolerance in GD&T. Depending on datum feature references, profile of a surface can control size, form, orientation and location of feature surfaces. The main use of profile of a surface is to locate surfaces and replaces plus/minus location tolerances.

Profile tolerance defines a tolerance zone relative to a defined datum reference frame within which all points on the surface must lie. Of course, it is impossible to check *all the points*. However, the same can be said about *all the points* with a plus/minus tolerance and *all the points* with a surface finish. How many points are verified is based on a cost versus risk balance and is defined in the measurement plan. Defining a feature with profile tolerance does not mean it is more important or more difficult. Instead, the tolerance value is the determining factor for manufacturing capability.

There are many ways to verify a profile tolerance depending on the tolerance value, geometry, and equipment available. Profile may be checked with a CMM, micrometer, calipers, gages, optical comparator, height gage, dial indicators, functional gages, or visually. Verification procedures depend on many variables, such as how many parts need to be checked, is it for a first article or within a large production run, or is it a final check or an in-process check? The tightness of the tolerance, the method of manufacture, acceptable level of risk and other factors are all taken into account. The theoretical profile tolerance boundaries are defined in the drawing by the design engineer, and the method of verification should be defined in the quality dimensional measurement plan and documented by the quality engineer. See examples in this unit of the profile specifications and methods for verifications and reporting.

Basic dimensions define the true profile (perfect geometry) and the profile tolerance zone is centered around true profile. In inspection, profile may be treated as a pass/fail requirement or variable data may be recorded. In a variable data inspection report, the measurement points are recorded as deviations from true profile.

The circle U modifier makes the profile tolerance zone unequally distributed. The note NONUNIFORM can allow the tolerance zone to be any desirable shape.

A large profile tolerance may be applied in a general note to control unimportant surfaces and replace a plus/minus general title block tolerance. All dimensions must then be basic with boxes or a general note: UOS (unless otherwise specified) ALL DIMENSIONS BASIC.

Profile tolerance may be applied to the 3D model according to ASME Y14.41 without the display of basic dimensions. Profile tolerancing as a replacement of plus/minus is certainly the future direction of industry and in modern mathematically defined CAD, CAM and CMM software.

Profile of a Surface - Bilateral

By default, profile tolerance specifies a uniform tolerance zone equally distributed about the true profile defined by the basic dimensions. All elements of the surface must lie within the tolerance zone. An arrow from the feature control frame must point to the surface or extension line.

This on the drawing

Profile - Default Equal Bilateral

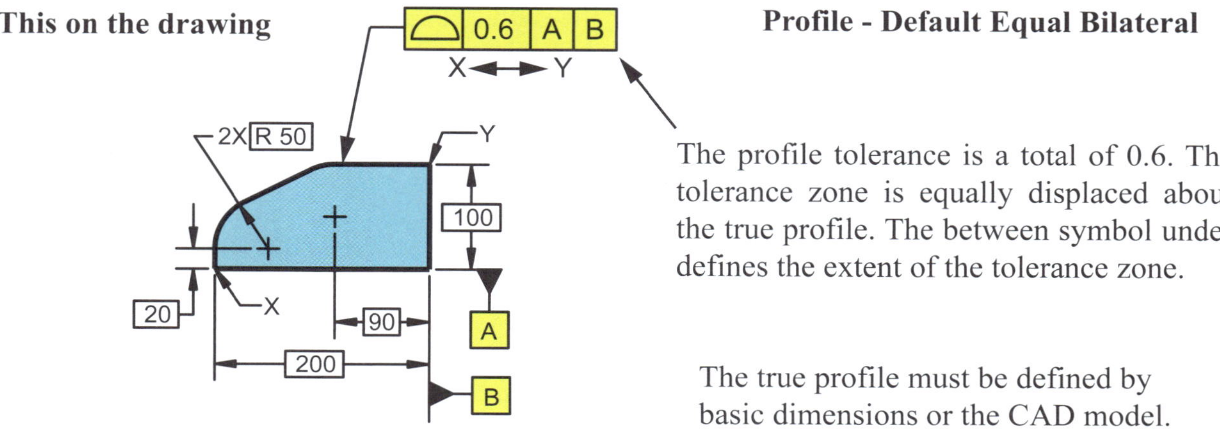

The profile tolerance is a total of 0.6. The tolerance zone is equally displaced about the true profile. The between symbol under defines the extent of the tolerance zone.

The true profile must be defined by basic dimensions or the CAD model.

The tolerance zone established by the profile of a surface control is 3D and extends the full depth of the feature. The between symbol extends the tolerance to all surfaces between points X and Y.

Means this

2D View

A profile zone of 0.6 allows the surface to vary within ±0.3 of the true profile

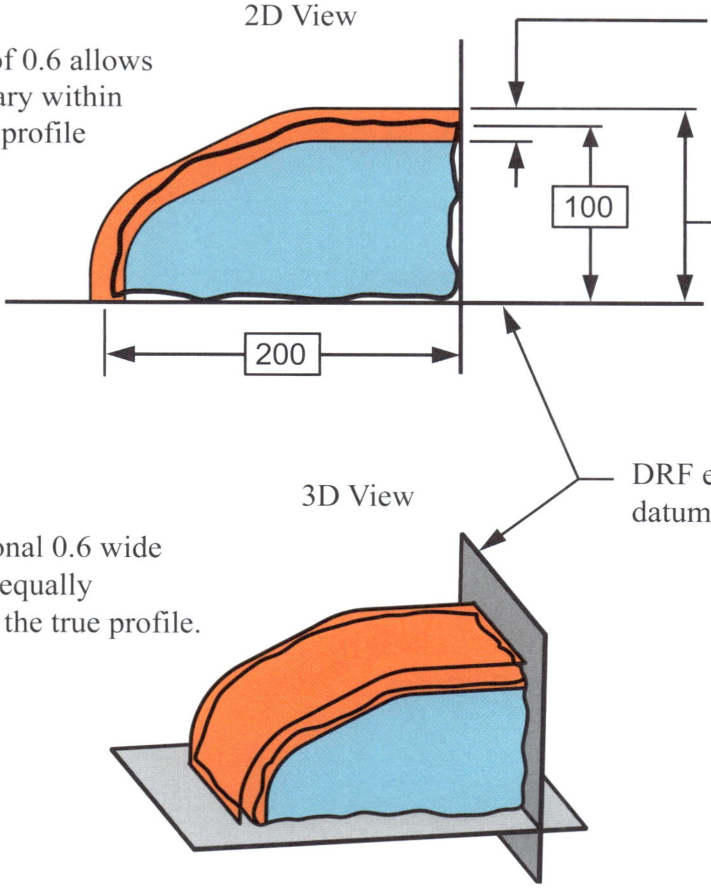

0.6 tol zone equally displaced about the true profile.

100

Allowable feature height is 100±0.3

200

3D View

DRF established by datum features A and B.

Three dimensional 0.6 wide tolerance zone equally disposed about the true profile.

Profile of a Surface - Unequal Modifier

By default, profile tolerance specifies an equally disposed tolerance zone about the true profile. However, the ASME Y14.5-2018 standard allows profile tolerance to be an unequal distribution with a circle U modifier.

Specification of unequal profile tolerance: The first value is the total tolerance. The circle U designates an unequal tolerance. The value after the modifier is the displacement outside of the true profile (direction that adds material).

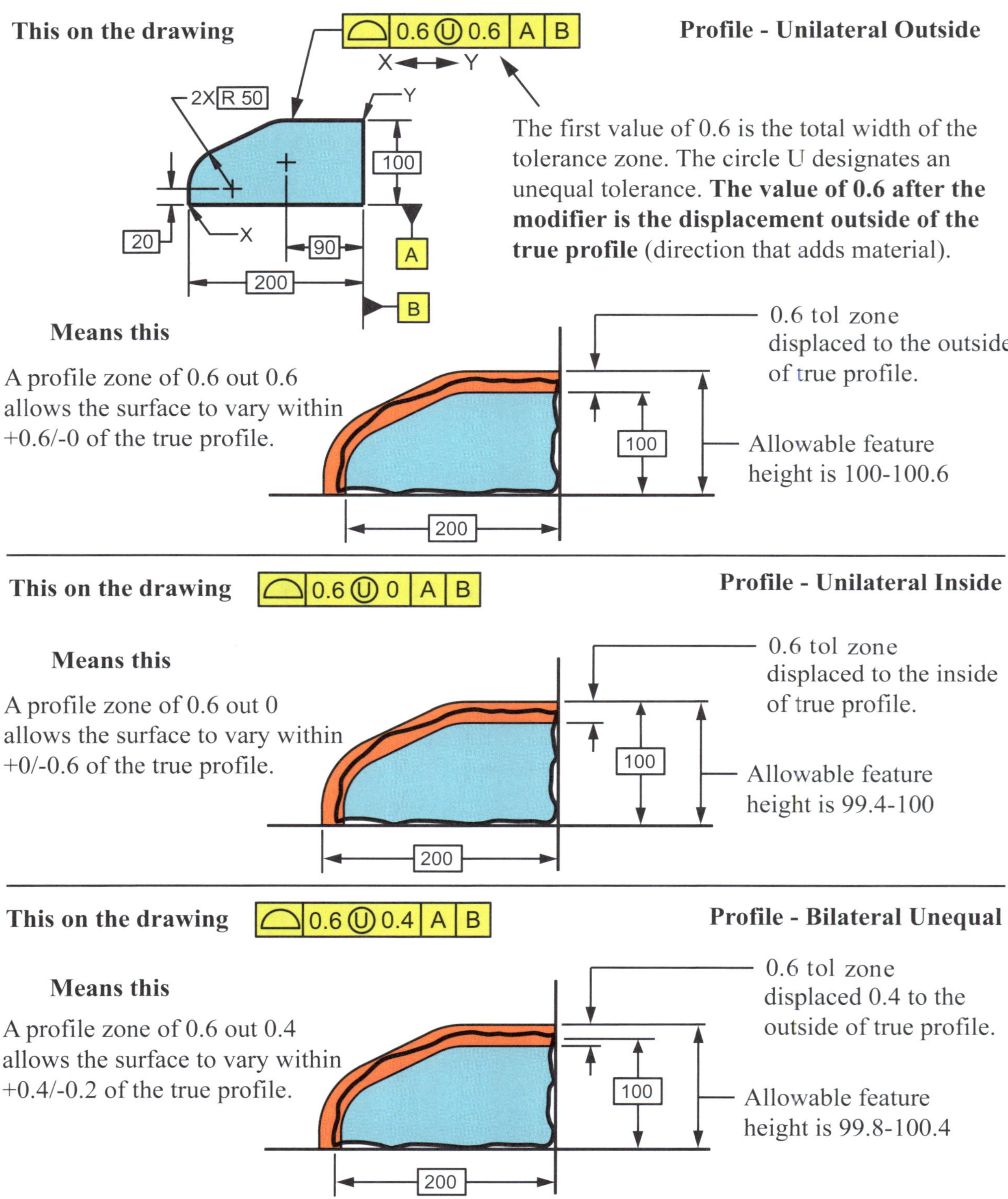

Profile - Unequal ASME Past Practices and ISO UZ Modifier

Unequal Profile Past ASME Y14.5 practices: The circle U modifier was first introduced in the ASME Y14.5-2009 standard. The earlier 1994 standard instead used a pictorial representation for unequal profile tolerances shown below. The pictorial method was not easily applied in model based definition (MBD) and was difficult to make machine readable. The 2009 standard allowed both methods, but the Y14.5-2018 has phased out the pictorial option, and circle U is the now the only method for unequal profile.

This on the drawing in ASME Y14.5-1994 and 2009

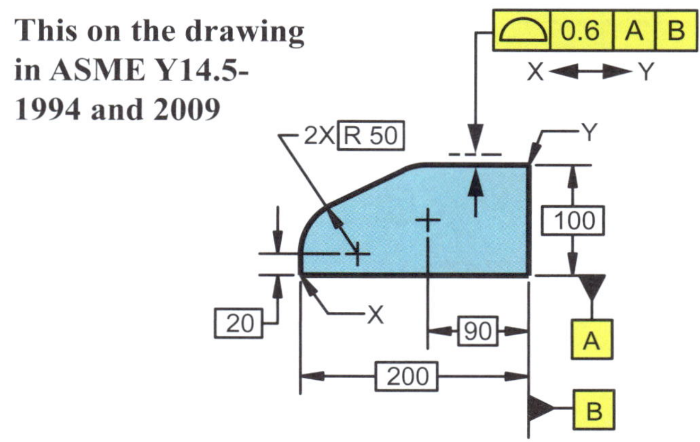

Profile - Unilateral

The feature control frame leader line needs two arrows drawn normal to the true profile. A phantom line is drawn to show the direction of the displacement.

This allows the surface to vary within +0.6/-0 of the true profile.

This on the drawing in ASME Y14.5-1994 and 2009

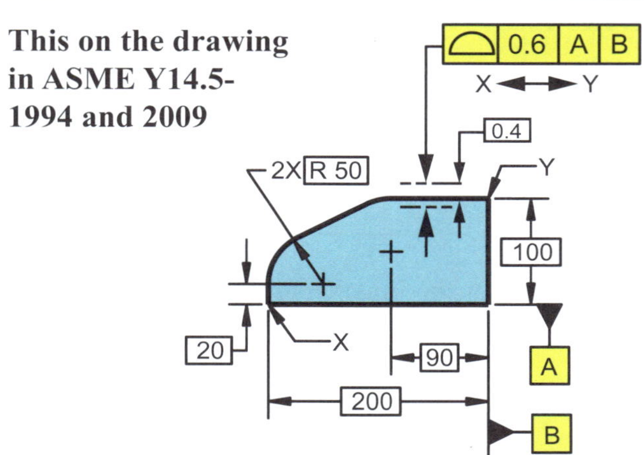

Profile - Bilateral Unequal

The feature control frame leader line needs two arrows drawn normal to the true profile. Two phantom lines are drawn along with an exaggerated basic dimension to show the direction and magnitude of the displacement.

This allows the surface to vary within +0.4/-0.2 of the true profile.

ISO 1660-2017 has a different way of defining an unequal profile zone. Instead of offsetting one of the boundaries, ISO instead offsets the center of the tolerance zone. The first value is the total zone followed by UZ. The second value is the displacement of the tolerance zone center. Positive and negative indicate the direction of the offset.

This on the drawing in ISO 1660-2017

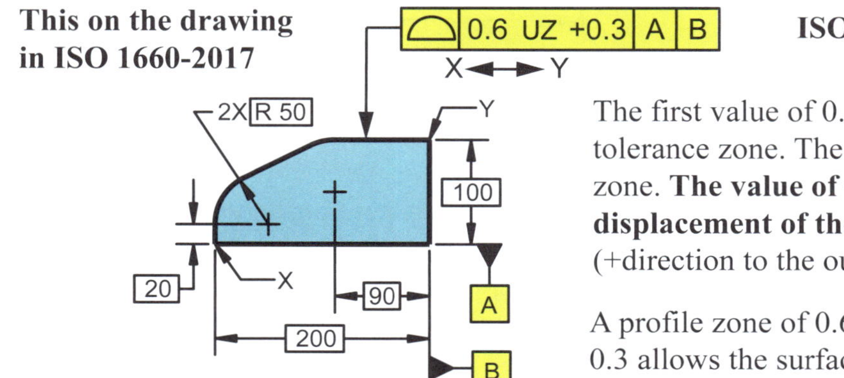

ISO Profile - Unilateral Outside

The first value of 0.6 is the total width of the tolerance zone. The UZ designates an unequal zone. **The value of +0.3 after the modifier is the displacement of the tolerance zone center** (+direction to the outside, -direction to the inside).

A profile zone of 0.6 with its center displaced out 0.3 allows the surface to vary within +0.6/-0 of the TEF (theoretically exact feature).

Workshop Exercise 11.1 - Unilateral Profile

Profile can be applied on a unilateral basis with a circle U modifier following the total tolerance. The value behind the modifier specifies how much the tolerance applies out from true profile (direction that adds material). The example below illustrates a unilateral profile applied to an internal feature and a external feature. On the produced part below, calculate the possible min and max distances allowed by the profile tolerance zones.

This on the drawing

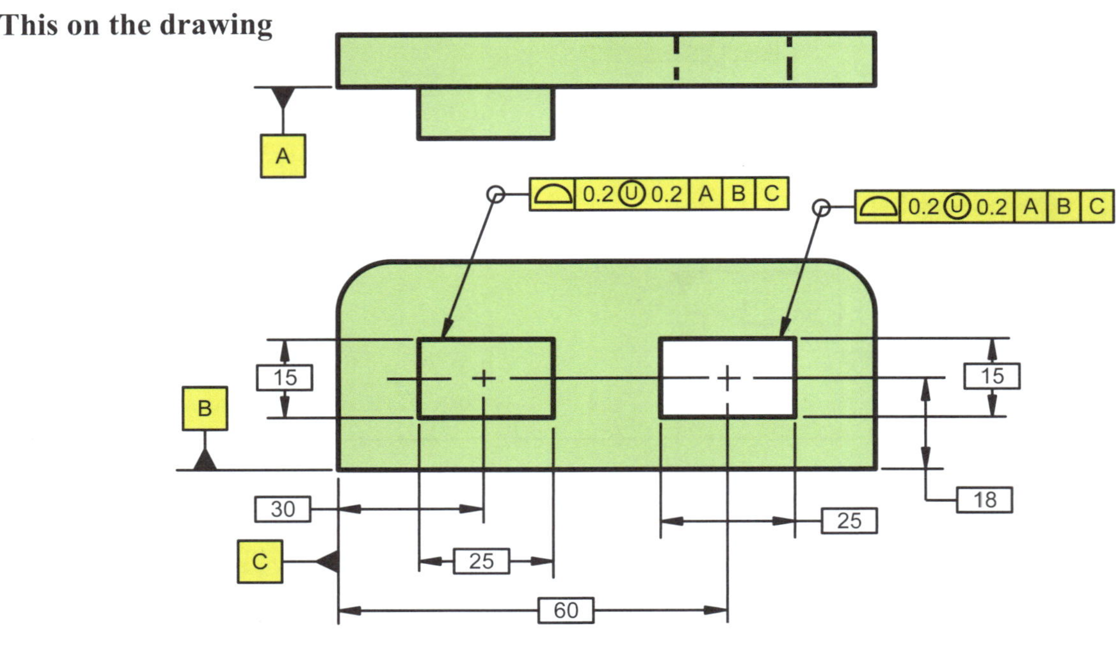

Means this Calculate the four min/max distances for the internal and external features.

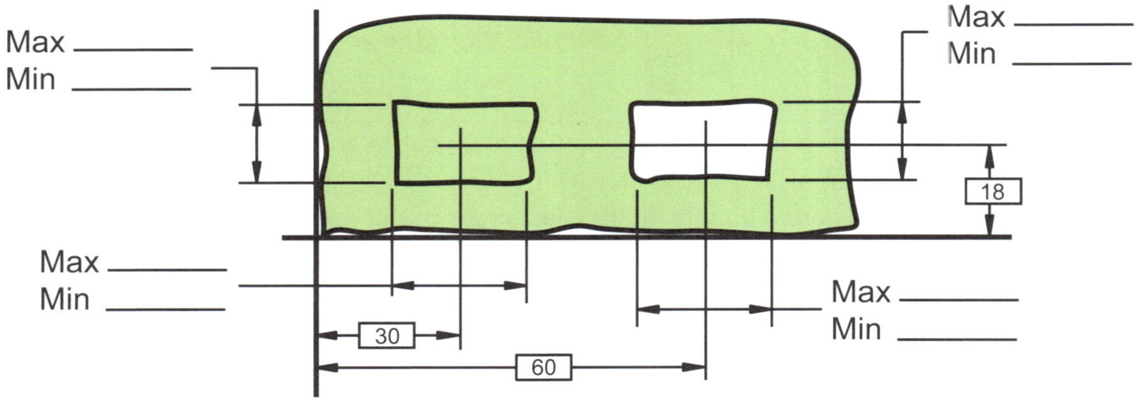

This example is to show how the internal/external unilateral can be tricky for a new learner. Unilateral and unequal profile tolerances should be used with caution and is generally not recommended. Design, manufacturing, and inspection often share the same CAD model. If the tolerance zones are artificially pushed to one side by a unilateral tolerance zone, manufacturing also needs to shift their model data to manufacture to the middle of the tolerance zone. This can be easily missed with cause for defects. It is simpler when design adjusts the basic dimensions and uses a regular bilateral profile tolerance zone instead.

Profile of a Line

Profile of a line specifies a series of 2D cross-sectional uniform tolerance zones along the true profile, within which each 2D surface element must lie. The cross-sections are not compared to each other as a single entity. Profile of a line in the Y14.5 standard refines the shape of cross-sections of the feature. Profile of a line without datum references is sometimes used on extruded shapes with constant cross-section. An example might be a rubber/plastic molding or metal track. When used with datum references and as a refinement of profile of a surface (see example below), it may be necessary to clarify the cross-sections are only oriented to the referenced DRF. In the feature control frame, following each datum feature reference, define only the u, v, and w rotational degrees of freedom constrained (see customized DRF in unit 9).

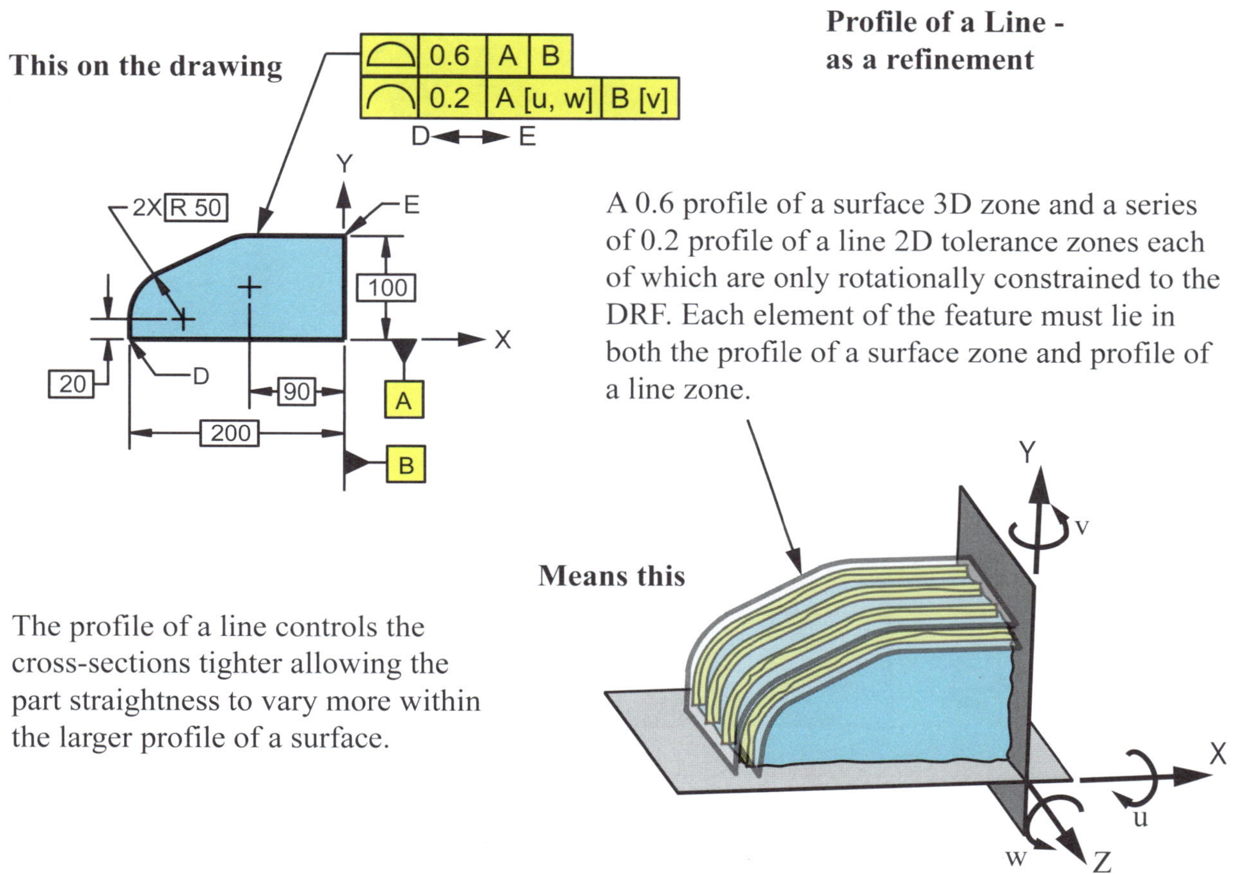

Note: profile of a line is not a well-defined tool in ASME Y14.5. The Y14.5.1 (mathematical definitions standard) does not give a mathematical definition for this symbol because there are different interpretations of its meaning. There is some controversy over how the cross-sections of the surface are taken for evaluation. Some say it is in the view in which the symbol is specified (normal to the drawing view). While others say the cross-sections are taken relative to the specified DRF or relative to the true profile. There is also controversy on how the 2D tolerance zones are established. Are the tolerance zone boundaries normal to the surface element, normal to the drawing view in which the symbol is applied, or normal to the referenced DRF? The pictorial examples in the Y14.5 standard are simplistic with shapes of constant cross-section and the word definitions are vague without a concrete rule set. Notes or a company addendum may need to be added when using this symbol on a more complex application with varying cross-section such as an aircraft wing or curved computer housing.

Profile of a Surface - Cam Wheel

Below is a cam wheel with two profile tolerances applied. The upper 0.4 profile specifies a tolerance zone that is equally disposed about the true profile between points X and Y. The lower 0.6 profile between points X and Y is a unequal control because of the circle U modifier. The 0 value following the circle U designates displacement outside (direction that adds material). Therefore the 0.6 profile zone is all to the inside of the true profile. The surface of the part must fall within the profile zones.

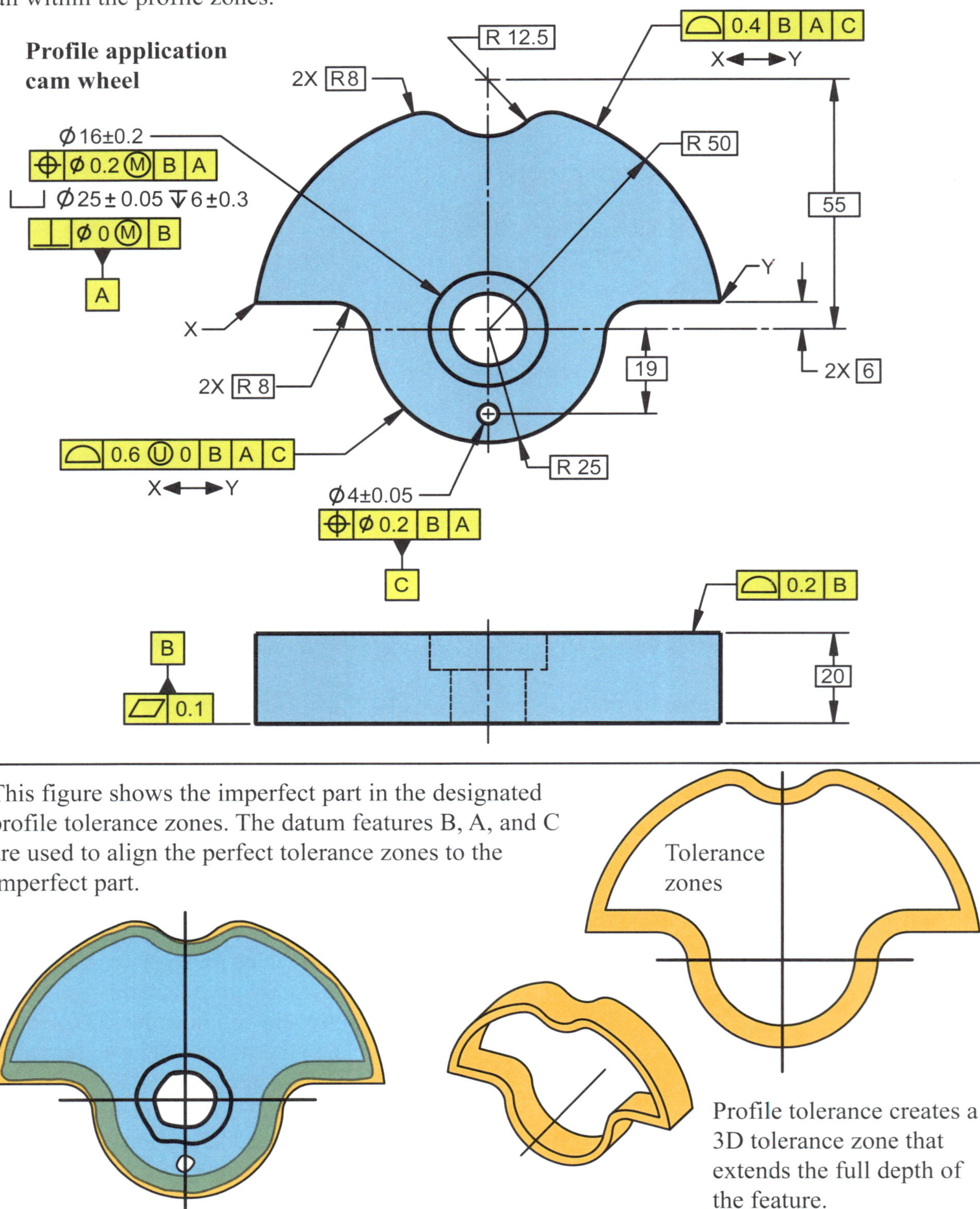

This figure shows the imperfect part in the designated profile tolerance zones. The datum features B, A, and C are used to align the perfect tolerance zones to the imperfect part.

Profile tolerance creates a 3D tolerance zone that extends the full depth of the feature.

Profile of a Surface - Inspection Reporting

A sample inspection report is shown for the two profile specifications. Characteristic identifiers are placed next to the specifications to correlate with the report. An electronic height gage and a surface plate are used to collect data. Four points were selected for feature 2 because of its relatively small size and large tolerance. Six points were selected for feature 1 because of its larger surface area and relatively small tolerance.

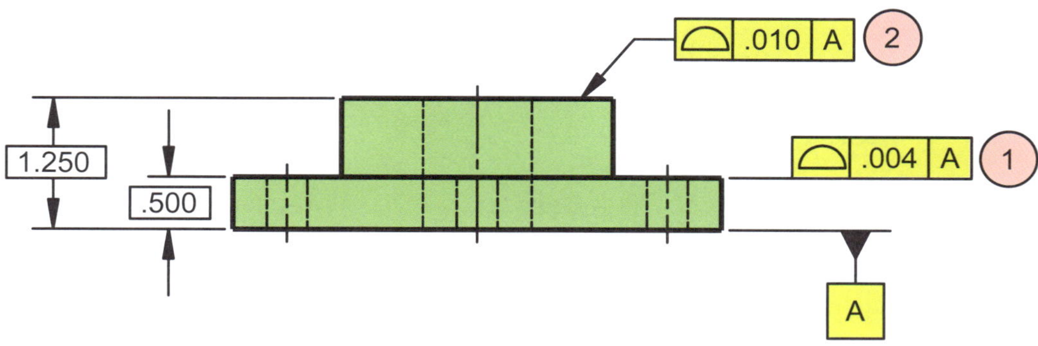

Feature	Allowed Profile	# of Pts Measured	Min/Max Deviation	Measured Profile	Accept Reject
1	.004	6	-.0005/ +.0015	.003	A
2	.010	4	+.001/ +.003	.006	A

Depending on the complexity of the measurement plan, the value of each measured point may be included in the report. When reporting, all values are converted to deviations from true profile (basic). They are reported as plus material or minus material.

The measured profile is recorded as a total zone about basic. The extreme deviation in either direction is doubled for this value. This allows it to be compared to the allowed profile.

Raw measured values

1 .5010
2 .5002
3 .5015
4 .4998
5 .5004
6 .4995

Reported Values

Pt.	Deviation from Basic
1.1	+ .0010
1.2	+ .0002
1.3	+ .0015
1.4	- .0002
1.5	+ .0004
1.6	- .0005

2

1 1.253
2 1.252
3 1.253
4 1.251

Pt.	Deviation from Basic
2.1	+ .003
2.2	+ .002
2.3	+ .003
2.4	+ .001

1.1 1.2 1.3 1.4 1.5 1.6 2.1 2.2 2.3 2.4

The locations of the points may also be defined. They may be shown in a simple picture or with exact x, y, z coordinates included in a table.

Track Pad - Profile Measurement Data

Below is an assembly of a laptop case and touch pad. The visual gap between these pieces is important to show a quality product.

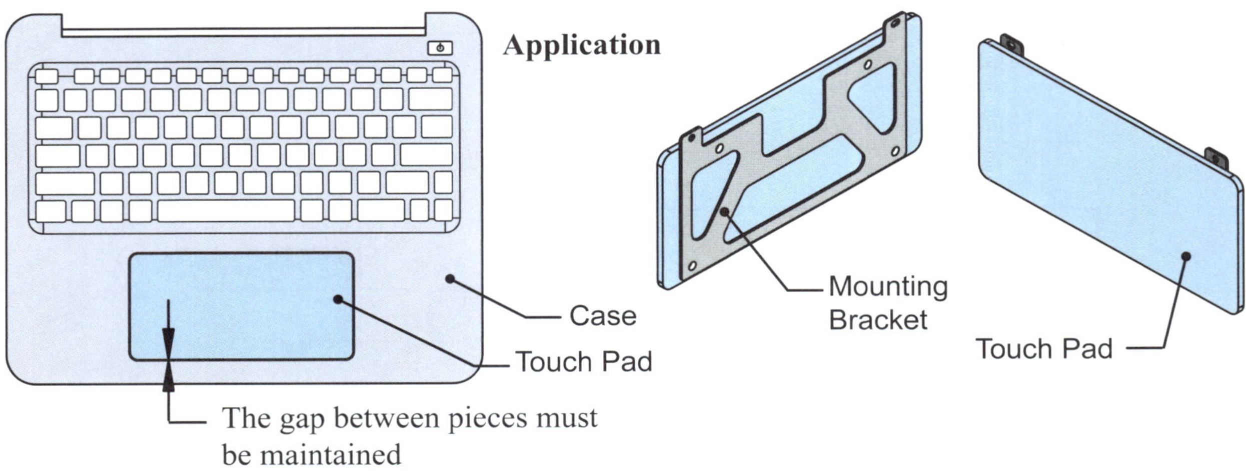

A profile tolerance relative the datum reference frame is used on the outside contour. The size, form, orientation, and location of this surface all have an effect on the gap. The profile zones make it easy to determine the worst case gap with the mating part.

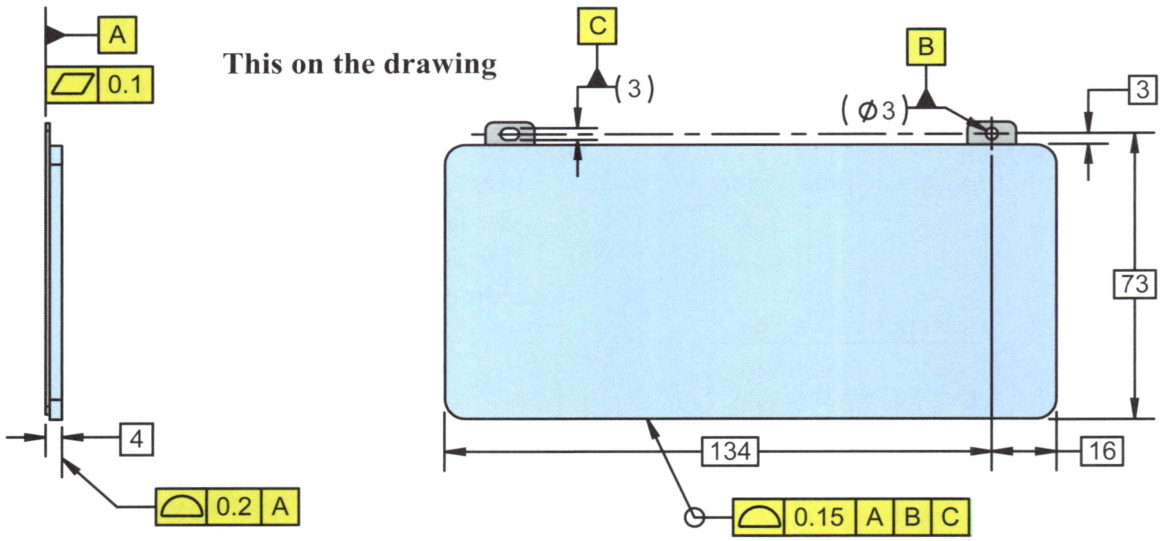

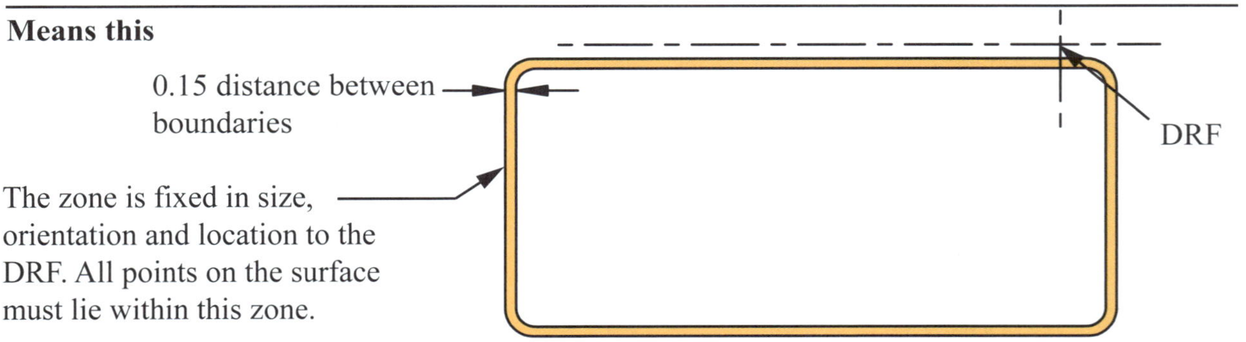

This on the drawing

Means this

0.15 distance between boundaries

The zone is fixed in size, orientation and location to the DRF. All points on the surface must lie within this zone.

DRF

Track Pad - Profile Measurement Data

A CMM first aligns to the ABC datum reference frame and measures 20 points at the locations shown on the quality plan.

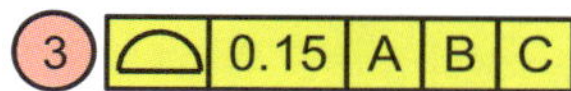

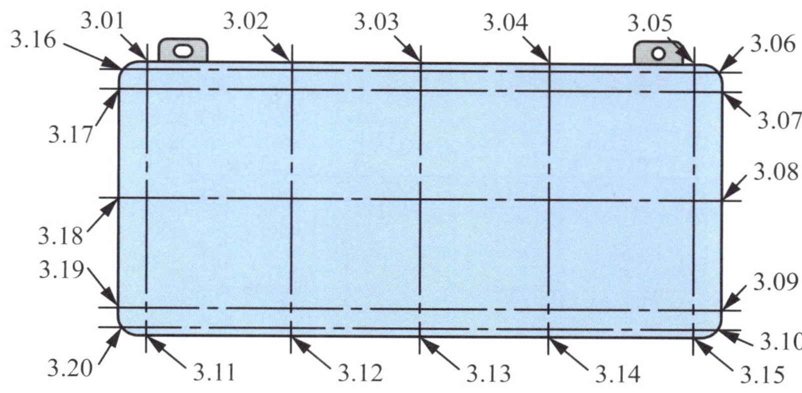

The quality plan may show exact locations where measurements are to be taken. They may be dimensioned on a drawing view or shown with X,Y,Z coordinates in a chart.

The profile zone is fixed relative to the datum reference frame and basic dimensions. The surface measurement points are reported as deviations from the true profile.

Measurement data (deviations from true profile)

3.01	+0.02	3.11	+0.03
3.02	+0.03	3.12	+0.02
3.03	+0.05	3.13	+0.05
3.04	+0.07	3.14	+0.05
3.05	+0.09	3.15	+0.07
3.06	+0.03	3.16	+0.03
3.07	-0.01	3.17	+0.05
3.08	-0.03	3.18	+0.05
3.09	-0.01	3.19	+0.02
3.10	+0.05	3.20	+0.05

Inspection Report

ID#	Tolerance Type	Allowed Tolerance	Min/Max Deviations	Measured Value	Pass/ Fail
3	Prof	0.15	-0.03/+0.09	0.18	Fail

Measured profile value = 2x | max deviation |

Measured profile value = 2x | 0.09 | = 0.18

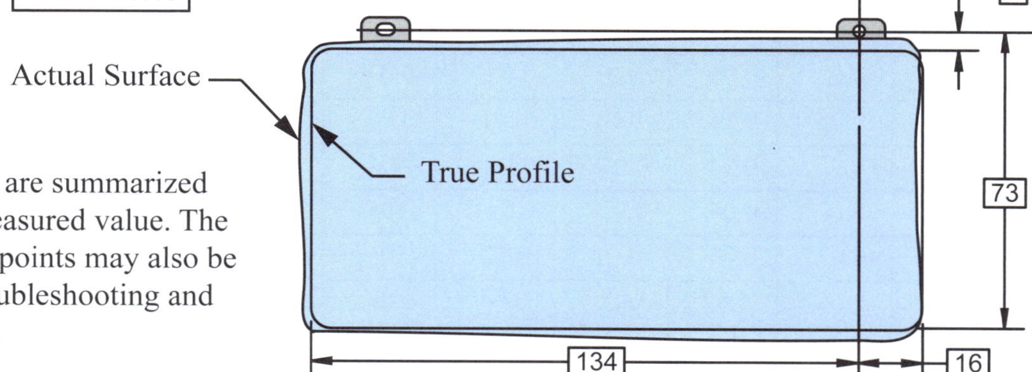

The data points are summarized into a single measured value. The individual data points may also be reported for troubleshooting and process control.

The inspection report shows a failure for the outside profile. After looking at the individual data points, it is only failing at one location (point 3.05). From the measurement data and the exagerrated surface drawn above, we can visualize the actual part. The surface is mostly produced larger than the true geometry. There is also a small cutout on the right side. The gap with the mating part will be bigger than expected on the right side and smaller on the other three sides.

Workshop Exercise 11.2 - Profile Measurement Data

A sample and 4 other Track Pads have been measured based on the drawing from the previous pages. The data from these inspections were imported into a spreadsheet below. This can be used to track trends and evaluate capabilities based on statistics. Summarize the profile data for each part into a min/max value and measured profile zone. Evaluate pass or fail.

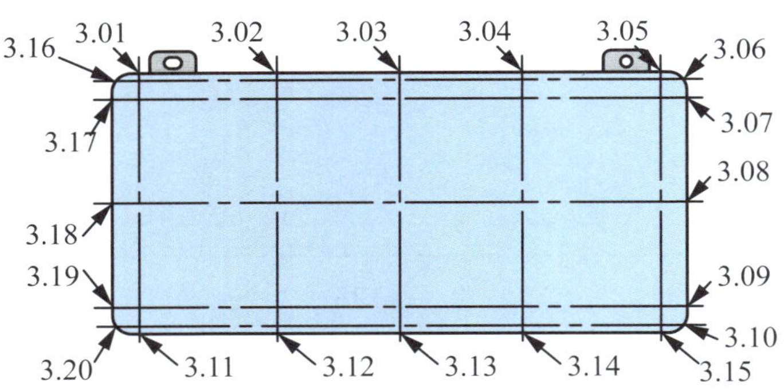

Oops, someone mixed up the parts! Match the data in the spreadsheet with the exaggerated produced part shape below. Which shape below is part 1, 2, 3 & 4?

Point No.	Sample	Part 1	Part 2	Part 3	Part 4
3.01	+0.02	-0.02	+0.00	+0.02	-0.03
3.02	+0.03	+0.05	+0.02	+0.02	-0.02
3.03	+0.05	+0.12	+0.01	+0.02	-0.01
3.04	+0.07	+0.06	-0.01	-0.01	-0.03
3.05	+0.09	+0.02	-0.01	-0.01	-0.03
3.06	+0.03	-0.03	-0.01	-0.07	-0.06
3.07	-0.01	+0.01	+0.08	-0.08	-0.02
3.08	-0.03	-0.02	+0.08	-0.06	-0.03
3.09	-0.01	-0.02	+0.07	-0.05	-0.03
3.10	+0.05	-0.04	-0.03	-0.08	-0.06
3.11	+0.03	-0.03	-0.04	-0.02	-0.03
3.12	+0.02	-0.06	+0.01	-0.02	-0.03
3.13	+0.05	-0.14	+0.01	+0.01	-0.03
3.14	+0.05	-0.06	-0.03	-0.02	-0.04
3.15	+0.07	-0.04	-0.02	-0.04	-0.05
3.16	+0.03	-0.03	+0.01	+0.02	-0.06
3.17	+0.05	+0.02	+0.07	+0.04	-0.03
3.18	+0.05	+0.01	+0.08	+0.09	-0.06
3.19	+0.02	-0.02	+0.08	+0.04	-0.06
3.20	+0.05	-0.05	-0.01	+0.01	-0.06
Max Min	+0.09 -0.03				
Meas Zone	0.18				
Pass/Fail	Fail				

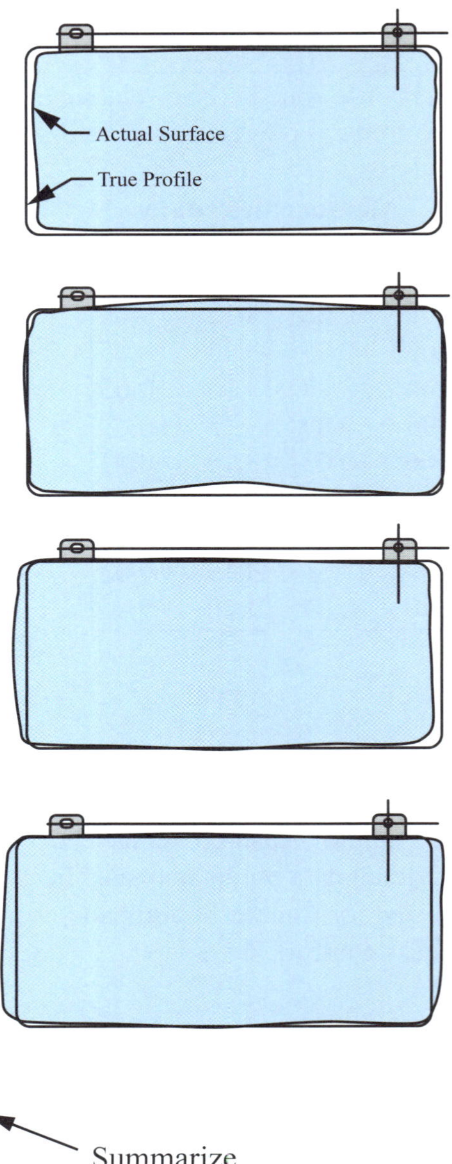

Summarize the data

Armor Plate Design Drawing

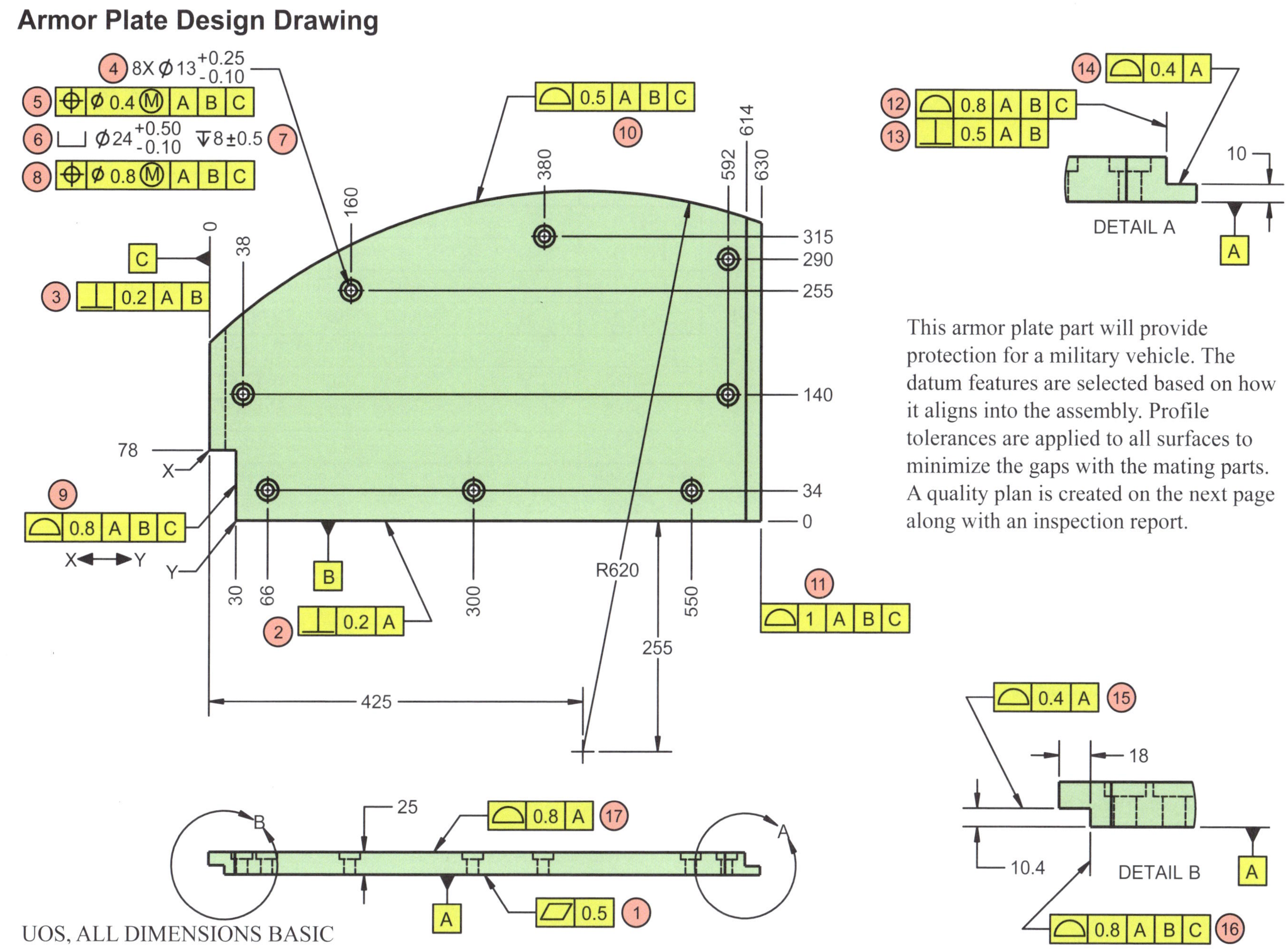

This armor plate part will provide protection for a military vehicle. The datum features are selected based on how it aligns into the assembly. Profile tolerances are applied to all surfaces to minimize the gaps with the mating parts. A quality plan is created on the next page along with an inspection report.

Measurement Plan for Armor Plate

Part Name: Armor Plate	Part Number: 00380212
Machine: CMM Articulating arm	Machine number: 02 A
Stylus: 4mm ruby, 465-4R	Program: Armor380212.3
Datum Establishment: Use L2 constrained algorithm for all.	

ID #	Type	Inspection Requirement	Reporting Method	Equipment
1	FLAT	16 locations, random	B	CMM
2	PERP	10 locations, random	B	CMM
3	PERP	8 locations, random	B	CMM
4	MMC	go gage	A	gage pin
4	LMC	no-go gage	A	gage pin
5	POS	functional gage	A	gage 1344
6	MMC	go gage, measure 3 of 8	A	gage pin
6	LMC	no-go gage, measure 3 of 8	A	gage pin
7	DEP	depth gage, measure 3 of 8	A	calipers
8	POS	not measured, (drilled with 5)	-	-
9	PROF	5 locations, (2 on top, 3 on side)	B	CMM
10	PROF	8 locations shown, 10.1-10.8	C	CMM
11	PROF	3 locations, equally spaced	B	CMM
12	PROF	5 locations, equally spaced	C	CMM
13	PERP	same as 12	B	CMM
14	PROF	6 locations, top, middle, bottom	B	CMM
15	PROF	6 locations, top, middle, bottom	B	CMM
16	PROF	depth gage, 3 locations	A	calipers
17	PROF	10 locations, random	B	CMM

The profile specification requires all points on the surface to be within the profile zone. It is not possible to verify “all points” without more complex scanning technology or spending a lot of CMM time/money. Therefore a quality measurement plan is created to document how each specification is to be verified and reported. A quality engineer must devise a plan to catch the bad parts within a certain time/money budget. The equipment to measure and number of points is decided based on many factors: how tight the tolerance, size of the surface, time and money constraints, trust in the manufacturing process. More than one measurement plan may exist for a drawing (one for first article and another for a production run.) During the product life cycle, the measurement plan may adjust the number or location of the measurement points based on past data. Guard-banding techniques (artificially reducing the spec limits to curb risk) may also be used with a lower number of measured points.

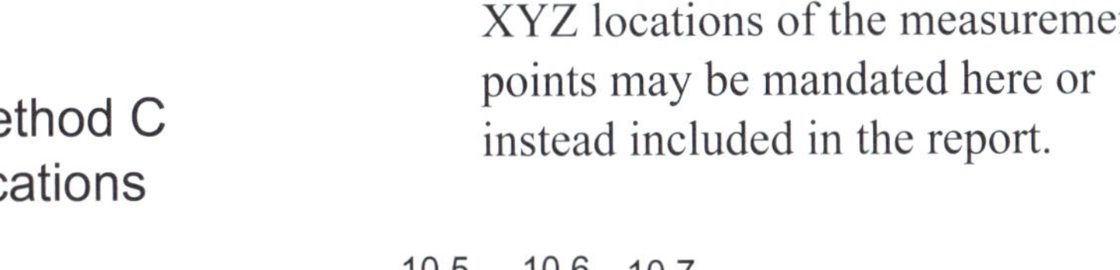

XYZ locations of the measurement points may be mandated here or instead included in the report.

Method C locations

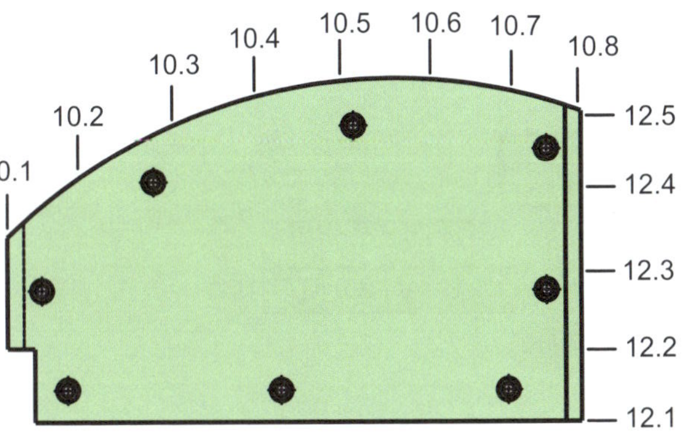

Inspection Report for Armor Plate

ID #	Type	Allow	Meas Value	Pass/ Fail	Comments
1	FLAT	0.5	0.36	Pass	
2	PERP	0.2	0.12	Pass	
3	PERP	0.2	0.08	Pass	
4	MMC	12.9	-	Pass	
4	LMC	13.25	-	Pass	
5	POS	0.4 M	-	Pass	
6	MMC	23.9	-	Pass	
6	LMC	24.5	-	Pass	
7	DEP	8±0.5	-	Pass	
8	POS	0.8 M	-	-	
9	PROF	0.8	0.36	Pass	+0.18/+0.12
10	PROF	0.5	0.62	Fail	+0.31/-0.16
11	PROF	1.0	0.88	Pass	+0.44/-0.14
12	PROF	0.8	0.62	Pass	+0.31/+0.21
13	PERP	0.5	0.10	Pass	
14	PROF	0.4	0.32	Pass	+0.16/+0.14
15	PROF	0.4	0.32	Pass	-0.12/-0.16
16	PROF	0.8	-	Pass	
17	PROF	0.8	0.52	Pass	+0.26/+0.10

The measured value represents the smallest size of the profile zone centered on the basic true profile that just contains the worst deviation point.

The comments show an optional reporting method that can show the direction of the deviations. This is in addition to the single measured value.

Method C Data

Pt #	Dev
10.1	-0.16
10.2	-0.08
10.3	-0.06
10.4	+0.06
10.5	+0.12
10.6	+0.05
10.7	+0.31
10.8	+0.16

Pt #	Dev
12.1	+0.31
12.2	+0.26
12.3	+0.21
12.4	+0.27
12.5	+0.30

The number of measurement points are set by the quality plan and recorded as deviations from true profile. The XYZ locations of the measured deviations may also be mandated in the quality plan or recorded in the inspection report.

An actual surface has variations that cannot be reported as one "measured dimension". Instead, points on the surface are measured and reported as deviations from true profile. These can be summarized as a single measured value representing the smallest size of the profile zone that is just large enough to contains all the measured points.

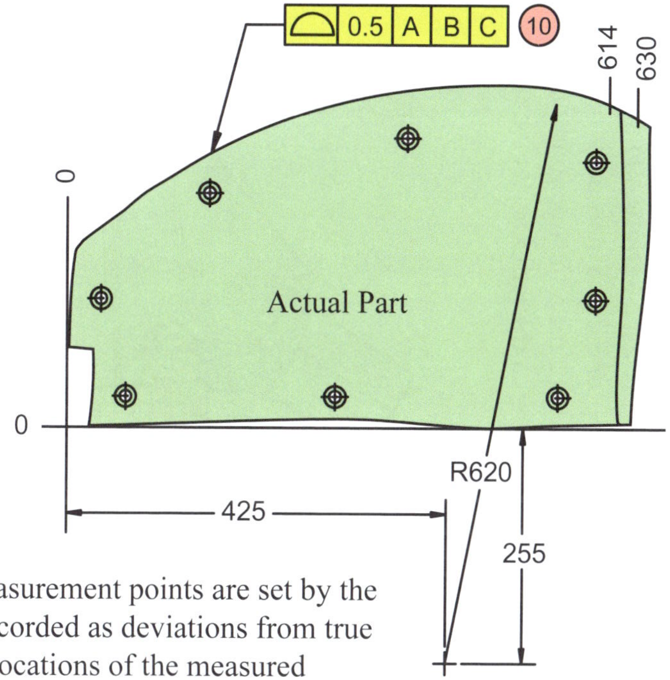

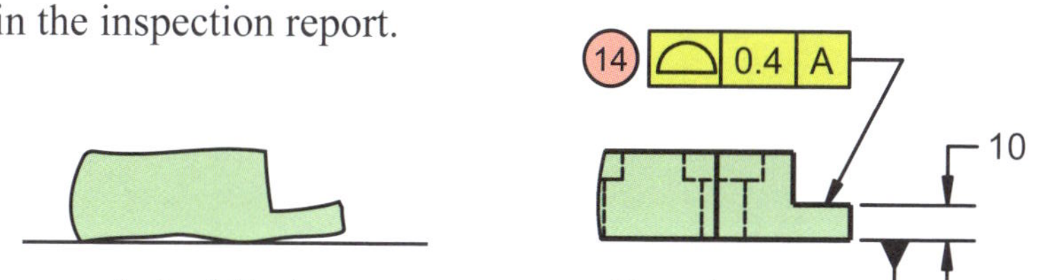

Actual Part

Drawing

Profile of a Surface - Fuel Line Bracket

The assembly below shows a bracket and clamp that secures a fuel line in place relative to the engine. The bracket mounts to the engine on the back surface and by screws in the hole and slot. The periphery of the bracket must clear the engine in one area but the remaining contour is unimportant. The slotted holes on the bracket are for adjustment and must line up with the clamp holes. The drawings for the Fuel Line Bracket and Clamp on the next pages illustrate functional geometric tolerances.

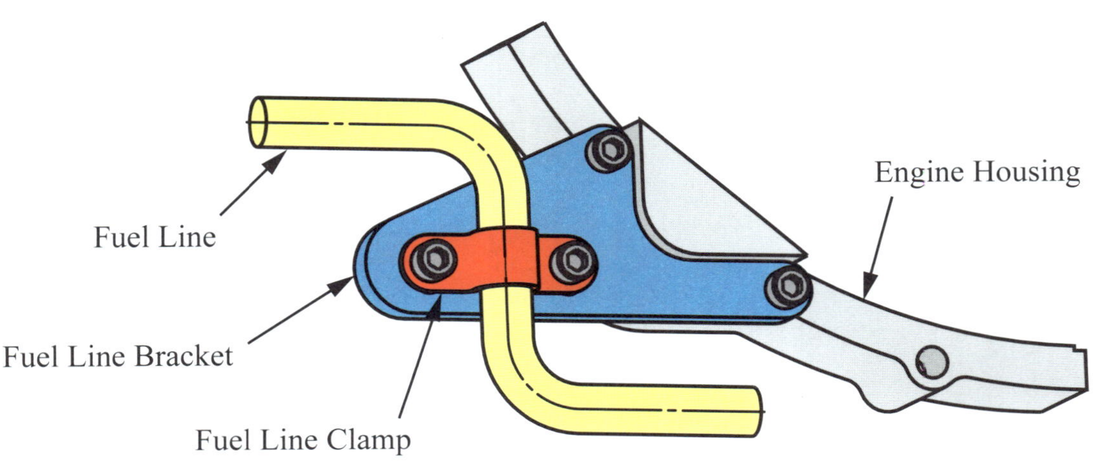

Fuel Line Bracket with model based definition (MBD) The model is toleranced to the right. See the next page for the 2D toleranced drawing instead.

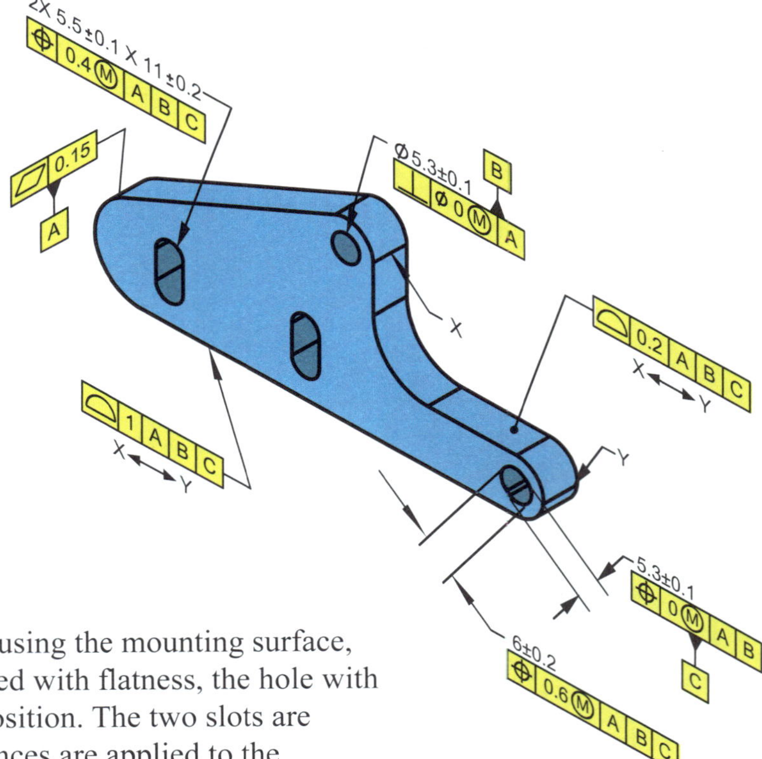

Fuel Line Bracket
A DRF is established on the bracket using the mounting surface, hole and slot. The surface is controlled with flatness, the hole with perpendicularity, and the slot with position. The two slots are positioned to the DRF. Profile tolerances are applied to the remaining features. Notice the profile tolerance is held closer on the right upper side area of the bracket to clear the engine housing. The remaining outside contour has a larger profile tolerance.

Fuel Line Bracket 2D drawing

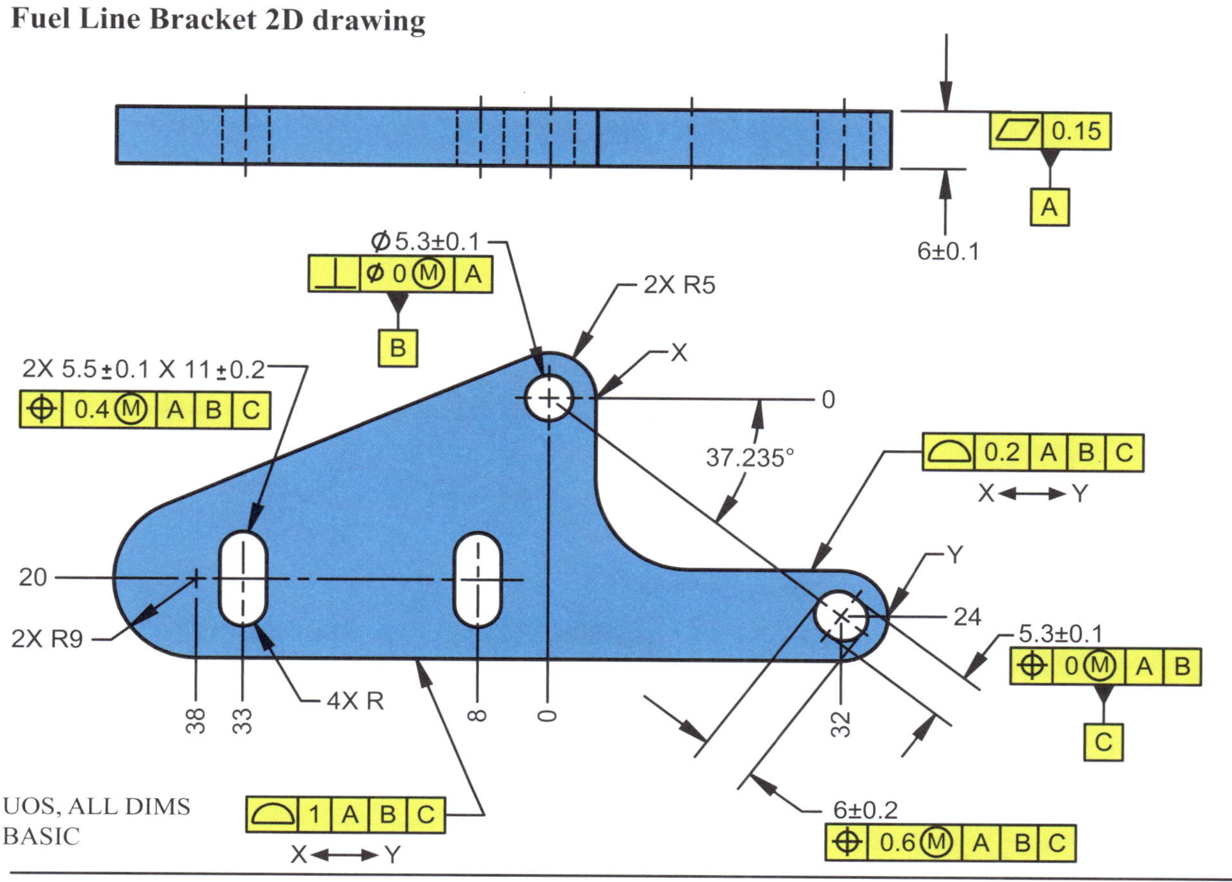

Rotational Offset

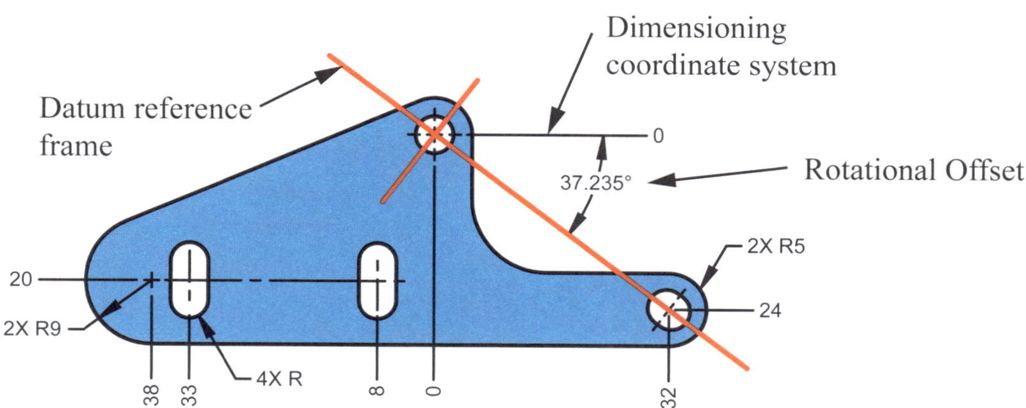

On the fuel line bracket above, the DRF is aligned thru the mounting hole and slot. However, it would be awkward and complicated to dimension from this angled coordinate system. Instead, the part is dimensioned from the axis of datum feature B and aligned horizontal. The basic dimension of 37.235 degrees is the rotational alignment back to the DRF. Inspection first aligns to the DRF and then uses the 37.235 degrees as a "rotational offset" before measuring the locations of features. Since the dimensions are all theoretically-exact basic dimensions, the DRF and dimensioning scheme do not always have to align. Dimensional and rotational offsets are often used on complicated geometry. Also see unit 8 for more examples.

Profile of a Surface - Fuel Line Clamp

The fuel line clamp has multiple profile controls applied. The datum features are selected as the two mounting surfaces and holes. The two surfaces are controlled for coplanarity with a profile tolerance. The two holes are positioned to each other relative to datum A. The inside formed radius contour is located with a relatively tight profile of 0.5 where it clamps to the mating tube. The outside surfaces are relatively unimportant and a large profile tolerance is applied.

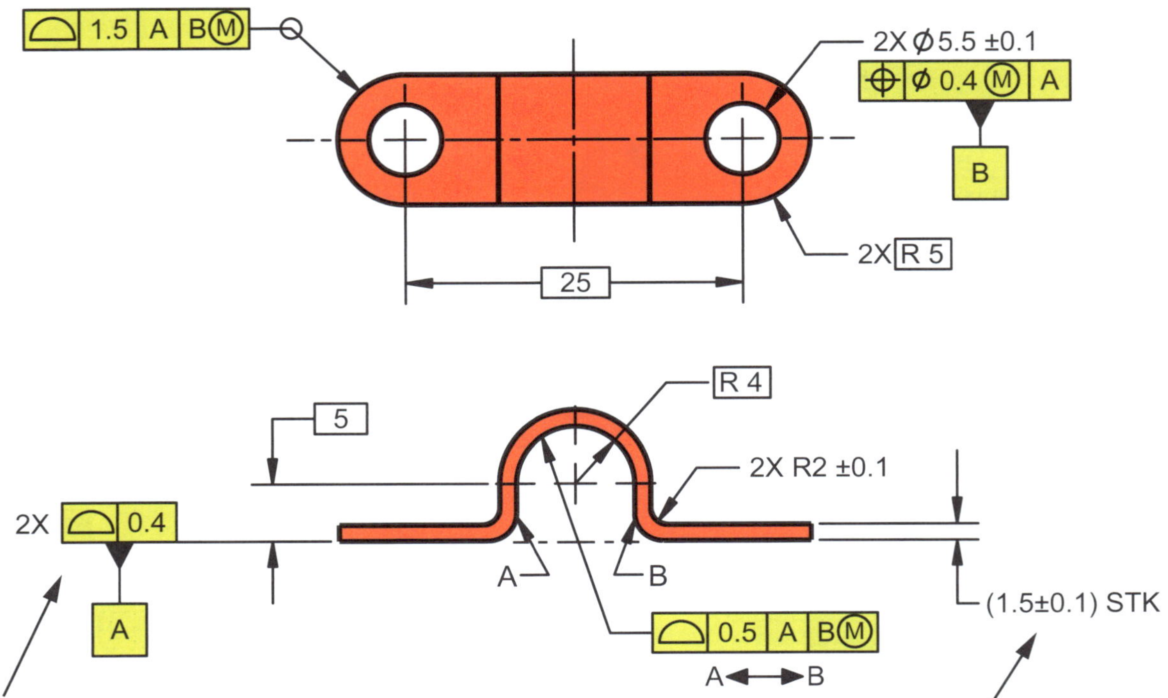

Profile is used to control coplanarity of multiple surfaces.

Sheet metal is produced from stock (STK) material that has a thickness requirement. Profile tolerance applies to only one side of the formed material. The bend radii of 2 are also controlled with plus/minus.

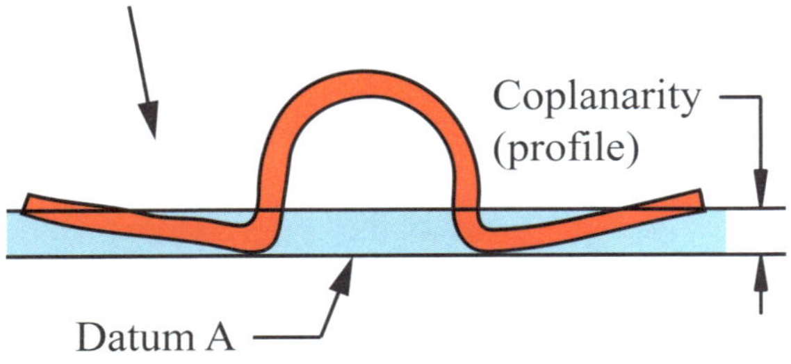

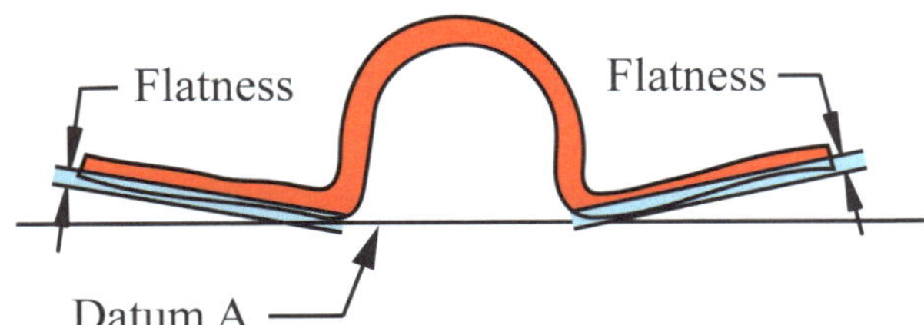

Flatness only controls the form of surfaces individually. A 2X flatness requirement would not control coplanarity between the two surfaces.

Workshop Exercise 11.3

Often in the verification process, it is only necessary to monitor a few simple distances on the part. On the three parts below, calculate the min and max of the designated distances. See the drawings earlier in the unit for the basic dimensions and tolerances.

Cam Wheel

See page 11-8

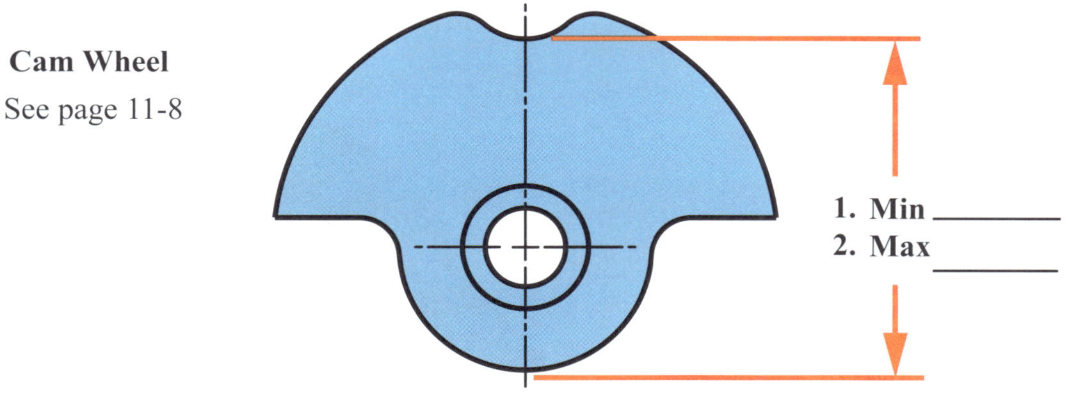

Fuel Line Bracket

See page 11-17

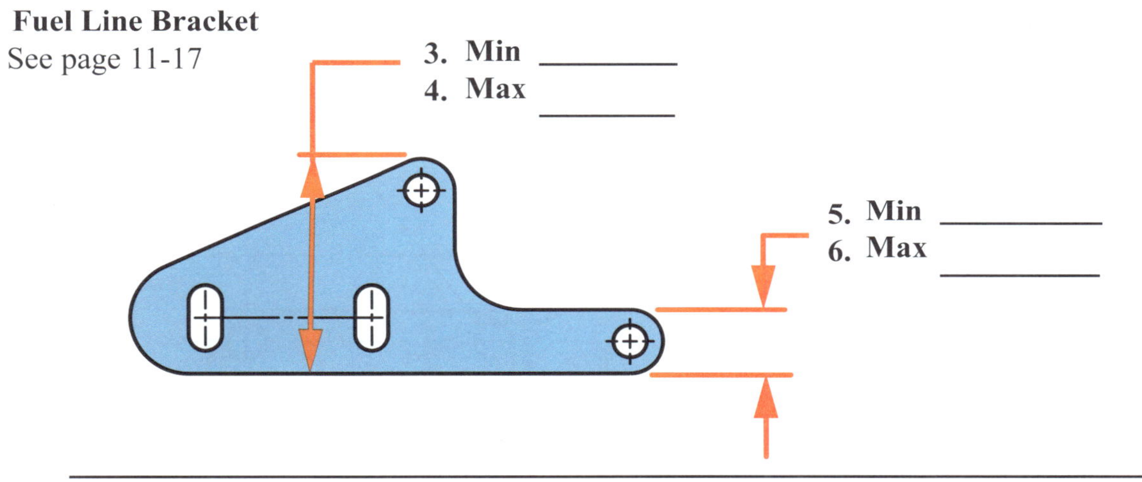

Fuel Line Clamp

See page 11-18

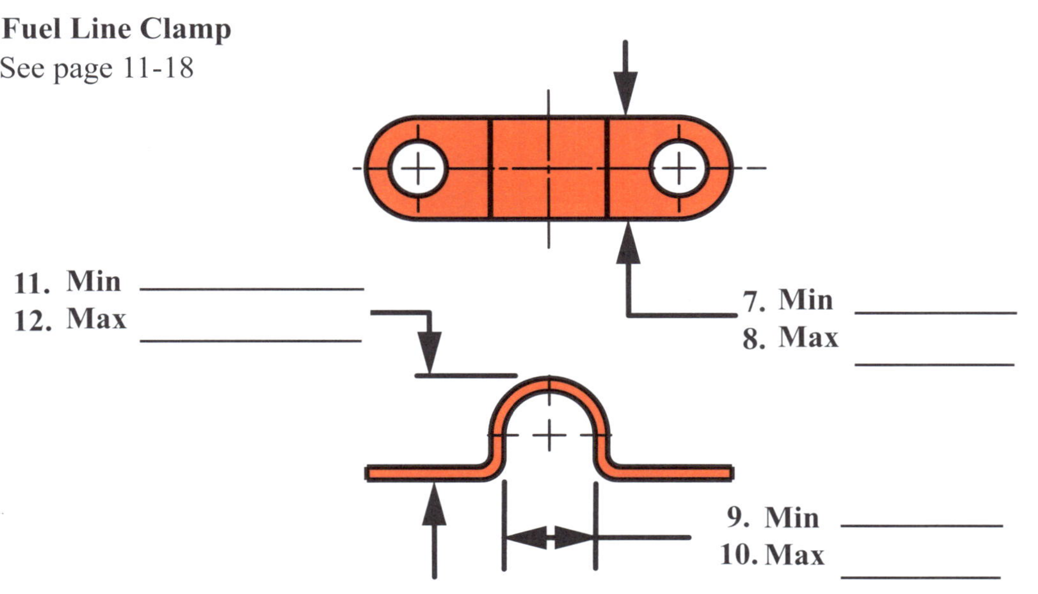

Profile of a Surface - Hat Bracket

The sheet metal Hat Bracket drawing below has geometric tolerances applied. The datum features are selected based on the mounting conditions. Profile tolerances control the surfaces, and position tolerances control the holes.

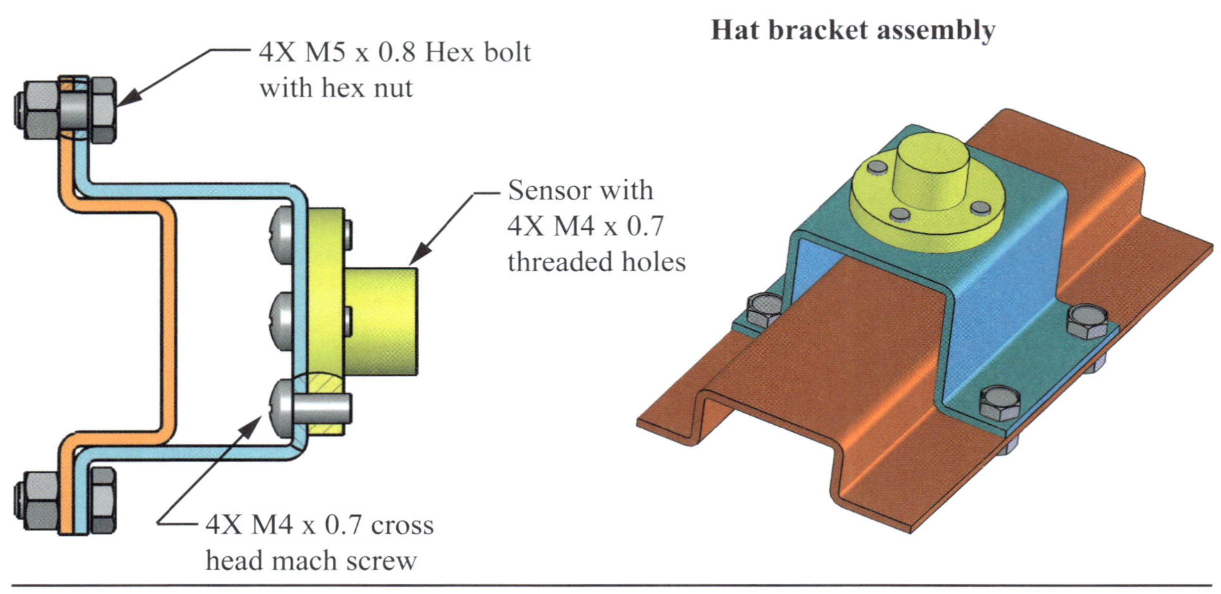

Hat bracket drawing

UNLESS OTHERWISE SPECIFIED:

DIMENSIONS ARE BASIC

PART IS TO BE RESTRAINED ON DATUM FEATURE A WITH 4 M5 SCREWS

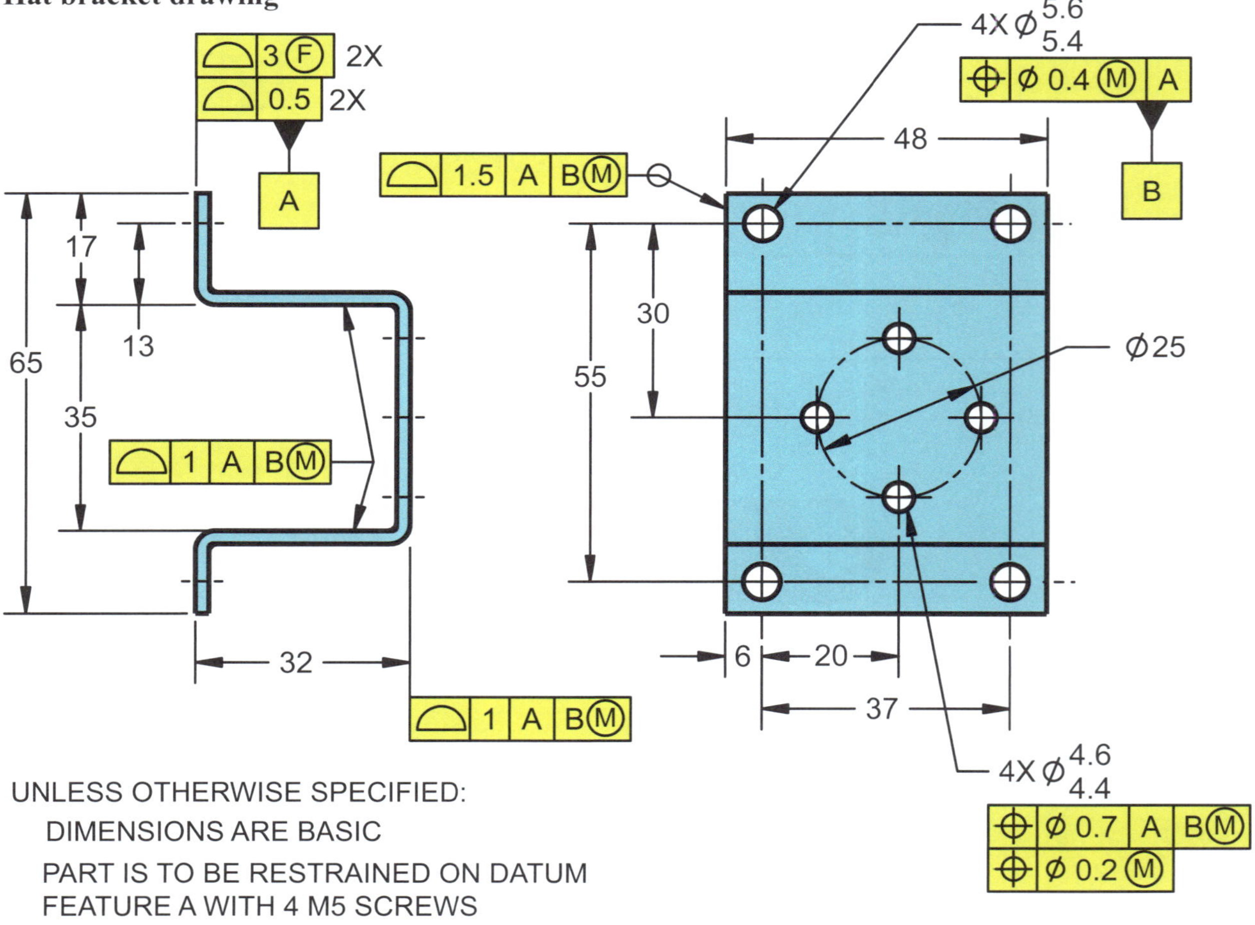

Profile of a Surface - Hat Bracket

The hat bracket mounts on the bottom two flanges and four hole pattern which establish the DRF. The default restraint for parts is the free state condition. This means all measurements are taken in the free state without any external forces applied. Since the part is flexible, a UOS note is added for all tolerances to instead apply in a restrained condition. However, tolerances with the free state symbol (circle F) are exempt from this note and apply in the free state. Also see Non-Rigid Parts in unit 8.

The mounting surfaces have two coplanarity requirements. The 3 profile tolerance with the circle F modifier is verified with the part in the free state to insure the part is not twisted beyond an initial limit. The second 0.5 profile tolerance is verified in the restrained condition per the requirements in the note.

The figure below illustrates the MMB and LMB of the profile and position tolerances in the restrained condition. Note how simple it is for design to evaluate the worst-cases between the features. Inspection may use a number of techniques to verify the conformance: A functional gage could be built using gage pins and scribed lines. The part could be verified in an open set-up using a height gage, angle plate, clamps, and the paper gage concept shown in unit 9. Or a CMM can be used with a holding fixture to align to the hole pattern and probe the surfaces to get variable data.

Hat bracket tolerance zones

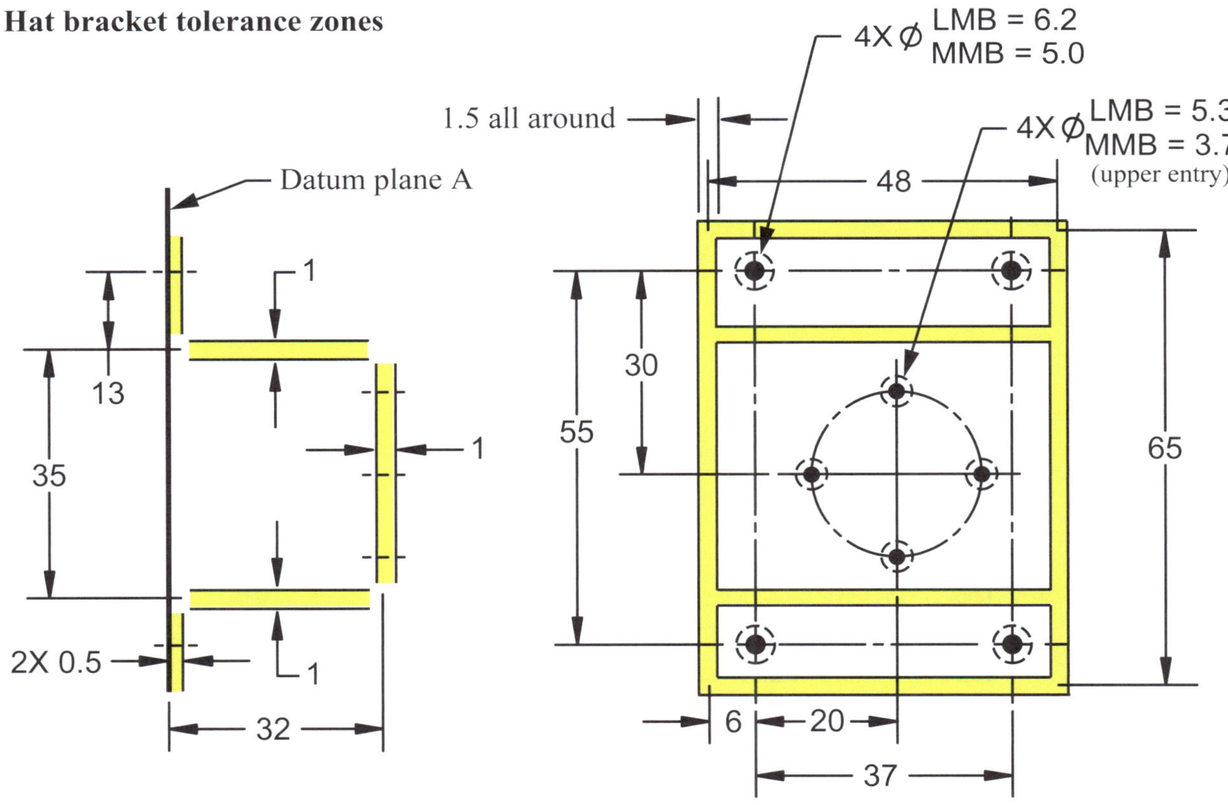

Workshop Exercise 11.4

Calculate the min and max distances in the restrained condition on the hat bracket below. Enter your answers in the table.

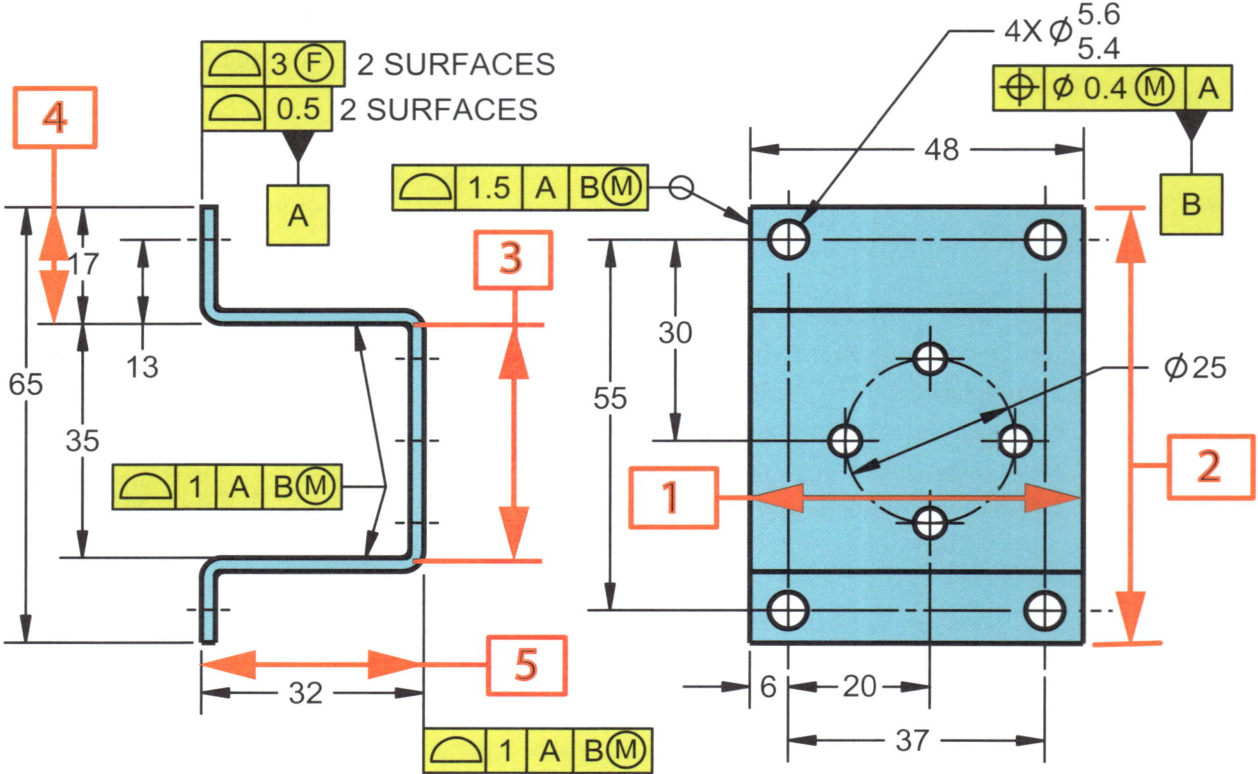

UNLESS OTHERWISE SPECIFIED:
ALL UNTOLERANCED DIMENSIONS BASIC
PART IS TO BE RESTRAINED ON DATUM FEATURE A WITH 4 M5 SCREWS

Calculate the Min and Max Dimensions		
No.	Min	Max
1		
2		
3		
4		
5		

Composite Profile Tolerancing

A group of surfaces may have multiple levels of profile tolerance applied. Sometimes the location to the datum reference frame (DRF) is less important than the size or shape of the feature. This requirement could be specified with either composite profile or multiple profile frames depending on the requirements. Each segment may be verified separately, but the lower segment is a subset of the upper segment.

In composite profile tolerancing, the profile symbol is entered once for both horizontal entries and is different than two single segmented feature control frames. With a composite feature control frame, the tolerance zones in the upper segment are constrained in translation and rotation to the specified DRF (like normal). The tolerance zones in the lower segment still control form, size and relationships between the features in the group, but are constrained in rotation only to the specified DRF.

In contrast, all single segment profile frames control the location between the features and are constrained in translation and rotation to the specified DRF. This is interpreted as two separate profile requirements.

The next pages will go into the details of these two different methods of grouping features.

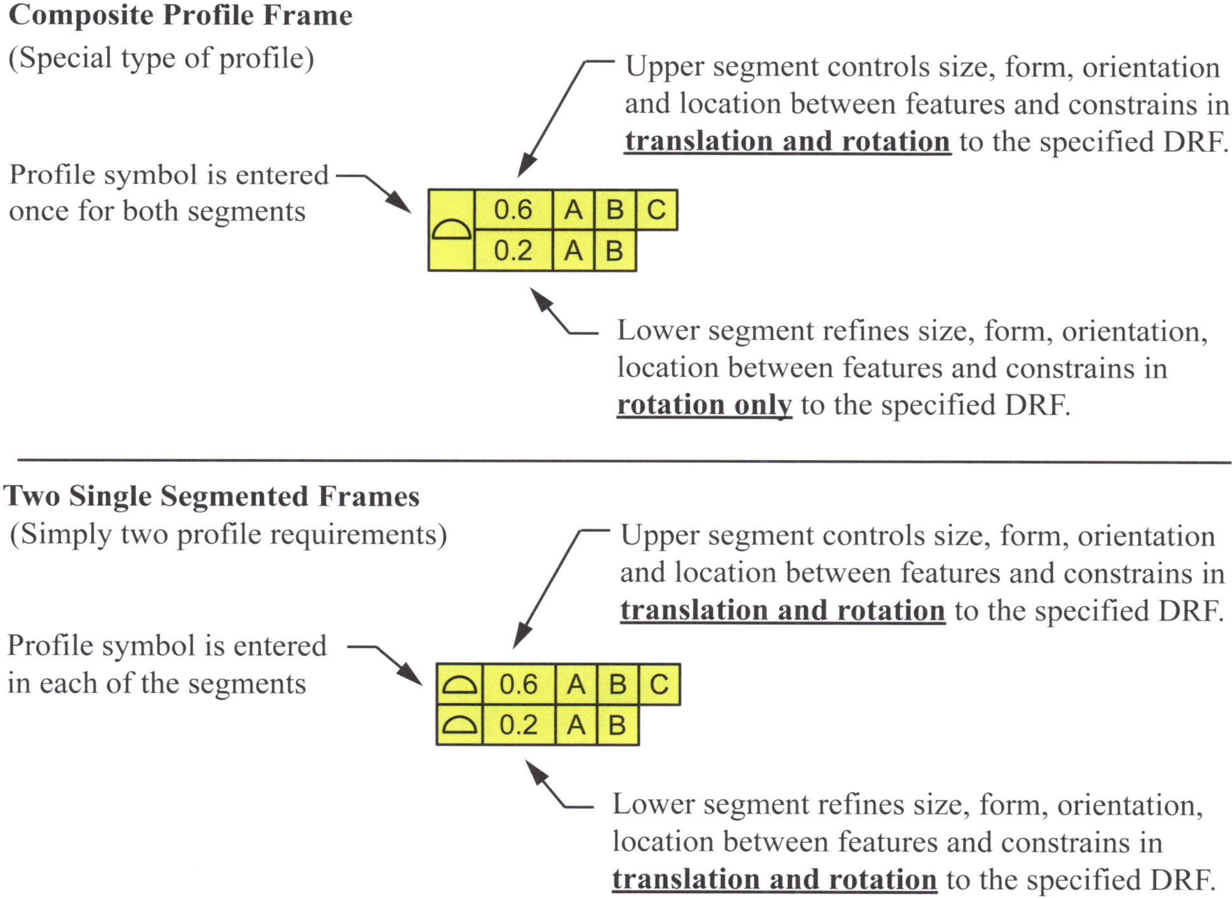

Another technicality defined by ASME Y14.5: Both composite and multiple profile segments used with nX on multiple irregular shapes also constrains the shapes to each other within the lower profile specification. If these multiple shapes should be evaluated separately, the notation INDIVIDUALLY is placed under the feature control frame.

Composite Profile - One Datum Feature

Trim piece

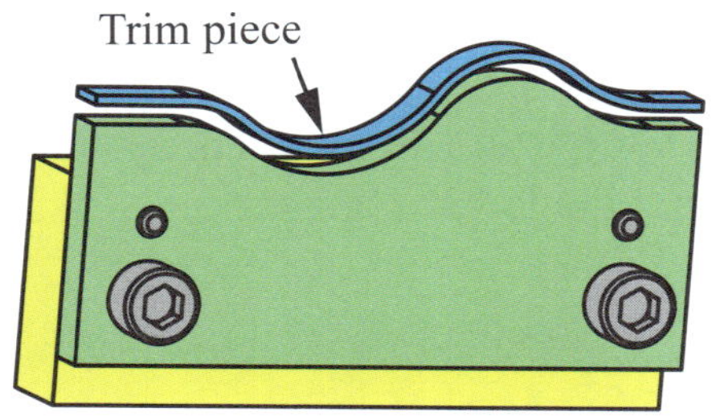

The part mounts on the back surface and two dowels. These features establish the DRF. The top surface contour mates with a trim piece and the gap between them is important. The location of this surface to the DRF is not as important.

The upper segment of composite profile locates and orients the contour to the DRF within 0.5. The lower specification of 0.1 refines the form and orients it only to datum A to control the gap with the floating trim piece.

This on the drawing

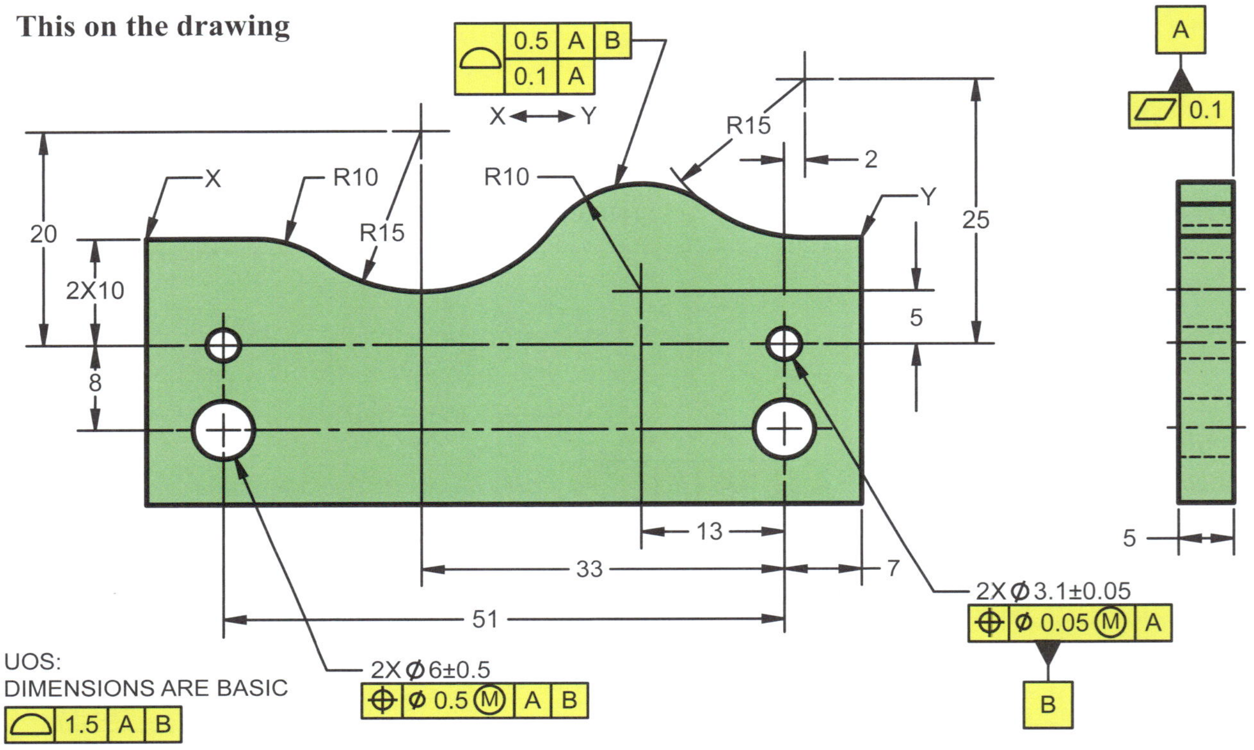

0.5 A B
0.1 A
X ←→ Y
A
0.1
X
R10
R15
R10
R15
2
Y
25
20
2X10
5
8
13
33
7
51
5
2XØ3.1±0.05
Ø 0.05 M A
B
UOS:
DIMENSIONS ARE BASIC
1.5 A B
2XØ6±0.5
Ø 0.5 M A B

Means this

The 0.5 profile zone is fixed and fully constrained to the AB DRF.
10
DRF
The 0.1 profile zone is only constrained in rotation to datum A. The zone may float up/down, left/right and rotate horizontally.
10
DRF

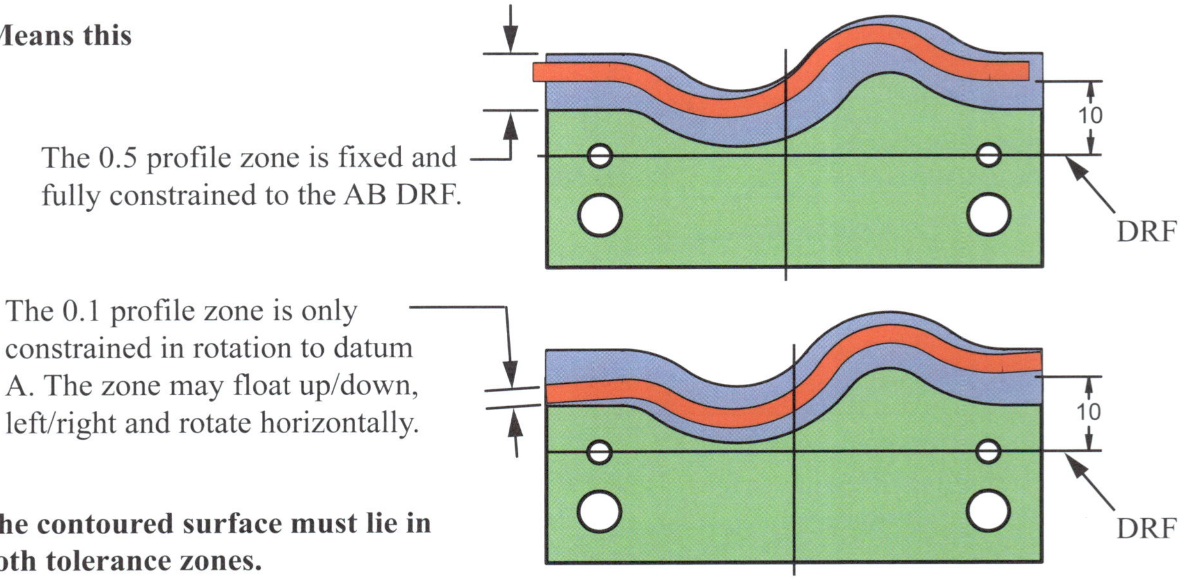

The contoured surface must lie in both tolerance zones.

Composite Profile - Two Datum Features

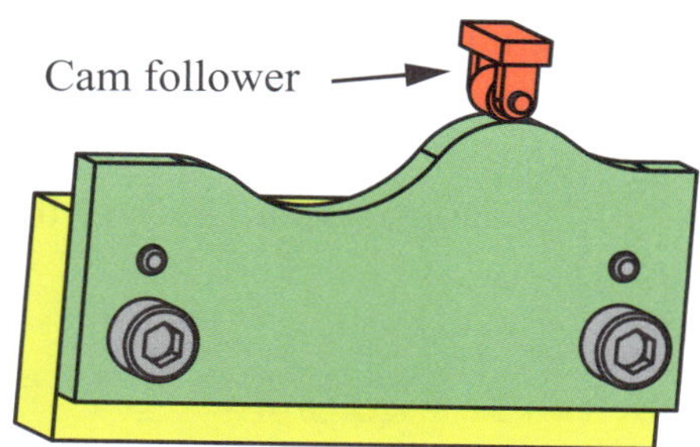

The part mounts on the back surface and two dowels. These features establish the DRF. A cam follower rides on the top surface contour and can adjust up and down for locational error to the the DRF, but it has no adjustment for a bad shape or tilted surface.

The upper segment of composite profile locates and orients the contour to the DRF within 0.5. The lower specification of 0.1 refines the form and orientation to the DRF to control the "ride" with the cam follower.

This on the drawing

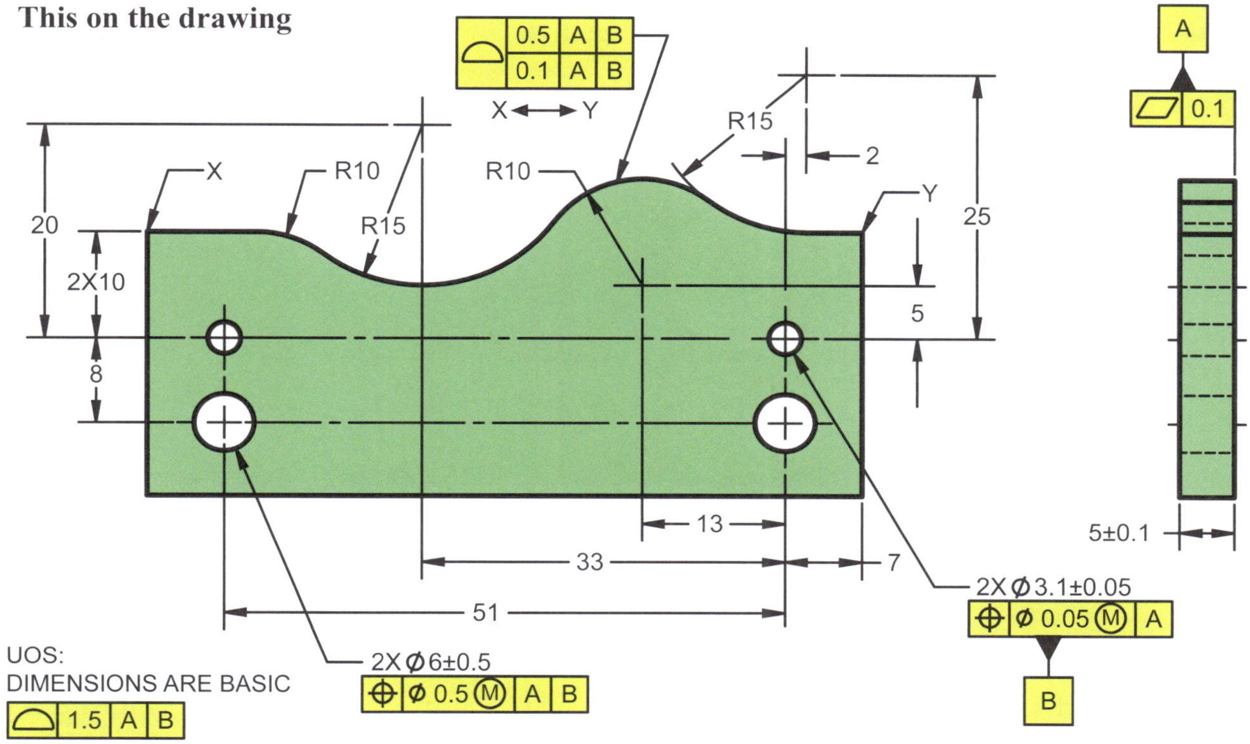

UOS:
DIMENSIONS ARE BASIC

Means this

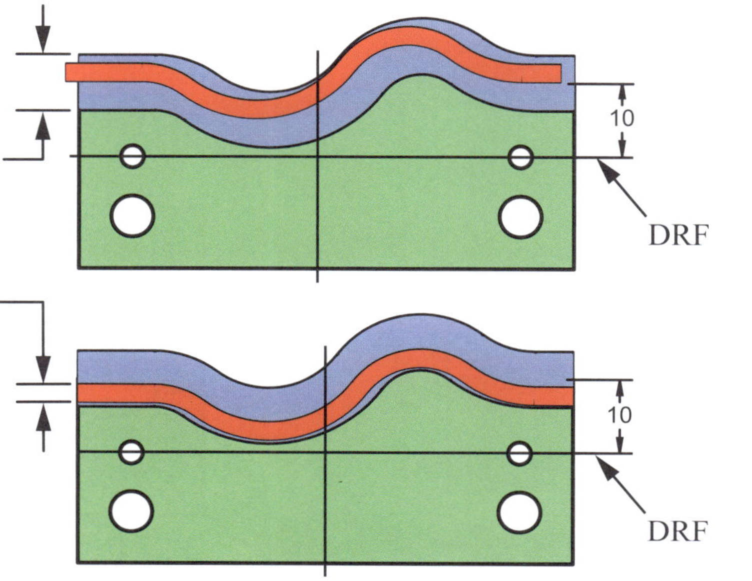

The 0.5 profile zone is fixed and fully constrained to the AB DRF.

The 0.1 profile zone is only constrained in rotation to the DRF. The zone may float up/down and left/right, **but may not rotate**.

The contoured surface must lie in both tolerance zones.

Composite Profile of an Irregular Feature of Size

A composite profile is applied to the irregular feature below. The tolerance zone defined by the upper segment is fixed in translation and rotation to the ABC DRF. This tolerance of .030 locates the feature on the part while also controlling orientation, form, and size. The smaller .004 tolerance zone defined by the lower segment is fixed in rotation only to datum A. This refines the size and form to itself, and perpendicularity to datum A.

The lower segment of a composite profile can be used to refine size, form, or orientation an irregular feature.

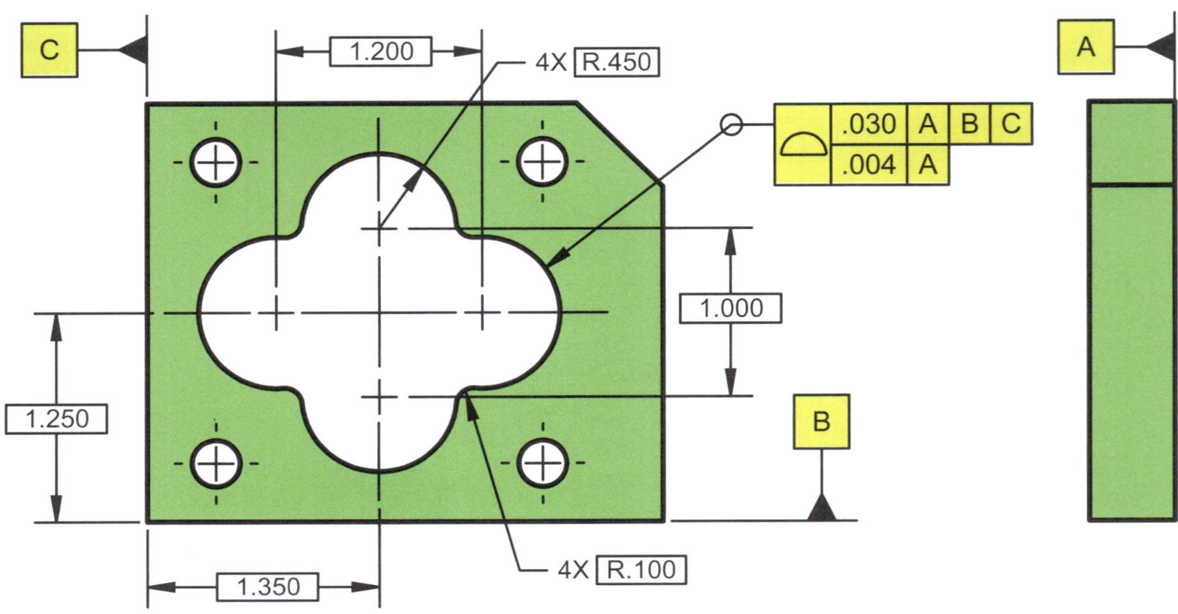

Note: Composite profile used for locating irregular features is similar to the position boundary concept shown later in unit 12. The difference is the upper profile specification establishes **both an MMB and LMB** within which the surface must lie and modifiers MMC or LMC are not allowed. However, position boundary applied at MMC or LMC establishes a **single MMB or LMB boundary** that the feature must clear. Using composite profile to locate an irregular feature is a more restrictive control than position boundary.

Calculate the min/max dimensions.

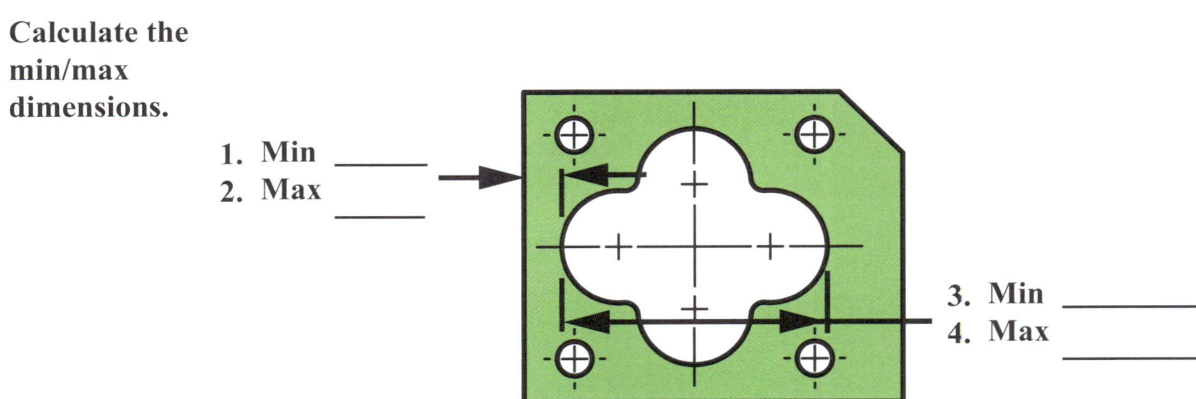

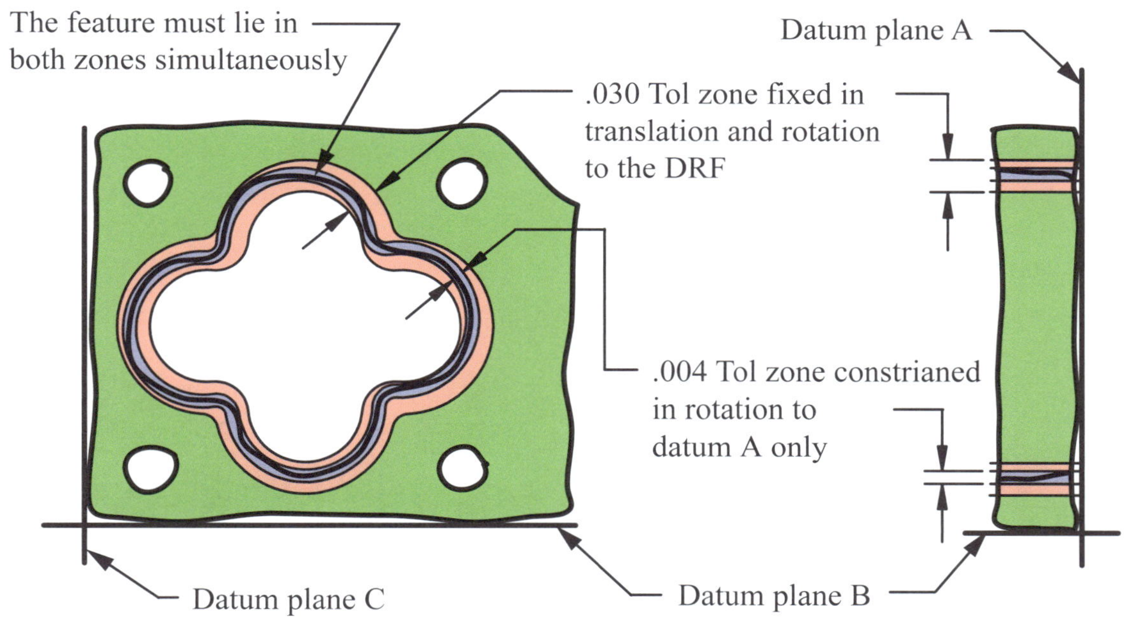

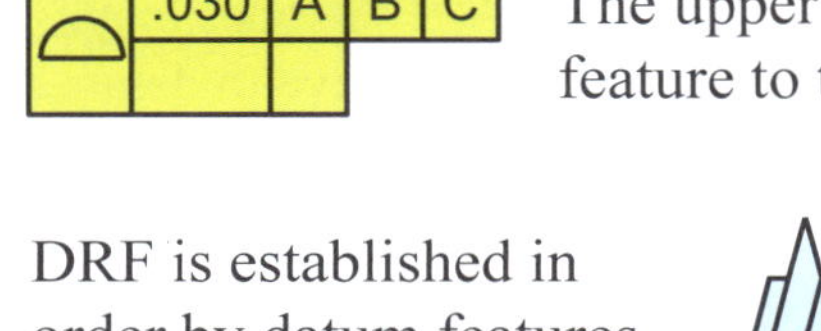

The upper segment specifies the location of the feature to the specified datums.

DRF is established in order by datum features A, B, & C

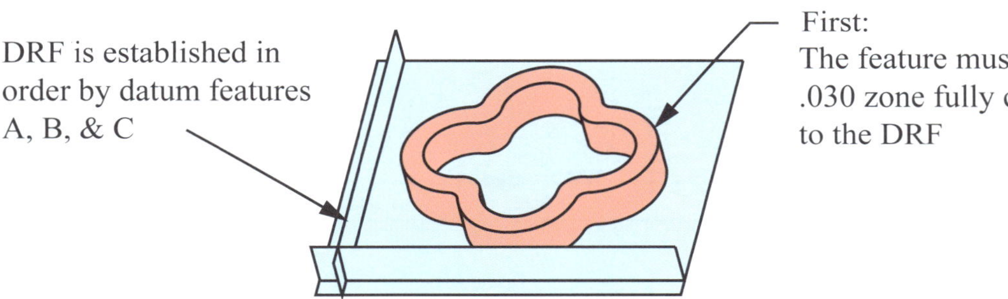

First:
The feature must lie within a .030 zone fully constrained to the DRF

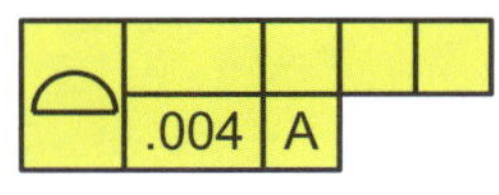

The lower segment refines the size and form of the feature and the orientation to the specified datums.

DRF is established by datum feature A. This is an orientation plane only.

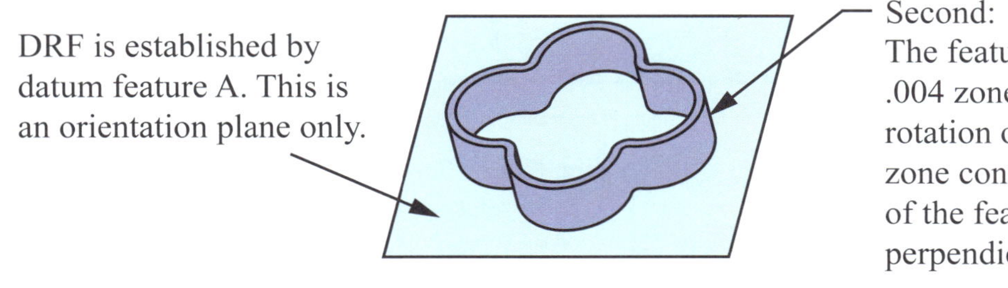

Second:
The feature must lie within a .004 zone that is constrained in rotation only to datum A. This zone controls the size and form of the feature to itself and perpendicularity to datum A.

The two segments in the composite profile feature control frame create two tolerance zones. The .030 zone locates the feature to the datum reference frame. The .004 zone refines the size, form, and orientation of the feature. This .004 zone may float up, down, left, right and rotate inside the .030 zone to accept the feature.

Profile - Coplanarity

The part below has a composite profile tolerance applied to the four top surfaces. The height of the pads must be located within .040. The pads must also remain coplanar and parallel within .010.

The upper segment creates four .040 wide tol zones that are fixed in translation to datum A. This controls form, orientation, and location to datum A.

The lower segment creates four .010 wide tol zones that are located to each other and fixed **in rotation only to datum A**. This refines form, location between the pads (coplanarity), and also orientation (parallelism) to datum A.

A comparison of composite profile with other tolerance combinations are shown below.

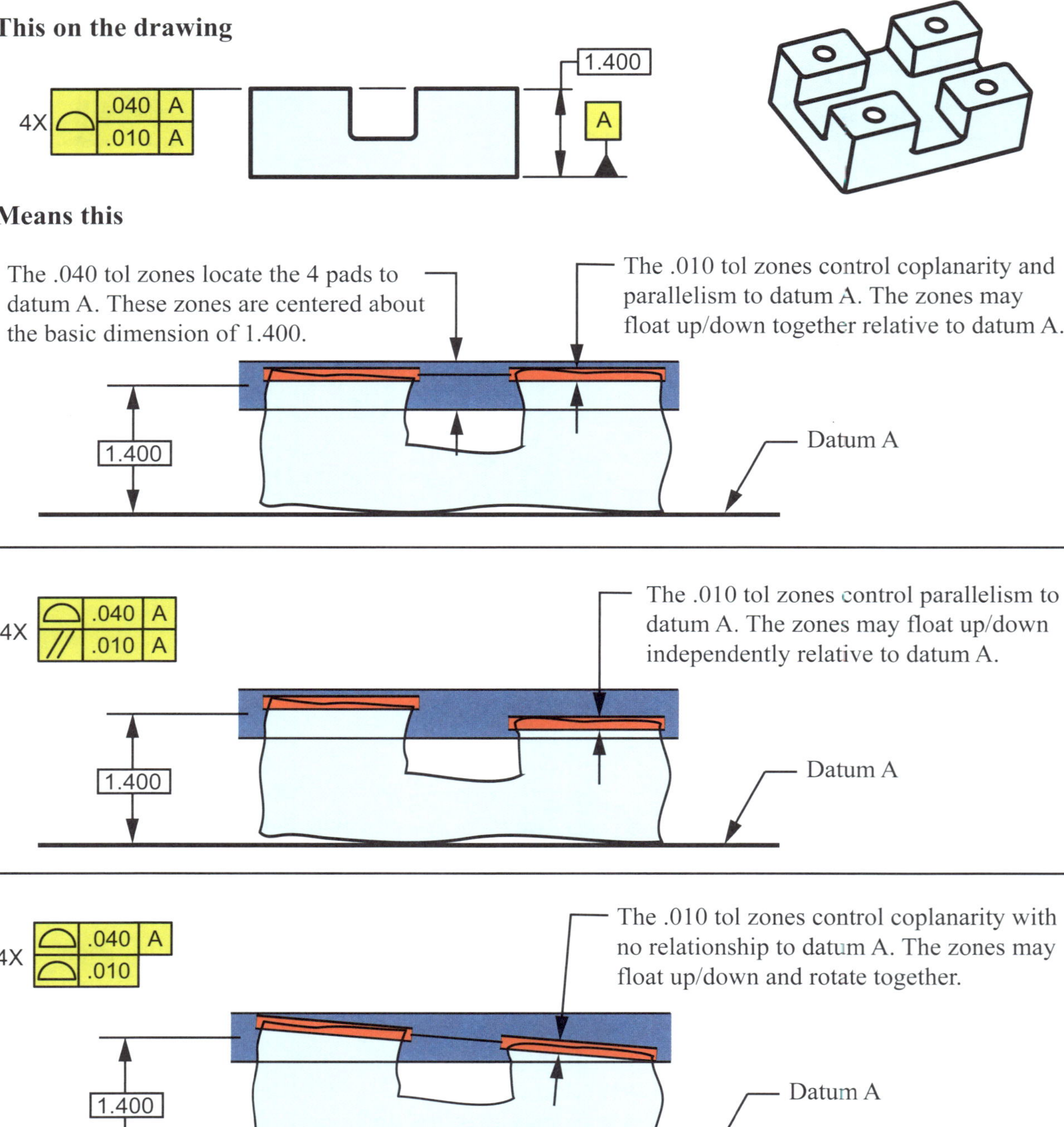

Workshop Exercise 11.5 - Coplanarity

Use the drawing below to answer the following questions according to ASME Y14.5-2018.

This on the drawing

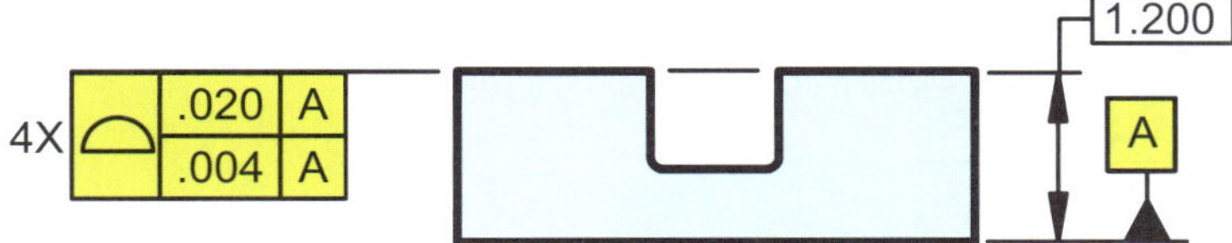

1. What is the maximum height of the four surfaces to datum A? ______________________

2. What is the parallelism tolerance on the top surfaces to datum A? ____________________

3. What is the flatness tolerance on each top surface? ______________________________

4. What is the maximum offset (coplanarity) allowed between the top surfaces? ___________

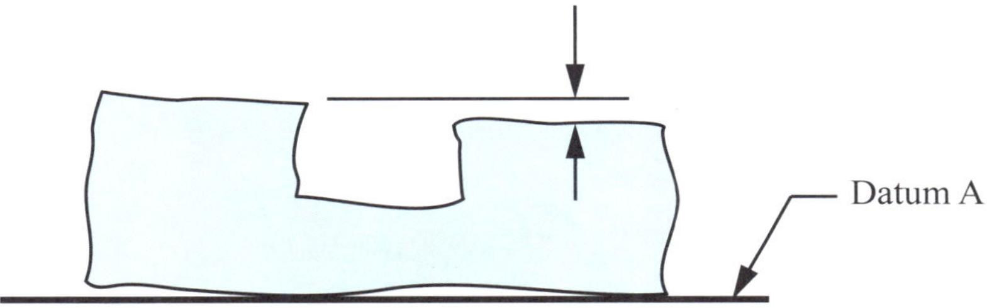

5. If the composite profile were replaced with a profile and flatness, what is the maximum offset (coplanarity) allowed between the top surfaces?

4X ⌓ .020 A
4X ⏥ .004

____

6. If the datum feature reference A in the lower segment of the composite profile were removed, what is the parallelism tolerance on the top surfaces?

7. The term "coplanarity" refers to what type of tolerance?
   - a. size
   - b. form
   - c. orientation
   - d. location

Tangent Plane Symbol

The tangent plane symbol may be added to profile, runout, or orientation tolerances on planar surfaces to filter out flatness error. The tangent plane symbol (circle T) is shown below applied to a parallelism specification. Only a plane contacting the high points of the surface (not all points on the surface) must lie within the tolerance zone.

This on the drawing

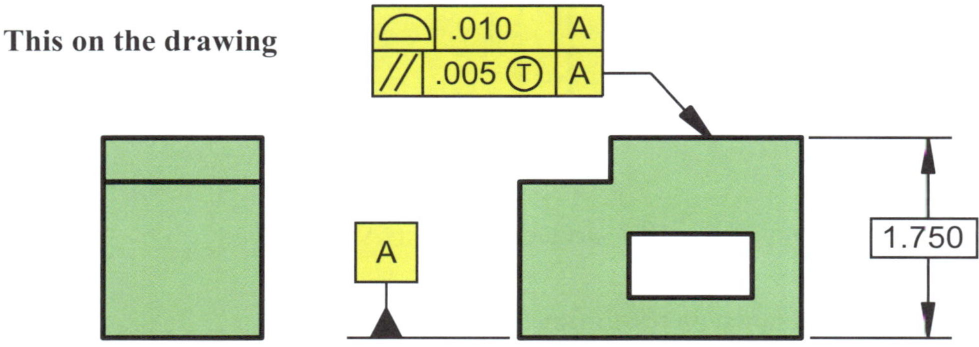

The tangent plane contacting the high points of the surface must lie within two parallel planes .005 apart which are parallel to datum plane A. **The parallelism with tangent plane modifier does not control the flatness on the surface** (the profile tolerance controls the flatness).

Means this

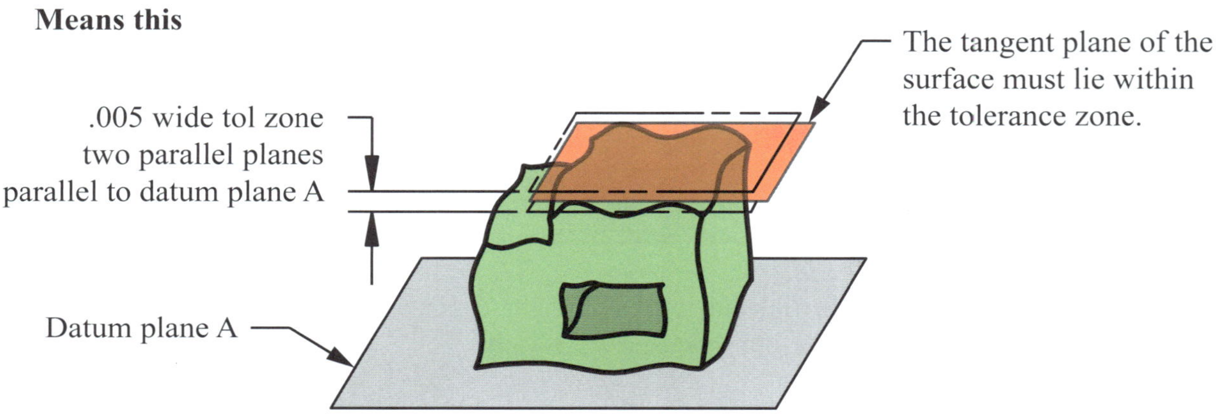

The tangent plane symbol may also be used with profile of a surface. Profile with a tangent plane modifier is sometimes used for surfaces in a weldment. The flatness of the surface is controlled on the individual piece part drawing, and the profile only locates the high points of the surface.

Sample Inspection

Part is mounted on datum feature A with a parallel bar placed on the surface. As the indicator moves on the parallel bar, the full indicator movement (FIM) can be no more than .005

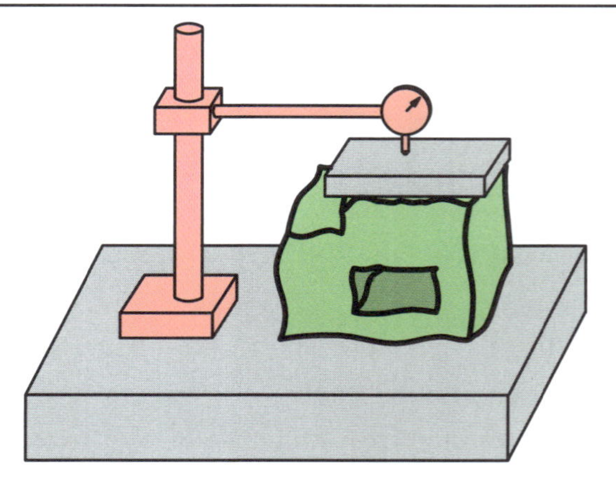

Profile Tolerance on Sharp Corners

Below is a part with multiple designed sharp corners. The shape of the profile tolerance zone on sharp corners can be confusing and is clarified in the Y14.5-2018 and Y14.5.1-2019 standards. Also see ISO 1660 interpretations in the appendix.

Application

This on the drawing

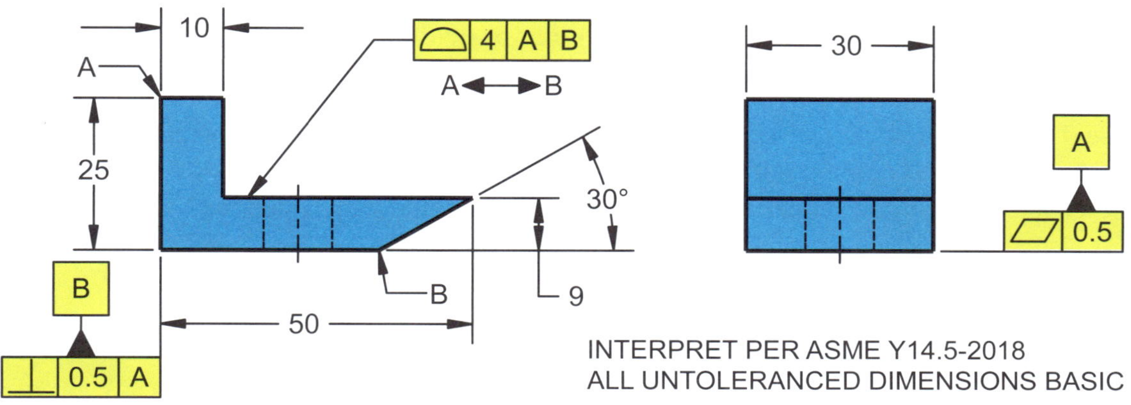

Means this

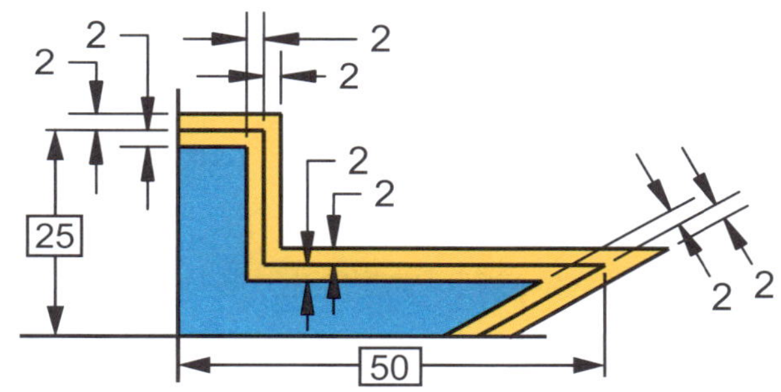

Profile tolerance zones apply along surface normals (lines perpendicular) to the true profile. Mathematically, sharp corner do not have a surface normal. Y14.5 clarifies in these cases the tolerance zone boundaries for adjacent surfaces extend to intersect each other. The actual surface must be within the tolerance zones.

Calculations to sharp corner

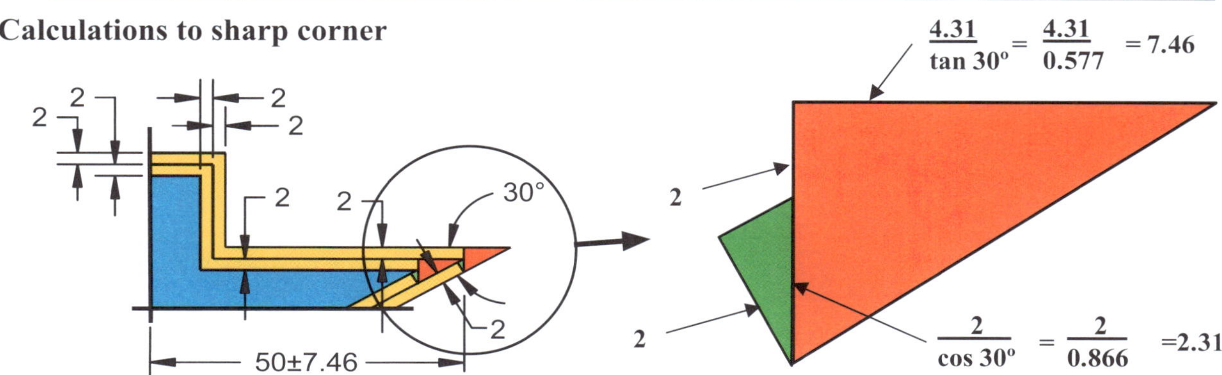

Since the profile tolerance zone extends to the intersection of the boundary lines. The overall length of the part measured from the datum to the end of an acute angle can vary more than ±2. As seen from the right angle geometry calculations, the overall length to the corner can vary as much as 50±7.46. If necessary, the corner zone can be refined by adding a min or max radius or modified by using a nonuniform profile tolerance (see next page).

Profile Tolerance - Nonuniform Zone

Application

The profile non-uniform tolerance zone was new for the ASME Y14.5-2009 standard. The nonuniform zone modifies the shape of a standard profile tolerance zone. The leader line from the feature control frame is directed to the surface, and the term "NONUNIFORM" replaces the tolerance value.

A nonuniform profile tolerance zone is represented by an MMB and LMB of unique shape that encompasses the true profile. These boundaries may either be defined by a CAD file or basic dimensions on a drawing with phantom lines to indicate the tolerance zone.

On the drawing below, the MMB and LMB boundaries of the nonuniform profile zone are shown in phantom lines and defined with basic dimensions. Nonuniform profile is a specialized tool that may be used on complex shapes that are difficult to tolerance with a standard profile.

This on the drawing

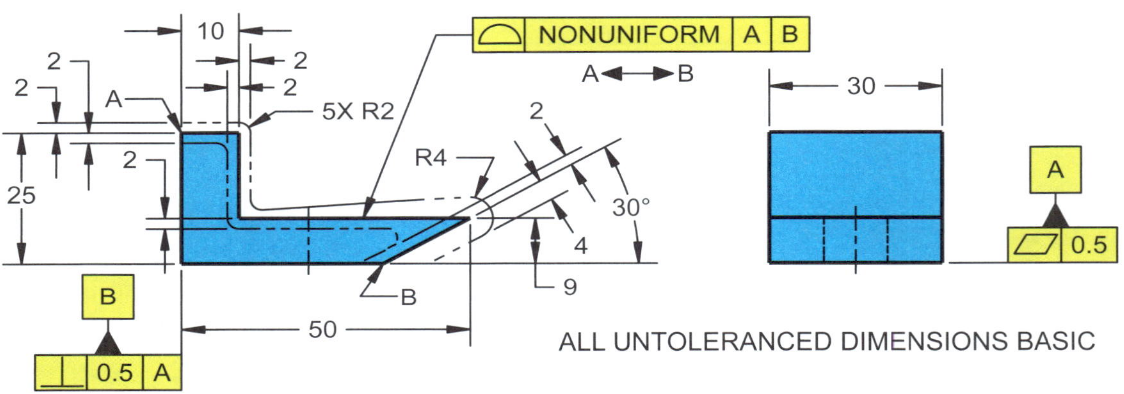

Means this

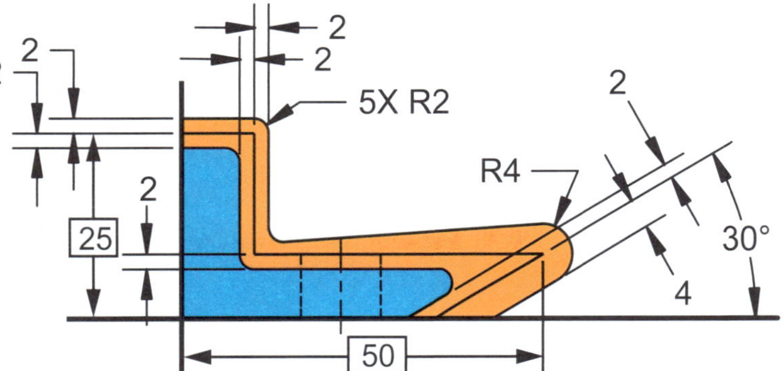

Basic dimensions define the size and shape of the tolerance zones.

Dynamic Profile Modifier - Form Only

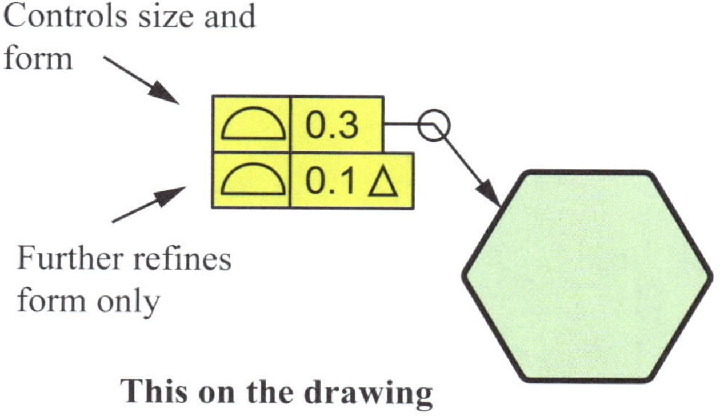

This on the drawing

Dynamic profile is a new concept for ASME Y14.5-2018. The modifier is the Greek letter delta that may be placed behind the tolerance value. This allows the profile boundaries to expand or contract while maintaining the specified constant distance between the boundaries.

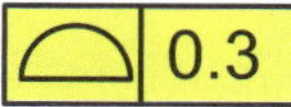

Means this

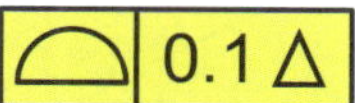

By default, profile controls size and form of a non-planar feature

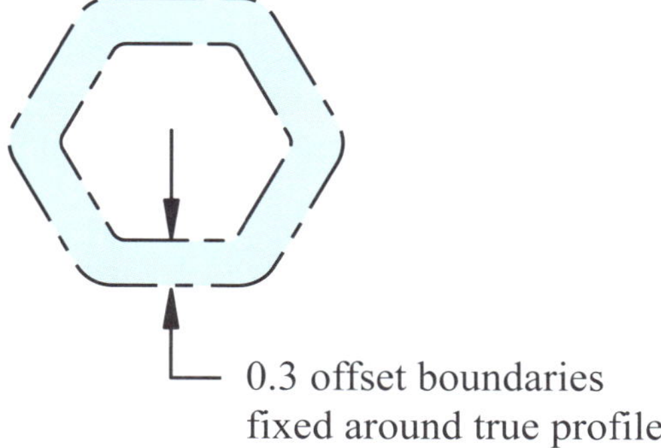

0.3 offset boundaries fixed around true profile

Profile with the dynamic modifier unlocks the size control

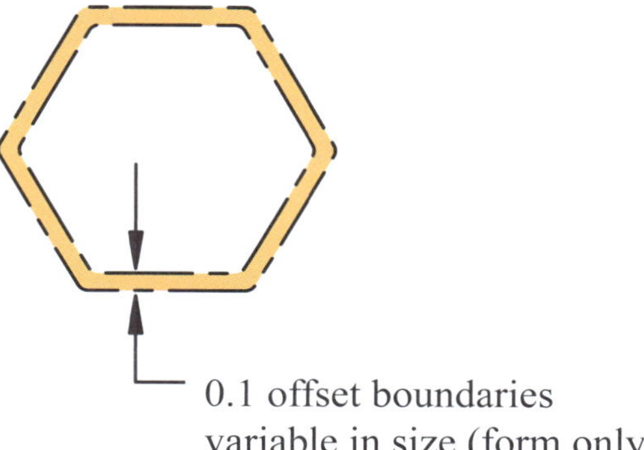

0.1 offset boundaries variable in size (form only)

The dynamic profile modifier may also be used with datum feature references to control form, orientation, and location but unlocking the size requirement.

The dynamic profile modifier without datum references is similar to cylindricity on a shaft controlling form but not size.

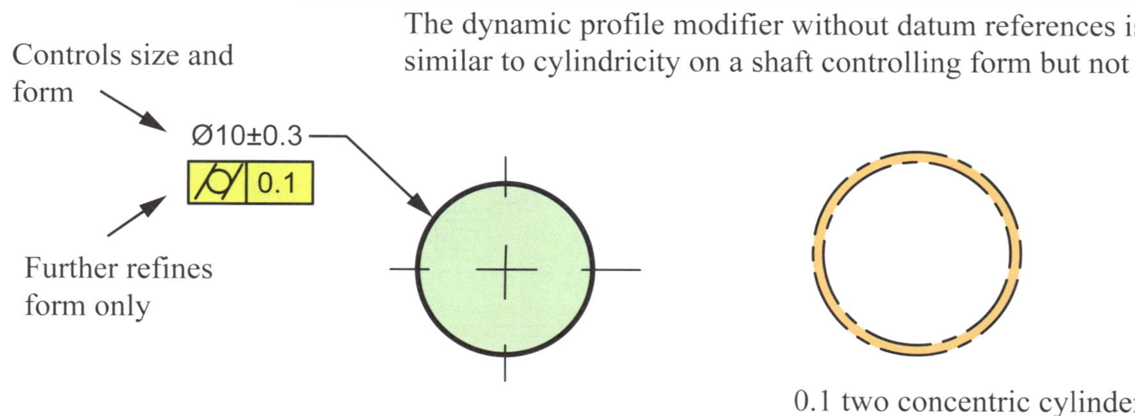

0.1 two concentric cylinders variable in size (form only)

Dynamic Profile Modifier - Form, Orientation, Location

Below is the assembly of a laptop case and touch pad shown earlier in this unit, but a change is made to the assembly requirement: The visual gap between parts may be big or small but it must be a near consistent size gap all around.

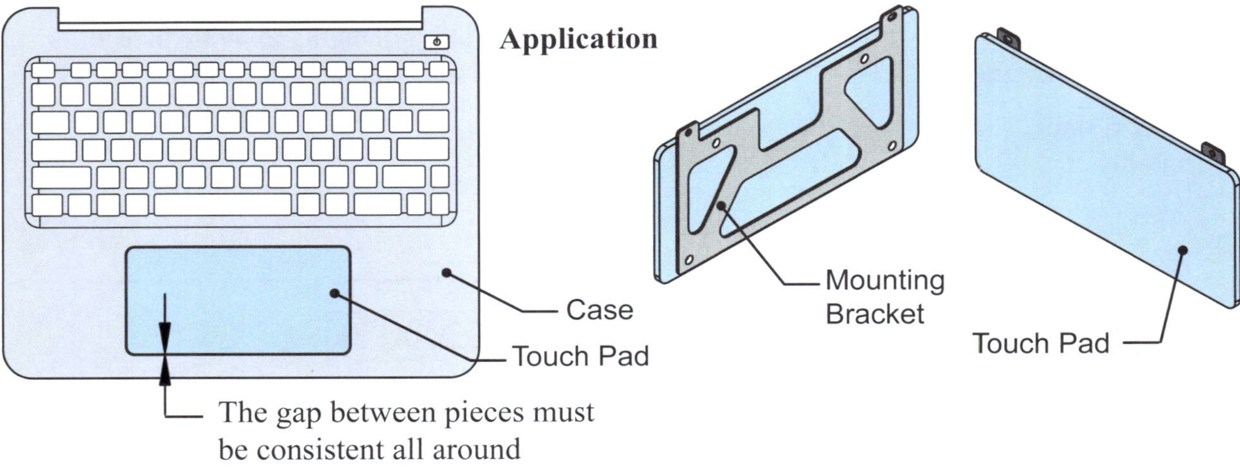

A profile and dynamic profile relative the datum reference frame (DRF) are both used on the outside contour. The size, form, orientation, and location all have an effect on the gap and are controlled with the 0.3 profile. A dynamic profile tolerance is added to refine the more important consistency of the gap. The 0.1 zone has the size requirement unlocked while still controlling form, orientation and location of the surface relative to the DRF.

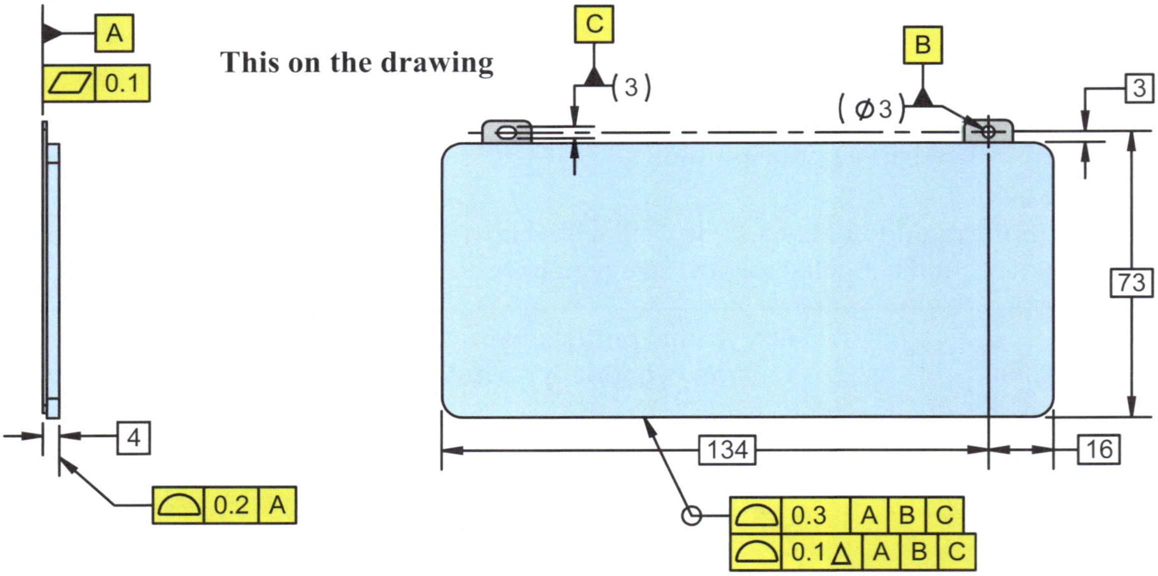

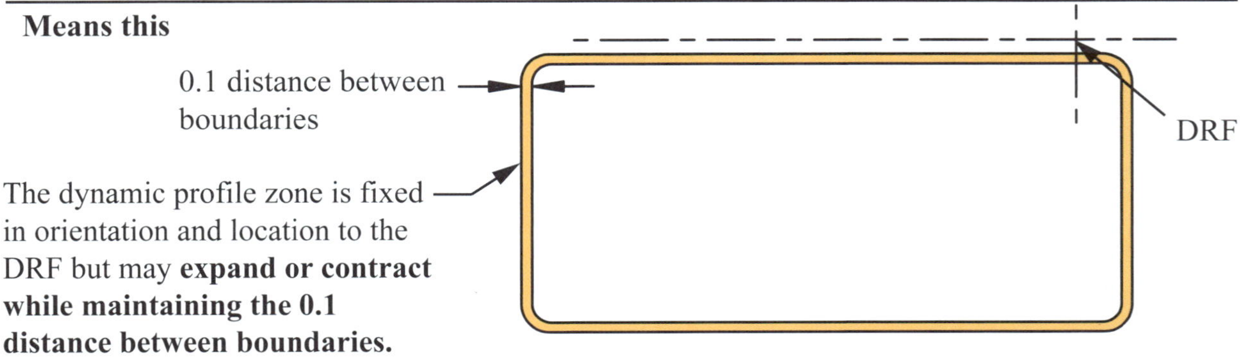

This on the drawing

Means this

0.1 distance between boundaries

The dynamic profile zone is fixed in orientation and location to the DRF but may **expand or contract while maintaining the 0.1 distance between boundaries.**

DRF

Dynamic Profile Modifier - Measurement

A CMM aligns to the ABC DRF and measures 20 points at locations shown on the quality plan.

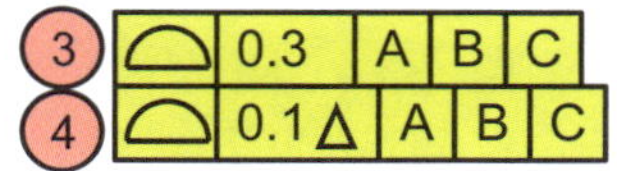

The quality plan may show exact locations where measurements are to be taken. They may be dimensioned on a drawing view or shown with X,Y,Z coordinates in a chart.

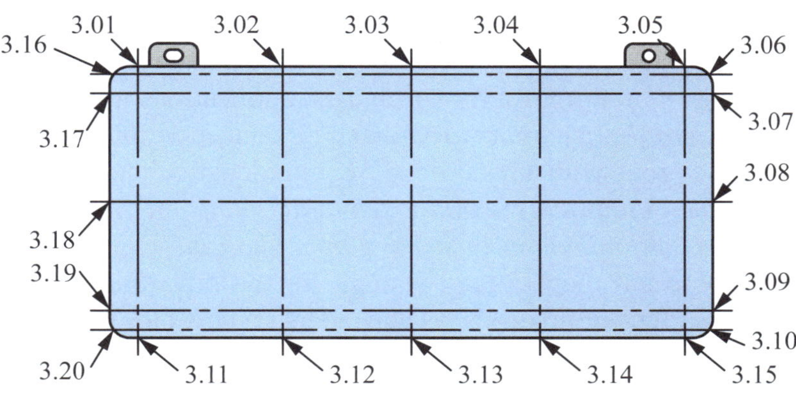

The top profile zone is fixed relative to the DRF and basic dimensions. The surface measurement points are reported as deviations relative to the true profile.

Measurement data (deviations from true profile)

Point	Deviation	Point	Deviation
3.01	+0.02	3.11	+0.03
3.02	+0.03	3.12	+0.02
3.03	+0.05	3.13	+0.05
3.04	+0.07	3.14	+0.05
3.05	+0.09	3.15	+0.07
3.06	+0.06	3.16	+0.03
3.07	+0.03	3.17	+0.05
3.08	+0.03	3.18	+0.05
3.09	+0.02	3.19	+0.02
3.10	+0.05	3.20	+0.05

Inspection Report

ID#	Tolerance Type	Allowed Tolerance	Min/Max Deviations	Measured Value	Pass/ Fail
3	Prof	0.3	+0.02/+0.09	0.18	Pass
4	Prof dyn	0.1	+0.02/+0.09	0.07	Pass

Measured profile value = 2x | max deviation | 2x | 0.09 | = 0.18

Measured dynamic profile value = max - min   0.09 - 0.02 = 0.07

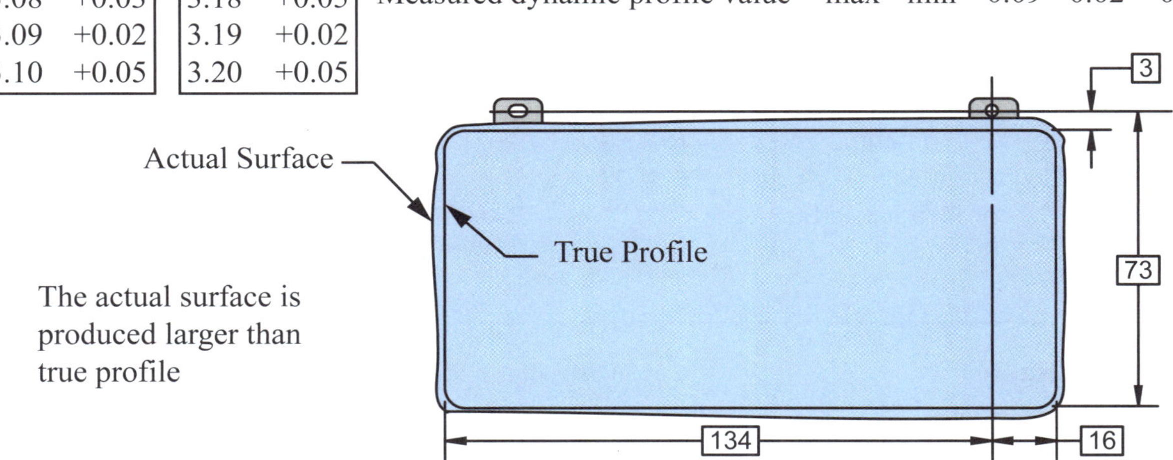

The actual surface is produced larger than true profile

From the measurement data and the exagerrated surface drawn above, we can visualize the actual part. The surface is well aligned to the DRF and has a good shape but is produced larger than the true geometry. This meets the design requirements with the larger profile and tighter dynamic profile. The gap with the mating part will be smaller than expected but will also consistent within 0.07 at the measured locations.

Radius and Controlled Radius

There are two types of plus/minus radii in ASME Y14.5: radius (R) and controlled radius (CR). CR was first defined in the 1994 standard.

The radius symbol (R), dimension, and plus/minus tolerance together create a crescent shaped tolerance zone within which the surface must lie. It was clarified in Y14.5M-1994 that this tolerance zone allows the surface to have flats and reversals within its boundaries. However, a more restrictive control for specialized applications was needed when the shape of the radius is to stay free of sharp corners to avoid stress concentrations. CR symbol also creates a crescent shaped tolerance zone with an additional requirement that the surface must be a *fair curve with no flats or reversals. Additionally, radii taken at all points on the part contour shall be neither smaller than the specified minimum limit nor larger than the maximum limit.* This definition was vague and subjective but maybe good enough for the time. But now we ask, how "fair" is a fair curve? "Without flats or reversals" is dependent on how close you zoom in. "Radii taken at all points" can not be described mathematically. There needs to be some sort of filter defined for this requirement or a tighter form tolerance specified. The Y14.5.1 standard (mathematical definitions) does not give a mathematical definition for CR. Both R and CR are pass/fail requirements and variable data is not possible without resorting to CMM averaging formulas. Y14.5-2018 added to the CR definition:

NOTE: It is recommended that the controlled radius only be used if its meaning is clarified by a general note, a company or industry standard, or another engineering specification. This clarification should define the limits of allowable imperfections, and should be referenced on the drawing, annotated model, or elsewhere in the data set.

See next page for possible alternatives.

This on the drawing | **Means this**

Radius

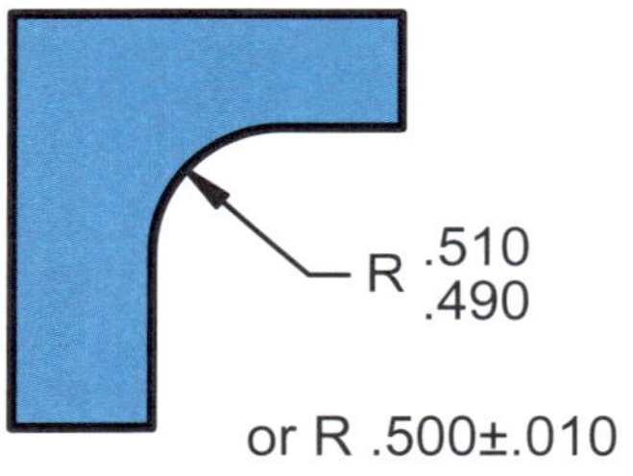

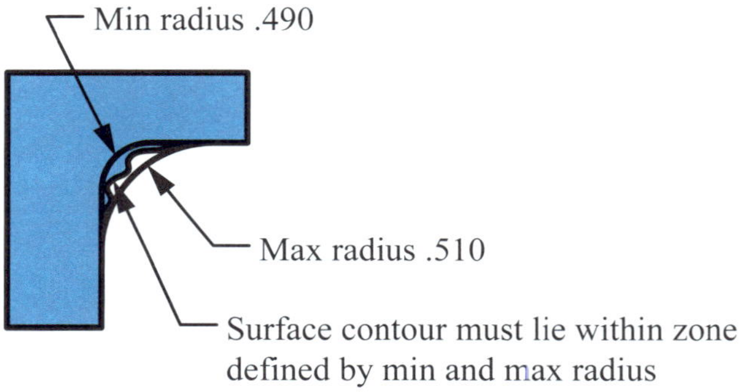

Controlled Radius

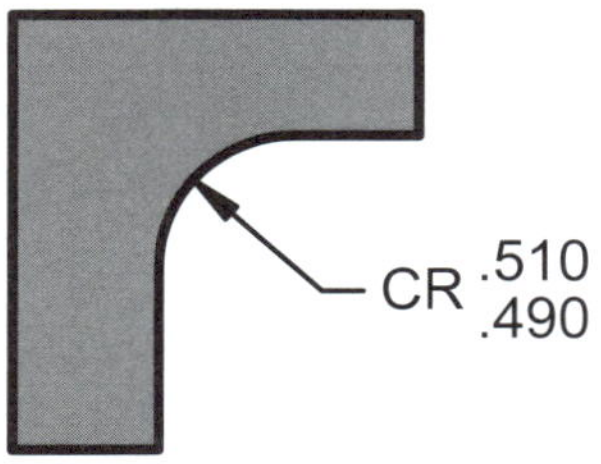

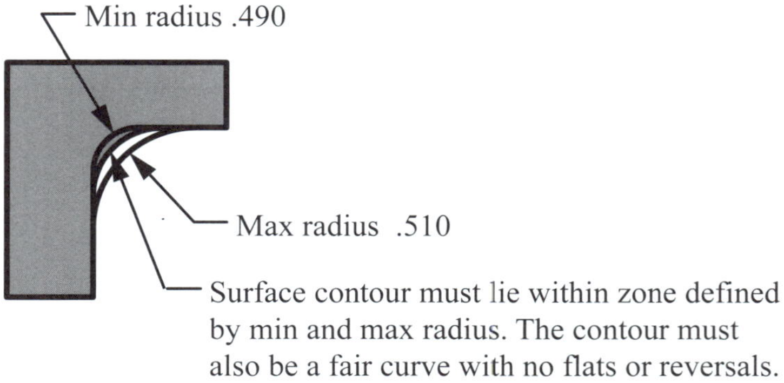

Dynamic Profile Instead of Controlled Radius

The last page discussed the controlled radius (CR) symbol and its ambiguous Y14.5 definition. However, there still is a design need for a specification that allows a radius large size tolerance but keep it a "fair curve without reversals". This can be specified with a form control and a value for the allowed variation.

Profiled Radius

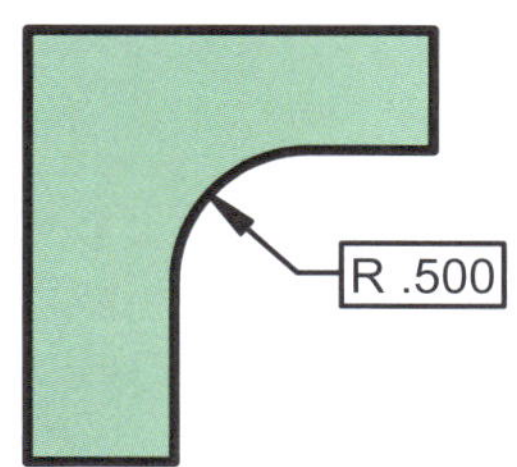

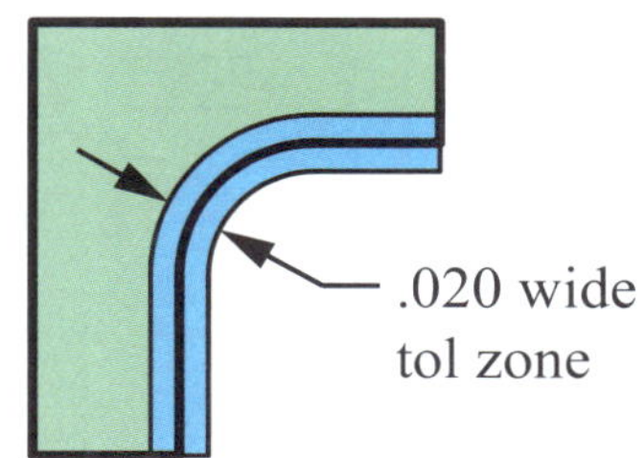

UNLESS OTHERWISE SPECIFIED:

ALL SURFACES | ⌓ | .020 | A | B | C |

A large profile tolerance controls the size, form, orientation, and location of unimportant radii. However, because the tolerance is large, it allows form variations big enough for stress concentration concerns.

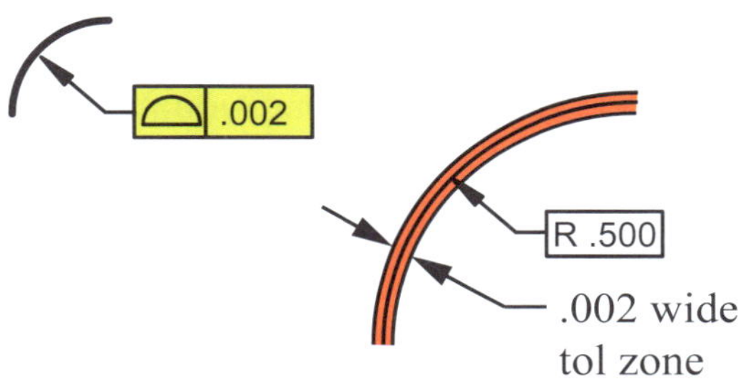

A tighter profile tolerance with no datum references may be added to refine the size and form of the radii. However, this tolerance is too restrictive for the design requirement. Because the tolerance zone must be equally distributed around the basic dimension, the radius size is being tightened to ±.001.

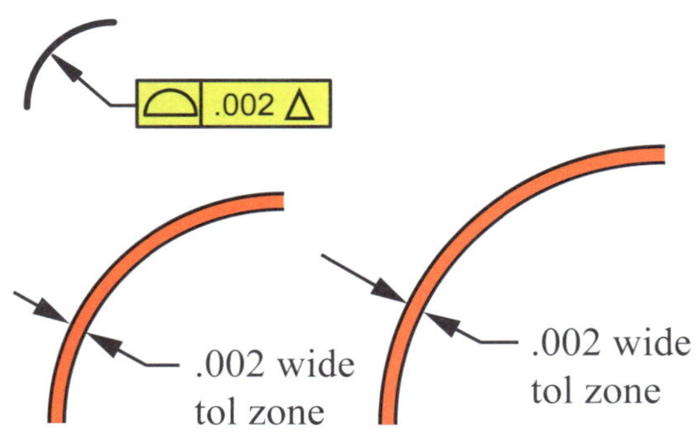

A tighter dynamic profile tolerance with no datum references refines only the form of the radius feature. The width of the tolerance zone must remain at .002 but may expand or contract normal to the true profile.

UNLESS OTHERWISE SPECIFIED:

ALL SURFACES: | ⌓ | .020 | A | B | C |

ALL RADIUS SURFACES: | ⌓ | .002 Δ |

The dynamic profile refinement may be added directly to a radius feature of stress concern or included in a note with the general profile. This creates better definition than a plus/minus CR . It creates a mathematical and machine readable requirement with a defined limit for the form variation.

Profile of a Surface - Per Unit Area

Profile tolerancing specifies a uniform boundary along the true profile within which the surface must lie. The rate of change on the profile variation may be further refined by using profile per unit area with a more restrictive tolerance.

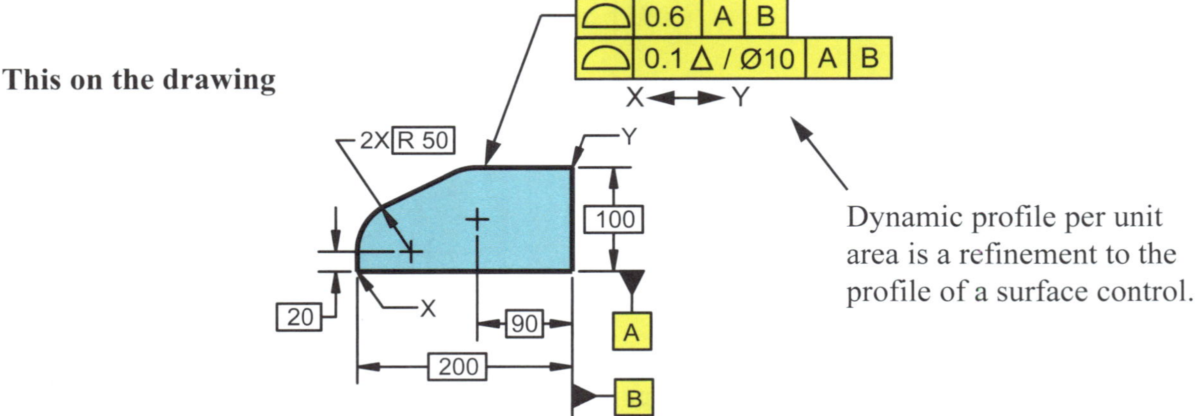

The tolerance zone established by the 0.6 profile is three dimensional and extends the full depth and between points X and Y. It is fully constrained to the AB DRF. The profile per unit area is a series of overlapping Ø10 tolerance zones that are 0.1 wide and float within the 0.6 profile zone.

The profile per unit area refines the rate of change within the larger 0.6 zone profile zone. It limits abrupt changes such as bumps, wrinkles, dimples, machine mis-match etc. Profile per unit area is used with a fully defined DRF and a dynamic profile modifier. This allows the partitioning of the surface to be well defined. The zones are allowed to expand and contract independently relative to the true profile. The max-min deviation of the points must be no more than 0.1 in a distance of 10 mm. This specification can be a replacement for such notes as "NO DINGS AND NO DENTS IN THE SURFACE" and "SURFACE MISMATCH NO MORE THAN 0.1".

Note: An explicit example of this combination is not shown in Y14.5-2018 although dynamic profile and per unit flatness/straightness explanations are shown separately. This combination does provide a quantified value for max allowances of abrupt changes over a set distance on complex surfaces. See next page for possible inspection methods.

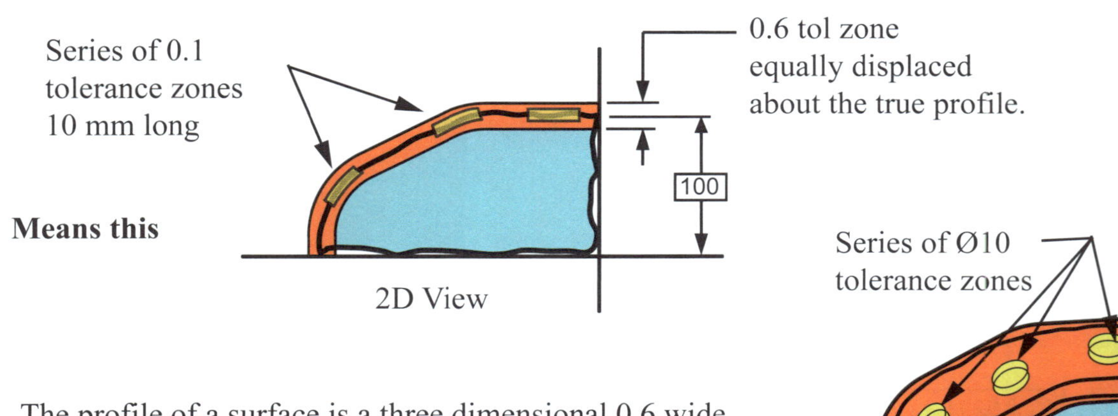

The profile of a surface is a three dimensional 0.6 wide tolerance zone equally disposed about the true profile. The profile per unit area additionally specifies each Ø10 unit must fall within a 0.1 tolerance zone.

Profile of a Surface - Per Unit Area

The dynamic profile per unit area may be evaluated in many ways. One method could be an inspector visual or fingernail check looking for quick interruptions in the surface. An optical comparator may be used to enlarge the view. A CMM could partition the surface into random samples and evaluate each dynamic profile sample separately. Below shows a method using deviation points collected from the regular profile and post-processing that data to evaluate the dynamic profile per unit specification.

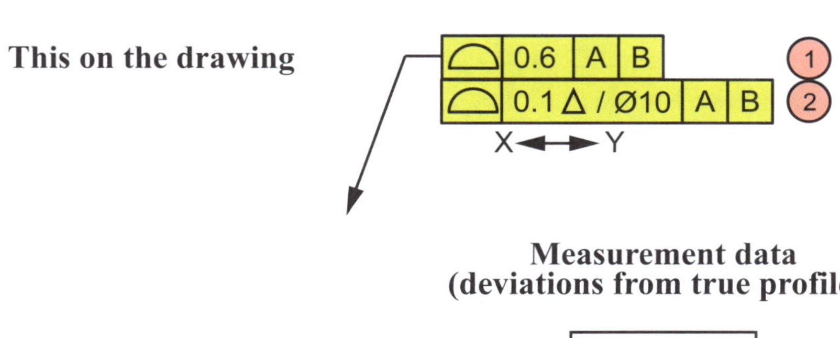

Measurement data (deviations from true profile)

Inspection chooses to measure the 0.6 profile with points every 5 mm along the surface. All points must be within ±0.3.

1.01	+0.22
1.02	+0.18
1.03	+0.20
1.04	+0.19
1.05	+0.18
1.06	+0.15
1.07	+0.14
1.08	+0.02
1.09	+0.03
1.10	+0.05
1.11	+0.01
1.12	-0.02
1.13	-0.05
1.14	-0.05
1.15	-0.07
1.16	-0.03
1.17	-0.05
1.18	+0.03
1.19	+0.02
1.20	+0.05

The deviation on points 1.06 to 1.08 dropped too quickly and fails the per unit area

The dynamic profile may be checked by evaluating each spread of 3 points (since they were taken at 5 mm increments). The difference in the spread shall not vary more than 0.1.

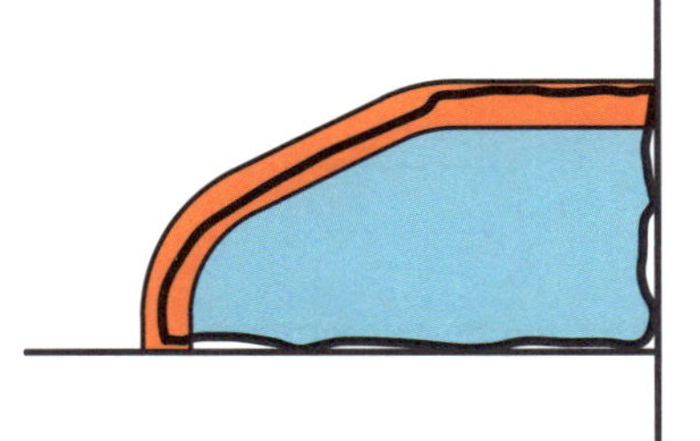

The reporting of the XYZ locations for each of the deviation points could be helpful for the rate of change evaluation.

Inspection Report

ID#	Tolerance Type	Allowed Tolerance	Min/Max Deviations	Measured Value	Pass/ Fail
1	Prof	0.6	-0.07/+0.22	0.44	Pass
2	Prof dyn	0.1	+0.15/+0.02	0.13	Fail

Measured profile value = 2x | max deviation | 2x | 0.22 | = 0.44

Measured dynamic profile value = max - min   0.15 - 0.02 = 0.13

Workshop Exercise 11.6 - Composite Profile Stack

Calculate the min and max values for the indicated distances below. All distances with an asterisk (*) should be calculated as originating from the DRF established by the datum targets. All other distances should be calculated as the relationship between the features.

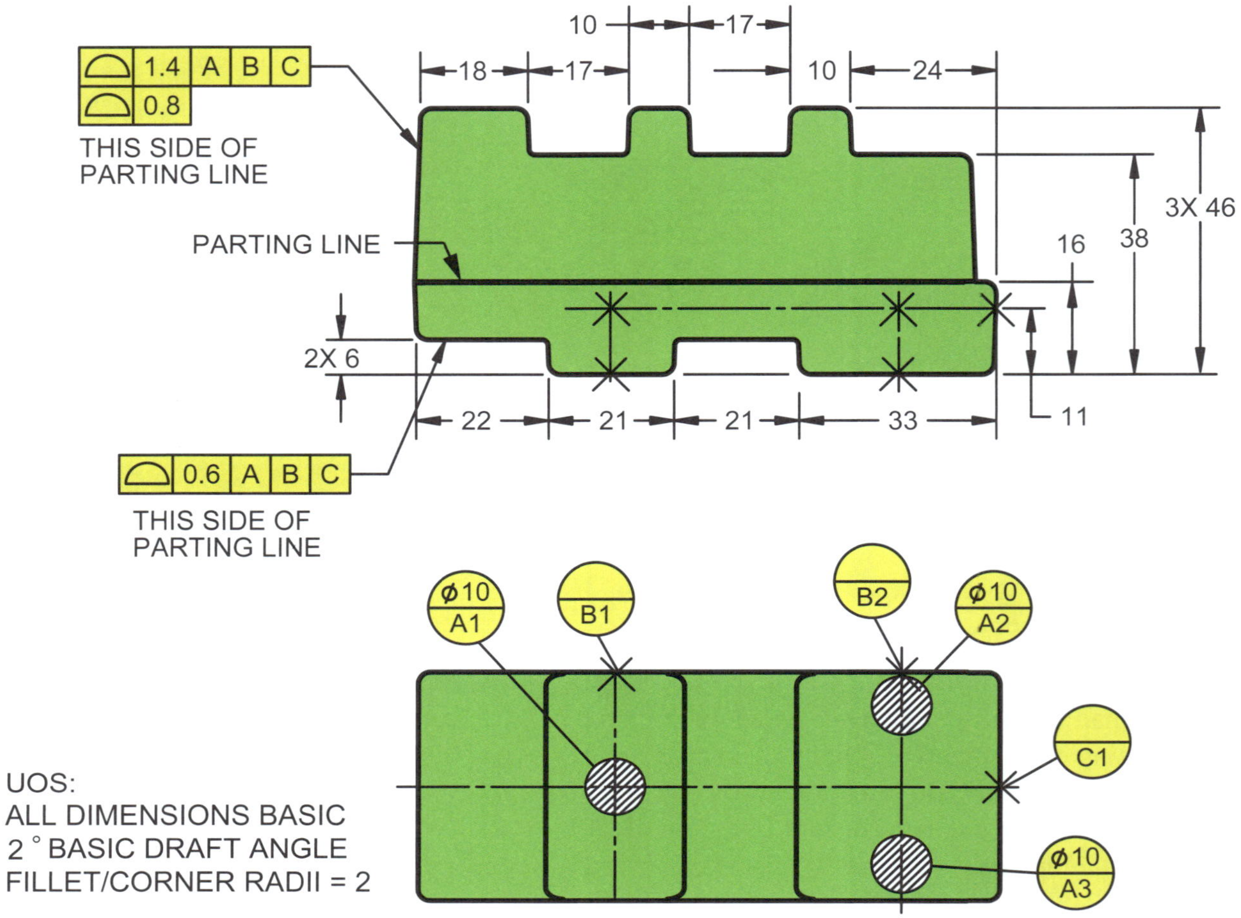

1.4 A B C
0.8
THIS SIDE OF PARTING LINE
PARTING LINE
0.6 A B C
THIS SIDE OF PARTING LINE
10
17
18
17
10
24
3X 46
38
16
11
2X 6
22
21
21
33
Ø10 A1
B1
B2
Ø10 A2
C1
Ø10 A3
UOS:
ALL DIMENSIONS BASIC
2 ° BASIC DRAFT ANGLE
FILLET/CORNER RADII = 2

Min
Max
Min
Max
*Min
*Max
Min
Max
Min
Max
*Min
*Max
*Min
*Max
Min
Max

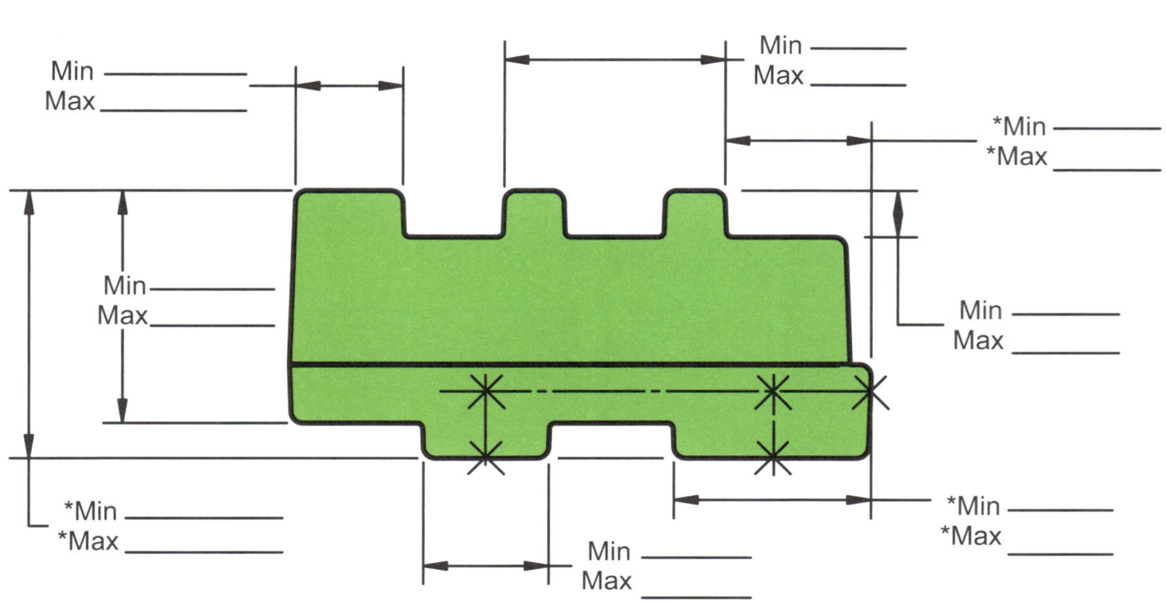

Unit 12

Position Tolerances

Position Tolerancing

Symbol	Tolerance	Common Shape of Tolerance Zone	2D / 3D	Application of Feature Modifier
⌖	Position	Cylindrical 2 Parallel planes Spherical Conical Boundary	3D	Yes

Overview:

The basics of position tolerance have already been explained in earlier units of this text. Position tolerances on holes/pins with RFS, MMC and LMC modifiers are in Unit 3. Position inspection and reporting methods are in Unit 5. Virtual condition boundaries (combination effects of size and position at MMC) are explained in unit 7. This unit 12 only has a short review of the basics before exploring the more advanced and specialized applications of position tolerancing. See these other units and familiarize yourself with those basic concepts before reading this unit.

Position tolerances locate features of size. They define the tolerance in which the center points, axes, median planes, or surfaces may vary from the true (theoretical exact) position. The true position is established with basic dimensions from a datum reference frame.

Position tolerance is a three dimensional control and by default the tolerance zone or boundary extends the full length/depth of the feature. The shape of the tolerance zone depends on the geometry of the feature and other symbols in the feature control frame. The diameter symbol in the frame defines a cylindrical shape tolerance zone. If no symbol is used, the tolerance zone defaults to two parallel planes. The tolerance value always represents a total wide or diameter value, plus/minus values are not allowed in the feature control frame.

Position tolerance values for clearance and threaded holes are often calculated using the floating and fixed fastener formulas shown in this unit.

Position tolerances may be applied at MMC, LMC or RFS. If no modifier is specified, tolerance is implied at RFS (regardless of feature size). Where MMC or LMC modifiers are desired, the symbol is applied in the feature control frame following the feature tolerance. See modifier rules and effect of these modifiers in Unit 3.

Position tolerances may also locate irregular shaped features at MMC or LMC that have no discernible axis or median plane. This does not create a tolerance zone but rather a virtual condition boundary located at true position in which the surface must not violate.

Position tolerances are usually referenced to a datum reference frame. However there are cases, where a group of features have an interrelationship to each other and datum feature references are not necessary. Sometimes multiple position tolerances may be applied to patterns of features to control grouping tighter than to the DRF. This is called composite position and multiple segment position.

Axis Method Versus Surface Method

Position tolerance at MMC is often described as locating the axis or center plane of a feature. The axis of a hole is derived by using the unrelated actual mating envelope (unrelated AME). As the feature departs from MMC, additional location tolerance (bonus) is allowed for the axis. This is called the *axis or center plane method* in ASME Y14.5 (called the *resolved geometry interpretation* in Y14.5.1).

Another method to explain position tolerance with an MMC modifier is through a *surface method* (called the *surface interpretation* in Y14.5.1). The surface of the hole may not violate a virtual condition boundary located at true position. (A virtual condition is the single worst case boundary created by the collective effect of the size and geometric tolerance, see unit 7).

Because of unsymmetrical form variations on a hole (key-hole shaped) the axis method and surface method are not equivalent. The unrelated AME may find the axis outside of the tolerance zone, however the hole may still clear a virtual boundary. The difference in the two interpretations is usually a minor concern, and the axis method is always a more conservative approximation.

The ASME Y14.5-2018 states that if there is a conflict between the two methods, the surface interpretation shall take precedence with geometric tolerances at MMC or LMC. Geometric tolerances at RFS are defined with the axis or center plane method.

The axis method is most often used in industry for position at MMC because of past history and ease of explanation. Another big reason is the collection of variable data. A CMM or open set up inspection measures the feature and reports the size and XY locations of the axis for process control. The surface method for inspection does not give this type of data, but is most commonly used in functional gaging. Either method for inspection is fine, but understand the axis method may reject conforming features with extreme form deviations.

This concept of axis versus surface was first recognized in the ANSI Y14.5M-1982 standard. The latest ASME Y14.5-2018 has revised a lot of figures to show the virtual boundaries for the hole surfaces rather than the tolerance zones to be more in line with the actual definition.

See Unit 7 in this text for more information on the definition of virtual condition and the inspection method. See the Y14.5-2018 and Y14.5.1-2019 for more on the differences between these methods.

ISO Position Interpretations

In ISO, geometric tolerances with MMR and LMR modifiers require the surface to clear a MMVC or LMVC boundary (same as ASME). For geometric tolerances applied RFS, the integral feature (derived center) must be within the tolerance zone.

The default condition to establish a derived center of a feature is different than the ASME Y14.5 standard. ASME uses the unrelated actual mating envelope for extracting a feature axis. ISO 14660, part 1 and 2 defines the default extraction process for a derived median line as the centers of a series of least squares circles perpendicular to the axis of the least squares cylinder. If another method is desired, such as minimum inscribed, maximum circumscribed, or global least squares, a modifier must be used. See the appendix for more information of the differences between ASME and ISO definitions.

ISO standards also permit the position symbol to locate planar surfaces. The surface must lie between a tolerance zone of two parallel planes. However, curved surfaces must be located with profile tolerance. ASME standards do not allow position to locate surfaces.

Position - Cylindrical Tolerance Zone

Position tolerance locates features of size. It defines a tolerance zone within which the feature axis or centerplane must lie. The size of this tolerance zone is equal to the amount of variation allowed from the true (theoretically exact) position. Basic dimensions establish the true position from the specified datum reference frame, which also controls the interrelationship between the features.

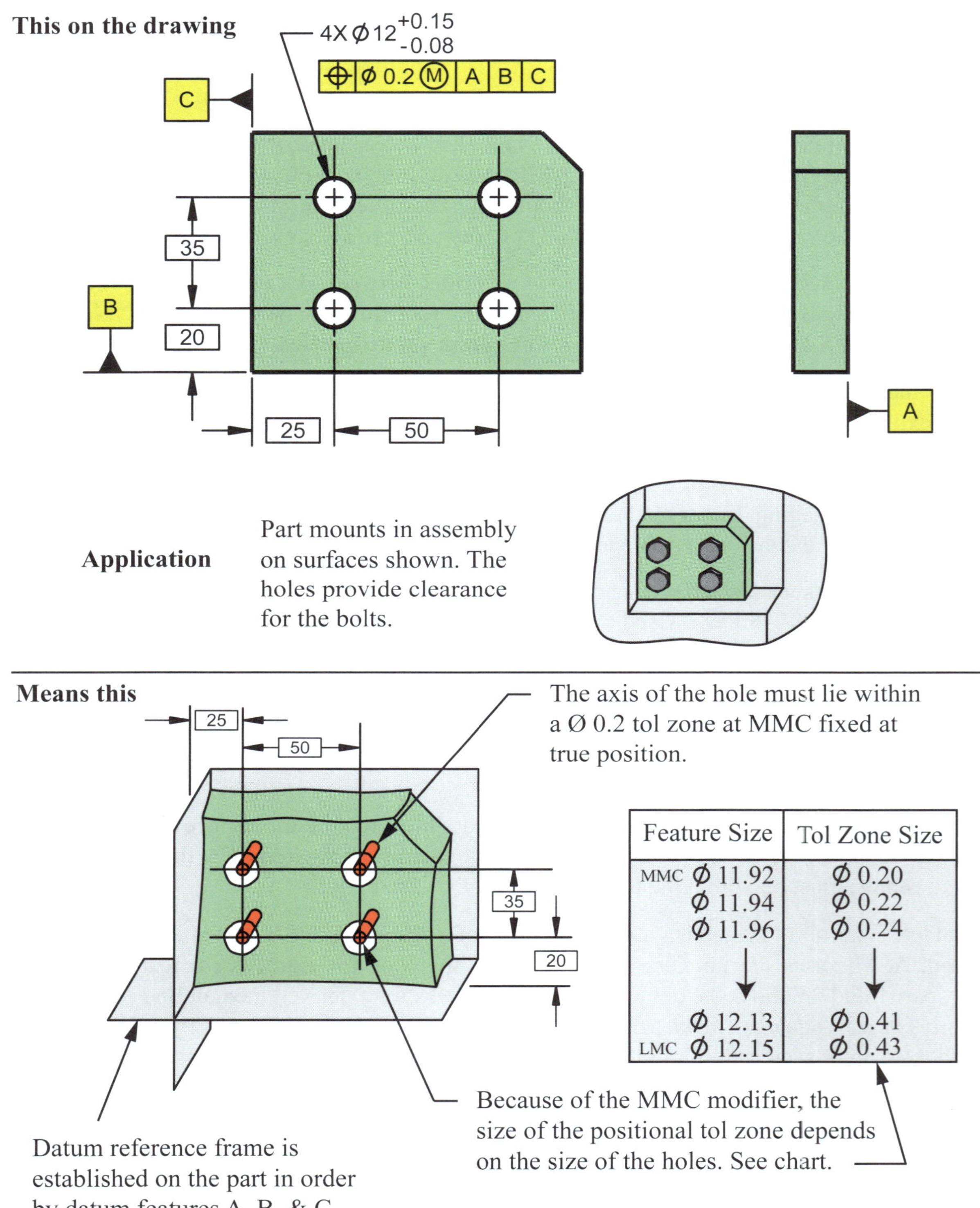

Feature Size	Tol Zone Size
MMC Ø 11.92	Ø 0.20
Ø 11.94	Ø 0.22
Ø 11.96	Ø 0.24
↓	↓
Ø 12.13	Ø 0.41
LMC Ø 12.15	Ø 0.43

The graphic below shows the sectioned imperfect part from the previous page. The theoretical 3D cylindrical tolerance zones control the location and orientation of the hole axes. These axes can be simulated with a gage pin, CMM, or other methods.

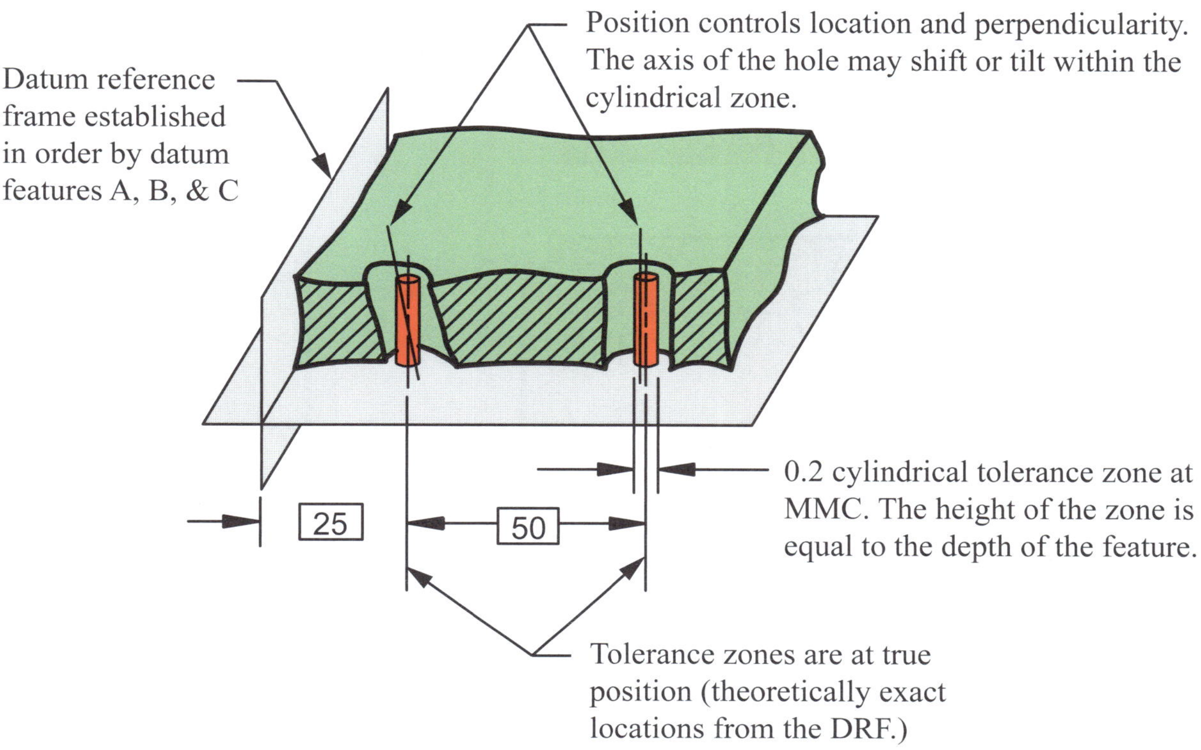

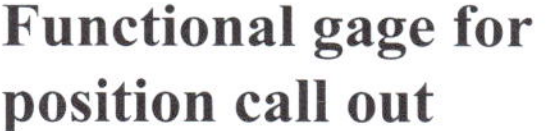

Functional gage for position call out

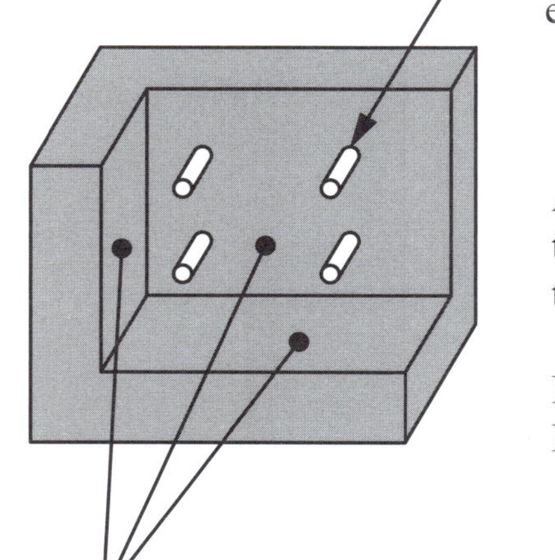

A functional gage is a good tool to understand a position tolerance at MMC. The gage pins are 3D boundaries at true position that the holes must clear.

Position can be checked by other methods also. See Position Verification in unit 5 and 7, for more information.

Floating Fastener Formula

The floating fastener formula is used by the designer to calculate position tolerance for mating features. A floating fastener case is when both parts have clearance holes and the fastener can "float" and is not fixed in either part. Common floating fastener examples are assemblies that use bolts with nuts, or rivets. See the drawings and example calculation below. See the next page for more explanation.

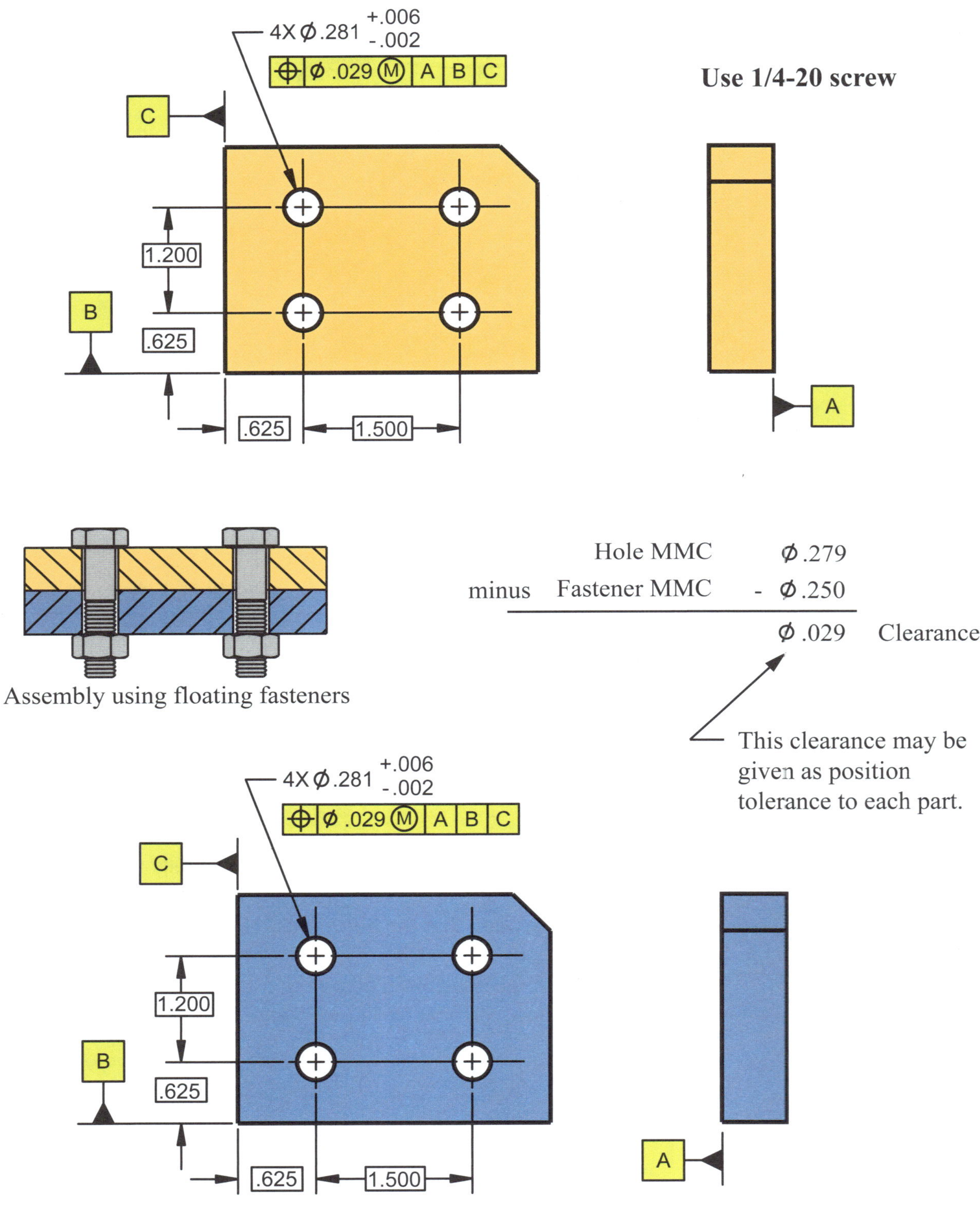

Assembly using floating fasteners

Floating Fastener Formula

A floating fastener case is in an assembly where all parts have clearance holes and the fastener is a bolt with nut (or rivet).

The floating fastener formula is used to determine the position tolerances of mating features to ensure assembly. It will give a "no interference and no clearance" fit when all features are at MMC and at the extreme position. Additional consideration may need to be given for variables not accounted for in this formula, such as non-matching datum reference frames to mating parts.

The two flat plates on the previous page fasten together using four .250 screws and nuts. Basic dimensions define the location of the holes.

To determine the position tolerances, calculate the difference between the smallest hole (MMC) and the biggest bolt (MMC). This clearance is the allowable position tolerance that may be applied to each part. The MMC modifier is also applied to allow additional positional tolerance (bonus tolerance) as the features depart from MMC.

Use standard hole sizes: The floating fastener assembly uses four 1/4-20 UNC screws. These .250 MMC screws have clearance holes in the mating parts at .279-.287 diameter. The clearance holes are produced by a standard drill size of .281 (1/32 larger) with +.007/-.002 size tolerance. This standard tooling size helps reduce cost in manufacturing.

Unequal size tolerance: Standard drilled holes usually have a nominal size, with the plus tolerance larger than the minus tolerance. As a drilling tool wears, it wobbles/wanders making the hole larger. The designer uses this unequal size tolerance to give more life to the tools and reduce manufacturing cost. It also works in the design's favor because the MMC size is used for the fastener formula.

Exercise: The shim below fits in the floating fastener assembly on the previous page. Use the formula to calculate the max position tolerance and insure assembly. Also apply the correct material condition modifier.

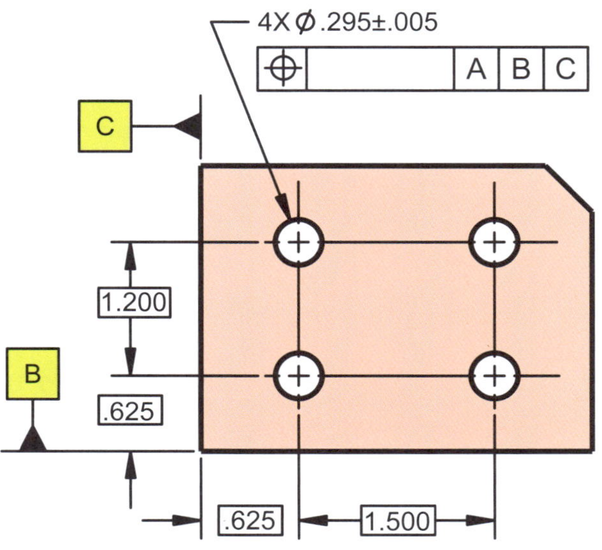

Shim fitting in **floating** fastener assembly on previous page.

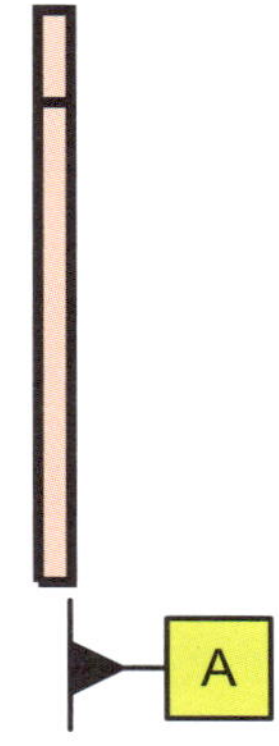

Fixed Fastener Formula

The fixed fastener formula is used by the designer to calculate position tolerance for mating features. A fixed fastener case is where one part uses clearance holes and the other uses tapped holes, studs, formed or pressed fit pins. The fastener is "fixed" in one part. See the drawings and example calculation below. See the next page for more explanation.

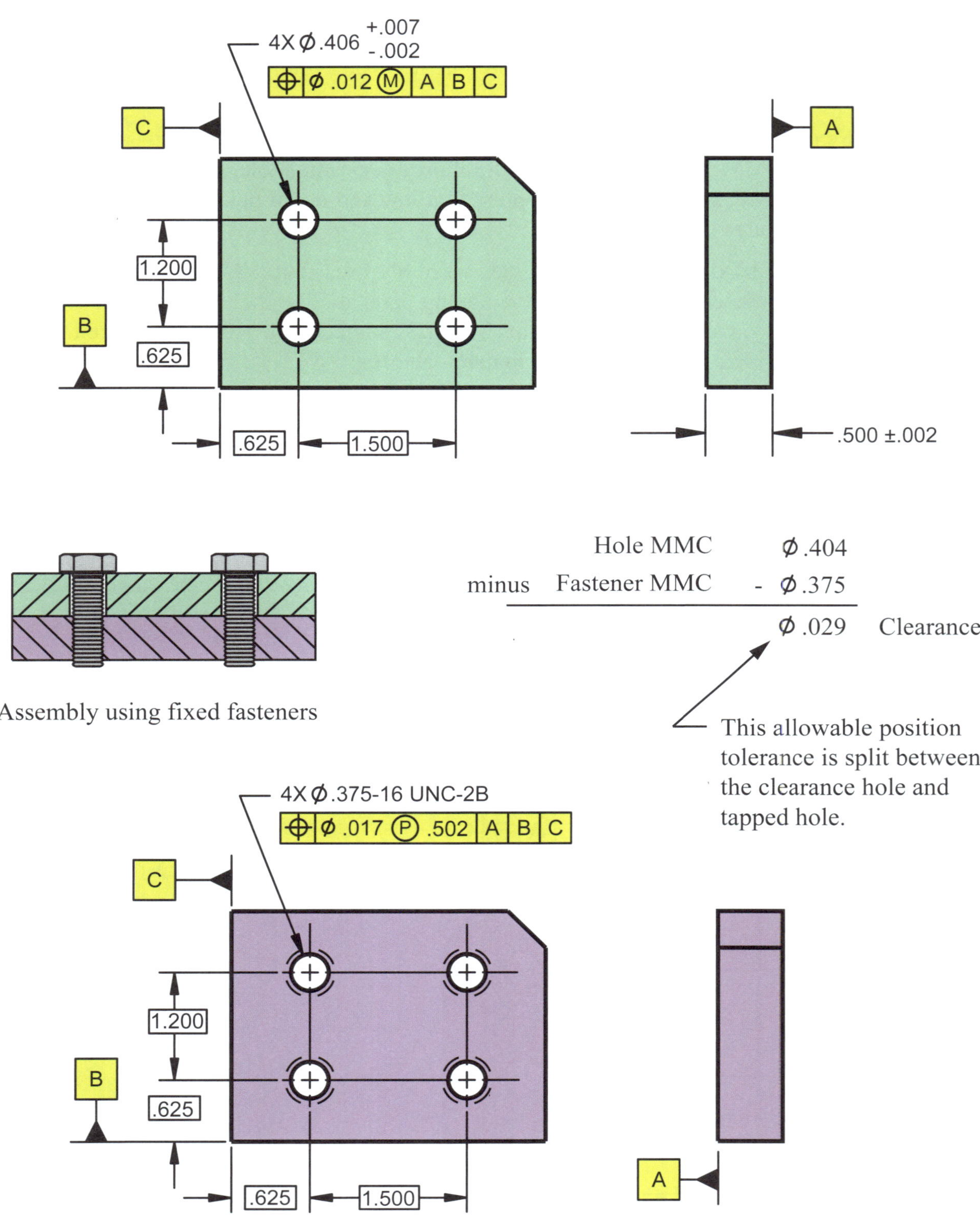

Assembly using fixed fasteners

Fixed Fastener Formula

The fixed fastener formula is used to determine the position tolerances of mating features to ensure assembly. It will give a "no interference and no clearance" fit when all features are at MMC and at the extreme position. Additional consideration may have to be given for variables not accounted for in this formula, such as non-matching datums to mating parts.

The two flat plates on the previous page are fastened together using four .375 screws that fix into tapped holes on one part. Basic dimensions define the location of the holes.

To determine the position tolerances, calculate the difference between the smallest hole (MMC) and the biggest bolt (MMC). This clearance is the allowable position tolerance that must be divided between the two parts in any combination. The tapped hole is usually given a larger share of the position tolerance split for two reasons:

First, the tapped hole is usually two operations - the tap drill and then the tap. This more difficult manufacturing operation could need more tolerance.

Second, and most importantly, the tapped hole is positioned RFS and does not get the benefit of the bonus tolerance provided by the MMC modifier. When the MMC modifier is applied to the clearance hole, it will allow additional positional tolerance as the feature departs from MMC. A threaded hole cannot take advantage of the departure from MMC. Position tolerance for a tapped hole applies to the pitch diameter of the thread. When the bolt is tightened (because of the incline on the threads), it creates a centering effect and negates any extra position tolerance from an MMC departure.

The clearance hole usually has a large size tolerance and because of the MMC modifier, it results in more position tolerance at nominal and mean sizes. To make the positional tolerance more equal, a larger positional tolerance is given to the tapped hole RFS. As a general rule, split the tolerance 60/40. The tapped hole receives 60%, and the clearance hole receives 40%.

To account for perpendicularity problems with the mating bolt, a projected tolerance zone is usually applied to a tapped hole. More explanation of this is shown on the next page.

Exercise: The shim below fits in the fixed fastener assembly on the previous page. Use the formula to calculate the max position tolerance and insure assembly. Also apply the correct material condition modifier.

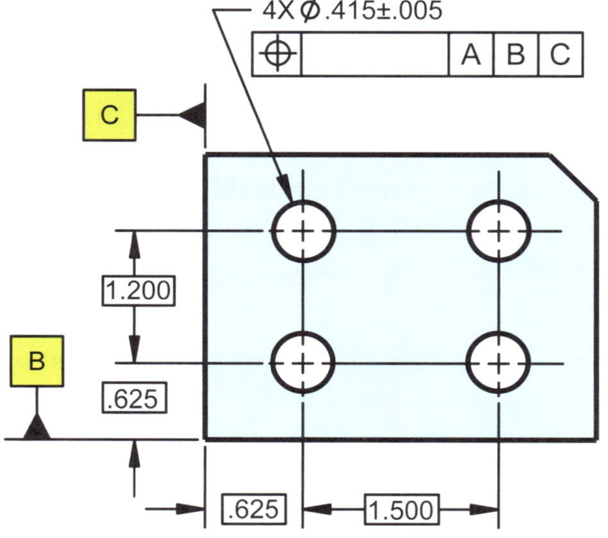

Shim fitting in **fixed** fastener assembly on previous page

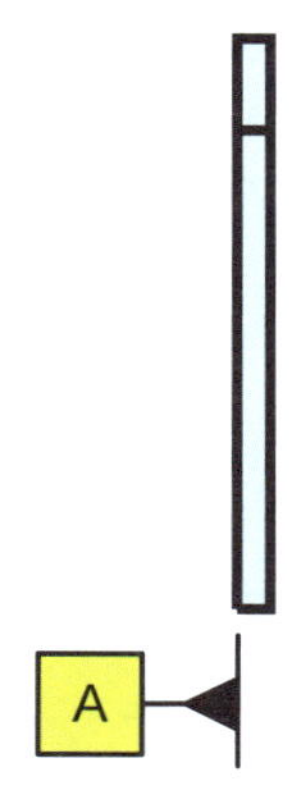

Projected Tolerance Zone

By default, position and perpendicularity tolerance zones extend for the full length/depth of the feature. A projected tolerance zone modifier, circle P, instead projects the tolerance zone outside the hole to a specified height.

The calculations in a fixed fastener formula are assuming the tolerance zones are extending the full depth of the clearance hole and the full length of the mating pin. However, the position tolerance is not always applied to the bolt (pin) but instead the empty threaded hole. When a threaded hole is produced tilted inside its position tolerance zone, the bolt will take the same attitude and project this error as it extends out of the hole to cause interference.

The projected tolerance zone modifier projects the threaded hole position tolerance zone out to match the length of the extended fastener (usually the mating part thickness). This modifier is needed with the calculations in the fixed fastener formula to ensure interchangeability. The location of the threaded holes are only of importance to the extended portion of the engaging fastener.

The height of the projected tolerance zone is usually the thickness of the mating part including any gaskets or shims. The thickness of washers is usually not included because they may float to follow the bolt. If a stud or pin is toleranced as an assembly with the pin or stud installed, a projected tolerance zone is not necessary, as the tolerance extends for the full length of the feature. If the hole is toleranced without the studs or pins installed, then the hole should have a projected zone applied equal to the height of the studs or pins.

Where the direction of the projected tolerance zone is clear, only circle P and height dimension is required in the feature control frame. Where the direction of the projected tolerance zone is not clear, only circle P is placed in the feature control frame, and the dimensioned height value of the projected zone is included on the drawing view with a heavy chain line that is drawn closely adjacent to the center line of the hole.

More on Screw Threads, MMC or RFS?

Position tolerance on a tapped hole applies to the pitch diameter of the thread. This pitch diameter technically has size, and therefore an MMC modifier may be applied. However, when the bolt is tightened (because of the incline on the threads), it creates a centering effect and negates any extra position tolerance from an MMC departure. It is for this functional reason, the position tolerance on a screw thread applies RFS.

Functional gaging of threads

It is often stated that MMC is applied to threads to make it easier to gage. However, the drawing should only define the functional requirements and not the method for verification. If an MMC modifier is applied to the thread, the designer must artificially reduce the position tolerance to account for the functional centering effect of the bolt. Instead it should be positioned RFS with the max calculated position available. Quality then analyzes the measuring equipment available and determines the verification method (documented in the quality plan) with the corresponding measurement uncertainty.

A functional gage shown on the next page can be used to check positioned threads modified at RFS. The threaded gage has "go" threads built at MMC of the pitch diameter. The shoulder on the threaded gage pin is increased to reduce the allowable position tolerance by the amount of the pitch diameter size tolerance.

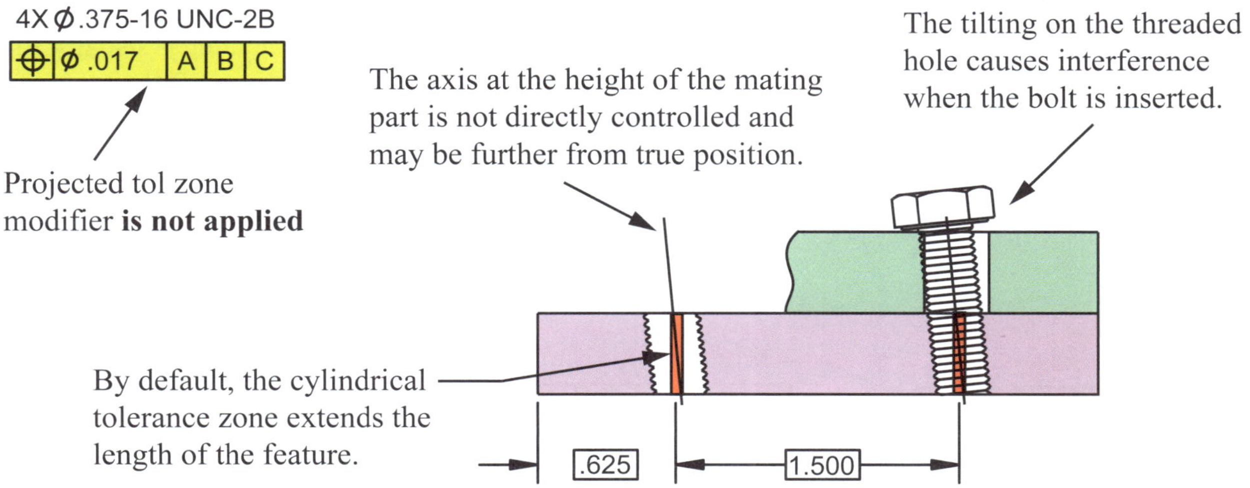

4X Ø.375-16 UNC-2B
⌖ Ø.017 A B C
Projected tol zone modifier **is not applied**
The axis at the height of the mating part is not directly controlled and may be further from true position.
The tilting on the threaded hole causes interference when the bolt is inserted.
By default, the cylindrical tolerance zone extends the length of the feature.
.625
1.500

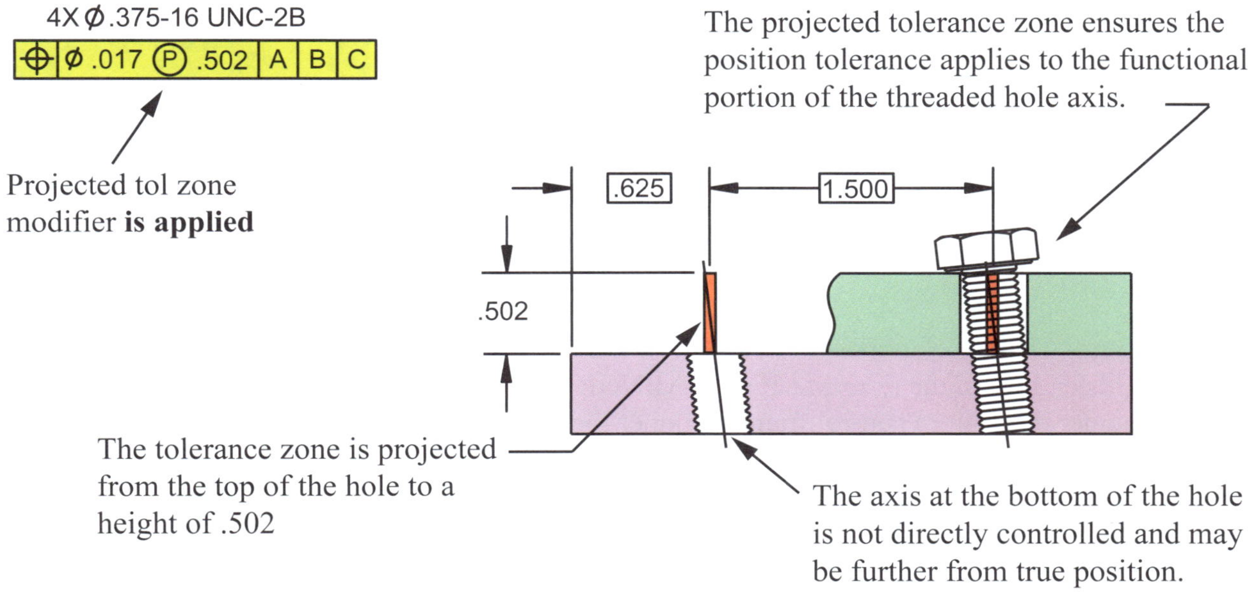

4X Ø.375-16 UNC-2B
⌖ Ø.017 Ⓟ .502 A B C
Projected tol zone modifier **is applied**
The projected tolerance zone ensures the position tolerance applies to the functional portion of the threaded hole axis.
.625
1.500
.502
The tolerance zone is projected from the top of the hole to a height of .502
The axis at the bottom of the hole is not directly controlled and may be further from true position.

Functional Gage

Inspection uses a thread gage to simulate a "perfect" bolt in the threaded hole.
Clearance between gage shoulder pin and hole = Ø .017 (tapped hole position tol)
.502 min
Thread gage with slits to expand in the tapped hole. (RFS)
Fixed MMC size thread "go" gage, may "wiggle" in actual tapped hole.
Gage has edges to simulate datums A, B, & C
4X Ø.375-16 UNC thread

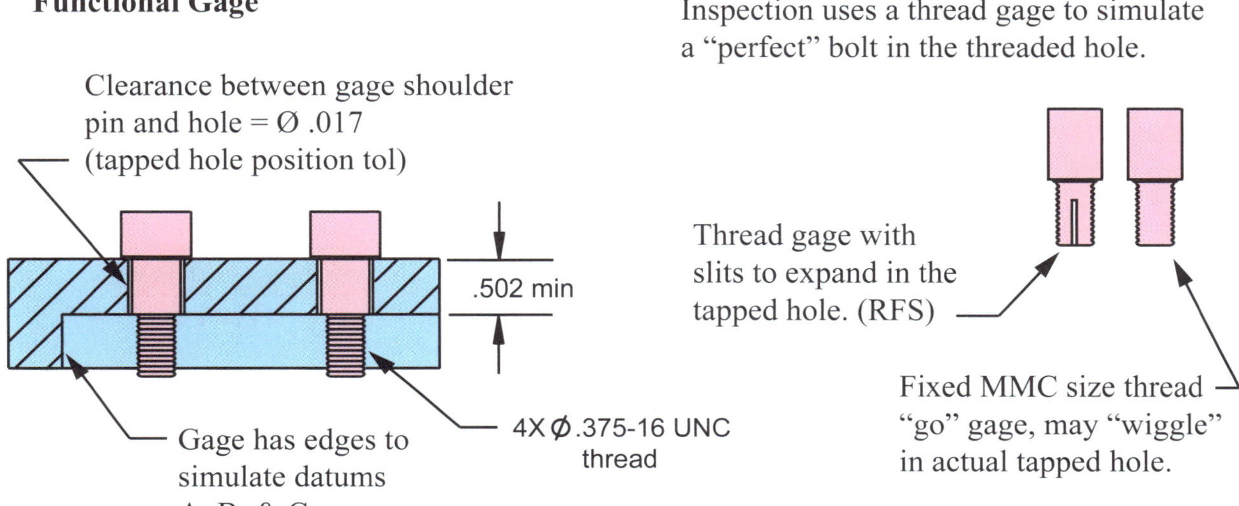

Screw Thread Rule - Gear and Spline Rule

Screw Thread Rule:

A screw thread has three diameters: major, minor, and pitch. The pitch diameter is usually the theoretical functional mating diameter, and according to both the ASME Y14.5-2018 and ISO 1101 standards, geometric tolerances apply to this pitch diameter by default.

Thread wires, thread gages or CMM thread traces may be used to establish this axis in inspection. However, with a large enough tolerance, sometimes quality will measure from the major or minor for ease of inspection and reduce the allowable tolerance (guard-band the tolerance limit).

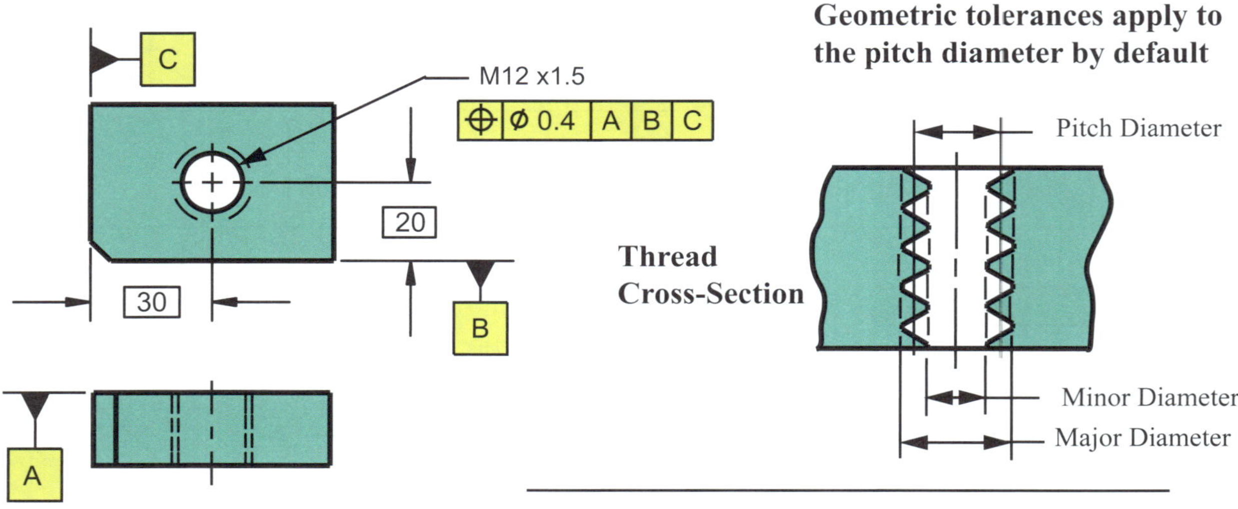

The geometric tolerance applies to the major or minor diameter instead when the term MAJOR or MINOR diameter is stated under the feature control frame or under the datum feature symbol. The example to the right illustrates a position tolerance applied to the major diameter and a datum feature reference applied to the pitch diameter.

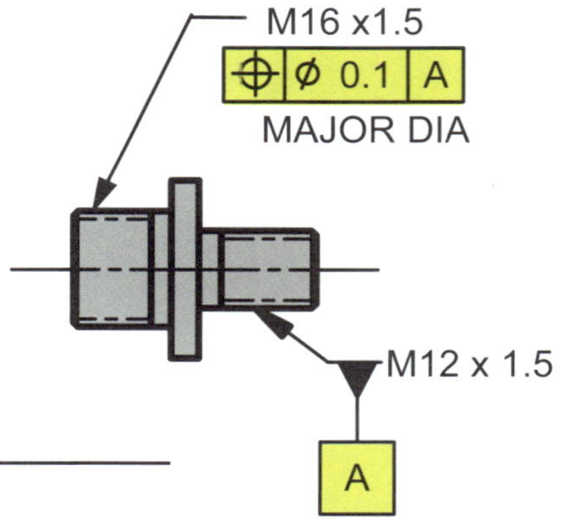

Gear and Spline Rule

According to the ASME Y14.5-2018 and ISO 1101 standard, each geometric tolerance specified for gears and splines shall designate the specific feature to which each applies. The required diameter (MAJOR DIA, PITCH DIA, or MINOR DIA) should be stated beneath the feature control frame or beneath or adjacent to the datum feature symbol. (ISO: MD, LD, PD)

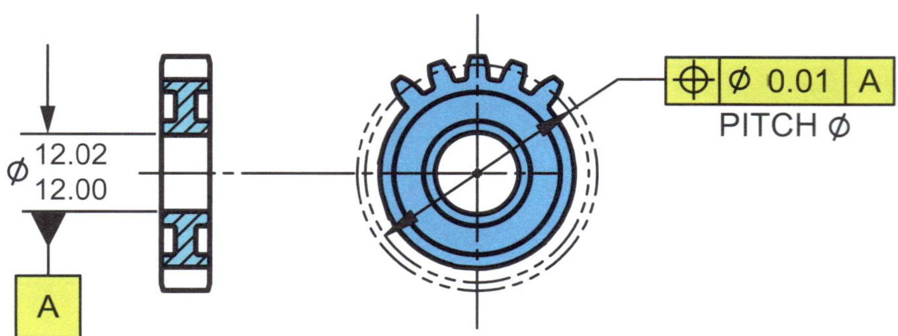

Workshop Exercise 12.1 - Fastener Formula

Fill out the feature control frame on each part drawing below to ensure interchangeability during assembly. Calculate the tolerance using the correct fastener formula. Be sure to include any applicable modifiers.

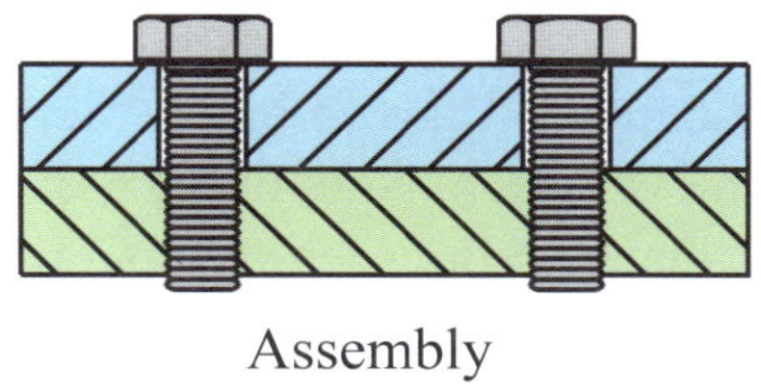

Assembly

Part 1

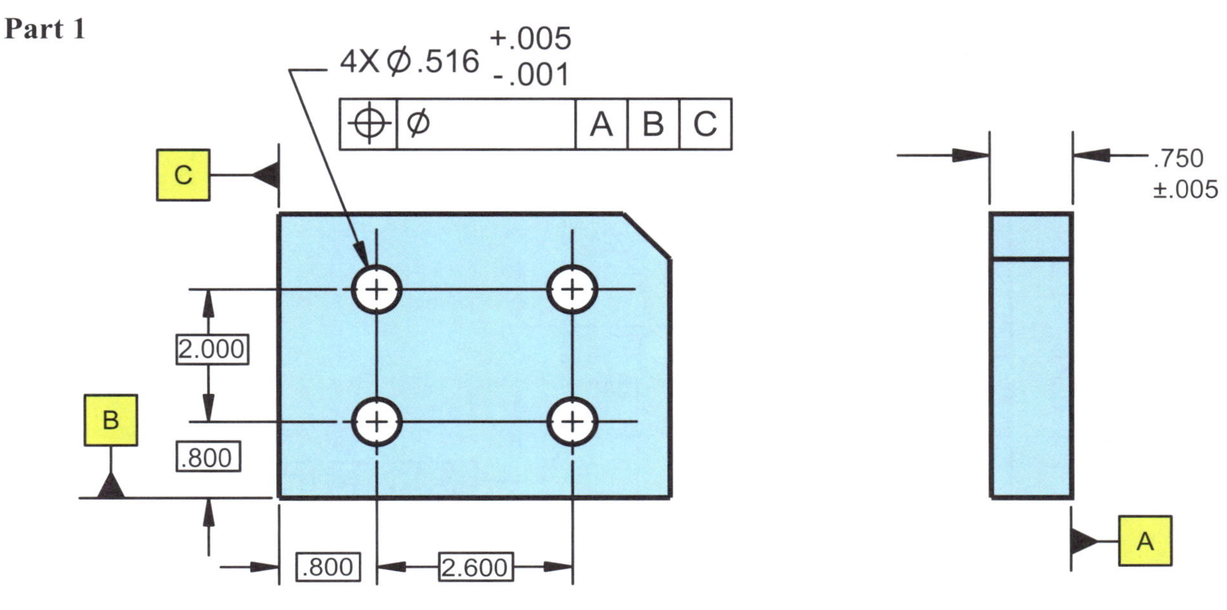

Part 2

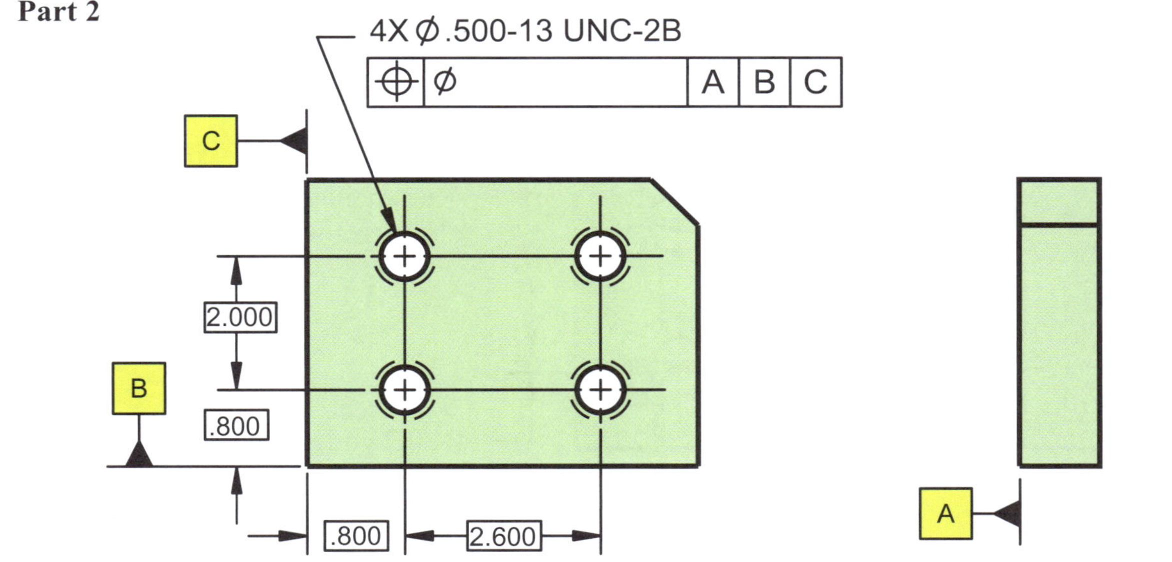

Position - Rectangular Tolerance Zone

A feature may be located or oriented within a tighter tolerance in one direction than the other by the method shown below. Separate feature control frames indicate the direction and magnitude of the variation. Note that the diameter symbol is not present in the feature control frames indicating a distance between two parallel planes. An MMC modifier may also be used. This is a common way to locate slotted holes.

This on the drawing

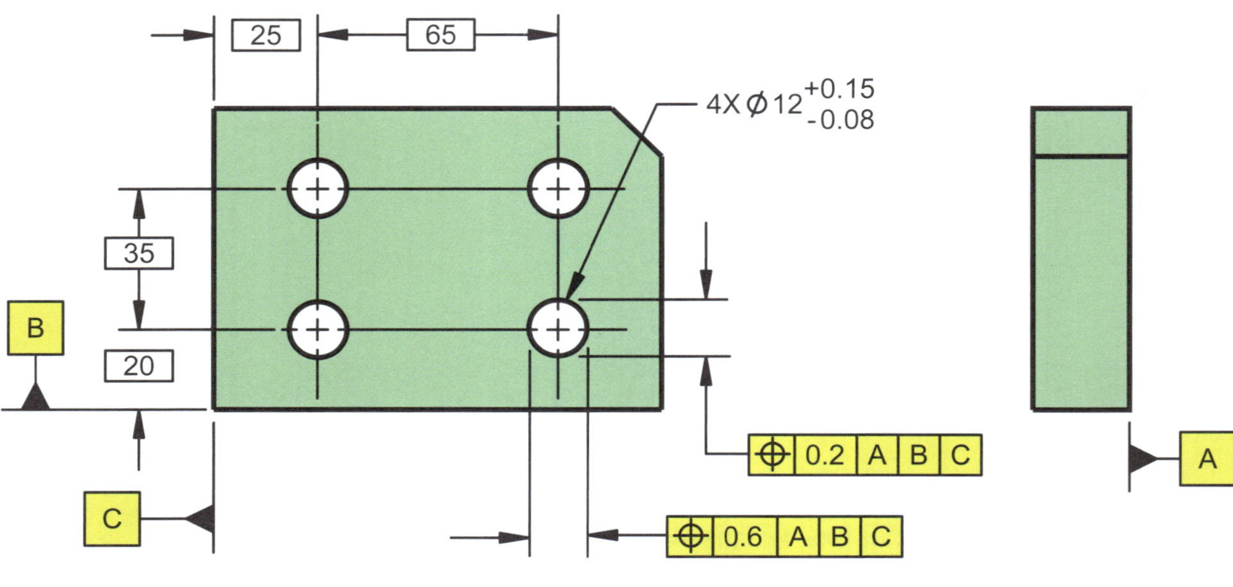

Means this

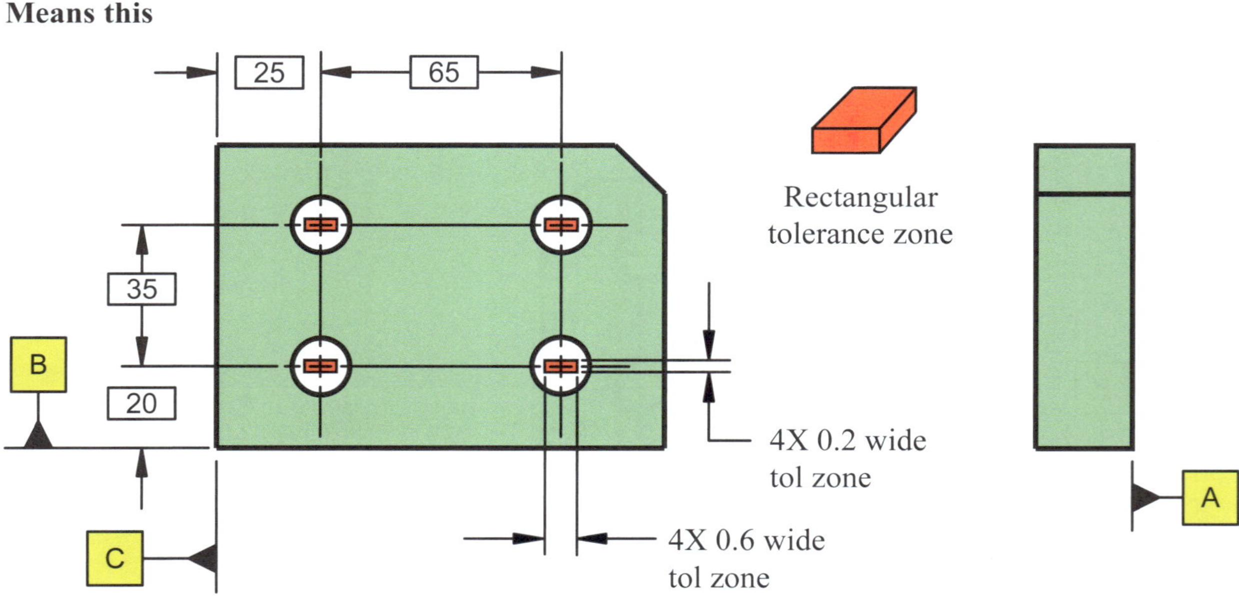

The axes of the holes must lie within the 0.2 X 0.6 rectangular tolerance zones basically located to the datum reference frame.

Position - Two Parallel Planes Zone - Location of Slots

Slot features may be located with either position or profile. A slot is a feature of size and the center plane may be located with position, or one side of the slot may be located with profile. Compare the examples below. The function of the part should dictate the method.

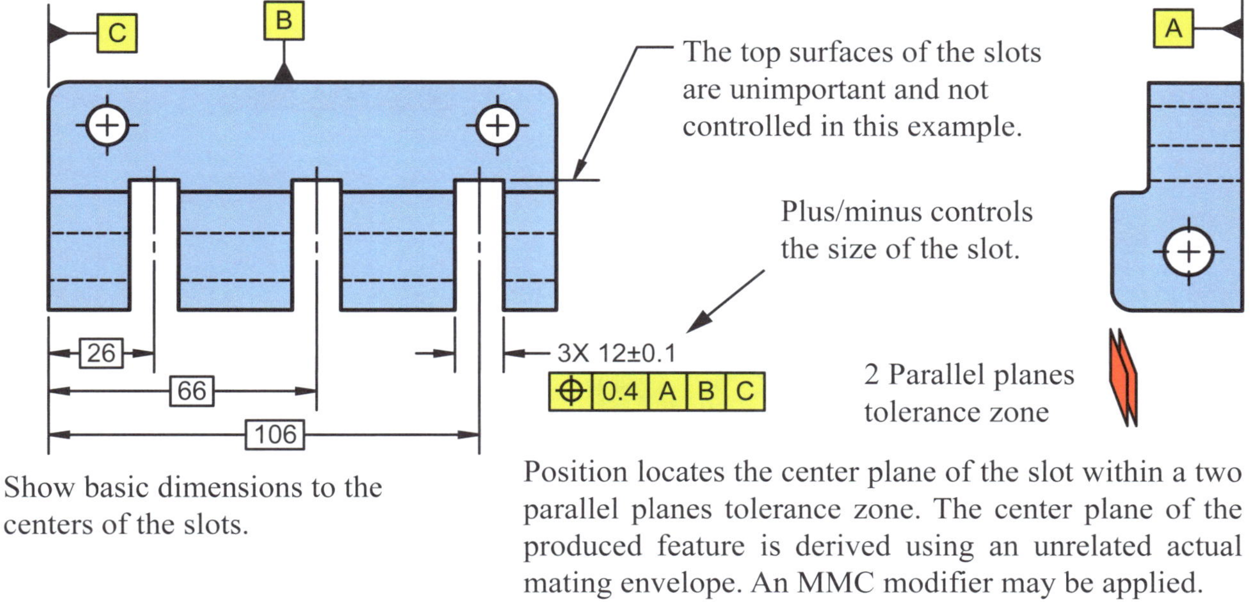

Show basic dimensions to the centers of the slots.

Position locates the center plane of the slot within a two parallel planes tolerance zone. The center plane of the produced feature is derived using an unrelated actual mating envelope. An MMC modifier may be applied.

Use this method when the mating part must be centered in the slots. One side is not more important than the other. This is common in symmetrical parts.

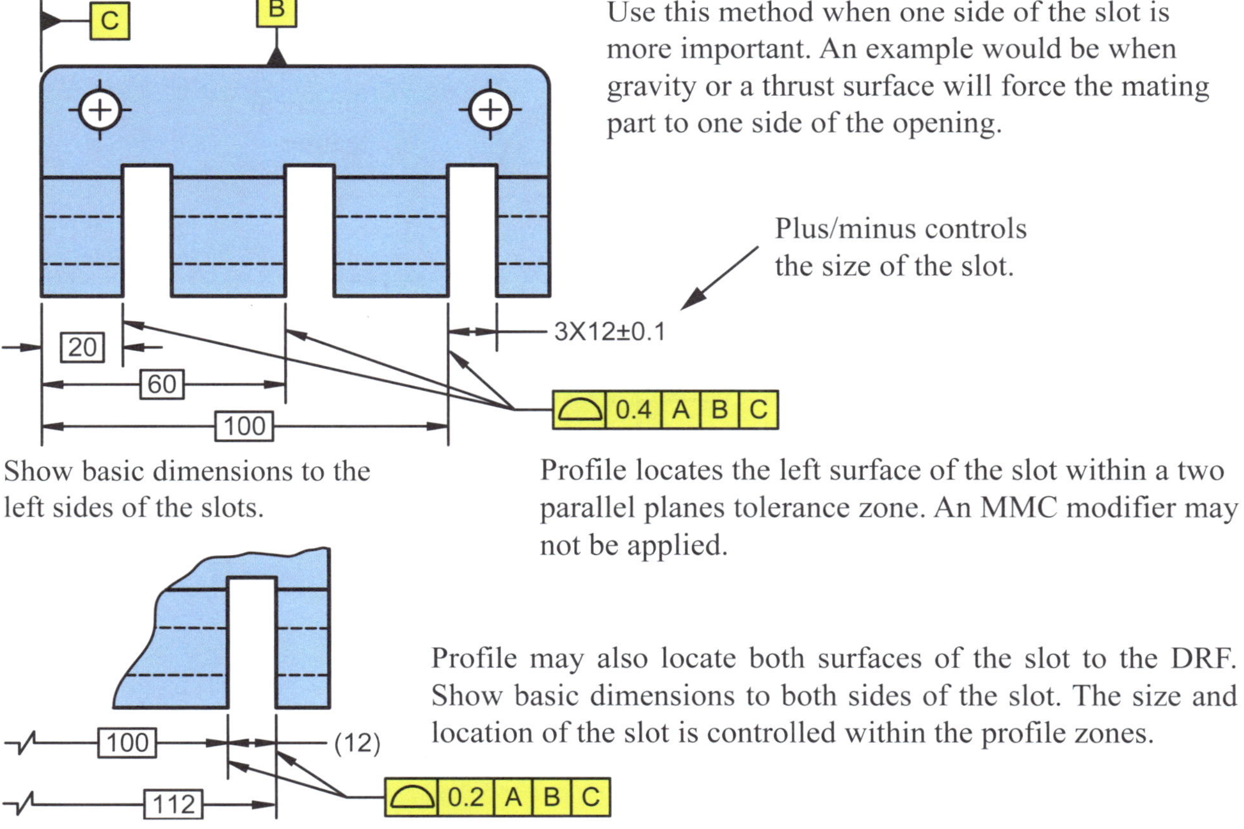

Use this method when one side of the slot is more important. An example would be when gravity or a thrust surface will force the mating part to one side of the opening.

Show basic dimensions to the left sides of the slots.

Profile locates the left surface of the slot within a two parallel planes tolerance zone. An MMC modifier may not be applied.

Profile may also locate both surfaces of the slot to the DRF. Show basic dimensions to both sides of the slot. The size and location of the slot is controlled within the profile zones.

Position - Spherical Tolerance Zone

Position tolerancing may be used to control the location of a spherical feature. The symbol for spherical diameter precedes the size dimension to indicate a spherical feature. The SØ is also entered before the feature tolerance in the feature control frame to indicate the shape of the position tolerance zone is a sphere.

This on the drawing

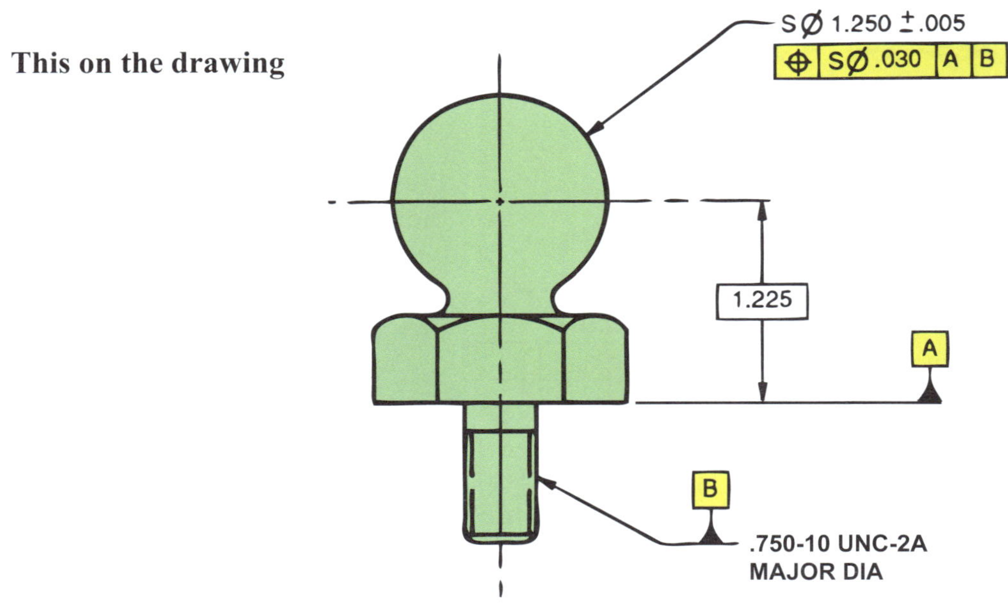

Means this

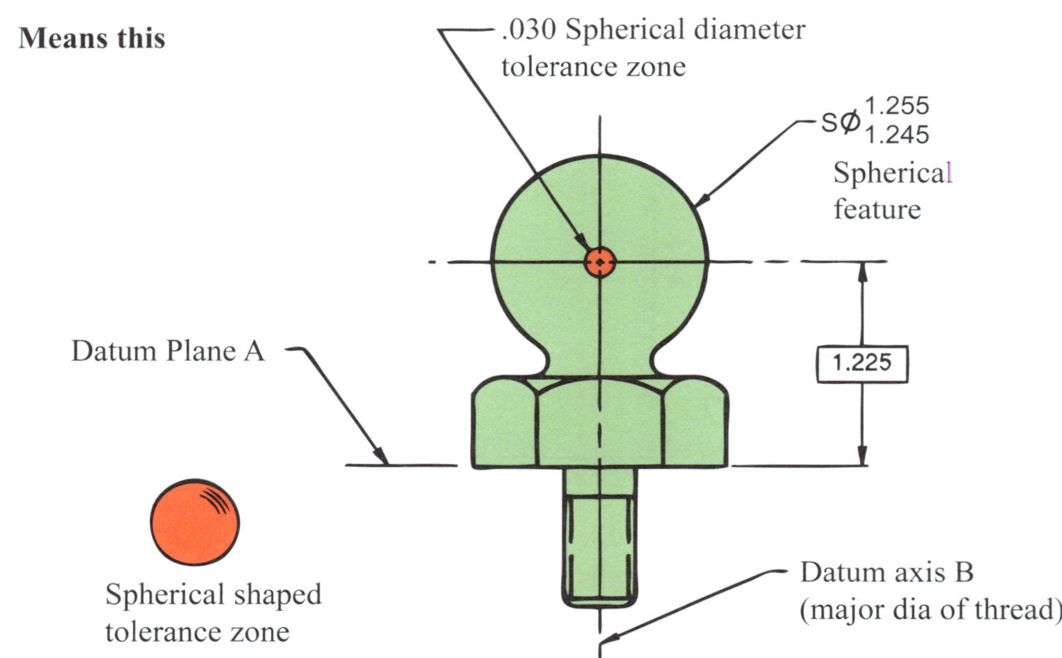

The center point of the spherical diameter must lie within a spherical diameter zone of .030 basically located to the datum reference frame.

$$\text{Actual position} = 2\sqrt{\Delta x^2 + \Delta y^2 + \Delta z^2}$$

Position - Conical Tolerance Zone

Position tolerance may control a feature tighter at one end than the other. The center hole in the manifold below needs to be closely located where it meets a port but can be allowed more location tolerance at the far end. Two surfaces are labeled on the drawing as SURFACE X and SURFACE Y and two feature control frames are shown under the feature size. One defines a small .010 circular tolerance at Surface Y, the other defines a larger .060 circular tolerance at Surface X. The result is a conical shaped tolerance zone for the feature axis.

Application

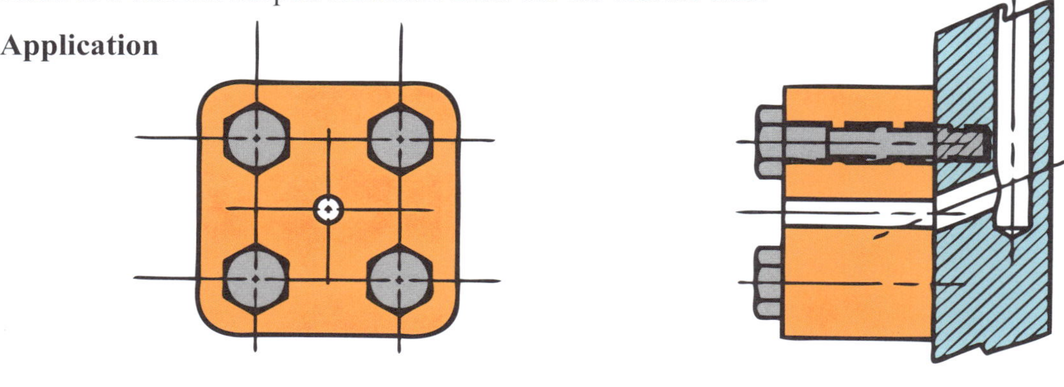

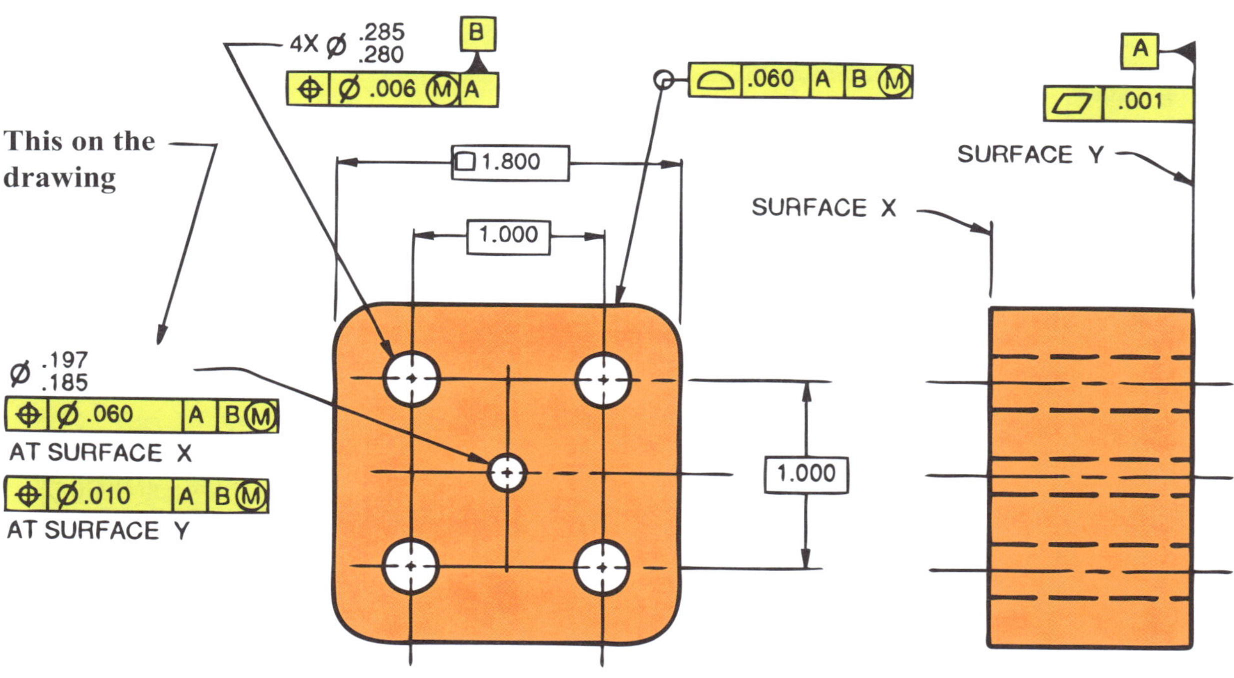

Means This

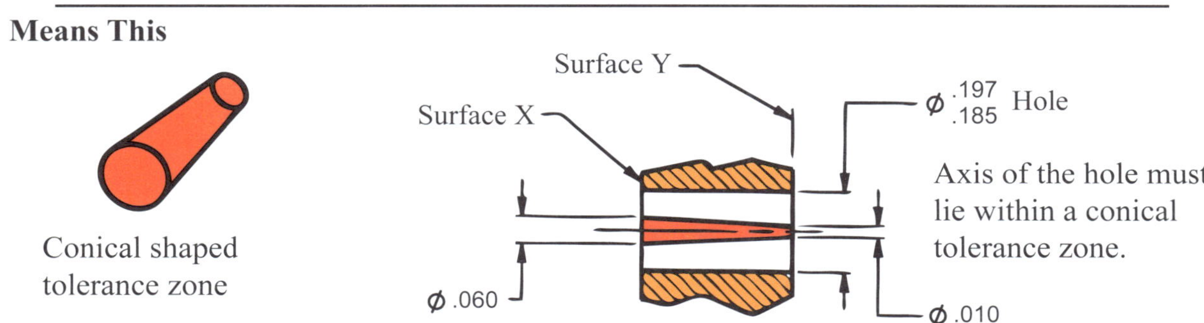

Position Boundary

Position tolerance may locate irregular features of size. Rather than locating the axis or median plane of the feature, a virtual condition boundary is established that the feature surface may not violate. In the drawing below, a DRF is established by the back surface, height, and width. The profile tolerance on the irregular opening defines the size, form, and orientation to datum A. The position tolerance controls the location of the feature. It defines a virtual condition boundary in which the surface must clear. The MMC or LMC modifier should be applied. Position of an irregular feature of size at RFS is not supported (consider a composite profile instead).

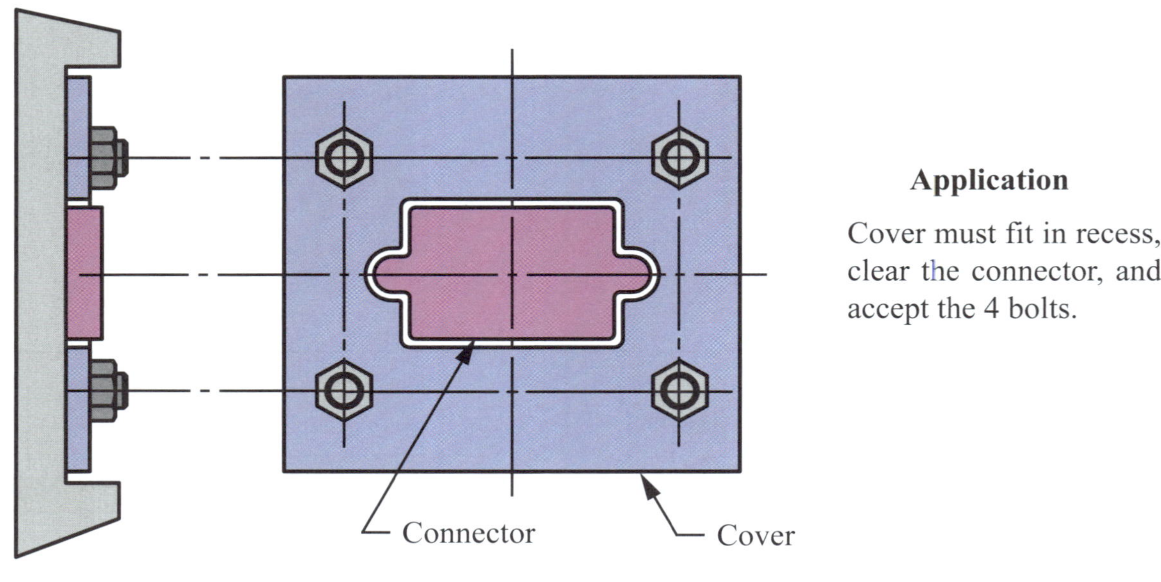

Application

Cover must fit in recess, clear the connector, and accept the 4 bolts.

This on the drawing

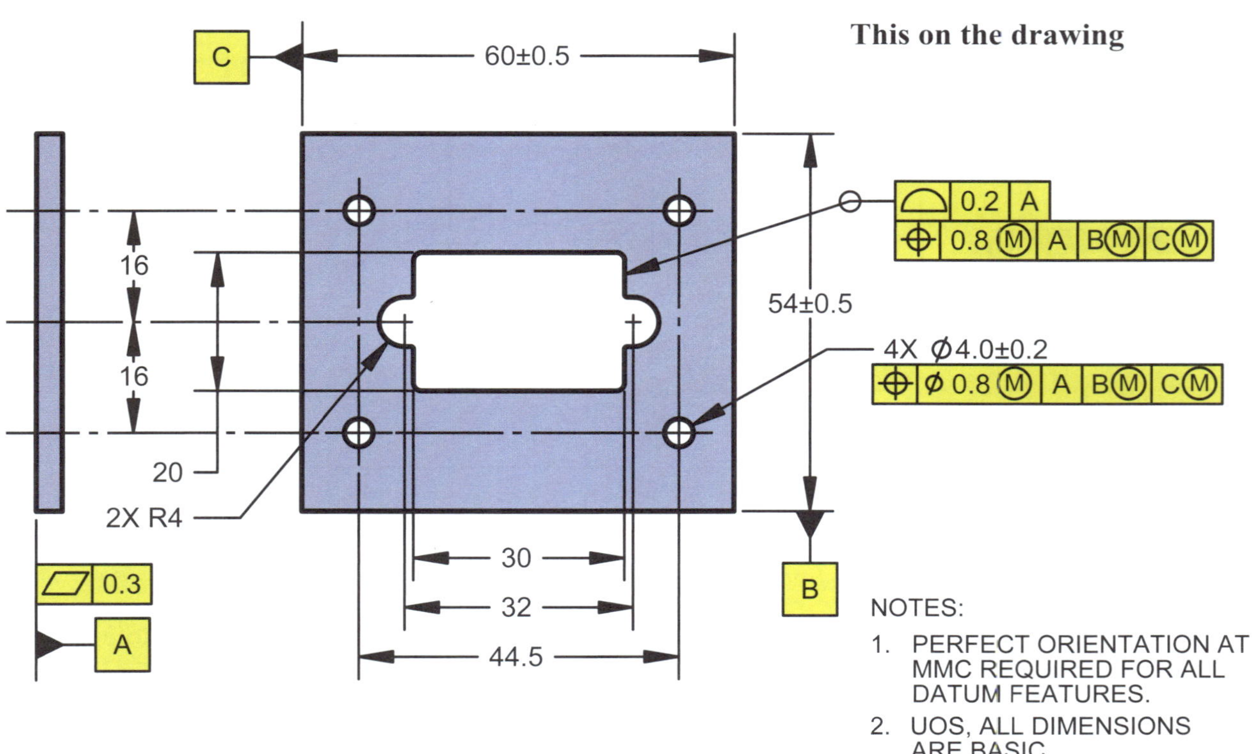

NOTES:

1. PERFECT ORIENTATION AT MMC REQUIRED FOR ALL DATUM FEATURES.
2. UOS, ALL DIMENSIONS ARE BASIC.

Means this

⌓	0.2	A

The profile requirement controls the size, form, and orientation of the feature.

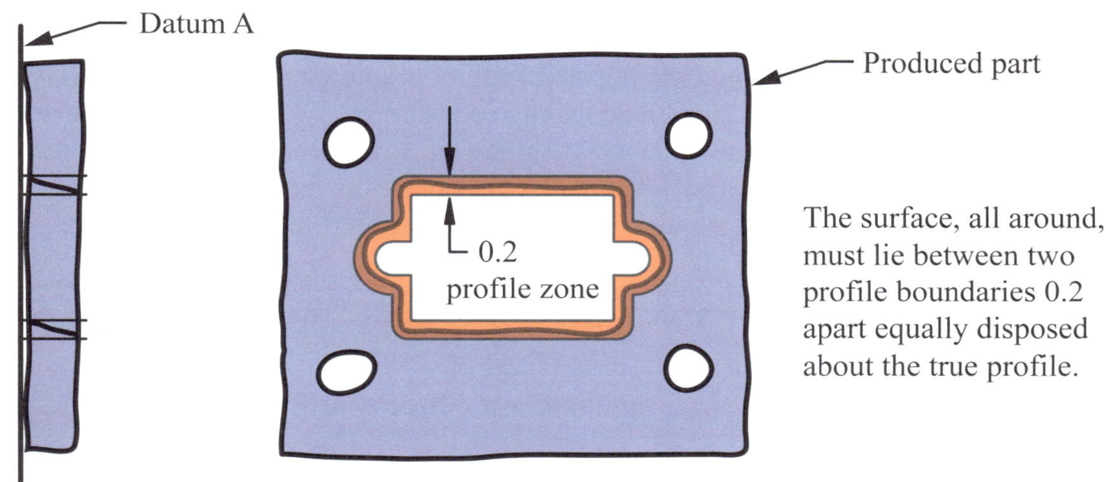

⌖	0.8 Ⓜ	A	BⓂ	CⓂ

The position requirement locates the feature to the DRF.

No portion of the surface may lie inside the virtual condition boundary created by the smallest profile boundary minus the position tolerance. This boundary is located at true position to the DRF.

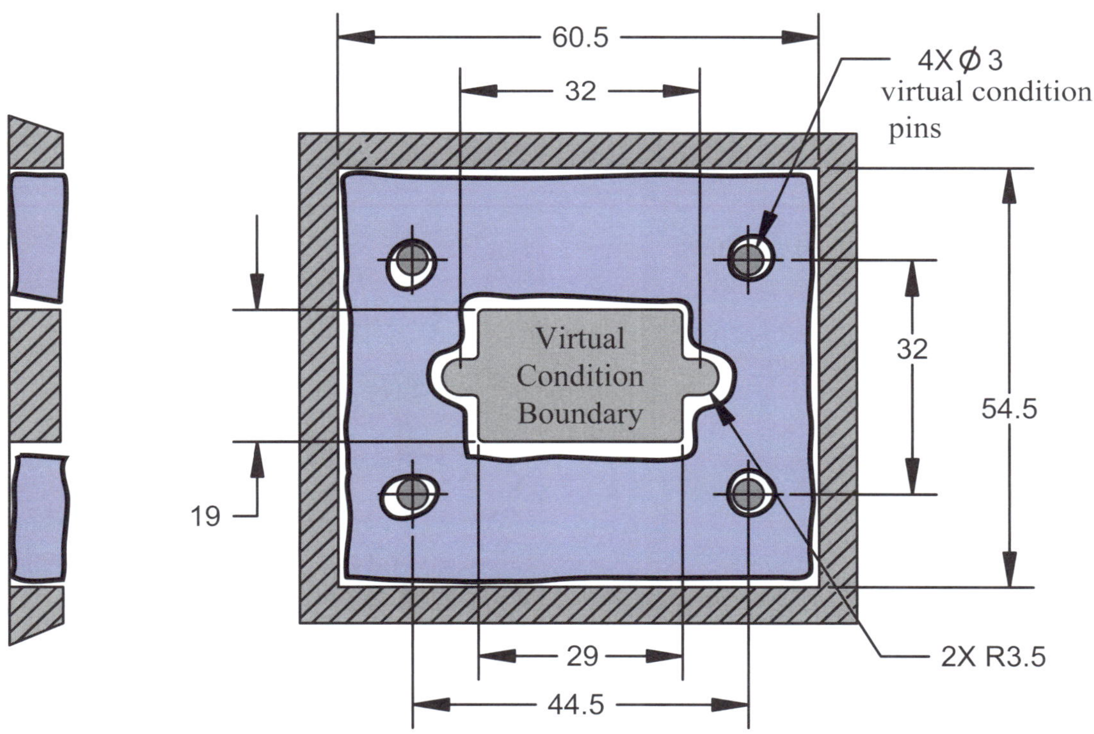

Position boundary for locating irregular features of size is a similar concept to composite profile. However, position with an MMC or LMC modifier defines only a single virtual boundary that the surface may not violate. While composite profile creates both an MMB and a LMB in which the feature must lie. See composite profile in unit 11.

Composite Tolerancing vs. Two Single Segments

A pattern of features of size may have multiple levels of positional control required. The pattern of features may require a larger tolerance relative to the datum reference frame and a smaller tolerance within the pattern. This may be accomplished with a composite feature control frame or with multiple separate position frames. Each segment may be verified separately, but the lower segment is a subset of the upper segment.

In composite position tolerancing, the position symbol is entered once for both horizontal entries and is different than two single segmented feature control frames. With a composite feature control frame, the tolerance zones in the upper segment are constrained in translation and rotation to the specified DRF (like normal). The tolerance zones in the lower segment still control location between the features, but are constrained in rotation only to the specified DRF.

In contrast, all single segment position frames control the location between the features and are constrained in translation and rotation to the specified DRF. This is interpreted as two separate position requirements.

The next pages will go into the details of these two different methods of grouping features.

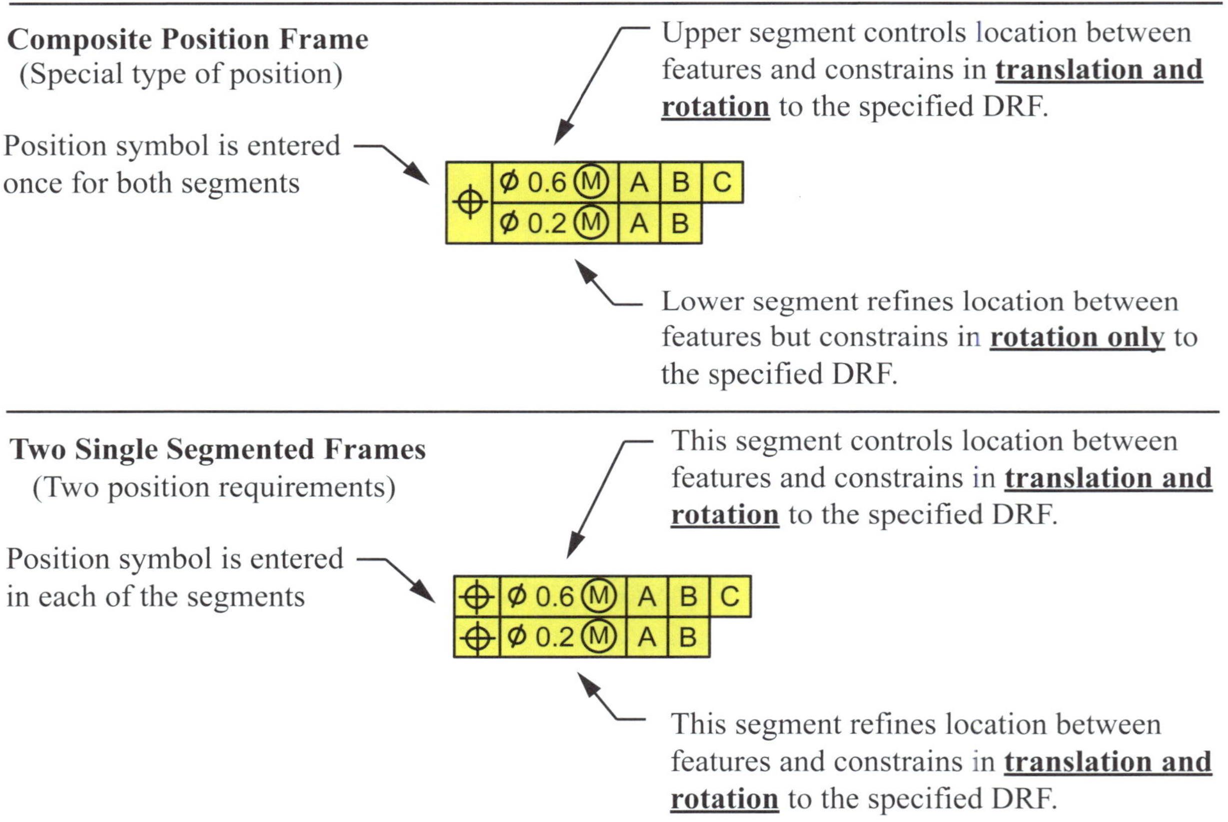

Another notable difference between these two specifications is with simultaneous requirements. The lower segments of composite tolerancing are exempt from the default simultaneous requirement. If lower segments of different composite feature control frames must be linked, the notation "SIM REQT" must be placed next to the lower frame.

Conversely, the stand-alone lower positions of different patterns are still linked with a simultaneous requirement. They may be separated with the notation "SEP REQT".

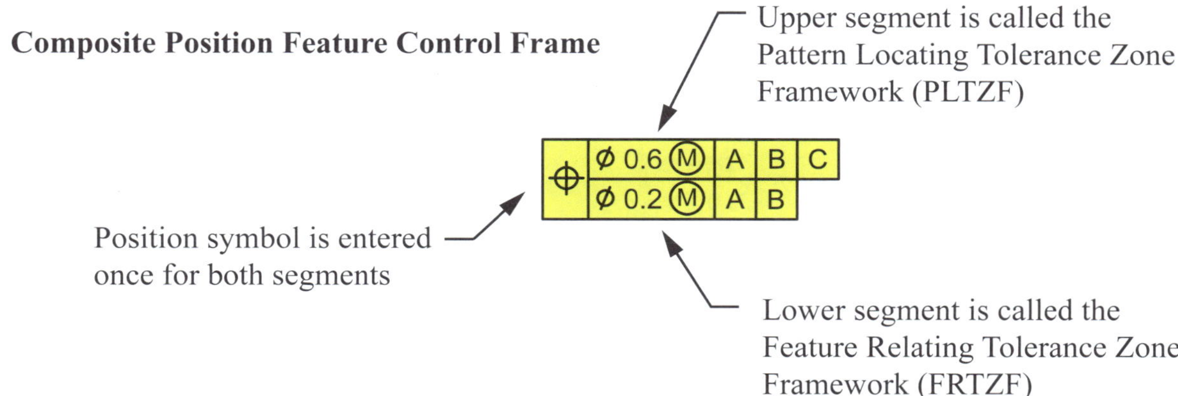

The upper segment of a composite position feature control frame is called the Pattern Locating Tolerance Zone Framework (PLTZF). The PLTZF is constrained in translation and rotation to the DRF. It specifies a larger positional tolerance which locates and orients the features to each other and to the specified DRF. (The upper segment is identical to a normal single position tolerance).

The lower segment of a composite feature control frame is called the Feature Relating Tolerance Zone Framework (FRTZF). The FRTZF specifies a smaller position tolerance to refine the feature-to-feature relationship within the pattern. When datum feature references are specified in a lower segment, the FRTZF is constrained only in rotation relative to the DRF which controls orientation of the pattern.

The order of precedence may not be changed in the FRTZF from the PLTZF, although datum feature references may be omitted.

The composite frame may be explained by stating the constraints (degrees of freedom) of each datum feature reference. The upper segment locates the features to each other and constrains translations (x,y,z) and rotations (u,v,w) to the specified DRF. The lower segment(s) refines the location between features, but constrains only rotations to the specified DRF.

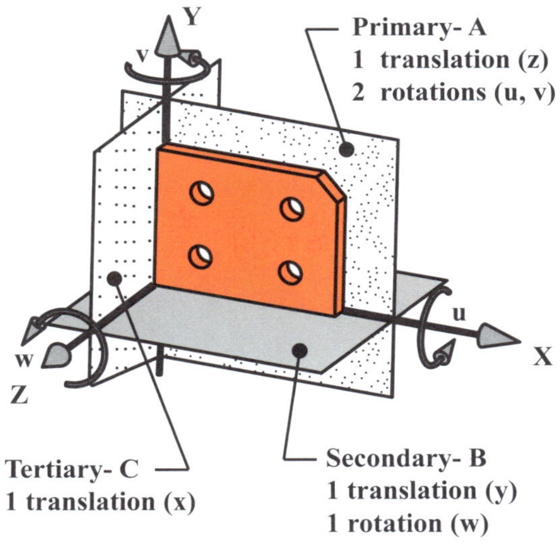

The datum reference frame constrains the 6 degrees of freedom for a part.

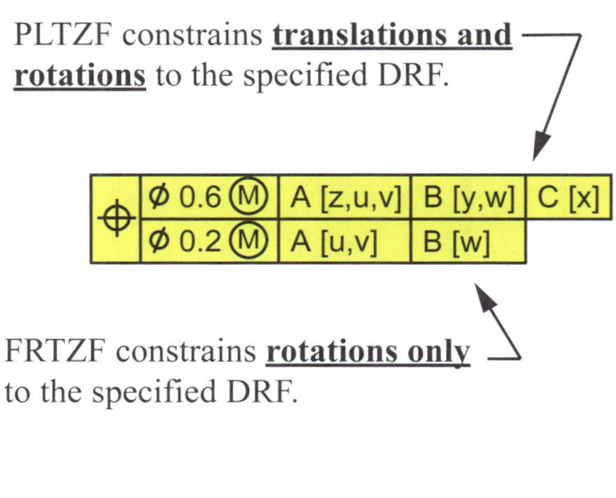

Note: These constraints do not need to be listed in a composite frame. This is only to show the effect for explanatory purposes.

Composite Position - One Datum Feature Reference

A pattern of features may require a larger tolerance relative to the datum reference frame and a smaller tolerance within the pattern. This may be accomplished with a composite feature control frame or with multiple separate position frames. Each segment may be verified separately, but the lower segment is a subset of the upper segment.

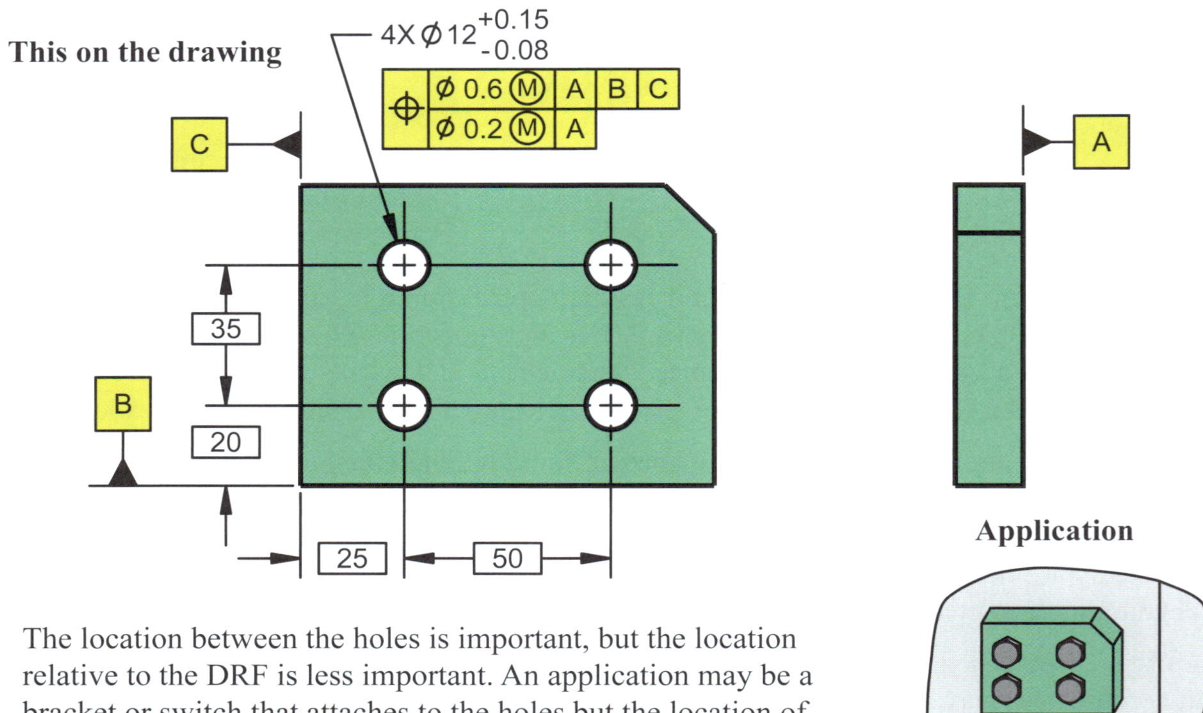

The location between the holes is important, but the location relative to the DRF is less important. An application may be a bracket or switch that attaches to the holes but the location of the bracket to the edges is not important.

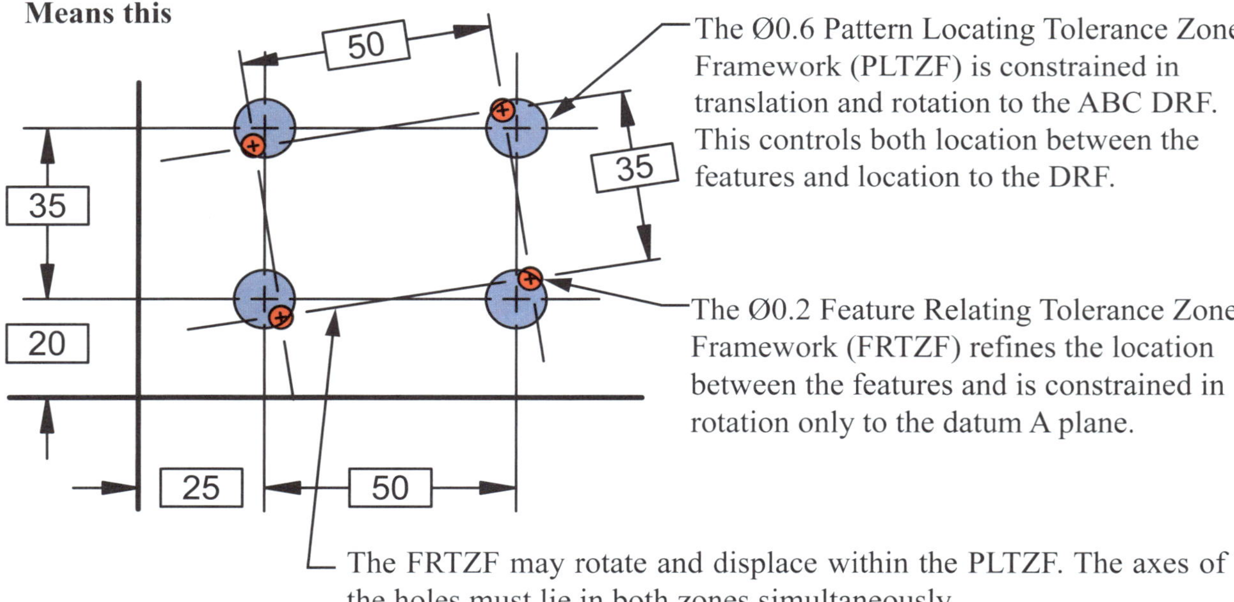

Note: Composite and two single segments would yield the same result in this case because of the single datum A in the lower frame. The tolerance zones are perpendicular to this plane and may only be constrained in rotation to it.

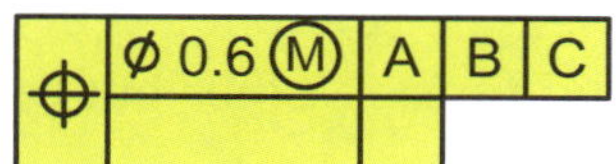

The upper segment specifies the location of the pattern to the specified DRF.

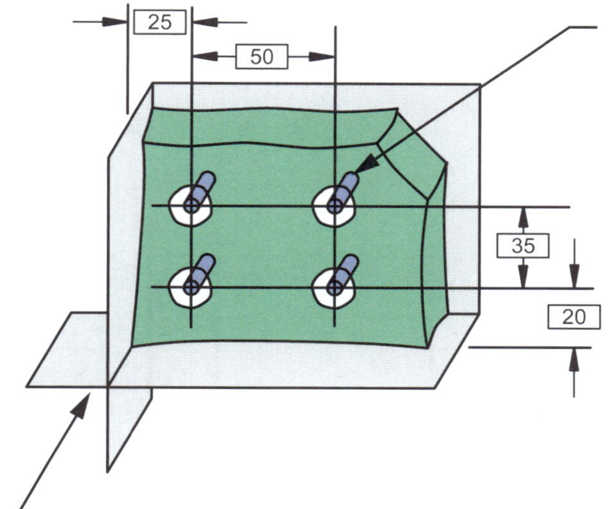

The axes of the holes must lie within a set of Ø0.6 at MMC tolerance zones that are basically located to each other and the upper DRF.

4X Ø 11.32 virtual size pins basically located to each other and the DRF.

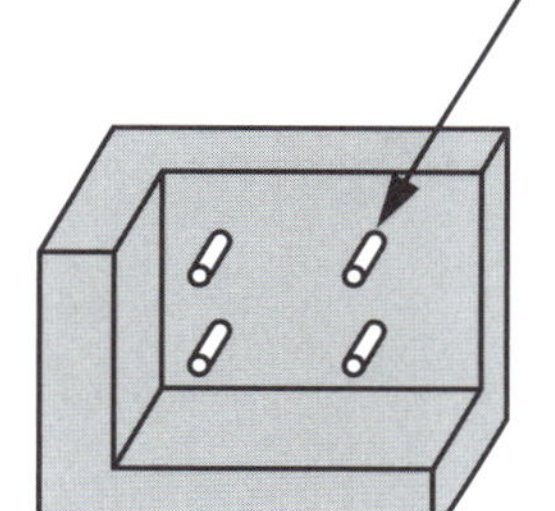

Datum reference frame is established in order by datum features A, B, & C.

Sample functional gage for the upper segment. The size of the holes must also be verified.

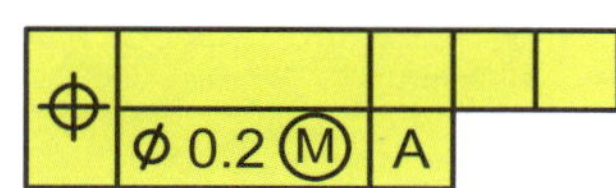

The lower segment refines the location between the features (hole-to-hole) and orientation to the specified DRF.

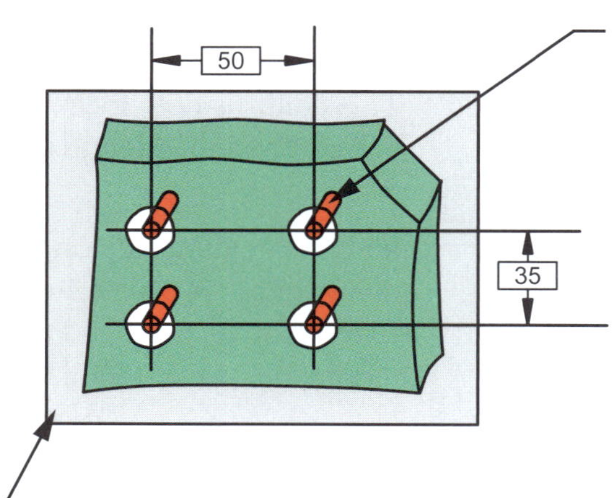

The axes of the holes must lie within a set of Ø0.2 at MMC tolerance zones that are basically located to each other but constrained in rotation only to the lower DRF.

4X Ø 11.72 virtual size pins basically located to each other and perpendicular to the face.

DRF is established by datum feature A. This is an orientation plane only.

Sample functional gage for the lower segment. The holes must meet both requirements.

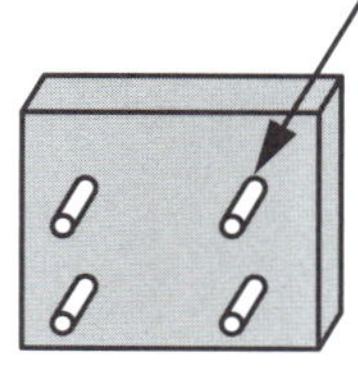

Composite Position - Two Datum Feature References

Below is the same part as the last example but with an additional datum feature reference B in the lower frame. Since it is composite, the lower tolerance zones are located to each other but only constrained in rotation to the specified DRF.

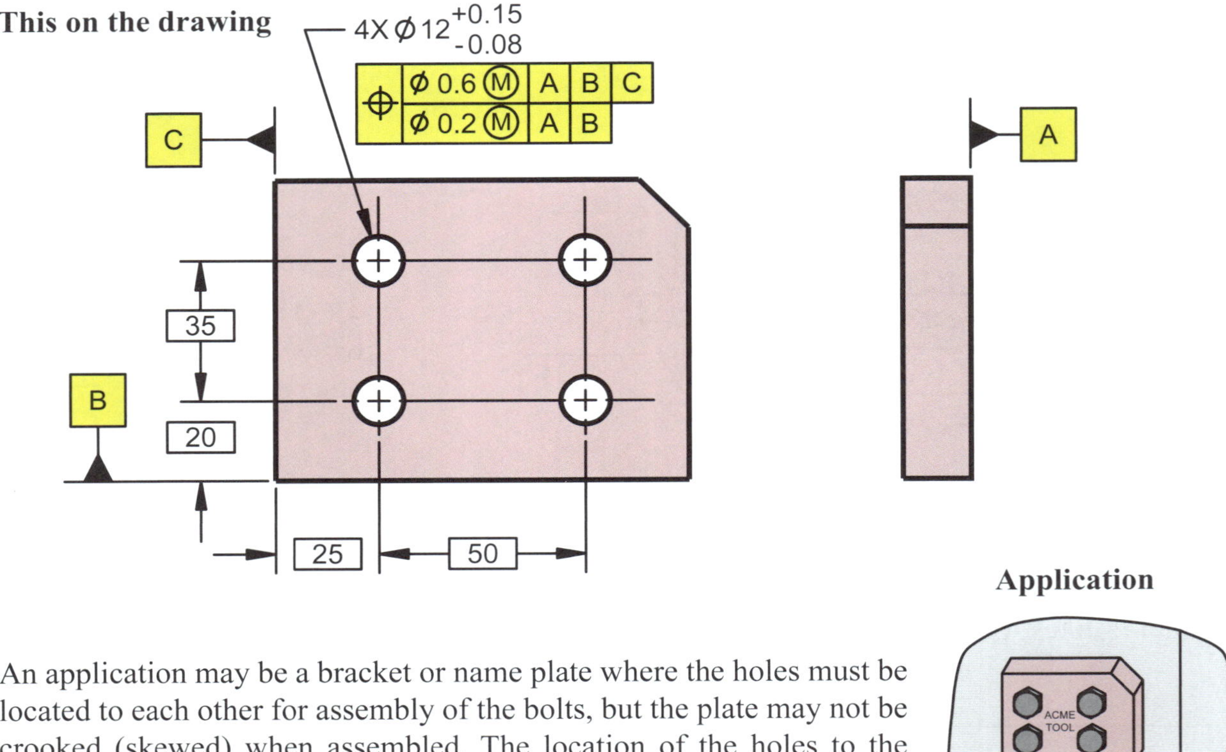

Application

An application may be a bracket or name plate where the holes must be located to each other for assembly of the bolts, but the plate may not be crooked (skewed) when assembled. The location of the holes to the edges is unimportant.

Means this

The Ø0.6 Pattern Locating Tolerance Zone Framework (PLTZF) is constrained in translation and rotation to the ABC DRF. This controls both location between the features and location to the DRF.

The Ø0.2 Feature Relating Tolerance Zone Framework (FRTZF) refines the location between the features and is constrained in rotation only to datum planes A and B.

The FRTZF may displace up, down, left, and right within the PLTZF, but it may not rotate. The axes of the holes must lie in both zones simultaneously. (The axes of the holes may only rotate within the confines of the FRTZF.)

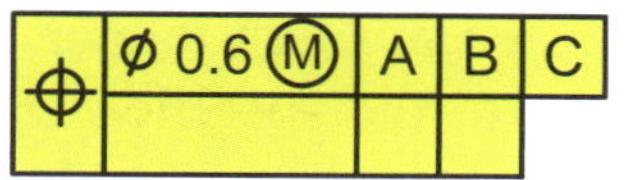

The upper segment specifies the location of the pattern to the specified DRF.

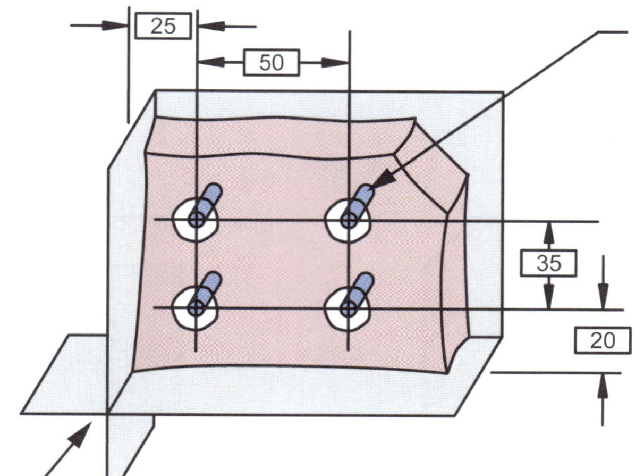

The axes of the holes must lie within a set of Ø0.6 at MMC tolerance zones that are basically located to each other and the upper DRF.

4X Ø 11.32 virtual size pins basically located to each other and the DRF.

Datum reference frame is established in order by datum features A, B, & C.

Sample functional gage for the upper segment. The size of the holes must also be verified.

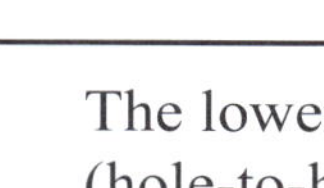

Ø 0.2 Ⓜ A B

The lower segment refines the location between the features (hole-to-hole) and orientation only to the specified DRF.

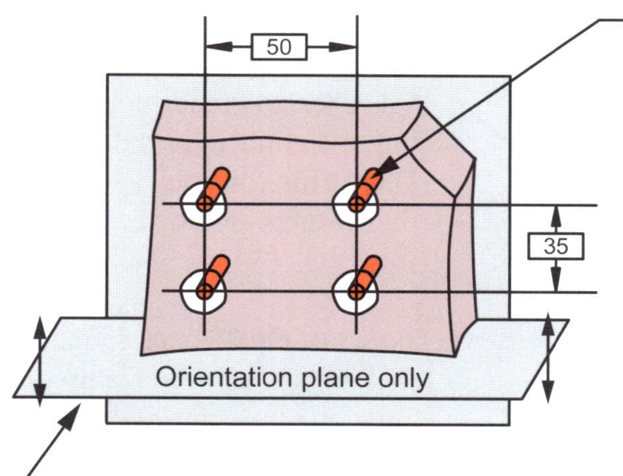

The axes of the holes must lie within a set of Ø0.2 at MMC tolerance zones that are basically located to each other but **constrained in rotation only** to the lower DRF.

4X Ø 11.72 virtual size pins basically located to each other and perpendicular to the face.

DRF is established by datum features A and B. These are orientation planes only. Basic dimensions to the datums are unlocked.

Sample functional gage for the lower segment. The sliding gage rail allows part movement up, down, left, and right, but only constraining rotation to datum B.

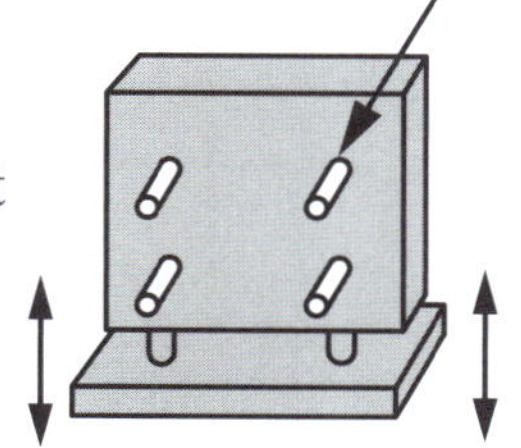

Note: If datum feature C were added to the lower segment, the interpretation would be the same. The lower segment is only constrained rotationally to the DRF. Datums features A and B are enough to constrain all 3 rotations.

Position - Two Single Segments

This drawing is not using composite tolerancing but rather two segmented position tolerances. Each tolerance controls the location between the holes and the location to the specified DRF. Lower frames may also reference a completely different DRF or rearrange the order as required.

This on the drawing

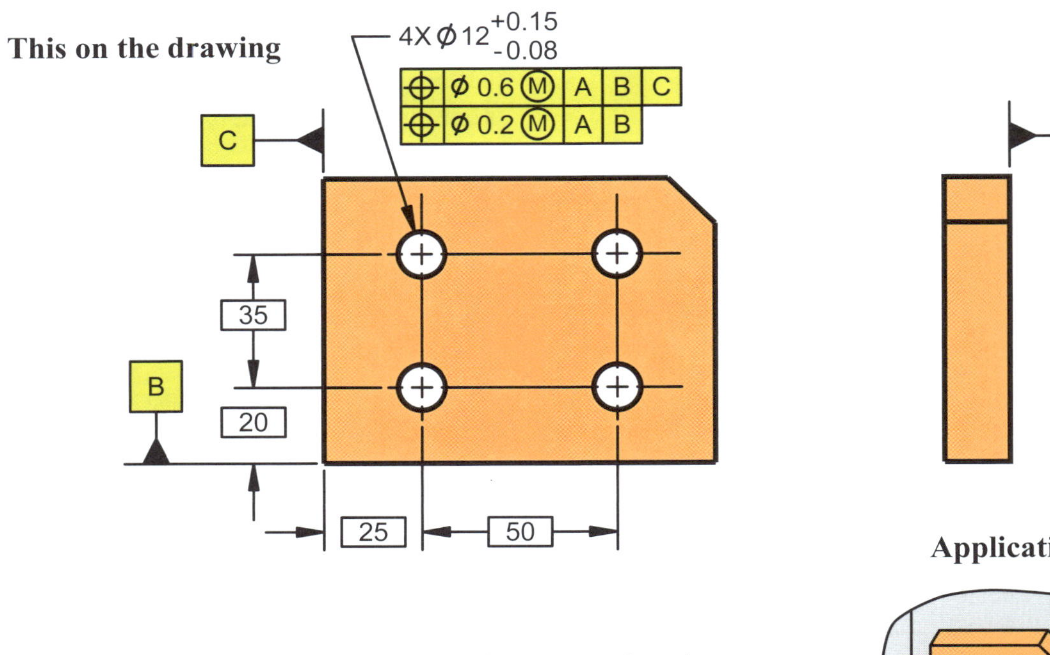

Application

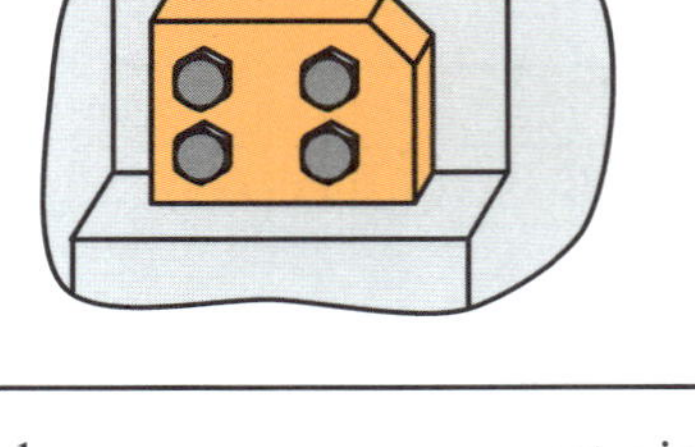

The location between the holes is important, but the location relative to the C datum feature is less important. The holes may move in the left/right direction more (as a group) than in the up/down direction.

Means this

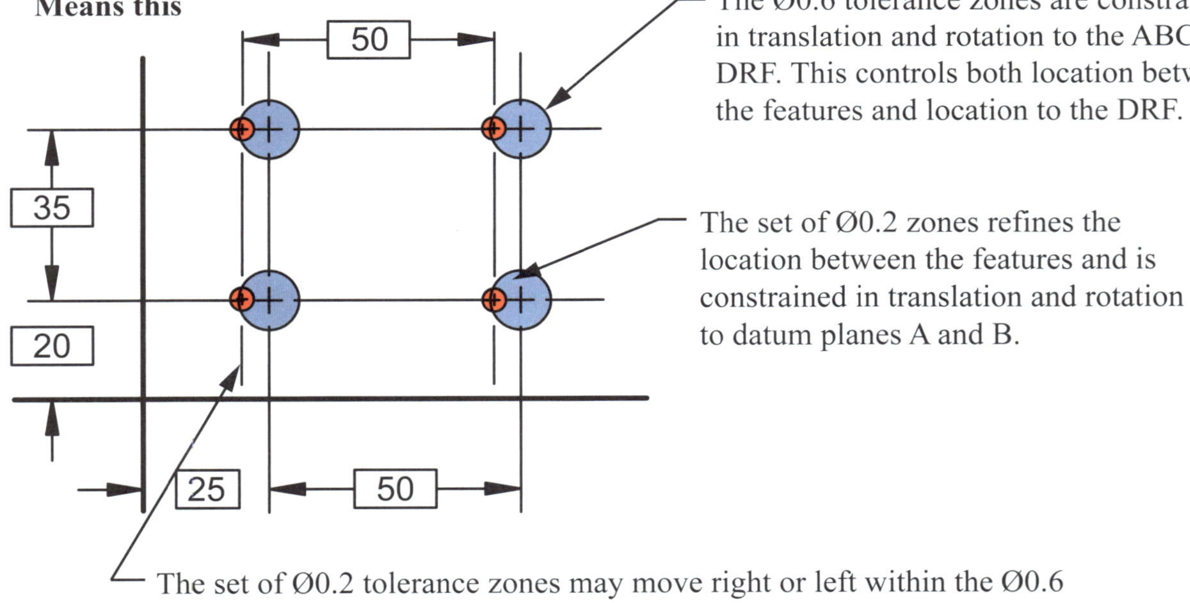

The Ø0.6 tolerance zones are constrained in translation and rotation to the ABC DRF. This controls both location between the features and location to the DRF.

The set of Ø0.2 zones refines the location between the features and is constrained in translation and rotation to datum planes A and B.

The set of Ø0.2 tolerance zones may move right or left within the Ø0.6 tolerance zones. The axes of the holes must lie in both zones simultaneously.

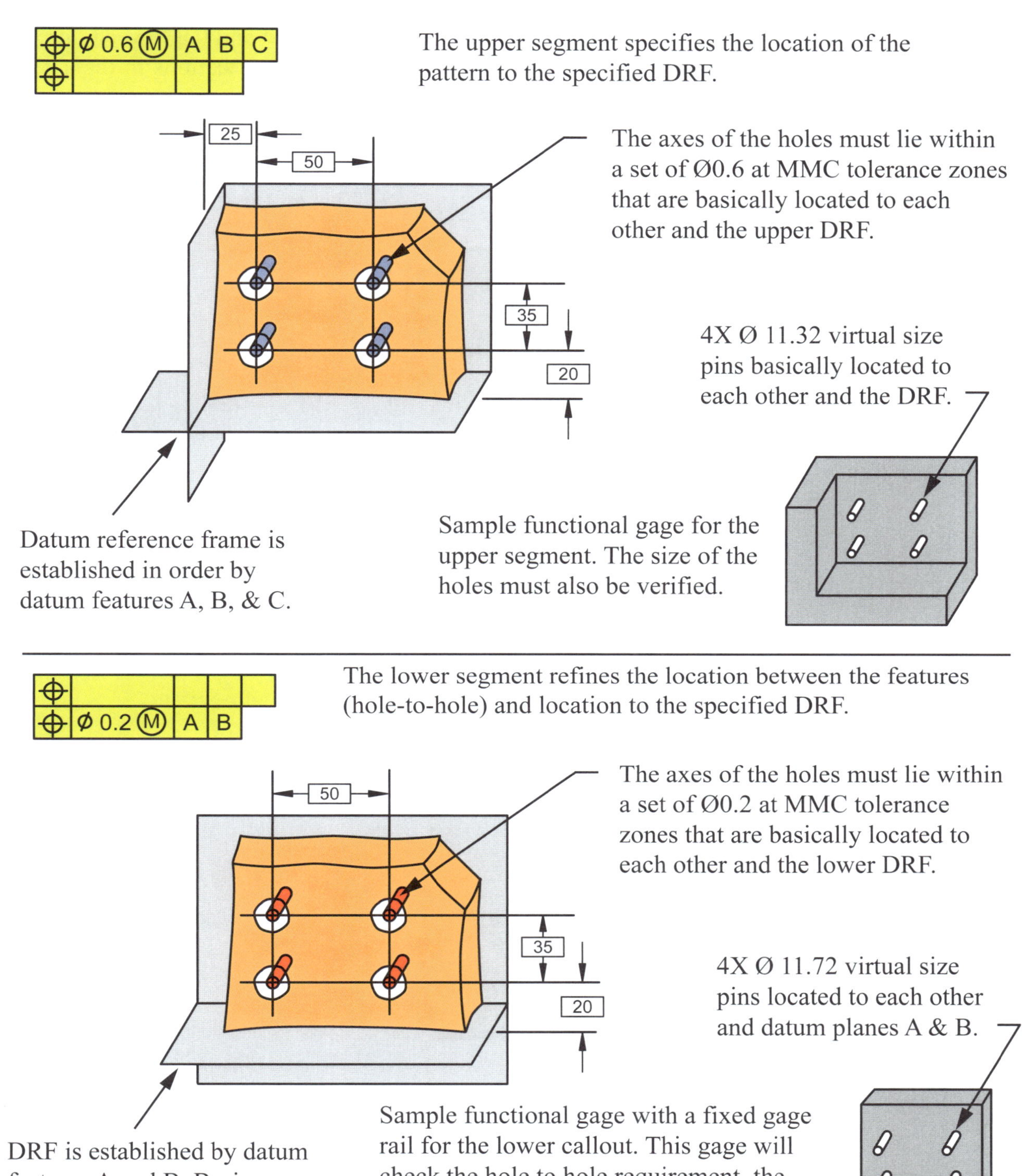

Note: If datum C were also entered in the lower segment, there would be a conflict. Both the upper and lower callouts would control location to all three datums, there would be no need for the larger tolerance in the upper feature control frame.

Composite Position - Paper Gage Verification

The top drawing is a plate with a composite position tolerance applied and the lower figure is the produced part. The upper segment can be evaluated using the x/y deviations in the actual position formula (as shown in unit 5). The lower segment can be evaluated by processing this XY data using a paper gage or appropriate CMM software (see next page).

This on the drawing

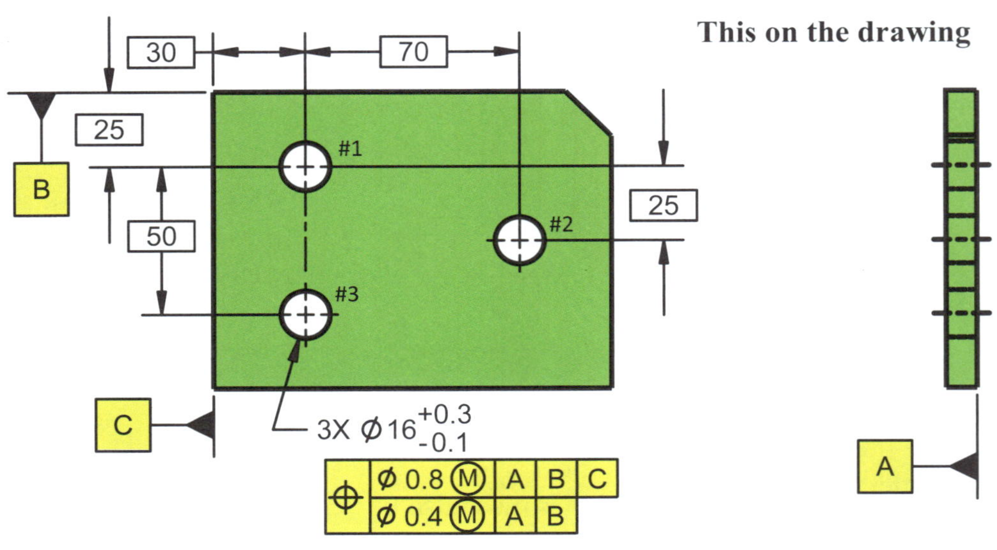

Produced part

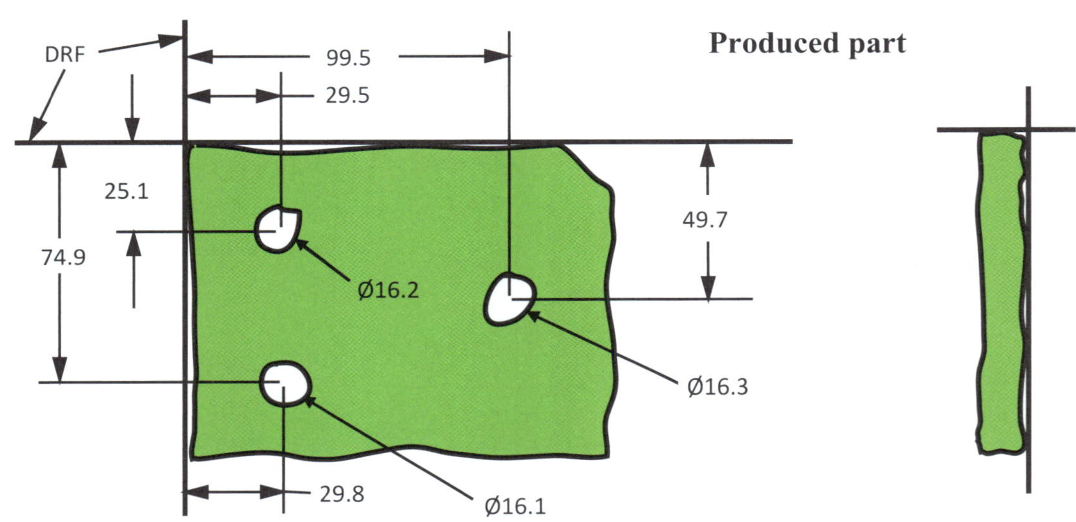

Upper segment calculations | Lower segment calculations

Hole No.	MMC Size	Act Size	Pattern Locating Allowed	"X" Dev	"Y" Dev	Pattern Relating Actual	Acc Rej	Feature Relating Allowed	Feature Relating Actual	Acc Rej
1	15.9	16.2	1.1	-0.5	-0.1	1.02	A	0.7	0.5	A
2	15.9	16.3	1.2	-0.5	+0.3	1.17	A	0.8	0.5	A
3	15.9	16.1	1	-0.2	+0.1	0.45	A	0.6	0.5	A

The actual value of the upper segment on the composite position can be calculated using the x/y deviations in the actual position formula or with the paper gage as shown below. The deviation from basic for each hole is plotted out on the graph, taking care to note positive and negative direction. The circles represents the position tolerance zones and must be coincident with the center of the Cartesian coordinates. The axes of the holes must lie within the upper segment tolerance.

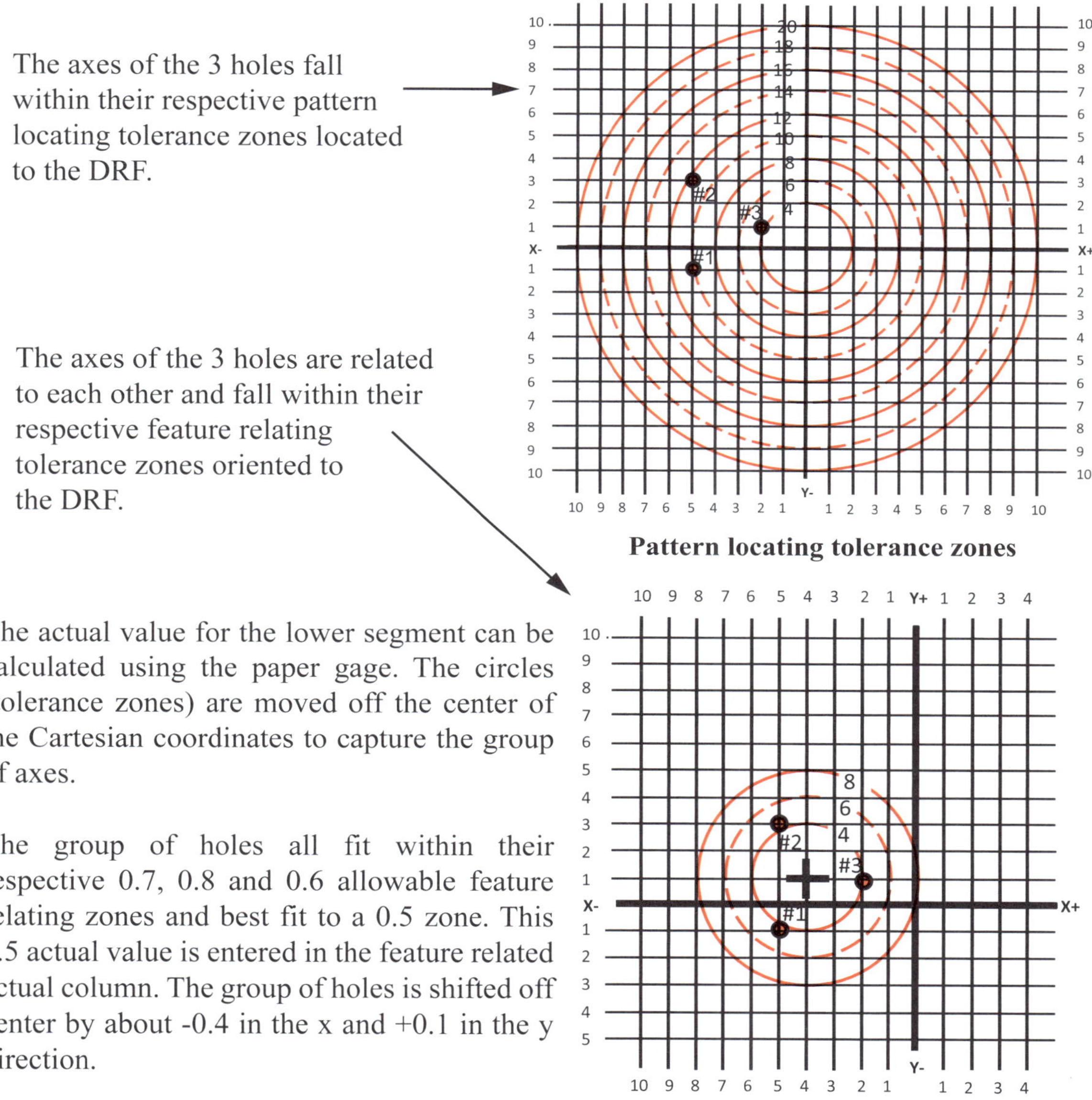

Pattern locating tolerance zones

The actual value for the lower segment can be calculated using the paper gage. The circles (tolerance zones) are moved off the center of the Cartesian coordinates to capture the group of axes.

The group of holes all fit within their respective 0.7, 0.8 and 0.6 allowable feature relating zones and best fit to a 0.5 zone. This 0.5 actual value is entered in the feature related actual column. The group of holes is shifted off center by about -0.4 in the x and +0.1 in the y direction.

Feature relating tolerance zones

The collection of XY data is done while the part is constrained in translation and rotation to ABC. The lower entry is constrained in rotation only to datums A and B, therefore the tolerance zones are unlocked in translation and may be shifted up/down and left/right to accept the features. If the datum feature B reference were removed from the lower entry, the set-up could change. The part may be reoriented to balance rotationally to the holes and re-measure the XY deviations. In other words, the removal of the B reference would also unlock the rotational constraint to allow the acceptance of the hole locations to each other.

Composite Position - Application

The sheet metal Base Tray drawing below shows an application for composite position tolerance. The part has mounting locations to a mating frame on datum features A, B, and C. Two components mount to it on two sets of holes. The location of the components are not important to the DRF but the holes in each group must be tightly controlled to each other for the mating rivets. It is also important the components stay well oriented (parallel) to the DRF.

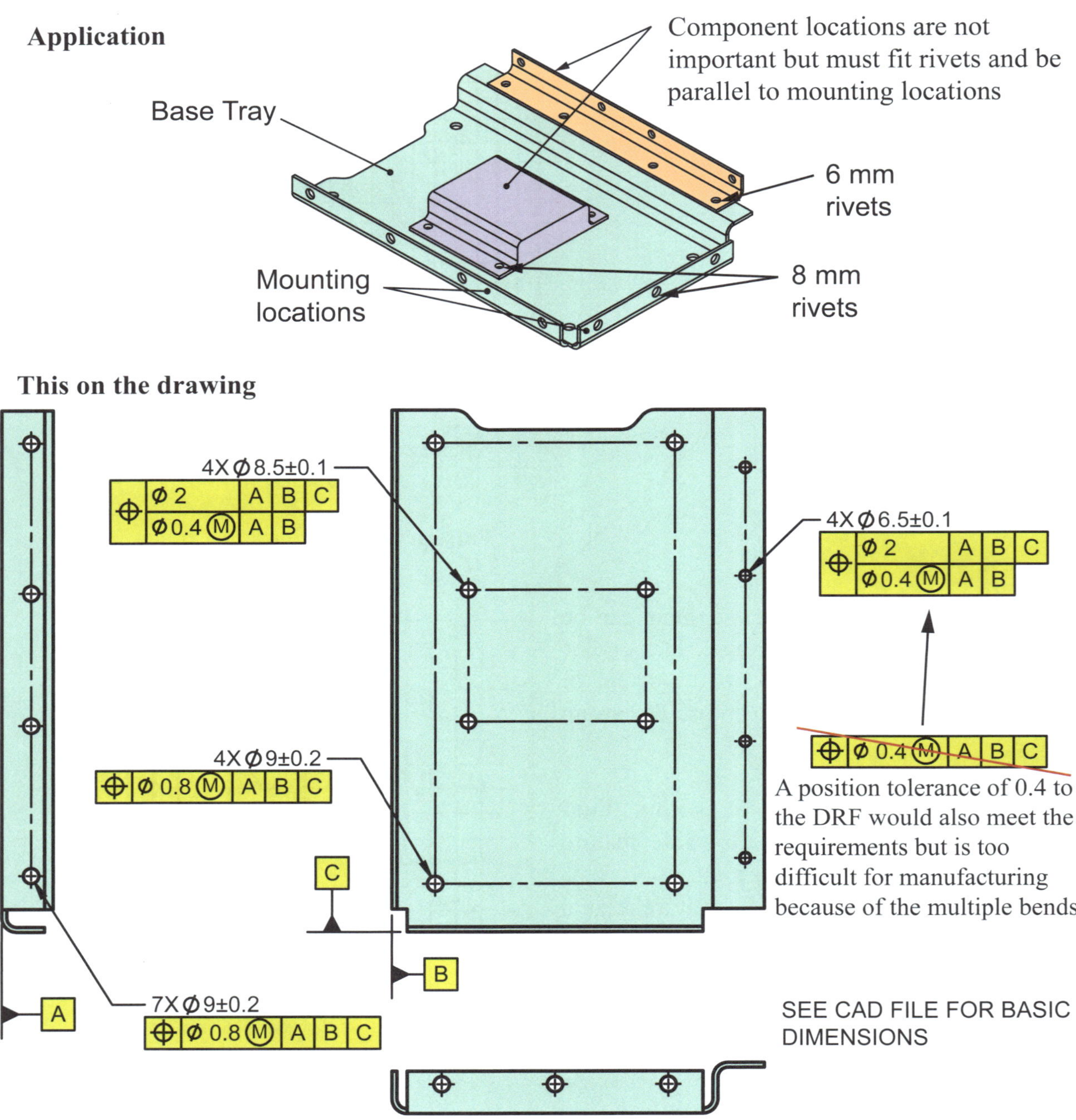

The upper segment position tolerance must be large (2) because of the multiple bends between the holes and datum features. The grouping of the holes controlled by the lower segment must be held tight for the rivets to fit and is calculated thru the floating fastener formula (0.4). A reference to A and B is added to the lower frame to constrain the rotational degrees of freedom of the tolerance zones. This keeps the hole patterns oriented (parallel) to the DRF. Note: the datum features were not qualified with flatness and perpendicularity for simplicity.

Workshop Exercise 12.2 Composite Position

(44)
A
(102)
B
(58)
C
(12)
G
(70)F
(204)
D
(45)
E

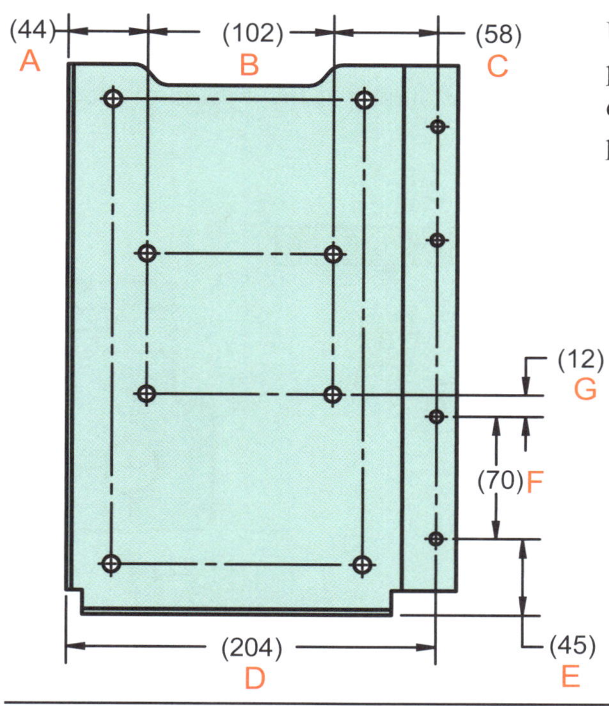

Using the position tolerances on the previous page, what are the max distances of the dimensions to the left. Assume all holes are produced at MMC (no bonus tolerance).

A	a. 44.2	b. 44.4	c. 45	d. 46
B	a. 102.2	b. 102.4	c. 103	d. 104
C	a. 58.2	b. 58.4	c. 59	d. 60
D	a. 204.2	b. 204.4	c. 205	d. 206
E	a. 45.2	b. 45.4	c. 46	d. 47
F	a. 70.2	b. 70.4	c. 71	d. 72
G	a. 12.2	b. 12.4	c. 13	d. 14

Both sets of holes were measured relative to ABC and pass the upper position tolerance of 2 mm. Use the X,Y measurement deviation data given to plot the hole axes on the graphs. Sketch the actual tolerance zones for the lower frames and estimate the measured value. Do the holes pass or fail the lower specifications?

5 4 3 2 1 Y+ 1 2 3 4 5
X-
X+
Y-

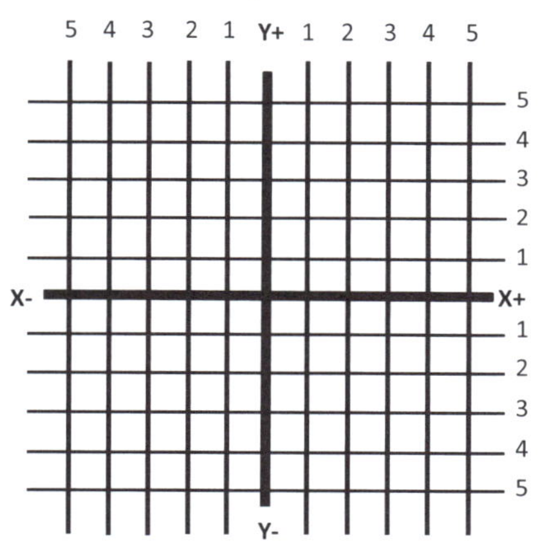

4X Ø8.5±0.1

⌖	Ø 2	A	B	C
⌖	Ø0.4 Ⓜ	A	B	

Hole #	Allwd ⌖	XDev	YDev	Meas ⌖	Pass/Fail
1	**2.0**	**+0.4**	**+0.4**	**1.131**	Pass
2	**2.0**	**+0.4**	**+0.5**	**1.281**	Pass
3	**2.0**	**+0.3**	**+0.3**	**0.849**	Pass
4	**2.0**	**+0.2**	**+0.3**	**0.721**	Pass
Group	**0.4**	**---**	**---**		

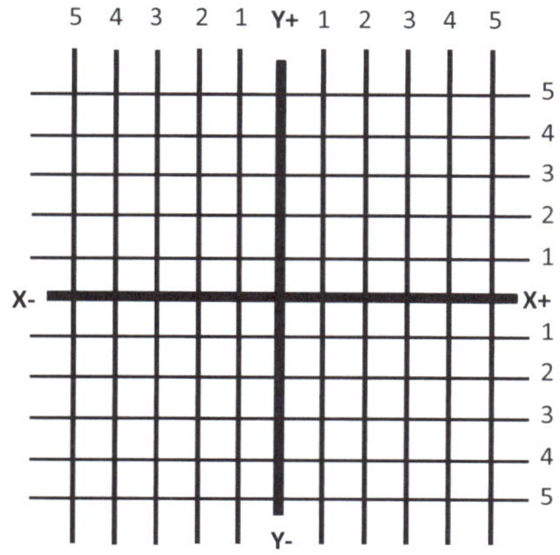

5 4 3 2 1 Y+ 1 2 3 4 5
X-
X+
Y-

4X Ø6.5±0.1

⌖	Ø 2	A	B	C
⌖	Ø0.4 Ⓜ	A	B	

Hole #	Allwd ⌖	XDev	YDev	Meas ⌖	Pass/Fail
1	**2.0**	**-0.4**	**+0.2**	**0.894**	Pass
2	**2.0**	**-0.2**	**+0.1**	**0.447**	Pass
3	**2.0**	**+0.2**	**+0.2**	**0.566**	Pass
4	**2.0**	**+0.4**	**+0.1**	**0.825**	Pass
Group	**0.4**	**---**	**---**		

Composite Position Application - Coaxial Holes on a Hinge

Composite position tolerancing may be used for coaxial holes. Shown below are four examples of composite and segmented position frames to help illustrate the differences when adding and additional datum references. The explanation of scenario #1 is shown at the bottom of the page. Scenarios #2 - #4 are shown on the next page.

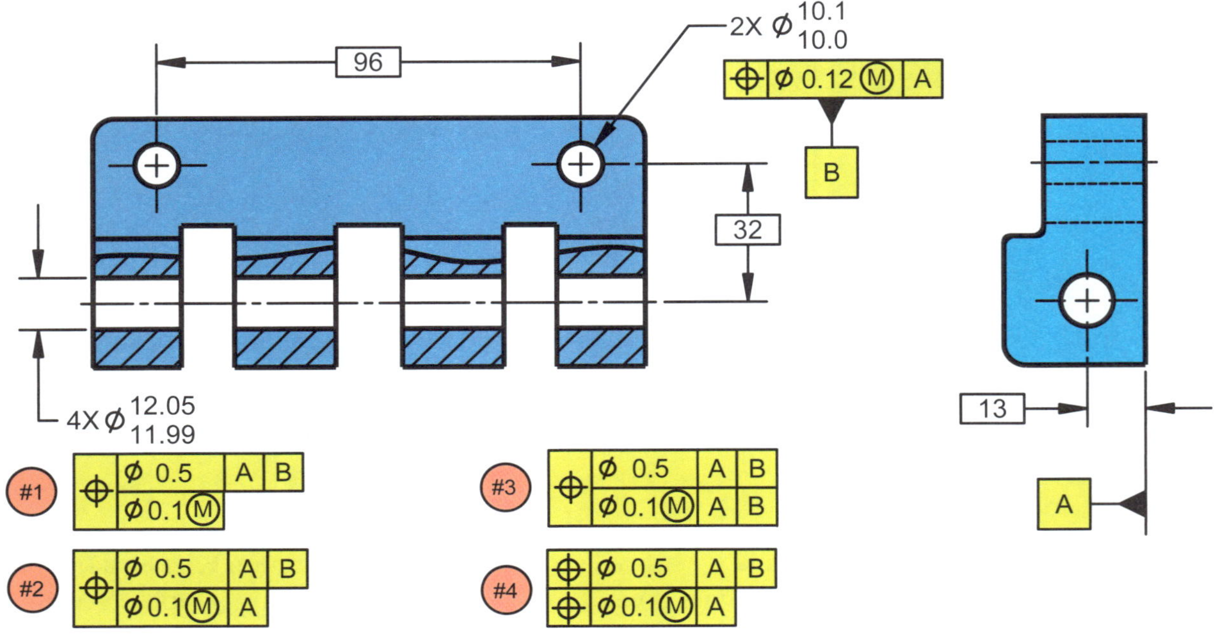

Scenario #1- There is a composite frame with the position symbol entered once for both segments. The upper segment controls the location and orientation of the four holes to the A, B reference frame within four fully constrained Ø0.5 tol zones. The lower segment refines the location between the holes (coaxiality) within the tighter Ø0.1 tol zones. Since there are no datum feature references in the lower segment, these zones are free to translate and rotate together within the upper tol zones. The hole axes must lie within both zones simultaneously.

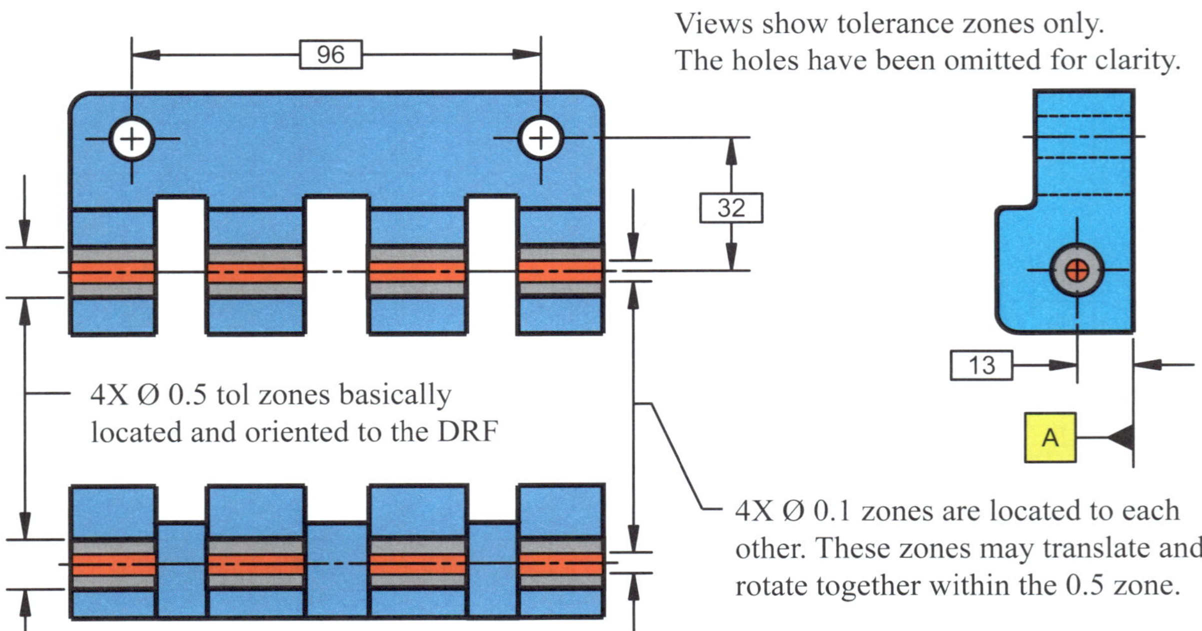

Scenario #2 - The composite position tolerance is revised and a reference to datum feature A is added to the lower segment. The lower segment constrains the tolerance zones in rotation only to datum A plane. The Ø0.1 zones may translate up/down and left right together, and rotate in one direction together but must remain parallel to datum plane A.

The lower segment refines the location between the holes (coaxiality) and orientation to datum A.

Scenario #3 - The composite position tolerance is revised and references to datum features A and B are added to the lower segment. The lower segment constrains the tolerance zones in rotation only to the full DRF. The Ø0.1 zones may translate up/down and left/right together, but may not rotate to the DRF.

The lower segment refines the location between the holes (coaxiality) and orientation to the DRF.

> **Note:** A parallelism tolerance would not yield the same results as the lower segment of the composite position tolerance. Parallelism is an orientation tolerance for individual features. It will not control the location between the holes (coaxiality). A parallelism specification will require each hole to be parallel separately. If there were only one hole, as shown in the example in Unit 6 of this text, a position and parallelism tolerance would be used instead of composite position.

Scenario #4 - The tolerance is revised to two separate position frames and reference to datum feature A is added to the lower segment. The lower segment constrains the tolerance zones in rotation and translation to the datum A plane. In the side view, the Ø0.1 zones may translate up/down and rotate up/down, but may not translate left/right or rotate left/right. They must remain located and oriented to datum A.

In other words, the basic dimension to datum A remains locked, but the basic dimension to datum B is unlocked for the lower segment.

The lower segment refines the location between the holes (coaxiality), location and orientation to datum A.

After all these scenarios, #1 and #3 are probably the most common. Coaxiality of a set of holes is important but the location to the datum reference frame is not. Adding datum feature references to the lower segment of composite constrains only rotations and forces the tolerance zones to also be oriented (parallel).

Workshop Exercise 12.3

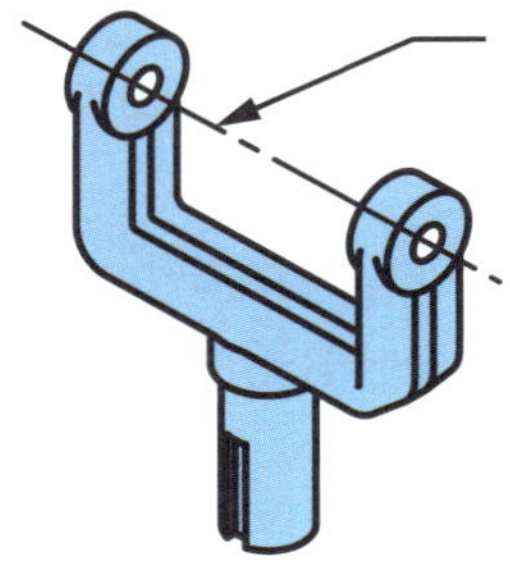

Function:

The location of the holes to the ABC datum reference frame is not important. However, the holes must be coaxial and oriented to ABC (not tilted or twisted).

Which set of specifications would match the design function best?

A. | ⌖ | Ø .015 | A | B | C | / | ⌖ | Ø .003 | A | B | C |

B. | ⌖ | Ø .015 | A | B | C | / | ⊥ | Ø .003 | A | B | C |

C. | ⌖ | Ø .015 | A | B | C | / | ⌖ | Ø .003 | A | B |

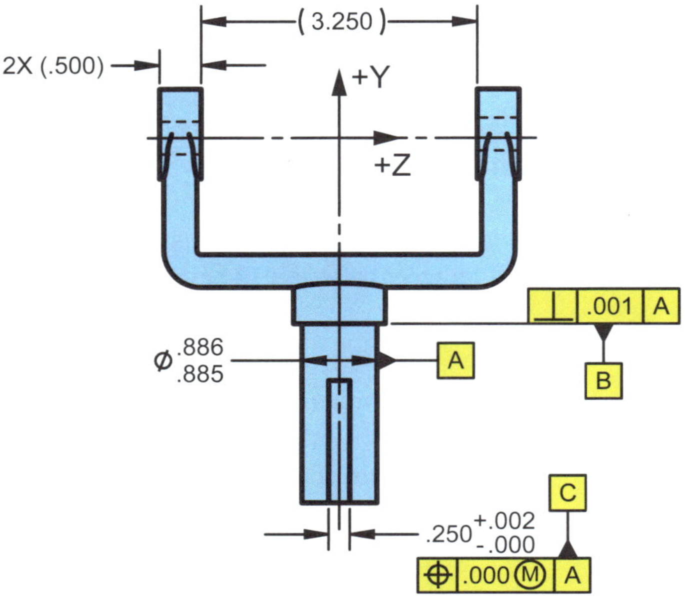

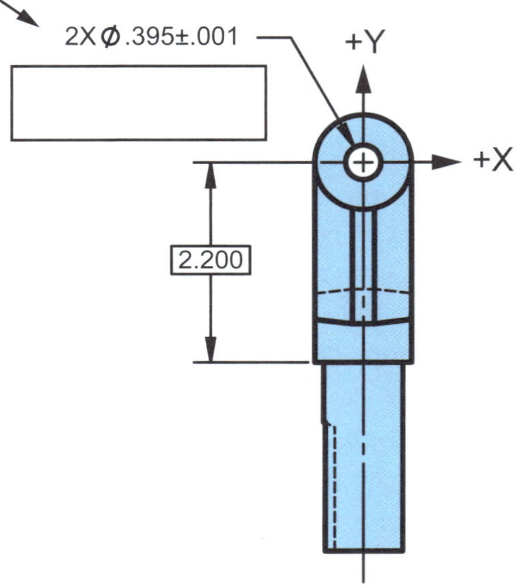

2X (.500)
(3.250)
+Y
+Z
⊥ .001 A
B
Ø .886 .885
A
C
.250 +.002 -.000
⌖ .000 Ⓜ A

2X Ø .395±.001
+Y
+X
2.200

Measurement data for two holes relative to ABC

2X Ø .395±.001

| ⌖ | Ø .015 | A | B | C |

		Allowed ⌖	XDev	YDev	Actual ⌖	Pass/Fail
Hole #1	Z= -1.625	.015	+.003	+.004	.0100	Pass
	Z= -2.125	.015	+.004	+.005	.0128	Pass
Hole #2	Z= +1.625	.015	+.002	+.002	.0072	Pass
	Z= +2.125	.015	+.003	+.003	.0072	Pass

Use the X,Y measurement deviation data above to plot the hole axes on both of the graphs below. Sketch the actual tolerance zones for each of the lower frames. Would the holes pass or fail the lower specifications?

2X Ø .395±.001

| ⌖ | Ø .015 | A | B | C |
| | Ø .003 | A | B | C |

2X Ø .395±.001

| ⌖ | Ø .015 | A | B | C |
| ⊥ | Ø .003 | A | B | C |

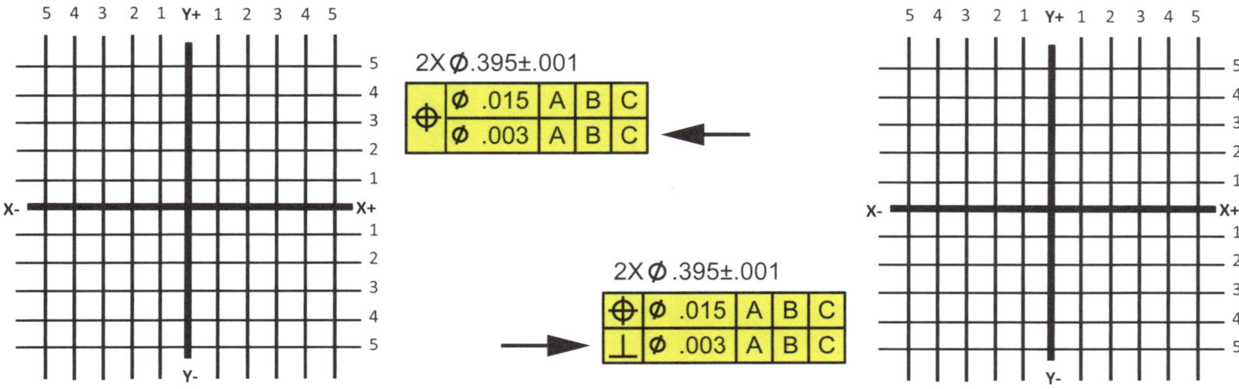

Continuous Feature

Size tolerances apply to individual features, and through rule #1, require the feature to have perfect form at MMC. Size tolerances by themselves do not control relationships between features. Extension lines may define the nominal relationship between multiple features but do not control the location tolerance between them.

The location between features is usually controlled with a position tolerance (coaxiality). However, if the features are the same size, a continuous feature symbol may be used instead. This makes the group of features act like a single feature of size, and the size tolerance will control the form and location relationship. It is not required to state the number of features (3X) with CF, but it may be helpful to clarify.

The continuous feature symbol was new for the ASME Y14.5-2009 standard. The concept was expanded in Y14.5-2018 and now may also be applied next to a geometric tolerance (like a flatness) on interrupted surfaces. This treats the multiple surfaces as a single continuous surface.

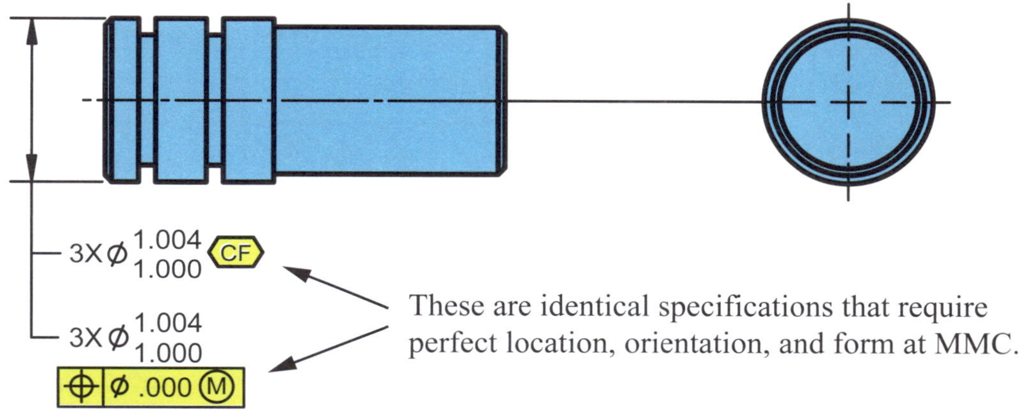

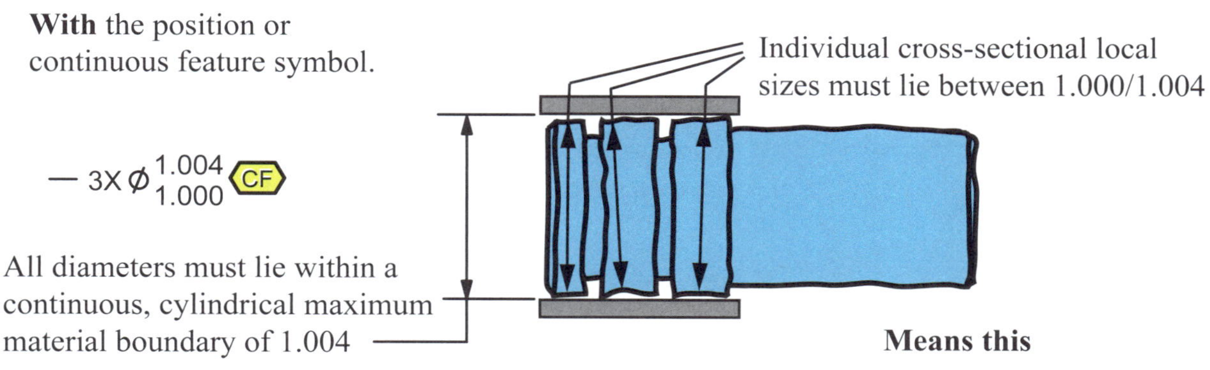

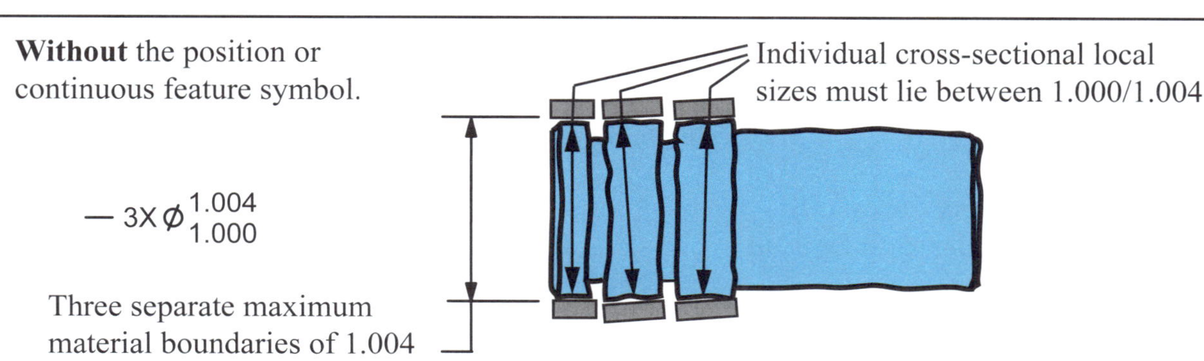

Two Single Segments - Rotational Control

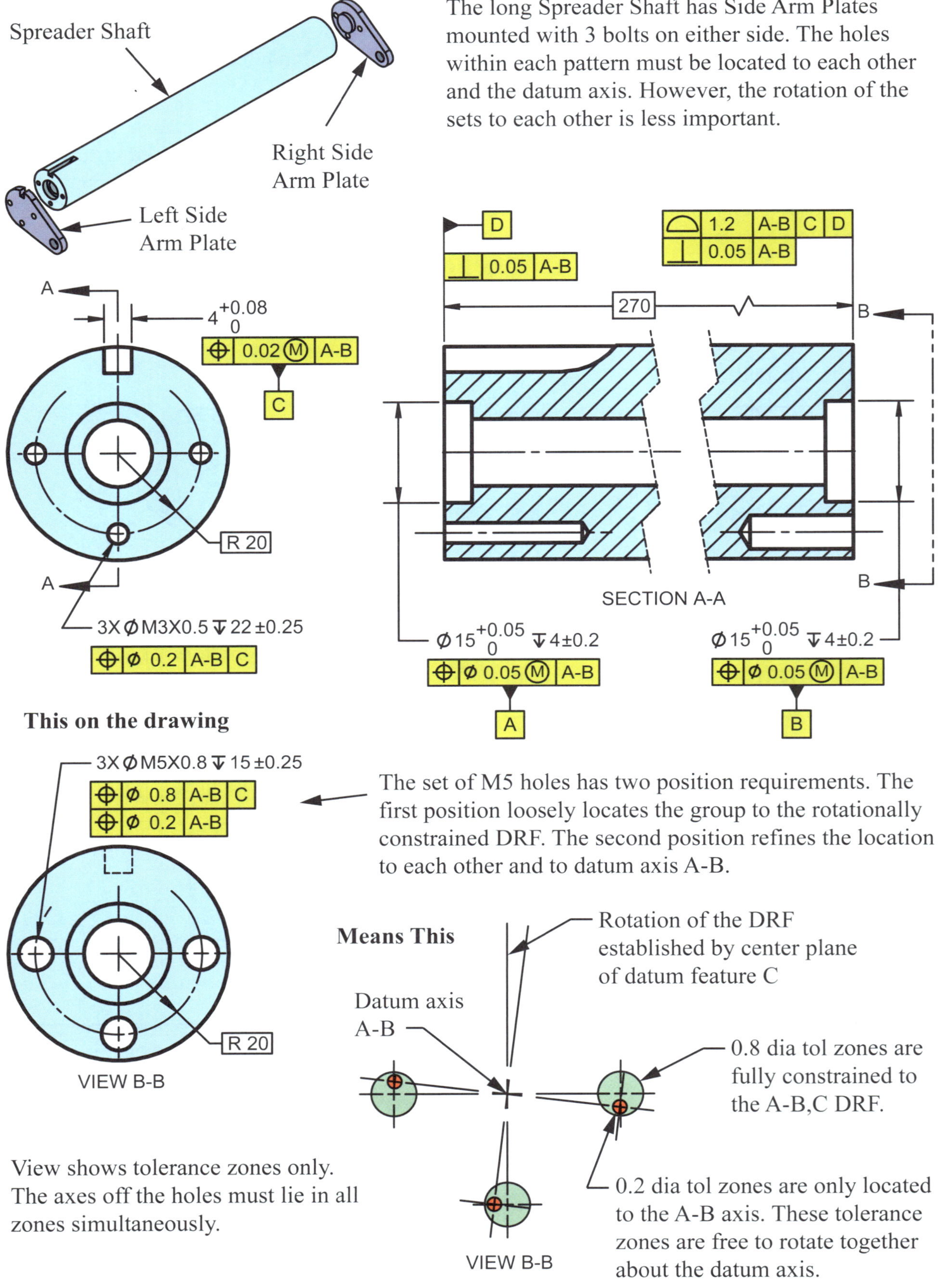

Workshop Exercise 12.4

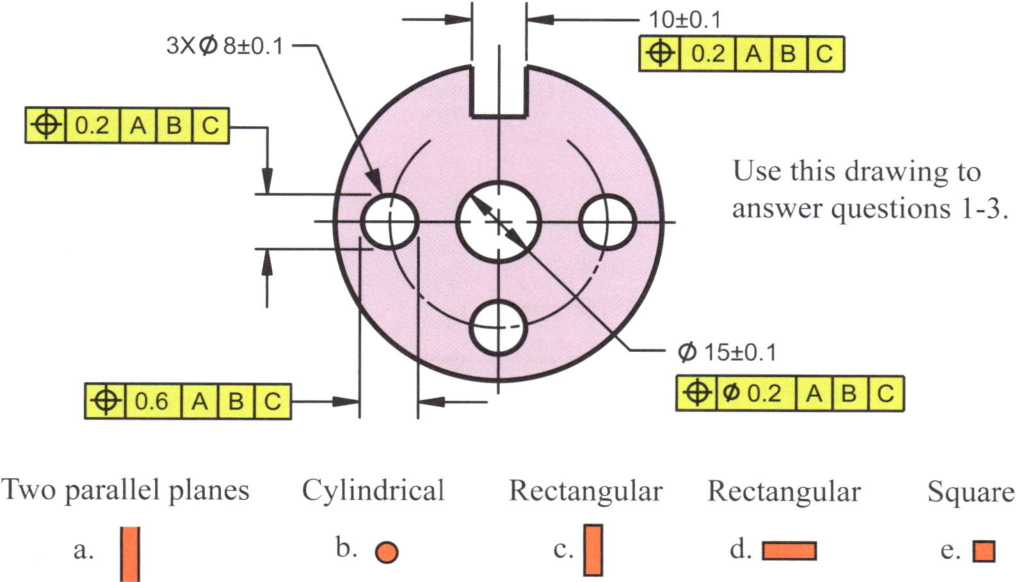

Use this drawing to answer questions 1-3.

Two parallel planes	Cylindrical	Rectangular	Rectangular	Square
a.	b.	c.	d.	e.

1. The 15 mm feature above has which shaped position tolerance zone shown above?

2. The 10 mm feature above has which shaped position tolerance zone shown above?

3. The 8 mm feature above has which shaped position tolerance zone shown above?

4. By default, when a position tolerance applies to a threaded hole, does it control the axis of the major, minor, or pitch diameter?

5. True or False? A position tolerance may be applied to a planar surface in ASME Y14.5-2018.

6. True or False? A position tolerance may be applied to an irregular feature of size.

7. What is the name of this symbol? 

a. contacting feature b. continuous feature c. controlling feature d. complex feature

8. Which of the following specifications represent a composite position tolerance?

a. only i
b. only ii
c. both i and ii
d. all

i
⌖	⌀0.8 Ⓜ	A	B	C
	⌀0.1 Ⓜ	A	B	

ii
⌖	⌀0.8 Ⓜ	A	B	C
⌖	⌀0.1 Ⓜ	A	B	

iii
⌖	⌀0.8	A	B	C

iv
⌖	⌀0.8 Ⓜ	A	B	C
⊥	⌀0.1 Ⓜ	A	B	

9. The tolerance zones created by the lower segments of a composite position
   a. are constrained in rotation only to the specified datum reference frame
   b. are constrained in translation only to the specified datum reference frame
   c. are constrained in translation and rotation to the specified datum reference frame
   d. are unconstrained to the specified datum reference frame

Workshop Exercise 12.5

On the rectangular hole in the part below, apply a profile of 0.1 all around in relation to datum A to control the size and form. In addition, apply a position to the hole within a 0.5 boundary at MMC in relation to the datum reference frame ABC to control the location.

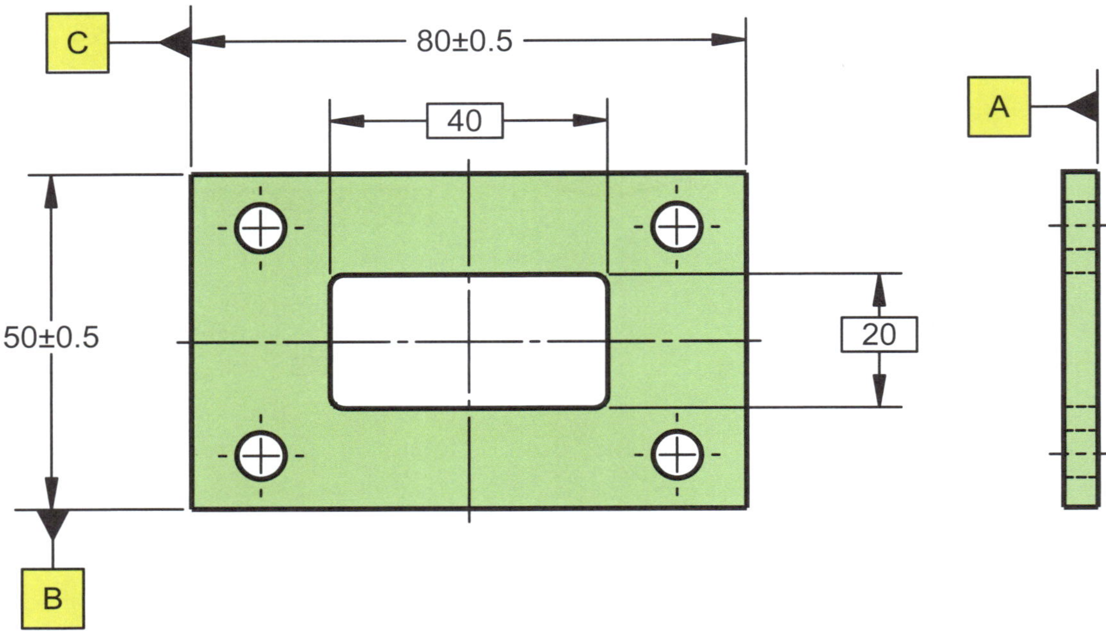

On the part below, calculate the allowable min and max hole sizes from the profile tolerance as well as the size of the virtual condition boundary created by the position at MMC.

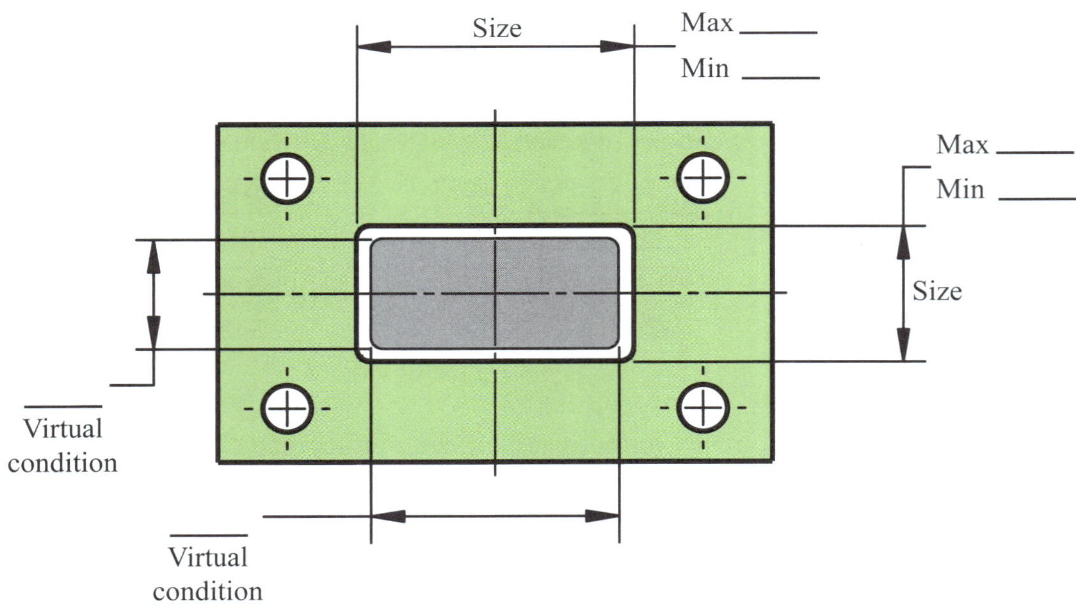

Workshop Exercise 12.6

The two position tolerances on the drawing below may be verified with two functional gages. Calculate the pin sizes for these gages to help explain the two requirements. Also see unit 7 for calculations of MMB and virtual condition.

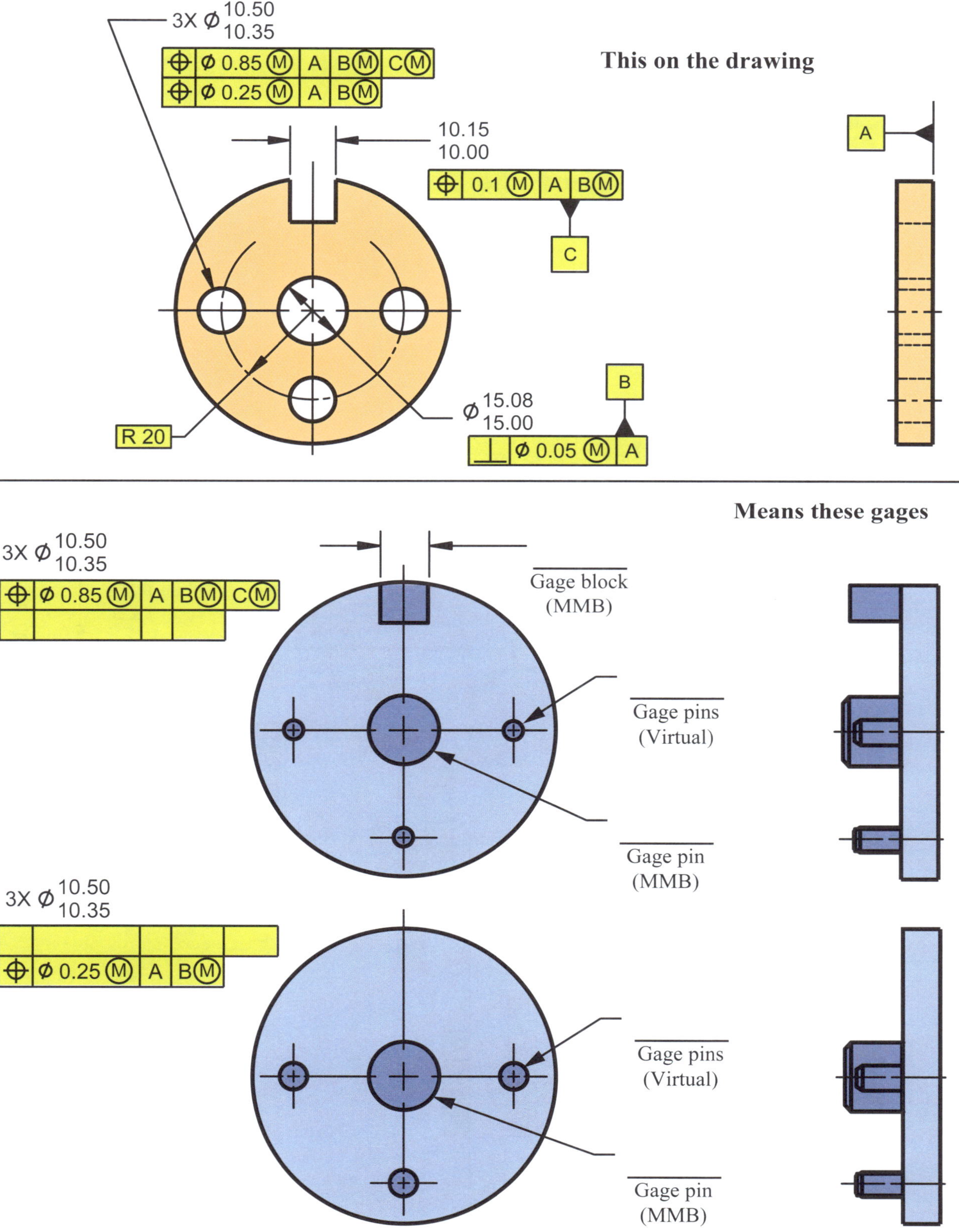

Workshop Exercise 12.7 What is Wrong?

The drawing is so bad, it looks like a ransom note. See if you can find any mistakes. Look for missing symbols, misused symbols, improper datum feature symbol placement, incorrect feature control frames, etc. If you think the drawing looks good, take the course again.

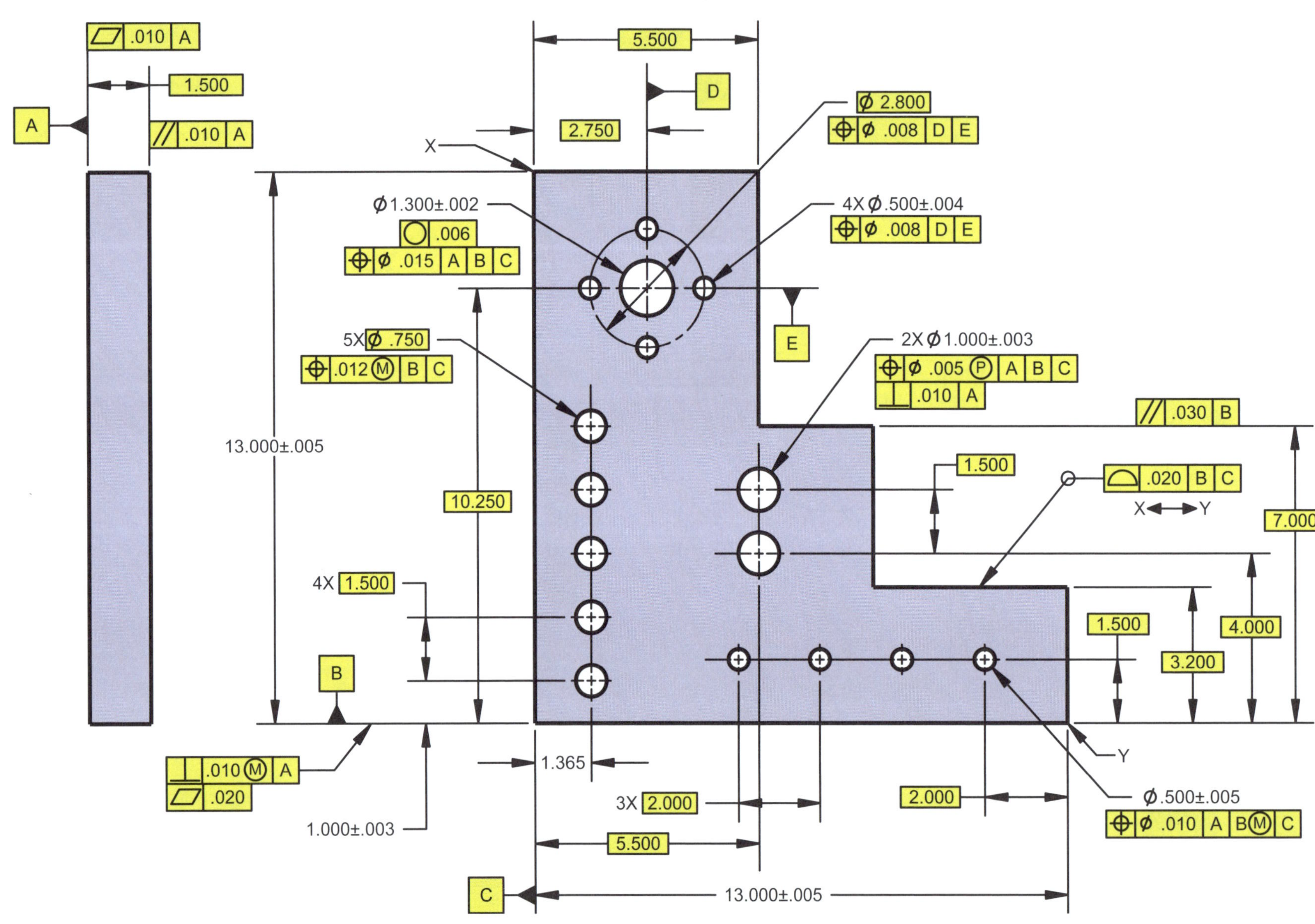

Unit 13

Coaxial Controls

Runout, Position, Profile

Coaxial Tolerances Overview - Keeping Diameters Centered

There are four geometric characteristics that control a coaxial relationship between features: position, circular runout, total runout, and profile. Each characteristic has a different definition and will control a different aspect of the feature. The drawing below illustrates these coaxial specifications and a quick summary of their definition. The goal for applying any tolerance is to maintain part function while providing maximum manufacturing allowance.

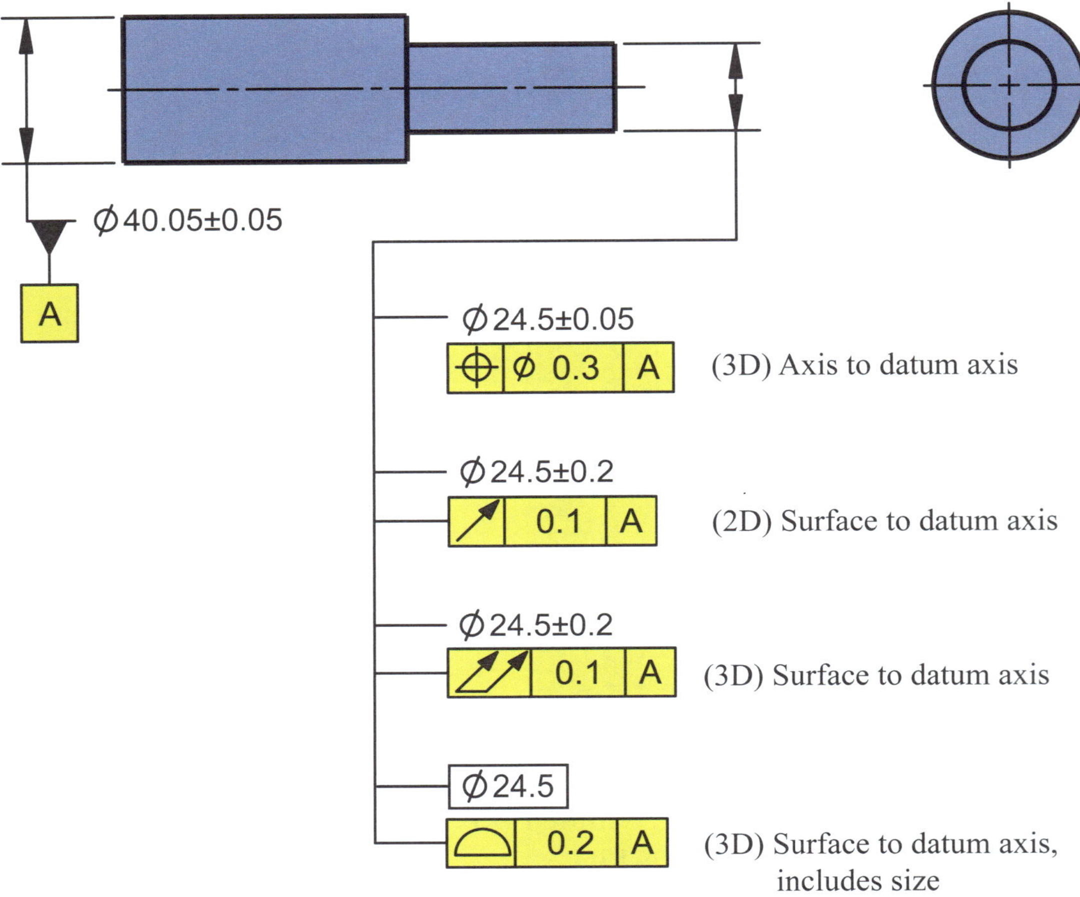

The actual manufactured part will never be as good as its depiction in the drawing or CAD model. Datum features and tolerances must be selected to control the variation between features.

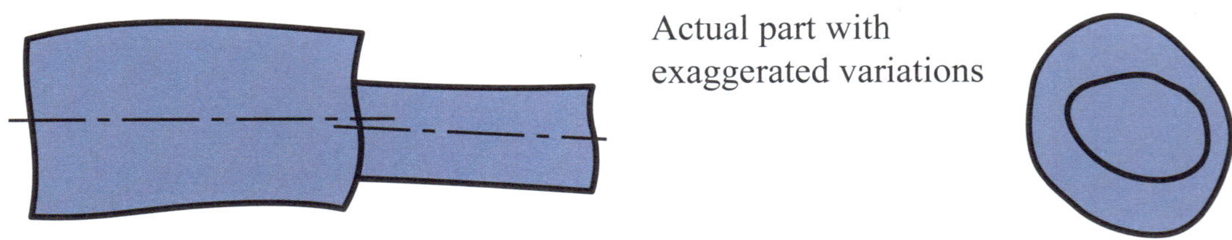

The same part is shown four times over the next pages to illustrate the definition of each specification. The geometric specification is chosen based on the functional application, therefore a sample practical application for each is also shown.

Position - Coaxial Features

Position tolerance for coaxial features is a 3D axis to axis control. It defines a cylindrical shaped tolerance zone concentric to the datum axis that the axis of the unrelated actual mating envelope (unrelated AME) must lie within. This controls orientation and location to the datum axis. It does not control size or form, and therefore requires a separate size tolerance for the feature. The MMC or LMC modifier may be applied to the feature, and MMB or LMB modifiers may be applied to the datum feature.

This on the drawing

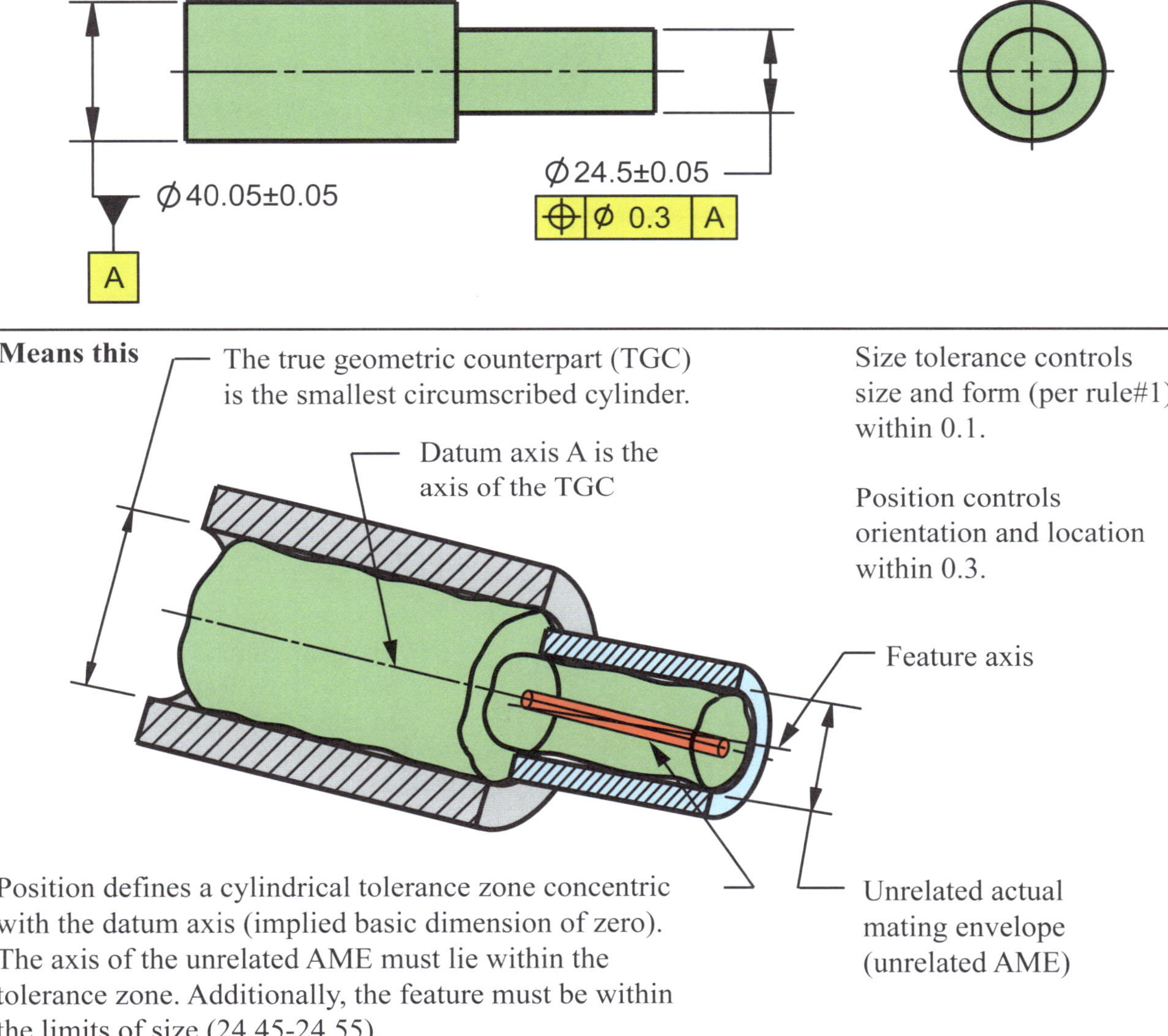

Inspection: Datum feature A is mounted in a collet, chuck, or vee block. A dial indicator is placed on the Ø24.5 surface at various locations along its length. As the part rotates, if the full indicator movement (FIM) does not exceed 0.3, the feature passes. If the FIM exceeds 0.3, the feature is not necessarily bad. As the indicator rides the surface, it also picks up form (circularity and straightness) error. Since position is only an axis to axis control, surface variations are not included in the requirement. A mapping of the surface to exclude these form errors may be necessary to accept features beyond 0.3 FIM. This also may be checked with a CMM, optical comparator, height gage, functional gage or other methods.

Position - Coaxial Application

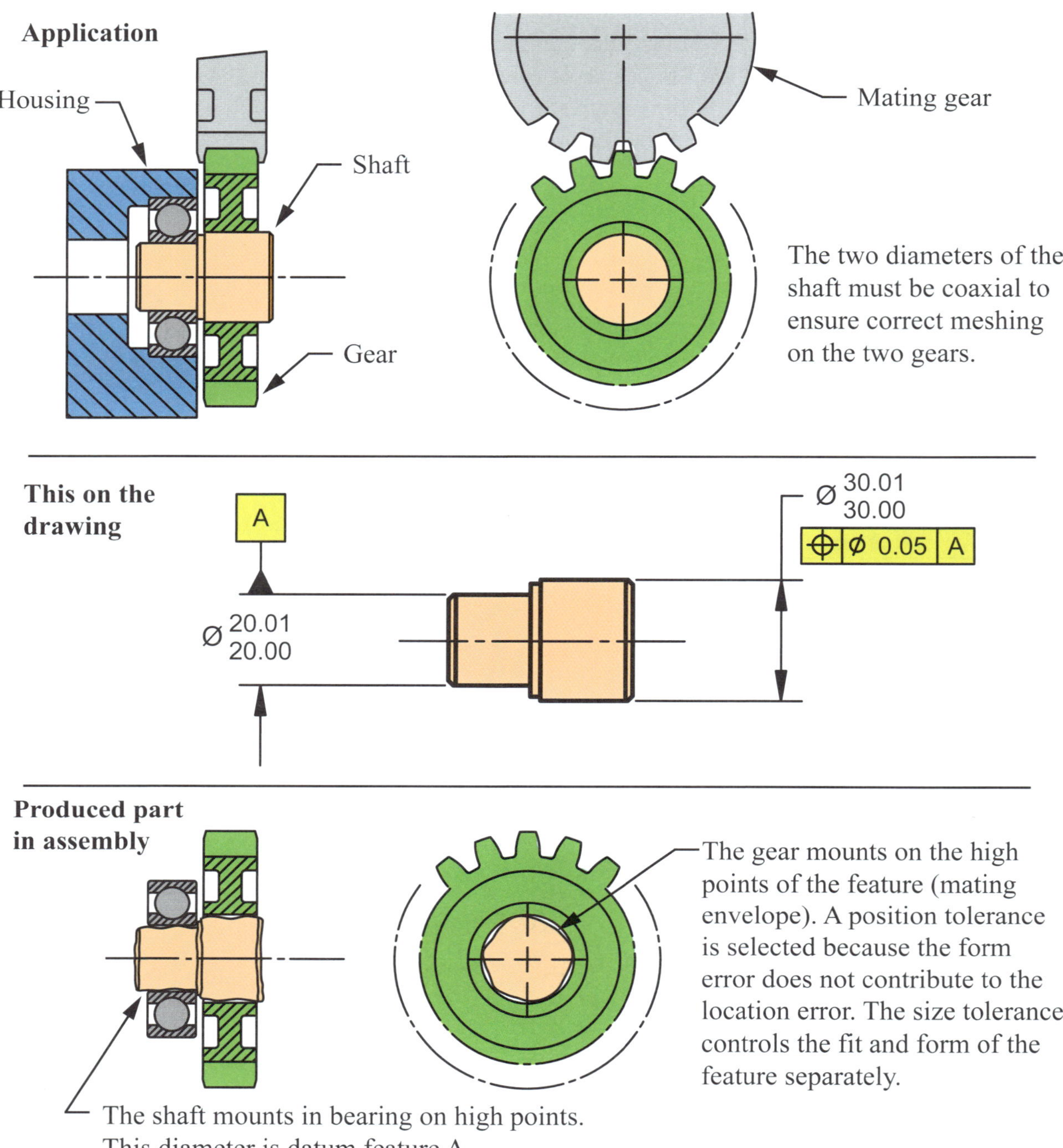

A runout tolerance is not selected because the form error of the surface does not affect the location of the gear axis. Runout requires the form to be included in the location tolerance, while position allows full location tolerance regardless of the form error.

A profile tolerance is not selected because the size of the feature is important for the fit in the gear, while a separate larger location tolerance is allowed. Profile combines both of these requirements into a tighter profile tolerance and requires a basic diameter dimension.

Runout Tolerances

Symbol	Runout Tolerance	Common Shape of Tolerance Zone	2D / 3D	Application of MMC Modifier
↗	Circular Runout	2 Concentric circles about a datum axis 2 Concentric circular line elements about a datum axis	2D	No It is a Surface Control
⌰	Total Runout	2 Concentric cylinders about a datum axis 2 Parallel planes perpendicular to a datum axis	3D	No It is a Surface Control

Overview:

The runout tolerances of circular runout and total runout control form, orientation, and coaxiality of surfaces constructed about a datum axis. Runout must always be referenced to a datum axis or a datum reference frame that establishes an axis of rotation.

Runout tolerances do not control the size of a feature, therefore a separate size tolerance or profile must also be applied. Rule #1 states that a size tolerance controls form, therefore any form control from the runout specification is in addition to the size tolerance (usually as a refinement).

The two runout tolerances are near identical controls. Total runout defines a single 3D tolerance zone for the surface, while circular runout defines a series of 2D tolerance zones for each circular element controlled separately. On a cylindrical feature, total runout also controls 3D form (cylindricity), but circular runout only controls 2D form (circularity).

Older versions of the Y14.5 standard and engineering drawings used terms like *total indicator reading (TIR)*, and *full indicator movement (FIM)* in the definition of the symbols. Y14.5-2018 instead defines only tolerance zones to separate inspection methods from the mathematical requirements. The quality plan should designate the inspection tool and number of cross-sections or points to measure.

These are both surface controls. Therefore, the material condition modifiers of MMC, LMC, and RFS are not applicable. Datum feature references are only applicable RMB.

Runout tolerances may also control surfaces at a right angle to a datum axis. In these applications, total runout controls perpendicularity and flatness. Circular runout controls perpendicularity of 2D circular elements of the surface and does not control flatness.

In the past, runout tolerances were often used on all rotating components. This is not always needed and can unnecessarily tighten manufacturing tolerances. The other coaxial controls of position and profile of a surface should be considered as well. The best applications for runout are for features with mating parts that ride on the surface, such as a wheel or pulley with adjustments for larger size tolerances. Examples of applications are shown later in this section.

Total Runout - Coaxial Features

Total runout is a 3D surface to axis control. It creates one tolerance zone that all surface elements must lie within. When applied to a cylindrical feature, the tolerance zone is the radial separation between two cylinders concentric with the datum axis. This controls 3D form (cylindricity), orientation and location to the datum axis. It does not control size, and therefore requires a separate size tolerance for the feature. Total runout may only be applied to surfaces constructed around a datum axis or surfaces at right angles to a datum axis.

This on the drawing

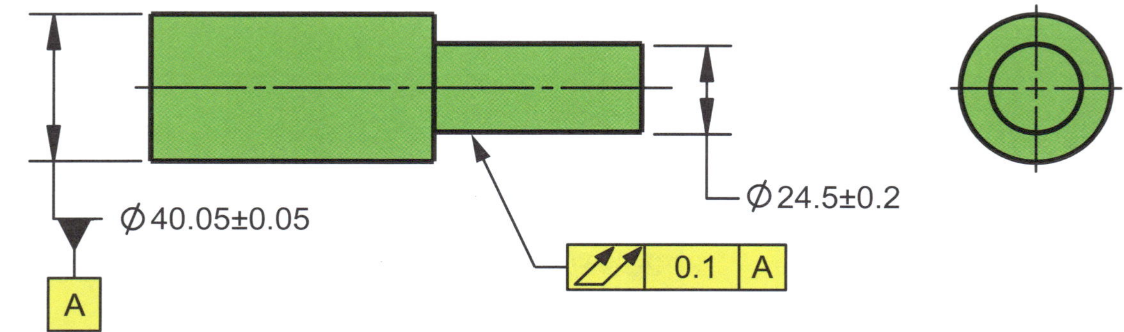

Means this

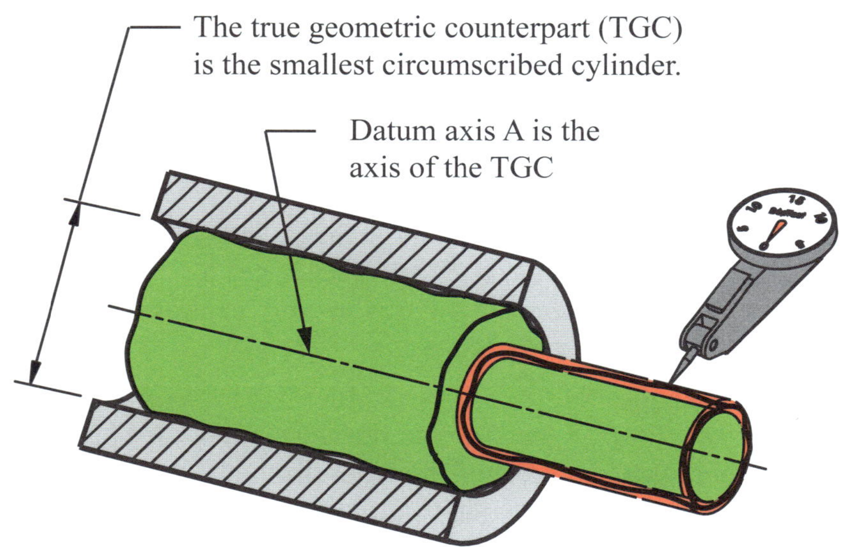

Size tolerance controls size and form (per rule#1) within 0.4.

Total runout refines cylindricity, and controls orientation and location within 0.1.

Total runout defines a tolerance zone between two cylinders, one having a radius of 0.1 larger than the other, concentric with the datum axis. Additionally, the feature must be within the limits of size (24.3-24.7).

Inspection: Datum feature A is mounted in a collet, chuck, or vee block. A dial indicator is placed on the Ø24.5 cylinder surface at various locations along its length. At each location, the part is rotated a full revolution about the datum axis. The full indicator movement (FIM) shall be no more than 0.1. Because this is a 3D callout, the indicator is not reset at each cross-section along the length. Although the specification requires all cross-sections to be within tolerance, a quality plan should define the number of places to be verified. This also may be checked with a CMM, optical comparator, or other methods.

Circular Runout - Coaxial Features

Circular runout is a 2D surface to axis control. It creates a series of 2D tolerance zones that apply independently to each other. When applied to a cylindrical feature, each tolerance zone is the radial separation between two circles concentric with the datum axis. This controls 2D form (circularity), orientation and location to the datum axis. It does not control straightness, taper, or size, and therefore requires a separate size tolerance for the feature. Circular runout may only be applied to surfaces constructed around a datum axis or surfaces at right angles to a datum axis.

This on the drawing

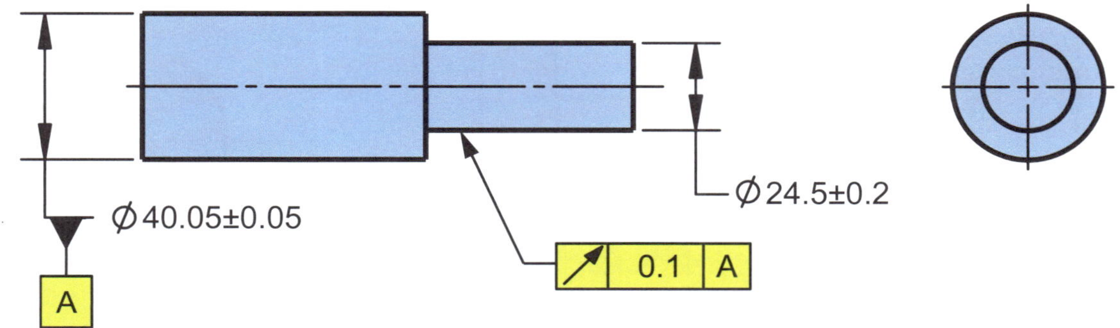

Means this

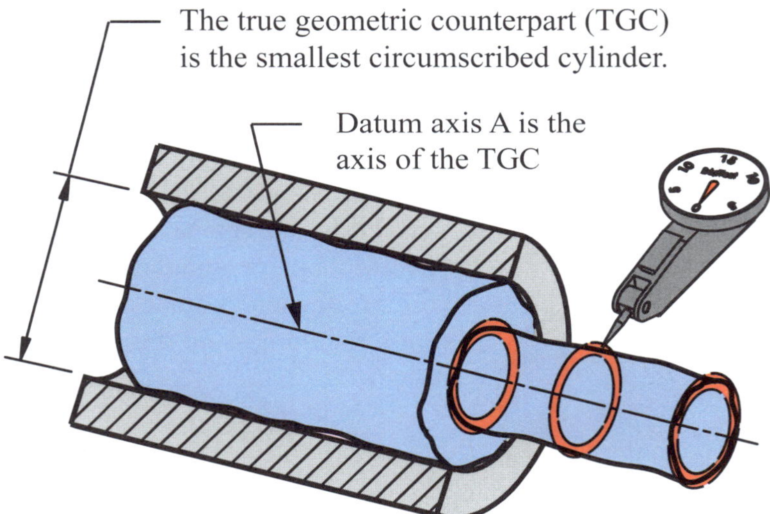

Size tolerance controls size and form (per rule#1) within 0.4.

Circular runout refines circularity, and controls orientation and location within 0.1.

Circular runout does not control taper or surface straightness. Each cross-section is evaluated separately.

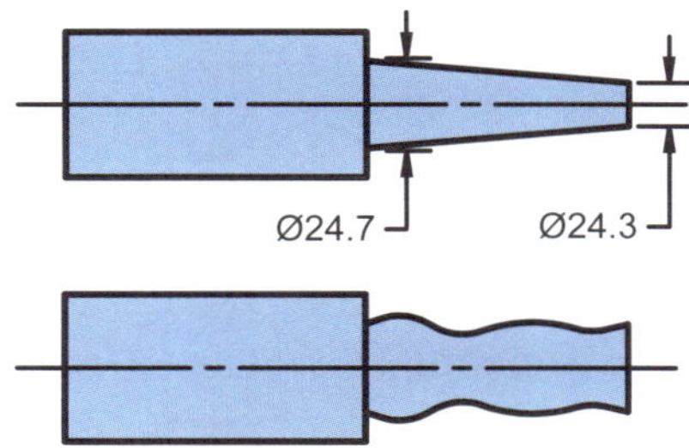

Parts with perfect circular runout

Circular runout defines a series of tolerance zones that each cross-sectional element of the surface must be within. Each tolerance zone is between two circles concentric with the datum axis, one having a radius of 0.1 larger than the other. Additionally, the feature must be within the limits of size (24.3-24.7).

Inspection: Datum feature A is mounted in a collet, chuck, or vee block. A dial indicator is placed on the Ø24.5 cylinder surface at various locations along its length. At each location, the part is rotated a full revolution about the datum axis. The full indicator movement (FIM) shall be no more than 0.1. Because this is a 2D callout, the indicator is reset at each cross-section along the length. Although the specification requires all cross-sections to be within tolerance, a quality plan should define the number of places to be verified. This also may be checked with a CMM, optical comparator, or other methods.

Runout - Applied to Flat Surfaces

Both total runout and circular runout may be applied to surfaces at right angles to a datum axis. These callouts are refinements of the location (profile) tolerances. Total runout on a right angle surface provides an identical requirement to perpendicularity. Circular runout controls a series of 2D circular elements within separate tolerance zones about the axis. This allows the surface to be concave or convex within the location tolerance.

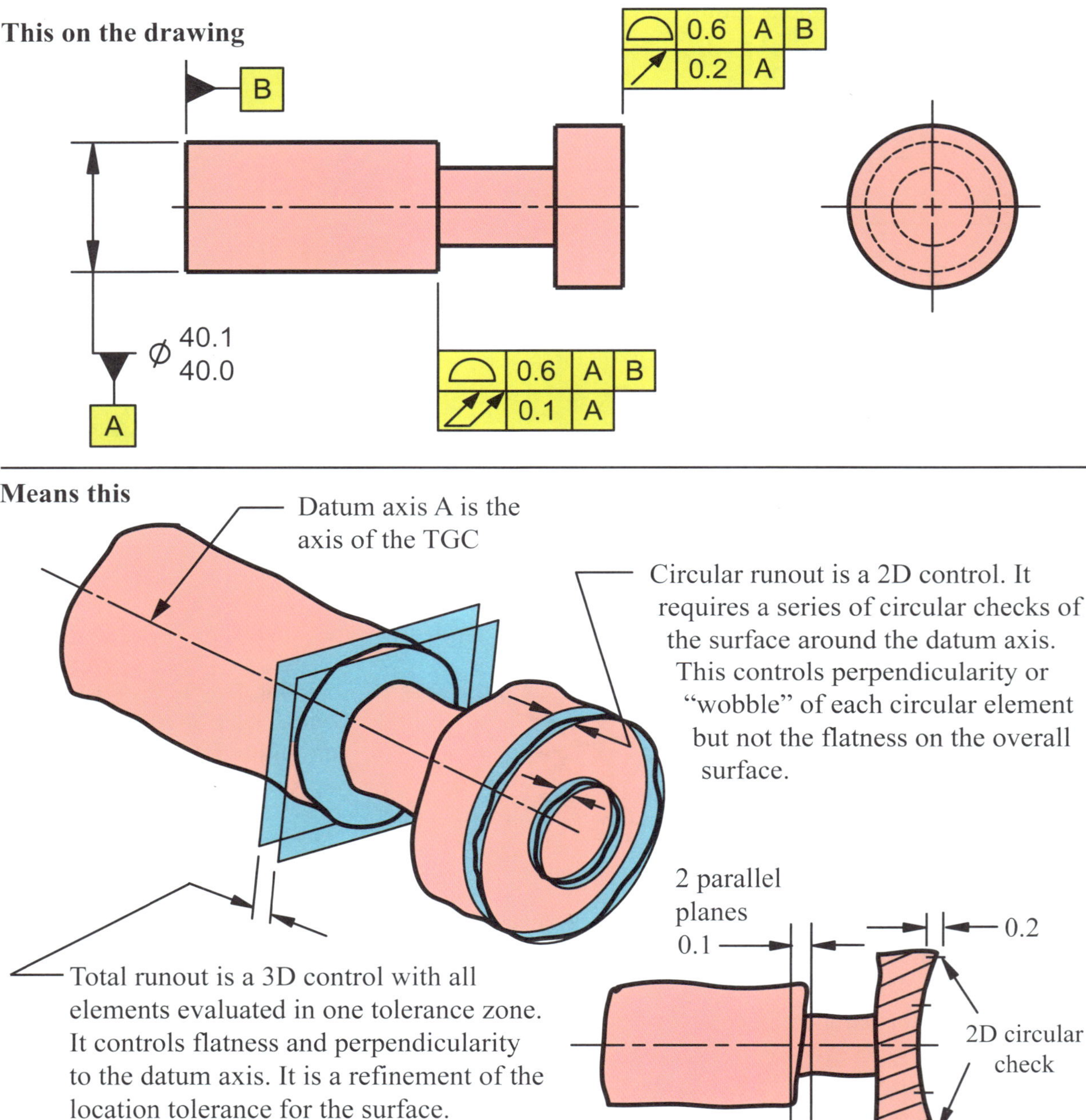

Inspection: A dial indicator is placed normal to the surface at various distances from the axis. At each location, the part is rotated a full revolution about the datum axis. The full indicator movement (FIM) shall be no more than the tolerance value. Total runout requires all elements to be within tolerance without an indicator reset. With circular runout, the indicator is reset to zero after the indicator is moved radially. In addition, the surfaces must also be within the profile tolerance.

Runout - Coaxial Application

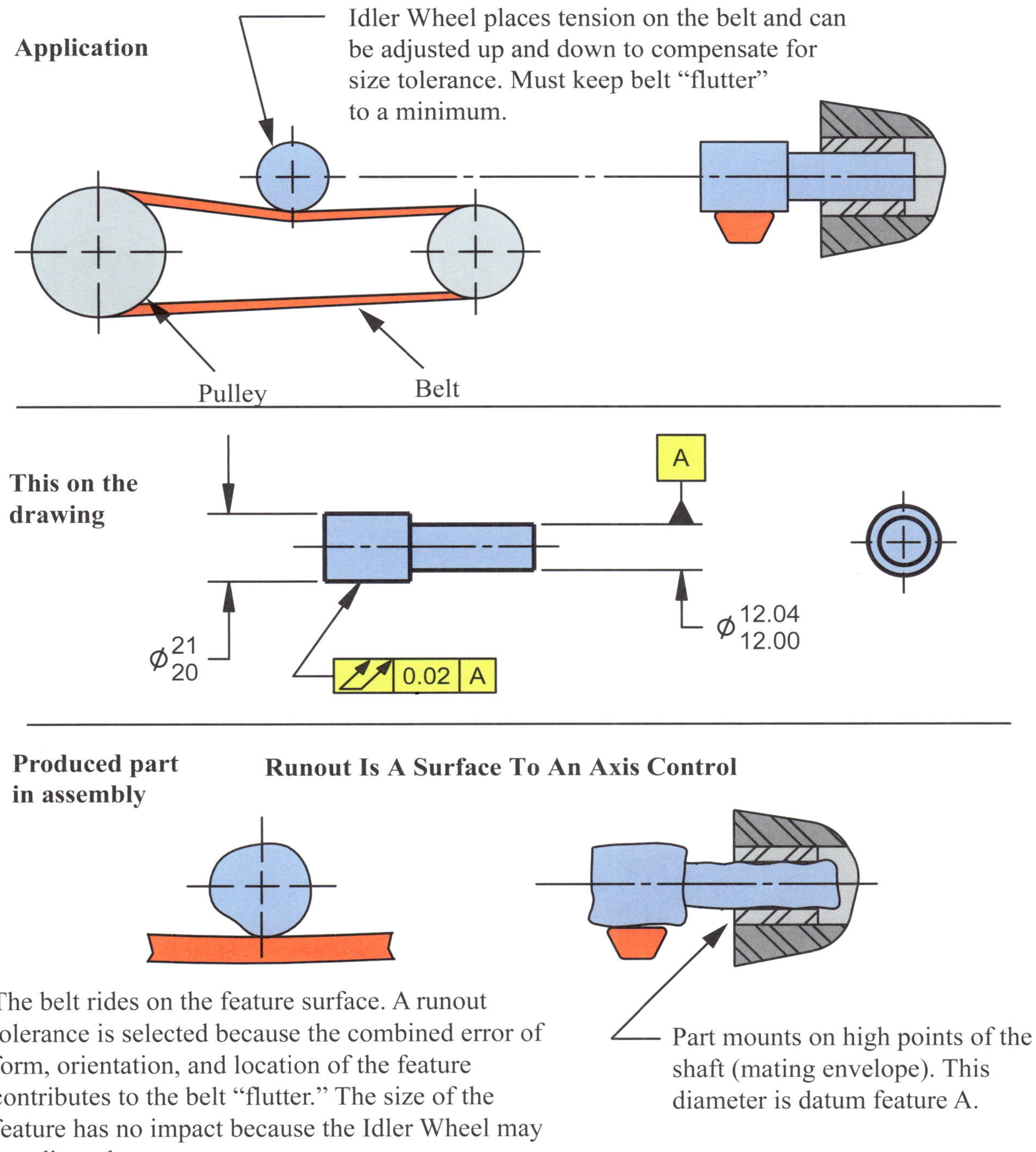

The belt rides on the feature surface. A runout tolerance is selected because the combined error of form, orientation, and location of the feature contributes to the belt "flutter." The size of the feature has no impact because the Idler Wheel may be adjusted.

Part mounts on high points of the shaft (mating envelope). This diameter is datum feature A.

Position is not selected because the belt rides on the surface of the feature and not on the mating envelope (high points). The circularity error of the feature contributes to the belt "flutter." Position does not control form.

Profile is not selected because the wheel may be adjusted for the size tolerance. Profile requires a basic dimension for the diameter and tightens the size tolerance more than necessary. If the Idler Wheel were not adjustable in location, profile would be used.

Profile - Coaxial Features

Profile of a surface for coaxial features is a 3D surface to axis control. It defines a tolerance zone that is equally disposed about the basic diameter. When applied to a surface constructed around a datum axis, profile of a surface controls the variations of size, form, orientation, and location (coaxiality). A basic dimension must be used for the diameter.

This on the drawing

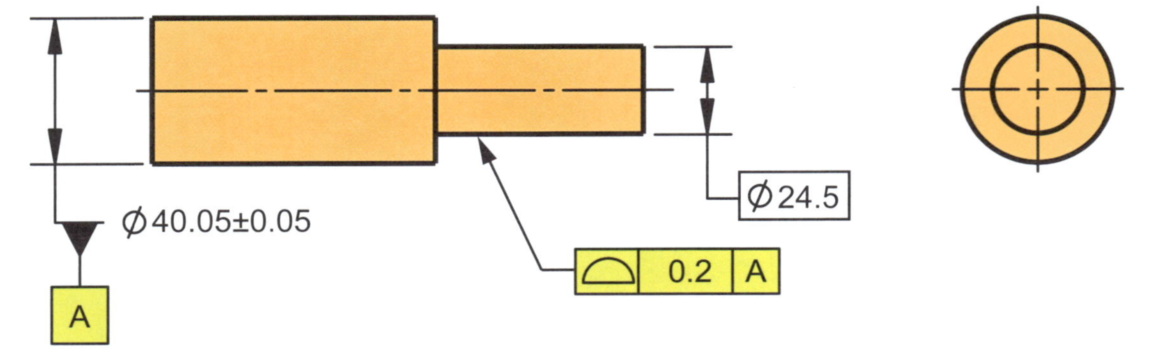

Means this

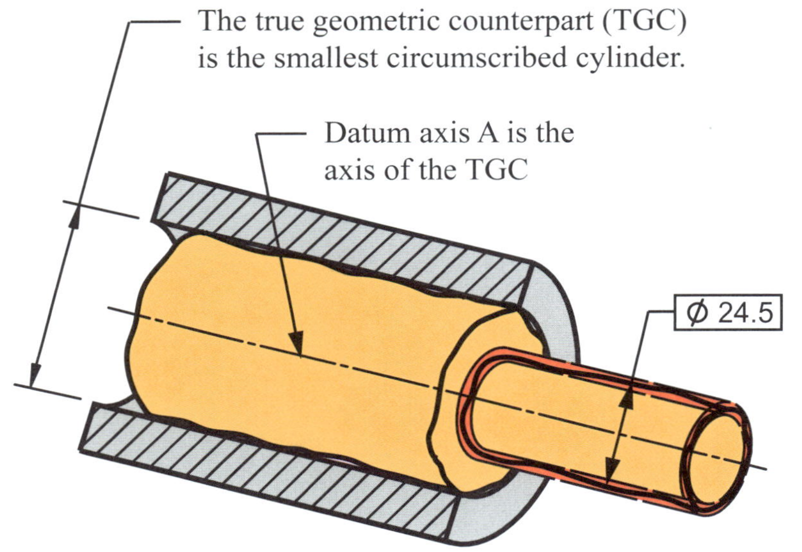

The diameter dimension is basic.

Profile controls the size, form, orientation and location within 0.2.

Profile defines a tolerance zone between two cylinders, one having a radius of 0.2 larger than the other, concentric with the datum axis. The two cylinders are equally disposed about a basic cylinder of Ø24.5.

The MMB is a diameter of 24.7

The LMB is a diameter of 24.3

Inspection: Datum feature A is mounted in a collet, chuck, or vee block. A dial indicator is mastered/set at the radius of 12.25 (half of basic 24.5) from the datum axis. All points on the surface may not vary any more than ±0.1 from the basic radius. Although the specification requires all points to be within tolerance, a quality plan should define the number of places to be verified. This also may be checked with a CMM, optical comparator, or other methods. See profile in unit 11 for methods of verification and measurement data reporting.

Profile - Coaxial Application

Application

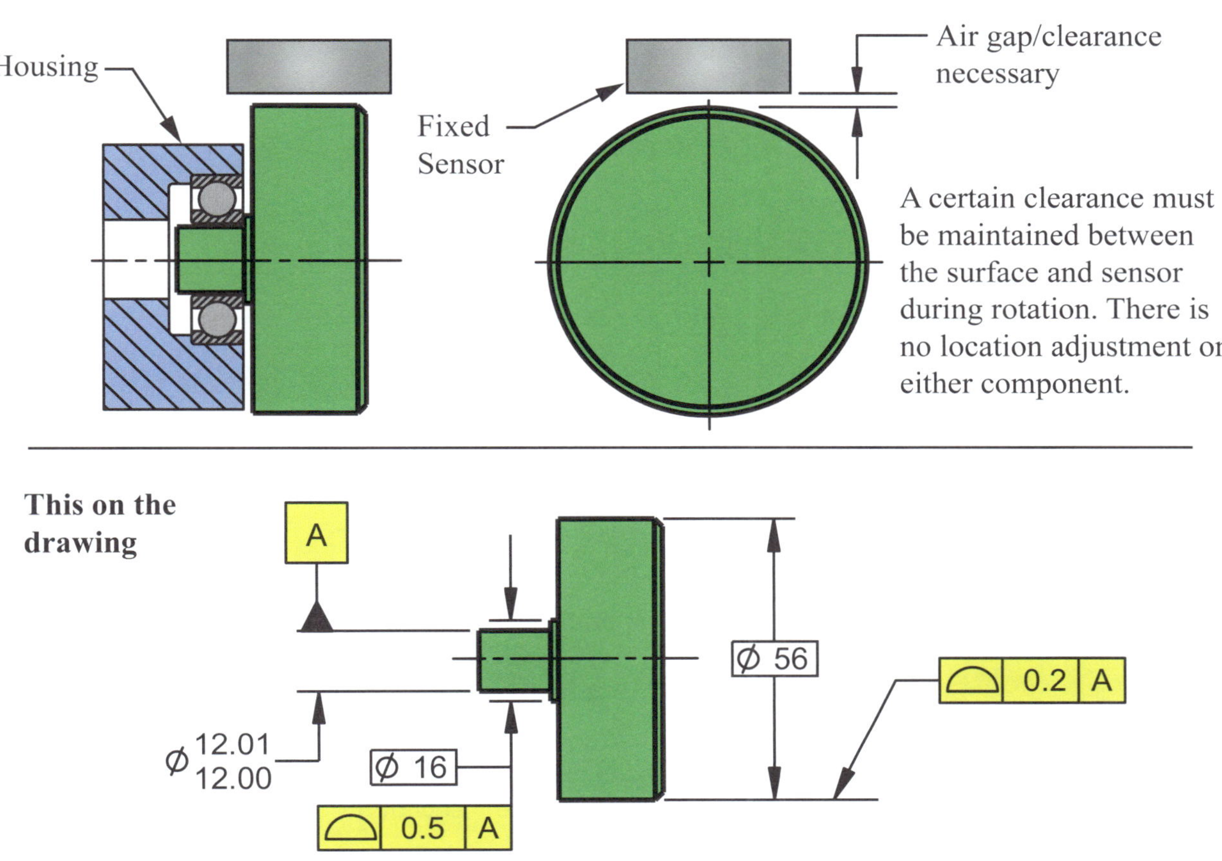

Produced part in assembly

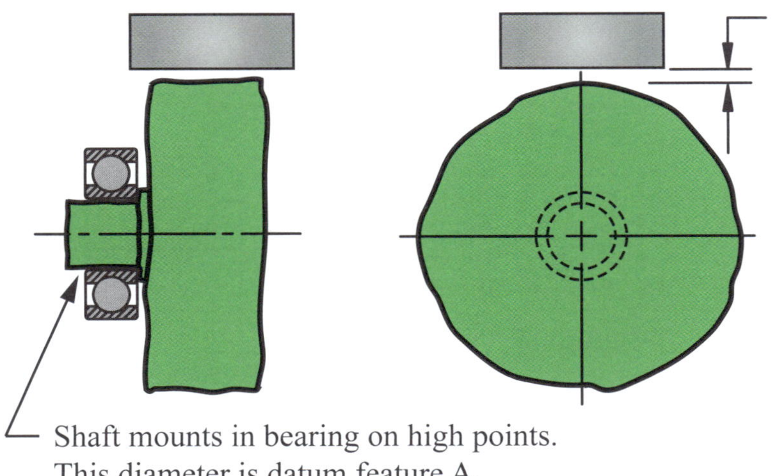

The clearance is dependent on the location of the surface from the mounting datum axis. A profile tolerance is selected because it combines size, form, orientation, and location in one specification. It is simple to calculate and verify, and it provides maximum tolerance while still preserving the function.

MMB = 56.2
LMB = 55.8

A runout or position tolerance is not selected because a separate size and location tolerance is required. Separating into two tolerances unneccesarily tightens the requirement and allows manufacturing less flexibilty.

Coaxial Tolerances Review

This is a review of the four coaxial tolerances and their controls.

Position  **Axis to axis**

Ø24.5±0.05

⌖	Ø 0.3	A

Controls: Orientation, Location

Feature diameter must have a separate size tolerance*

Runout  **Surface to axis**

Ø24.5±0.2

↗	0.1	A

Ø24.5±0.2

⌰	0.1	A

Controls: Form, Orientation, Location

Feature diameter must have a separate size tolerance*

Circular Runout 

Controls: 2-D Form (Circularity)
Orientation, Location

Total Runout 

Controls: 3-D Form (Cylindricity, Straightness, Taper)
Orientation, Location

Profile  **Surface to axis, includes size**

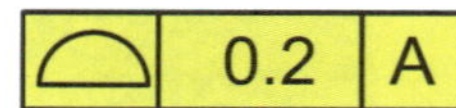

Controls: Form, Orientation, Location, Size

Feature diameter dimension is basic

---

*The size tolerance controls the size and form of the feature.
(Rule #1 requires perfect form at MMC.)

Concentricity and Symmetry Symbols Removed from Y14.5-2018

Symbol	Tolerance	Common Shape of Tolerance Zone	2D / 3D	Application of Feature Modifier
◎	Concentricity	Cylindrical about a datum axis	3D	No
⌯	Symmetry	2 Parallel planes about a datum median plane	3D	No

Overview:
Concentricity and symmetry symbols are no longer defined in ASME Y14.5-2018. In Y14.5-2009, concentricity controls opposing median points of cylindrical features relative to a datum axis, and symmetry controls opposing median points of widths/slots relative to a datum center plane. However, it is not exactly clear how these median points are established on a produced part. The figures depict multiple median points at each circular cross-section. Even if this is functionally needed, why are these complex requirements named with simple/generic terms and symbols of concentricity and symmetry? The definitions were deceivingly more complex than the symbols.

The concentricity and symmetry definition of controlling opposing median points is not usually functional and not in agreement with dictionary and general conversational definitions. This disagreement in the definitions caused misapplication of these symbols for the novice user. Concentricity and symmetry define complex requirements when instead a simple position coaxiality or runout tolerance would suffice.

The Y14.5 committee decided to remove these symbols and concepts rather than amend the definitions or change the symbols. This simplifies the tool-set for coaxial/symmetrical features:

-Use position for control of an axis/center plane
-Use runout or profile for control of a surface.
-If another more complex analysis of the feature is required, detail this requirement in a note.

ISO Definitions:
These symbols do not have the same definition in ISO 1101:2017. The concentricity symbol is called coaxiality when applied to a full shaft or hole. It has the same definition as ISO position but used exclusively for features nominally centered with the datum axis. The symbol is called concentricity only when the symbol is applied to any cross-section (notation ACS) of a shaft or hole. Symmetry has the same definition as ISO position but used exclusively for features with a center plane nominally centered on the datum.

Workshop Exercise 13.1

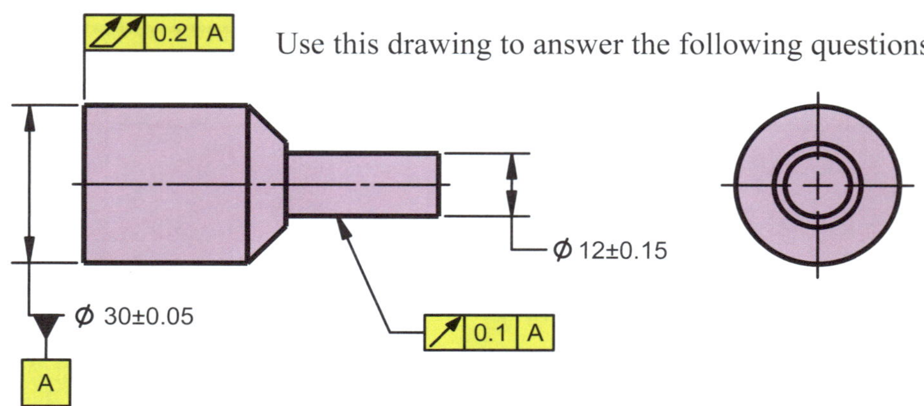

Use this drawing to answer the following questions.

1. What coaxiality tolerance is implied between the two diameters if no geometric tolerances are applied?
   - a. within the size tolerance
   - b. within half the size tolerance
   - c. no coaxiality tolerance implied

2. With the circular runout specification applied, how much taper is allowed on the 12 mm diameter?
   a. 0.05 b. 0.1 c. 0.3 d. not defined

3. If the 0.1 circular runout specification were replaced with a 0.1 total runout specification, how much taper would be allowed per side on the 12 mm diameter?
   a. 0.05 b. 0.1 c. 0.3 d. not defined

4. With the circular runout specification applied, how much circularity tolerance is allowed on the small diameter?
   a. 0.05 b. 0.1 c. 0.3 d. not defined

5. With the circular runout specification applied, how much location, on a diameter, is allowed on the small diameter relative to datum axis A?
   a. 0.05 b. 0.1 c. 0.3 d. not defined

6. What is the difference between a circular runout and a circularity tolerance on a shaft?
   - a. circularity controls only the form, runout controls the form and location
   - b. circularity controls the surface, runout controls the axis
   - c. there is no difference

7. What is the difference between the tolerance zone created by the total runout on the left face and a perpendicularity specification?
   - a. perpendicularity does not control flatness
   - b. perpendicularity does not have a datum reference
   - c. there is no difference

8. True or False: Total runout may only be applied to surfaces constructed around a datum axis or at right angles to a datum axis.

Workshop Exercise 13.2

There are four coaxial controls: position, circular runout, total runout, and profile. Answer questions below for each type to show the differences in the requirements.

1. **Position** ⌖ Axis Control or Surface Control?

Controls what types of variation on the feature? Circle all that apply.

Form Orientation Location Size

Is a basic dimension used for the diameter or is a size tolerance required?

2. **Runout** ↗ ⌰ Axis Control or Surface Control?

Controls what types of variation on the feature? Circle all that apply.

Form Orientation Location Size

Is a basic dimension used for the diameter or is a size tolerance required?

3. **Profile** ⌓ Axis Control or Surface Control?

Controls what types of variation on the feature? Circle all that apply.

Form Orientation Location Size

Is a basic dimension used for the diameter or is a size tolerance required?

4. Explain the difference between total runout and position on a cylindrical part. Assuming the numbers are the same, which is a more restrictive requirement?

____

____

5. Which one of these tolerances may have a material condition modifier (MMC/LMC)?

____

6. Which two symbols may only be applied to surfaces constructed about (or at right angles to) a datum axis?

____

Workshop Exercise 13.3

1. Application Requirements

The wheel mounts on the axle which may be adjusted up and down to compensate for the variation in size. The "ride" of the shaft axis must be controlled to move no more than .005 total.

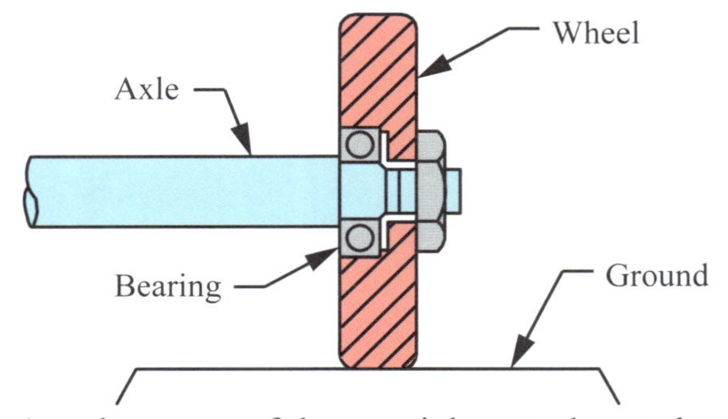

On the drawing below, select the datum feature A and use one of the coaxial controls to tolerance the other diameter and meet the application requirements.

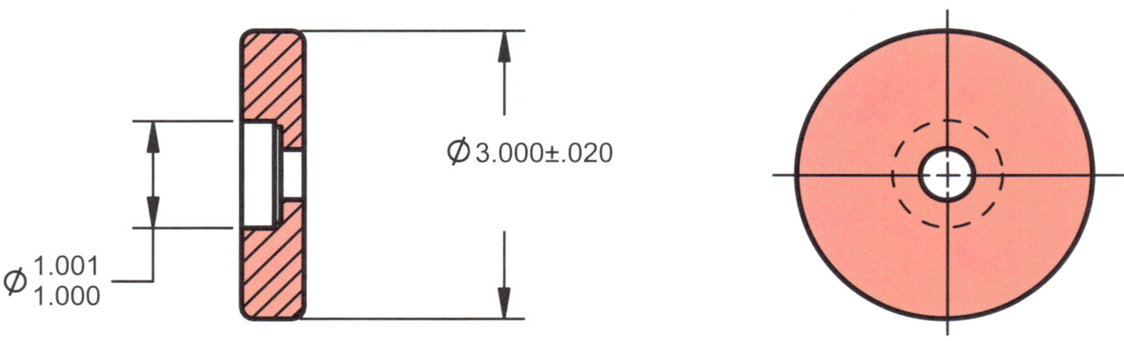

2. Application Requirements

The wheel mounts on the axle and cannot be adjusted up and down. The gap with the mating part must be within .015±.005

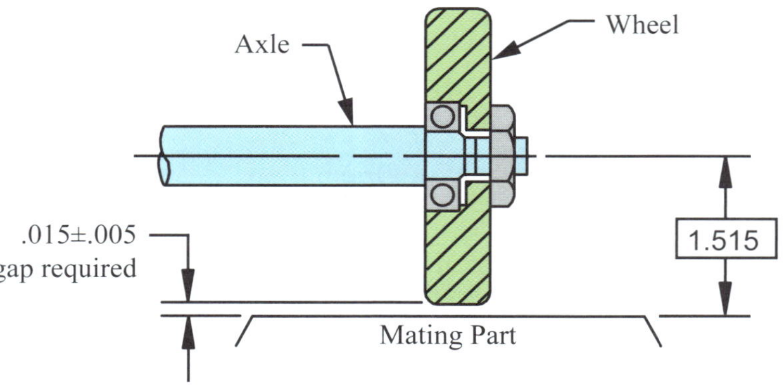

On the drawing below, select the datum feature A and use one of the coaxial controls to tolerance the other diameter and meet the application requirements.

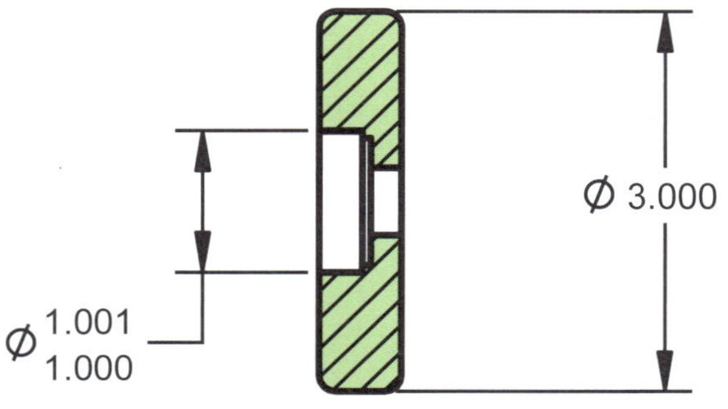

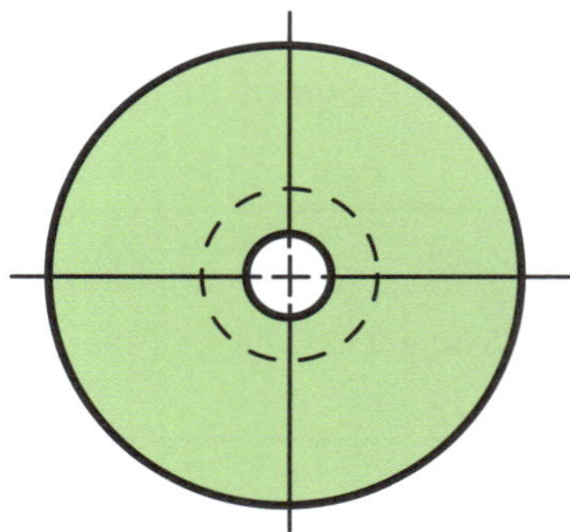

Unit 14
Application Exercises

Workshop Exercise 14.1 - Corner Bracket
Workshop Exercise 14.2 - Flange Bearing
Workshop Exercise 14.3 - Reinforcement Tube Assembly
Workshop Exercise 14.4 - Powder Case
Workshop Exercise 14.5 - Link

Workshop Exercise 14.1 - Corner Bracket

This corner bracket reinforces the table assembly as shown below. The 12 mm surface radius must clear a pin that is pushed through the assembly. The four 8 mm holes mount with 7.2 mm max rivets. The three 9 mm holes mount to the mating cover with M7 screws into tapped holes. The tapped holes on the mating cover have a 1 mm position tolerance. The top flange surfaces must not be above the 30.5 min height of the table edges. Specify datum features, qualify the datum features, and apply necessary geometric tolerances.

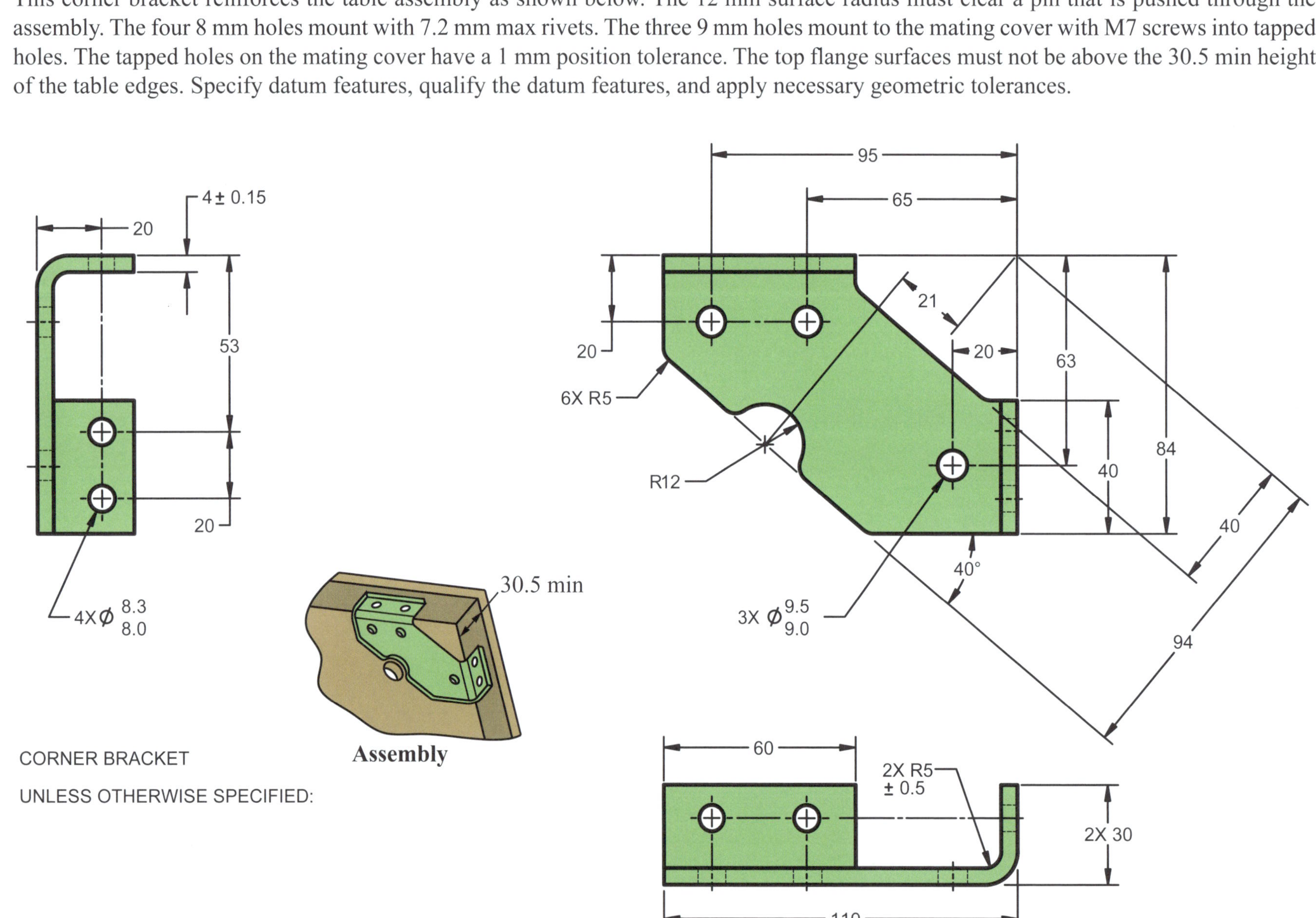

Workshop Exercise 14.2 - Flange Bearing

The flange below has a bearing pressed into the large dia 2.2390 hole. Four .4375 bolts attach the flange to a frame. Select datum features to establish a DRF and qualify the datum features with any necessary form, orientation and/or location tolerances. Make necessary dimensions basic. Calculate the allowable position tolerance for the 4 holes. The mating frame has tapped holes with .017 position tolerance. In this problem, just estimate the remaining tolerances based on realistic expectations.

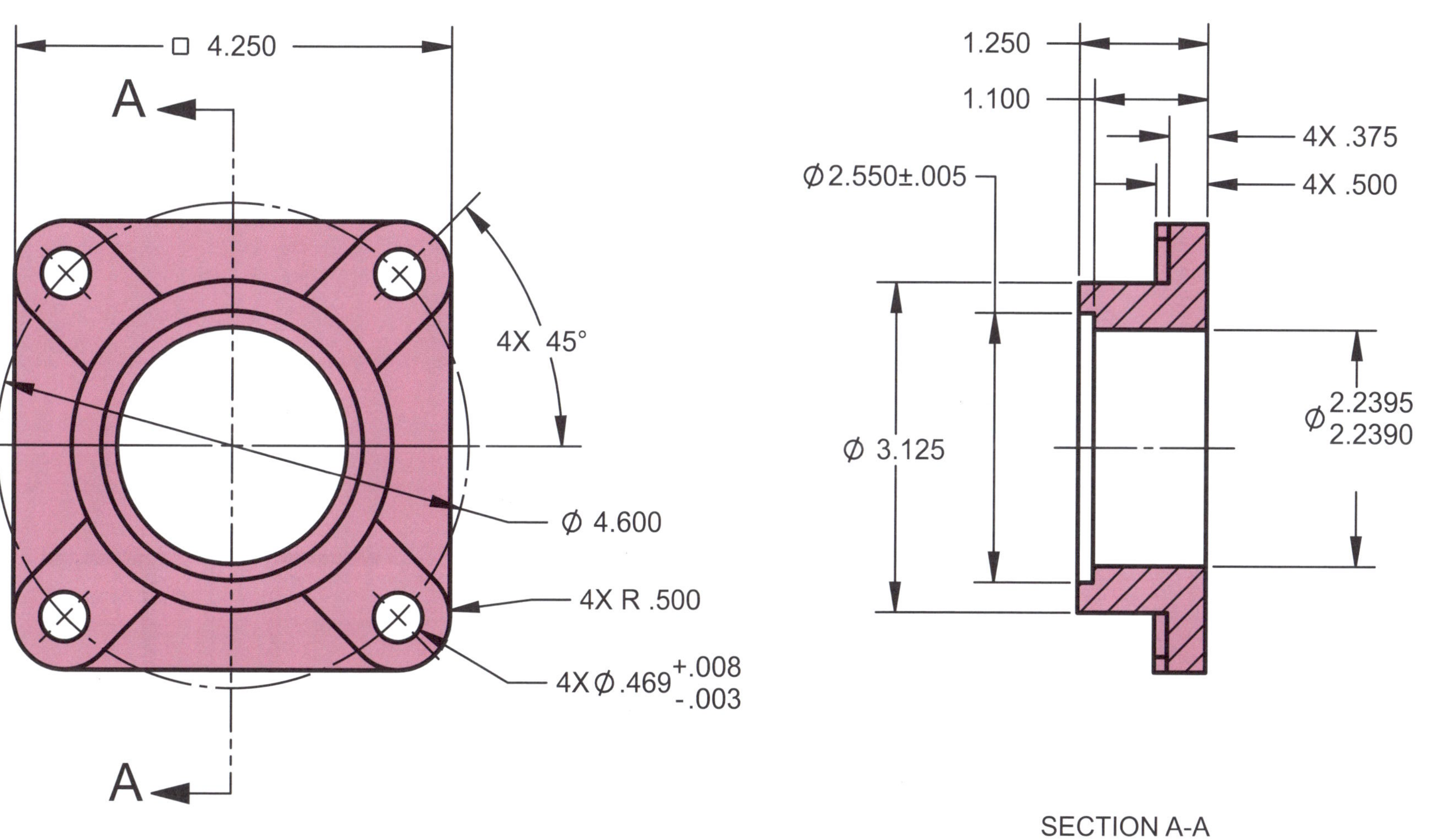

Workshop Exercise 14.3 - Reinforcement Tube Assembly

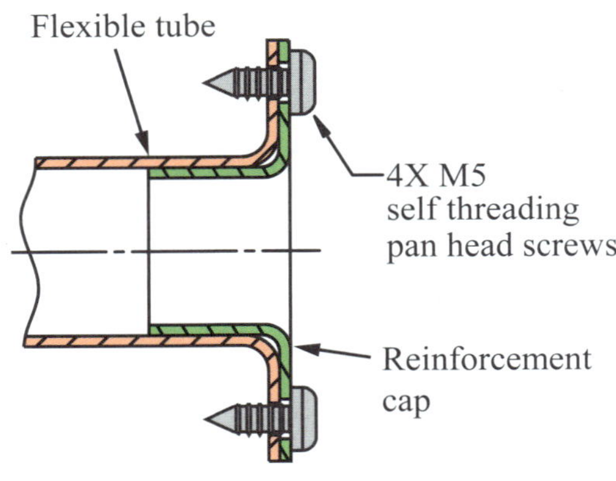

The sheet metal assembly to the left consists of two main parts: a flexible tube and reinforcement cap. They are attached with four self-threading M5 screws.

Select datum features based on the mating condition. Qualify these features with flatness and perpendicularity.

Calculate position tolerances using either the floating or fixed fastener formula.

Apply a geometric tolerance to the outside diameters to minimize mismatch of the edges.

Flexible tube

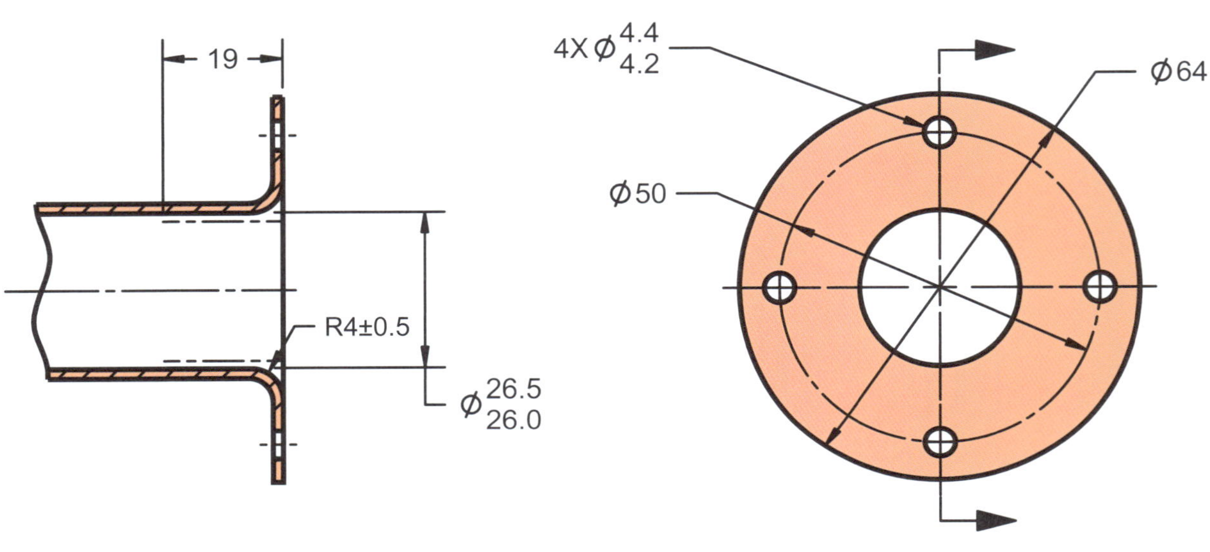

Reinforcement cap

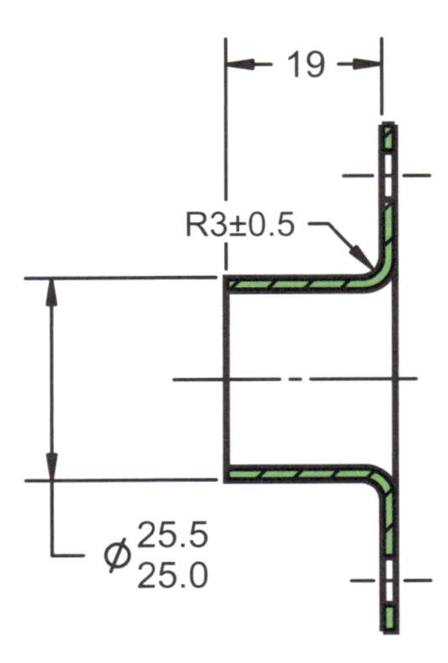

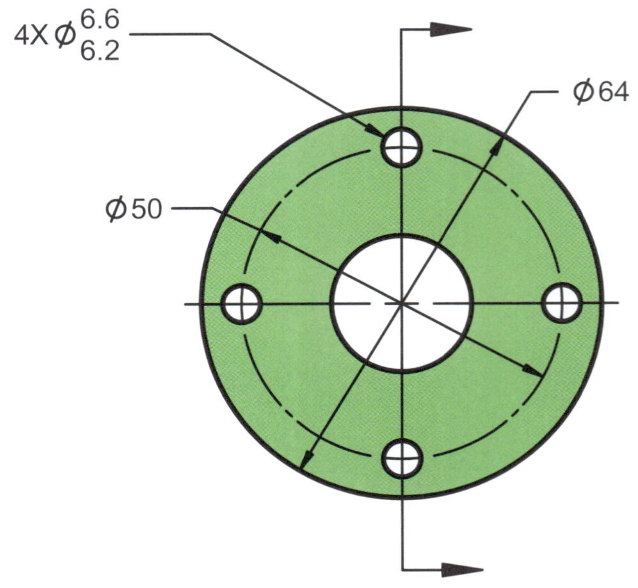

Workshop Exercise 14.4 - Powder Case

The two parts below fit together and must seal in powder with .006 min diameter. The mismatch on the outer diameters may be no more than .020 per side. The overall thickness on the assembly may be no more than 1.800. Select datum features and apply necessary geometric tolerances.

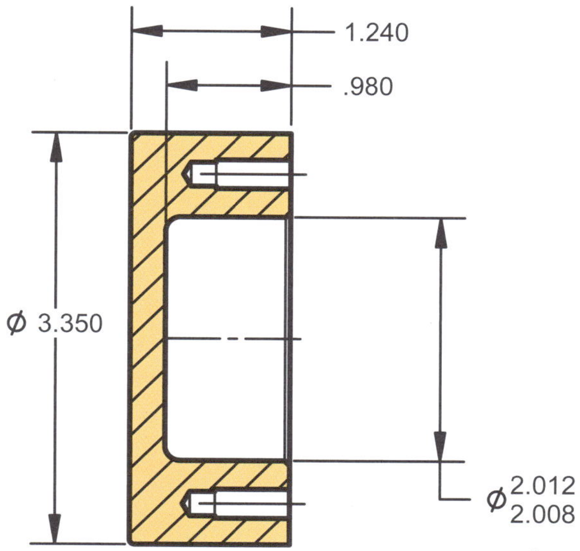

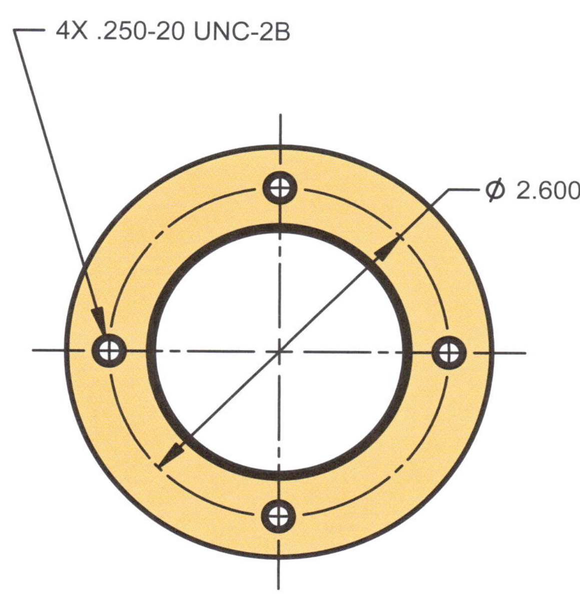

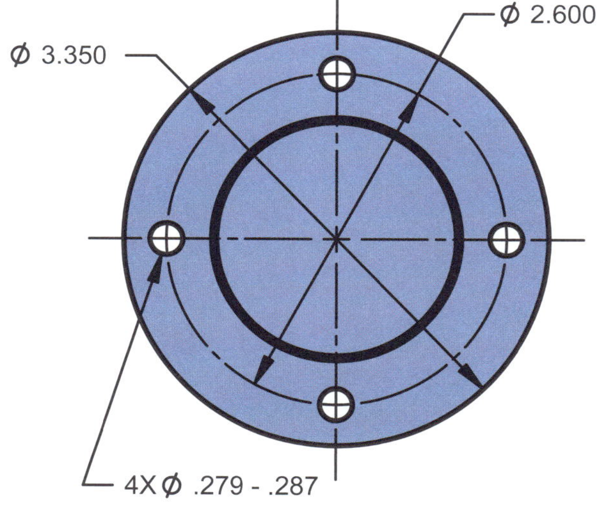

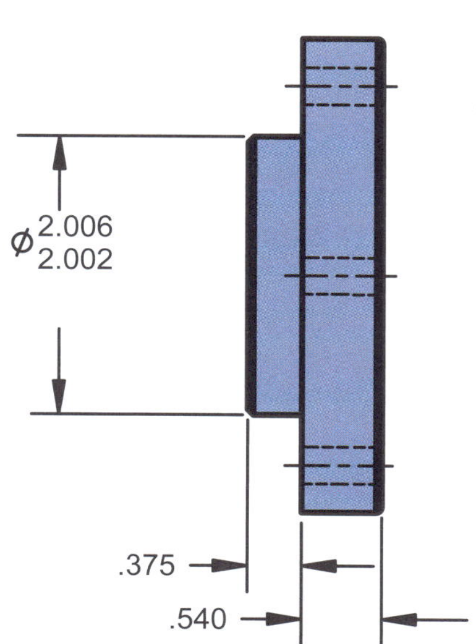

Workshop Exercise 14.5 - Link

Study the assembly at the bottom of the page. Label the datum features to create a datum reference frame. Then fill in the feature control frames to locate the features to the DRF. The tolerance value for the 6 mm holes, 3.05 mm slot and 12 mm width can be calculated, but other values in this exercise may be engineering estimations. Make any necessary dimensions basic. Also choose the most functional material condition modifiers (MMC, LMC, or RFS) with the position tolerances.

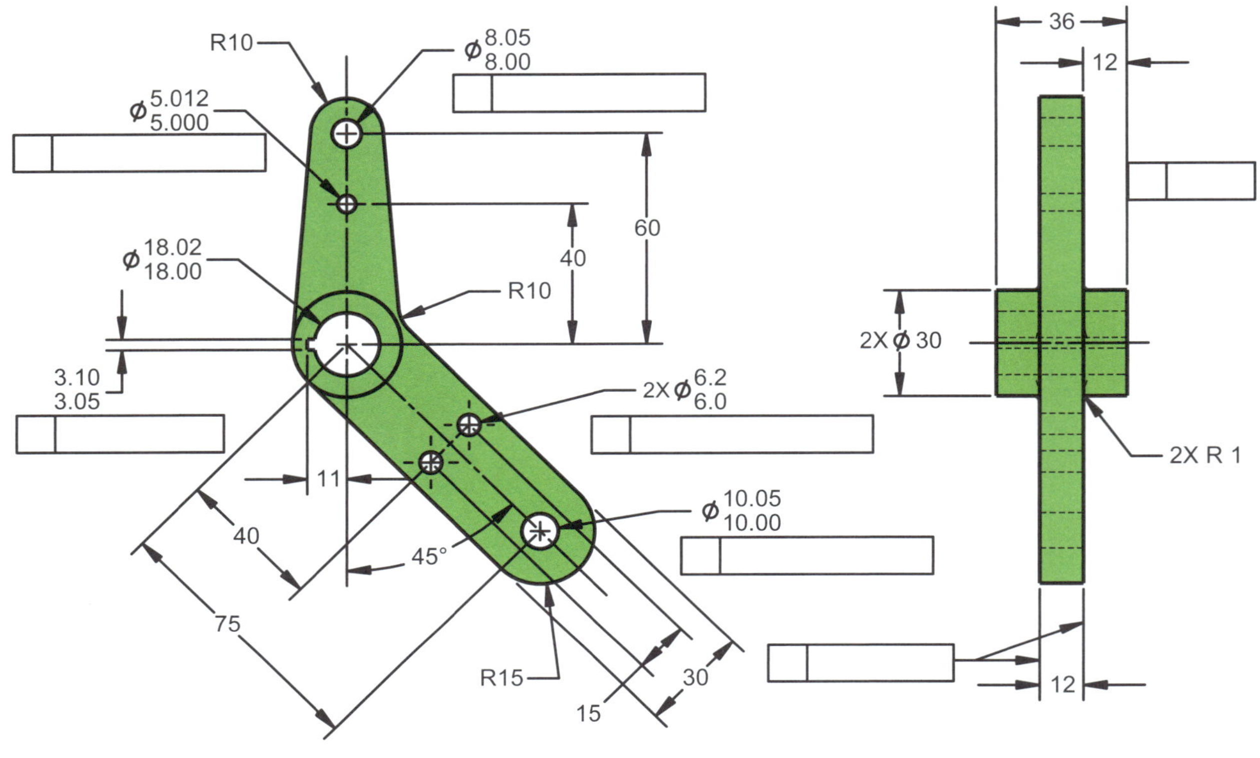

Use the switch drawing below to help calculate the position tolerance for the 6 mm holes.

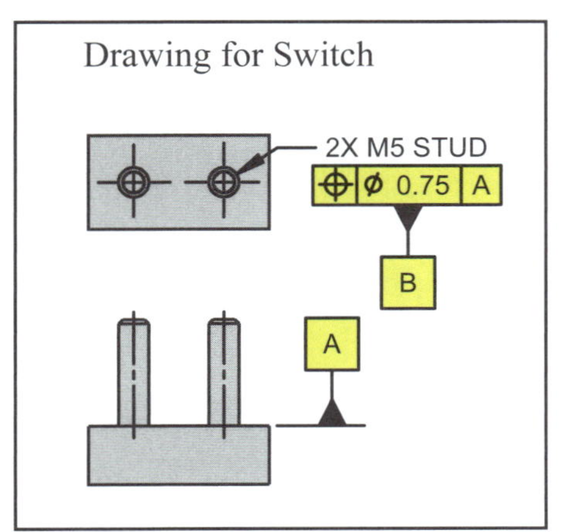

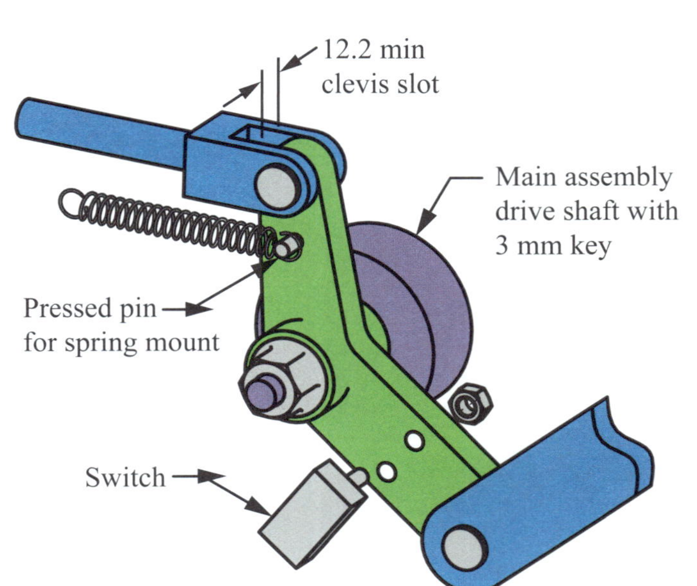

Appendix A - Part 1

Principle changes, improvements, clarifications and enhancements in the ASME Y14.5-2018 from the earlier ASME Y14.5-2009 standard

Part 1 of this appendix shows the changes in the ASME Y14.5-2018 from the previous Y14.5-2009. Although we cannot show every word or paragraph change in the standard, we will address the most noteworthy. If you are upgrading from Y14.5M-1994, part 2 of this appendix covers changes from 1994 to 2009.

The new standard does hold the title of the 2018 completion date even though it wasn't released until February 2019. The sections are renumbered to match ASME's new formatting. All new ASME standards must now start with sections 1-3 as Scope, References, and Definitions. The digital .pdf version of the standard now has hyper-links to the correct figures when reading text in the paragraphs. This makes it easier to flip between the words and figures. The extra thickness of the book seems like a lot has been added, as the book went up from 214 to 326 pages. This is mostly due to the extra 3D figures for most of the concepts. Y14.5 is starting to absorb the 3D representation for model based tolerancing from the Y14.41 standard. At least half of the 2D figures now have a matching 3D figure.

The core concepts of Dimensioning and Geometric Tolerancing have not changed. You will find minor tweaks to definitions and clarifications of concepts with new figures. Two new symbols have been added. A couple terms have been renamed. Some outdated or misused concepts have been removed to streamline the document and reduce confusion. Application of tolerancing in 3D models is gaining more traction and a lot of the definition updates in Y14.5-2018 have been to accommodate model-based applications.

A Notable Change

The Default Stabilization for Datums

The biggest change in the standard relates to the establishment of a datum from a datum feature that is unstable (i.e. a convex surface "that rocks"). This applies to a planar datum feature or a datum feature of size referenced at RMB. In previous versions of Y14.5, *the candidate datum set* is used to derive multiple permissible datums (rock the part and find the datum that works). The 2018 version is now using a default *stabilized single solution*: "the part is to be adjusted to a single solution that minimizes the separation between the feature and the true geometric counterpart". This can be done with shims on a surface plate or with an official algorithm further outlined in ASME Y14.5.1-2019, Mathematical Definitions of Dimensioning and Tolerancing Principles. See Default Stabilization in unit 4 of this book for more info.

Concept and Symbol Removal

Concentricity and Symmetry

The concentricity and symmetry symbols have been removed. These two concepts shown in the 1994 and 1982 versions of Y14.5 have always been controversial and complicated. These symbols control the opposing median points of a feature (not the axis or center plane) relative to a datum. This is rarely a functional requirement and often gets confused with axis to axis, center-plane to center-plane requirements set by position tolerancing. This was a good move by the Y14.5 committee to remove confusion and simplify the toolset.

Unequal Profile Graphical Representation

In the 2009 standard, unequally distributed profile tolerance may be indicated in two ways:

1. Graphically showing the distribution with the use of a phantom line offset from the surface
2. The circle U modifier in the feature control frame with a value in the plus material direction

The 2018 standard has closed the door on the first graphical method. The circle U modifier is now the only way to show unequal profile tolerance. This allows easier readability in the model-based definition and digital inspection world.

Ambiguous Plus/Minus

All plus/minus tolerances defining the relationship between features have been removed from figures and their use discouraged even more. This type of tolerancing has always been ambiguous and the Y14.5 standard did not give definitions even though some were still displayed on figures. The standard recommends the use of geometric tolerancing symbols of position, profile, orientation, and runout tolerances as the proper way to define relationship between features. This has been a long time coming, with each new version of Y14.5 removing more and more ambiguous plus/minus. It is good to see the complete removal in 2018 even with an appendix showing the previous examples and ambiguity.

Notable Changes to Definitions:

Fundamental Rules

Here is an example of a simple but important change to the Fundamental Rules:

> ASME Y14.5 -2009 Paragraph 1.4 Fundamental Rules (a)
>
> *"Each dimension shall have a tolerance. The tolerance may be applied directly to the dimension (or indirectly in the case of basic dimensions) ..."*
>
> ASME Y14.5 -2018 Paragraph 4.1 Fundamental Rules (a)
>
> *"Each feature shall be toleranced. Tolerances may be applied directly to size dimensions. Tolerances shall be applied using feature control frames when feature definition is basic ..."*

Notice the subtlety in this change. The standard is now focusing on "feature based tolerancing" rather than "dimension based tolerancing". Plus/minus tolerances are only used to control size of features and geometric tolerances control relationships of features.

Controlled Radius

The definition of controlled radius now recommends to clarify the limits of allowable imperfections with a note on the drawing. See CR in this book for more information.

Orientation of a Line Element around a Datum Axis

The 2009 standard defined the orientation of multiple line elements around a datum axis with an orientation tolerance and a note underneath: EACH RADIAL ELEMENT. The 2018 standard now shows this with a profile of a line referenced to the datum axis. This is a rarely used concept and a minor change.

Term changes

Common Datum Features

A set of datum features used to create a single datum (notated A-B) is now called "common datum features" in 2018. This used to be called "multiple datum features" in 2009.

True Geometric Counterpart

The term "true geometric counterpart (TGC)" in 2018 replaced "datum feature simulator (theoretical)" in 2009. True geometric counterpart was the term used in 1994 for the theoretical device used in extracting a datum from a datum feature. This term was switched to datum feature simulator in 2009. Now 2018 has switched it back to the true geometric counterpart.

Expansion and Clarification of Concepts

Restrained Condition and Free State modifier

Restrained condition notes in the datum reference frame section has been expanded and clarified. Explanation of the free state modifier was also moved to this section from the form section to link the concepts. The 2018 standard gives more guidelines for the use of a restrained condition note on a non-rigid part. It lists important parameters that may be included in the note such as: magnitude, location, direction, sequence, and area of restraint. Gravity affecting a non-rigid part is addressed. Examples and rules for a restrained note and datum targets have also been added. The free state symbol may now be used on individual datum references without affecting the restraint of the rest of the part.

Axis vs. Surface Interpretation for Position at MMC/LMC

Historically, position tolerance at MMC has been explained in terms of the feature axis within a cylindrical tolerance zone (called the axis method). The Y14.5 also states that position at MMC creates a virtual condition boundary that the surface may not violate (called the surface method). It was documented as early as the 1982 standard that the two methods are not equivalent because of unsymmetrical form deviations on the feature, and UOS the surface method shall take precedence. The 2018 standard has revised a lot of figures to show the surface instead of the axis interpretation and sometimes both. Nothing has changed here in 2018 but the explanation in the figures to reduce contradictions. See unit 12 for more information.

Profile in a note

The 2009 standard allowed a profile to be placed in a general note by this paragraph:

> *3.5 FEATURE CONTROL FRAME PLACEMENT*
> *A feature control frame is related to a considered feature by one of the following methods*
> *(e) placing in a note, chart, or the general tolerance block*

The 2018 standard has clarified this in the application of the all over profile requirement:

> *11.3.1.5 Profile All Over Specification:*
> *A profile tolerance may be applied all over the three-dimensional profile of a part UOS. It shall be applied in one of the following ways:*
> *(c) place the profile tolerance requirement in the general tolerance block or general notes*

Other examples of profile blocks in notes were also included in other sections of the document. This is another push for replacement of plus/minus in title blocks to profile of a surface relative to a datum reference frame, which has been an industry practice for years.

Runout

Runout did get a substantial overhaul in its 2018 definitions without really changing anything. In previous versions of the standard, runout was mostly defined by the dial indicator inspection device. Throughout the past decades, the Y14.5 has been transitioning out of inspection-based definitions and into more theoretical tolerance boundaries. This allows quality to choose the best inspection method based on equipment available, expertise, capability, cost and risk. Runout was the last hold-out on the inspection-based definition and was changed in 2018.

Size tolerances are added to the figures to clarify the use of size and runout together.

Tangent plane modifier is clarified for use on runout.

Runout clarified for use on assemblies that do not rotate about the datum axis.

Continuous Feature

The continuous feature symbol is first explained in 2009 and unites two or more features of size as a single feature; the size tolerance also controls coaxiality. The 2018 standard made it optional to include nX next to the CF symbol for clarification on the number of features involved. In 2009, it was a bit unclear whether this symbol could be applied to surfaces, but in 2018, there are now two types of continuous features: continuous feature and continuous feature of size. The implications of applying CF to surfaces is still unclear and may have opened a door into a different way of controlling relationships. Some say a flatness and continuous feature may be used to control coplanarity (usually done with profile tolerance) although there are not any examples of this in the standard. It may also replace composite tolerancing in some cases. There are a couple examples in the standard of CF being used in place of 6X or 6 surfaces, but the benefit is not easily seen. This symbol may cause more confusion than our classic position or profile tolerances with nX or multiple leader lines to control locational relationships between features. Be careful with this slippery symbol, especially on surfaces.

New Symbols

From-to

This symbol may be used with profile tolerance in place of the between symbol. Two values are also added in the feature control frame. Instead of the profile tolerance being a fixed value across the surface, the tolerance offset gradually changes from one point to another. This same concept could have been applied in 2009 with "non-uniform profile" and sketching the boundaries. Be careful with this application. This can be complicated to understand the tolerance at any given point and should be used only in specialized situations. A single measured value for the measured data cannot be determined and the specification drops to a pass/fail requirement or variable data only.

Dynamic Profile

The dynamic profile tolerance modifier is the shiny new symbol in 2018. Profile has always been a powerful symbol, able to control size, form, orientation, and location based on datum feature references. By default, on a non-planar feature, profile always controls size and form of the surface. When this modifier is added, the profile controls the form of the feature without size. The offset between the profile boundaries remain fixed but the size of the boundaries is now variable.

Profile with no datum feature references and the dynamic modifier would be the equivalent of cylindricity on a hole but for more complex shapes (think trianglicity and hexagonicity). Datum feature references may also be used with this concept to allow profile to control form, orientation, location without the size. This is usually used as a refinement of a regular profile specification. On another note, this modifier could be the solution for fixing the definition of CR. See unit 11 for more examples.

Final Notes on ASME Y14.5-2018

Most of these changes and additions are minor, but Y14.5-2018 does clarify and expand the tool-set to control the size, form, orientation, and location of part features. Ever since the first Y14.5 standard in 1957, the committee has strived to reduce ambiguity in the definition of the worst-case variations of a part while also allowing maximum manufacturing tolerance. The standard has been an evolving document advancing our understanding of the subject, like a big Wiki-document passed through the generations. In addition, it has sprung new committees of recognized experts to create other related Y14 documents including mathematical definitions in Y14.5.1, measurements in B89 standards, gaging requirements in Y14.43, casting/plastic part specific symbols in Y14.8, model-based definitions in Y14.41 and Y14.47, additive manufacturing definition in Y14.46, measurement data reporting in Y14.45 to name a few. Even though the concepts in the Y14.5 document are coming to a maturity, the work is never done. ASME Y14.5 still stands as the core document that defines the most complicated portion of documentation on engineering drawings: tolerancing!

Appendix A - Part 2

Principle changes, improvements, clarifications and enhancements in the ASME Y14.5-2009 from the earlier ASME Y14.5M-1994 standard

The ASME Y14.5-2009 standard on dimensioning and tolerancing reflects a culmination of effort extending over 15 years. It is a revision of the ASME Y14.5M-1994 standard. The M in the title which reflected the standard was written in metric was deemed no longer necessary because all ASME standards are now written in metric. There are many changes, improvements and enhancements from the earlier 1994 standard. The chapters in the standard have been reorganized to present the foundational principles first and then build on the foundations. Many of the changes are simple rearrangements or definition clarifications.

The standard has been revised to emphasize and encourage the use of basic dimensions and geometric tolerancing as the preferred method of controlling the form, orientation, and location of features. The use of plus/minus tolerancing should be used to control the size of features only.

Many major enhancements and clarifications have occurred in the datum section. The degrees of freedom concept has been introduced and a table has been added defining the constrained degrees of freedom for primary datum features. This enhancement also allows any feature to become a datum feature. As a result, datum feature modifiers have been expanded using new datum feature modifier terms such as Maximum Material Boundary (MMB), Least Material Boundary (LMB) and Regardless of Material Boundary (RMB). These new terms replace the term MMC and virtual condition for datum features to provide a better definition of the boundary established by related datum features.

The set of rules for the establishment of a datum reference frame have been clarified. Datum feature simulator requirements along with a new datum feature translation modifier was added. These requirements along with the translation modifier clarify the process of establishing datums and datum reference frames from datum features. It also clarifies the establishment of a secondary or tertiary datum relative to a higher precedence datum axis (known as the tertiary datum problem).

The profile section also has significant enhancements. A non-uniform profile zone was added where the user can specify the applicable tolerance zone with basic dimensions or CAD geometry. The symbol, circle U, was added and can be used in as feature control frame to identify a unilateral or unequal unilateral tolerance zone. This will make the unilateral symbol more model friendly.

Since the release of the former ASME Y14.5M-1994 standard there have been major advances in technology in CAD, CMM, CAM and CNC type equipment. The standard has also advanced to take advantage of these changes. There is a trend towards applying geometric tolerancing to the model called model based definition (MBD). The ASME Y14.41 illustrates how to apply the geometric tolerancing symbology but ASME Y14.5 still defines the basic principles of tolerancing.

The ASME Y14.5.1-2019 Mathematical Definitions of Dimensioning and Tolerancing provides the solid mathematical foundation for Y14.5-2009. The ASME Y14.5.2-2017 Certification of Geometric Tolerancing Professionals has also been updated to the Y14.5-2009 standard. The Y14.43-2011 Dimensioning and Tolerancing Principles for Gages and Fixtures also has an update to the 2009 standard. A new standard Y14.45, Measurement Data Reporting, is in the works to standardize the reporting of measurement data.

In this short outline, it is impossible to address the implication of all the changes and only the major changes are shown. Many of the changes are woven through the fabric of the document. In order to understand the impact of these changes, it is assumed the reader has knowledge of the earlier 1994 standard. The reader can find detailed information on the changes in the GeoTol Pro workbook released in 2009. Appendix A of the ASME Y14.5-2009 standard also has a listing of the principle changes.

Significant New and Revised Terms and Definitions

Least Material Boundary, (LMB)

Maximum Material Boundary, (MMB)

Regardless of Material Boundary (RMB)

Actual Mating Envelope

Unrelated Actual Mating Envelope

Related Actual Mating Envelope

Feature of Size

(a) Regular Feature of Size

(b) Irregular Feature of Size

Fundamental rules revised:

A zero basic dimension applies where axes, center planes or surfaces that are shown congruent on a drawing and geometric controls establish the relationship between the features.

General Tolerancing Principles

The standard has been revised to emphasize and encourage the use of basic dimensions and geometric tolerancing as the preferred method of controlling the form, orientation, and location of features. The use of plus minus tolerancing should be used to control the size of features only.

Rule #1 for individual features of size has been expanded to include irregular features of size.

Continuous feature concept and new symbol added.

New symbology added

All Over
Spotface
Continuous Feature
Independency
Unequally Disposed Profile
Datum Reference Frame
Moveable Datum Target
Datum Translation
Degrees of Freedom
MMB, LMB, BSC

Datum Reference Frame (DRF)

The concept of degrees of freedom constrained by the primary, secondary, and tertiary datum features has been added. Degrees of Freedom Table for primary datum features.

The terms virtual condition and resultant condition to define datum feature boundaries has been replaced and clarified with the new terms:

Maximum Material Boundary (MMB)

Least Material Boundary (LMB)

Regardless of Material Boundary (RMB)

The term datum feature simulator has been revised and expanded into two types.

Datum Feature Simulator (Theoretical) is defined as theoretically perfect for use in the standard and has replaced the term **true geometric counterpart.**

Datum Feature Simulator (Physical) is defined as the practical embodiment of the theoretical datum feature simulator used in manufacturing, inspection or tooling.

Requirements for datum feature simulators are defined to clarify the establishment of a DRF.

Translation datum feature modifier and new symbol added.

Customized datum reference frames have been added to allow the user to override the requirements of a standard DRF and selectively and specifically state the degrees of freedom constrained by each datum feature.

Calculations of various datum feature simulator boundaries are explained and clarified.

Values of the datum feature simulator may be added in the feature control frame with dimensions or the term BASIC or BSC for clarification.

Datum Feature Shift is clarified.

The establishment of a secondary or tertiary datum relative to a higher precedence datum axis has been clarified and expanded.

Datum feature modifiers MMB, LMB and RMB may be applied to surfaces in certain cases.

Datum reference frame symbol added to identify the datum reference frame labeled with the x,y, z translational degrees of freedom.

Contoured surface established as a datum feature is clarified.

Moveable datum target symbol added and adopted from ASME Y14.8 and ASME Y14.41.

Form Tolerances

Flatness of a center plane replaces straightness of a center plane.

Orientation Tolerances

The use of the angularity symbol to control all orientation is introduced as an alternative practice to using the perpendicularity and parallelism symbols.

Position Tolerance

Clarification that the surface interpretation takes precedence over the axis interpretation for positional tolerance.

Multiple segments to a composite tolerance feature control frame are explained and clarified.

Position tolerance applied without a datum feature reference to control coaxiality is clarified.

The term BOUNDARY placed under a feature control frame is now optional when applying position tolerance to an irregular feature of size.

Profile Tolerance

The use of profile tolerancing is encouraged for locating surfaces instead of plus/minus tolerancing. The use of direct tolerancing methods which includes limit dimensioning and plus minus tolerancing should be used to control the size of features only.

A new symbol, circle U, is used in a feature control frame as a preferred method of indicating that a profile tolerance is either unilateral or unequally disposed bilateral.

The application of a profile "all over UOS" can be applied with a new double circle symbol placed at the elbow of the leader line from the feature control frame.

The application of a profile non-uniform tolerance zone has been added. The term "NON-UNIFORM" replaces the tolerance value in the feature control frame and the extent of the tolerance zone is dimensioned. This can also be used to control abrupt changes in the tolerance zone.

The nX symbol (example 2X) has replaced the note designation (example 2 SURFACES) for a number of surfaces when using profile tolerance.

Coplanar profile for controlling two or more offset surfaces has been enhanced and clarified.

Addition of multiple segments to a composite tolerance feature control frame are explained and clarified. Composite profile tolerancing has been expanded to include multiple features in a pattern.

Profile tolerancing is clarified as a method to control coaxiality.

Appendix B

Differences between the ASME Y14.5 and ISO-GPS standards

Table of Contents:

The ASME and ISO Standards Committees

ASME Y14/B89 and ISO-GPS/ISO-TPD series standards have similar content that establish symbols, rules, definitions, requirements, defaults, and recommended practices for stating and interpreting dimensioning, tolerancing, and related requirements for use on engineering drawings. To understand the differences between ASME and ISO standards, it is first important to understand how the standards are structured and who creates them.

	ASME		ISO	
Committees	Y14 divided into subcommittees	B89 divided into subcommittees	TC/10 divided into working groups (WG)	TC/213 divided into working groups (WG)
Standards	Y14 standards	B89 standards	Technical Product Documentation (TPD)	Geometrical Product Specifications (GPS)
Scope	Presentation, Dimensioning, and Tolerancing	Measurement	Presentation and Dimensioning	Tolerancing and Measurement

ASME combines dimensioning and tolerancing together in one document (Y14.5) written and revised by one subcommittee every 10-15 years. There are more standards in the Y14 series written by different subcommittees that cover other aspects of the engineering drawing such as drawing views (Y14.3), Mathematical Definitions of Y14.5 (Y14.5.1), casting symbols (Y14.8), Digital Product Definition Data Practices (Y14.41) etc. The Y14 standards are all about product definition and documentation. There is a separate group of subcommittees that writes the B89 series of standards on metrology and measurement of the specifications.

The people that make up the ASME subcommittees are from companies, universities and government agencies representing the mechanical engineering industry in the US.

ISO combines tolerancing with measurement in the GPS series of documents written by the Technical Committee (TC) 213. While the dimensioning and presentation (drawing views, line conventions, etc.) is covered by the separate TPD series written by TC/10. The GPS series break the tolerancing spectrum into smaller standards written by Working Groups (WG) to focus on narrower areas. Datums in ISO 5459 is separate from Profile in ISO 1660, separate from form, orientation, and location in ISO 1101. This makes the standards easier to revise, but there are complaints with them being less cohesive and hard to follow. Most ISO-GPS standards have been updated recently and will be staying on a 5 year revision cycle to keep them more unified.

The ISO working groups consist of people representing standards institutes from different countries (the countries are called member bodies). Some of these people work for the countries' standards institute but some also work for private companies and government agencies. The US is a member body in these ISO standards called the US TAG (Technical Activity Group) through ASME and ANSI. Only a handful of member bodies participate in the TC/10 and TC/213 meetings, but many will comment and vote on drafts and proposals remotely. Although many people from one country may attend the meetings, there is only one vote per member body.

To focus the discussions, this book will only talk about the differences in the definition of the tolerancing specified by ASME Y14.5 and the related documents in ISO-GPS.

Introduction to the Differences in ASME Y14.5 and ISO-GPS system

Although the dimensioning and tolerancing concepts of ASME Y14.5 and ISO-GPS are probably 95% similar, the notable differences are outlined in this unit. These differences are slight and sometimes cannot be compared symbol for symbol because of the structure of the rule sets. Similar to the way English and German may not be directly translated word for word because of the sentence structure and word definition differences. There may not be a direct ISO symbol for some ASME ones and vice versa, but we can usually find a way to communicate our design intent nonetheless.

Both Y14.5 and ISO-GPS standards are big complicated documents written by large groups of people over a long period of time, and the history of these creations plays into the applications and definitions. Y14.5 is written from a design and functional standpoint. The standards also began in the era of functional gaging and dial indicators as the prime way to evaluate the boundaries of a feature. Significant overhaul of the definitions has been done in the 2009 and 2018 revisions to overcome this, however the flavor of gaging and old-school measurement is still there. The standard also often weaves the definitions in with guidance on why a symbol may be selected. Although this is helpful, it can sometimes be difficult to separate the guidance from the official rules. Figures are often used to define the rules of a concept rather than have the words stand alone.

Conversely, ISO-GPS standards are newer and written more from a digital metrology point of view. Function sometimes takes a backseat to the options and ease of measuring with a CMM or other digital equipment. ISO symbols and concepts are defined with short and direct rules. The figures are simple and little guidance is given on when or why a symbol is applied or how it plays into the bigger picture. Often many options and modifiers are made available even though the function of a part would rarely (if ever) need such concepts.

Both of these writing styles have their pros and cons. ISO is probably more powerful with all the options available, however it takes a highly experienced user to filter through to the useful content and create functional tolerancing. ASME is more user friendly on application with a simpler tool-set and examples that are similar to real parts. However, Y14.5 reads more like a story, and it can be difficult to fix on the hard rules for a concept.

Apply ISO standards to your drawing with ISO 8015:2011---section 5.1 Invocation principle:

> *Once a portion of the ISO GPS system is invoked in a mechanical engineering product documentation, the entire ISO GPS system is invoked, unless otherwise indicated on the documentation, e.g. by reference to another document.*
>
> *"Tolerancing ISO 8015" can optionally be indicated in or near the title block for information, but is not required to invoke the ISO GPS system.*

ASME Y14.100-2017 has a similar statement that Y14 series applies to an unreferenced drawing. Since both ASME and ISO have invocation principles that high-jack an unreferenced engineering drawing, always include a reference on the drawing to the desired standard.

Unit 1 of this workbook has a comprehensive list of the latest ISO-GPS standards. To start with the differences between ASME and ISO definitions, it is recommended to also look at Unit 1 for charts that show the ASME symbol and concept name along with the corresponding ISO symbol and concept name. Note that this appendix is not meant to teach geometric tolerancing, but instead show the differences in ISO to someone already familiar with ASME Y14.5.

Term Differences

Below are the differences in the terms used in the ASME and ISO standards. This can be helpful when you know one system but need to understand the vocabulary used in the other. The following are terms that have no notifiable differences except for the name change:

ASME term	ISO term
Geometric Dimensioning and Tolerancing (GD&T)	Geometrical Product Specifications (GPS)
Basic Dimension	Theoretically Exact Dimension (TED)
True Profile True Position	Theoretically Exact Feature (TEF)
Datum Reference Frame	Datum System
Feature Control Frame	Tolerance Indicator
Datum Feature Symbol	Datum Feature Indicator
MMC modifier for features MMB modifier for datum features	Maximum Material Requirement (MMR)
LMC modifier for features LMB modifier for datum features	Least Material Requirement (LMR)
Virtual Condition	Max Material Virtual Condition (MMVC) Least Material Virtual Condition (LMVC)
Datum Feature Simulator	Associated Feature

Definition of a Size Tolerance

One of the major differences in the ASME and ISO standards is the default defintion of a size tolerance for holes, shafts, slots, tabs and spheres. ASME requires **perfect form at MMC** (rule#1) in addition to the min max of the cross-sectional sizes. ISO only requires min/max cross sectional sizes. Modifiers are available to change the default in both standards.

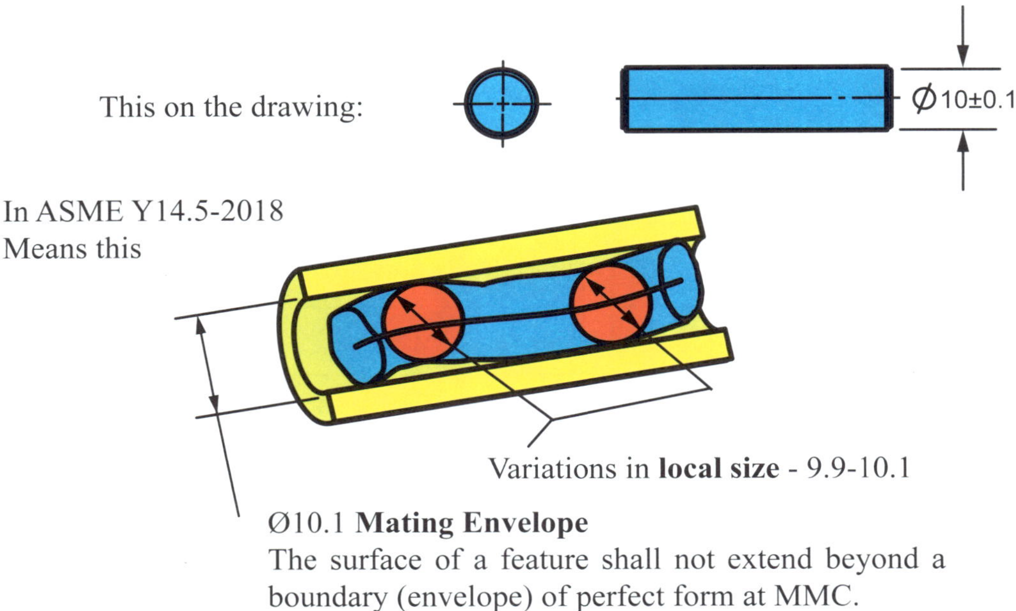

The ASME Y14.5.1-2019 (Mathematical Definitions) defines the local size by a spherical cross section (also controls lobing effects). The mating envelope is defined as the smallest circumscribing cylinder for a shaft, largest inscribed for a hole.

The independency principle may be invoked by the circle I symbol placed next to the size tolerance. This indicates that perfect form at MMC is not required.

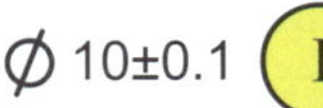

The Independency Principle in ISO 8015

"By default, every GPS specification for a feature shall be fulfilled independent of other specifications." This means size tolerance does not control form. and the two requirements are treated as being unrelated. If a particular relationship of size and form is required, it shall be specified on the drawing.

The envelope principle may be invoked on an ISO drawing by placing a circle E symbol next to the size tolerance. **This is the same perfect form at MMC requirement as the ASME default.**

Linear Size according to ISO 14405-1

By default, a size tolerance is defined as local two point distances across the feature. There are many modifiers that can be placed next to the size tolerance to change the default. Most of them will probably never be used. Below are a few that could be useful:

Maximum Inscribed	GX	Spherical Size Cross Sec	LS	All least squares circles of the shaft must lie within 10±0.1
Least Squares	GG	Calculated from Volume	CV	
Minimum Circumscribed	GN	Any Cross Section	ACS	Ø 10±0.1 GG ACS

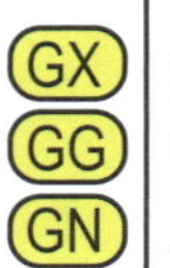
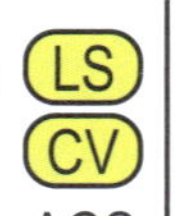

The Similarities between ASME and ISO

Before showing the differences between the two standards, let's look at the similarities. The top drawing is to ASME and the bottom to the ISO. Even though the symbols are attached and dimensions are presented in slightly different ways, the meaning of the geometry and tolerances is nearly identical. The datum features must fall within the respective flatness and perpendicularity tolerance zones. All holes must clear virtual condition boundaries created by the size and position at MMC. The profile tolerances create offset boundaries for the surfaces. The only difference is the definition of the hole size tolerances. ASME requires all features of size to have perfect form at MMC (rule#1). ISO GPS requires only two point size. This difference would be negligible on a shallow sheet metal hole. Since these are clearance holes for fasteners, perfect form at MMC is unnecessary.

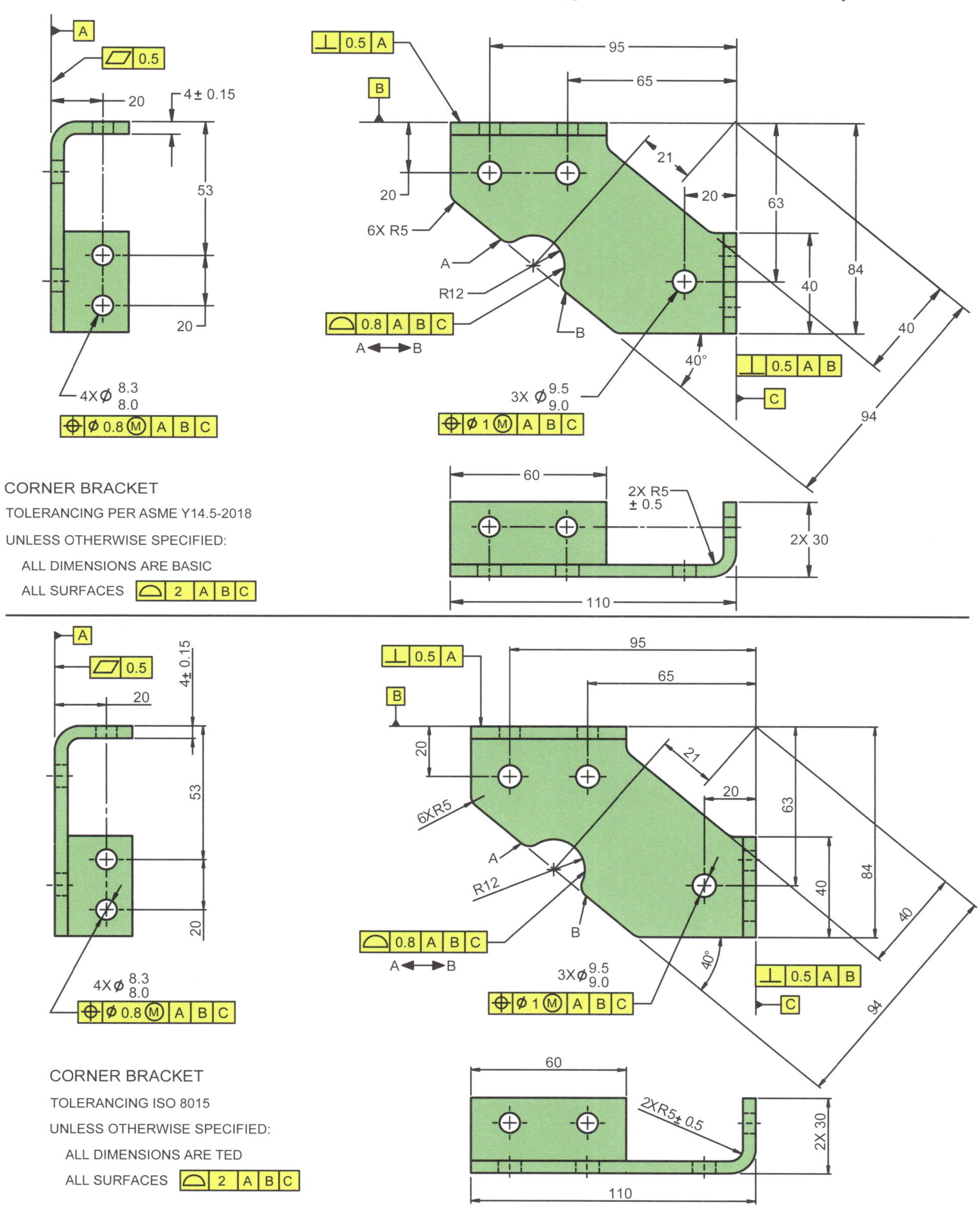

The Definition of a Feature and the Extraction

ASME Y14.5

A feature is a physical portion of a part
There are two types of features:
- -Features of size (hole, slot, shaft, width)
- -Features without size (surfaces)

Tolerances control the surface when the feature control frame is attached to the surface or extension line. The tolerance controls the feature's center (axis, center plane or point) when floating under the size tolerance.

The axis of the feature must lie within the 0.6 diameter tolerance zone

The feature's axis is established from the unrelated actual mating envelope (largest inscribed cylinder for a hole)

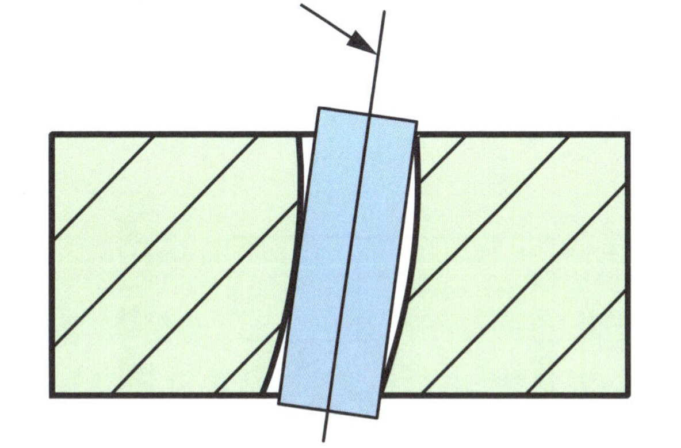

If something other than the axis of the mating envelope is to be evaluated, it must be specified with a note.

ISO-GPS

A feature is a portion of a part
There are two types of features:
- -Derived features (median line, median surface, center point)
- -Integral features (surfaces)

The median line of a cylinder is a derived feature obtained from the cylindrical surface, which is an integral feature.

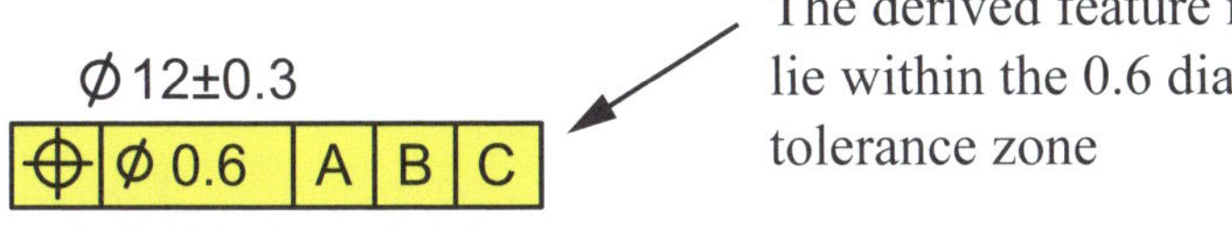

The derived feature must lie within the 0.6 diameter tolerance zone

By default, the median line is extracted from a series of least squares circles in cross sections perpendicular to the least squares cylinder

default extraction set by ISO 17450

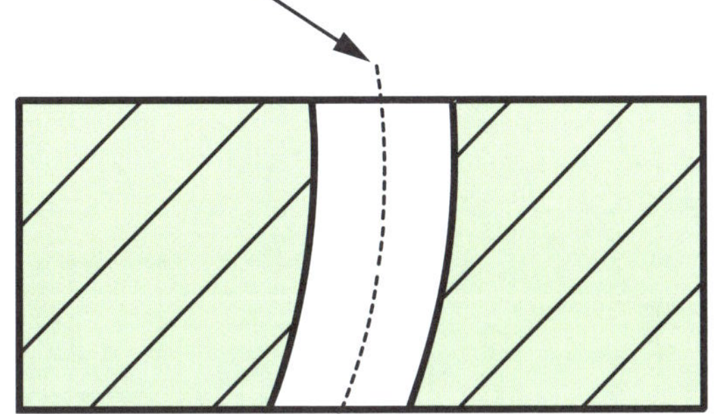

ISO 1101 allows other extraction processes with modifiers:
N - min circumscribed
X - max inscribed
G - least squares axis

Profile Tolerance per ASME

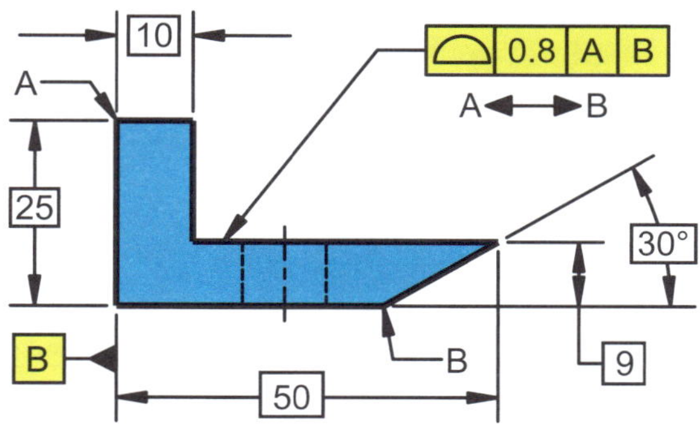

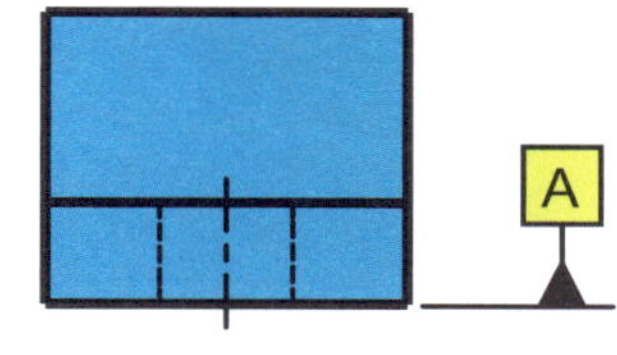

By default in the ASME Y14.5, profile tolerance zones are defined as two boundaries equally disposed about the true profile. These boundaries extend through the surfaces to create sharp cornered limits.

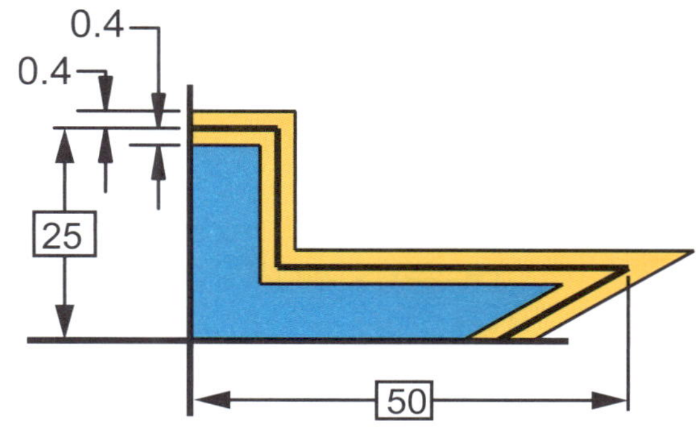

The profile tolerance only defines the tolerance zones. The actual surface does not have to be this same shape. It only must lie inside the tolerance zone. An additional requirement such as min radius (MIN R X.X) or max radius (MAX R X.X) may be specified.

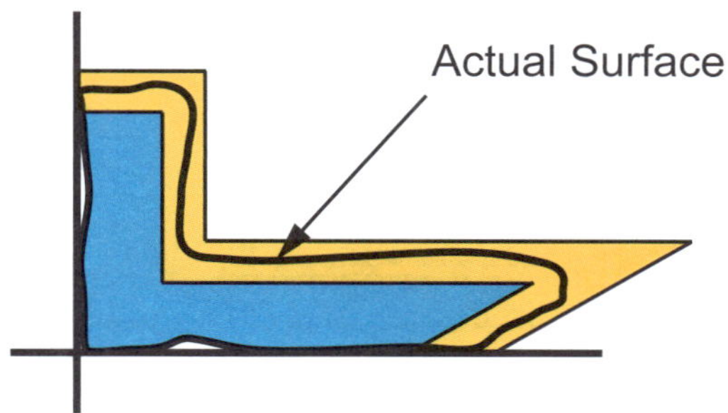

Profile Tolerance per ISO

Profile Tolerance per ISO GPS

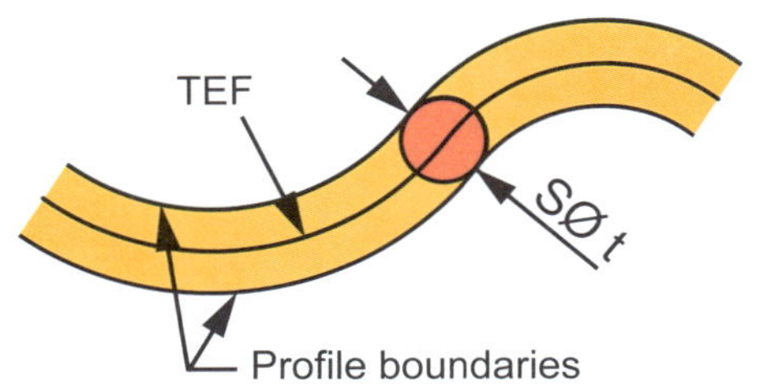

In ISO 1660:2017, profile tolerance zones are defined as two boundaries enveloping spheres with a diameter equal to the tolerance value (t). By default, the centers of the spheres are situated on the TEF (thoeretically exact feature).

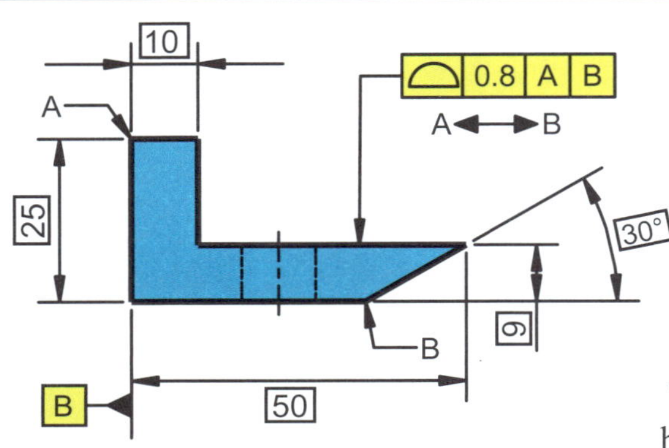

Tolerancing per ISO 8015

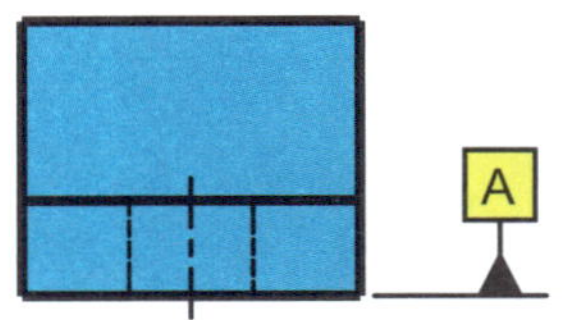

The profile tolerance evaluates each surface between points A and B separately to the datum system. This will create sharp cornered tolerance boundaries for the part (the same as ASME).

Surfaces evaluated separately to the datum system

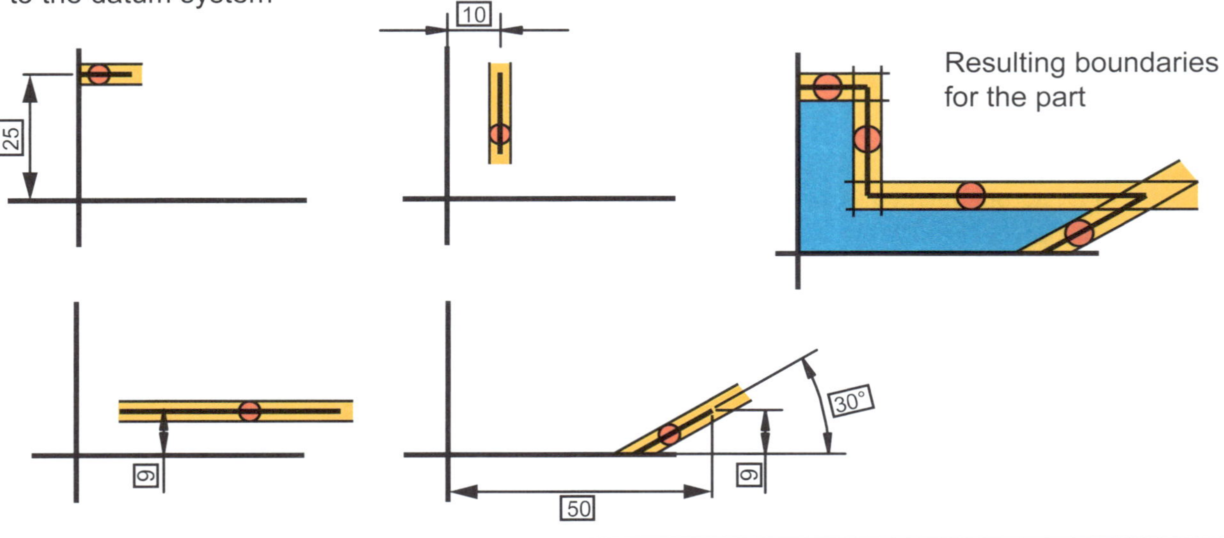

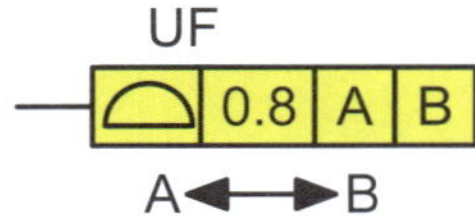

The UF (United Feature) modifier considers the multiple surfaces identified between points A and B as one feature. The spheres creating the profile boundaries will now create rounded corners.

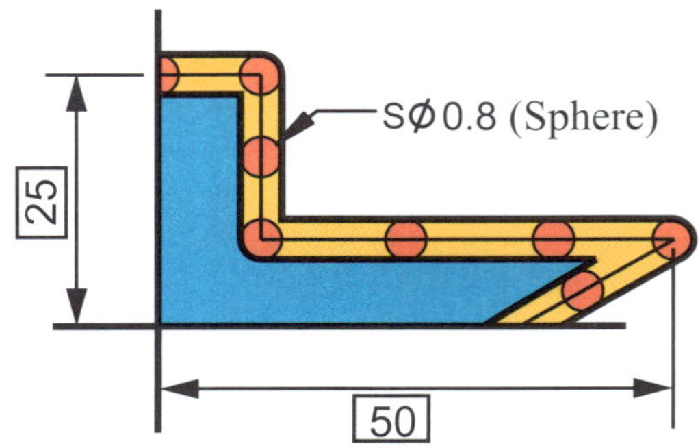

Profile Tolerance Without Datum References

Profile Tolerance per ASME

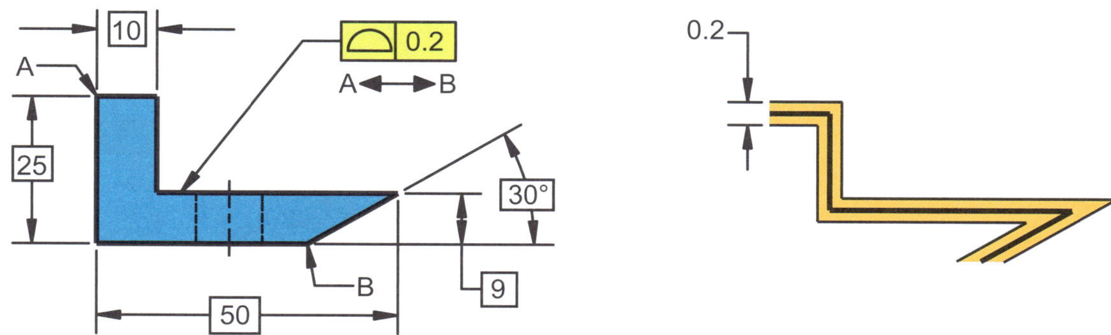

In the ASME Y14.5, profile may be used without datum feature references along with grouping mechanisms: nX, between, all around, all over, or multiple leader lines. The profile zones are connected as if they were one feature and centered on the true profile.

Profile Tolerance per ISO GPS

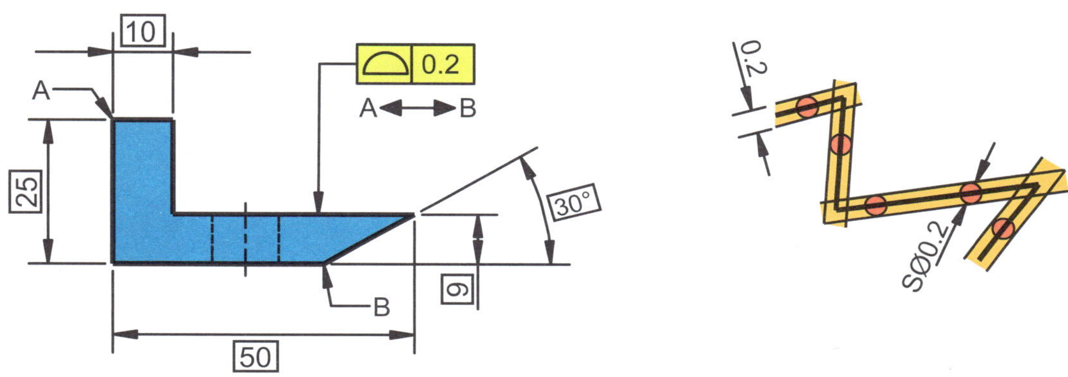

According to ISO 1101, nX, between, all around, all over, or multiple leader lines do not group features. They are only a way to identify multiple features. The profile zones are evaluated separately. In this case, the profile has the same meaning as four flatness tolerances.

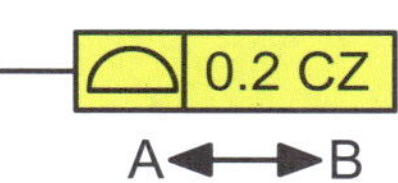

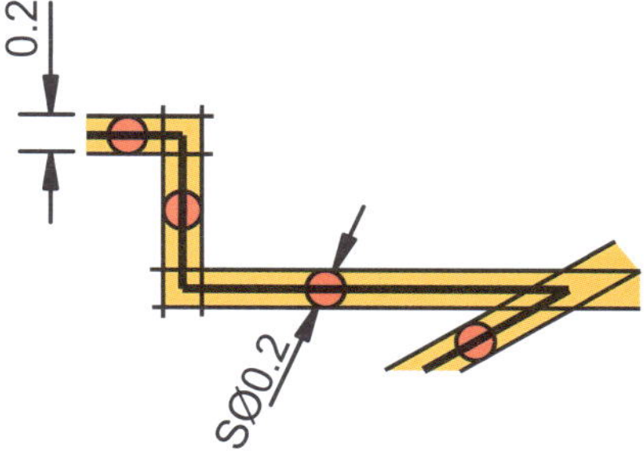

The CZ (combined zone) modifier combines all four tolerance zones and are bound by the TEF. Since each feature should satisfy its own zone, the resulting combined zone has sharp corners.

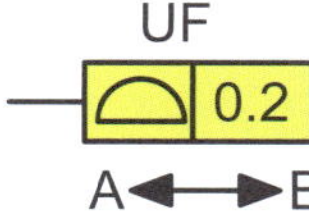

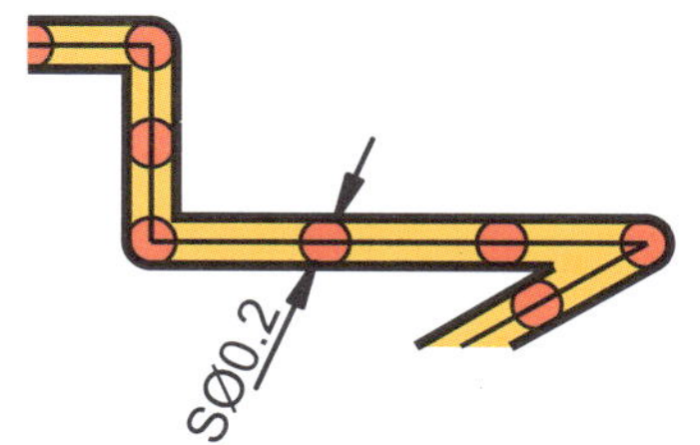

The UF (United Feature) modifier considers the multiple surfaces identified between points A and B as one feature. The spheres creating the profile boundaries are centered on the TEF and will result in rounded boundary corners.

ASME Simultaneous Requirement

The drawings below reference the ASME Y14.5-2018. All the features are related with feature control frames using the same datum reference frame. This constitutes a **simultaneous requirement** and all the features must be within their tolerances zones as a group simultaneously.

Simultaneous requirement is implied by default

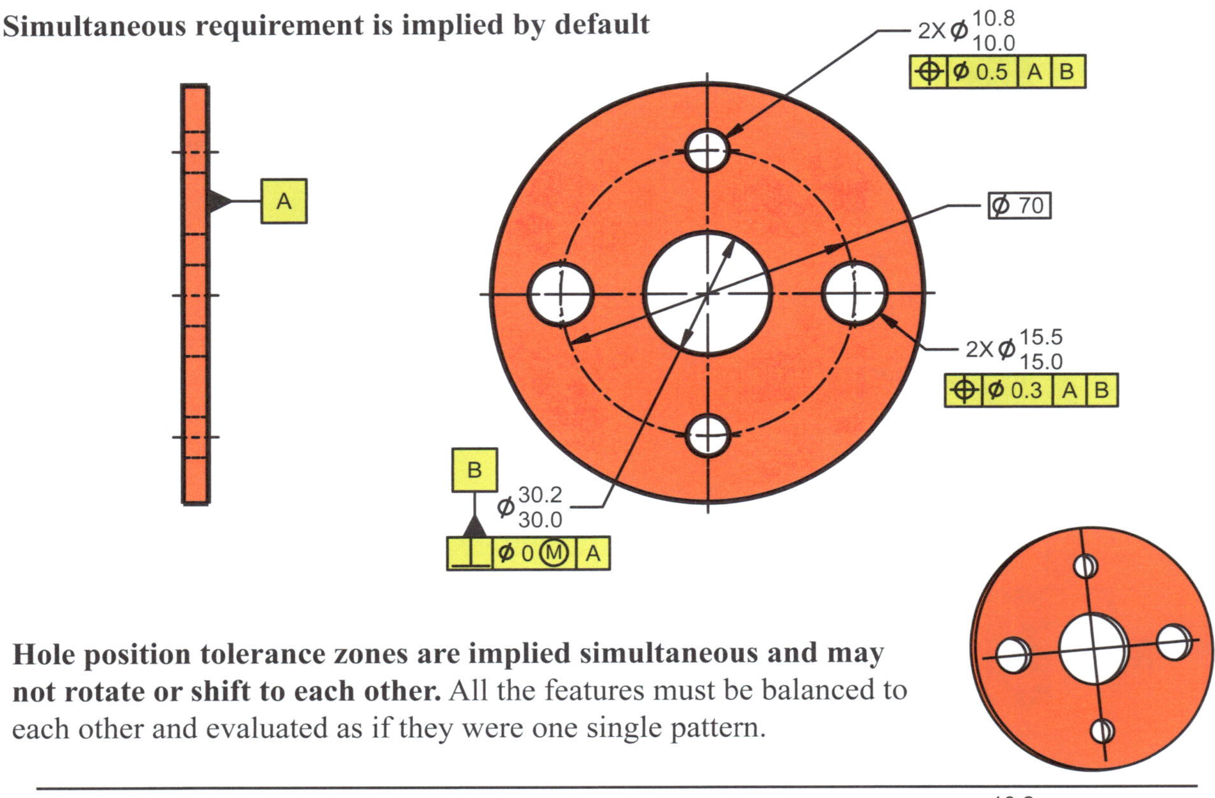

Hole position tolerance zones are implied simultaneous and may not rotate or shift to each other. All the features must be balanced to each other and evaluated as if they were one single pattern.

Separate requirement must be stated

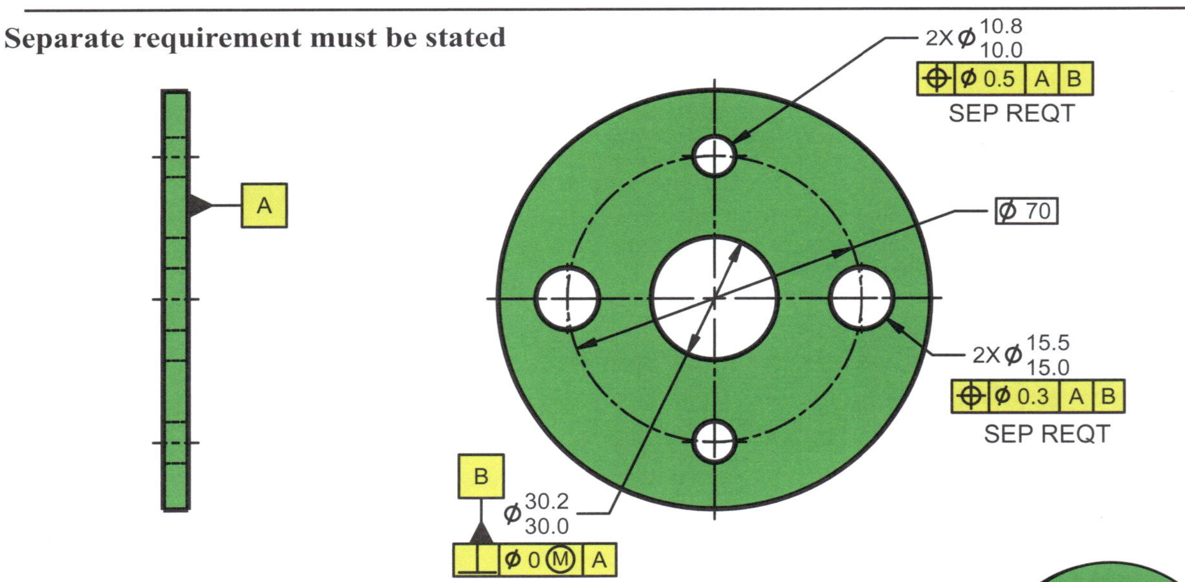

The specified separate requirement, means the hole position tolerance zones between the patterns are not rotationally related. The 2X grouping mechanisms still tie the two 10mm holes to each other and the two 15mm holes to each other, but the relationship between the two patterns is no longer controlled.

ISO Simultaneous Requirement with CZ

The parts below are toleranced to ISO-GPS standards. According to ISO 1101:2017 and ISO 5458:2018, the 2X symbol does not group features into a pattern. According to the independency principle in ISO 8015: simultaneous requirement is not the default, and each feature must meet its geometric specification independently.

Simultaneous requirement is not the default

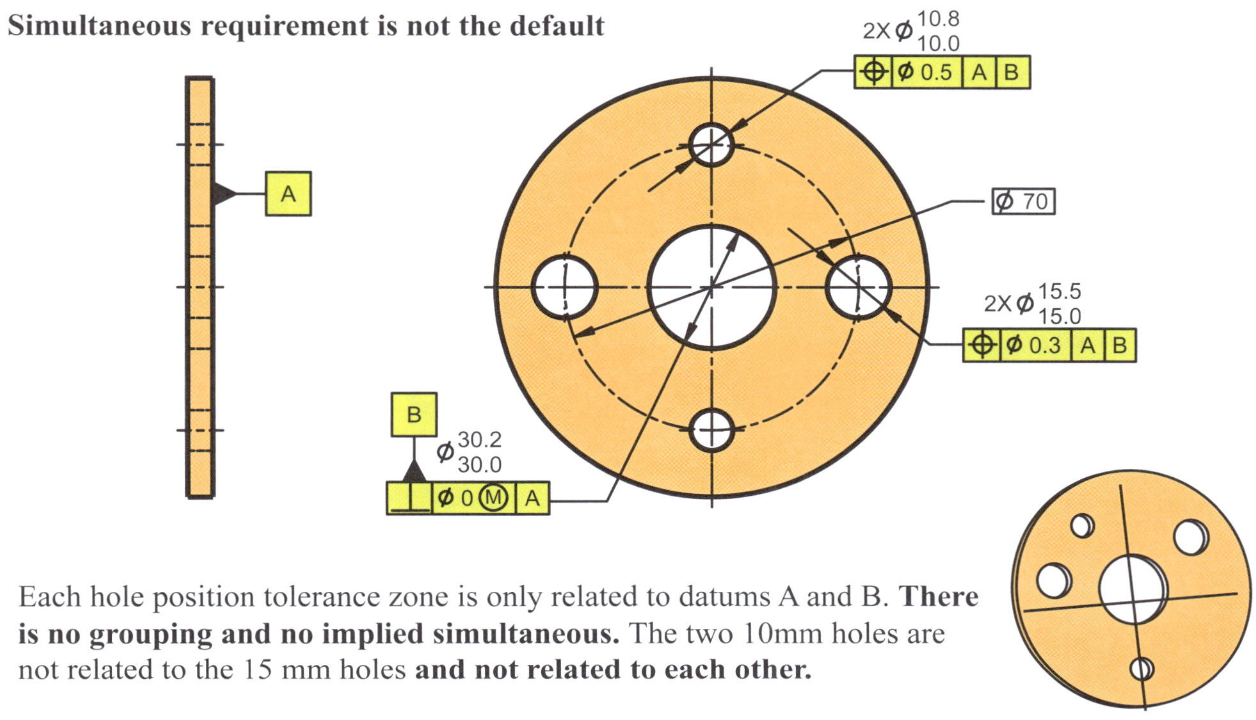

Each hole position tolerance zone is only related to datums A and B. **There is no grouping and no implied simultaneous.** The two 10mm holes are not related to the 15 mm holes **and not related to each other.**

The modifier CZ (combined zone) in ISO 1101 and ISO 5458 links the features in that specification. However, the CZ modifier does not connect to other specifications.

CZ connects the features in the specification

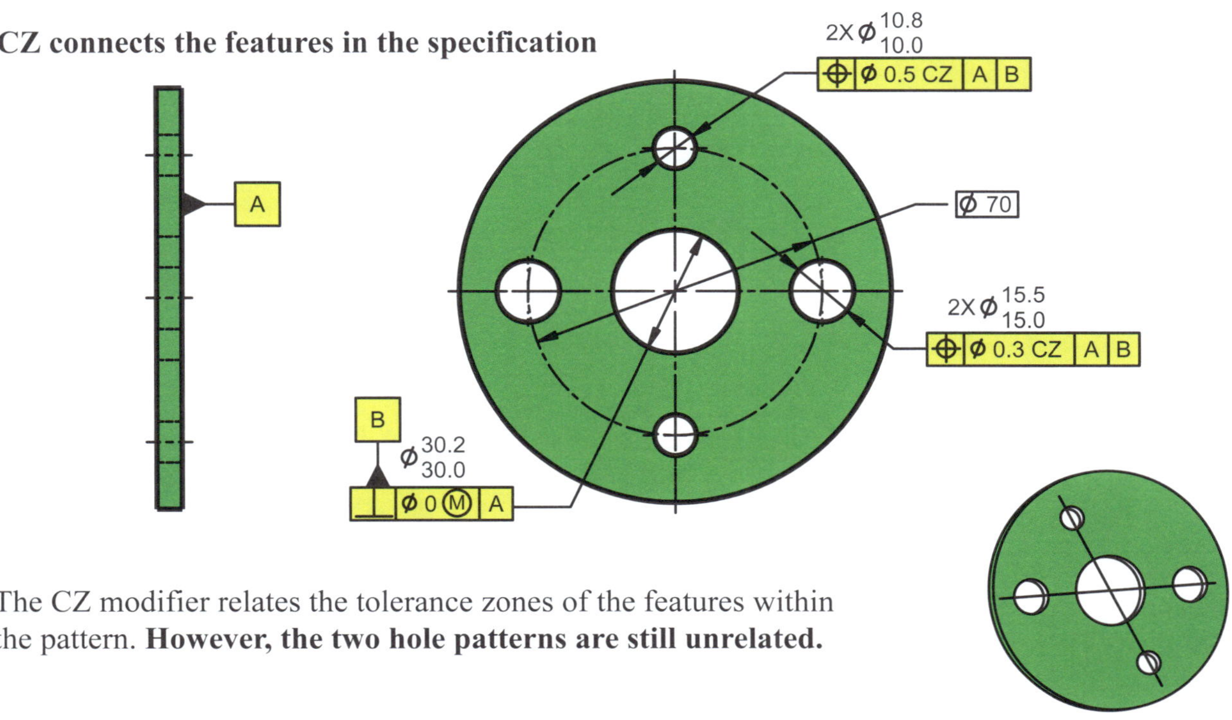

The CZ modifier relates the tolerance zones of the features within the pattern. **However, the two hole patterns are still unrelated.**

ISO Simultaneous Requirement with SIM

According to ISO 5458:2018, the modifier CZ (combined zone) links the features in the specification, but does not connect it to other specifications. The additional modifier "SIM" links the specifications to others creating a simultaneous requirement.

SIM designates a simultaneous requirement

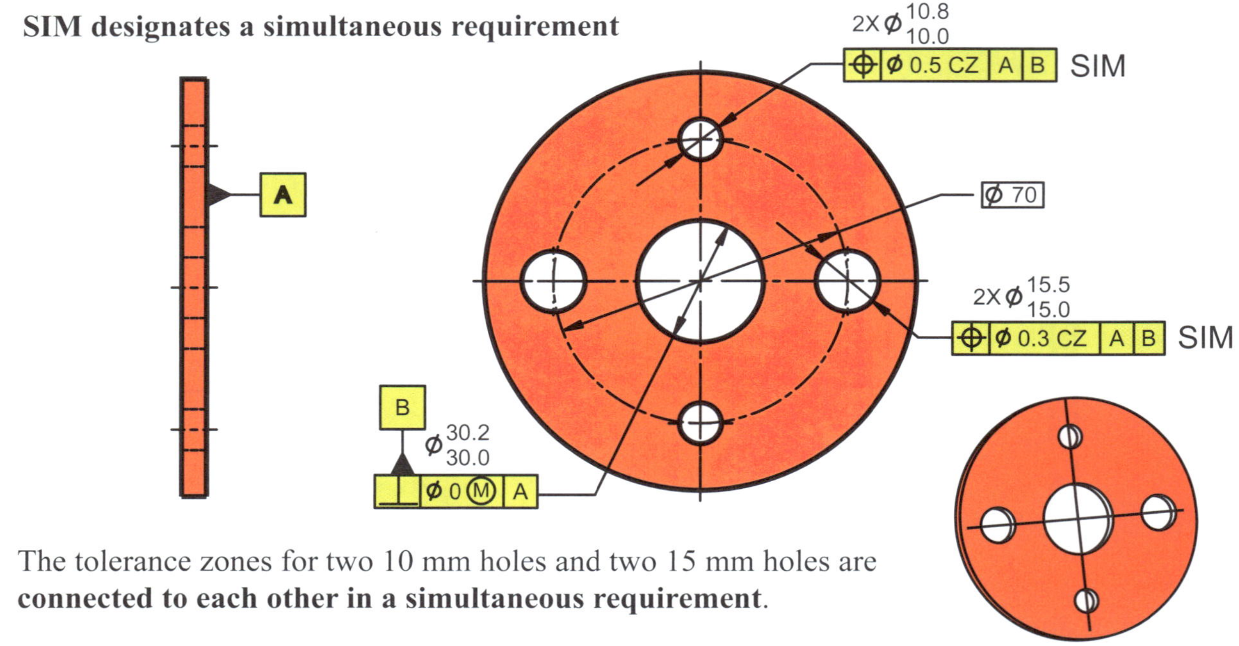

The tolerance zones for two 10 mm holes and two 15 mm holes are **connected to each other in a simultaneous requirement**.

According to ISO 2692:2014, the principle of independency defined in ISO 8015 does not apply when the maximum material requirement Ⓜ or least material requirement are used. These modifiers connect the features within the specification but do not link them to other specifications. The features must clear the MMVC (maximum material virtual condition).

Principle of Independency does not apply within the specification when Ⓜ is used

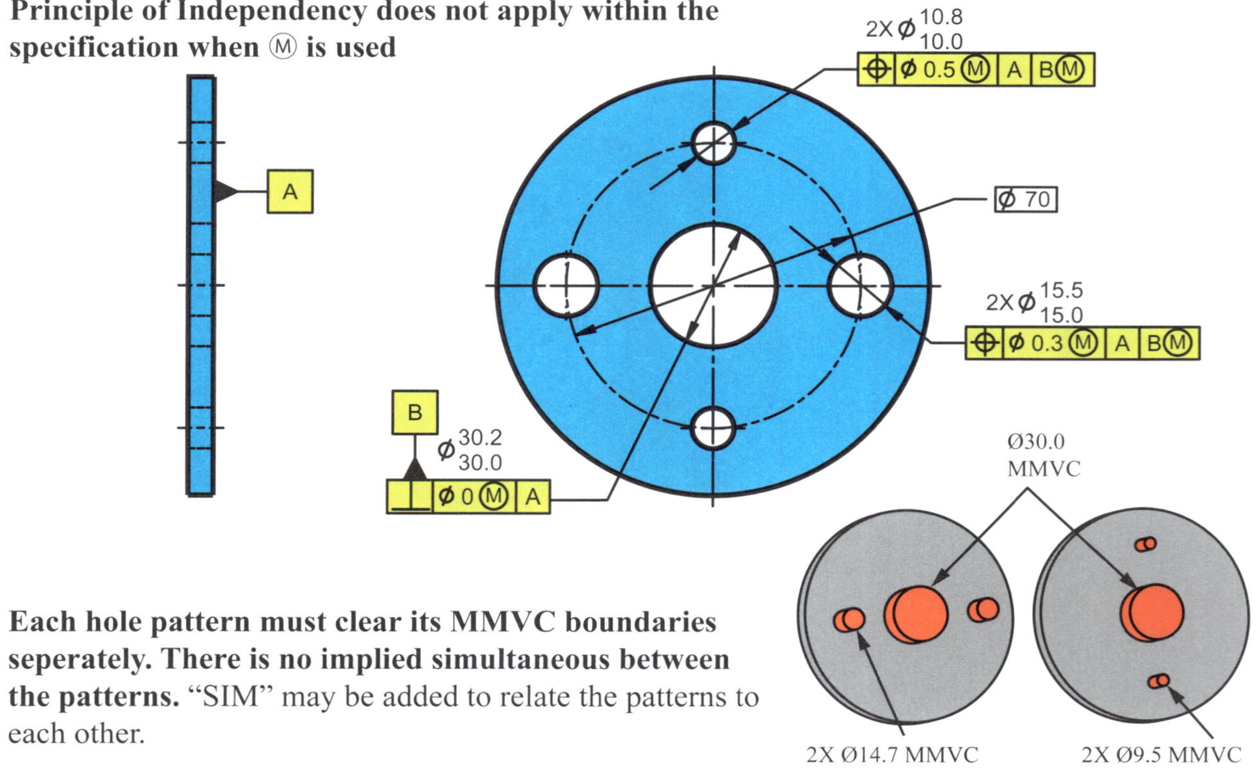

Each hole pattern must clear its MMVC boundaries seperately. There is no implied simultaneous between the patterns. "SIM" may be added to relate the patterns to each other.

Common Datums in ISO

When all features are related to the same fully defined datum reference frame, there are only small differences in notation between ASME Y14.5 and the ISO-GPS standards.

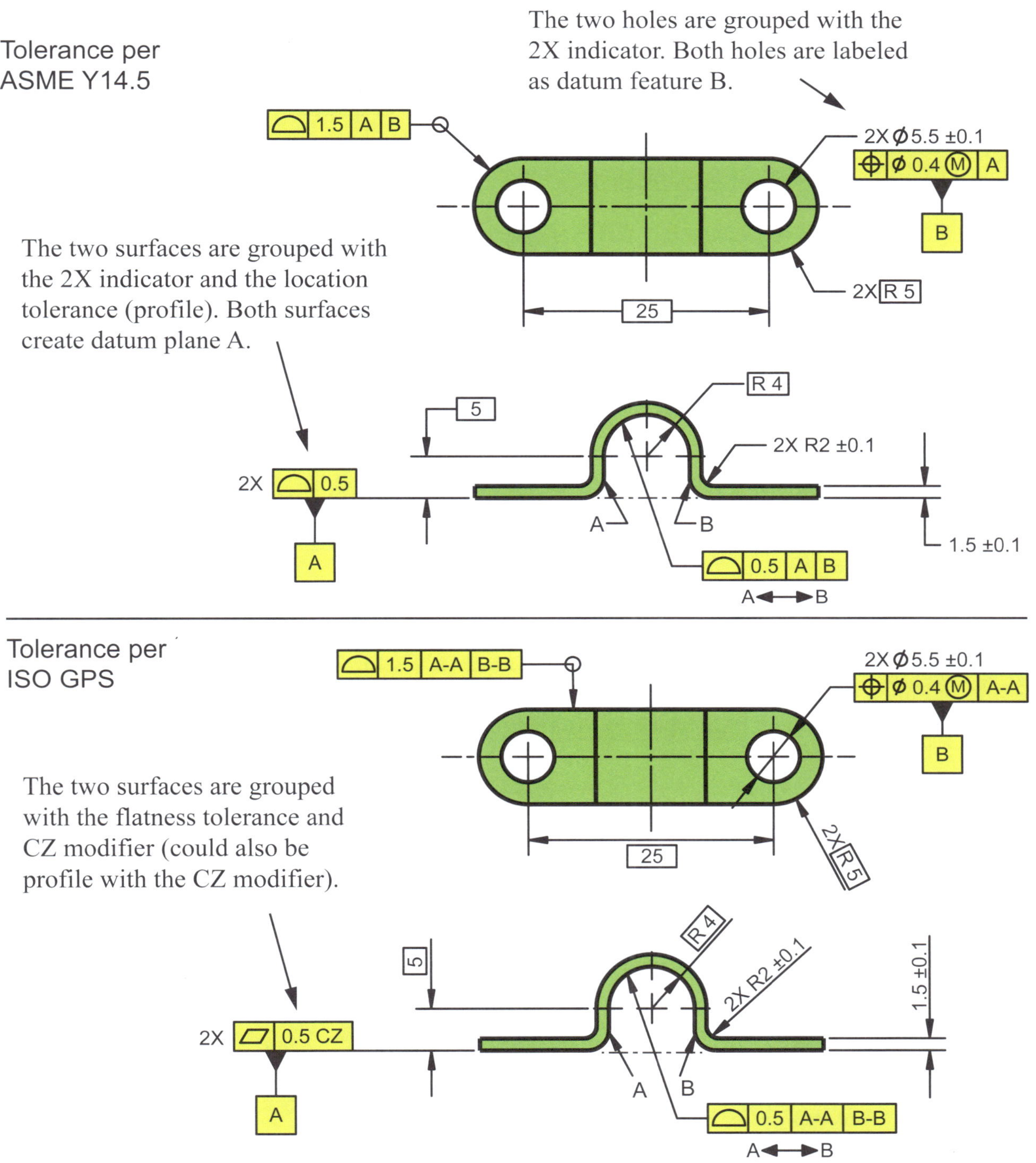

According to ISO 5459:2011, a datum established from two or more datum features considered simultaneously is called a *common datum.* This is notated in the tolerance frame with n-n. Since the primary datum is established from two surfaces, the notation is A-A. It could have also been indicated A-B with one surface labeled as datum feature A and the other as B. The secondary datum is created from two holes, the notation in the feature control frame is B-B.

Modifiers on Datum Features

The notation in the ISO-GPS gets more complicated when the datum reference frame is partially constrained or when modifiers are used on datum features. Remember the Independency Principle in ISO 8015 states that all specifications are evaluated separately. Datum modifiers allow datum feature shift when evaluating the specification. This would allow multiple set ups to evaluate the features and cause stack up issues. The CZ modifier is used to combine features within a specification and "SIM" to combine multiple specifications into one simultaneous requirement.

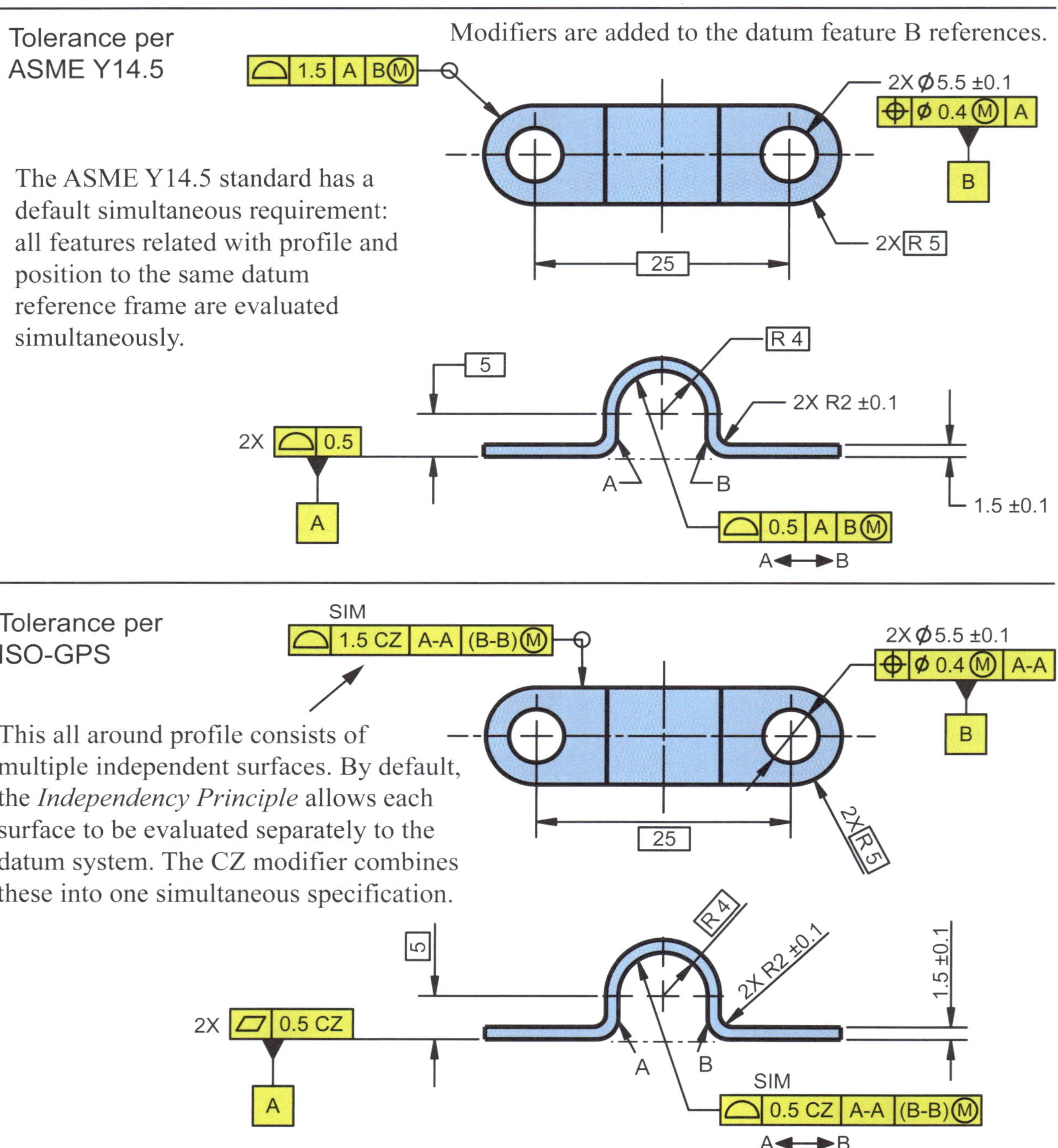

When a *common datum* (A-A or A-B) is modified with the MMR, the notation in the tolerance frame is (n-n)Ⓜ. The SIM modifier above the tolerance frames connects two profile specifications into one simultaneous requirement.

Other Notable Differences

- In ASME, profile controls surfaces. Position locates features of size.

  In ISO, profile controls surfaces (ISO 1660:2017). Position may also be used to control nominally flat surfaces (ISO 1101:2017)
- In ASME, circle U modifier is used to indicate unequal profile tolerance.

  In ISO, UZ (unequal zone) modifier is similar but with different notations. (ISO 1660:2017) (See unit 11 for an example of ISO UZ modifier and differences with ASME circle U)
- In ASME, dynamic profile modifier unlocks the size control of profile.

  In ISO, OZ (offset zone) modifier is similar (ISO 1660:2017)
- In ASME, the lower segments of composite position and composite profile control orientation only to the DRF.

  In ISO, composite tolerancing is not supported. Orientation only for a datum feature reference may be specified by >< behind the datum reference in the tolerance indicator (ISO 5459:2011)
- In ASME, degrees of freedom constraints can be specified in a customized datum reference frame using notations: X, Y, Z, u, v, w in the feature control frame.

  In ISO, degrees of freedom constraints can be specified using Tx, Ty, Tz, Rx, Ry, Rz, T=Translation, R=Rotation (ISO 5459:2011)
- In ASME, datum targets may indicate partial datum features or the datum feature simulator.

  In ISO, datum targets are portions of surface. If the datum target is indicating the fixture, the modifier [CF] (contacting feature) is used. (ISO 5459:2011)
- In ASME, the movable datum target symbol is always oriented horizontally, the leader line indicates the direction of the movement.

  In ISO, the triangle on the symbol rotates to the direction of movement. (ISO 5459:2011)
- In ASME, all true geometric counterparts have a default fixed at the basic location. The translation modifier is used to make the distance between them variable.

  In ISO, the associated datum features have a default fixed location with A-B and A-A. Modifier [DV] changes it to distance variable. The secondary and tertiary simulators have a default variable distance. Modifier [DF] changes it to distance fixed. (ISO 5459:2011)
- In ASME, the size of the true geometric counterpart may be specified with B (M) [10.2]

  In ISO, the size may be specified with B[SF 10.2] (size fixed) (ISO 5459:2011)
- In ASME, Continuous Feature (CF) is used when a size tolerance applies across multiple features or a broken feature. In ISO, Continuous Tolerance (CT) is used (ISO 14405-1:2016)

ISO concepts not covered in ASME

- Reciprocity - make any tolerance at MMR to a zero at MMR (ISO 2692:2014)
- Any Cross Section (ACS) - a tolerance or datum applies at any cross section (ISO 1101:2017)
- Circle A - Alternate way to indicate a tolerance applies to the median feature not the surface (ISO 1101:2017)
- A complicated datum feature (cone, two holes, etc) will create only a datum Axis [SL], Plane [PL] or Point [PT] (ISO 5459:2011)
- Directional indicators for cutting planes indicated for form, orientation, profile of a line (ISO 1101:2017)

ASME versus ISO Defaults

There are a set of underlying rules in both standards that influence the rest of the respective tolerancing systems. Some of the default rules are opposite in both standards, however there are ways to change these defaults. In both standards, all features are considered separate until related with tolerances.

ASME Defaults

Rule #1 (envelope principle):
Regular features of size create a boundary of perfect form at MMC.
(Size controls form)

Exceptions to the Rule #1 default:
- -Application of median line straightness or median plane flatness
- -Independency principle
- -Stock materials

Simultaneous requirement - Applies to separately specified position and profile tolerances related to common datum reference frame. These two or more geometric tolerances are **grouped as a single pattern**, and the tolerance zones are related with basic dimensions.

Toleranced features may be grouped in a pattern with the following:
- -nX multipliers with profile and position
- -Between, all around, all over symbols for profile
- -Continuous Feature

Exceptions to the simultaneous requirement default:
- -lower segments of composite feature control frames
- -Features with the notation "INDIVIDUALLY" or "SEP REQT"

ISO Defaults

The Independency Principle in ISO 8015
By default, every GPS specification for a feature shall be fulfilled independent of other specifications.

- -Size does not control form
- -Simultaneous Requirements are not the default.
- -nX multipliers do not group features
- -Between, all around, or all over symbols for profile do not group features

Exceptions to the independency default:
- -Ⓜ modifiers according to ISO 2692,
- -CZ, UF modifiers according to ISO 1101
- -Ⓔ modifiers according to ISO 14405-1
- -SIM, CZR according to ISO 5458

Ⓔ envelope requirement: Requires perfect form at MMC (size controls form)
Ⓜ modifier creates virtual condition boundaries controlling location between nX features
UF United Feature- multiple surfaces indicated as one feature. With profile, the sphere defining the tolerance will move in a continuous path to create a single tolerance zone
CZ Combined Zone- tolerance zones for multiple features are linked together with basic dimensions
CZR - separate features creating tolerance zones that are linked together with basic angles
SIM - makes multiple specifications as a simultaneous requirement

Index

Bibliography:

Dimensioning and Tolerancing, ASME Y14.5-2018. NY: American Society of Mechanical Engineers. 2018

Dimensioning and Tolerancing, ASME Y14.5-2009. NY: American Society of Mechanical Engineers. 2009

Mathematical Definition of Dimensioning and Tolerancing Principles, ASME Y14.5.1-2019. NY: American Society of Mechanical Engineers. 2020

ISO-GPS Standards. Geneva, Switzerland: ISO. 2020

For the Introduction and History:

Foster, Lowell. Geo-Metrics III. Upper Saddle River, NJ: Pearson Education. 1993

Hounshell, David A. *From the American System to Mass Production, 1800-1932*. Baltimore: John Hopkins University Press. 1984

Liggett, John V. *Fundamentals of Position Tolerance,* 1st ed. Dearborn, MI: Society of Manufacturing Engineers. 1970

Roser, Christoph. *"Faster, Better, Cheaper" in the History of Manufacturing: From the Stone Age to Lean Manufacturing and Beyond*, 1st ed. Productivity Press. 2016